The Fate of
Place

The Fate of Place

A Philosophical History

Edward S. Casey

University of California Press

Berkeley / Los Angeles / London

The publisher wishes to thank Bernard Tschumi Architects for
permission to reproduce three images in this volume
(all appear in this volume's chapter 12).

University of California Press
Berkeley and Los Angeles, California

University of California Press
London, England

First Paperback Printing 1998

Library of Congress Cataloging-in-Publication Data

Casey, Edward S.
    The fate of place : a philosophical history / Edward S. Casey.
        p.   cm.
    Includes bibliographical references and index.
    ISBN 978-0-520-21649-5 (pbk : alk. paper)
    1. Place (Philosophy)   2. Space and time.   I. Title.
B105.P53C36   1997
114—dc20   96-6411
                                                        CIP

Printed in the United States of America

12   11   10   09
9   8

The paper used in this publication is both acid-free and totally chlorine-free (TCF).
It meets the minimum requirements of ANSI/NISO Z39.48-1992 (R 1997)
(*Permanence of Paper*). ♾

In Living Memory of Three Extraordinary Mentors

*Mikel Dufrenne (1910–1995), William Earle (1919–1988),
John Niemeyer Findlay (1903–1987)*

*Whose Exemplary Practice, in Speech
and Writing, Taught Me the Force and Value
of Taking Philosophical History Seriously*

Contents

    Newton   137

7 Modern Space as Extensive: Descartes   151

8 Modern Space as Relative: Locke and Leibniz   162

9 Modern Space as Site and Point: Position, Panopticon,
    and Pure Form   180

Part Four   The Reappearance of Place

                 Transition   197

10 By Way of Body: Kant, Whitehead, Husserl, Merleau-
     Ponty   202

11 Proceeding to Place by Indirection: Heidegger   243

12 Giving a Face to Place in the Present:
     Bachelard, Foucault, Deleuze and Guattari, Derrida,
     Irigaray   285

     Postface: Places Rediscovered   331

     Notes   343
     Index   479

Preface: Disappearing Places

The power of place will be remarkable.
—Aristotle, *Physics*

No man therefore can conceive anything, but he
must conceive it in some place.
—Thomas Hobbes, *Leviathan*

The present epoch will perhaps be above all the
epoch of space. . . . The anxiety of our era has to do
fundamentally with space, no doubt a great deal
more than with time.
—Michel Foucault, "Of Other Spaces"

I

Whatever is true for space and time, this much is true for place: we are immersed in it and could not do without it. To be at all—to exist in any way—is to be somewhere, and to be somewhere is to be in some kind of place. Place is as requisite as the air we breathe, the ground on which we stand, the bodies we have. We are surrounded by places. We walk over and through them. We live in places, relate to others in them, die in them. Nothing we do is unplaced. How could it be otherwise? How could we fail to recognize this primal fact?

Aristotle recognized it. He made "where" one of the ten indispensable categories of every substance, and he gave a sustained and perspicacious account of place in his *Physics*. His discussion set off a debate that has lasted until the present day. Heidegger, for example, contends with Aristotle as to what being *in* a place signifies for "being-in-the-world." More recently still, Irigaray has returned to Aristotle's idea of place as essential to an ethics of sexual difference. Between Aristotle and Irigaray stretch more than two millennia of thought and teaching and writing about place—a period that includes such diverse debating partners as Iamblichus and Plotinus, Cusa and Bruno, Descartes and Locke, Newton and Leibniz, Bachelard and Foucault.

Yet the history of this continuing concern with place is virtually unknown. Unknown in that it has been hidden from view. Not deliberately or for the sake of being obscure, much less to mislead: unlike the unconscious, place is not so controversial or so intrusive or embarrassing as to require repression. On the contrary, just because place is so much with us, and we with it, it has been taken for granted, deemed not worthy of separate treatment. Also taken for granted is the fact that we are implaced beings to begin with, that place is an a priori of our existence on earth. Just because we cannot choose in the matter, we believe we do not have to think about this basic facticity very much, if at all. Except when we are disoriented or lost—or contesting Aristotle's *Physics*—we presume that the question is settled, that there is nothing more to say on the subject.

But there is a great deal to say, even if quite a lot has been said already by previous thinkers. Yet this rich tradition of place-talk has been bypassed or forgotten for the most part, mainly because place has been subordinated to other terms taken as putative absolutes: most notably, Space and Time. Beginning with Philoponus in the sixth century A.D. and reaching an apogee in fourteenth-century theology and above all in seventeenth-century physics, place has been assimilated to space. The latter, regarded as infinite extension, has become a cosmic and extracosmic Moloch that consumes every corpuscle of place to be found within its greedy reach. As a result, place came to be considered a mere "modification" of space (in Locke's revealing term)—a modification that aptly can be called "site," that is, leveled-down, monotonous *space for* building and other human enterprises. To make matters worse, in the course of the eighteenth and nineteenth centuries place was also made subject to time, regarded as chronometric and universal, indeed as "the formal *a priori* condition of all appearances whatsoever," in Kant's commanding phrase.[1] Even space, as the form of "outer sense," became subject to temporal determination. Place, reduced to locations between which movements of physical bodies occur, vanished from view almost altogether in the era of temporocentrism (i.e., a belief in the hegemony of time) that has dominated the last two hundred years of philosophy in the wake of Hegel, Marx, Kierkegaard, Darwin, Bergson, and William James.

I say that place disappeared "almost altogether." It never went entirely out of sight. Part of its very hiddenness—as Heidegger would insist—includes being at least partially unhidden. In bringing out the concealed history of place, I shall show that place has continued to possess considerable significance despite its discontinuous acknowledgment. Thus Plato's *Timaeus*, though stressing space as *chōra*, ends with the creation of determinate places for material things. Philoponus, taken with the idea of empty dimensions, maintains nonetheless that three-dimensional space is always in fact filled with places. Descartes finds room for place as volume and position within the world of extended space. Even Kant accords to place a special privilege in the constitution of what he calls "cosmic regions," thanks to the role of the body in orientation—a role that, a century and a half later, will provide a key to twentieth-century conceptions of place in the work of Whitehead, Husserl, Merleau-Ponty, and Irigaray. But in every such case (and in still others to be discussed in this book) it is a matter of drawing place out of its latent position in the manifest texts of Western philosophy, retrieving it from its textual tomb, bringing it back alive.

The aim of *The Fate of Place* is to thrust the very idea of place, so deeply dormant in modern Western thinking, once more into the daylight of philosophical discourse. This will be done in four parts. In Part I, I shall first examine mythical and religious narratives of creation—with an eye to discerning the primordiality of place at the beginning of things. I will then focus on Plato's quasi-mythical cosmology in the *Timaeus,* as well as on Aristotle's detailed treatment of place in the *Physics.* In Part II I follow the sinuous but fascinating thread that leads from Hellenistic and Neoplatonic thought to medieval and Renaissance consideration, and in Part III I take a close look at early modern theories of place and space, ranging from Gassendi to Kant. This sets the stage for the final part, which explores a recrudescence of concern with place—no longer subordinate to Space or Time—in an array of late modern and postmodern thinkers.

An earlier volume of mine, *Getting Back into Place,* described concrete, multiplex, experiential aspects of the place-world.[2] The present book carries forward the project of regaining recognition of the power of place. But it does so in a very different way: by delineating doctrines of place as these have emerged at critical moments of Western rumination as to the nature of place and space. My purpose here is to set forth what these doctrines actually say— and, just as often, do not say. I shall trace out, not the history of place per se, that is, its ingrediency in the actualities of art or architecture, geography or world history, but the story of how human beings (mainly philosophers) have regarded place as a concept or idea. This is an essay, therefore, in intellectual history and, more specifically, in the history of philosophical thinking about place. Merely to realize how much intelligent and insightful thought has been accorded to place in the course of Western philosophy is to begin to reappreciate its unsuspected importance as well as its fuller compass.

II

The present historical moment is a propitious one for assessing the fate of place. This is so even though there is precious little talk of place in philosophy—or, for that matter, in psychology or sociology, literary theory or religious studies. It is true that in architecture, anthropology, and ecology there is a burgeoning interest in place, but this interest leaves place itself an unclarified notion. This is an extraordinary circumstance, one that combines magnitude of promise with dearth of realization. As this book will amply demonstrate, place has shown itself capable of inspiring complicated and variegated discussions. Even if it is by no means univocal, "place" is not an incoherent concept that falls apart on close analysis, nor is it flawed in some fundamental manner, easily reducible to some other term, or merely trivial in its consequences. And yet in our own time we have come to pass over place as a thought-worthy notion. In part, this has to do with the ascendancy of site-specific models of space stemming from the early modern era. It also reflects the continuing miasma of temporocentrism that draws much of the complex and subtle structure of place into its nebulous embrace.

At work as well in the obscuration of place is the universalism inherent in Western culture from the beginning. This universalism is most starkly evident in the search for ideas, usually labeled "essences," that obtain *everywhere* and for which a particular *somewhere,* a given place, is presumably irrelevant. Is it accidental that the obsession with space as something infinite and ubiquitous coincided with the spread of Christianity, a religion with universalist aspirations? Philoponus, a committed Christian, was arguably the first philosopher in the West to entertain the idea of an absolute space that is not merely a void. Thomas Bradwardine, Archbishop of Canterbury, was a leading theorist of such space in the fourteenth century: for him, God's immensity is coextensive not only with the known universe but also with the infinite empty space in which it is set. By the next century, the Age of Exploration had begun, an era in which the domination of native peoples was accomplished by their deplacialization: the systematic destruction of regional landscapes that served as the concrete settings for local culture.

In our own century, investigations of ethics and politics continue to be universalist in aspiration—to the detriment of place, considered merely parochial in scope. Treatments of logic and language often are still more place-blind, as if speaking and thinking were wholly unaffected by the locality in which they occur. On the eve of World War I, Russell and Whitehead composed *Principia Mathematica,* which explored the universal logical foundations of pure mathematics with unmistakable allusion to Newton's *Philosophiae naturalis principia mathematica.* Whitehead and Russell's epoch-making book appeared during the very years when de Saussure was lecturing on a systematic "general linguistics" that sought to provide synchronic principles for all known languages irrespective of their diachronic and local differences. Herder and Humboldt, early-nineteenth-century philosophers of language, knew better; but the success of de Saussure, followed by that of Jakobson and the Prague school, and later (in a quite different vein) by Chomskian linguistics, reinstalled a formalist universalism at the heart of the theory of language.

Other reasons for the shunning of place as a crucial concept are less point-edly logical or linguistic, yet even more momentous. These include the cata-clysmic events of world wars, which have acted to undermine any secure sense of abiding place (in fact, to destroy it altogether in the case of a radical anti-place such as Auschwitz); the forced migrations of entire peoples, along with continual drifting on the part of many individuals, suggesting that the world is nothing but a scene of endless displacement; the massive spread of electronic technology, which makes irrelevant *where you are* so long as you can link up with other users of the same technology. Each of these phenomena is truly "cosmic," that is, literally worldwide, and each exhibits a *dromo-centrism* that amounts to temporocentrism writ large: not just time but speeded-up time (*dromos* connotes "running," "race," "racecourse") is of the essence of the era.[3] It is as if the acceleration discovered by Galileo to be inherent in falling bodies has come to pervade the earth (conceived as a single scene of communication), rendering the planet a "global village" not in a positive sense but as a placeless place indeed.

In view of these various theoretical, cultural, and historical tendencies, the prospects for a renewed interest in place might appear to be bleak indeed. And yet something is astir that calls for a return to reflective thought about place. One sign of this auspicious stirring is found in the fact that Bergson, James, and Husserl, all apostles of temporocentrism, accorded careful attention to space and place in lesser-known but important writings that were overshad-owed by their own more celebrated analyses of lived time. Similarly, Heideg-ger, an outspoken temporocentrist in his early work, affirmed the significance of place when he pondered the destiny of modern technological culture.

Still more saliently, certain devastating phenomena of this century bring with them, by aftershock as it were, a revitalized sensitivity to place. Precisely in its capacity to eliminate all perceptible places from a given region, the prospect of nuclear annihilation heightens awareness of the unreplaceability of these places, their singular configuration and unrepeatable history. Much the same is true for any disruptive event that disturbs the placidity of cities and neighborhoods. Perhaps most crucially, the encroachment of an indifferent sameness-of-place on a global scale—to the point where at times you cannot be sure which city you are in, given the overwhelming architectural and com-mercial uniformity of many cities—makes the human subject long for a diver-sity of places, that is, difference-of-place, that has been lost in a worldwide monoculture based on Western (and, more specifically, American) economic and political paradigms. This is not just a matter of nostalgia. An active desire for the particularity of place—for what is truly "local" or "regional"—is aroused by such increasingly common experiences. Place brings with it the very elements sheared off in the planiformity of site: identity, character, nu-ance, history.

Even our embroilment in technology brings with it an unsuspected return to place. Granting that the literal locus of the technologically engaged person is a matter of comparative indifference, this locus is still *not nowhere*. As I watch television or correspond by e-mail, my immediate surroundings may not matter greatly to the extent that I am drawn into the drama I am watching or into the words I am typing or reading. But a new sense of place emerges from this very circumstance: "virtual place," as it can be called, in keeping with current discussions of "virtual reality." In inhabiting a virtual place, I have the distinct impression that the persons with whom I am communicating or the figures I am watching, though not physically present, nevertheless present themselves to me in a quasi face-to-face interaction. They are accessible to me and I to them (at least in the case of e-mail or call-in radio shows): I seem to share the "same space" with others who are in fact stationed elsewhere on the planet. This virtual coimplacement can occur in image or word, or in both. The comparative coziness and discreteness of such compresence— its sense of having boundaries if not definite limits—makes it a genuine, if still not fully understood, phenomenon of place.[4]

As for the philosophical scene—which is most explicitly at stake in this book—even within the most rebarbative purlieu there lurk more than echoes and ghosts of place. Both "politics" and "ethics" go back to Greek words that signify place: *polis* and *ēthea,* "city-state" and "habitats," respectively. The very word "society" stems from *socius,* signifying "sharing"—and sharing is done in a common place. More than the history of words is at issue here. Almost every major ethical and political thinker of the century has been concerned, directly or indirectly, with the question of *community*. As Victor Turner has emphasized, a *communitas* is not just a matter of banding together but of *bonding together* through rituals that actively communalize people— and that require particular places in which to be enacted.[5] When Hannah Arendt proclaims—or, rather, reclaims—the *polis* as an arena of overt contestation, she invokes a bounded and institutionally sanctioned *place* as the basis for "the public sphere of appearance."[6] John Rawls's idea of "the objective circumstances of justice" in human society entails (even if his discussion does not spell out) the concrete specificities of implacement.[7] More surprising still, certain developments in language and logic are promising from a placial point of view. I am thinking of investigations into the structure of informal argumentation, a structure likely to reflect local custom and culture; a renewed interest in rhetoric, alike among epigones of Leo Strauss as well as followers of Jacques Derrida and Paul DeMan; not to mention the notion of family resemblance first introduced by Wittgenstein, a notion that implies (even though it does not espouse) the special pertinence of locality and region to basic issues in epistemology and philosophy of language and mind.

And yet "place," despite these auspicious directions in contemporary thought, is rarely named as such—and even more rarely discussed seriously. Place is still concealed, "still veiled," as Heidegger says specifically of space.[8] To ponder the fate of place at this moment thus assumes a new urgency and points to a new promise. The question is, can we bring place out of hiding and expose it to renewed scrutiny? A good place to start is by a consideration of its own complex history. To become familiar with this history is to be in a better position to attest to the pervasiveness of place in our lives: in our language and logic as in our ethics and politics, in our bodily bearing and in our personal relations. To uncover the hidden history of place is to find a way back into the place-world—a way to savor the renascence of place even on the most recalcitrant terrain.

Acknowledgments

The most direct inspiration for this book stems from a graduate seminar I taught at Emory University in the spring of 1992, held under the auspices of the philosophy department and at the instigation of its chairman, David Carr. The intense interest in the history of place that was palpable in that seminar— animated by the keen questioning of the remarkably responsive students who were present—brought home to me the need for a book on the subject. The story of philosophical accounts of place has not yet been told, and I decided (in the wake of my earlier descriptive efforts to discern place more accurately) to tell this story in a comprehensive format. Other graduate seminars substantially aided my efforts: one at the New School for Social Research (1993) and one at the State University of Stony Brook (1994). In each case, my tentative formulations were increasingly refined, thanks to the intense scrutiny of my students. I also presented my views at a week-long seminar on "The Senses of Place" at the School of American Research in Santa Fe, New Mexico, where a number of anthropologists gave me renewed direction and purpose; I especially wish to thank Keith Basso and Steven Feld for their hosting of this event and for the guidance of their pioneering work. I was the beneficiary as well of public audiences when I lectured on the topic, most notably at Vanderbilt University, SUNY at Binghamton, New School for Social Research, Duquesne University, and Yale University.

A number of individuals made essential contributions to my ongoing research into the hidden history of place. Janet Gyatso read many parts of the manuscript and offered invaluable advice, particularly with regard to clarity of argumentation, substance, and style. Without her congenial and warm encouragement, the book might not ever have seen the light of day. The entire manuscript profited from Kurt Wildermuth's discerning and disciplined look.

I also benefited from exchanges with Robert Gooding-Williams, Iris Young, Tom Flynn, David Michael Levin, Elizabeth Behnke, Henry Tylbor, Bruce Wilshire, Glen Mazis, and, especially, Elizabeth Grosz.

My colleagues at Stony Brook were generous in their assistance. Tom Altizer discussed with me my fledgling formulations of mythical accounts of place, and Peter Manchester led me to reconsider my interpretation of the *Timaeus*. Irene Klaver was of immense help in my treatment of Plato, Husserl, Merleau-Ponty, and Irigaray. I learned a great deal from Lee Miller's comments on my treatment of medieval figures (especially Nicholas of Cusa), Walter Watson's close reading of my treatment of Aristotle, Robert Crease's remarks on my treatment of Leibniz, David Allison's perusal of the chapter on Descartes, François Raffoul's and Jeffrey Edwards's sagacious insights into Kant, and Mary Rawlinson's rectifying of my discussion of Irigaray. I thank Celian Schoenbach for diligently typing in final changes to the manuscript, and Ann Cahill for preparing the index.

I am grateful to Brenda Casey for help on a number of perplexing points that were evading me even at the end. Constance Casey was an important presence throughout. Consulted at critical moments was Eric Casey, whose knowledge of the languages and cultures of the ancient world proved indispensable to the completion of this book.

James Hillman urged me to pursue place into its most recondite corners so as to convey its story fully and effectively. Conversations with him on aspects of place—particularly its neglected importance in our own time—have been of continuing inspiration. I was fortunate to be so effectively supported in this project by the intelligent, sensitive efforts of Edward Dimendberg, philosophy editor at the University of California Press. He asked me to put this book together in the first place, and he gave me sound direction at every point. To Michelle Nordon of the same institution I am indebted for her caring and responsive supervision of the entire publication process.

Part One

From Void to Vessel

1

Avoiding the Void

Primeval Patterns

But, first, they say, there was only the Creator, Tai-owa. All else was endless space, Tokpela. There was no beginning and end, time, shape, and life in the mind of Taiowa the Creator.

—Hopi creation myth

At first there was neither Earth nor Sky. Shuzanghu and his wife Zumiang-Nui lived above. One day Shuzanghu said to his wife, "How long must we live without a place to rest our feet?"

—Dhammai legend

I

Following Nietzsche's admonition, in *The Genealogy of Morals,* that "man would sooner have the void for his purpose than be void of purpose,"[1] there is an area of human experience in which, indeed, the void plays a constitutive and recognized role. This occurs in theories of creation that concern themselves with how things came into being in the first place. "In the first place": a quite problematic posit. For if there is a cosmic moment in which no *things* yet exist, it would seem that *places* could not exist at that "time" either. Although places are not things in any usual (e.g., material) sense, they are *some* kind of entity or occasion: they are not nothing. If, at this primeval moment (which might last an eternity), absolutely nothing exists, how could anything like a place exist, even if that place were merely to situate a thing? Such a situation is not only one of *non*place but of *no-place-at-all:* utter void.[2]

It is by dint of this distinctive "cosmologic" that the notion of no-place becomes something with which any thoughtful account of creation has to contend. Despite its status as an apparently ineluctable inference from cosmological reasoning, the notion of sheer void is akin to the empty place that gives rise to so much existential angst among human beings. It has even been proposed that the Judeo-Christian creator God may have experienced an analogue of this anxiety: a divine separation that is just as intolerable as the predicament of a person separated from secure place. If so, the creator might well have been as desperate to populate the cosmic void with plenary presences as mortals are to fill in their own much more finite voids. Indeed, He or She might well have been willing to engage in an act of self-emptying in order to generate contents available nowhere else. In this paradoxical action of *kenosis* (from *kenon,* "void"), the creator would have created a void within as a first step toward filling the void without.

Place is especially problematic from a cosmological perspective if the world or universe is held to be something created to begin with. On doctrines of noncreation that affirm the permanent presence of things, place—along with everything else—will have been in existence forever. "Know that the world is uncreated" runs a passage from the Jain *Mahapurana.*[3] Despite its espousal of eternal plenitude, such a claim characteristically adverts to the notion of varying manifestations of a single uncreated universe, thereby allowing for change and development. For instance, in Hindu cosmogony we find that "no original creation of the universe can be imagined; but there are alternations, partial and complete, of manifestation and withdrawal."[4]

Far from offering an exception to the pervasiveness of place, doctrines of noncreation only reinforce place's necessity. For if neither creation nor a creator is responsible for the way things are, then the existence, concatenation, and fate of things will owe much to place. Archytas of Tarentum maintained that *to be (at all) is to be in (some) place.*[5] Modifying this Archytian axiom only slightly, we may say that if the things of the world are already in existence, they must also already possess places. The world is, minimally and forever, a place-world. Indeed, insofar as being or existence is not bestowed by creation or creator, place can be said to take over roles otherwise attributed to a creator-god or to the act of creation: roles of preserving and sustaining things in existence. For if things were both uncreated *and* unplaced, they could not be said to *be* in any significant sense. Given a primal implacement—a genuine "first place"—that is independent of creation or creator, things would fulfill at least one strict requirement for existing. If separation is a condition for creation, implacement is a sine qua non for things to be—even if they have never been created.

But let us focus on the cosmogonic circumstance in which the universe considered as a topocosm is held to come forth from an act of creation. I borrow the word "topocosm" from ethnologists, who use it to designate the comparatively stable world system, the cosmology, of traditional societies.

The word fortuitously brings together "place" and "cosmos," thereby suggesting that in the complete constitution of a cosmos, that is, a well-ordered world, place has a prominent role to play. In fact, as we have just witnessed, place figures centrally even in scenarios of noncreation; and (as we shall soon see) it is indissociable from the notion of utter void. In all of these instances, place presents itself not just as a particular dramatis persona, an actor in the cosmic theater, but as the very scene of cosmogenesis, the material or spiritual[6] medium of the eternal or evolving topocosm. Cosmogenesis is topogenesis—throughout and at every step.[7]

"Cosmogony" names this double genesis. It means an account of how the created universe came to be. "Genesis" (a word that lies buried in "cosmogony" itself) implies becoming in the most capacious sense, and is not to be reduced to temporal development alone. This is why cosmogonic myths and tales are rarely consecutive in any consistent, much less chronometric, manner. The narration they proffer is not chronological; their logic is a cosmo-logic, not a chronologic. Cosmologic deals with the elemental interpenetration of simultaneously present entities rather than with their successive evolution from one stage to another. For this reason, the transition from cosmogony to cosmology—a transition I shall trace out in the next chapter—is somewhat less abrupt than certain historians of ideas have suggested. For the genesis of the *cosmos* already contains highly configured and densely conjunctive elements that at least portend *logos,* or rational structure. Place is basic to such protostructuring, since it is place that introduces spatial order into the world— or, rather, shows that in its formative phases the world is already on the way to order. In this way place provides the primary bridge in the movement from cosmogony to cosmology.

Nor is this merely a matter of speculation—of theogony or theology. Concrete rituals of implacement often serve to reaffirm and reinstate the cosmogonic accounts. Upon moving into a new place, as Mircea Eliade recounts, many native peoples perform ceremonies that amount to a reenactment of a cosmogony. For example, the nomadic Australians of the Achilpa tribe carry with them a *kauwa-auwa,* a sacred pole that they implant in each new campsite. By this act, they at once consecrate the site and connect—by means of a situated *axis mundi*—with the cosmic force of their mythic ancestor Numbakula, who first fashioned a *kauwa-auwa* from the trunk of a gum tree. As a result, "the world of the Achilpa really becomes *their* world only in proportion as it reproduces the cosmos organized and sanctified by Numbakula."[8] Such a ritual bears on a particular place not in its idiosyncrasy or newness but in its capacity to stand in for a preexisting cosmogonic Place. If it is true that "settling in a territory is equivalent to founding a world,"[9] the settling is a settling *of place in terms of place.* It is a modeling and sanctifying of *this* place in view of, and as a repetition of, *that* place—that primordial Place of creation (and not just the primordial Time of creation: *in illo tempore*).

Such concrete actions of primal place-instauration stand midway between the abstractions of cosmogonies/cosmologies and the existential predicament of place-bereft individuals. That predicament is one of place-panic: depression or terror even at the idea, and still more in the experience, of an empty place. As some people find the prospect of an unknown place—even a temporary stopping place on an ordinary journey—quite unsettling, many others experience a wholly unfamiliar place to be desolate or uncanny. In both cases, the prospect of a strict void, of an utter no-place, is felt to be intolerable. So intolerable, so undermining of personal or collective identity is this prospect, that practices of place-fixing and place-filling are set in motion right away. In the one case, these practices amount to public rituals reenacting cosmogenesis; in the other, they occur as private rituals of an obsessive cast—efforts to paper over the abyss by any means available. The aim, however, is much the same in both cases: it is to achieve the assurance offered by plenitude of place. The void of no-place is avoided at almost any cost.

It is evident that in any thorough cosmogony the issue of place, and in particular, of no-place, will arise. For one of the most fundamental cosmogonic questions is, *where* did things begin to be? The response "nowhere" is tempting, especially if the cosmogony is conceived as a strict ex nihilo theory of creation. If the *nihil* is to be in full force—if there is to be an entirely clean slate before the moment of creation—there can be no whereabouts to begin with: nowhere, *nusquam,* for to-be-created things to be located. Rather than being a merely nugatory notion, the void here plays the positive (and quite economical) role of satisfying a demand of ex nihilo theorizing.

Such theorizing has two operative premises. First, the universe of things is not permanent or eternal; there was a time when the things we know did not exist. As a consequence, a separate creative force had to bring things into existence: *ex nihilo nihil fit.*[10] Second, there was a corresponding state of being so strictly void of anything at all that it can be described only as a condition of no-place. To progress from this initial state of no-thing-cum-no-place to the state of created existence—to *ens creatum*—calls not only for cosmically creative acts but also for a sequential temporality within which the transition from void to plenum can occur. The story of that transition is the narrative of cosmic creation, of cosmogony, itself. Not only does this narrative supervene upon, and express in words, the movement from placelessness to a place-filled existence; it is itself part of the cosmically creative process and inseparable from it: "In the beginning was the Word." This claim is by no means limited to the Old Testament. The Dogon of Mali also attribute cosmogonic powers to the Word. They conceive of creation as a process of word weaving:

> The Word is in the sound of the block and the shuttle. The name of the block means "creaking of the word." Everybody understands what is meant by "the word" in that connection. It is interwoven with threads: it fills the interstices in

the fabric. It belongs to the eight ancestors; the first seven possess it: the seventh is the master of it; it is itself the eighth.[11]

Wherever cosmo*genesis* is taken seriously—that is, wherever it is not presumed that things simply are as they always were—we are likely to find a narrative of creation.

A cosmogonic narrative is not only a recounting of events in time. Of course, it does relate the act or acts of creation and thus presupposes a cosmic temporality whose minimal structure is that of Before/After: prior to creation/ posterior to creation. But such a narrative also tells of things *in place*, how things occupy or come to acquire places. It tells, too, of *events* in place. Events, those prototypical temporal occurrents, call for cosmic implacement: no event can happen unplaced, suspended in a placeless *aithēr*. This includes the event of creation itself. It, too, must have its place. Integral to cosmic creation is the creation not just of places for created things as such but of a place for creation (and thus for the creator). Inseparable from topogenesis is cosmogenesis itself.

To create "in the first place" is to create *a first place*. Perhaps it is true that in the beginning was the Word. But is it not equally likely that in the beginning was a Place—the place of creation itself? Should we assume that the Word precedes Place and brings it into being? Or does not the Word itself presuppose Place? Whichever direction we may prefer to take, it is evident that narrative accounts of creation must bear on place even as they rely on time and language. It behooves us to consider these accounts with an eye to place— and to no-place, that from which places themselves, along with all other things, are so often thought to arise. But how then does the placelessness of nonbeing give way to the placedness of beings? How do these beings gain their existence as well as their place from a primal act of creation that is itself self-placing in character?

II

> So things evolved, and out of blind confusion
> each found its place, bound in eternal order.
> —Ovid, *Metamorphoses*

Might everything have come from chaos? This idea has perennial appeal. Contemporary "chaos theorists" carry on a chain of speculation that stretches backward to some of the earliest extant accounts of creation. The Pelasgian narrative of creation, dating from at least 3500 B.C., runs like this:

> In the beginning, Eurynome, the Goddess of All Things, rose naked from Chaos, but found nothing substantial for her feet to rest upon, and therefore divided the sea from the sky, dancing lonely upon its waves.[12]

The insubstantiality of Chaos, its elemental confusion and gaping character,[13] is what gives rise to the terror with which it is characteristically experienced—a terror closely affiliated with the place-panic occasioned by no-place. But is the "nothing substantial" of Pelasgian Chaos the same thing as nothing whatsoever? Is it equivalent to the sheer void? The proper name "Eurynome," the creator Goddess of All Things, hints that we must answer both questions in the negative. For Eurynome, taken literally, means "the wide wandering." A wanderer, even a cosmogonic primal wanderer, cannot wander amid nothing: to wander is to roam *between places* of some kind. Indeed, that Eurynome "rose naked *from* Chaos" indicates that Chaos has at least enough substantiality to be something from which to arise in the first place. If this substantiality is not sufficient for surefootedness, it can be made more determinate—as Eurynome proceeds to do when she "therefore divided the sea from the sky," so as to dance "lonely upon its waves." The "therefore" is revealing; it possesses the special cosmogonic force of something *having to be the case* if other things are to obtain.

Suddenly we recall that in I Genesis the separation of the heavens from the earth—and all that ensues from this separation—requires the primordial scission of "the waters from the waters," that is, the creation of the firmament in an otherwise undifferentiated Deep. We shall return to Genesis presently, but for now let us only note that in the Old Testament and the Pelasgian account alike *for creation to proceed differentiation must occur.* Moreover, this differentiation is *of one place from another.* Could "chaos" be another name for this obligatory action of primeval differentiation of places? The opening lines of Hesiod's *Theogony,* a text whose composition occurred between the Pelasgian narrative and the writing of Genesis, intimate that this is indeed so:

> Verily first of all did Chaos come into being, and then broad-bosomed Gaia [earth], a firm seat of all things for ever, and misty Tartaros in a recess of broad-wayed earth, and Eros, who is fairest among immortal gods, looser of limbs, and subdues in their breasts the mind and thoughtful counsel of all gods and all men. Out of Chaos, Erebos and black Night came into being; and from Night, again, came Aither and Day, whom she conceived and bore after mingling in love with Erebos. And Earth first of all brought forth starry Ouranos [sky], equal to herself, to cover her completely round about, to be a firm seat for the blessed gods for ever. Then she brought forth tall Mountains, lovely haunts of the divine Nymphs who dwell in the woody mountains. She also gave birth to the unharvested sea, seething with its swell, Pontos, without delightful love; and then having lain with Ouranos she bore deep-eddying Okeanos.[14]

The surprising affinity between this text of the seventh century B.C. and Genesis, in regard to the deferred separation of earth from sky, has been remarked on by several commentators.[15] Most striking, however, is the suggestion in

Hesiod's account that Chaos came into being *first*—not as a settled state, that is, as something that (as one interpreter puts it) "coexisted with the undifferentiated state of the universe from eternity,"[16] but as *itself both differentiated and differentiating.*

The ancient notion of chaos as a primal abyss or gap points in this same direction: a gap is both an opening *between* two already existing things (e.g., earth and sky) and an *opening* between them (i.e., that which brings about the differentiation of these two things in the first place). A gap has boundaries and thus a form, however primitive; it is not an indefinite, much less an empty and endless, space. As John Burnet remarks, Chaos for Hesiod "is not a formless mixture, but rather, as its etymology indicates, the yawning gulf or gap where nothing is as yet."[17] Nothing may yet be *in* Chaos, but Chaos itself is not nothing. As a gap, Chaos is a primordial place within which things can happen. Aristotle, who cites the first several lines of the *Theogony* with approval, comments that "things need to have space first, because [Hesiod] thought, with most people, that *everything is somewhere and in place.*"[18]

Chaos, then, is not a scene of disorder—of what moderns shortsightedly call "the chaotic."[19] It is a scene of *emerging* order. Such a scene cannot be an utter void, a merely vacant space. It is a scene of spacing, not just gaping but "gapping" in a cosmogonically active sense. To be chaotic in this sense is not to destroy order but to create it. Indeed, on the Hesiodic account Chaos is the very first stage of creating; it is what makes the rest of created order possible in the first place. Indeed, it *is* the first place of creation. As G. S. Kirk, J. E. Raven, and M. Schofield put it, Chaos is "not the eternal precondition of a differentiated world, but a modification of that precondition."[20] As an action and not a permanent state, Chaos is not eternal. It occurs. But it occurs as a place—a place for things to be.

What kind of a place is this? As the Pelasgian cosmogony, Genesis, and the *Theogony* all insist, it is *a place of separation.* Occurring not as an empty place but as a scene of separation, it acts to distinguish—and first of all to distinguish earth from sky (or, alternately, sea from sky). Thus to say *chaos genet* (in transliterated Greek) is to "imply that *the gap between earth and sky came into being;* that is, that the first stage of cosmogony was the separation of earth and sky."[21] After this inaugural separation has taken place, other more delimited separations—"local differentiations"[22]—can occur: Night from Day, Mountains from Earth, Sea from Ocean. A sequence of increasingly specific differences arises from the primordial Difference, that is to say, from what Aristophanes (in a playful parody of Hesiod) calls the "first gap":

first Gap   Night   deep Dark   abyss   Tartaros
                        no air earth or sky
then in deep Dark's bottomless wombs
Night on black wings laid the wind egg.[23]

Even though Chaos qua Gap is neither disorder nor void (some early Greeks held that the primal gap contained air), as cosmic separation it remained threatening enough to call for filling. Aristophanes thus deposits a primordial wind-borne egg in it. Hesiod himself tries to fill the gap first with Eros—who acts to reunite earth and sky, his dissociated parents—and then with Kronos and Zeus, to whose glorification the *Theogony* is devoted.[24] In these various ingenious moves to plug up the Gap, we already witness the phenomenon of *horror vacui,* that is, the intolerability of no-place-at-all.

That the cosmogonic Gap is most often conceived as the gulf between heaven and earth is not accidental. We may speculate that the separation between these latter regions is the *first* separation for a quite concrete phenomenological reason. If you look around in almost any outdoor situation, you discover the stark difference between land and sky (or at sea, between water and sky). These are the separate protoregions of ordinary perception; they divide up the perceptual landscape *from the beginning.* This beginning confirms the cosmogonic beginning—and may well provide the model for the latter, especially if we include the fact that dawn, the allegorical origin for many creation stories, arises literally in the opening between earth and sky. If our ordinary perceptual lives are as "gapped" as they are because they are filled with "obtrusions" (in Husserl's word for objects as they are given at the primary level of perception),[25] can it be surprising that ancient cosmogonies single out the very gap that is the most obtrusive of all?

Such singling out is not limited to early Mediterranean cosmogonies. A southern Chinese creation myth has it that the creator god P'an Ku "went to work at once, mightily, to put the world in order. He chiseled the land and sky apart."[26] P'an Ku himself was born from a cosmic egg that contained Chaos—as if to show that Chaos is not boundless.[27] Quite different traditions place the scission between Heaven and Earth at the beginning of things. These traditions include those of the Celts, the ancient Japanese, and the contemporary Navajo.

> The Navajo world or universe consists of a shallow, flat disk in the form of a dish, topped by a similar form which covers it like a lid. The lower part is the Earth, while the upper part (the lid, so to speak) is the Sky. . . . [B]oth are represented as human or anthropomorphic forms, lying down in an arching stretched manner, one on top of the other. . . . The things were placed on the Earth and in the Sky in the Holy Way.[28]

For the Navajo, Earth and Sky are the two great regions in which any particular thing must be "placed" if it is to become created. As in ancient Mediterranean and Far Eastern accounts, an initial period of Chaos, imagined by the Navajo as a time of primal mists, gives way to (or, more radically, occurs as) the primeval separation of Earth from Heaven.[29] As if to underline the importance of this separation, the Navajo believe that around the edges of the double-dished structure of Earth and Sky is an opening: "The Sky does not really touch the Earth at any place, not even at the horizon."[30] If Sky and Earth were ever to touch, it would mean the destruction of the world—as if to say that the original act of separation must be continued *as horizon* if the created world is to retain its identity as a coherent cosmos.

What is the horizon but that factor in everyday perception that embodies the cosmogonic separation of Earth from Sky? The strange power of the horizon to distinguish these two regions from each other in the course of daily existence—a power to which we rarely attend as such—is the dynamic basis of the gap between Heaven and Earth. As painters know, it is anything but a mere "horizon line," the spatial equivalent of the time line; the experienced horizon is a central creative force in the field of visual perception, especially when beheld at the beginning or the ending of the day.[31] Without its differentiating action—which the Navajo symbolize by variegated coloration—we would be lost indeed in a primal mist of indifferentiation, a perceptual morass, a "slush" of indetermination such as the Ainu people of Japan posit as the first state of things: "In the beginning the world was slush, for the waters and the mud were all stirred in together. All was silence; there was no sound. It was cold. There were no birds in the air. There was no living thing."[32] A world without a horizon would be a most inhospitable environment—if it could still be considered *environing*. It would be a world without a distinction between Heaven and Earth, and thus no world, no "cosmos," at all. No wonder a creator must be invoked to bring such slush, such chaos, into the minimal order that being a world (and being-in-the-world) requires. On the way from Chaos to Cosmos the horizonal differentiation between Earth and Sky is of crucial importance.

We need not live in the American Southwest (or any other particular place) to grasp the world-creating character of the horizon, its unique capacity to bring earth and sky into active contiguity with one another while respecting their differences as distinct cosmic regions. Just by looking at photographs of the earth taken from the moon, we see the globe of the earth horizoned against an all-encompassing sky. In these remarkable images—at once disturbing and inspiring—we observe the earth itself as a place of places, as a "basis body" for more particular bodies.[33] In fact, we observe the primal separation of Earth from Heaven, the differentiation of an ordered Cosmos out of Chaos. Before our eyes is something like an icon of Creation.

III

> The mountains rose, the valleys sank down to the place which thou didst appoint for them. Thou didst set a bound which they should not pass.
>
> —Psalm 104

Contrary to popular belief, 1 Genesis, the first Book of Moses, does not tell a story of creation ex nihilo. That it is believed to be such a story is a tribute not so much to misinterpretation as to the power of a certain cosmologic, which dictates that nothing *should* or *must* precede the act of creation. But the celebrated opening lines of Genesis suggest otherwise:

> In the beginning God created the heavens and the earth. The earth was without form and void, and darkness was upon the face of the deep; and the Spirit of God was moving over the face of the waters.[34]

Not only does "the deep"—*tehom,* a term to which we shall have occasion to return—preexist creation, but it already has a "face." The face itself is not superficial: it is the face "of the waters," that is, of something quite elemental, and it is determinate enough to be *moved over.* In the beginning, then, was an elemental mass having sufficient density and shape to be counterposed to the movement of the spirit (or, alternately, the "wind") of God. If the Deep is nothing, it is, like Chaos, the "nothing substantial," a strangely substantial nothing!

It is true that the earth is said to be "without form and void." Is this a reference to the absolute void that cosmological reasoning relentlessly posits? I think not. The void at stake here is the relative void of shapelessness—of something devoid of form. This becomes evident when the text adds, several lines later,

> And God said, "Let the waters under the heavens be gathered together into one place, and let the dry land appear." And it was so. God called the dry land Earth, and the waters that were gathered together he called Seas. And God saw that it was good. (Gen. 1:9–10)

This passage makes it clear that the first allusion to "earth" is to an indeterminate entity that gains its full identity only when it has become separated from the oceans and other waters. When it has become "dry land," it deserves the designation "Earth." From a preformative state, it has come into its own; and at just this moment, God celebrates the fact of its formation as something determinate: He "saw that it was good." It is notable that the latter clause is used for the first time at just this point in the text, that is to say, when the primordial act of distinguishing land from sea has occurred.

By this act, *two* places have been created, thereby illustrating a basic principle of cosmo-topo-logy: there is never merely *one* place anywhere, not even in the process of creation. It is as if cosmogony respected the general rule enunciated by Aristotle in another connection: "the minimum number, strictly speaking, is two."[35] To create in the first place is *eo ipso* to create two places. This principle is at work in the very first sentence of 1 Genesis ("God created the heavens *and* the earth"), and it recurs twice again even before the description of the separation of sea and land. First, God "separated the light from the darkness" (1:4), thereby creating two great domains that are not only temporal but spatial in character. Second, the creation of the "firmament," that is, the vault of the sky, or Heaven, calls for separating "the waters from the waters" (1:6), those of the sea from those of the sky. Two aqueous realms signify two distinct places for water to be.

In the space of a few lines and following the bivalent logic of place-creation, then, we witness a surprisingly complicated beginning of the known world. In effect, Genesis maintains that a twice redoubled doubling of place occurs in the course of creation. For Heaven to become separate from the Earth, the creation of the firmament requires the prior dissociation of two regions of water; and the earth, to be truly Earth, in turn requires a distinction of land from sea. No simple matter this! In particular: no lack of place to begin with!

Thus there is no creation *from* a void or creation *as* a void. God is not creating from a preexisting abyss of nothingness. Things are already around when He begins to create—things in the guise of elemental masses, the watery Deep, darkness upon the face of that Deep, the predeterminate earth. Nor does God empty Himself in a kenotic move to constitute a void within His own being. In the germinal account of Genesis there is neither void without nor void within.

In place of the void are places, and all the more so if regions count as places, as surely they must. Already extant are domains of deepness and darkness. Indeed, at play here is the Spirit of God, which in "moving over the face of the waters" must ineluctably be moving among places. For there is no movement without place. As Aristotle says, "There cannot be change without place,"[36] and movement is certainly a kind of change. God, in moving over the dark Deep, is already moving over a place as well as between places. He is moving, for example, between the beginning-place and the end-place of his own cosmogonic journey. These ur-places, though unnamed in the text, preexist the more particular places that *are* named.

In fact, we may distinguish three levels of place within the first chapter of Genesis: (1) the ur-places presupposed by the very activity of God Himself, as sources of His movements; (2) the elemental regions of darkness, the Deep, and the unformed Earth; and (3) the formed regions of Earth as dry land, the Seas as the waters that have been "gathered together into one place," and the regimes of Day and Night. It is clear that the Old Testament account gives us a picture of creation as arising in an already given plenitude of places; and it describes as well a certain cosmic progression from one place to another—or, more exactly, from one *kind* of place to another. Creation, in short, is not only *of* place (and of things stationed in places) but cannot occur *without* place, including its own place-of-creation. The act of creating takes place in place.

This is not, of course, the whole story. As creation continues, yet other sorts of places emerge. These subsequent or consequent places are progressively more definite in character. They include the places of the sun and the moon, "the two great lights" that "rule over the day and over the night and separate . . . the light from the darkness" (1:14–18); of the birds that "fly above the earth across the firmament of the heavens" (1:20); of sea monsters "with which the waters swarm" (1:21); of the "beasts of the earth" (1:25); of "every plant yielding seed which is upon the face of all the earth" (1:29); and of the human beings who are given dominion over all of these creatures and things" (1:26–28). When it is added in the second Book of Genesis that "a mist went up from the earth and watered the whole face of the ground" (2:6) and that "God planted a garden in Eden, in the east" (2:8), we attain a still more definite degree of place-determination, one that now includes quite particular places (i.e., patches of ground) that have proper names and even cardinal directions.

In the progression just sketched, a pattern of cosmogenesis emerges which is common to many theories of creation: rather than from no-place to place *simpliciter,* the movement is from less determinate to more determinate places. It is only a step farther to call for measurable place as well—as happens, for example, in Job.

Where were you when I laid the foundation of the earth?
  Tell me, if you have understanding.
Who determined its measurements—surely you know!
  Or who stretched the line upon it?
On what were its bases sunk,
  or who laid its cornerstone,
when the morning stars sang together,
  And all the sons of God shouted for joy?[37]

The origin of "geometry"—literally, earth-measurement (*geō-metria*)—lies in place: above all, in its ever more precise delimitation as natural boundaries give way to the imposed and regular configurations, the "limit-shapes," of the builder and the surveyor.[38] This is not to say that on this paradigm measuring is merely posterior to creation: it is itself an act of creation. *To measure is to create.* This bold equation will be repeated in other texts concerning creation, as we shall observe in one particular case in the next chapter.

For the moment, I want only to draw attention to the fact that in the inaugural creation text of the Judeo-Christian tradition, place is both ubiquitous and multifarious—and that its unfolding is even presented in a quasi-progressive (but not simply successive) manner. The void is evaded, and in its stead we find a proliferation of cosmogonically significant places, each of which is essential to the progress of the narrative of creation. Does this narrativized proliferation of places betray an effort to paper over the abyss of the void? If it does, it only repeats a gesture found elsewhere—beginning with the way we handle our own place-panic. For who can face the void? An absolute void cannot be faced (in either sense of this term). God Himself, as Genesis avers, can move only over a Deep that already possesses a face. He faces the Deep only insofar as its own face is already traced out upon its dark surface.

IV

> It gives as great a shock to the mind to think of pure nothing in any one place, as it does to think of it in all; and it is self-evident that there can be nothing in one place as well as in another, and so if there can be in one, there can be in all.
> —Jonathan Edwards, "Of Being"

Is this to say that cosmogonic accounts *never* begin expressly with a void? The citation from a Hopi creation myth that stands as an epigraph to this chapter shows that such a beginning indeed can be made. For the Hopi, "the first world," that is, the first state of the world, is precisely that of Tokpela, "endless space." Tokpela is conceived as an "immeasurable void" that has no beginning or end; no time, shape, or life. Once given the prospect of endless space, however, no time is wasted in the attempt to change that space into something less appallingly empty. The awesome void is just what creation must transmute—which is precisely what Taiowa, the Hopi creator-god, proceeds to do.

> Then he, the infinite, conceived the finite. First he created Sotuknang to make it manifest, saying to him, "I have created you, the first power and instrument as a person, to carry out my plan for life in endless space. I am your Uncle. You are my Nephew. Go now and lay out these universes in proper order so they may work harmoniously with one another according to my plan."
> Sotuknang did as he was commanded. From endless space he gathered that which was to be manifest as solid substance, molded it into forms.[39]

The task is so immense that Taiowa creates a younger and stronger person to undertake it: his nephew Sotuknang. To "lay out these universes in proper order" Sotuknang engages in an action of *gathering*. Just as in Genesis the waters are "gathered together in one place" (Gen. 1:9), so in the Hopi creation story solid substances or parts of the earth are gathered together and given form. In both cases, the giving of form entails the bestowal of place: *where else* are formed things to be? The cosmogonic gathering is in effect a formation of place. Thus, even if the beginning is characterized as a situation of no-place, the ineluctable nisus is toward place—and toward an ever-increasing specificity of place, its laying out in the right (and ultimately a measurable) order. If the void is not itself a place, it must become one.

Despite their considerable diversity, all the accounts of creation examined so far agree on one basic cosmo-axiom: only from place can created things come. The known universe, albeit originating in a void, evolved from place to place. It follows that creation is a process of progressive implacement.

V

We have observed, then, a set of quite diverse cosmogonic models. Place figures in each of these, though with important nuances of difference. Genesis begins from a diffusely regionalized place made ever more determinate by the several stages of creation. In the chaos model of Hesiod's *Theogony,* no preexisting regions are presumed—only the cosmomonstrosity of a primal Gap, whose action of scission brings about places of many sorts. Whereas scission in Genesis is subsequent to the initial state of things—acting to divide what is already there—separation itself is the first state in Hesiod's story: or, more exactly, the first state proves to be no state at all but an action of dissociation that is place-creative by its very nature. Much the same is true of the Navajo creation myth, which imputes to the fateful horizon between the disks of Sky and Earth a special cosmogonic significance. In the case of the Hopi legend, creation opens with a situation of endless space in which neither regions nor actions are possible. (Elsewhere, cosmic emptiness is recognized as a *second* state of the universe situated between the first beginning and the plenitude of creation proper.)[40] But the radical no-place of this inaugural moment in the Hopi myth is immediately succeeded by an act of deputized filling, a filling that recalls the gap-plugging presence of Eros, Kronos, and Zeus in the *Theogony.* Even apart from this remedial action, the cosmogonic void is not wholly devoid of place-properties in its aboriginal state. However empty it may be, it is still a place of, and for, creation. In it, from out of it, creation occurs—and first of all, in most cases, the creation of heaven (or sky) as a domain distinct from earth or sea.

There is no creation without place. This is so whether place is considered to preexist (as does the dark Deep in Genesis or the underworlds from which the primal mists arise in Navajo belief);[41] or is brought forth out of Chaos as one of "ten thousand creations" (as the Taoists would put it); or is an emptiness that, precisely *as* emptiness, is necessary to world-creation (as we see dramatically enacted in kenotic models of the self-emptying of a creator god); or is the very place of creation and, more particularly, of the creator (as in the case of the ancient Babylonian account).[42] Whether it is presumed or produced, given as simultaneous with creation or subsequent to it, place figures throughout. It is the continuing subtext of narratives of creation, the figured bass of their commingled melody.

VI

> In being said—or not said—the void is voided.
> —Edmond Jabès, *The Book of*
> *Resemblances*

But the void, the *strict* void, does not vanish easily, not even under the most unrelenting efforts to eliminate it. It keeps returning, in creation myths as in personal life. The Maori people speak of "the limitless space-filling void,"[43] while the Zuñi point to "void desolation everywhere"[44] as the original state of things. Anaximander's notion of *to apeiron,* "the Boundless," is tantamount to "the Placeless"—given that places, even cosmically vast places, require boundaries of some sort. The notion of the Boundless anticipates modern ideas of infinite space that expressly exclude places from their ambit (or if including them, then only as indifferent areas). From the perspective of place, to be without bounds of any kind, to be limitlessly empty, is to enter into dire straits indeed: "straits" despite the fact that there are no effective enclosures in these troubling unlimited waters.[45] In cosmogonies that posit the utter void, water itself may not yet exist—not even in the form of the Deep, primal mists, or the "chaos-fluid" posited in the Egyptian Book of the Dead:

I am (bowl   lord all   fluid   owl) ATUM   completing-rising
                           of all
the only one
in Nun/chaos-fluid/[46]

Without an aqueous life-inducing element, and especially without its separation from earth or from sky, we reach that extremity of emptiness that seems to be sine qua non for those aporetic cosmogonies in which creation must come "from nothing." About this extremity, this zero point, we must ask, do we here finally encounter a void so radical that it cannot offer place in any sense whatsoever?

In this aporia—this literal im-passe—Aristotle makes a most puzzling claim: "The theory that the void exists involves the existence of place; one could [even] define void as place bereft of body."[47] If Aristotle is right, the void itself is not without place, and may be itself a kind of place. Difficult as it may be to conceive, anxiety provoking as it certainly is to experience, even the strictest void is not unrelated to place. At the very least, the void may possess certain residual place-properties: for example, "*bereft of* body." To be devoid of body is nevertheless to be *capable of containing a body*—even if the body in question does not yet exist, or no longer exists. Aristotle here qualifies Archytas: to be (a body) is to be in place, but there can also be a (void) place without (any) body. Although void and place usually are construed as antonymic, they may not be antinomic: they may share in some common *nomos*, or law, some shared structure.

   What void and place share is the common property of being *the arena for the appearance of bodies* (and thus for the events of which bodies form part). But while a place is the immediate arena for such appearance—a body appears precisely *in a particular place*—the void is the scene for this kind of place. As a precreationist entity, the void is empty of place primarily and of bodies secondarily. It is empty of the place that is empty of bodies. Thus we need to emend Aristotle's dictum: not merely is void "place bereft of body" but "void is bereft of place that is bereft of body." The void is doubly bereft. As a scene, it is an empty stage that is not yet specified as to places *or* bodies. ("Scene" in its origins meant an empty tent or booth before it came to signify a theatrical stage.)

   Regarded as a scene of places and things to come, the void may thus play a positive and not a merely nugatory role in cosmogony. It figures precisely as the scene named "Tokpela" (endless space) by the Hopi, or as "Taaora," literally "immensity" or "void," by the ancient inhabitants of Hawaii, the Tuamotuans.[48] Neither of these void-scenes is an inert pregiven entity. According to Hopi tradition, Taiowa the Creator immediately occupies Tokpela; indeed, far from inertly preexisting, the endless immensity of Tokpela is said to exist already *in Taiowa's mind* and thus to be part of an active agency from the start. Tokpela is "an immeasurable void that had its beginning and end, time, shape, and life in the mind of Taiowa the Creator."[49] Conversely, for the Tuamotuan people the creator-god exists *in the void,* thereby assuring its dynamism from within: "It is said that Kiho dwelt in the Void. It [is] said that Kiho dwelt beneath the foundations of Havaiki [i.e., in a particular place] which was called the Black-gleamless-realm-of-Havaiki."[50] To dwell in the void in this immanent manner is to dwell in the active scene of creation, the scene of what-is-to-come. It is to dwell *in the void as place-giving;* to be placed in the void. The lines that follow in the Tuamotuan epic spell out this curious topology.

   > That place wherein Kiho dwelt was said to be the Non-existence-of-the-land; the
   > name of that place was the Black-gleamless-realm-of-Havaiki.
   > It was there that Kiho dwelt; indeed, in that place he created all things whatsoever.
   > Hereafter [I give] the names of his dwelling places.
   >
   > Kiho dwelt in his heaven at the nadir of the Night-realm.
   > Kiho dwelt in his heaven in the Black-gleamless-realm.
   > Kiho dwelt in his heaven in the Many-proportioned-realm-of-night.
   >
   > These places were situated within the Night-sphere.[51]

This night-sphere of creation is a scene of becoming-place; it is a "many-proportioned" arena of possible places-to-come. The cosmogonic void, far from being place-indifferent or simply place-bereft, proves to be place-productive, proliferating into place after place.

The Tuamotuan text illustrates a principle that can be designated "topo-reversal." Void is posited as no-place, only to be succeeded by the immediate positing of place. Or more exactly: no-place is succeeded by something that, precisely as *something,* brings places with it. Nowhere is this reversal so dramatically evident as in a Jicarilla Apache creation tale.

> In the beginning nothing was here where the world now stands; there was no ground, no earth—nothing but Darkness, Water, and Cyclone. There were no people living. Only the Hactcin [personifications of the powers of objects and natural forces] existed. It was a lonely place.[52]

Here the reversal is marked by the sudden transition from "nothing" to "nothing but." While the first stage represents a radically empty state, the second populates it with at least three natural things and several personified forces. The volte-face occurs even within one and the same sentence, and is expanded in subsequent sentences. Saturation is by no means reached—the place in question is still quite "lonely"—but the changeover from nothing at all to just barely something is cosmogonically progressive. Nonplacement gives way to implacement: cyclones, darkness, and water come clinging to their cosmic locations.

The topo-reversal can move in the opposite direction as well: from something to nothing. In the Han dynasty text *Huai-nan Tzu,* the Great Beginning gives way to emptiness. Or else something and nothing may be considered as coexisting. Thus Chuang Tzu writes, "There is being. There is nonbeing."[53] An ancient Mayan text proclaims that in the beginning "there was nothing standing; only the calm water, the placid sea, alone and tranquil. Nothing existed."[54] Nothing stands—and yet water and sea are already standing there. The chiasmatic turn whereby even a minimal nothing-but or an "only" (i.e., a bare something) is denied existence, yet is nevertheless *given* existence, also receives expression in one of the Upanishads: "In the beginning this world was merely non-being. It was existent."[55] To *exist* as *non*being: a self-complicating assertion of convoluted cosmologic.

Despite such reversals and twists, indeed *through* them, we witness the persistence of place in the face of the nothing—a nothing that one might have assumed to be the very death of place. Whether as the sheer something of a "Black-gleamless-realm" or as the still sheerer nonbeing that nevertheless *exists* (and thus literally "stands-out"), place abides. In the context of cosmogony—that is to say, in an account of the *becoming* of the world—*there is no place for no-place.* Dearth of place, even literal nonplace, we may acknowledge: such is the "lonely place" of the Apache creation myth. But this is not tantamount to the death of place, no-place-at-all: rather than dealing with its demise, cosmogony has to do with the birth of place itself.

Even the utter void, then, retains the dynamic property of being a scene of emergence, a proscenium on which things can arise as taking place and as having their own place. Much as we have found that chaos is not entirely empty of form, so we now discover the empty no-place of the void to have more shape and force than we might have imagined. Indeed, if chaos can be regarded as predeterminate place, the void is best construed as the scene of emergent place. Cosmogonically considered, the void is on its way to becoming ever more place-definite. It is the scene of world-creation and thus the basis of an increasingly coherent and densely textured place-world.

VII

The foregoing construal of the void does not retrieve it for place. Indeed, it deprives void of place—particular place—and place of void. But it makes room for the *possibility* of place in the void by maintaining that the void may itself *become* devoid of its own initially unimplaced and unimplacing character. By speaking of "possibility" and of "become," I am keeping the void within a cosmogonic context. It is important to retain this context in the face of the temptation to offer a transcendental deduction of place as that which *has to be* presupposed if experience or knowledge of certain kinds is to be possible. This temptation must be resisted. The only thing that can be deduced from a transcendental argument—of a Kantian sort—is the presupposition of *empty space.* Such space, especially when located in (or, more exactly, *as*) a form of intuition, is not only mental in status; more seriously still, it is a merely objective posit, a present-at-hand entity. As such—as categorial, or *vorhanden* in Heidegger's nomenclature—it fails to capture what is specific to place, namely, the capacity to hold and situate things, to give them a local habitation. Such holding action proffers something ready-to-hand (*zuhanden*), something concretely palpable, to which attachment can be made. This palpability belongs properly to place and not to space.[56]

A deductive, relentless cosmologic is driven to presuppose an empty and boundless no-place—not yet named "space" in many mythic accounts—that is as abstract and barren of holding-locating properties as is space on the modern conception. To parry this cosmologism (whereby an entity is posited as cosmically necessary yet is unable to play any constructive role), the void is quickly filled with various places. Navajo cosmogony lays down places of emergence, "underworlds" that are both located (*under* the visible upperworld) and locating (of all that is *on* and *in* the upperworld). These subworlds are concrete holding environments that do what the void, taken by itself alone, cannot do: they offer palpable implacement to things. The advantage in this literally topocosmic move is that the role of place is made central and explicit from the beginning. It need not be inferred as something surreptitiously supposed. The transcendental deduction of space stands instructed by a cosmogonic espousal of place.

By interpreting the void as a scene of emergent implacement, we pursue a middle path, one that is neither covertly transcendental nor expressly mythical. This middle way regards the void as the scene of the becoming of place. To take up this view is neither to transform the strict void into infinite isotropic space nor to populate it in advance with determinate mythical places. Neither the indeterminate nor the determinate but the predeterminate is what is cosmogonically formative. The strict void is avoided by recognizing the void as *already on the way to place.* Such a void is not presupposed, much less deduced as cosmologically or epistemologically necessary. It is posited in the first place—not *as* the first place but as *the first becoming of place itself.* Just as the space posited in a transcendental deduction shows itself capable of providing particular places, the void of cosmogonic accounts is on its way to the determination of particular places. The void makes provision for places. It is place in its provisionality.

In pursuing this last line of thought, am I not papering over the abyss of the cosmogonic void by my own discursive considerations? If so, I shall not have been the first philosopher to have averted place-panic by proposing the massive preplacement of the world-in-the-making. In the next chapter, we shall witness Plato doing something similar. In the face of the void, and in the absence of the deducibility of space, recourse to place becomes tempting indeed.

Yet, even apart from concerted (and quite possibly defensive) steps to assure the abiding prepresence of place, in the end we may take a certain comfort in the very void itself. We have seen that even in the face of the utter void, of no-thingness itself, place is already prefigured. Place configures and situates the face of the dark Deep. Even a cosmogonically rigorous account that sets down no-place as a necessary beginning point—or one that discovers chaos at the origin—is never without the resources of place. At no place is such an account altogether destitute of these resources. Even the void yields place: if it is *now* bereft of body and place (i.e., is no-place for no-body), it promises to give way to both body and place *then,* after the work of creation has been done.

In fact, as we reflect on all the cosmogenetic moments in which place is of import (moments, however, not arranged in any strict chronological sequence), we begin to savor a different prospect. This is a prospect of an aboriginal preplacement, and an ongoing implacement, of the created world. Whether as nonbeing that exists, or as chaos on the way to cosmos, or as an orderly progression of stages of creation, cosmogenesis creates (or discovers) place at the origin, thereby becoming topogenesis. *Cosmos* and *topos* conjoin in the becoming of the topocosm.

Shuzanghu's question to his wife, "How long must we live without a place to rest our feet?" was posed when "at first there was neither Earth nor Sky." But once Earth and Sky have separated from each other—once creation has begun, as it always already has—the answer to Shuzanghu's question is evident: there will be somewhere to rest your feet if only you will look in the right place— in the first place. As Aristotle assures us that "time will not fail,"[57] so Shuzanghu can be certain that place will not lack.

2
Mastering the Matrix
The *Enuma Elish* and Plato's *Timaeus*

That which is far off, and exceeding deep, who can find it out?
—Ecclesiastes 7:24

[Marduk] crossed the sky to survey the infinite distance; he stationed himself above Apsu, that Apsu built by Nudimmud over the old abyss which now he surveyed, measuring out and marking in.
—*Enuma Elish*

Before that, all these kinds were without proportion or measure. . . . Such being their nature at the time when the ordering of the universe was taken in hand, the god then began by giving them a distinct configuration by means of shapes and numbers.
—Plato, *Timaeus* 53b

Everyone says that place is something; but [Plato] alone attempted to say what it was.
—Aristotle, *Physics* Book 4

I

Once we admit that the panic-producing idea of the void is always (in advance) a matter of place—and is thus not reducible to the daunting nothingness, the strict no-place, that occasions the panic—we must face a second major issue. This is the propensity not merely to fill the void as a way of allaying anxiety but, more especially, to *master* the void. To master is not to bring into being in the first place but to control and shape that which has already been brought into existence. It is still a matter of creation, at least in that sense of creation inherent in the Hebrew word *bará* used in I Genesis: a word whose cognate meanings include "to carve" (e.g., the tip of an arrow) or "to cut up" (e.g., a carcass).[1] What is now at stake is not creation ex nihilo—an action we have discovered to be as rare as it is problematical—but creation *ex datis,* "out of the given." Yet how is creation carried forward once we are willing to acknowledge that the void has content, that something is already given in and with (and even *as*) the void itself?

What is pregiven is usually considered to be material, a matter of matter. But in ancient and traditional cosmogonies, "matter" does not signify anything hard and fast—anything rigorously *physical* in the manner of determinate and resistant "material objects." On the contrary: matter connotes *matrix,* one of its cognates and certainly something material (even if not something completely definite in its constitution). In its literal sense of "uterus" or "womb," the matrix is the generatrix of created things: their *mater* or material precondition. As such, it is the formative phase of things—things that will become more fully determinate in the course of creation. Vis-à-vis the generative matrix, the task of creation becomes that of crafting and shaping, ultimately of controlling, what is unformed or preformed in the matrix itself. Creation becomes a matter of mastering matter.

Just as chaos has proved to be a place, so a cosmogonic matrix is a place as well. Beyond its strictly anatomical sense, matrix means "a place or medium in which something is bred, produced, or developed," "a place or point of origin and growth." In the matter of the matrix, place remains primary. As the *Oxford English Dictionary* informs us, the definitions just cited are traceable to at least the middle of the sixteenth century A.D. But they are seen to possess a still more ancient lineage if we reflect that a text such as Genesis opens with the description of a state of affairs that is neither chaos nor void but a matrix: "Darkness was upon the face of the Deep." As the initial moment of cosmogenesis, the dark Deep is a material, or more precisely an *elemental,* matrix. The world starts with an "embedding or enclosing mass" (in yet another *OED* definition of "matrix") that is aqueous in character; it starts with "the waters" as the generative matrix of things-to-be, things-to-come.

We may trace things even farther back. *Tehom,* the Hebrew word for "deep [waters]," itself stems from Tiamat, the Mesopotamian proper name for that primordial oceanic force figuring at the very beginning of the *Enuma Elish,* a tale of creation that predates the reign of Hammurabi (ca. 1900 B.C.). Tiamat is in place as an elemental matrix from time immemorial, and therefore creation must begin with her antecedent and massive presence.

When there was no heaven,
no earth, no height, no depth, no name,
when Apsu was alone,

the sweet water, the first begetter; and Tiamat
  the bitter water, and that
return to the womb, her Mummu,
    When there were no gods—

    When sweet and bitter
mingled together, no reed was plaited, no rushes
  muddied the water,
the gods were nameless, natureless, futureless, then
  from Apsu and Tiamat
in the waters gods were created, in the waters
  silt precipitated.[2]

Unlike Genesis, the Babylonian text does not mention earth, not even an earth "without form and void." Nor do we find any gods—certainly not "God," or Yahweh—much less any words by which a god could summon up creation. In this nameless scene, no one says "Let there be light."

On the other hand (and here in contrast with Hesiod's *Theogony*),[3] in the *Enuma Elish* there is no chaos to start with, nor is there any primal separation between heaven and earth. All that *is* present is water: two kinds of water, salt and fresh, "Tiamat" and "Apsu." Even Mummu, the originary mist, is aqueous. All begins with/in water. The gods themselves are created from it: creation occurs without creators. Instead of arising from a decisive act of scission, creation takes place with the imperceptible mixing of waters; everything begins with the *merging of two regions of water in an elemental commixture*. For Apsu and Tiamat are less the names of gods than of primeval places; they are cosmogonic place-names. "Bitter water" is one kind of place and "sweet water" another kind of place. When they merge, they create a common place—a matrix—for more particular places, including the places of particular gods.

The silty mass precipitated in the intermixed waters is the first definite place to emerge from the Apsu-Tiamat matrix, and it brings with it the naming of the first four gods. Place and name are here coeval.

  Lahmu and Lahamu,
were named; they were not yet old,
  not yet grown tall
When Anshar and Kishar overtook them both,
  the lines of sky and earth
stretched where horizons meet to separate
cloud from silt.[4]

From the place of silt, "primeval sediment,"[5] comes the separation of earth and sky. Lahmu and Lahamu, barely distinguishable from each other as names (except insofar as the former is male, the latter female), are overtaken by the

more distinctly differentiated figures of Anshar and Kishar, gods of the horizons of sky and earth, respectively. The comparatively belated distinction of
earth from sky constitutes separation between heaven and earth that we have
observed elsewhere—most notably in Genesis, where God "separated the waters which were under the firmament from the waters which were above the
firmament." Unlike the Old Testament account, however, the *Enuma Elish*
explicitly builds the feature of horizon lines into the proper names Anshar and
Kishar, remarking oxymoronically that these gods are found "where horizons
meet to separate cloud from silt." The oxymoron is merited: every horizon at
once conjoins and separates. In particular, the horizon at land's end both holds
earth and sky together as two contiguous domains of the same surrounding
space and teases them apart as two conclusively different regions.

That Anshar and Kishar are indeed decisively different places is confirmed
by the fact that the immediately following generations replicate the earth/sky
distinction that these two gods embody. Anu, son of Anshar, is the god of
"empty heaven," and he begets Nudimmud-Ea, god of sweet waters and of a
wisdom that is "wider than heaven's horizon."[6] Nudimmud-Ea in turn slays
his aqueous ancestor Apsu when the latter schemes with Tiamat to destroy the
clamorous gods who have been born to them. In so doing, Ea "sounded the
coil of chaos and against it devised the artifice of the universe."[7] Then, in an
action that would not have surprised the Freud of *Totem and Taboo,* Nudimmud-Ea builds a memorial to Apsu.

> When Ea had bound Apsu, he killed him. . . . Now that his triumph was com-
> pleted, in deep peace he rested, in his holy palace Ea slept. Over the abyss, the
> distance, he built his house and shrine and there magnificently he lived with his
> wife Damkina.[8]

The "artifice of the universe" here appears in the form of Ea's palace-shrine,
the first constructed dwelling place. The construction itself takes place over
an abyss, and by this very fact it is a memorial to Apsu: *apsu* is the Semitic
equivalent of Sumerian abzu, signifying "deep abyss," "ocean," and "outermost limit." To build over an abyss is not only to create cosmos out of chaos.
It is to bring constructed or "devised" place out of an unconstructed material
matrix, and thereby to memorialize the matrix itself.[9]

It is out of this same abyssal matrix that Marduk, the ultimate architect of
creation and the nemesis of Tiamat, is born from Ea and Damkina.

> In that room, at the point of decision where what is to come is predetermined,
> he was conceived, the most sagacious, the one from the first most absolute in
> action.
> In the deep abyss he was conceived, Marduk was made in the heart of the
> apsu, Marduk was created in the heart of the holy apsu.[10]

To be conceived *in* the abyss is to be generated in the matrix of creation—"in that room" where "what is to come is predetermined." The depth of this matricial abyss is resonant with the depth of Tiamat, the depth of her womb (she is continually bringing forth new gods and monsters) and the depth of her oceanic being (Tiamat means literally "primeval waters," including stretches of water, sea, or lake). "The coil of Tiamat," the Sumerian gods admit, "is too deep for us to fathom."[11]

It is precisely because Tiamat's coil—her troublesome tumult—is too deep to fathom that Marduk must rise up against her. For Marduk can only deal with *measurable* depth. His confrontation with Tiamat is thus foredoomed: their difference is literally "cosmic." The confrontation itself comes when "he surveyed her scanning the Deep."[12] He surveys *her*—makes her into an object of conquest—while she is embroiled in scanning something that never can become an object and with which she is ultimately identified. Precisely as an amorphous nonobject, that is, as herself the Deep, Tiamat can be conquered in a cosmomachia wherein the architectonic triumphs over the unstructured and the mastery of the matrix is asserted. If Ea is the first architect in this cosmogony—"archi-tect" signifying "first builder"—Marduk is the master builder.[13]

Marduk proves himself master of the matrix by brutally crushing Tiamat in battle. He "shot the arrow that split the belly, that pierced the gut and cut the womb."[14] Marduk's arrow, symbol of his phallic manhood, invades the womb-matrix: death penetrates to the seat of life. Only by destroying an organic matrix, source of generation, can the inorganic work of building proceed. As Paul Ricoeur remarks apropos of Marduk, it is "by disorder that disorder is overcome; it is by violence that the youngest of the gods establishes order."[15]

As master builder—as "Lord of the Land," as "Son-of-the-Sun"[16]—Marduk must construct *out of* something: nothing ex nihilo here! He finds his building materials in Tiamat's slain body, whose corporeal depths become the (re)source of the civilized cosmos.

> The lord rested; he gazed at the huge body, pondering how to use it, what to create from the dead carcass. He split it apart like a cockle-shell; with the upper half he constructed the arc of sky, he pulled down the bar and set a watch on the waters, so they should never escape.[17]

In this violent action—which takes place precisely as *bará,* or cutting up—Marduk repeats the initial separation between Anshar and Kishar by creating the horizon line or "bar" that distinguishes sky from sea. To "set a watch on the waters" is to take a definitive step toward delimiting them by placing a cosmic boundary over them. Such delimitation is place-making in its power—as is the creation of the "arc of the sky," a bowlike outer limit that makes the sky into a region of its own. Thanks to this new place-setting, we no longer need to refer to the open sky as "Anu," or to the shared horizons of earth and heaven as "Anshar" and "Kishar." The evolution from primeval elements to gods has given way to cosmic places no longer requiring mythical names.[18] But the story goes on.

> He crossed the sky to survey the infinite distance; he stationed himself above apsu, that apsu built by Nuddimud over the old abyss which now he surveyed, measuring out and marking in.
>
> He stretched the immensity of the firmament, he made Esharra, the Great Palace, to be its earthly image, and Anu and Enlil and Ea had each their right stations.[19]

Following the creation of gods earlier in the epic—theogony proper—we are now presented with the creation of *places for the gods,* their "right stations." Through Marduk's actions, the gods "are assigned their places."[20] Once again, topogenesis follows from cosmogenesis. As a condition of this locatory action, the "infinite distance" of the abyss must be surveyed and the "immensity of the firmament" stretched out. To stretch out is the corporeal equivalent of visual survey: in both cases, the full scope of something is swept out in advance, "sized up" as we say, by a preliminary action of literal circumspection. To do this, Marduk must establish a stable position from which to do the stretching and sizing. Such a position is found in the station assumed by Marduk "above *apsu*": above the abyss. His stationing there is in effect a double superpositioning: first over Ea's house and shrine and then over "the old abyss" of the elemental Apsu, an action now surveyed in its infinite extent. More than survey is at stake here. Marduk also sets to work by "measuring out and marking in" the abyss. He moves to mensuration, a measurement at once spatial and temporal.

> He projected positions for the Great Gods conspicuous in the sky, he gave them a starry aspect as constellations; he measured the year, gave it a beginning and an end, and to each month of the twelve three rising stars.[21]

Just as the gods are given spatial positions, so temporal positions are also marked out—positions primarily taken by the sun and the moon in their respective cycles.[22] In addition to these positions (which are in effect visible and countable places), Marduk bestows basic directionalities on the new world: "Through her ribs he opened gates in the east and west, and gave them strong bolts on the right and left; and high in the belly of Tiamat he set the zenith."[23] An entire landscape is drawn out from the dismembered Deep.

> Then Marduk considered Tiamat. He skimmed spume from the bitter sea, heaped up the clouds, spindrift of wet and wind and cooling rain, the spittle of Tiamat.

With his own hands from the steaming mist he spread the clouds. He pressed hard down the head of water, heaping mountains over it, opening springs to flow: Euphrates and Tigris rose from her eyes, but he closed the nostrils and held back their springhead.

He piled huge mountains on her paps and through them drove water-holes to channel the deep sources; and high overhead he arched her tail, locked-in to the wheel of heaven; the pit was under his feet, between was the crotch, the sky's fulcrum. Now the earth had foundations and the sky its mantle.[24]

Marduk here creates the very topography of the earth, its atmosphere and terrain, from the megabody of Tiamat. Originally a sea region, this gigantic body is displaced and transmuted into the created earth, an earth no longer hanging in the abyss but endowed finally with firm "foundations."

The last two things to be fashioned by Marduk are human beings and their dwelling places. It is striking that the latter are created *before* the former—as if to say that housing is a precondition of being human. Ea is employed as architect of temples and in particular of the city of Babylon.[25] Humankind is then created out of the sacrificial blood of Kingu, Tiamat's second spouse and the captain of her monstrous forces. It is at this point that Marduk makes his strongest claim to be a creator-god.

Blood to blood
I join,
blood to bone
I form
an original thing,
its name is MAN,
aboriginal man
is mine in making.[26]

Despite this possessive and self-congratulating proclamation—and others like it earlier[27]—Marduk is not altogether omnipotent in his creative powers. He certainly does not create anything out of *nothing*. Humankind, his proudest *ens creatum,* is created out of the blood of a preexisting god: even here, he "moulded matter."[28] Marduk does not bring forth matter out of the nothing of nonmatter: "From the wreck of Tiamat's rout, from the stuff of fallen gods he made mankind."[29] Everything is created out of the body of Tiamat—a body that is the primal stuff of creation.

Tiamat's body is not only primal. It is inexhaustible—so much so that it is not entirely consumed in the course of creation. At the very end of the *Enuma Elish* a propitiatory prayer implores

let her recede into the future
far-off from man-kind

till time is old, keep her
for ever absent.[30]

Tiamat may have been "disappeared" from the current scene of creation—her
intact body does not survive—but she is not completely vanquished. Her matter, her matrix, persists. Any subsequent act of creation will have to draw
upon it.

    N. K. Sandars, the English translator of the *Enuma Elish,* is certainly right
to claim that in this epic "matter is eternal, [and] Tiamat and Apsu provide,
from within themselves, the material of the whole universe; a universe which
will evolve into ever greater complexity."[31] But it does not follow from this
(as Sandars also claims) that "in the Babylonian poem there is, strictly speaking, *no creation at all.*"[32] As we have seen abundantly from Sandars's own
translation, creation takes place, indeed it occurs continually, throughout the
poem. The creation itself, however, is subject to two constraints. First, it is
always a creation *from something,* that is, from a material matrix (and in particular Tiamat's own body). Second, it is a creation primarily *of places.* The
evolution of the created world into "ever greater complexity" is an evolution
into ever more particular kinds of places, as the world becomes increasingly
habitable for humankind.

    In fact, the *Enuma Elish* proposes three major stages of creation, each of
which is distinctively place-specific. (1) To begin with, we are presented with
a watery world composed of two fluids, sweet and bitter, in intimate conjunction. From this aqueous admixture the early gods emerge—gods of the horizons of sky and earth, of the waters of the earth, and of the empty heaven.
Theogony occurs as a differentiation of regions out of the primal scene of
parental intercourse between Apsu and Tiamat. (2) Places of antagonism and
conflict supervene as an Oedipal drama is enacted among the gods: Ea kills
Apsu, and Marduk slaughters Tiamat. (3) Finally, the creation of the cosmos
per se happens in and through Tiamat's hulking carcass as the place-of-creation. Marduk, assuming his preordained role as "King of the cosmos,"[33] constructs an ordered universe in which everything, gods and heavenly bodies,
earth and human beings, has its proper place. "His glory touched the abyss"[34]
by virtue of the fact that he builds elaborately over the abyss itself. He fills it
in with the plenary presences of particular places.

    Throughout the *Enuma Elish,* place figures as a generative matrix. Al-
though there is one reference to the "void" and two references to "chaos" in
the text, each of these occurs as a retrospective interpretation of what has
already taken place.[35] What actually takes place, that is, arises *as place,* occurs
in the form of a matrix—or, more exactly, of place-as-matrix. Just as there is
no strict void at the start of this cosmogony (the void in question is the relative
void of a not-yet-existent earth; but waters already exist), so there is no genuine chaos either: Tiamat is fluid but not chaotic. Nor is she disorderly—except

when routed by Marduk![36] Taken on her own terms, she is an orderly being: orderly enough to give rise, thanks to Marduk's eventual shaping actions, to the cosmos, the ordered world.

Order, and especially the order of place, is nascent in the matrix. Not just at the stage of elemental waters but also at the subsequent stages of conflict and creation, place occurs as matrix. Indeed, creation itself arises in the very place of destruction, the bloody scene of Marduk's res gestae: "The creative act, which distinguishes, separates, measures, and puts in order, is inseparable from the criminal act that puts an end to the life of the oldest gods, [and is] inseparable from a deicide inherent in the divine."[37] In the final stage of this cosmogony, the two previous matrices, the elemental and the destructive, give way to the built matrix inherent in Marduk's construction of a fully ordered world from the materials furnished by Tiamat's dead body. A superfetation of gods, goddesses, and monsters from Tiamat's womb-matrix is replaced by a superproduction of human beings and buildings on Marduk's phallogonic part: continual birthing gives way to assiduous architectural ordering.[38] Instead of void or chaos, everywhere there is plenitude and place, a plenitude of places, indeed plenitude-as-place, arranged as an ascending series of ever more specific matrices.[39]

And there is, to end with, the place of *re*enactment. For the *Enuma Elish* was recited at the beginning of the New Year festival at Babylon. It was recited not just anywhere in Babylon but "in a particular place, the inner room or holy of holies of the god Marduk, where his statue lived throughout the year."[40] This room was regarded as identical with the Ubshukinna, the Chamber of Destiny wherein Marduk was proclaimed "Great Lord of the Universe."[41] The Ubshukinna, too, is a matrix—a matrix of reenactment. In the complete ceremony, actors staged the combat between Marduk and Tiamat, the officiating priest crying out, "May Marduk continue to conquer Tiamat and to shorten her days!" More than a mere representation or recollection of aboriginal confrontation was at issue in this ritualized performance. The reenacted combat brought the world, as it was entering a new year, from a state of perilous preorder or nonorder, more radical than disorder, back to a renewed state of order. As Eliade remarks,

> This commemoration of the Creation was in fact a *reactualization* of the cosmogonic act. . . . The battle between two groups of actors . . . [re]actualized the cosmogony. The mythical events became *present* once again. . . . The combat, the victory, and the Creation took place *at that instant, hic et nunc.*[42]

To this we need only add that the reactualized events also took place *at that place,* Marduk's inner room at Babylon. Much like Tiamat's own fertile body, this room served as a womb for continual rebirth—and not just as a scene of destruction and creation. The generative and the architectural, the primal matrix and the master builder, otherwise so fiercely antagonistic, combined forces in a common room of reenactment.

II

Much like Marduk, the Demiurge in Plato's *Timaeus* has the unenviable task of converting an originally refractory space into a domain of domesticated places. Just as concertedly "male" as Marduk, the Platonic power figure substitutes the straight lines of geometry for the lethal arrows of pitched combat. But in both instances, a precosmic "female" body is at once the source and the limit of creation, and its massive preexistence demonstrates that the intervening god is far from omnipotent. Both epics make it clear that creation takes place only under certain circumstances—precisely those embodied in the hulk, the heft, of the world-body as it is initially given. Creation must occur *in* and *with* this body, which Plato names Necessity (*anankē*)—and also Space (*chōra*).

Space, then, is what *must* be there in the beginning, even before the act of creation occurs. In this respect, Plato only formalizes what we have found to be true in many previous accounts: the necessity of preexisting spaces (i.e., places, regions) for the occurrence of creation. For whatever comes to be must "come to be in a certain place."[43] Compared with such spatial necessity, time is secondary in status—merely a "moving *image* of eternity"[44] that is devised by the Demiurge to keep track of the circular motions of the heavens. No more than in the first stanzas of the *Enuma Elish* is time essential to the primal state of the Platonic universe. In both cases, time is a distinctly *late* addition to the scene of creation. What matters first and foremost is the fate of space, its original standing and its subsequent vicissitudes.

Plato also uses the term "Receptacle" to designate the pregiven space with which the Demiurge must begin. As "the 'nurse' of all Becoming,"[45] the Receptacle is no less deep, and no less fertile, than Tiamat. And it is no less maternal, since both the mythic and the philosophic entities require that creation involve a return to the womb, the womb of Nature (*phusis*) itself. It is altogether by and in the Receptacle construed as "mother"[46] that the phallogonic paternal action of the Demiurge occurs—occurs within a matrix.

> It never departs at all from its own character; since it is always receiving all things, and never in any way whatsoever takes on any character that is like any of the things that enter it: *by nature it is there as a matrix for everything*, changed and diversified by the things that enter it.[47]

The Platonic matrix is not, however, strictly material in character. Although it takes on material qualities, it is not itself composed of matter. As exhibiting or reflecting these qualities, it is more like a mirror of the physical than a physical thing itself.[48] It has no qualities of its own, for, if it did, it could not be altogether receptive of the qualities of the things that occupy it, nor would it reflect them faithfully: "that which is to receive in itself all kinds must be free from all characters" (50e). Thus we cannot even characterize the receptive matrix as aqueous—as we are certainly encouraged to do at the beginning of the *Enuma Elish* and in Genesis. In fact, none of the four elemental qualities can be said to characterize the Platonic matrix: "the mother and Receptacle of what has come to be visible and otherwise sensible must not be called earth or air or fire or water" (51a). If the Sumerian and Old Testament matrices are expressly elemental, this is no longer possible in the Greek instance. As preelemental, Space or the Receptacle is "a nature invisible and characterless" (51b). Yet the Receptacle is neither a void nor placeless.

The Receptacle not a Void. Plato's primary opponents in the *Timaeus* are the ancient Atomists, who held that cosmogenesis occurs by the interaction of discrete bits of matter within a circumambient empty space (*kenon*). Empty space itself possesses no predetermined routes, much less any qualities of its own. Nor does it possess places or regions; in its radical placelessness, it is a prime candidate for what I have called the "strict void" and "no-place."[49] In contrast with this model, the Receptacle is richly plenary. The only emptiness it knows occurs in the form of the tiny interstices at the edges of the regular figures that come to fill it out.[50] Neither outside itself (for there is nothing *outside* the Receptacle) nor within itself is there any sheer emptiness.[51]

The Receptacle not Placeless. The Receptacle "*appears* to have different qualities at different times" (50c; my emphasis). To appear at all requires a *place-of-appearance.* In other words, the Receptacle, even if it has no place of its own (i.e., being Space itself, it is not located in some more extensive space), offers place to sensible qualities. Just as the initial state of things in the *Enuma Elish* is place-providing, so the Receptacle proffers place, thereby "providing a situation [*hedran*] for all things that come into being."[52] Such place-provision occurs for both formal and substantive reasons.

(1) *Formally,* even sensible qualities (and a fortiori the material bodies they will inhabit) must be exhibited *somewhere.* F. M. Cornford remarks that "the Receptacle is not that 'out of which' [*ex hou*] things are made; it is that 'in which' [*en hō*] qualities appear, as fleeting images are seen *in* a mirror."[53] Plato echoes Archytas here, and even seems to be paraphrasing him when he says that not just appearances but "anything that is must needs be in some place and occupy some room. . . . [W]hat is not somewhere in earth or heaven is nothing" (52b). Some kind of place must therefore always be on hand— *and already on hand within the Receptacle itself.* But what sort of place is this?

We have just seen that, in contrast with the body of Tiamat, the Receptacle cannot be a strictly material locus of creation, a physical realm of the sort that is at stake when Marduk "piled huge mountains on her paps and through them drove water-holes." Intrinsically characterless, the Receptacle can contain no features comparable to mountains or water holes. Not only must it not be designated as "earth" or "water," but, Plato adds shrewdly, it does not even consist of "any of their compounds or components" (51a). Of what then does it consist? The answer is *regions,* that is, primal zones in which elementary sensibilia cling to each other in momentary assemblages. Thanks to the cosmological rule that like seeks like, groups of these qualities gather into primeval regions.

> Now the nurse of Becoming, being made watery and fiery and receiving the characters of earth and air, and qualified by all the other affections that go with these, had every sort of diverse appearance to the sight; but because it was filled with powers that were neither alike nor evenly balanced, there was no equipoise *in any region of it;* but it was everywhere swayed unevenly and shaken by these things, and by its motion shook them in turn. And they, being thus moved, were perpetually being separated and carried in different directions. . . . [The Receptacle] separated the most unlike kinds farthest apart from one another, and thrust the most alike closest together; whereby the different kinds *came to have different regions,* even before the ordered whole consisting of them came to be.[54]

I cite this long passage to underscore the fact that in the Platonic cosmology regions, or perhaps better, protoregions, arise in the very beginning. The shaking or "winnowing"[55] action of the Receptacle, carrying like into the company of like, is itself an action of *regionalization:* it renders the Space of the Receptacle regional in status.

(2) A region is not just a formal condition of possibility. It is a *substantive* place-of-occupation. *Chōra,* translated both as "region" and as "space" by Cornford, connotes *occupied place,* for example, a field full of crops or a room replete with things. A region includes both the container and the contained—terms Aristotle insists on keeping separate—and we can make ostensive reference to it as "this region" (whereas, as Plato insists, we cannot refer to a merely evanescent sensible quality as "this"). A choric region is substantive without being a substance: rather than a thing, it is a locatory matrix *for* things.[56] Such a region is finally a matter of place rather than of space—if "place" implies finite locatedness and "space" infinite or indefinite extension. Despite its curious adumbration of the modern idea of space as something invisible, the Receptacle remains above all a scene of implacement.[57]

The Receptacle is place-providing twice over. First, as we have just seen, it is inherently regionalized and regionalizing. In this capacity, it "clears space for" groups of similar qualities, furnishing them with their "leeway."[58] Regions in this sense are primal zones—not altogether unlike the major "zones" of psychosexuality identified by Freud. Just as the psychosexual zones are located on (or, better, *in*) the lived body while not being sharply demarcated there, so the cosmological zones structure the body of the Receptacle and are not strictly bounded (in a region, like draws to like; but likeness is a matter of degree and so cannot be rigorously delimited). Second, the openness and vagueness of a region call for a much more particular sense of place: place as *topos*. Although Plato does not always bother to distinguish between *chōra* and *topos*, he needs this very distinction when he comes to discuss the "primary bodies" constructed by the Demiurge. For each such body, formed as it is from sensible qualities and regular geometrical shapes, "is something coming to be in a certain place" (52a)—that is, in its own *topos* as determined by its outer form along with its volume. But this *topos* is in turn located in a region, an encompassing but delimited portion of choric space.[59]

Just as *chōra* precedes creation—it is what the Demiurge encounters upon his intervention into the scheme of things: hence its Necessity—so particular *topoi* ensue from creation. *Demiurgic creation consists in the configuration and specification of things in particular places within a pregiven (and already regionalized) Space.*

III

In the *Enuma Elish* as well creation consists in the production of particular places out of preexisting regions, even if it is true that the *kind* of particularity differs in the two cases: in the Sumerian epic the particularity belongs to architectural and civic entities, not to simple physical bodies. Where the *Enuma Elish* is resolutely finite and historical—being finally about the founding of Babylon—the *Timaeus* purports to be transfinite and nonhistorical. Moreover, the kind of *generality* varies in the two accounts: the down-to-earth materiality of the precosmic regions (e.g., sweet and bitter waters) posited in the earlier text is superseded by the purely receptive regions of the Greek tale of creation. Yet the overall movement from diffuseness of region to concision of place is found in both stories—as is the root notion of matrix, which characterizes the notion of region in each case.

The deeper difference between the two epics, one composed before the second millennium and the other in the fourth century B.C., is found elsewhere: the transition from cosmogony to cosmology. Where genesis is the constant concern of a cosmo*gonic* text such as the *Enuma Elish*, "becoming" (by which one may translate *genesis*) is only one of three main concerns in the *Timaeus*. Put most pithily, these concerns are "Being, Space, Becoming—three distinct things" (52d). A thing that becomes (*to gignomenon*) is distinguishable from that in which it becomes (*to en hō gignetai*), that is, Space; and both in turn are distinguishable from the Form that supplies the timeless pattern of the becoming-thing. While sensible things are perishable and Space is "everlasting,"[60] Forms are eternal. The mere fact that Forms are expressly considered as equiprimordial with Space and Becoming indicates that we have now entered the domain of cosmology, moving from *muthos* to *logos*. For the created *cosmos* is what it is only insofar as it is permeated by a *logos*, a permanent structure; and the proper account of such a cosmos is a "rational account" (another of the basic meanings of *logos*). Philosophy furnishes such an account, and it is in this respect that it differs most markedly from myth. Even if Plato himself considered the *Timaeus* as no more than a "likely story" (29a), and even if contemporary philosophers may take him at his word and despair over the status of such a story,[61] it remains undeniable that with the *Timaeus* we have taken a fateful step into cosmology. What is merely "likely" (*eikos*) about the account is precisely what survives within it of the cosmogonic: for example, the matricial status of the Receptacle, the role and actions of the creator, the quasi-narrative ordering of the tale, the stress on material qualities. When we read that the Receptacle "was everywhere swayed unevenly and shaken by these things, and by its motion shook them in turn" (52e), we can *almost* imagine this to be a description of Tiamat herself (especially in her monstrous, sea-serpent phase). But the lack of proper names—the fiercesome "Marduk" has been replaced by a faceless "Demiurge"—is a sign that we are in a different genre of discourse with different aims and different stakes. If the Receptacle is said to be, much like Tiamat herself, "watery and fiery," still the Receptacle only *receives* these qualities and *reflects* them: not actually characterized by the qualities it receives, the receptacle is not what it appears to be. Since it is the prelogical collocation of regions where such qualities appear, the Receptacle certainly can *seem* monstrous and chaotic, a matter of wild sensibility; but it *is not* sensible, indeed it is not even matter. As Derrida remarks, "*Chōra* receives all the determinations, so as to give [a] place [to them], but it does not possess any of them properly. It possesses them, it has them (since it receives them), but it does not possess them as properties, it possesses nothing properly."[62]

What then is the Receptacle in the end? *Hupodochē*, one of its names in Greek (besides *dechomenon*, literally "the recipient"), gives a crucial clue. The Receptacle is what lies *under* (*hupo*) that which appears in the physical world. It is an underlying "region of regions"—to borrow a concept from Husserl (who, however, applied it to consciousness, not to the material world).[63] Not being that "out of which" (*ex hou*) things are made (as is Tiamat), it is the "in which" (*en hō*) *on which* things (qualities, powers, motions: ultimately perceptible things) come to appearance, exchange positions, and gain their place. Not strictly heterogeneous itself (for it is not material enough to *be* diverse), it nevertheless underlies the heterogeneity of the physical universe and makes this heterogeneity possible. Its violent rocking guarantees that its occupants will be changing places continually.

> All are changing the direction of their movement, this way and that, towards their own regions; for each [primary body], in changing its size, changes also

the situation of its region. In this way, then, and by these means there is a perpetual safeguard for the occurrence of that heterogeneity which provides that the perpetual motion of these bodies is and shall be without cessation.[64]

This passage makes it clear that even the primal regions of the Receptacle are by no means stationary or secure. For the region of a given kind of body cannot be considered a fixed sector to which it adverts as to something settled: "There [is] no equipoise in any region of it."[65] In fact, both the generic region and the particular place of a given body are in a state of ongoing mutation. This is due to the character of the Receptacle as "all-receiving (*pandeches*)" (51a), that is, reflecting every kind of change: changes in motion, quality, quantity, and so on.

The Receptacle is accordingly the bearer (but not the begetter) of all that occurs in the sensible world.[66] It bears up (under) all that is located in (elemental) regions and (particular) places, thereby "providing a situation for all things that come into being" (52b). But despite its considerable locatory power, the Receptacle remains the referent of a bare cosmological "this." There is, after all, no Form of Space.[67]

A strange beast, a half-bred hybrid, this Receptacle. It is at once locatory and yet not itself located, permanent and yet invisible, underlying and yet nonsubstantial. Plato avers that it is "apprehended without the senses by a sort of bastard reasoning, and [is] hardly an object of belief" (52b), and he analogizes its perception to that of a dream.[68] The Receptacle is also a hybrid entity in another, still more encompassing, sense. It stands between, even as it combines, myth and science. In particular, it stands between the *Enuma Elish* and Aristotle's *Physics*. It has too much "reasoning" and too little "belief" for the Sumerian epic, and yet exhibits too desultory a form of thinking and possesses too little materiality for the Aristotelian treatise. If Tiamat gives way to *chōra* in the *Timaeus, chōra* will cede place to Topos in the *Physics*. The Platonic cosmology of regionalized Place precariously and provocatively straddles the tenebrous middle realm between the mythics of elemental matrices and the physics of pinpointed places.

IV

Imagine the shock of the Demiurge, that eminently rational creator who intends to model the world on the pattern of an unchanging Form, when he confronts the crazy-quilt, irregular motions of the Receptacle: motions generated by "errant causes" (48a). Given his wish "to make this world most nearly like that intelligible thing which is best and in every way complete" (30d)— that is, a Form—he cannot but be chagrined by the tumultuous spectacle, indeed threatened by it in ways that recall the disorientation and fear that an angry and defiant Tiamat occasioned in the objects of her wrath. In the

Mesopotamian legend, Tiamat had to be killed and her carcass transmuted before ordering could begin. In the Platonic tale, however, persuasion rather than physical force is invoked to bring the unruly Receptacle into rationally regulated behavior: "Reason overruled Necessity by persuading her to guide the greatest part of the things that become towards what is best" (48a). The mastery of the matrix arises from the rule of reason rather than by the application of brute force.

It was just because of the nondistinction between primordial space and material body—between Tiamat-as-place and Tiamat-as-body—that her body had to be destroyed, physically obliterated, in order to make way for a world-ordering use of space such as Marduk instituted in building Babylon. Insofar as *chōra* and the sensible qualities appearing in it are distinguished in the *Timaeus* from the start, there can be an ordering of these qualities without recourse to acts of outright obliteration. Furthermore, even before the intervention of the Demiurge a significant amount of structuring—if not rational ordering—has already taken place, thanks to the apportioning of the sensible qualities in accordance with the assimilation of like to like. Rough and ready as this assimilation is (it never reaches a settled state), still it does present the Demiurge with a prospect that is not utterly chaotic. The prospect remains challenging, however.

> Desiring, then, that all things should be good and, so far as might be, nothing imperfect, the god [i.e., the Demiurge] took over all that is visible—not at rest, but in discordant and unordered motion—and brought it from disorder into order, since he judged that order was in every way the better. (*Timaeus* 30a)

But if the motion in the Receptacle is indeed tumultuous, it is nevertheless a *local* motion, that is to say, a motion that occurs in distinctive places and regions.[69] Such "locomotion" guarantees a minimal coherency in the precreationist moment. (Conversely, at least some of this same wandering motion, this errant causation, survives creation: the errancy continues to haunt the created cosmos as well.)[70]

However ill- or unordered the aboriginal state may be, the Demiurge must set to work with what he is given. Not being omnipotent, he is constrained by this pregivenness: he can introduce only "as much order and proportion as Necessity allows."[71] The act of creation thus brings about structure and not simply things that did not previously exist. Creation is the creation of order. *The Demiurge urges*—urges Necessity to bring forth order, if not "with the greatest possible perfection" (53b), at least to the extent of an ordering that is effected by the infusion of the mathematical into the sensible.

It is striking that both Marduk and the Demiurge have recourse to mathematics at approximately the same critical point. Once Marduk is able to survey the scene of his triumph over Tiamat, he can "measure out and mark in" positions and directions within "the immensity of the firmament." In the case of the Demiurge, the inspiration and source of mathematics also reside in the sky, that is, in the periodicity of celestial motion.[72] The special power of mathematics to shape a *cosmos* proceeds from the sky downward: "The operation of Reason is carried, so far as may be, into the dark domain of the irrational powers."[73] Seemingly against all odds, what Aristophanes had called "deep Dark's bottomless wombs"—the womb of Tiamat's generativity as well as the womb of *chōra's* agitated motion—come to yield order, a distinctively mathematical order at that.

If creation is to work, it must bring together—must literally *articulate*—the most advanced state achievable by the Receptacle "even before the Heaven came into being" (52d) with the most elementary form of mathematical ordering. As Cornford comments, "from the abyss of bodily 'powers' in complete abstraction from the works of Reason, we now ascend to the lowest level at which the element of order and design contributed by the Demiurge can be discerned in the turbulent welter of fire, air, water, and earth."[74] To depict this situation graphically, we can imagine two triangles touching at their respective tips. The bottom triangle ("N" for Necessity) represents the "abyss" and "turbulent welter" of the Receptacle—recalling the abyss of Apsu and the tumult of Tiamat—and the upper triangle ("R" for Reason) the "order and design" of mathematical rationality.

The point of overlap ("d")—that is, where the two factors of Necessity and Reason touch at their tips—is "depth" (*bathos*), which Merleau-Ponty has termed "the dimension of dimensions."[75] For depth is a dimension of every spatial span and spread, no matter how such a stretch may be determined or measured. It is even an important dimension of motion, including that primal

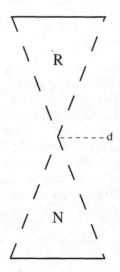

motion by which, in the Receptacle, like seeks like and unlike drifts away from unlike.

Depth is also a feature of every surface, and it is by virtue of depth-of-surface, even more than by depth-of-motion, that the fateful step is taken from the realm of sheer sensible qualities (the proper constituents of the Receptacle) to the material bodies whose stereometric shapes are supplied by the Demiurge in his first and most definitive world-creative act. Depth is at once the mediatrix between sensible quality and body *and* that which enables the application of geometry to material body itself.

> In the first place, then, it is of course obvious to anyone that fire, earth, water, and air are bodies; and *all body has depth.* Depth, moreover, must be bounded by surface; and every surface that is rectilinear is composed of triangles.[76]

It is from the combination of two such triangles—the right-angled isosceles and the half-equilateral—that all four of the solid geometrical figures of the primary bodies are constructed. For the pyramid (fire), octahedron (air), icosahedron (water), and cube (earth) are each three-dimensional figures whose surfaces are constituted from these triangles (the surfaces of a cube from the isosceles; those of the other figures from the half-equilateral). What matters in such applied mathematics is less its intrinsic plausibility—for which a convincing case can in fact be made[77]—than its earnest effort to mathematize what in the original state of the Receptacle remains rudely rough in character. It is this effort that is the proper work (*ergon*), the sole creative task, of the Demiurge (construed literally as a "working for the people").[78] It is the mathematizing of the Receptacle that counts, for here alone Reason is able to win over Necessity to its own aims.[79]

V

We witness in Plato's "likely story" a general movement from a space that is radically heterogeneous to a space that is on its way to becoming homogeneous. In Eliade's terms, this is a movement from a "sacred space" of discontinuity and difference (e.g., between a temple and the profane space outside it) to a "secular space" of homogenized and all-too-predictable equiformity.[80] On Heidegger's assessment, it is an adumbration of a distinctly modern conception of space.[81] In the language of the *Timaeus* itself, it is a movement from the erratic (and rectilinear) motions of sensible qualities to the regular (and circular) trajectories of geometrized physical bodies that imitate the motions of the heavenly bodies. But likely or not, prophetic or not, where does this story leave us with regard to the question of place? What does the Timaean cosmogenesis have to say about topogenesis?

What it has to say is that place itself—*topos*—is a derivative and comparatively late moment in a sequence of three stages whose first two moments are concerned with *chōra*.

> *Space:* a matrix for particular places that is ingredient in and coextensive with the Receptacle as a whole; to be placed herein is to be placed in Space (*chōra*), that is, to be placed *somewhere* (but at no specific place or region) in the Receptacle regarded as a massive spatial sphere, beyond which there is Nothing, not even the Void. Thus Space "signifies total implacement"[82]—but only in the most nascent state.
>
> *Primal Regions:* areas within the Receptacle constituted by the changing clusterings of like sensible qualities—areas that never attain strict homogeneity; were they to do so, motion would cease: "Motion will never exist in a state of homogeneity" (57e); such stasis is in any case precluded by the continual transformation of one primary body into another.[83]
>
> *Particular Places within Primal Regions:* the discrete *topoi* that fully formed sensible bodies occupy. Each such place is thus a locus within a primal region composed of similar bodies; the locus itself is not stationary but is in effect the traced trajectory of the movement of these bodies as they *change place* from moment to moment.

The Timaean tale is thus a story of increasing implacement. The first two stages both preexist and *succeed* the intervention of the Demiurge: choric spatiality and regionality remain throughout. The last stage is not so much created by the craftsman-god as fashioned by him out of the material supplied by the first two. For the shape-bestowing geometrism of the Demiurge affects only the *form* of sensible bodies—not their quality, power, depth, matter, or motion. In endowing these bodies with stereometric form, the Demiurge is more of a micro-manager than a creator-god. His efforts are restricted to forming the exact fit required by any particular *topos,* since the shape and size of a material body situated in a given place cannot be incompatible with the surfaces of surrounding bodies. The Demiurgic action is mainly a matter of the configuration and covariation of an already (and always) existing choric Necessity.

The pertinacity of *chōra* illustrates a quite general point. In the *Timaeus* we find—in keeping with a classical Greek concern for maintaining well-ordered equilibria, usually in the form of means between extremes—a delicate but firm balance between such polar terms as Reason and Necessity, homogeneity and heterogeneity, the disorderly and the mathematized. This balance is most saliently seen in the complementarity that exists between the irregularity

of aberrant bodily motions before the Demiurge intervenes and the regularity
of geometric shapes grafted onto the erratically moving bodies. As Albert
Rivaud remarks,

> The theory of elementary figures is destined to explain how order is introduced
> into the moving chaos of qualities. By their definite and invariable properties,
> these figures infuse a certain fixity into Becoming. But they do not form its
> substance, which remains constituted by changing qualities.[84]

It is not so much that the initially wild motions are "subordinated"[85] by the
Demiurge—such a term would be more suitable in describing the martial confrontation between Marduk and Tiamat—as that errancy and regularity coop-
erate in the constitution of a world that is a conjoint product, a literal bi-
product, of their disparate tendencies. For this reason, it is difficult to say
whether the Demiurge *imposes* order on the Receptacle or *draws out* what is
already immanent in its pregiven necessities. Perhaps, as Alfred North
Whitehead suggests, both claims are true.

> Plato in the *Timaeus* affords an early instance of wavering between the two
> doctrines of Law, [i.e. between] Immanence and Imposition. In the first place,
> Plato's cosmology includes an ultimate creator, shadowy and undefined, impos-
> ing his design upon the Universe. [But] secondly, the action and reaction of the
> internal constituents is—for Plato—the self-sufficient explanation of the flux of
> the world.[86]

VI

when everything was   sunless desert   downcast soundless night
things-not-things   unfilled
by the still empty MotherTimberStuff
for this was a slack time her lovely bodyforms had yet to employ

then WorldMother Start worked everything into her fashion
drawing them for safety and health into her body
to give them birth
she bore the universe her beauty's/*cosmos* which is also order
unhooked earth from sky unfurled endless land and sea
untangling them from each other

after she'd considered everything
before shuffling each into place
the god . . . since she had no clear choice
separated into shape her once aimless body[87]

This Hellenistic poem of creation sets forth an important variant. "Mother-
TimberStuff" (*hulē*), the matrix of creation, fills herself with things that are

not yet fully things—with what "had not yet had its character struck"[88]—and proceeds to create. She creates first by separating regions from each other, dislodging earth from sky and dissevering land from sea. Thanks to this primal *diairesis* (division), she is able to find determinate places for created things, "shuffling each into place." As in Genesis and the *Theogony,* the *Enuma Elish* and the *Timaeus,* creation of the world occurs as the creation of regions and of places; and in every instance as well the creation of regions (*chōrai*) precedes the creation of places (*topoi*). But there is a decisive difference in the above text of Heraclitos the Grammarian. Instead of calling for the intervention of another figure—a male creator-god, a master of creation: Yahweh, Zeus, Marduk, the Demiurge—the "WorldMother" does the creating on her own and from her own. She creates the world out of her own "lovely body-forms." It is a matter of autochthonous birth, birth from a self-ingesting and self-generating matrix. This *mater*-mother, far from needing the external assistance of an independent master, creates sui generis. She separates *herself* "into shape," mastering her own matrix.

The disparity between this account and previous phallogocentric versions of creation is momentous (it bristles with gender issues), but the choice between them may be as undecidable as whether the *Timaeus* presents us with a paradigm of Imposition or Immanence. Just as we may wonder indefinitely which of these latter is the truer term, so we may inquire without respite as to whether a matrocentric or phallogocentric model is the truer one. In keeping with the logic of undecidability, we may very well be led to say: neither one nor the other, *and* both.[89]

The same undecidability pertains to a still more pressing question: Does place precede the creation of the world—being presupposed by it—or is place a result of creation itself? Place is definitely *not* precedent if by "place" is meant something like a particular locale or spot: anything of this order of specificity, that is, of the order of *topos* or of *thesis* (position), misses the mark. For it would be manifestly absurd for world-creation to be inaugurated in a scene in which places already existed in complete determinacy: creation then would be superfluous, since the world would be *already* constituted in large measure *as a world,* being place-ordered in advance. Just as there is no place without a world for, and of, places, so there is no world without places, without definite loci in which things and events can appear: every world is a place-world. (This latter claim is merely an extension of the Archytian axiom.) Given the intrinsic, internal relationship between place and world, it is senseless to say that place precedes world or is presupposed by the creation of the world (whether this creation is autogenous or interventionist in character).

Yet, by the same token, it is not the case that place is a mere *product* of such creation. We have found, massively, that place in one sense or another is continually at stake *throughout* the process of creation: if not in the form of discrete *topoi*, then as predeterminate (and often quite indeterminate) parts of the scene of creation. Such pregivenness can be thematized as such—as occurs precisely in the *Timaeus,* which posits a precosmic Space (the Receptacle) and various regions (*chōrai*) within this Space. But it also can be left quite implicit, as happens in Hesiod's allusions to a primal Chaos, a state we have found to possess its own peculiar place-predicates. Even when the role of place seems to be expressly denied—as at the beginning of the *Enuma Elish* ("no heaven, no earth, no height, no depth") or in a Sumero-Akkadian purification ritual that begins with the words "No place for the bright house . . . no land [or] sea"[90]—we may still detect the presence of place in a prospective or residual sense. Close inspection reveals a primordial process of implacement at work, whether by claiming that "in the waters gods were created" or by referring to "motion in sea cunt."[91] Indeed, wherever an "in" is employed, place is already at stake—if not literally, then as an active force all the same. This is what we learn from Plato's careful description of the Receptacle as a Space *in which* things happen and appear, including the event of creation itself. If places are thus always part of creation and coextensive with it, they cannot be regarded as its mere outcome—as on a par with, say, the creation of the human species in Genesis or the city of Babylon by Marduk. In these latter cases, something is brought forth that was not present beforehand, not even in an amorphous format.

But we can also say, and for a not dissimilar set of reasons, that place is both presupposed *and* produced in the course of creation. On the one hand, there can be no altogether ex nihilo act of creation if by this is meant an act of creation taking place *nowhere at all.* As we have seen, the very same lines of Genesis that are so often cited to confirm ex nihilo cosmogonies contain the unambiguous conditional clause that even the most exalted monotheistic God can create only if He moves *over* "the face of the Deep." Just as depth implies place—depth brings with it depth-of-place, qualifying distance, motion, surface, size, and shape—so place implies depth, something of sufficient extent into which to step. No wonder that Tiamat, that creature of cosmogonic depth par excellence, continues to haunt the Old Testament.[92] In this instance, place is presupposed conceptually *and* linguistically *and* mythically (not to mention religiously). If other instances are less dramatic or overdetermined, they are no less crucially dependent on place as a condition of creation.

On the other hand, it is *also* true that place is an *ens creatum;* it is something set forth by creation, where by "set forth" I do not mean brought into existence for the first time (i.e., as a new product) but endowed with enhanced emphasis or structural specificity. Such endowment is just what happens in the *Timaeus,* where the ingression of geometrical shapes gives greater exactitude to the primal regions occupied by emergent material bodies within the circumambience of the Receptacle. To the extent that a given *topos,* that is, a discrete place, fits and reflects precisely (and only) what it holds and locates—and thus is changed decisively if what it situates changes shape, however minutely—then indeed we can speak of the literal production of places out of resident regions. In the Platonic text, this drawing forth is less ontological than geometrical, since it consists in the grafting of formal shapes onto vagrant entities. It is this engrafting that pro-duces the determinate places whose pregeometrized forebears are found in the loosely assembled and spontaneously engendered regions of the Receptacle.

Neither/nor, both/and: not only can we not decide in any definitive manner between these two options as ways of expressing the relationship between creation and place, but, still more significantly, we must affirm each option. The either/or of a forced choice between such alternatives, either one *or* the other, yields to the inclusive "or" of affirming both together. It follows that creation is at once *of* place and *from* place. From creation, place proceeds; but it, creation itself, takes place only in place.[93]

VII

If the immediately preceding reflections seem to rely too readily on the undecidable, I would suggest that they in fact only carry forward into reflective discourse what is already present, at least implicitly, in various texts examined in this and the previous chapter. Even in quite fragmentary utterances, such as the text of Heraclitos with which I began the last section, we find a stance of "having it both ways." There, too, place (the WorldMother's body) was both presupposed and produced (i.e., as earth and sky, land and sea, and more particular places). And we see the same dual cosmologic at work even in the following suggestive lines from the *Orphic Argonautica.*

everything was born
        everything pulled apart
    from one another.[94]

If *everything* has been born, this must apply to place as well as to things-in-places. Place itself would have to be a created product. But if everything is born as "pulled apart from one another," then equally everything is born *in some place* (for there can be no pulling apart except from or into a place). Everything is born placed: to be born at all is to be born as a separated being with its own place. The process of birth itself is no exception to this rule, since there is parturition only *from within place.* This is not only to presume place at the origin of things, along with other pregivennesses; still more audaciously, it is to posit it *as* this origin.

It is evident that the frequent invocation of water or waters as there from the beginning—most conspicuously in Genesis and in the *Enuma Elish,* but also in many other ancient accounts of creation ("in the beginning there was nothing but water, water, water")[95]—is an invocation as much of a place or a region as of a generative source. It is an invocation of place-as-source. The same is true of such other nonaqueous elements as the "sunless desert" in Heraclitos's "Homeric Allegory" or the earth on which there was not "even a wild bush" in the older Hebrew cosmogony of the Yahwist tradition.[96] In both of these latter cases, a precosmic Place is posited as/at the very source of the creation that will take place *on* it. Such a place is indispensable to the taking-place of creation itself. In and from this place will come myriad items of creation that will at once populate the created world and occupy singular *topoi* within it. In this manner places will be added to Place; or, better, the latter will be seen as harboring the former.

Could it be that this is what Plato had in mind when he in effect deconstructed the idea of obdurate physical body—the focus of earlier physiocratic speculation—as a candidate for the elementary unit of the Receptacle? Could it be that the most primordial items are not elements, much less atoms, but choric regions? Is this not what Aristophanes meant when he placed the "deep Dark" *before* "air earth or sky"? Could it be that Place (e.g., *chōra* as Space and Region)[97] provides, perhaps ultimately *is,* deep Dark's own "bottomless wombs"—matrices, however unillumined, that are place-bearers?

If the answers to such questions are in the affirmative, Archytas would be vindicated again, and even twice over. For place indeed would be (as Archytas put it pithily) "the first of all things."[98] It would be this not only for the formal reason that every physical thing must occupy *some* particular place but also for the substantive reason that the generation of the world itself must take place in, from, and as place. If so, place is cosmically and even precosmically privileged.

To affirm this privilege is to reinforce the quite basic idea, which emerged in the first chapter, that the notion of no-place, and in particular the conception of a sheer void preceding the creation of the world, is highly problematic. The facility of the rhetorical gesture by which such a void—whether termed "Gap" or "abyss" or "interval"—is assumed to constitute the aboriginal state of things should not obscure the fact that on close examination few, if any, accounts of world-creation consistently maintain a strict nowhereness at the origin of things. Consider these famous lines of Milton's in *Paradise Lost:*

The secrets of the hoary deep, a dark
Illimitable ocean, without bound,
Without dimension, where length, breadth, and highth,
And time and place are lost; where eldest Night
And Chaos, ancestors of Nature, hold
Eternal anarchy, amidst the noise
Of endless wars, and by confusion stand.[99]

At first glance these lines seem to offer a straightforward ex nihilo version of the state of the universe before Creation. To be "without bound" and "without dimension" is to be without depth—and thus to be, as I have just argued, without place. And yet Milton's explicit allusions to Chaos and Night[100] as well as to the "hoary deep" and to "a dark illimitable ocean"—to what the Romans called *immensi tremor oceani*—point us unmistakably to primal regions that precede any act of creation. It is also revealing that the poet says that "time and place are *lost*": he does not say that they *do not exist* in this precreationist moment. To be lost is still to exist, however amorphously or covertly. In the Miltonic account, place is still very much around—as much as it is in Hebraic or Platonic cosmogonies. In no instance is the comparative shapelessness of place—its lack of "length, breadth, and highth"—a reason for doubting its preexisting and persisting being.[101]

I single out Milton because the account he presents in the above passage illustrates the continuing power of anxiety before the void. In the opening pages of this part I referred to the extreme measures we take to avoid confronting the possibility of there being no place at all in our lives—or even, as we may now add, in our speculation about the origin of the world. Milton's elegant poetic-mythic synthesis is itself one such extreme measure, filling up the looming void with the "confusion" of Chaos and Night. Other extremes include those accounts of creation that posit places as existing from the beginning. In the latter case, the very intolerability of no-place influences the account itself, an account that, circuitously or directly, indicates that we never need fear reaching actual placelessness, not even at the very start of the known universe. For *if creation is itself an ur-scene,* it is ineluctably a Place of considerable cosmogonic significance.

Is this not the lesson of the Pelasgian myth that (as we saw in chapter I) states, "In the beginning, Eurynome, the Goddess of All Things, rose naked from Chaos, but found nothing substantial for her feet to rest upon, and therefore divided the sea from the sky, dancing lonely upon its waves"? Does not any such primal creation-and-division of place express an effort to escape, at all costs, from a situation of being altogether without place? Deeper than what Friedrich Nietzsche calls a "will to nothingness"—"man would rather will *nothingness* than *not* will"[102]—may be an effort *to will place itself in place of the void.* Such a will, I suspect, is the Ariadne's thread connecting all the disparate views of creation we have considered: disparate in historical and geographic location, in conscious intention, and in explicit textuality.

This is not to say, however, that place is simply the opposite of void, as if it were merely a matter of replacing the void with a plenum. Even the place-proffering Receptacle, though it is expressly designed as a critique of the void of the Atomists, is not, strictly speaking, a plenum.[103] Place includes much indissociable absence—as depth, as distance, as difference of location, as dislocation itself. Place neither fills up a void nor merely papers over it. It has its own mixed, ambiguous being. But one of its essential properties is its *connectivity*—its power to link up, from within, diversely situated entities or events.[104] The placefulness of the Receptacle, "providing a situation for all things that come into being" (*Timaeus* 52b), is at one with its connectiveness, its choric capacity for furnishing an ongoing ambience for like and unlike alike. Although the Receptacle must appear to the rational mind of the Demiurge as "discordant and unordered," we have found Plato's actual account to allow for massive preordination: for an entire immanent order of things "even before the Heaven came into being." This in-dwelling order is the basis for the Receptacle's considerable connectiveness.

In the end—or more exactly, in the beginning—the Receptacle offers what Whitehead calls a "community of locus" for its various inhabitants, a "real communication between ultimate realities."[105] The Receptacle thus furnishes what I have elsewhere called "in-gathering."[106] Thanks to its connection-making capacity, the precosmic Receptacle gathers heterogeneous constituents into the arc of its Space, *giving place* to what otherwise might be depthless or placeless—thus allaying the most acute metaphysical anxiety. Its action creates implacement for everything, in-gathered within its encompassing embrace. In Plato's own words, "it is always receiving all things" (50b).

In this way we rejoin the idea of place as matrix with which this chapter opened. If we have had to reject the notion of place as a material begetter, as a physical *fons et origo*—these literalistic meanings of "matrix" being questioned by the working of the Receptacle, which, unlike Tiamat's monster-begetting body, lead us to distinguish between sensible quality, material body, and place—there has emerged a valid matricial sense of place that consists in the sheer connectiveness that place in all its guises uniquely affords. From Plato we learn that receptivity is connectivity.

But we are by no means restricted to the Receptacle as a paradigm of implacement, evocative and suggestive as this paradigm remains still today. Other models are possible if it is indeed true that *placing and being placed are matters of connecting,* whether in the context of cosmogony or cosmology, of phenomenology or metaphysics, or in everyday life. Just as there is no place without depth, so there is no place that does not connect the disparities of being and experience, of perception and language, of chaos and cosmos. And if it is also true that (as Kierkegaard said) "existence separates," then we need to heed E. M. Forster's celebrated counsel: "only connect!"[107] Both Kierkegaard and Forster were thinking more of people than of places. But it is in and by places that the most lasting and ramified connections, including personal connections, are to be made.

If place is "there as a matrix for everything" (*Timaeus* 50c), it tempers any fear that a matrix of places—whether this be conceived as primordial waters, as night, as chaos, as earth, or as Receptacle—is a devastating void, an abysmal *atopia.* If we can *think* of the Receptacle as some kind of no-place, this is only because, as a reservoir of connections yet to come, or at least yet to be

specified, its place-full and place-filling potentiality is always still to be realized in time-to-come. There is, after all, a right and full time for places to
come into being, and even if we have found places to be pervasively present
at the creation of things, their destiny is also to be ongoing and ever-increasing
in their connectivity.

Place is thus, in Plato's own word, "ever-lasting." And, just as this last
locution—*aei on,* the source of *aiōnios,* means literally "always in being"—
brings together time and place, so the same two forces are conjoined in a
telling Neoplatonic fragment of the sixth century A.D.:

everything you see PLACE or
TIME

which separate in Two
making a double pair

OROMESDES   who is Light
Ahura-Mazda

AREIMANIOS   who is Dark
Ariman

       PLACE
       (Topos)

                    ——Zerauné akerené

       TIME
       (Chronos)[108]

3

Place as Container

Aristotle's *Physics*

Everything remains naturally in its proper place.
                    —Aristotle, *Physics* 212b34–35

No one thinks or speaks—even when the thought or
word is erroneous—without recognizing, from this
very fact, the existence of place.
        —Henri Bergson, "L'Idée de Lieu chez Aristote"

I

That place was a continuing cynosure of ancient Greek thought is abundantly
evident in Aristotle's treatment of the topic: for Aristotle, *where* something is
constitutes a basic metaphysical category.[1] Except for the extraordinary cases
of the Unmoved Mover and the heavens (*ouranos*) taken as a single whole,
every perishable sublunar substance (including the earth as a whole) is place-
bound, having its own "proper place" as well as existing in the "common
place" provided by the heavens.[2] Thanks to this stress on the importance of
place for each particular "changeable body"—that is, changeable with respect
to motion or size—the Stagirite situates his most scrupulous examination of
place in the context of physics rather than of cosmology. Cosmology is of
decidedly less interest to Aristotle than to Plato; and of cosmogony only the
barest traces survive in Aristotle's text, typically in the form of bemused and
skeptical citations from pre-Socratic figures. The at least quasi-mythical aura
of the *Timaeus*—its ambiguous status as a mixed "third genre" (*triton genos*)
of discourse (*Timaeus* 48e, 52a)—gives way to the sturdy, no-nonsense attitude of the *Physics,* wherein place is conceived in the cautious, finite terms

of container and limit, boundary and point. Chōra yields to Topos, the bountiful to the bounded.

It is precisely because of its indispensable role within the physical world that, for Aristotle, place "takes precedence of all other things" (*Physics* 208b35). In particular, it assumes priority over the infinite, void, and time.[3] Place is requisite even for grasping change itself (*kinēsis*), with which the study of physics is always concerned; for "the most general and basic kind [of] change is change in respect of place, which we call locomotion."[4] Locomotion, after all, is movement *from place to place.*[5] On Aristotle's view, one simply cannot study the physical world without taking place into account: "A student of nature must have knowledge about place" (208a27). For wherever we turn in the known universe—outside of which there is "neither place, nor void, nor time" (*De Caelo* 279a18)—we find place awaiting us and shaping any move we might wish to make. Remember that even a void, were it to exist, would be a "place bereft of body" (208b26).

Given this perception of the pervasiveness of place, it is not surprising to find Aristotle offering his own version of Archytas's archetypal argument for the primacy of place—an argument whose other advocates include Zeno, Parmenides, Gorgias, Plato, and, much more recently, Whitehead. Aristotle puts it this way:

> For everyone supposes that things that are are somewhere, because what is not is nowhere—where for instance is a goat-stag or a sphinx?[6]

It is at this very point that Aristotle makes a rare gesture toward *muthos* by citing the *Theogony* as an early testimonial to the inevitability of implacement. Having just argued for this inevitability from the various phenomena of *antiperistasis* (i.e., the replacement of one body by another: despite the exchange of bodies, the place remains the same), natural movement (whereby different kinds of bodies move to "distinct and separate" regions [208b18]), and the void (in its empty placelikeness), Aristotle observes,

> These are the reasons, then, for which one might suppose that place is something over and above bodies, and that every body perceptible by sense is in place. Hesiod, too, might seem to be speaking correctly in making Chaos first; he says
>
> > Foremost of all things
> > Chaos came to be
> > And then broad-breasted Earth
>
> suggesting that it was necessary that there should first be a space (*chōra*) available to the things that are, because he thinks as most people do that everything is somewhere (*pou*) and in place (*en topō*). (208b27–33)

Here Aristotle rejoins the analysis of chaos at stake in the last two chapters. Rather than a species of no-place, of sheer void, chaos is for Aristotle a kind of place, however inchoate and formless it may be. Indeed, it is just because chaos is some sort of place and *not* a void that Aristotle can exclaim that "the potency of place must be a marvelous thing, and take precedence of all other things." For, adds Aristotle, "that without which nothing else can exist, while it can exist without the others, must needs be first."[7] In these last words, the Archytian axiom is literally reinscribed in Aristotle's text as he prepares to make his own case for the primacy of place in the physical world.

Before he can make this case, however, he must come to terms with Plato on the subject of place. He does so by an ambivalent admixture of praise and critique. The praise is straightforward: "While everyone says that place is something, [Plato] alone tried to say *what* it is" (209b16–17). The critique, however, is less than straightforward. For one thing, it rests on the supposition that for Plato "matter and space are the same thing" (209b12) and thus that place is also reducible to matter: inasmuch as "place is thought to be the extension of the magnitude [of a physical thing occupying that place], it is the matter" (209b6–7). For another, in the *Physics* "space" as *chōra* is no longer an independent term designating a vast extent such as that found in the Receptacle. Considered as "magnitude" (*megethos*), space is brought down to the scale of "place" qua discrete *topos*—given that place is coextensive with the magnitude of a particular thing-in-place.[8] As W. D. Ross puts it bluntly, "The doctrine of place in the *Physics* is not a doctrine of space. Neither here nor elsewhere does Aristotle say much about space, *chōra,* and he cannot be said to have a theory about it."[9] Not to have a theory of *chōra,* to replace it with considerations of *megethos* and *topos,* is tantamount to a rejection of what had been most important, or in any case most challenging, in Plato's cosmology.

Beyond this, Aristotle levels at Plato the general charge that "we should ask Plato why the Forms and numbers are not in place, if place is the 'participative' (*to metalēptikon*), whether 'the participative' is the great and the small or whether it is matter, as he writes in the *Timaeus*" (*Physics* 209b34–36). The charge is unanswerable; not only does the term "the participative" not occur in the *Timaeus* (which limits itself to claiming that the Receptacle "partakes in some very puzzling way of the intelligible" [*Timaeus* 51a–b]), but, more important, the Forms and Space, along with the items of Becoming, are posited by Plato as ultimate metaphysical givens, necessary postulates of any adequate cosmology. Elsewhere, notably in *On Generation and Corruption,* Aristotle takes Plato to task for failing to "say clearly whether the omnirecipient [i.e., the Receptacle as all-receiving (*pandeches*)] is separated from the elements" (*Physics* 329a14–15; see also 329a23–25) and for "making no use of it" in that Plato does not show precisely how, apart from Demiurgic intervention, the matrix of Becoming is transubstantiated into the geometrically configured primary bodies (*Physics* 329a15–23).[10]

II

> Place is thought to be some surface and like a
> vessel and surrounder.
>
> —*Physics* 212a28–29

Having laid Plato to rest—albeit in an unquiet grave—Aristotle proceeds to
make his own case for the priority of place. Although he makes this case in
the text entitled *Physikē akroasis* (Hearkening to Nature), a text considered
by Heidegger to be "the basic book of occidental philosophy," [11] Aristotle
operates as much like a phenomenologist as a physicist, carefully investigat-
ing "in what *way* [place] is." [12] In so doing, he inaugurates an alliance between
physics and phenomenology that extends into the recent past: the very word
"phenomenology" was coined by Lambert in 1764 to designate the study of
physical phenomena as they appear to the senses; Mach and Einstein continued to draw on this sense of the term. [13] What is unique in Aristotle's enterprise
is its concern for general principles of change and motion—a concern combined with a scrupulous description of concrete phenomena. As Aristotle says
in opening the *Physics,* "Start from the things which are more knowable and
obvious to us and proceed towards those which are clearer and more knowable
by nature" (184a17–18). To be "more knowable and obvious *to us*" is to be
the potential object of a descriptive, phenomenological investigation, since
such an investigation considers how things present themselves to the human
observer in his or her immediate life-world.

A first instance of Aristotle's protophenomenological description is found
early in book 4 of the *Physics.*

> These are the parts and kinds of place: above, below, and the rest of the six
> dimensions. These are not just relative to us. Relatively to us, they—above,
> below, right, left—are not always the same, but come to be in relation to our
> position, according as we turn ourselves about, which is why, often, right and
> left are the same, and above and below, and ahead and behind. But in nature
> each is distinct and separate. 'Above' is not anything you like, but where fire,
> and what is light, move. Likewise, 'below' is not anything you like, but where
> heavy and earth-like things move. So they differ not by position alone but in
> power too. [14]

Notice the fine balance here struck between matters of physics proper—which
considers place as something "distinct and separate" and as having its own
"power" (*dynamis*) when considered "in nature" (*en de tē phusei*)—and matters of phenomenological description: for example, the relativity of right versus left to our own particular position at a given moment. A complete consideration of place will have to take both matters into account: how place is "in
itself" and how it is relative to other things.

Much the same dual focus is evident in Aristotle's treatment of two basic aspects of place: (a) just as in Husserlian phenomenology the method of "free variation" helps to discern how many basic kinds of a given phenomenon there are, so Aristotle does not hesitate to project two variant kinds of place: the "common place" (*topos koinos*), "in which all bodies are" (209a33), and the "special place" (*topos idios*) that is "the first in which a body is" (209a34); (b) since each kind of place involves an "in" as an integral component, Aristotle proceeds to specify eight senses of being *in* something.[15] Two of these can be considered logical or classificatory, two are metaphysical, one is political, two delineate part-whole relations, and a final one is expressly descriptive: "as [a thing is] in a vessel and, generally, in a place" (210a23–24). It is striking that this last sense of "in," the most manifestly phenomenological sense, is also declared to be "the most basic of all" (ibid.).[16] To be in a place is very much like being in a vessel, and the question becomes just *how* this is so—thereby calling for further descriptive refinement.

 It is the analogy of the vessel that allows Aristotle to refute the persisting temptation to regard either form or matter as providing the key to the nature of place: "Since the vessel is nothing pertaining to that which is in it (the primary 'what' and 'in which' are different), place will not be either the matter or the form, but something else" (210b27–30). Matter and form inhere in the body that is located in a given place—the matter furnishing the substratum, the form providing shape. The form belongs primarily to the surface of the located body, not to the place locating it, even if the two are contiguous and coextensive.[17] As Aristotle states with phenomenological precision,

> It is because it surrounds that form is thought to be place, for the extremes of what surrounds and of what is surrounded are not in the same [spot]. They are both limits, but not of the same thing: the form is a limit of the object, and the place of the surrounding body. (211b10–14)

But this leaves unanswered just how place is "thought to be some such thing as a vessel" (209a27–28). The answer is clearly to be sought in the containing and, more specifically, the surrounding, capacity of vessels: their power to *hold (things) in.* By carefully describing this capacity of holding-in, Aristotle is able to determine the exact definition, the "what-is-it" (211a8: *ti estin*) of place. The definition itself is set forth in two stages. In the first, Aristotle concentrates on the factor of containment as such by observing that we are located in the celestial system by virtue of being surrounded by air, which is in turn surrounded by the heavens. We are placed in this system by being located "in the air—not the *whole* air, but it is because of the limit of it that surrounds us that we say that we are in the air."[18] Place in its "primary" sense is thus "the first thing surrounding each body."[19] It is this immediately environing thing taken as a limit. But the limit here belongs to the surrounder, not to the body surrounded (the limit of the latter is determined by its form, i.e., its outer shape: see 209b3–6). As a vessel, such as a glass or a jug, surrounds its content—say, air or water—so place surrounds the body or group of bodies located within it. "Surround" translates *periechein,* which means "to circumscribe without including as a component part"; literally, it signifies to "hold" (*echein*) "around" (*peri-,* as in perimeter). As a vessel holds water or air within it, so a place holds a body or bodies within it in a snug fit.

But Aristotle does not rest content with this first definition of place. For one thing, the analogy with a vessel is imperfect. While a vessel can be transported, a place cannot: "Just as the vessel is a place which can be carried around, so place is a vessel which cannot be moved around" (212a14–15). Still more serious, there is the problematic fact that a river is a place for a boat and yet the content of the water immediately surrounding a boat continually changes. Hence the inner surface of the surrounding water, that which delimits the boat's place, is not selfsame from moment to moment. Since a minimal requirement of place is to be selfsame—to be the *same* place for different things located in it—Aristotle must add to the first definition the rider that a place cannot itself be changing or moving: it must be "unchangeable" (*akinēton*). This allows him to move to his most definitive formulation: "That is what place is: the first unchangeable limit (*peras*) of that which surrounds" (212a20–21). In the case of the river, it is thus "the whole river" that is the place: a phrase that Simplicius and others interpret to mean the banks and bed of the river, its fixed inner surrounding surface.[20]

Place thus construed is "the inner surface of the innermost unmoved container of a body."[21] As such, it contains-and-surrounds the body by furnishing to it an environment that, if not always stable (the immediate "spot" of a boat in the river is only a momentary locale, not a lasting locus), is nevertheless a defining locatory presence. Thanks to this presence, place is actively *circumambient* rather than merely *receptive.*[22] It is just here that Aristotle's departure from Plato becomes most manifest. In the *Timaeus,* space qua *chōra*—including both regions and particular places—is held to be receptive: indeed, it is "omnirecipient." Precisely as such, it can be qualified by sensible qualities and can serve as the medium in which physical bodies will appear. But these bodies receive their definition, that is, their limit or shape, from geometric figures. Hence the limiting factor comes from the active infusion of forms by the Demiurge.

On Aristotle's account, the limiting power is *already in place;* it is of the essence of place itself to provide this delimitation by its capacity to contain and to surround: to contain by surrounding. Where Plato's interest lay in the shaping of the outer surface of physical bodies, Aristotle's concern is with the fixed contour of the inner surface of environing places. For Aristotle, the limit is found within place, indeed as part of place itself. Limit is ingredient in place from the beginning—indeed, *as* the beginning of an ordered natural world—and is not imposed by an external ordering agent. Hence there is no need to invoke a deific regulator, a divine inseminator possessing a *logos spermatikos*. Places have their own independent potency. As Aristotle puts it in a characteristic understatement, place "has some power" (208b11). But the result of this modest proposal is quite sweeping: the world is always already fully implaced; it is never without those determinate *topoi* whose limits circumlocate particular things within their immediate environments.

III

Given the choice between Whitehead's two models of creation—"Immanence" versus "Imposition"—Aristotle, in revealing contrast to Plato, opts unambiguously for a model of immanence. This is to be expected, for the Aristotelian scheme of things does not contain anything even remotely resembling chaos (the word itself appears in the *Physics* only as a vestigial term). Only by a process of conceptual prescinding does Aristotle reach the level of "prime matter" (*prōtē hulē*), which is as close as he allows himself to come to chaos. But prime matter is too indefinite in status to exist by itself. Instead, in the physical world—and that means effectively *everywhere,* since "everything is in [this] world" (212b18)—we encounter only matter that is already informed. In this world, material bodies have their own integrity thanks to their indissociably hylomorphic character. There is thus no need to explain the infusion of form *into* matter, much less the generation of an entire well-formed cosmos. The invocation of the Demiurge may have been essential in a situation in which sheer sensible qualities had to be transformed into full-fledged material bodies with stereometric shapes, but any such invocation is now pointless. Since the physical world takes care of itself by appearing from the start as fully formed, the only pertinent deity is an utterly stationary Mover who is (despite the appellation) eternally at rest *outside the world* and thus in effect *nowhere at all.* All places belong to the world, but the world-all itself has no place of its own.[23] We have come a long way from the temptation to posit a primordial no-place: now the only philosophically legitimate null place is located neither *before* creation (as in ex nihilo accounts) nor *between* bits of created matter (as in the infinite void of the Atomists) but in the very being of the Unmoved Mover. If it is indeed true that there is "no place or void or time outside the heaven" (*De Caelo* 279a12–13), then the Mover itself is placeless.

A crucial paradox emerges from this situation.[24] In a text such as the *Timaeus,* a quasi-diachronic account of creation leads both to the positing of a preexisting Space (along with its various regions and places) and to the need for demiurgic intercession in order to give regular shape to formless sensible qualities. Space is thematized in an account whose narrative nature entails Time. In the *Physics,* a nonnarrative account plays down place at the origin:

placelessness obtains "outside the universe" (212b18). The paradox is thus double-sided: where a time-bound tale such as that told in the *Timaeus* requires deity to interpose itself literally *in place*—to give shape to qualities in particular places so that "the ordered whole consisting of them [can come] to be" (*Timaeus* 53a)—the timeless tale told in the *Physics* gives to its deity *no place to intervene*, given that this deity exists outside the world-whole of perceptible bodies in a metaphysical Erewhon of its own. In the one case, time and place conspire to draw deity into the world—at least during the critical event of creation. In the other, deity remains out of the world in a timeless and placeless state. The conception of a richly regionalized and still unordered world, spatially inchoate even if not strictly chaotic, gives way to the idea of a world at once coherently placed and formally shaped—a world having an immanent order that is the rigorous counterpart of the independence of the Unmoved Mover.

One important corollary of this shift in outlook concerns the role of mathematics and of geometry in particular. If the created world of the *Timaeus* involves what might be called an "ingrafted geometrism"—that is, the introduction of plane triangular figures as the primary structures of the surfaces of solids—there is no trace of any such externally infused geometrization of material things in the *Physics*. What had been essential to Platonic cosmology (creation necessarily includes geometrization in the Timaean account) is viewed with deep skepticism by Aristotle, who might well have applied to this cosmology Eugène Minkowski's sardonic pathognomonic label "morbid geometrism."[25] If the world already possesses an inherent ordering that includes form or shape as well as place, to call for a separate act of geometrizing is an otiose gesture.[26]

I dwell thus on the disparity between Plato and Aristotle—especially in the contrasting terms of imposition versus immanence, geometrism versus physicalism—in an effort to indicate that two deeply different ways of regarding place are already present in ancient Greek thought. Moreover, in contrast with the two other most important early Greek paradigms—Hesiodic Chaos and the Atomistic void—the Platonic and Aristotelian conceptions of place have a significant posteriority in contemporary nonscientific thinking on the subject. Geometry provides a model for several early modern notions of space that are even today, in the twentieth century, pervasively operative at the level of common sense, if not of scientific thinking. And the Aristotelian alternative is the active ancestor of those phenomenological approaches that, in the writings of Husserl and Merleau-Ponty, question the superimposition of geometry and call for a recognition instead of the world's immanent shapeful order.

The critical question for Aristotle as a protophenomenologist is how (not *why*) the world possesses such deeply inherent placeful order. The answer is: "Place is together with [every] object," for "the limits are together with what is limited" (212a30–31). It is the "together" (*hama*) that is the clue to the

58 From Void to Vessel

"how" of place, to the manner in which place is "the most basic way" in
which one thing can be *in* another: "Things are 'together' in place when their
immediate or primary place is one."[27] A material thing fits snugly in its proper
place, a place that clings to that thing, since thing and place act together in
determining a given situation. I say "*act* together" in view of the power of
place to actively surround and to situate what is in it—that is, a physical thing
or body, which is not there as a mere passive occupant: as actually or potentially changing or moving, and as changing or moving precisely in/to its
proper place, it, too, has power.

The double immanence, the reciprocal belongingness, of thing and place is
summed up in an axiomatic formula that quite appropriately incorporates two
uses of "in": "Just as every body is in a place, so in every place there is a
body" (209a25–26). This is not a merely empty or redundant statement. The
Atomists were not the only ones to posit a place without a body (i.e., qua
void); Plato did so as well: none of the primal regions at play in the Receptacle
contains a full-fledged physical body. (Nor is it to be taken for granted that
there are no bodies without place: what of the circumstance of being *between*
places?) It remains that, according to Aristotle, to be in motion or at rest is to
be in place, however momentary or transitional that place might be. And this
continual implacement is itself the result of the closely cooperative action of
places and things. Just as things are always (getting) placed, places are themselves always (being) filled—and filled precisely with things.

Such cooperation is the main way in which the limit acts together, *hama,*
with what is limited: the outer limit of the contained body rejoining the inner
limit of the containing place. Not only can one limit not exist without the
other, but each actively influences the other, helping to shape a genuinely
conjoint space, a space of mutual coexistence between container and contained. This co-constituted, coincidental, compresent double limit is what defines place in its primariness.[28]

IV

A point is that which has no part.
—Euclid, *Elements,* Book 1, Definition 1

The point is projected in imagination and comes
to be, as it were, in a place and embodied in
intelligible matter.
—Proclus, *A Commentary on the First Book
of Euclid's Elements*

It is not necessary ... that there should be a
place of a point.
—Aristotle, *Physics* 212b24

Despite its double delimitation, place is something unchanging vis-à-vis the changing things that are its proper occupants. "For," as Aristotle warns us, "not everything that is, is in a place, but [only] changeable body" (212b27–28). In fact, four things lack place within the Aristotelian system: not only the heavens and the Unmoved Mover but also numbers and points. The most exalted physical and metaphysical entities join forces with the minimal units of arithmetic and geometry in a common circumstance of placelessness. The specter of no-place that haunts cosmogonic accounts of creation now charac-terizes not just a God who is impassively (and impassably) beyond changing and moving things—and even beyond the heavens that encompass these things—but the very numbers and points by which these same things come to be grasped arithmetically and geometrically. Contributing to the strangeness of the situation is the double paradox that (a) God as the Unmoved Mover might seem to be the *ultimate place* since, existing outside the heavens or at its outer edge, He might be thought to contain or surround (and thus to provide place for) the physical universe itself; (b) numbers and especially points, as formal constituents of a material world that is knowable scientifically, might seem to require a certain intrinsic *placelikeness* in order to play their proper roles in any mathematical understanding of this world: roles that rely on order and position. But if metaphysical and mathematical "places" are thus strongly suggested within the system of Aristotelian physics, they just as surely are denied within that same system.

Without trying to resolve this doubly perplexing circumstance—leaving God and numbers for the delectation of the Neoplatonists and the heavens for the construal of Copernicus, Kepler, and Galileo—I want to focus in this sec-tion on Aristotle's treatment of the point in relation to place. The question of whether points have places (or, alternatively, *are* places) is more complex and intriguing than it first appears. To begin with, there is the basic question of how to distinguish point from place.

> Since a body has a place and a space, it is clear that a surface does too, and the other limits, for the same argument will apply: where previously the surfaces of the water were, there will be in turn those of the air. *Yet we have no distinction between a point and the place of a point;* so that if not even a point's place is different [from the point itself], then neither will the place of any of the others be, nor will place be something other than each of these.[29]

The premise in this line of reasoning is that the series of "limits" (*perata*) represented by lines, surfaces, and solids is ultimately dependent on the point as their *non plus ultra* constituent or progenitor. Where Plato prefers the indi-visible *line* as a basic unit in cosmology, Aristotle states that "it is common ground that a point is indivisible."[30] But if points lack places, how will places accrue to everything constructed out of points: lines, surfaces, and three-dimensional bodies? No one, least of all Aristotle, wishes to deny that solid bodies lack place.

Inasmuch as "a point is that which *has no part*,"[31] we might think that it cannot occupy space at all, much less be surrounded by a container, since to contain or surround normally requires that what is encompassed possesses at least one part. A passage from Plato's *Parmenides* is illuminating in this connection.

> If it [the one] were in another thing, it would presumably be surrounded all around by that in which it was, and that would be in contact with it, with many parts, at many places; but it is impossible to be in contact all around in many ways with something that is one and without parts and that does not partake of a circle.[32]

But, isn't a point something that is *always* surrounded—indeed, *totally* surrounded in the space in which it is placed and thus as fully ensconced in its own surrounder as any sensible body? Is not the point a paradigm of being in place, precisely on Aristotle's own view of place as a matter of strict containment? What could be *more* completely contained or surrounded than a point, whether it occurs in isolation or as part of a line or a surface or a solid?[33]

In attempting to resolve the issue, it will not help to claim that points are simply nonphysical, as is suggested by the idea of their indivisibility and by their status as a "limit." Such may well be true of Euclid's notion of point: " 'Point', then . . . is the extreme limit of that which we can still think of (*not observe*) as a spatial phenomenon, and if we go further than that, not only does extension cease but even relative *place,* and in this sense the 'part' [of a point] is nothing."[34] This may hold for points as they figure into plane geometry proper—Euclid's primary concern—but it is hardly adequate to their role in the physical world, where they certainly can be observed: for example, as the center or at the extremity of a given perceptual phenomenon (to cite instances given by Aristotle himself).[35] If it is the case (as Proclus asserts in the exergue to this section) that a place for points can be projected by our imagination into "intelligible matter," places for points surely can be discerned in physical matter as well.[36] Indeed, does not Aristotle's own ingrained immanentism and physicalism—his conviction that "spatial magnitudes cannot exist apart from things" (*Metaphysics* 1085b35) and thus his antipathy to any imposed geometrism—require us to find a valid role for points precisely within the physical world?

Indeed it does, and Aristotle's preferred solution to the present predicament—whereby points are at once indispensable (as the minimal units of any plane or solid figure), observable (in physical nature itself), and yet placeless—is found in his distinction between *place* and *position.* If points do not possess place *stricto sensu,* they do exhibit location or "position" (*thesis*). In this respect, they are to be contrasted with the "one" (*monas*) to which Plato alluded in the passage cited above from the *Parmenides;* the one, as the basic arithmetical unit, is definable as "substance without position," whereas the point is "substance with position."[37] This view, whose ultimate roots are to be found in the Pythagoreans,[38] allows Aristotle to accord to points a spatial determinacy that exists despite their placelessness. Beyond sheer locatedness, this determinacy consists in an inherent bipolarity of direction, as when points aid us in distinguishing right from left, above from below, front from back. The determinacy is also evident in the way that points demarcate the limits of given spatial intervals as well as the shapes of figures of many kinds (including nongeometric figures).

That the determinacy yielded by position is limited in scope, however, is indicated by (i) the linguistic fact that the word *thesis* can mean merely "convention" or "orientation" as well as "position";[39] (ii) the geometric fact that intervals between points call for lines to connect them, as do also the bipolar directions mentioned above (if not explicitly drawn, then at least imputed); (iii) the phenomenological fact that directions, and even intervals, are usually relative to the percipient's own position: "Relatively to us, they— above, below, right, left—are not always the same, but come to be *in relation to our position,* according as we turn ourselves about" (*Physics* 208b14–16; my italics), where "our position," being the position of a physical body, is a position with its own proper place.

There are three telling arguments against the implacedness of points that Aristotle does not set forth but that are worth considering here.

1. The first of these bears on *position:* if position is a necessary condition of place, it is not a sufficient condition; thus points, having position alone, are still not full-fledged places. This is not to deny that points can *characterize places:* for example, boundary markers at the edges of fields (ranging from Mesopotamian *kudduru* to concrete posts of more recent times), the points where the walls of a room come together, or the corners of a basketball court or a football field. In each of these cases, points establish determinate positions—they "pinpoint" them—and are invaluable, indeed indispensable, in this very role. (In fact, it is thought that Pythagorean points or dots were at first representations of boundary stones.)[40] But it would be straining the point to say that they *establish the place itself.* For this to happen, something *else* must occur or be present within the interior of the field, the building, or the court, whether this be a specific activity of raising crops or playing a sport, a generalized action such as dwelling, or a sheer potentiality (e.g., a forthcoming event scheduled to occur in that very place). Points, then, as physically determinate—that is, as fixed in world-space—can serve as crucial demarcators of place even if they

do not, *solus ipse,* bring about place as such. Thus we can agree with Proclus's encomium that the point "unifies all things that are divided, it contains and bounds their processions, it brings them all on the stage and encompasses them about"[41]—so long as we do not go on to claim that the action of points is sufficient to bring about places themselves.

2. Points cannot constitute *depth,* an uneliminable dimension of all places.[42] Points, taken by themselves alone, do not give rise to depth as an actual dimension of surfaces, much less solids composed of surfaces, or fields populated by solids; and by the same token they only rarely give rise to the *perception* of depth on such surfaces or solids or fields. Thus even in perceiving a highly complex composition of city lights seen from an airplane, I still may not grasp the recession in depth of the city below me: it remains a sheerly pointillistic scene. The perception of depth requires the co-perception of several shapes qua surfaces, for example, the profiles of city buildings in the distance.[43] In making this observation, I am only rejoining a familiar passage from the *Timaeus:* "All body has depth. Depth, moreover, must be bounded by surface" (*Timaeus* 53c). We need not claim (as Aristotle imputes to Plato) that all physical masses are generated from a dialectic of the "deep and shallow"[44] to concede the basic point: that a minimal requirement of depth is surface and that a precondition of surface in turn is line. And even if we concede that "a moving line generates a surface and a moving point a line" (*De Anima* 409a4–5), the point remains only indirectly constitutive of a surface and hence even more indirectly constitutive of the depth that a surface brings with it.[45]

3. If we grant that points are capable of being wholly contained—strictly surrounded by their immediate environment and thus themselves fully *in* place on Aristotle's own criterion of implacement—we cannot aver the converse: namely, that points contain in turn. In fact, points, regarded as discrete entities, do not contain anything other than themselves; they are, quite literally, *self*-contained. As such, they cannot be analogized to "a vessel which cannot be moved around" (*Physics* 212a15). To fail the test of this analogy is to fail the Aristotelian test of place, for it is to fail to embody the criterion of containership. A point can be extended, that is, at once manipulable and visible, and yet, in its very compactness and density, still be incapable of surrounding in the manner of a vase or jug or river.[46] For surrounding to arise, two conditions must be met: there must be both a plurality of units, and it must be possible to draw lines between them. Either way, we must move beyond any *single* point if a circumstance of containing is to obtain. Though sine qua non for containership (i.e., as constituents of surfaces), points are not themselves containers.[47]

This discussion leads us to distinguish between *boundary* and *limit.* We can grant that a point is a "limit of localization" [48]—precisely the *lower* limit, beneath which we cannot (and need not) go. For limit, like shape,[49] belongs primarily to what is limited and only secondarily to what does the limiting (e.g., a container). At least this is so in Aristotelian physics, given its resistance to any externally imposed mathematization. In such a physics, as Proclus suggests, "the limits surrender themselves to the things they limit; they establish themselves in them, becoming, as it were, parts of them and being filled with their inferior characters." [50] Indeed, in a properly Aristotelian physics, the point can even be regarded as a paradigm of the limit because of its compressed and self-contained state. As Proclus says, "All limits . . . subsist covertly and indivisibly in a single form under the idea of the point." [51]

To be a boundary, by contrast, is to be exterior to something or, more exactly, to be *around* it, *enclosing* it, acting as its surrounder. As such, a boundary belongs to the container rather than to the contained—and thus properly to place conceived as the inner surface of the containing vehicle, that is, as (in Aquinas's formulation) "the terminus *of the container.*" [52] Like place itself, a boundary "shuts in and closes off something from what lies around it" [53]—*which is precisely what a point cannot do.* Even if it is composed of points, a boundary must be at the very least linear in character if it is to function in this simultaneously en-closing and closing-off manner: hence its affinity with the idea of a "borderline." But, as linear, a boundary is the boundary of a surface or a solid, *not* of a point. A point is surrounded by space as immersed *in* it, not as bordered *by* it; to be itself part of a boundary, a point must be conjoined with other points so as to constitute a line.

Two possible outcomes are suggested by the distinction I have just made between boundary and limit. On the one hand, the case for Aristotle's denial that a point is itself a place is strengthened: if a point is indeed a limit, it does not constitute a boundary; and since it is the latter that is essential to place on Aristotle's own model, a point cannot be a place or perhaps even an integral part of place. Self-limited in its splendid isolation and other-limiting only as part of a continuous line, a point lacks the crucial criterion of containership. On the other hand, place itself is more like a boundary than like a limit. Not only is a place two-sided in the manner of a boundary—insofar as it is inclusive and exclusive at once—but it is also like a boundary in the special signification that Heidegger detects in the ancient Greek conception of *horismos,* "horizon," itself derived from *horos* (boundary): "that from which something *begins its presencing.*" [54] For a place is indeed an active source of presencing: within its close embrace, things get located and begin to happen.

In view of place's considerable boundarylikeness,[55] one move seems clearly indicated: if Aristotle's definition of place is to avoid leaking like a sieve, that is, like a vessel that has been moved one time too many, we ought to substitute "boundary" (*horos*) for "limit" (*peras*) in its formulation. Then the definition might hold water once again, and in so doing it would also put point itself finally in its proper place. But what is this place?

V

> Now in imagined and perceived objects the very points that are in the line limit it, but in the region of immaterial forms the partless idea of the point has prior existence. . . . Thus it is at once unlimited and limited—in its own forthgoing unlimited, but limited by virtue of its participation in its limitlike cause.
>
> —Proclus, *A Commentary on the First Book of Euclid's Elements*

> A point is a nexus of actual entities with a certain "form."
>
> —Alfred North Whitehead, *Process and Reality*

> Suppose no feeling but that of a single point ever to be awakened. Could that possibly be the feeling of any special *whereness* or *thereness*? Certainly not. . . . Each point, so far as it is *placed*, [exists] . . . only by virtue of what it *is not*, namely, by virtue of another point.
>
> —William James, *Principles of Psychology*

The comparison of point and place has more of a point than the skeptical reader might imagine. For one thing, point is at stake in any cosmogenesis of place that is of recognizably geometric inspiration, whether by way of conspicuous presence (as in Pythagorean accounts and in Euclid as read by certain Neoplatonists) or because of an equally conspicuous omission (as in Plato's case). For another thing, points are invoked in concrete descriptions of place that lack any cosmological or geometrical overtones: as in such descriptive phrases as "meeting point," "the point of the peninsula," "the point of overlap [between two adjacent areas]," or "the point of no return." Indeed, Aristotle himself, ignoring his own precautions, sometimes adverts to point-language in describing movement between places.

> As it is with the point, then, so it is with the moving thing, by which we become acquainted with change and the before and the after in it. The moving thing is, in respect of what makes it what it is, the same (as the point is, so is a stone or something else of that sort); but in definition it is different . . . [i.e.,] different by being in different places.[56]

That the point is a unit by which place, and still other regions of space, can be conceived and even experienced has been of perennial interest. If Plato regarded the point as a "geometrical fiction"[57] contra the Pythagoreans, Aristotle reinstated the abiding importance of the point, considering it to be as indispensable in geometry as it is problematic in physics. By the time of Proclus (A.D. 410–485), the point had assumed an almost irresistible allure that has continued to capture the attention of thinkers as diverse as Descartes and Hegel, Leibniz and Bergson, Whitehead and Derrida—each of whom devotes himself to the fate of the point in space and time.

In this tradition of continuing attention to the topic, Proclus represents something of a watershed. For him, the point is both cosmically and geometrically generative. It is this not as something aggressively imposed on an underlying matrix by some theurgic power but as itself a procreative principle. As Proclus says, "Although its being is determined by the Limit, [the point] secretly contains the potentiality of the Unlimited, by virtue of which it generates all intervals; and the procession of all the intervals 'still' does not exhaust its infinite capacity."[58] "Intervals" include lines and distances of all kinds (i.e., the very basis of many modern conceptions of place as metrically determinate), and their dependence on the point represents a reversal of the Platonic view that a point is nothing but the beginning of a line.[59] No wonder that Proclus is able to proclaim, "We have expanded somewhat largely on these matters in order to show that points, and limits in general, have power in the cosmos and that they have the premier rank in the All."[60]

On this expansive view, points come to replace place itself as "the first of all things." Just as Aristotle reacts against Plato by espousing an immanent physicalism in which place and not space is paramount, so Proclus proposes a view of the created universe in which the point and not place is the most effective immanent generative principle. Indeed, we witness in Proclus the first appearance of a distinctive pointillism of place wherein points, regarded as cosmically primary, give rise to places as if by natural extension. For Proclus, the question is not *whether* there are such things as points (as Plato wondered), or whether points themselves are places or placelike (as Aristotle ponders), or whether points are superimposed on indifferent space (as Descartes will speculate), but instead *how* points generate lines, surfaces, solids, and ultimately places themselves by virtue of producing "all intervals."

Where Aristotle is concerned to *put point in (its) place*—to confine it to a status as a limit-concept in a geometry that reflects, rather than informs, the physical world—Proclus insists on the place-making power of the point, a power that exceeds what Aristotle calls "the power of place [itself]" (*Physics* 208b34). That which has (much less is) strictly no place at all in Aristotelian physics becomes a cosmogenetic force that "unifies all things that are divided,"[61] including all places and regions in the known universe. The point becomes a first principle, an *archē,* in the process of cosmic procreation.

Echoes of such a principle still resonate in Hegel's philosophy of nature, where the movement of space (conceived as Being-outside-itself), from an initial situation of sheer undifferentiation into a first moment of determinacy, is effected precisely by the point.

> The difference of space is, however, essentially a determinate, qualitative difference. As such [the point] is first the negation of space itself [insofar as] this is immediate, differenceless self-externality.[62]

Derrida comments tellingly on this passage.

> The point is the space that does not take up space, the place that does not take place; it suppresses and replaces the place, it takes the place of the space that it negates and conserves. It spatially negates space. It is the first determination of space.[63]

For Hegel, the point is determinative *from within* the spatial world itself and is not the result of any supervening action on the part of a separate deity. It is determinative of place in particular by its internal negation of sheer space; thus it precedes place, which comes *after* space and time in the Hegelian dialectic.[64] Point "replaces" place by its very position *before* place in the final scheme of things; it is thus pre-positional, not by being put *over* place but by being posited as the abstract moment that gives rise to place—to begin with.

We might contrast this Proclean-Hegelian vision of immanent point-power with the very different vision of Marduk, whose lethal pointed arrows "split the belly, pierced the gut, and cut the womb" of Tiamat. I have argued that Tiamat, whose writhing body is "too deep for us to fathom," is the mythic progenitor of the Receptacle. As such, she is deeply threatening to the world-ordering interests of Marduk, who must subdue her *from without* by martial maneuvers and by the pointed power of arrows. Only by the application of such power can the Tiamatian ur-place become a well-ordered place-world with determinate locales.[65] In this protogeometric act of creation—which we have seen to be remarkably analogous to the actions of the Demiurge in the *Timaeus*—we witness the point as an alien power, as something that ravages space, indeed annihilates it from a position of aggressive exteriority. Instead of respecting and preserving space—instead of taking "the place of the space that it negates *and conserves* [i.e., by an act of *Aufhebung*]"—it is as if Tiamatian space is too dangerous to live with, much less to conserve: thus it must be eliminated. This is accomplished by a sharp-tipped point that draws away the vital force of space qua primal Place. The dot destroys the matrix—in poignant contrast with the composite dot-matrix solutions proposed by Aristotle (who promotes place over point) and by Proclus (who makes point primary within place itself).

It is instructive to learn that Aristotle is the last of the early Greek thinkers who consistently used the word *stigmē* for "point." *Stigmē* connotes a *punctur-ing* point,[66] a point that includes the arrows of Marduk, punctuation points, and the insistent isolation of separated geometric points. Becalming the ambition and hostility of the stigmatic point—embedding stigmatism within the ambience of place—Aristotle inaugurates an astigmatic era in which a more irenic relation between dot and matrix will become possible.[67]

VI

> Yet how can there be a motion of void or a place for void? That into which void moves comes to be void of void.
>
> —*Physics* 217a3–5

> Aristotle repeatedly assimilates theories of void to theories of place.
>
> —Edward Hussey, *Aristotle's Physics,*
> *Books III and IV*

It is a striking structural fact that Aristotle, having disposed of infinity in the opening chapters of book 4 of the *Physics,* treats the void *in between* place and time in the same book. Void, then, exists between place and time: as if to say that to get out of place is to get into the void and to get into time is to get out of the void. Time is therefore one way of avoiding, indeed of *de*voiding the void—emptying its emptiness by introducing measured cadences and reliable rhythms into its abyss. These cadences and rhythms are dependent on motions and magnitudes that belong in turn to place.[68] Thus to go from place to void to time is in the end to return to place; it is to travel in a topoteleological trajectory that keeps coming back to place even as it departs from it.

In view of this circular topology it is hardly surprising that Aristotle argues for the indissociability of place and void.[69] He does so at two levels. First, at the level of *endoxa,* or common belief, "those who say there is a void suppose it to be a kind of place" (213a16). They do so because of a seemingly commonsensical (but in fact paralogical) line of reasoning: "People think that what is, is body, and that every body is in a place, and that void is place in which there is no body; so that, if anywhere there is no body, then there is nothing there" (213b32–34). Second, at the level of conceptual analysis, Aristotle takes over this paralogic of ordinary belief for his own purposes. He assumes the possible truth of this belief in order to discern its implications for place: void, *were it to exist, would be* placelike. As placelike, however, it cannot exist as "separated," that is, in its own right: for a place is always inseparable from its occupant. And yet an unseparated void—a void dependent on its contents—is no void at all. In short, to the extent that void is placelike, it cannot be a true void; conversely, insofar as a place is vacuous, it cannot be a true place. Referring to his own discussion of place in the immediately preceding chapters of the *Physics,* Aristotle concludes that "since an analysis of place has been made, and void, if it is, must be place deprived of body, and [as] it has been stated in what sense there is and is not place, it is manifest that in this sense there is no void" (214a16–18). Even when we regard void merely as "extension between bodies"—that is, as the *interval* (*diastēma*) posited by the Atomists—we find that it remains placelike, for such an extension is a place of possible occupancy by bodies.[70]

Consider the leading argument for the void as set forth by the Atomists: the void is "responsible for" change in that it provides the setting for all change (including motion), being "that in which change occurs."[71] But, given that the void is nondifferentially structured, it cannot explain the inherent directedness or the differential speed of natural motion—indeed, it cannot explain why anything moves to begin with—and its invocation in physics is otiose: "For what then *will* the void be responsible? It is thought to be responsible for change in respect of place, but for this it is not."[72] Place, on the other hand, explains any change—including velocity and direction—that involves locomotion. Thanks to its stationariness, it also explains rest. While the void renders motion as well as rest incoherent, for Aristotle place qua container accounts for both of these phenomena economically and effectively.[73] Similarly, if we consider condensation or rarefaction, or the displacement of substances, the void will explain nothing: worse, if it were in fact to exist, it would render such changes senseless.[74]

For all of these reasons, the void as a concept (and not merely as a belief) is regarded as dispensable by Aristotle. Fascinating as its idea may be and compelling to the Atomists as it doubtless was, it is finally a gratuitous fiction—a ghostly double of that which is not gratuitous at all, namely, *place.* Place suffices to account for all that the vaunted void purports to illuminate. As Edward Hussey comments, "The implication of the argument is that a void which is not an explanatory factor of anything is pointless and therefore cannot exist."[75]

Pointless as well is any effort to associate the point with the void—an effort stemming from the Pythagorean association between the point and the Unlimited.[76] As Aristotle says brusquely, "It is absurd, if a point is to be void; for [void] must be [place] in which there is an extension [within] tangible body" (214a4–6). Just as we can neither imagine nor think a void that is unplacelike, so we cannot imagine or think point as void—or, for that matter, void as point. Therefore, not only does Aristotle deconstruct the point as a candidate for place, but he ends by eliminating both point and void as competitors with place in the determination of location. In such determination, place takes first place; and in this privileged position it takes care of itself, needing neither the point nor the void as explanation or support. If everything is fully

placed—if nothing, at least nothing sensible, is without a place of its own—
then no void need exist, actually or potentially, and things do not require
points to specify their status.[77] Otherwise put: to be a physical body is to
occupy a determinate *topos,* a place-pocket as it were, that is filled by this
very body and that (at another time) can be reoccupied by another body of the
same dimensions. To Freud's dictum that "the finding of an object is in fact a
refinding of it," we can add Aristotle's rule that every implacement is in effect
a reimplacement.[78] And if everything in the physical world is not only placed
but also displaceable and replaceable, then we have to do with a world in
plenary session—a lococentric world-whole. This is a world in which points
and the void are not so much absent (particular points and discrete vacua may
still occur) as superfluous. As Bergson says, "All is full in Aristotle's world."[79]

Aristotle conceives this place-world not by expanding but by *restricting*
his field of inquiry. In contrast with the logical and rhetorical excesses of
Zeno, Parmenides, and Gorgias—each of whom extols the ubiquity of place
without ever telling us anything specific about place itself—Aristotle's nuanced descriptions attempt to say just what place is and how it differs from
other constituents of the physical world. And in contrast with Plato, Aristotle
confines his efforts to describing the exact characteristics of just *one* of the
three sorts of spatial entities distinguished in the *Timaeus.* The *Physics* concerns itself only with the most particular such entity, that is, *topos,* while
general regions and *chōra* are made marginal. The amplitude of the Receptacle
gives way to the stringency of the container; and within place-as-container,
concrete issues bearing on boundary and limit, line and surface, point and
void, are addressed in scrupulous detail.

VII

> It is obvious that one has to grant
> priority to place.
>
> —Archytas

This is not to claim that Aristotle's idea of place is without complications and
difficulties. To begin with, there is the fact that he changed his model of place
in a major way in the period between the early composition of the *Categories*—where place qua *chōra* is construed as equivalent to empty "interval"
(*diastēma*)—and the text of the *Physics,* where this very model is decisively
rejected.[80] More important, there are at least four serious problems in Aristotle's mature view of place as the immobile inner surface of a container.
(1) By its emphasis on surface (*epiphaneia*), this view is confined to a two-
dimensional model of place, despite the fact that place itself is manifestly
three-dimensional inasmuch as it surrounds *solid* objects. (In comparison,

Aristotle's fascination with the point can be taken as an incursion into one-dimensional or even zero-dimensional space and, for all its interest, is fore-doomed as a fitting model for volumetric containment.) (2) There is an unre-solved tension between the *localism* of the container model—which points to physical things as "place tight" in their immediate environs—and the *glob-alism* implicit in certain of the Stagirite's descriptions of the physical uni-verse.[81] Even if it is true that "everything is in the world" (212b17) and that there is nothing *outside* the world—no external void—the world-whole en-compasses any particular place of any given changeable body and must be a global Place for that place-cum-body. (That the total world is a Place follows from the fact that it contains and surrounds all more particular places within it.) A place is not only a place *for* a body but a place *in* the larger world-Place.[82] In addition, only such a cosmic Place can make sense of Aristotle's insistence on the irreducibility of the up/down dimension. Construed as cos-mic, this dimension signifies that the earth is at the center of the universe and the heavens at its outer limit.[83] But to make this latter claim—to say that the earth is always and only at the center of the universe—is to call for a sense of space as absolute or global that is not allowed, strictly speaking, by the con-tainer model in its constrictive, localizing character. (3) The full determination of the "first unchangeable limit of that which surrounds" remains moot. In the case of the floating vessel, is this limit the immediately surrounding water regarded as an ideal perimeter (yet as flowing water, it is constantly changing, with the result that the place of a stationary boat will be *continually changing*), or is it the river's bed-and-banks or even the river itself as a whole (in both of these last cases, two boats equidistant from two banks but heading in opposite directions will occupy *the same place*)?[84] This seemingly trivial but in fact momentous question was to engage over two thousand years of debate in Western philosophy: it is still a live issue for Descartes in the seventeenth century A.D. (4) Finally, we must inquire as to what it means to *contain* some-thing. Is it merely a matter of "holding," as is implied by the verb *periech-ein*—in which case, the emphasis is on the act of delimitation, that is, of *surrounding*? Or is it a question of establishing a boundary—which stresses the *surrounder*? Where the former interpretation directs us to what is sur-rounded, the latter points to what is other than, and beyond, the surrounded object (and perhaps even beyond the surrounder itself). How are we to choose between these two interpretations—one of which stresses the container as *limit,* the other the container as *boundary*? And if we cannot choose effec-tively, are we not confronted with an essentially undecidable phenomenon?

Despite these perplexities and still others,[85] we need to retain what is most original—and most lasting—in Aristotle's mature vision of place. This is the acknowledgment of place as a unique and nonreducible feature of the physical world, something with its own inherent powers, a pre–metric phenomenon (thus both historically and conceptually pre-Euclidean in its specification), and above all something that reflects the situation of being in, and moving between, places. It is just this accommodating and yet polyvalent model of place that became lost in Euclidean and post-Euclidean theories of strictly measurable space.[86] Aristotle was able to resist this mensurational view even as he was drawn to it early in his career: he came to realize that, regarded as extension or interval, place becomes merely an item of exact quantitative determination. For what matters most is not the measurement of objects in empty space but the presence of sensible things in their appropriate and fitting places.

In effecting this tour de force—whereby a focused, forceful description yields what may well be the most astute assessment of place to be found in Western philosophy—Aristotle proceeds with a phenomenologist's deft sensibilities.[87] This is most evident in his resolute refusal to restrict the phenomenon of place to atomistic or formal properties. Just as he rejects Plato's attempt to regularize sensible bodies by the imposition of elementary geometric figures (he takes such bodies to be straightforwardly "what is extended in three dimensions"),[88] so he approaches place on its own terms. His preoccupation with the propriety of place is evident in his telling remark that "each thing moves to its own place" (*Physics* 212b29), that is to say, to its proper natural place. That each such place is encompassed by the common place of the firmament—and that this latter is conceived as having constant circular curvature—does not mean that Aristotle has "spatialized" place in the manner of the spatialization of time decried by Bergson and Heidegger alike.[89] Problematic as we have just seen it to be, the very nesting of special *topoi* within an overarching *Topos* has the virtue of conceiving the cosmos not as an empty and endless Space but as an embracing Place, filled to the brim with snugly fitting proper places. The firmament that encircles the world-whole is at once a paradigm for all lesser places and filled with these very same places. Everything, or almost everything, is in place. To be an existing sensible thing is never *not* to be in some place. Place prevails. Archytas stands vindicated.

Aristotle surpasses Archytas, however, in his eagerness to show just how "it is obvious that one has to grant priority to place" and just why "it is the first of all things."[90] He does so by demonstrating that place, beyond providing mere position, gives bountiful aegis—active protective support—to what it locates. Defined as a bounding container, place in Aristotle's sure hands takes on a quite dynamic role in the determination of the physical universe. Place indeed "has some power." It has the power to make things be *somewhere* and to hold and guard them once they are there. Without place, things would not only fail to be located; they would not even be *things:* they would have *no place to be the things they are.* The loss would be ontological and not only cosmological: it would be a loss in a *kind* of being and not merely in the number of beings that exists.

Part Two

From Place to Space

Interlude

In Part I we witnessed a development—or, more in keeping with Aristotle's thinking, an "envelopment"—of remarkable scope. The scope is impressive not just in terms of time (a period of approximately two thousand years) but also in terms of theme: all the way from *muthos* to *logos*. Yet Plato's *Timaeus* combines both of these latter extremes in a single text: hence its position in the middle of Part I, flanked on one side by imaginative mythicoreligious accounts of creation and on the other side by Aristotle's sober descriptions. Nevertheless, this progression in time and theme is no simple matter of progress. Anticipations and retroactions abound: Aristotle's closely containing *topos* is foreshadowed in the final stage of Plato's tale, while the Stagirite's concern with the importance of the point rejoins the stress in the *Enuma Elish* on the deadly edges of weapons of war. Nor can it be said that Plato "improves upon" myth, given that the language of his dialogue is so deeply indebted to earlier mythical traditions. Indeed, Aristotle himself, "the Master of Those Who Know," is by no means free from mythical borrowings and infusions. We have seen that Hesiod is an important source in his opening, "exoteric" discussion of place in the *Physics* (Hesiod is reinvoked in the first book of the *Metaphysics*).[1] More crucially, Aristotle illuminates the role of place in the concreta of everyday life—a life that, despite historical and social vicissitudes, is recognizably similar across the centuries that separate Aristotle from the anonymous authors of the Sumerian epic. Instead of progression, in his case we are better advised to speak of a *regression* into the immanent structures of daily life: the same structures that characterized the experience of earlier generations of people in the Mediterranean world.

Another continuity that binds together an otherwise disparate and far-flung

picture is that of the relation between cosmogenesis and topogenesis. We have
seen that this relation is two-way in its directionality. Cosmogenesis, that is,
the generation of the (or *a*) world, entails topogenesis, the production of particular places with which the world—in becoming a place-world—is to be
populated. Places punctuate a world and serve to specify it. On the other hand,
the proliferation of places requires a world, a coherent and capacious cosmos,
in which and in order to occur. But *cosmos* and *topos* hardly exhaust the
question of place. Neither term does justice to the middle realm of *chōra*,
which is not well ordered enough to be a world yet is too extensive to be a
single place or set of places. No wonder that Aristotle, threatened by the prospect of such an incommodious middle term, could not admit it into his *Physics:* if not absurd (he takes it too seriously for this to be the case), it is surd
(i.e., it does not fit into his scheme of things). Consequently, he restricts the
range of *chōra* severely, attempting to identify it with his own notion of matter. Yet, as we have seen, he cannot do without the idea of the universe at
large, "all that is" (*to pan*), and in this way one basic property of choric space
(i.e., its indefinite expansiveness) is reimported into his physical theory. Becoming (*genesis*), another attribute of such space, reappears in Aristotle's emphasis on change (*kinēsis*), with which his *Physics* is concerned throughout.
As a result, the interplay between Aristotle and Plato, their embattlement, is
as complex and revealing as the interaction between *cosmos* and *topos* when
mediated by *chōra* as a third term.

The primary issues that emerge in ancient treatments of place have to do
with genesis and purpose on one side and with form and embodiment on the
other. It is striking that the first two issues bear on questions of causation and
teleology, whereas the latter two concern such things as location and containment: thus, not where place comes from or where it is tending, but how it
operates in the present. In terms of the analytical categories employed elsewhere in the *Physics* and in the *Metaphysics,* we have to do with efficient and
final causes (*aitia,* also "explanations") in the first case and with formal and
material explanations in the second. Efficient causes concern origins, and final
causes constitute ends: both are aspects of becoming as it affects and characterizes place. In contrast, location, especially location accomplished by secure
containment, raises questions of the formal and material structuring of the
phenomenal world: such structuring is inherently stabilizing, a matter of *stabilitas loci.* The ancient world, including many of Aristotle's own predecessors
(indeed, including Aristotle himself),[2] considered place in all four ways,
thereby leaving a rich and lasting legacy for future explorations in post-
Aristotelian philosophy.

In Parts II and III we shall explore this legacy as it is assimilated and
transformed in the more than two millennia that extend from 400 B.C. to A.D.
1800. In this enormous epoch, Aristotle's Archytian emphasis on the primacy
of place is deepened and broadened—especially in the Hellenistic and Neopla-

tonic periods—and yet finally curtailed and limited, as occurs most dramatically in medieval and early modern times. In this complex transition a preoccupation with place gradually gives way to a stress on space—where "space" connotes something undelimited and open-ended: a conception first posited by Aristotle's antagonists, the ancient Atomists. While place solicits questions of limit and boundary, and of location and surrounding, space sets these questions aside in favor of a concern with the absolute and the infinite, the immense and the indefinitely extended. If place bears on what lies *in*—in a container, dwelling, or vessel—space characteristically moves *out,* so far out as to explode the closely confining perimeters within which Aristotle attempted to ensconce material things. In this unequal battle, spacing-out triumphs over placing-in.

What we shall observe in the two chapters constituting Part II is part and parcel of the overall transformation from a mostly secular and naturalistic worldview—in which the vernacularity of place, its habitability and idiosyncrasy, is predictably prominent—to a theological Weltanschauung in which the infinity of space becomes a primary preoccupation. If God is limitless in power, then His presence in the universe at large must also be unlimited. Divine ubiquity thus entails spatial infinity. It further follows that the physical universe itself must be unlimited if it is to be the setting for God's ubiquity as well as the result of His creation. Not surprisingly, the increasing hegemony of Christianity supported both forms of infinity: that of God as the ultimate monotheistic being and that of His universe as the ultimate monothetic entity.

Nor is it surprising that this theological background set the stage for a comparable concern with the spatial infinity of the physical universe on the part of the natural scientists and philosophers who began to mathematize nature in the sixteenth and seventeenth centuries. This resecularization of the world via quantification, which will be the subject of Part III, would not have been possible without the theological reflections of the preceding several centuries. Theology and physics are closely allied in their common effort to conceive of space in utterly maximal terms: a marriage epitomized in the intimate intertwining of Isaac Newton's physical and theological writings. If theology, especially Christian theology, is universalist in its aims, why should not the new physics—standing on the shoulders of this ambitious theology—proclaim truths that hold for every material object in the universe? The colonizing tendency of Christianity is echoed in the attempts of Galilean, Cartesian, and Newtonian physics to appropriate whole realms formerly consigned to alchemy and "natural philosophy," not to mention local custom and history. In both instances, the power of place, uncontested in the ancient world (and still potently present in medieval times), was put into abeyance—indeed, often literally abolished, and with as much relentless force as that with which native peoples were subjected to Christian indoctrination. By the end of the eighteenth century, the idea of universal space came to be regarded as obtaining

not just for the external world and for God but also for the mind of the knowing subject. Immanuel Kant, with whose rigorous philosophy of space Part III
shall close, internalized the very spatial infinity that had been located either
in God or in the natural world in the twelve hundred years that preceded his
work. Yet this act of incorporation (or, rather, inpsychicalization) is no less
insistent on the infinity—and the absoluteness—of the space thereby located
within the pure intuition of the knowing subject.

The saga about to unfold is a tale of the gradual ascendancy of the universe
over the cosmos. "Uni-verse," *universum* in its original Latin form, means
turning around *one* totalized whole. The universe is the passionate single aim
of Roman conquest, Christian conversion, early modern physics, and Kantian
epistemology. In contrast, "cosmos" implies the particularity of place; taken
as a collective term, it signifies the ingrediency of places in discrete place-
worlds. (The Greek language has no word for "universe"; instead, it speaks of
to pan, "all that is," "the All.") In its aesthetic being—"cosmetic" and "cosmos" are second cousins linguistically via the sharing of *aisthēsis,* that is,
bodily sensing—cosmos brings with it an essential reference to the experiencing body that is in close touch with it, takes it in, and comes to know it. The
limit of a place is specified by what a body can do in that place, that is, by its
sensory activity, its legwork, its history there. The universe is mapped in physics and projected in theology: it is the transcendent geography of infinite
space. The cosmos is sensed in concrete landscapes as lived, remembered, or
painted: it is the immanent scene of finite place as felt by an equally finite
body.

Where the universe calls for objective knowledge in the manner of a unified physics or theology, the cosmos calls for the experience of the individuated subject in its midst—with all of the limitations and foreclosures this experience brings with it. To have substituted the spatial infinity of the universe
for the placial finitude of the cosmos is to have effected the fateful transition
from ancient to modern thinking in the West. To this transition we must now
turn.[3]

4
The Emergence of Space in Hellenistic and Neoplatonic Thought

All that is is place.

—Lucretius, *De rerum natura*

All there is is place.

—Richard Sorabji, *Matter, Space, and Motion*

I

The nature of the universe is bodies and void [*to pan esti sōmata kai kenon*].

—Epicurus, *Peri phuseōs* (On Nature)

One's thought of the void does not give out anywhere.

—attributed to Cleomedes

Part of the perennial appeal of Aristotle's conception of place as something confining and confined is doubtless the philosophical support it offers to human beings' longing for cozy quarters—not merely for adequate shelter but for boundaries that embrace, whether these boundaries belong to decorated rooms in the home or to indecorous glades in the forest primeval. But human beings (and doubtless other animals) also long for wide open spaces and thus for lack of containment, perhaps even for limitlessness. The cozy can be *too* confining, and just to peer out beyond thick walls or through dense treetops into the sky is to discover the inviting and intriguing presence of empty spaces and unoccupied places.

One way to sanction this different longing is to posit a cosmological model radically divergent from that of Aristotle—or, indeed, from those of Plato and

Anaximander, the thinker of the Boundless, *to apeiron*.[1] The ancient Greek
world knew such a model: put in crude but compelling terms, the Atomists
held that there is nothing but "atoms and the void." Atoms are incredibly
condensed and indivisible bits of matter (*a-tomos* means "uncuttable"), and
the void is the open space, the free leeway, required for their random motions.
Consider the cosmogony of Leucippus, the earliest Atomist and the presumed
mentor of Democritus (both lived in the fifth century B.C., approximately two
generations before Plato).

> The coming to be of the worlds (*cosmoi*) is thus: (1) In severance from the
> infinite, many bodies, of all varieties of shape, move into a great void. (2) These,
> being assembled, create a single vortex, in which they collide, gyrate in every
> way, and are sorted like to like. (3) When because of the number they are no
> longer able to move round in equilibrium, then the fine ones move into the void
> outside, as if sifted, while the remainder stay together, become intertwined, join
> courses with each other, and bring about a first system, in the shape of a sphere.[2]

This cosmogony is said to proceed by "necessity" (*anankē*). Unlike Plato's
account in the *Timaeus,* however, this likely story includes no formative
Demiurge, since "all varieties of shape" are present from the start. Also present are "the infinite" (again *to apeiron,* but now construed not just as bound-
less but as a positive being), "the great void," and "many bodies." These three
crucial constituents of the universe—that is, of *to pan*—are uncreated and
pregiven. From them, everything else ensues: regions of "like" things as well
as the earth, the sun, the moon, the stars, and all other celestial bodies. The
great void is the gathering area for those bodies that will form "a first system,"
that system being our own *cosmos*.[3] Other *cosmoi* will form in what Leucippus calls "the void outside." Taken together, the great void and the void outside constitute the infinite void, and this all-encompassing void is differen-
tially populated throughout by those compact indivisible material bodies
called "atoms."

The Atomist model entails a double infinity: the infinity of space and the
infinity of the atoms that populate this space. Just as there can be no end to
space in the universe, so there is no end to the number of atoms (and thus, as
a corollary, to the number of worlds to which atomic combinations in turn
give rise). As Epicurus (341–270 B.C.) put it, "The totality is infinite both in
the quantity of atomic bodies and in spatial magnitude."[4] Instead of there
being a fixed number of elements that make up material bodies—as Emped-
ocles, Plato, and Aristotle all believed—the elements and bodies themselves
are constituted from an unlimited number of atoms in diverse configurations.
In fact, the two Atomist infinities here in question are closely related. On the
one hand, an infinite number of atoms requires an infinite space in which to
move; anything less would curtail their motions. (Also required is that this
infinite space be essentially *empty* [*kenon*] or at least "porous" [*manon*].)[5] On

the other hand, an infinite space calls for an infinite number of bodies within it; otherwise, it would be merely the region for a few, or even many, bodies—but not for *all possible* bodies.[6]

The Atomists would agree with their archrival Parmenides that what is real is a plenum, adding only that what is real is plural and not singular. Since the void per se is empty of any material body, this means that the void in any of its three basic guises is necessarily "unreal" or "not real" (*mē on*). Yet the void *exists* (*einai*); indeed, as we have just seen, it *must* exist—exist as providing space—if the motion of the atoms is to be possible.[7] As Aristotle is reported to have said concerning this double ontology: "The real exists not a whit more than the not real, empty space no less than body."[8] Atoms and the void, the ultimate constituents of the physical universe, both exist, although only one is real in any strict sense. Even if one has "being" (*to on*) and the other does not, they rejoin each other in the co-necessity of their common existence.

The ingrained wholism of Aristotle and Plato—their passionate desire for perfection, especially of a teleologically ordered sort—ends in a cosmographic picture of a closed and finite world with no further universe around it. In contrast, the Atomists seek, beyond minuscule atoms, that which is infinitely large—a universe of empty space. In the first case, an overriding concern with formal, rational order (an order that, if not found initially, has to be added to the precosmic matrix) eventuates in a world of discrete places, whereas in the second case a commitment to "saving the appearances" (and especially the appearances of particular perceptual objects) calls for a vision of an infinite spatial universe, populated by sporadic and endlessly varying combinations of atomic units—both universe and atoms sharing in a like imperceptibility.[9] This difference of vision suggests that a radical departure from the primacy of place (first evident in Hesiod) occurred in the thought of the inaugural Atomists. For does not classical Atomism—a thousand years before Philoponus and two thousand years before Newton—plunge us into an unaccommodating, placeless space? Is there any place for *place* within the Atomistic void?

Democritus and Leucippus will not help us directly with these questions. Not only is the surviving evidence of their full-scale systems—called intriguingly the *Great World System* and the *Little World System*—extremely scanty, but these founding figures were not alive to answer Aristotle's scathing critique of the void. Epicurus, who visited Athens at the time of Aristotle's death in 322 B.C., was in a better position to answer this critique. This latter-day Atomist conceded to Aristotle that void is indeed placelike in certain basic respects. The concession was so striking that modern editors of Epicurus have been tempted to alter the standard Atomistic phrase "bodies and space" (*sōmata kai chōra*)" or "bodies and void" (*sōmata kai kenon*) to "bodies and place" (*sōmata kai topos*). However controversial this emendation has proven to be,[10] the temptation is based on a substantive point. For the more Epicurus pondered Aristotle's objections to the void as superfluous—superfluous precisely insofar as it duplicates what is already accomplished by place qua *topos*—the more he came to conceive of the void as locatory in nature. Void is that "in which" (*hopou*) atoms are located and that "through which" (*di' hou*) they move.[11] Precisely as such, it is what immediately situates any given atom. Does this mean that void *surrounds* the atoms it situates? One recent commentator draws our attention to

> the striking similarity of Epicurean void, [regarded] as place, to Aristotle's fluid, immediate place for moving objects. . . . [This void] is not a sort of extension that could be filled or not filled. It was simply an *anaphēs phusis* ("intangible substance") surrounding the distinct, constantly moving atoms. . . . Void is accepted as the absence of body, but not, on that account, as the unoccupied part of an extended space. . . . For Epicurus, an atom did not strictly speaking occupy space; it was simply surrounded by the absence of body.[12]

If this characterization of Epicurus is right, then the mere existence of atoms does not, after all, entail the existence of open and empty, much less infinite, space. No such amplitude, no such vacuity, is required. To each atom there corresponds only a quite particular *place* in which it is located at any given moment. The fact that atoms are always moving means only that their places are continually changing. On this view atomic motion does not demand an abiding space that is "a continuous entity subsisting everywhere in the same degree and manner, both where bodies are and where they are not."[13] In short, we can retain the basic Atomist cosmologic that says "if there were no void, there would be no motion; but there is motion; therefore, there is void"[14]—*without* having to interpret such a void as continuous or empty, not to say infinite. The void is finite; it is the very place of each and every atom.

Epicurus rejoins Democritus and Leucippus by maintaining that a distinction is to be made between genuinely empty space or "void proper" (as we can call the original sense of void in the phrase "atoms and the void") and what ought to be termed "vacuum," that is, an empty part or portion of a compound entity constructed of atoms, for example, an empty stomach in a hungry human being. A vacuum is a form of nonbeing, even a nothing, but it exists within the compound—which in turn exists within the void proper. This is why we can speak intelligibly and not merely oxymoronically of a vacuum as a nonbeing that exists: here the ancient paradox is seen to apply to a more discrete entity. The vacuum exists precisely as a "space-filler" in the apt term of David Sedley, who remarks that a vacuum "occupies some parts of space just as effectively as body occupies others."[15] The Archytian axiom is undisturbed by this claim: for a vacuum exists just to the extent that it has a place in which to exist.[16] Void proper—redescribed as "intangible substance" by Epicurus—is what provides such a place, its source as it were. Yet neither

void nor vacuum is place in Aristotle's strict sense of an always already occupied locus for fully formed material objects.[17]

Nevertheless, Epicurus, unlike Leucippus and Democritus, explicitly identifies void proper with what we must begin to call *space.* The best account of
this momentous step is given by Sextus Empiricus.

> Therefore one must grasp that, according to Epicurus, of "intangible substance,"
> as he calls it, one kind is named "void" (*kenon*), another "place" (*topos*), and
> another "room" (*chōra*), the names varying according to the different ways of
> looking at it, since the same substance (*phusis*) when empty of all body is called
> "void," when occupied by a body is named "place," and when bodies roam
> through it becomes "room." But generically it is called "intangible substance"
> in Epicurus' school, since it lacks resistant touch.[18]

This remarkable passage supports the contention that Epicurus was "the first
ancient thinker to isolate space in the broadest sense."[19] If Sextus is right, Epicurus does so by positing a generic space—that is, what is coextensive with
intangible substance (*anaphēs phusis*)—and then recognizing at least three
roles or functions of such space. "Void" (*kenon*), true to its sense as "empty,"
names the circumstance of unoccupied space; it is tantamount to what I have
just called "vacuum." "Place" (*topos*) names the situation of occupied space; it
refers to the location of a sensible thing *in* space. The thing thus located in a
topos is so far stationary, and to account for the different sense of localization
possessed by a moving thing Epicurus posits a third avatar of space: "room"
for something to move in. "Room" translates *chōra,* one of whose affiliated
verbs is *chōrein,* "to go," especially in the sense of "to roam."[20] From its initial
role as matrix in the *Timaeus, chōra* here becomes a much more delimited
power—yet a critical one, since for all the Atomists the primary bodies are in
constant motion, a motion that requires room in which to move. Such room,
affording leeway to solid objects (atoms, even if imperceptible, are "impassi-
ble" magnitudes), is literally voluminous. Aristotle's confining two-dimensional model of place—two-dimensional insofar as it limits itself to the surfaces of things—is surpassed in a three-dimensional roominess.

Thanks to its considerable dynamism, Epicurean space is the *Spielraum* of
atomic bodies, the very medium of their situatedness and movement, the scene
of their multiple occupation. Such space "provides these bodies with location,
with the gaps between them, and with room to move."[21] Expansive as such
space is—giving place and room for everything—it does not pertain to *parts*
of atoms (assuming that atoms have parts), nor does it exist as *intervals* among
atoms of a given body, nor does it even furnish the very *position* of a given
atom.[22] Epicurus might respond that this triple limitation follows from the
basic premise that atoms "have no share in the void."[23] Yet if atoms have
parts and intervals and positions and if they do indeed exist—and if to exist
is to exist in space—then these three aspects of atomic existence will have to

be spatially specified. One suspects that Epicurus has not thought through the full implications of his own idea of a sheerly intangible space. If space construed as *anaphēs phusis* is to be taken seriously, its scope will encompass both the utterly large (the infinite) as well as the utterly small (the infinitesimal), including the most diminutive parts, intervals, and positions.

Lucretius (ca. 99–55 B.C.), Epicurus's devoted and eloquent disciple, adds this thought: "Whatever will exist will have to be in itself something with extension (*augmen*), whether large or small, so long as it exists."[24] Here Lucretius is drawing on an entire heritage of thought concerning "extension," a notion of critical importance in the Hellenistic period. *Diastēma*, the Greek word for "extension," implies *standing/through* (*dia-* signifies "through," and *stēma* derives from the Indo-European root *sta-*, "stand") and, more particularly, *threading/through* (*stēmōn* means "thread"). To be in space is to stand through it, to stretch through it as a thread might stretch over a surface—except that more than surface is at stake here. The "through" is not only entailed by motion in a void but also is implied in all ways of being spatial.

For Epicurus and Lucretius alike there is an intimate link between the noun "extension," the preposition "through," and the concept "space."[25] If placial being is mainly a matter of the "in"—this much we may grant to Aristotle—spatial being is a matter of the "through," that is, a matter of being "extended," stretched *out* such that something exists *through* the interval or gap that space provides. Instead of being something turned in, en-closed, as in the case of Aristotelian place, space is something turned out; it is something that exists *throughout* whatever interval is at stake—an interval that can be infinitely large or infinitely small. Atoms may well have a different "order of being," a different way of existing, than the void proper; the former are essentially plenary, the latter is essentially unoccupied.[26] Even so, both atoms and the void must meet certain requirements of existing spatially. These are the requirements of diastemic space as first clearly glimpsed in the Atomism of Epicurus.

II

> Some say that *chōra* is the place of the larger body.
> —Sextus Empiricus, *Against the Professors*

One ancient thinker—not an Atomist but an Aristotelian—thought long and hard about the microphysics of space. I refer to Strato of Lampsacus, the third head of the Peripatetic school, who died ca. 269 B.C. and thus was an exact contemporary of Epicurus. Ancient tradition credits Strato with being the first thinker to proclaim space to be extended in three dimensions, also holding that any part of it always *in fact* contains a body—even though, in principle, it might not.[27] Stobaeus attributes to Strato the following definition: "Place (*topos*) is the interval in the middle of the container and the contained."[28] At first glance this appears quite Aristotelian, but on closer inspection it turns out that Strato takes place to be something that Aristotle explicitly rejects: the empty pockets found in the interstices of material bodies. These pockets riddle such bodies: "Strato of Lampsacus tries to show that the void exists interspersed in every body so that it is not continuous."[29] Places are thus void spaces: "microvoids," as we might call them. Even if microvoids are never actually vacuous—Atomists' claims notwithstanding—they are instances of extension at the most elementary level. Microvoids exist not only between container and contained (which for Strato are far less snugly fitting than Aristotle had imagined) but also *within* a given material body. Hence they pertain to two of the three aspects of atomic extension neglected by Epicurus: interiors and parts of primary bodies. In fact, they are coextensive and isometric with the interiors and parts of actual bodies that fill them. At the limit, the totality of microvoids may even be coextensive with the "cosmic body" that is equivalent to the complete physical universe.[30] It is not certain that Strato espoused this extreme position, but he did maintain that any given microvoid is an integral part of cosmic extension and not a mere lacuna in this extension. Hence he managed to put together what Epicurus failed to combine: the extension of the infinitely large and the extension of the infinitesimally small.

Strato also was known in the classical world for having devised the most convincing denial of Aristotle's notion of natural places, that is, places proper to given elements. According to Strato, *every* element is heavy and thus falls downward by its sheer weight. If fire and air escape upward, this movement is due to a process of *ekthlipsis,* that is, being "squeezed" up by the compression of other more forceful elements. By thinking this way, Strato agreed with Epicurus and the earlier Atomists in rejecting the idea of preexisting places in the void. There is indeed differential direction in the void, but this is determined by chance collisions of atoms and not by the power of extant cosmic places.[31] And if there are no places carved out of the cosmos in advance, then it is all the more likely that the universe lying beyond the world is something infinitely extended: and this universe is more aptly characterized in spatial rather than placial terms. Just as for Aristotle there is no space apart from place, for Strato there is no place apart from space—no place that is not merely a portion of a much more encompassing whole whose spatiality is both incredibly large and unimaginably small.

If the unimaginably small is a distinctive concern of the Atomists and of Strato, the incredibly large is what increasingly preoccupies ancient philosophers in the wake of Aristotle and Epicurus. One exemplary form of this preoccupation is found in the Stoic proposal that an endless empty void surrounds the finite and place-bound cosmos. The explicit reason for this proposal—which continued to be widely influential in the Middle Ages and the

Renaissance—is that the excess fire generated in periodic cosmic conflagra-
tions has to *go somewhere,* since the volume of this fire is greater than the
finite cosmos can contain. This "somewhere to go" is termed "room" (*chōra*),
where "room" connotes spaciousness, that is, unoccupied space to which to
flee.[32] The extramundane void is what provides room for world-destructive
conflagratory fires.[33] Does this mean that such a room-giving void is a *place*?
Cleomedes, writing in the first century A.D., claimed that the void must be
"capable of receiving body."[34] This would seem to make it some kind of
place. Yet the Stoics took seriously Aristotle's admonition that the void is
"that in which there is no body,"[35] and such a void would be a very tenuous
place indeed. Perhaps we may say that something (e.g., the cosmic fire) can
be *received* by the extramundane void but cannot *occupy* it in any strict sense,
that is, cannot be implaced there. It can enter the void yet cannot remain
there—cannot find therein its own place.

It is an axiom of Stoic cosmology that the void is infinite and place finite.[36]
With no bodies strictly occupying it—in contrast with the ancient Atomist
"void outside"—the Stoic void is neither bounding nor bounded. According
to Chrysippus (280–206 B.C.), "the void beyond the cosmos is infinite, unbounded (*apeiron*) in the literal sense of the word; it has neither beginning nor
middle nor end."[37] In fact, the Stoic void lacks both bodies and boundaries: it
is "an interval empty of body, or an interval unoccupied by body,"[38] where to
be an "interval" (*diastēma*) is precisely *not to be a place for a body.*
Cleomedes characterizes such a void as something "very simple, since it is
incorporeal and without contact, neither has shape nor takes on shape, neither
is acted upon in any respect, nor acts."[39] In other words, void is an empty
extension that has taken the place of place itself: it has (de)voided place. If
this is beginning to sound like "negative cosmology"—as is already indicated
in the very word "in-finite" (and in *a-peiron*)—we can at least say, in a more
positive vein, that the Stoic void is infinitely large, infinitely absorptive, and
altogether external to the cosmos. It gives room, if not place proper, to an
expanding cosmos. It is a macrovoid outside the cosmos—the very converse
of a microvoid internal to the cosmos and to bodies in that cosmos.

Such an extramundane void is a *negatité* (to borrow a useful term from
Sartre): even if not (a) nothing, it is also not an entity, neither a thing nor a
place. It stands in stark contrast with the packed and plenary character of the
cosmos, which for the Stoics does not possess void of any kind—neither in
the form of microvoids nor as the tiny interstices between polygons that are
mentioned in the *Timaeus.* The cosmos has everything the void lacks; it is
full of places and bodies, and full of one in being full of the other—double
plenitude.

Chrysippus declared place to be "what is occupied through and through by
an existent, or what can be occupied by an existent and is through and through
occupied whether by one thing or by several things."[40] Nothing empty, noth-

ing lacking, nothing tenuous here! Place is a dense fabric in the even denser place-world it composes. Guaranteeing coherence and connection in this cosmic plenum is the *pneuma,* the cosmic breath or spirit that circulates throughout the plenary world. Composed of fire and air, the *pneuma* is an active force that transmutes Plato's and Aristotle's geometric continuum of discrete bodies-in-places into a dynamic network of implaced and interpenetrating bodies.[41] Proceeding by a combination of habit (*hexis*) and tension (*tonos*), connection (*sunecheia*) and sympathy (*sumpatheia*), the *pneuma* constitutes "the physical field which is the carrier of all specific properties of material bodies."[42] This field is a close concinnation of places; it is as place-full as the void is sheerly space-rich.

"Under Chrysippus's guidance," writes David Hahm, "the Aristotelian cosmos of elements, each moving by nature to its own concentric sphere, is finally given a comfortable home in the infinite void."[43] Yet there is a darker side to Stoic physics: isolation, not comfort, looms. The cosmos, the physical world as we know it, is "an island embedded in an infinite void."[44] To be an island, however replete with places and bodies, is to be sequestered in an ocean of indifference. Moreover, if the only void is the void "outside the world,"[45] this leaves precious little leeway for maneuver *in this world.*

The Stoics were not insensitive to the problems inherent in the bifurcation of the universe into empty and full, void and place, the incorporeal and the corporeal, with material bodies brought forcibly into place by inescapable pneumatic forces. To address this dilemma, some Stoics speculated that a *third* entity is required to break the gridlock of their fiercely dichotomous universe. Thus Chrysippus "distinguishes an unnamed entity, different from void or place, that is capable of being occupied by being, but is only partly occupied."[46] This third thing is none other than "room." Room is not just space for roaming—as it was for Epicurus—but extension allowing for possible occupation. Extension and room, *diastēma* and *chōra,* come together in a single complex, or more exactly a duplex, entity: cosmos-cum-void.[47] The duplexity is evident in Sextus Empiricus's assertion that for the Stoics the universe is "the external void *together with* the world."[48] Or we might say that void and place merge in space, and they do so in the room space furnishes.

Yet this leaves us wondering if "room" and "space"—both terms being translations of *chōra*—are not merely terms of compromise, posited to conceal the abyss opened up by the diremptive difference between place (*topos*) and the void (*kenon*) that lies at the heart of Stoic cosmology. This is not to say that the compromise in question represents an admixture of equal parts of place (or world) and of void. Void is given the major emphasis insofar as its infinity is presupposed by the very room that promises to heal the cosmologically troublesome dichotomy of void and world: "The 'whole' [i.e., *to holon*] is finite, since the world is finite, but the 'all' [i.e., *to pan*] is infinite (*apeiron*), *since the void outside the world is such.*"[49] For room or space to combine place and void, it must be at least as capacious as void; hence it must be as infinite as the void it coadunates with place. With the Stoics, therefore, we take a concerted step toward the view that space, affording room and as modeled on the void, is—properly and primarily—infinite.

III

> Place is animated through the primal soul and has a divine life.
>
> —Proclus, cited by Simplicius

> It is likely that place first enjoyed the divine illumination, especially the place of more complete and perpetual things.
>
> .   —Simplicius, with reference to Damascius

Neoplatonic notions of place and space take account of Stoic, Epicurean, and earlier Atomist conceptions—while always addressing themselves explicitly to Plato and even more especially to Aristotle. In many respects, then, Neoplatonists confirm ideas and distinctions that we have already encountered. Iamblichus (A.D. ca. 250–ca. 325), for example, distinguishes "limit" and "boundary" in a manner reminiscent of the distinction to which my discussion of Aristotle progressed in the last chapter.[50] Syrianus (active in the fifth century A.D.) speaks of "room" in a sense that directly recalls Chrysippus: "Extension goes through the whole cosmos and receives into itself the whole nature of body . . . conferring room (*chōra*) and receptacle and boundary and outline and all suchlike upon all things that fill up the visible cosmos."[51] The extension that gives room is designated by the same term (*diastēma*) as that used by many previous thinkers, but here its meaning is not restricted to mere "interval" construed as a span or gap or interstice *between* or *within* determinate entities (whether atoms or bodies). For a Neoplatonist such as Syrianus, *diastēma* refers to the boundless and immobile and (usually) incorporeal spread-outness that "goes through the whole cosmos," a cosmos no longer distinguished from the universe. Such extreme expansiveness is coextensive with what Syrianus calls intriguingly "a different body, the more universal one."[52] This body is in turn identified with "broad, shared place"—place so broad as to have no effective limits.[53] The more we push the roomfulness of extension, however, the closer we come to the quite modern idea of a *space* that in its uncompromised infinity is considered "absolute."

Thus far we find ourselves on more or less familiar terrain. What do the Neoplatonists introduce that is novel? At least two basic lines of thought.

(1) The first is that there are more *kinds of place,* each with more sorts of power, than Aristotle dreamed of. Plotinus strikes the opening note in his

Enneads: "The place of the intelligible world is the place of life and the very principle and source of the soul and the Intellect."[54] Both kinds of place here mentioned—that of the "intelligible world" and that of "life"—are unreducible to the physical surrounder made paradigmatic by Aristotle in the *Physics.* Once Pandora's box is opened in this fashion, there is no limit to the sorts of place one can consider as fully valid instances. When Aristotle spoke of the mind as "the place of forms" in the *De Anima,* he was speaking metaphorically. But when Iamblichus talks of "formal place," he is not ascribing place to forms by means of a trope. He means straightforwardly that forms—in the Platonic sense—possess their own proper sort of place, to be distinguished from physical place as well as from the place of life and from what Iamblichus calls "intrinsic place."[55] The claim of variety comes paired with a claim concerning the plurality of the powers of place. As Richard Sorabji remarks, "It is because the concept of place has so many other applications [than simply surrounding] that a dynamic conception is required to fit all the cases."[56] When Aristotle said that place "has some power," he meant the particular power of encompassing the physical things it contains. Iamblichus does not deny this power—especially if it is not merely an external delimiting function but one that bestows boundary (*horizein*)—yet he insists that place possesses a set of distinctive strengths beyond that of surrounding (*periechein*).

> One has to conceive place not only as encompassing and establishing in itself the things existing in place, but as sustaining them by one single power. Regarded thus, place will not only encompass bodies from outside, but will fill them totally with a power which raises them up. And the bodies sustained by this power, falling down by their proper nature, but being raised up by the superiority of place, will thus exist in it.[57]

Iamblichus's own list of the plenipotentiary powers of place includes, then, supporting, elevating, and filling up. Underwriting this list is the basic twofold action of

- *raising up* bodies that would otherwise fall into the degradation of prime matter, filling them with a power that elevates them;

- *drawing together* bodies and parts of bodies that are already dissipated from their contact with prime matter, the lowest form of existence in the Neoplatonic universe: "gathering together the scattered ones."[58]

"Up" and "together" are thus to be added to the "around" and "in" of the repertoire of placial powers. To be implaced is not just to be cozily contained by an encircling surface but to be *sustained* by powers that ensure that what is in place will be inherently stronger for having been there. If the Aristotelian model of containment makes possible definition and location, the Iamblichean model of sustaining engrafts the dynamism of implacement onto what exists in place. This is why Iamblichus says expressly that "place is naturally united with things in place"[59]—instead of just surrounding them or offering them "bare extension" (*diastēma psilon*), much less (as the Stoics are held to assert) merely "supervening upon them" (*paruphistasthai*). To be "united with" (*sumphuēs*) is to be dynamically linked with something—to make a difference not just in its shape or form but in its very being or reality (*ousia*). Place is thus "never separate from [a body's] first entrance into existing things and from the principal reality."[60] Through place, reality is reached. Through reality, place is maintained.

Indeed, place has its own being, on the basis of which it is a "cause" (*aitia*) and not something merely inert or passive (*argos, adranēs*)—something caused by something *else* in turn. As Simplicius points out in the sixth century A.D., the essence of something and its place are difficult to distinguish, driving him to posit an "essential place" that is "naturally united with substance [i.e., the substance of what is in place]."[61] For Iamblichus and Simplicius alike, a place "has reality in itself" and "has an active power as well as an incorporeal and definitive reality."[62] In attributing such power and reality to place, these authors contest Aristotle's denial of place's intrinsic *causal* power. Not only does place *have* such a power, it *is* a causal power: it is "a power that acts" (*drastērios dunamis*).[63]

(2) The second new line of thought is that the less material place is, the more powerful it becomes. This notion derives from the basic premise that "everywhere the incorporeal reality ranks as prior to the corporeal one."[64] It follows that places incorporeal in nature will be superior in effective power to material places. Another corollary is that incorporeal places will be more powerful than anything physical they can be said to contain: as Iamblichus says, "Place, being incorporeal, is superior to the things that exist in it; and as something more independent it is superior to those things which are in need of and wanting to be in place."[65] The power of incorporeal place is even exerted over extension itself: instead of being dependent on a pregiven cosmic or universal extendedness, place generates the very spread-outness of the things it serves to situate.[66] Iamblichus explicitly contrasts this view with that of the Stoics—who are said to hold that "place subsists upon bodies"[67]—and claims to have rejoined Archytas: "Clearly he assumes place to be of a higher rank than things that act or are acted upon."[68]

In Iamblichus—that exemplary Neoplatonic thinker of place—we see the "intellective theory" (*noētē theōria*) of implacement in its full-blown expression. The place something is in is not only more real than the implaced thing; it is itself situated in increasingly intellective and ever more elevated kinds of place: material things are in the world's body (i.e., the cosmos), which is in the World Soul, which is in the Intellect, and so on. There is a virtual shell game of steadily improving implacement in which each place-level is at once sustained and surpassed in the next until we reach the ultimate level of the One that provides (again in Plotinus's phrase) "the place of the intelligible world." This escalating model of implacement can be regarded as an attempt to reconcile Aristotelian encasement with Platonic ascension to the final forms of things.[69]

The intellective or noetic nature of place was a theme throughout the history of Neoplatonic thought, for which place was a central theme for four continuous centuries—from Plotinus (A.D. ca. 205–260) to Simplicius (who flourished after A.D. 529). The two thinkers who pursued this particular theme furthest, however, were Damascius and Proclus. For Damascius, who served in the sixth century as the last head of the Athenian branch of the Neoplatonic school, place in general exhibits its power and superiority by its ability to *measure* what is in place. The positioning of the parts of something as well as the size of that something are measured by the place it is in. The measure (*metron*) is conceived as a mold or outline into which the implaced thing is set: "Place is as it were a sort of outline (*proüpographē*) of the whole position (*thesis*) and of its parts, and so to say a mould (*tupos*) into which the thing must fit, if it is to lie properly and not be diffused, or in an unnatural state."[70] As the idea of mold indicates, far from being a measure that proceeds in terms of numbers, placial measure is more like a shaping force that acts to hold off the diffusion inherent in prime matter. Such measuring resembles measuring *through* more than measuring *out:* it is through the configuration of a given place that the measure of a thing-in-place is taken.[71] Rather than giving exact quantitative assessments—which require a rigid ruler of some sort—place as *metron* is more plastic than it is rigid, with the result that, as Sorabji comments, "it can allow for a variety of positionings, as it does in the case of the moving heavens."[72] Aristotle's obsessive question as to what kind of place the heavens occupy is here answered by the view that they occupy a nonrigid, molded place—not entirely unlike the receptive regions proffered by primordial *chōra,* which is also characterized by Plato as acting like a mold. Such a place, precisely by virtue of its measuring power, ranks as superior to all the particular places it encompasses. Simplicius, commenting on Damascius, brings out the assumption at stake here: "The nature of the measure is superior to the nature of the measured and is not in need of the same things as [the measured] is."[73] Given this assumption, it is clear why Neoplatonists tend to give priority to places that are noetic in nature.

But the matter is more complicated than this. Proclus (ca. 411–485), a quintessential Neoplatonist, considered place to be a *body* and not just something *around a body* (or *through which* a body moves, or *in which* it is located). Yet, despite its corporeality, place is at the same time immobile, indivisible, and above all immaterial. Place an *immaterial body*? Proclus is driven to this intriguing idea in an effort to imagine an adequate vehicle for the World

Soul. Such a vehicle must be immaterial—that is, must lack the dissipative effects of prime matter—if it is to escort anything as pure as the World Soul. Indeed, the place of the World Soul "must be the most immaterial of all bodies, of those that move as well as of the immaterial ones among those that move."[74] The only candidate for such a sheerly immaterial place is *light* and, more especially, supracelestial light. This latter, hinted at in Plato's Myth of Er, is luminous without being literal illumination. Proclus appropriates this most diaphanous of media as a model for place of all kinds and in particular for that place which is "the luminous vehicle of the World Soul."[75] This is not sheer spiritualism, for there is a distinctive geocosmic specificity in Proclus's model of the universe.

> Let us then conceive two spheres, one made of a single light, the other of many bodies, the two equal to each other in volume. But seat one concentrically with the other, and on implanting (*embibazein*) the other in it, you will see the whole cosmos residing in its place, moving in the immobile light.[76]

Instead of thinking of the cosmos as an isolated island in an empty universe, Proclus contends that the physical world is coextensive with the luminous supracelestial sphere. As a form of light, this sphere is bodily and elemental; but as a place, it is immaterial. To be immaterial in this manner, however, is to be quite dynamic: the sphere of light is "called place (*topos*) as being a certain shape (*tupos*) of the whole cosmic body, causing unextended things to be extended. . . . [Such a] place is animated through the primal soul and has a divine life, being stationary, self-moving intrinsically, [even if it is not] externally active."[77] The sphere of supracelestial light is a Place of places, for it is the vehicle of the World Soul as well as the very place of the cosmos—at once its center and periphery, situating everything in between. Nowhere is there not such light; wherever there is something, it is there in the light—there somewhere, there in a particular place within the absolute Place of the universe. I capitalize this Proclean Place to suggest that it is an adumbration of infinite space. As "supracelestial," the ultimate sphere of light has a peculiar standing: as bodily, it has sufficient density to count *as a place* (thus is able to mold, measure, etc.), and yet, as immaterial, it is not the positive infinity of the physical universe that will be the obsession of seventeenth-century speculation. If not yet strictly infinite, however, the supracelestial sphere can be considered *absolute:* it "forms a kind of absolute place against which the cosmos can rotate and other things move."[78]

What Proclus teaches us is that in Neoplatonic thinking there is no contradiction between the bodily and the noetic character of place. A place like the supracelestial sphere is composed of light—it is corporeal—and yet it ranks high in the ascending noetic scale of being. This vision is in many ways the exact converse of the Atomist view of place. Where place for the Atomists is mechanical and physical, that is, bodily *and* material (and nothing else), place for the Neoplatonists is dynamic and intellective—and one thanks to the other. Moreover, indivisibility now pertains to place, not to atoms: as Proclus puts it bluntly, "Place is an indivisible body."[79] The immateriality of place also allows Neoplatonists to escape the confines of the Aristotelian container model, whose resolute physicalism dictates that the encompassing surface of place has to be material if this surface is to secure sensible bodies in place. Once it is agreed that place need not be physical, place can effect more than delimitation and location: it can preserve and order, support and sustain, raise up and gather. The singular inertia of a material surface is replaced by the plural dynamics of an immaterial presence. The dynamics can be forceful— even holding up bodies from a quasi-gravitational downward pull—as well as subtle. The subtlety is evident both in the nonnumerical measuring power of place and in such ideas as the situatedness of all things in "the luminous vehicle of the World Soul."

A Neoplatonic approach to place vindicates the common conviction that place always implies *some* sort of quantity (i.e., some amount of "room") while also always involving a set of distinctive qualities (as is indicated in such expressions as a "pleasant place," a "dangerous place"). Just as it is advantageous not to have to tie the quantum of place to arithmetical determination (or else we find ourselves in the midst of land surveys, property lines, and the like), so it is helpful not to limit the qualitative aspects of place to literally sensible properties. Thus Proclus's idea of a preternatural "light above the Empyrean"[80] enables us to draw on the panoply of properties of a natural phenomenon such as light while not enclosing ourselves in the straitjacket of a reductive physics. The immateriality of the noetic notion of place also rejoins Epicurus's idea of "intangible substance"—without, however, exacting a commitment to a macro- or microvoid. As corporeal, the universe is plenary and not vacuous; but as immaterial, it enjoys the flexibility required for the empowerment and determination of things in place. This conception also artfully avoids the awkward dichotomy inherent in the Stoic view that the world is plenary whereas what lies beyond the world is vacuous. Moreover, when place is recognized as immobile as well as indivisible and immaterial, place can assume an absolute status: as when Syrianus, Proclus's master, proclaims that "an extension goes through the whole world and receives into itself the whole of corporeal nature."[81]

IV

> Place, too, not less than time, pervades everything; for everything that happens is in a place.
> —Simplicius, *In Aristotelis categorias commentarium*

Philoponus—born in A.D. 490, five years after Proclus was buried with Syrianus in a conjoint tomb—sought to refine the idea of extension (*diastēma*), whose full significance had become overshadowed by the more speculative ideas of his immediate Neoplatonic predecessors. For Philoponus, extension and not body, not even immaterial body, is the very essence of place: place is "a certain extension in three dimensions, different from the bodies that come to be in it, bodiless in its own definition—dimensions alone, empty of body."[82] The tie between extension (*diastēma*) and dimensions (*diastaseis*) is close, not just linguistically but conceptually: dimensions are what open out extension, delineating its outreach, giving bodies room through which to move. This is why Philoponus can define extension as "room (*chōra*) for body, *and [for] dimensions alone,* empty and apart from all substance and matter."[83] Extension is what provides room for things, and the fact that *chōra* signifies either "room" or "space" allows Philoponus to make a crucial move, namely, to distinguish "spatial extension" from "bodily extension." Bodily extension is equivalent to the particular place occupied by a given physical body. It is the room taken up by the matter of that body.[84] Spatial extension, in contrast, is the extension that need not, in principle, be occupied by any given body or group of bodies: rather than being the room *of* a body, it gives room *for* a body. Thus it is a matter of "dimensions alone" and as such is "empty and apart from all substance and matter." This is so even though such extension is always actually occupied by bodies. Both sorts of extension are alike in being three-dimensional, but bodily extension is filled both in principle and in fact, whereas spatial extension is empty in principle but full in fact.[85]

Furthermore, bodily extension fits into spatial extension but not vice versa.[86] There is always *more* spatial extension than bodily extension, and spatial extension can be said to consist precisely in this "more," in fact so much more that Philoponus is tempted to regard spatial extension as tantamount to void. Where void can be defined as "spatial extension extended in three dimensions," spatial extension is "bodiless and matterless—space without body."[87] Both void and spatial extension are incorporeal *and* immaterial. In making this quasi-equation, Philoponus is concerned to wipe the slate clean of any such suspicious hybrid entities as immaterial bodies. He replaces Proclus's idea of such bodies—or, for that matter, the quasi-material plenum of Stoic *pneuma*—with something genuinely "empty by its own definition,"[88] that is to say, with the conceptual equivalent of the void. To carry out this radical cleansing operation, Philoponus will even say that "in itself place is void" and that "void and place are in reality the same in substance."[89] Nevertheless, in the end, there is no actual void—void does not exist—and, rather than being the counterpart of place, void is Philoponus's "*name* for space."[90]

Philoponus here effects a genuine tour de force. He proposes a theory of place or space—the ambiguity is inescapable, given the distinction between bodily and spatial extension—that obviates Aristotle's most important criterion for being in place: to be enclosed by the surface of a surrounding substance. Philoponus argues persuasively that *no surface* can contain a solid body: "for the surface is extended in two dimensions and so could not receive in itself what is extended in three dimensions."[91] It follows that any adequate theory of place and/or space must include three-dimensional extension as a minimum requirement. Yet precisely such a requirement is met in the idea of a spatial extension that situates bodily extension. Furthermore, spatial extension satisfies all of Aristotle's *other* criteria for being in place: it encompasses what is in place just as much as a boundary (*peras*), is (at least) equal to the thing in place, is not part of this thing, and is itself immobile.[92]

From this point—and from his virtual equation of void with spatial extension—one might have expected Philoponus to move to a theory of infinite space. Indeed, the very immobility of spatial extension would seem to entail an unending spatial expanse.

> We conceive the [spatial] extension to be different from all body and empty in its own definition, but various bodies are always coming to be in it, now this one, now that, while it remains unmoved both as a whole and in its parts—as a whole, because the cosmic extension which receives the body of the whole cosmos can never move, and in its parts, because it is impossible for an extension that is bodiless and empty in its own definition to move.[93]

What is this "cosmical extension" (*cosmikon diastēma*) but the extension of the ultimately unbounded, thus of a universe that can no longer be set over against the world? Nevertheless, just at the point when Philoponus is most tempted to join his Neoplatonic predecessors in a common step toward the infinite, he draws back from the abyss. Admitting the allure of thinking that cosmical extension, "void by its own definition and capable of receiving bodies, must be infinite," since it does not have any effective boundary or delimiting surface of its own, he proceeds to argue that (i) you still might be able to *imagine* such a surface; (ii) even if you could not, cosmical extension "would not necessarily be extended to infinity for this reason," that is, just because one could not succeed in this thought experiment.[94] A principle of parsimony is also invoked: only so much of spatial extension need subsist as is coextensive with the outer boundaries of the bodies that actually occupy it.[95] Philoponus's ultimate motive for denying the infinity of space is doubtless theological—as a believing Christian Neoplatonist, he may have wished to restrict infinity to God—but his argumentation remains unconvincing, especially for someone whose own idea of cosmical extension seems to entail spatial infinity by its very nature.[96]

Not only is such infinity repudiated, but likewise the powers of place. Despite his endorsement of the Damascian position that place is "a measure of things in place,"[97] Philoponus is unwilling to admit any other power intrinsic to place. Sarcasm surfaces when he says that "it is quite ridiculous to say that place has any power in its own right."[98] No longer sustaining or upholding, gathering or supporting, spatial extension is void indeed in its lack of inherent dynamism. Gone as well is the basic Neoplatonic premise that place is superior in status to what is in place.[99] The disappearance of placial dynamism is paired with the demise of the noetic nature of place. Although spatial extension is neither bodily nor material, it is also not intellective. It is something sheerly spatial, where "spatial" connotes what is true of the physical universe even if not itself physicalistic in constitution.

We are left with the paradox that despite Philoponus's outright rejection of infinite space, he is decidedly protomodern in his notion of a spatial (and ultimately cosmical) extension that is three-dimensional, empty in principle, and incorporeal, and that "gives room for body" while remaining independent of any particular material substance. In their expansive and extending character, these aspects of a distinctively diastemic space open up the prospect of a spatiality that is positively infinite and not just in-finite by negation (e.g., bound-less, end-less, empty, etc.). The same aspects will continue to be rediscovered, often piecemeal, during the next millennium in the West, sometimes as influenced by Philoponus himself.[100] The space they collectively characterize is perhaps most properly termed "absolute space," a term I have already invoked in discussing Syrianus and Proclus and that will be employed explicitly by Newton in his *Mathematical Principles of Natural Philosophy.*

Not only was Philoponus on the verge of espousing an infinite space that he felt impelled to repudiate, but the spatial absolutism entailed by the idea of a purely dimensional spatial extension was accompanied by a concomitant relativism of place. This latter is evident in his concern for the proper *arrangement* of things in space: "It is not through desire for a surface that things move each to its proper place, but through desire for that station in the order which they have been given by the Creator."[101] "Station in the order" translates *taxis*—the very word that Theophrastus, the first theorist of the essential relativity of place, used in departing from Aristotle. I cite from a celebrated statement of Theophrastus.

> Perhaps place is not a substance in itself, but is predicated in relation to the order (*taxis*) and position (*thesis*) of bodies, according to their natures and powers, equally in the case of animals and plants and, generally, of things composed of different elements, whether animate or inanimate, that have a natural shape. For the order and position of these parts is relative to the whole being. Therefore each is said to be in its own space (*chōra*) through having its proper order, since each of the parts of a body would desire and demand its own space (*chōra*) and position (*thesis*).[102]

Theophrastus, Aristotle's immediate successor in the Lyceum, opened the Hellenistic period in Greek philosophy; Philoponus is often considered the last great thinker of the same period. In between, Stoicism, Epicureanism, Skepticism, and Neoplatonism flourished. Yet Philoponus, the primary advocate of a purely empty extensiveness, was widely regarded as "a true upholder of Theophrastus"[103]—given that both thinkers attribute power to things in place rather than to place itself, and both believe that the ordering of things in place is the most important single effect of implacement.

The more closely you look at the critical span stretching from Theophrastus to Philoponus—already a first millennium!—the more one becomes convinced that the increasing interest in absolute or infinite space is shadowed at every step by an equal, though often less salient, concern with the importance of order and position in the process of implacement. Damascius's conception of place as *metron,* for instance, entails an ordering of the "position" of the "parts" of something: the key words remain Theophrastian. Damascius gives the example of the head being situated above and the feet below in a human body, thereby illustrating that "the order and position of these parts is relative to the whole being."[104] Damascius also extends the relativist model to nonnatural places: "Even among incorporeal things there will be position according to their order."[105] Iamblichus as well, attests Simplicius, is Theophrastian in inspiration: "The divine Iamblichus bears witness to the same position [i.e., as adopted by Theophrastus],"[106] namely, in his view that "place is of like nature with things in place."[107] Such likeness both facilitates and reflects the ordering of things in place: the more place is *like* what is being implaced, the better it can operate as an immanent agency of arrangement, and the more such an arrangement is realized, the more it exhibits a likeness between the things so ordered. (Much the same isomorphism is manifest in the shaking together of like with like that takes place in the primordial regions of the Timaean Receptacle.) Proclus, too, pays close attention to the power of position.

> The cardinal points of the whole universe are fixed in it as a unity. For, if the oracles say that the cardinal points of the material universe are fixed in the aether above it, correspondingly we shall say, ascending, that the cardinal points of the highest universe are seated in that light.[108]

Indeed, not just cardinal points—which are relative to each other and to the directions they serve to specify—but the entire Neoplatonic universe of ascending/descending levels of being betokens a deeply relativist model of place. In this universe, where you are *at* in the scale of things—your being situated at a material or psychic or noetic level—has everything to do with the kind of being you possess. Position is relative not only to other members of the same level but to *other levels in the ontological scale as well.*

So powerful is the effect of this scalar model that Simplicius can claim that extension, far from being a universal feature of things, is found only at the lower levels. In the realm of intellective being, there are only unextended and incorporeal items, including the places of noetic items such as ideas and numbers. As descent is made into the realm of matter, extension becomes ever more crucial—an extension that applies to places as well as to things in places. This means that place *becomes extended with bodies,*[109] and is not simply extended on its own and independently of bodies, as is implied on the model of Philoponean spatial and cosmical extension. Extension is thus an *acquired* attribute of place: "As the body that has position became extended through its decline, so also place that is the measure of position became extended, in the way that is possible for a measure that has declined from the unextended measurer."[110] In this statement of Simplicius, the Damascian idea of place as measure—intrinsically tied to the relativism of internal positions—is set within an emanationism of levels that is no less relativistic in implication. Speaking of place and time alike, Simplicius can comment that "their extension is not like that of other things, seen as they are as a mean between the unextended measurer and the extended objects measured."[111] To be "a mean between" is to have a position in a hierarchy of at least three levels, and thus to have a cosmic position that determines the very character of place and time themselves. Instead of being "God's infinite sensoria" (Newton) or the universal forms of pure sensible intuition (Kant), place and time are creatures of the level of emanation on which they are situated.

Double positioning is at play, then, in the Neoplatonic universe: first, a structural positioning within the cosmic hierarchy (which determines, in turn, whether place is extended or not) and, second, the pinpointed positioning that is the work of extended place proper (about such place Simplicius says that "everywhere it is the position of bodies and the determination of their position").[112] Moreover, the first positioning makes possible the second: only when place becomes adequately extended at an intermediate level of the emanationist hierarchy can it begin to do its locational work. For only at this level is there a distinction to be made between the immediate, unique, and shared implacements that guarantee a complete positioning for any extended body.[113] As a result, the scalar model in its Neoplatonic format allows Simplicius to adopt a relativism that is finally more radical than that of Theophrastus. Where Theophrastus had made "natural shape" (*emmorphos phusis*) responsible for the "order and position" of bodies, Simplicius attributes this ordering force to *place:* "Place is a certain arrangement and measure or demarcation of position."[114]

V

> The signs of the gods are perpetually scattered in places.
>
> —Simplicius, *In Aristotelis physicorum libros quattuor priores commentaria*

Just as the Neoplatonic proclivity for absolutism in spatial matters harbors an unsuspected underside of place-relativism, so the latter tendency leads, by rebound as it were, to a proposal that encompasses both directions of thought. Only several sentences after the words quoted at the end of the previous paragraph—words that epitomize the relativistic position—Simplicius speculates that when particular positions are not just juxtaposed but "well arranged" (*euthetismenoi*), that is, "well positioned and well placed " (*euthetoi kai eutopoi*), they will contribute to the harmony of the whole of which they are parts. Ultimately, all bodies, once they are well arranged, will become inherent parts of the "whole universe," and this universe itself will have its *own place:* "so there is, in truth, the whole place of the whole universe (*holos topos tou holou kosmou*), but it has its supreme position through the good arrangement in respect of its parts and through its whole good arrangement in respect of its parts." [115]

This last claim is remarkable. On the one hand, there is a proper place of, or rather *for,* the entire cosmos. This place must be unique, since there is no *other* cosmos or anything else of comparable magnitude to which it could be relative. (The idea of multiple worlds, entertained by the Atomists and Epicurus, will not be taken seriously again for another thousand years.) In this regard, the single cosmic Place can be considered the "transcendent measure" of all other places, including those parts and places (and places-as-parts) of which it is composed. [116] Concerning such a cosmically distinctive Place, Simplicius can say that "the essential place of the universe has stored up all the varying places and produces from within itself the proper measure of every position." [117] In this monolithic capacity, it is not unlike the Philoponean idea of "cosmical extension." On the other hand, this same super-place remains relative. Even if the place of the cosmos is not dependent on any of its parts (or on their totality), its "supreme position" does depend on a good arrangement that involves these parts in the following ways.

- The parts must be well arranged among themselves; this is what Simplicius means by the simple phrase "through the good arrangement of its parts."
- The same parts must be well arranged in relation to the whole they compose—that is, the whole cosmos or universe (terms significantly not distinguished by Simplicius).
- Finally, the cosmos itself must be well arranged in relation to its *own* parts, both as particular parts and as a whole of parts. This is what Simplicius implies when he speaks of "its whole good arrangement in respect of its parts."

Simplicius sums up this line of thought by observing that "in general, we do not only say that the parts have a well-arranged position in relation to each other and to the whole, but also that the whole has it in relation to its parts." [118]

I single out this final position of Simplicius—himself the last great pagan Neoplatonist—for its special promise as an answer to a question that will preoccupy the rest of this chapter and the next three chapters: Is place, as well as space, essentially relative or absolute? Are they heteronomous in status, that is, dependent on *other* entities for their being and character, or autonomous, that is, able to stand on their own no matter what their parts (or constituents) and motions are? Simplicius's response is that place/space is both absolute and relative. Not just both in the sense of an indifferent mixture, but both in the sense of *one through the agency of the other.* The place of the universe would not be absolute unless it were also relative—and relative in the particular ways just described. And it would not be relative—relative to the parts of which it is composed—unless these were the parts that, in proper arrangement, make up the cosmic whole. Put otherwise, the place of the universe is absolute in certain respects (e.g., in its transcendent all-measuring role) and relative in certain others (i.e., the three modes of relativity just singled out).

Simplicius's model, ingenious and satisfying as it is in many respects, leaves us with two major unresolved questions. Is there a place of this world, the cosmos? Is there infinite space beyond the cosmos? Aristotle, of course, would respond negatively to both of these questions. Given that place on his view requires an unmoving and immediate inner boundary, the outer heaven cannot count as a place since it has no such boundary; and it is not set in any subsequent extracosmic space either, since there is "no place or void or time outside the [outer] heaven."[119] It was the audacity of Aristotle's archrivals, the Atomists, not only to propose an unbounded void but also to argue that *precisely because there is such a void* the cosmos can be located in it. The void gives room for the world to be found within it—just as the world in turn gives "space for body" (in Philoponus's phrase). It is clear that any such void is infinite in the sense of unbounded. As Hahm comments with reference to the Stoic void, "If there is any void at all beyond the cosmos, it is necessarily infinite, for there is nothing that can bound it."[120] But the void elicits its own disquieting questions: Is it necessarily empty (as its name, *kenon,* certainly implies and as the Stoics explicitly posited in the idea of a strictly external void)? If so, the cosmos will float in this void as an anchorless entity adrift in infinite space: "How can the cosmos remain intact though situated in an infinite void?"[121] Or is it empty only in principle, being always filled in fact (as Philoponus holds)? But then it threatens to become a redundant entity or, rather, nonentity.

Yet no sooner do we give up on the idea of void—or perhaps just restrict its domain of application, as in Strato's idea of the microvoid—than we run into other questions, at least equally difficult to resolve. Could the universe be at once infinite and plenary? If it were *entirely* full of bodies, there would then be no space for motion, and it would become a frozen Parmenidean One. Yet if it were not chock-full, we would need more than microvoids internal to bodies to allow for motion. Perhaps, after all (as the Atomists held), there are empty "intervals" between bodies. But how can we determine *just how big* such intervals would need to be in order to make motion possible? There seems to be no way of giving a generally satisfactory answer to this last question. Maybe because of this difficulty, the very idea of interval (*diastēma*) was expanded by the Neoplatonists to become *extension,* ultimately the "spatial extension" posited by Philoponus. Yet this latter idea, especially under the guise of "cosmical extension," returns us to the deeply perplexing issue of whether the cosmos itself has a place. A place for the cosmos may be asserted—as it is by Simplicius—but then we must ask: a place *where?* Is its place a place in the universe at large, that is, in a space that exceeds the world-place itself? And is such a space finite or infinite?

By this circuitous route, we return once again to Archytas, who is reported to have posed the following conundrum.

> If I came to be at the edge, for example at the heaven of the fixed stars, could I stretch my hand or my staff outside, or not? That I should not stretch it out would be absurd (*atopos*), but if I do stretch it out, what is outside will be either body or place. . . . If it is always something different into which the staff is stretched, it will clearly be something infinite.[122]

Alexander of Aphrodisias claimed that this thought experiment comes to naught, since what is outside the cosmos is *nothing at all,* not even a void.

> He will not stretch out his hand; he will be prevented, but prevented not as they say by some obstacle bordering the universe (*to pan*) on the outside, but rather by there being nothing (*to mēden einai*). For how can anyone stretch something, but stretch it into nothing? How can the thing come to be in what does not even exist?[123]

Simplicius insists similarly that Archytas's conundrum is question-begging: "In imagination it assumes in advance what it seeks to prove, that there is something, whether empty or solid, outside the universe."[124]

Despite these telling objections, Archytas's provocative puzzle kept arising in ancient and medieval debates, and it still haunts contemporary cosmological thinking. For it will always occur to the cosmologically curious to ask, what lies beyond the last boundary of the known world? If there is some *thing* there, then I can (at least in principle) get to this thing and even reach beyond it. If there is *no thing,* then there might be, not nothing (as Alexander assumes), but empty space. This observation indicates that Archytas's exclusive alternative of "body or place" needs to be supplemented. If place is always bounded—as it is for Archytas and Aristotle alike—then *it* is not what we encounter when we stretch out our hand or staff beyond the final frontier of the cosmos. What such extracosmic stretching gets us into is something else, and its increasingly unrefusable name is *space.* This word (or its equivalent in other languages: *spatium,* Raum, espace, etc.) is required if we are to designate a domain that, itself unbounded, affords sufficient room for motion of all kinds, including the modest motion of a hand or staff as it reaches out tentatively beyond the world's outer limit.

But space thus regarded is precisely what "infinite space" means—at least minimally. Infinite space is *space for* (motion) and *space without* (bounds). In its twofold character, such space brings together two of the most ancient terms in Greek philosophy, attributable to Plato and Anaximander, respectively: "room" (*chōra*) and "the boundless" (*to apeiron*). Their conjunction, which is conceptual as well as historical, suggests that if the cosmos indeed has a place, it is *a place in space:* space at once endlessly voluminous and boundaryless. Moreover, the world not only *has* a place, it is *in* place: it is *in the very place of infinite space,* occupying particular stations in the regions that make up the spatial universe. Just as Archytas's conundrum drives us to the idea of infinite space from the known fact of the cosmos, so this same space preserves a place—indeed, innumerably many places—for the world from whose edge we are asked to stretch out our hand or staff, or (in Lucretius's version) throw a long javelin. The Archytian axiom abides, but only as applicable to a much larger domain than Archytas himself envisioned. To be is still to be in place, but a place that is part of an unending space.

5

The Ascent of Infinite Space

Medieval and Renaissance
Speculations

> God, however, is infused into the world He makes,
> which is placed wherever He makes it.
> —Thomas Bradwardine, *De causa*
> *Dei contra Pelagium*

> Physical objects are not in space, but these objects
> are *spatially extended.* In this way the concept of
> "empty space" loses its meaning.
> —Albert Einstein, *Relativity, the Special and the*
> *General Theory, A Popular Exposition*

I

From Archytas's challenging conundrum we can derive a more momentous
question: not whether an outstretched hand or staff can reach out into something (or nothing) but whether *the whole world* (i.e., the physical cosmos as
one entity) can move. And if the world moves, *in what, into what,* does it
move? These questions vexed philosophers and theologians of the Middle
Ages—construing this period as the entire era stretching between A.D. 600 (a
date that marks the demise of Hellenistic and Neoplatonic philosophy) and
A.D. 1500 (when the Renaissance was fully alive in Italy). Whichever way you
answer such questions, the stakes are high. For if the world cannot move—if
it is bound forever to occupy the same place, that place being coextensive
with the outermost sphere, as Aristotle and Aristotelians assumed—then a surrounding space that exceeds the place of the cosmos, were such space to exist,
would be idle. But if the world does move (i.e., laterally by displacement,

rather than spinning in place like a top), then there must be an encompassing space in and through which to move, a space that extends beyond the discernible heavens. Once more, the issue is that of place versus space, only now on the grandest scale. Theologically considered (and everything in the Middle Ages was eventually, if not always immediately, so considered), this issue amounts to whether God has the power to create and occupy space sufficient to surpass the place of the cosmos—in short, space unbounded by any particular cosmic constraints and thus ultimately infinite in extent.

One form this discussion took was whether God could create something possessing infinite *magnitude*. Aristotle, predictably, denied any such ability, since for him there was only a finite amount of matter in the universe to begin with and this could not be increased; he could entertain the idea of the indefinitely small (though only *in potentia*), but the infinitely large was out of the question.[1] Far from taking this restriction as problematic, Aristotle regarded it as a sign of the perfection of the universe: its very delimitation in size, like the confinement of the places within it, was a matter for admiration. (Of course, for Aristotle the two delimitations are closely related, given that place is quantitatively determined on his own analysis: questions of place are matters of magnitude, and vice versa.) But Aristotle's espousal of this double finitude left a particularly puzzling question: Does the outermost sphere (which, as encompassing all lesser spheres, provides a place for them) *itself have a place*? Or is it an *unplaced placer*, not entirely unlike the Unmoved Mover posited at its periphery? Aristotle himself hinted at—and his Hellenistic commentator Themistius developed in the fourth century A.D.—the idea that the moving *parts* of this super-sphere have places, for these parts change place as they move in a perfectly circular fashion. But what of the final sphere itself? Does it have its own proper place? Aristotle was inclined to think not: "The heavens," he maintained, "are not, as a whole, somewhere or in some place."[2] Is this to say that the heavens are *nowhere*? Averroës (ca. 1126–ca. 1198) gave an ingenious analysis of this paradoxical situation. According to "the Commentator," the outermost sphere has a place, not in relation to anything more encompassing (there is not anything more encompassing than this sphere), but in relation to the earth as the fixed center of all the celestial spheres. The earth is the immobile body at the center that provides place to the otherwise unplaced outer sphere. Roger Bacon (ca. 1220–1292), building on Averroës, distinguished between "place *per se*"—this is what the final sphere lacks—and place *per accidens*: place that is parasitic on another, altogether fixed place. As Bacon put it pithily, "Heaven has a place *per accidens* because its center has a place *per se*."[3]

The Averroësan-Baconian solution to the dilemma inherited from the Stagirite accounts for the world's place by turning inward to its very center—to what, existing at this center (indeed *as* this center) is most immobile. Moreover, this inward/downward turn teases apart the two main Aristotelian criteria of place, containment and immobility, since, conceding that the final sphere is not contained in any surrounder, it relies exclusively on the second criterion, exemplified uniquely in the unmoving earth. But the earth is precisely what is contained and thus implaced, via intermediate spheres, by the outer heaven itself. Strange indeed to think that the place of this heaven is *dependent on that to which it itself gives place.* One place calls for another: celestial and sublunar entities are codependent in their very difference.

Thomas Aquinas (ca. 1224–1274) thought this solution strange enough to remark, "It seems ridiculous to me to maintain that the final sphere is accidentally in a place by the mere fact that its center is in a place."[4] Given the choice, the Angelic Doctor preferred to return to the Themistian model whereby the final sphere is in place thanks to its own constitution: "It is much more suitable to say that the ultimate sphere is in place because of its own intrinsic parts than because of the center which is altogether outside of its substance."[5] But despite adopting this expressly Aristotelian model for the implacement of the outer sphere, Aquinas came to espouse a quite different model for the implacement of everything else. The true immobility that is required if a place is to be more than a sheer container is not to be found in the centrated earth but in *a set of relations to the celestial spheres that surround earth itself.* Hence the place of something subcelestial is determined by these relations or, more exactly, by the "order and situation" (*ordo et situ*) they offer.

> Although the container is moved insofar as it is a body, nevertheless, considered *according to the order it has to the whole body of heaven,* it is not moved. For the other body that succeeds it has the same order and site in comparison to all of heaven that the body which previously left had.[6]

In other words, the place of anything other than the outermost sphere is determined by its position vis-à-vis the celestial spheres (i.e., "heaven" or "the heavens")—a position that can also be occupied by other bodies. The heavens, taken as a whole to which all other parts of the cosmos relate, furnish the very fixity or stable reference required by any given place in the cosmos. This radically relational view echoes Theophrastus's paradigm of place as a matter of the way the parts of a quasi-organic body relate to the whole of that body. It anticipates Leibniz, the most systematic Western thinker of place as relational and someone whose theory also depends on the substitutability of objects located "in the same place" considered in relation to fixed external referents. In between, and in the immediate wake of Aquinas, others were to take up a comparably cosmic relational model: for example, Giles of Rome (who said that "what is formal in place is its location with respect to the universe"),[7] John of Jandun (for whom it is the heavens that determine the very centrality of the earth),[8] and Duns Scotus (who held that formal or rational place, *ratio loci,* "is a relation with respect to the whole universe").[9]

Although they often go hand in hand, an absolutist model of space is not necessarily a model of infinite space. For if *this* world system is the *only* cosmos, it will be at once absolute and self-enclosed. But a relational model such as that proposed by Aquinas and the other theorists just cited is not self-contained; it leads beyond itself, beckoning toward spatial infinity. For it calls for a fixed referent located *somewhere external* to an implaced item: a stable point on the shore when at sea, a permanent object, an everlasting celestial sphere. In proposing that place is a matter of *ordo et situ* in regard to something immobile, Aquinas is driven to extend the scene of place itself to "the whole body of heaven." Refusing to rely exclusively on the earth's centrality and immobility as had Averroës and Bacon, Aquinas finds the more pertinent fixity to reside in the larger arena of the planets and stars—that is to say, an expansive domain that increasingly demands the term "spatial" rather than "placial." Where this latter term implies something strictly contained, the heavens, taken as a spatial whole, are *uncontained.* Regular and steady enough in their appearance and motions to provide a stable region of reference for everything here below, as unbounded they lead outward beyond themselves into what can be regarded only as unending space.

In this way we rejoin the second question raised above: In (or into) what would the cosmos move if it were to move at all? Where would the system of fixed reference be if it were itself to be displaced? If it is *anywhere,* it is in space. Moreover, in *infinite space:* if the world can be moved even once, it can be moved an indefinite number of times and will thus require an endless amount of space in which to move.

It follows that God's creative force, if it is to be truly omnipotent, must not be limited to constituting finite regions of the known universe, such as the earth or the planets or even the stars. This force must be equal to the task of creating infinite space—and not just of shaping an already existing space, as befits the Demiurge in the *Timaeus.* World-constitution is not enough when space-creation is called for.

II

> The infinite is an imperative necessity.
> —Giordano Bruno, *On the Infinite Universe*
> *and Worlds*

This brings us to the fateful year 1277, just three years after Aquinas's death. It is only fitting that shortly after the death of the very thinker who had so ingeniously pointed to the need for infinite space—if Thomas did not explicitly endorse such space, his relational model certainly entails it[10]—Etienne Tempier, Bishop of Paris, at Pope John XXI's request and after consulting with theologians of the Sorbonne, issued a series of 219 condemnations of doctrines that denied or limited the power of God, including the power to move the world into a different place than it currently occupies. These momentous condemnations were driven by a desire to make the intellectual world safe for Christian doctrine, its teaching and its theology. But in fact they marked a decisive turning point in medieval thought concerning place and especially space. Until then, the primary efforts had been to shore up Aristotle with the aid of sympathetic commentators such as Themistius and Averroës— in short, to patch up the system of the world first outlined in *Physics*, book 4, a text preserved in Arabic during the Dark Ages and then translated into Latin in the twelfth century A.D. by Gerard of Cremona. The massive translation of many texts authored by Aristotle and Averroës at this same time sparked a renewed passion for discussing questions of place and space that was to continue for four more centuries and that rivaled the Hellenistic and Neoplatonic preoccupation with many of the same questions.[11]

The availability of these translations also led to the incorporation of Aristotle into the official curriculum of the University of Paris by the middle of the thirteenth century. So successful was this revival of Aristotle that local theologians in Paris became disturbed: Did not the Aristotelian cosmology hamper God's powers unduly? Is the extent of God's creative force limited to *this* admittedly finite world? Are not other worlds possible? Could not God jostle our world sideways in space, moving it into a new place and leaving an empty place behind? These and affiliated questions fueled the Condemnations, which attempted to reinstate the omnipotence of God in the physical world— a world whose final description was not to be left to the hands of a pagan philosopher, like Aristotle, no matter how important he had been for Thomas Aquinas (who was at least indirectly indicted by the Condemnations: their retraction in 1325 was motivated mainly by an effort to effect his redemption).

For our purposes, the primary importance of the documents of 1277 lies in their reopening the vista of the possible infinity of space. For the Condemnations give virtual carte blanche to explorations of spatial infinity—so long as this infinity remains linked to God's omnipotence. But the explorations themselves soon exceeded their theological origins; directly or indirectly, they inspired the bold thought experiments of thinkers in the fourteenth and fifteenth centuries, engendering the conceptual ventures that laid down the foundations of modern physics, above all its commitment to the infinity of the physical universe. Pierre Duhem has termed 1277 "the birthdate of modern science."[12] Whatever may be the truth of this claim, there can be little doubt that one of the most fateful things condemned by the Condemnations was the primacy of place, thereby making room for the apotheosis of space that occurred in the seventeenth century. Yet place was not condemned outright— any more than it had been by Philoponus or Simplicius. As in the case of the Neoplatonists, space was allowed to triumph gradually over place by a steadily increasing affirmation of its supremacy.

Article 34 of the Condemnations states: "That the first cause [i.e., God] could not make several worlds." [13] But if God is truly omnipotent, reasoned Tempier, then there is no reason why He cannot make other worlds than *this* world. As Nicholas Oresme (ca. 1325–1382) put it straightforwardly in the fourteenth century: "God can and could in his omnipotence make another world besides this one or several like or unlike it." [14] Of most interest to us is not the question of world plurality as such; rather, it is the implication of such plurality: if there are several worlds that coexist with each other, then they must share a space larger than the place taken up by any one of them. If, moreover, there are an infinite number of such worlds—as the Atomists first speculated, and as ensues from God's omnipotence (for why should He stop at the creation of *one* or even a *few* worlds?)—then the space shared must be infinite in extent. Such intercosmic space is empty, a void, except where occupied by given worlds, as Oresme concludes: "Outside the heavens, then, is an empty incorporeal space quite different from any other plenum or corporeal space." [15] The indefinite plurality of worlds calls for such a space; thanks to its coherent imaginability, its real—its plausible—possibility (though *not* its actuality) is assured.

A second path to spatial infinity arises from article 49: "That God could not move the heavens [i.e., the world] with rectilinear motion; and the reason is that a vacuum would remain." [16] At stake here is the question, what would happen if the world were moved, even ever so slightly, in a lateral direction along an imaginary line? In moving from position *A* to position *B,* would it not vacate position *A,* leaving it strictly empty? Would it not move *into* position *B,* which must have been empty for it to be occupied by this movement? Extending the stakes further—as theologians are wont to do, given their desire to do justice to God's unlimited powers—are we not driven to ask, is not such emptiness endless in principle, if it is true that God could move the world *anywhere*? Oresme is again apt.

> But perhaps someone will say that to move with respect to place is to change one's position in relation to some other body which may, or may not, be in motion itself. Yet I say that this is not valid primarily because there is an imagined infinite and immobile space outside the world . . . and it is possible without contradiction that the whole world could be moved in that space with rectilinear motion. To say the contrary is an article condemned at Paris. Now assuming such a motion, there would be no other body to which the world could be related with respect to place. [17]

This is a particularly revealing statement. Not only does it posit "space" (*spatium*)—immobile, infinite, and extracosmic—as what is required for world-translation, but it does so in express contrast with "place" (*locus*). As the last sentence suggests, place is at stake in a delimited relational model wherein one body is situated vis-à-vis another body. But this model does *not* obtain in the case of article 49: at issue here is the movement of the world in and by itself *without reference to anything else,* including any fixed marker. It is a question of an isolated *motu recto,* a motion taken with reference to the moving thing alone. Such a sheer motion is a motion in an absolute space—a space in which locations are not relative to each other but intrinsic to the preestablished parts of that space itself. Which is to say: a literally ab-solute space. Oresme's espousal of such a model of space, occurring exactly a century after the Condemnations, looks forward to Newton—including his defender, Samuel Clarke, who argued against Leibniz that a relativist model of space could not explain world-translation: "If space were nothing but the order of things coexisting [as Leibniz holds], it would follow that if God should remove the whole material world entire, with any swiftness whatever, yet it would still always continue *in the same place.*"[18] The world would stay in the same place, since its relations with its own constituents would remain the same. If the world is to move into another place than the one it presently occupies, it must be with a motion that moves across the steady structure of an absolute space.

This last discussion makes it even more apparent that "absolute space" and "infinite space," though closely allied in thinkers such as Oresme and Newton, are not to be confused. "Absolute" implies something self-sufficient, "freed from" any dependency on its own parts, much less any relation to other things elsewhere; whatever is absolute stands apart—thus the *ab-,* 'away', 'off'—from any immersion (i.e., any "solution") in these extraneous factors, being genuinely independent of them. "Infinite" entails unending extent; here sheer quantity is at stake: what John Locke calls "expansion." Unlikely as it may seem to the modern mind—indebted as it is to Newton, who brought absolute and infinite space together in one consistent theory—it is perfectly possible to posit an absolute, *finite* space. This is precisely the space of Plato's *chōra,* of Aristotle's heavens with the earth at the center, of almost every other ancient model of a closed world, and of Philoponean "spatial extension."[19] It is also perfectly possible to think of an absolute and finite world set in an open sea of infinite space: such is the standard Stoic model.

Further evidence for the inherent dissociability of absolute and infinite space is found in the fact that medieval thought arrived at the infinity of space in two distinctly different ways. In the first, a relational model, pushed to an extreme in the manner I have discussed, yields spatial infinity: such is the way of Aquinas (and of Bacon, Scotus, and others). In the second, an absolutist model ends equally in infinity: such is the way of Oresme (and of Robert Holkot, Richard of Middleton, and others).[20] It is striking that articles 34 and 49 of the Condemnations point respectively to these two primary avenues to the infinity of space. On the one hand, the plurality of worlds at issue in article 34 encourages a relational model of infinite space inasmuch as these various worlds serve as reference points—that is, cosmic *places*—for each other's positions in a vast intercosmic void. On the other hand, the movement of a single world (and in particular *our* world), which is at stake in article 49, induces the spectacle of an endless space in which locations are not determined by reference to the positions of other entities.

Two problems of cosmological/theological scope; two solutions of physical/philosophical import. The result is two paths to infinite space: one keeps a role for place; the other dispenses with place altogether.

I do not mean to imply that there ever existed a perfect equilibrium between the two approaches to space in its infinity. The first approach, significantly inaugurated by Aquinas *before* the Condemnations, was not to be fully pursued again until Locke took it up in 1690 in his *Essay Concerning Human Understanding*. The second approach, which stemmed more directly from the Condemnations themselves, was more favored and influential during the next few centuries, culminating in the publication of Newton's *Mathematical Principles of Natural Philosophy* just three years before Locke's *Essay*. Despite the predominance of the second direction, both tendencies share one important thing in common: they both were conceived as ways in which infinite space can be *imagined.*

For philosophers and theologians alike in the wake of 1277, what had been liberated was not so much a revised picture of the physical world as the freedom to project purely possible cosmological scenarios: what the world and the universe *would* be like if God *were* to choose to alter things as they are radically. Concerning things as they are, Aristotelian cosmology and physics were still regarded as the most reliable modes of explanation; but suddenly there was occasion, indeed active solicitation, to imagine things differently. Even if God is unlikely to reverse course—He has, after all, quite an investment in a world He has *already* created—it is conceptually salutary to think how He might have proceeded otherwise. When one begins to think this "otherwise," one is approaching things *secundum imaginationem,* "according to imagination"—not according to how things in fact are, have been, or will presumably be. Pondering the imagined situation in which God might destroy everything within "the arch of the heavens or within the sphere of the moon"—thereby leaving "a great expanse and empty space"—Oresme remarks that "such a situation can *surely be imagined* and is definitely possible although it could not arise from pure natural causes, as Aristotle shows in his arguments in the fourth book of the *Physics.*"[21] By extension, infinite space is a matter of what can be imagined, of what *could be;* finite space is a matter of what *is* the case. Thus for Oresme's near-contemporary John Buridan (ca. 1295–1356), "although God *could* indeed create corporeal spaces and substances beyond the world, and to any degree he pleased, it did not follow that he had *actually* done so."[22] Buridan's statement makes it clear that, in the end, post-1277 thinkers wanted to *have it both ways:* what is possible and what is so are both valorized, albeit on drastically different grounds. Edward

Grant concludes that "because of the Condemnations, it became a characteristic feature of fourteenth-century scholastic discussion for authors to declare
that although something was naturally impossible, it was supernaturally
possible."[23]

The move to infinite space, whether it takes the "relativist" or the "absolutist" route, was thus a move to a posited or supposed space—not to an actual
space, as occurred later on in the Renaissance and in the seventeenth century.
But the move remains immensely significant, since it accustomed medieval
minds to think in terms of a space without end, whatever they held to be in fact
the case concerning the given material universe. Even if the Condemnations of
1277 do not represent the literal birth of modern science, they certainly prepared the way for a science significantly committed to the actual infinity of
physical space. And they did so by the promotion of pure possibilities projected by a cosmologically informed theological imagination.

The valorization of *secundum imaginationem* also prepared the way for an
important new development in the advancing conceptualization of infinite
space. Precisely because such space had been freely projected by the intense
discussions that followed the publication of the Condemnations, it could be
recharacterized in terms of divinity rather than sheer physicality. Oresme, for
instance, says expressly that "this space of which we are talking is infinite and
indivisible, and *is the immensity of God and God Himself.*"[24] The converse
also holds: God's immensity is "necessarily all in every extension or space or
place which exists or can be imagined."[25] This is so even though God Himself
is "without any quantity"[26] and thus dimensionless and unextended. Unlike
Philo of Alexandria (for whom God is Place) and such seventeenth-century
thinkers as More, Raphson, and Newton—all of whom consider God to be
identical with infinite physical space—Oresme makes God immanent to infinite space without being identical with such space in every respect, especially
not in its dimensional, extended character.

It is a remarkable fact that no medieval thinker, not even those who basked
in the euphoria unleashed by the Bishop of Paris, claimed that God creates an
infinite void space *separate from Himself.* The reason is that such a space,
existing apart from God, would be a rival and limit to God's own infinite
spatiality.[27] It is more plausible to maintain that *if there is* an infinite empty
space, it is at one with God, pervaded by Him (and He by it), and finally not
distinguishable from His own immensity. A crucial step in this direction had
already been taken by Hermes Trismegistus, that apocryphal Egyptian vatic
figure who was a numinous presence for the Middle Ages and the Renaissance
alike. Trismegistus was held to proclaim in the widely read *Asclepius* that the
extramundane space outside the cosmos is not filled with anything material or
even quasi-material (e.g., *pneuma*) but is packed with "things apprehensible
by thought alone, that is, with things of like nature with its own [i.e.,
thought's] divine being."[28] Thinking is divine, and it is this internal divinity

that allows "thought alone" to be akin to the noetic content of an imagined infinite space. But the divinity of human thought—an Aristotelian theme—was bypassed in the High Middle Ages in favor of God's much superior divinity. Hence it is God's divine presence, not human "active intellect," that was believed to fill any possible extramundane, unmoving infinite space.

This last, momentous step was first made by Thomas Bradwardine (ca. 1290–1349) in his *De causa Dei contra Pelagium*. In this text, Bradwardine sets forth five crucial corollaries.

1. First, that essentially and in presence, God is necessarily everywhere in the world and all its parts;
2. And also beyond the real world in a place, or in an imaginary infinite void.
3. And so truly can He be called immense and unlimited.
4. And so a reply seems to emerge to the old questions of the gentiles and heretics—"Where is your God?" And, "Where was God before the [creation of the] world?"
5. And it also seems obvious that a void can exist without body, but in no manner can it exist without God.[29]

Bradwardine presents us with a pure panentheism of the void. God's "presence . . . necessarily everywhere" converts the void from what had been a purely negative and imaginary entity for other thinkers into something at once positive and real: positive insofar as it is not simply a form of nonbeing (e.g., void as sheer nothing), real insofar as it is filled with God's being (which is not only real but *most* real). Where Oresme had attributed reality to the void solely on the basis that it is an object of reason or understanding (as opposed to sensation or perception), Bradwardine is unhesitating in his conviction that the reality of any extramundane void stems exclusively from God's ulterior reality.[30] It does not stem from any quasi-physical attributes such as extendedness or dimensionality. Indeed, the void in question may even *lack* extension or dimension—unacceptable as this thought would be to Philoponus or Descartes. In this regard, it is nonphysical and "imaginary." But in the regard that matters most—that is, God's immanence in this space—it is altogether real.

By the same token, however, we can ask: Is such a void "empty of everything except God"?[31] Perhaps this vast void is not dimensional or extended precisely because nothing else is there *but God,* who was considered dimensionless and unextended by Bradwardine, Oresme, and other fourteenth-century theologians. But if so, perhaps this new void is literally a deus ex machina, invoked *only in order to ensure that God has a proper place in which to exist.* The void would then be a "place" that, precisely in accommodating God as "immense and unlimited," must be an infinite "space." Its existence would be merely tautological in status, a conceptual redundancy, part of God's definition. This much seems implied by Bradwardine's fifth corollary: if the void can "in no manner exist without God," by the same token it need not have (perhaps it cannot have) any other occupants in it. This is hardly a suitable model for the known universe, filled as it is with innumerable and diverse things.

As if anticipating this skeptical line of questioning, Bradwardine singles out three respects in which the void is more than a scene for God's residence. First, the void has *parts,* which are not necessarily identical with God's parts and which can thus belong to things other than God. I take this to be the purport of the first corollary: "God is necessarily everywhere in the world and all its parts." Second, the void has *places,* which once again are not necessarily those of God Himself; as Bradwardine adds, "God persists essentially by Himself *in every place,* eternally and immovably everywhere."[32] Indeed, as if to drive the point home, he remarks that "it is more perfect to be everywhere in some place, and simultaneously in many places, than in a unique place only."[33] Thus God does not restrict his occupation of the universe to His own place (assuming that this place is somehow delimited)—any more than to one part of space. Third, and most convincing, is Bradwardine's explication of his second corollary. To say that God is "beyond the real world in a place, or in an imaginary infinite void," is coded language for a return engagement with the continuing issue of whether God can move the world *motu recto.* The place *beyond* the world is the place to which God moves this world; since God can move the world to an infinite number of such extramundane places, he moves it in an "imaginary infinite void" that is the whole of space in which such motions are possible. Indefinite displacing entails unending spacing. As Bradwardine is wont to put it, if God moves the world from place A to place B, then either He was already in B or not. If he was not, then his omnipresence is compromised. If he was, then he is necessarily *everywhere*—in A and B, but also in C, D, E, and so on, ad infinitum. "If he was there [in B], then, by the same reasoning, He was there before and can now be imagined as everywhere outside the world."[34]

Bradwardine's views, though forgotten in detail until the belated publication of his *De causa Dei contra Pelagium* in 1618, nevertheless spelled out an entire way of thinking about the void and infinite space—a way that was deeply persuasive in its general outlines. It was pursued not only by John of Ripa and Nicole Oresme in the fourteenth century but by subsequent generations of philosophers and theologians. As Grant observes, "It was some version of Bradwardine's conception of the relationship between God and infinite space that was adopted and explicated by numerous scholastics during the next few centuries."[35] Bradwardine's adventuresome view was also explored by the great Jewish thinker Crescas (1340–1410), though with a distinctly Stoic emphasis on the infinite deific void as *surrounding* the plenary finite world.[36] More momentous, this same view "helped shape nonscholastic spatial interpretations in the seventeenth century."[37]

The point is not that everyone shared the Bradwardinian vision. Some, like Albert of Saxony (d. 1390) and John of Jandun (d. 1328), decidedly did not, denying any significant sense of a *vacuum separatum*. Others, like Richard of Middleton (a contemporary of Bradwardine), vacillated by divorcing God's immensity from infinite void space. Still others were preoccupied with the ancient question as to whether there was voidlike space *within* the world (even Bradwardine conceded that "by means of His absolute power, God could make a void anywhere that he wishes, inside or outside of the world").[38] Certain thinkers, like Nicholas of Autrecourt (active in the first half of the fourteenth century), even attempted to revive an Atomist notion of internal, interstitial vacua. But it remains the case that the freedom of speculation first tasted on the issuance of the 219 condemnations by the Bishop of Paris in 1277 was not only satisfying theologically (since it acted to restore faith in God's uninhibited powers, hemmed in as they were by Aristotelian cosmology) but also intoxicating philosophically (since it allowed numerous thought experiments concerning infinite space as a *situs imaginarius*).[39] Most important, it led to a fresh vision of what infinite space might be like were it to be identical with God—and God with it. It was a vision, befitting the Middle Ages, that was nothing short of "the divinization of space."[40]

We can say, in fact, that the Middle Ages contributed two new senses of infinite space to the gathering field of forces that were gradually granting primacy to space over place. Beyond the distinctive spatial infinites already posited in the ancient world by Atomism, Epicureanism, Stoicism, and Neoplatonism, we must now take into account a sense of infinite space as (a) *imaginal-hypothetico-speculative,* a space projected in a series of bold *Gedankenexperimente* that were not idle excursions but disciplined and serious efforts to grasp what space would be like if it had no imaginable limits; (b) *divine,* that is, an attribute of God or, more strongly still, identical with God's very being as immense beyond measure. These two emerging senses of the spatially infinite are deeply coimplicated: the divinization of space makes what is otherwise merely imaginal and negative into something real and positive, while imagined projections of such space furnish a limitless scope to the divine that is lacking on Aristotle's model of God as a Unmoved Mover who has no choice but to deal with a self-contained cosmos.

Along with this extended foray into a divinized-imaginified space came a related effort to overcome the confinement of place—at least as this latter was conceived on the model of *Physics,* book 4. Place itself (*locus*) was conceived in three distinctive senses in the medieval period. The first of these senses remains at least partly Aristotelian, while the other two senses depart ever more radically from the paradigm of place as an immobile container:

- place *in* the cosmos: this is specified by the immediate surrounder of an object; it is termed "material" or "mobile" (this latter inasmuch as what surrounds the object may give way to another environing medium);

- place *of* the cosmos: this is the position of the world-whole itself; and the burning issue, as we have seen, is whether *this* place can be exchanged for *another* place—whether in particular the world can be moved from position *A* to position *B;* this is what is at stake in article 49 of the Condemnations, which concerns whether God can move the existing world from its apparently "immobile" position;
- place *between* worlds: here the issue is how one existing cosmos is related spatially to another also-existing cosmos—and to still others as well, ultimately to the entire universe; the debate is over article 34, that is, whether there can be plural worlds.

If the first conception keeps place securely in the wraps in which Aristotle and the Peripatetic school had left it—literally a wraparound position that the medievals euphemistically called "lodging"—the second and third conceptions begin to break away from this tight tethering. In both of these latter cases, we witness *place becoming space* under our very eyes. In the second case, this happens in the form of a concern with the absolute locus of the world: if this locus can be displaced, then there must already exist an encompassing scene of diverse possible loci, each such place preestablished in an absolute space that embraces them all and each an unchanging part of that all-embracing space. In the third case, the transformation occurs on a relativist paradigm in which the crucial connection is not with a single Space but with *other worlds in other places:* what matters most is what lies *between* these worlds, that is, their interplace.

Whether by the second or by the third route, the adventurous avenue toward infinite space opened up decisively after the thirteenth century in the West. The closely confining circuit of place-as-perimeter dissolved and the vista of a New World of Space began to captivate the ablest minds of the succeeding period. It seems hardly accidental that the great Age of Discovery in the fifteenth and sixteenth centuries—an age that set out expressly to explore a terra incognita of interconnected places within the larger space of the earth itself as well as the still larger space of the heavens—immediately followed upon the bold speculations of philosophers and theologians in the thirteenth and fourteenth centuries. From an entirely imagined and divine status that was fully gained by A.D. 1400, such spaces became actual in the form of an earth and a sky that lay ready for discovery and possession not only by thought and faith but also by arms and men. And with the advent of an endlessly challenging space of exploration, we have reached the threshold of the Renaissance.

III

> All things are in all things.
> —Nicholas of Cusa, *On Learned Ignorance*

> Henceforth I spread confident wings to space; I
> fear no barrier of crystal or of glass; I cleave the
> heavens and soar to the infinite.
> —Giordano Bruno, Dedicatory Poem to
> *On the Infinite Universe and Worlds*

"Renaissance" does not mean something entirely new but, instead, *re*newed, new again. The New World of Renaissance thinking about place and space, more often than not, carries forward an Old World of previous conceptions. Just as the Middle Ages—and before that, the Hellenistic period—looked back at Aristotle most insistently, so the Renaissance will return to Plato for comparable inspiration. It will also go back to other sources, for example, the Neoplatonists (especially Plotinus, Iamblichus, and Philoponus) and the unknown authors of the *Hermetica*. As Frances Yates, who has made the strongest case for the Hermetic origins of Renaissance thought, puts it,

> The great forward movements of the Renaissance all derive their vigour, their
> emotional impulse, from looking *backwards*. . . . [For the Renaissance] history
> was not an evolution from primitive animal origins through ever growing com-
> plexity and progress; the past was always better than the present, and progress
> was revival, rebirth, renaissance of antiquity.[41]

A primary case in point is the very idea of spatial infinity, sometimes assumed to have been a product of late Renaissance thinking. We have seen, however, that this idea, at once alarming and attractive, first arose in ancient Atomism, and was pursued vigorously by Epicurus and the Stoics, explicitly formulated by Lucretius and Sextus Empiricus, investigated with subtle fervor by many generations of philosophers in the wake of Aristotle (from Theophrastus and Strato to Philoponus and Simplicius), examined in Arabic commentaries on Aristotle, and forcefully revived after 1277 in medieval thought. It is a paradox of the history of ideas that a book as insightful and scrupulous as Alexandre Koyré's *From the Closed World to the Infinite Universe* contributes by its title, if not always by its explicit claims, to the mistaken view that spatial infinity was a belated invention of the fifteenth and sixteenth centuries in the West.[42]

Also quite fateful in its consequences was the famous claim that the universe has its center "everywhere" (*ubique*) and its circumference "nowhere" (*nullibi*). Although often attributed to Nicholas of Cusa (1401–1464), in fact the claim derives from a pseudo-Hermetic text of the twelfth century, "The

Book of the XXIV Philosophers."[43] This statement of early medieval origin was destined to become a *mot célèbre:* not only Cusa but Giordano Bruno and Blaise Pascal (in the sixteenth and seventeenth centuries, respectively) cite it without attribution, each as if he had composed it himself.

Bruno's version is unusually instructive: "Surely we can affirm that the universe is all center, or that the center of the universe is everywhere, and that the circumference is not in any part, although it is different from the center; or that the circumference is throughout all, but the center is not to be found inasmuch as it is different from that."[44] Considered as a challenge to Aristotle—to his closed and centered world—this complex proposition has two parts: (i) In saying that the center is everywhere, it proposes that there is no single privileged center such as the earth—or any other heavenly body, not even the sun (Copernicus's efforts, known to Bruno, notwithstanding). The Arisotelian cosmographic model of a hierarchical universe with an immobile earth situated at the still center gives way to the idea that *any part* of the universe can be considered a fully valid center: the universe is "all center." This in turn implies that *every place* is a center—a center of perspectival viewing from which all other places can (at least in principle) be seen. As Cusa was the first to insist, the perception of the universe is relative to the place of the observer.[45] In other words, place is anywhere you choose to take up a point of view, and the universe yields an indefinite number of such places. (ii) In holding that the circumference is "throughout all"—that is, not in any single region, not even at the delimiting edge of the universe—Bruno maintains that it is in effect *nowhere,* "not in any [single] part." The circumference is *all over the place,* which is tantamount to saying that it is located in pure space and not in a particular place or set of places. Nor is such space a mere composite of places that are parts of the whole. It is a radically open field that is coextensive with the universe in its totality. In terms of Archytas's conundrum, we would have to say that no one could ever get to the edge of the world in the first place: nothing is *at* the edge since nothing can serve *as* the edge, as a simple circumference. There is no outer limit, no end to space. As Bruno himself comments, "Outside and beyond the infinite being, there exists nothing that is, because [such being] has no outside and no beyond."[46]

What is remarkable, then, about the claim in question—whether in its initial or its Cusan version—is that it manages to combine recognition of the importance of place with an equal acknowledgment of the value of infinite space. In this respect, it reflects its historical origin at the *beginning* of the Middle Ages: at the very moment when Aristotle was being rediscovered, yet also when burgeoning interest in the possible infinity of space was colluding with theological speculation as to God's uncontainable immensity. That the Renaissance took up the pseudo-Hermetic saying so enthusiastically indicates that the tension between place and space was still very much alive centuries after its first formulation in the twelfth century. Aristotle's celebrated utterance retained its relevance: place still "has some power." And it was just because it continued to have this power that the triumph of space was so slow in coming and so hard won during this same period. A considerable part of the struggle was due to the sheer fact that the looking-back was to place in its confinement (perspective is as confining as surface), just as the looking-forward was to a space unencumbered by such confinement. The situation was Januslike, exhibiting all the tension that looking in two opposed direc-. tions always brings with it. Instead of being surprised, we should ask instead: How could it be otherwise?

Nevertheless, the finally "triumphant beast" of Renaissance cosmology and theology is, indisputably, infinite space.[47] This becomes evident in Cusa's conception of space as modeled on the Absolute Maximum (*absoluta maximitas*), that is, the unqualifiedly great, that than which there can be no greater. Earlier medieval notions of absolute magnitude and of God's perfection (especially as invoked in the ontological argument) are detectable in the Cusan idea of the absolutely maximal, but what is new in this idea is that it makes infinity and the finite radically incommensurate. For Cusa, whatever is finite is subject to degrees of greatness—thus to comparison—but what is infinite is *incomparably great:* "Where we find comparative degrees of greatness, we do not arrive at the unqualifiedly Maximum; for things which are comparatively greater and lesser are finite; but, necessarily, such a Maximum is infinite."[48] It follows that we can never get to the infinite from any addition or compilation of the finite, no matter how massive or prolonged our efforts may be.[49] "The absolutely Maximum *is* all that which can be, it is *altogether* actual."[50] It also follows that the Absolute Maximum is equivalent to the Absolute Minimum—a palmary instance of Cusa's celebrated principle of *coincidentia oppositorum.* (For example, neither extremity can tolerate anything greater or lesser, since each is complete in itself.)[51] Further, the Absolute Maximum is incomprehensible and "beyond all affirmation and all negation."[52] Such a Maximum is numerically one (i.e., it is unique) and logically necessary (i.e., cannot not exist) as well as infinite.[53] We are thus not surprised to be told that the Absolute Maximum is God—and vice versa. By a very different route, then, we attain the divinization of the infinite first encountered in Bradwardine and Crescas.

Yet the route and the result are very different. This becomes clear when we ask ourselves: Is the Cusan infinite divinity infinite *space*? With his usual subtlety, Cusa distinguishes between two kinds of infinite, one applicable strictly to God and the other to the universe. God—the absolutely Maximum—is "negatively infinite." God is infinite in a negative mode insofar as He is *not* the sheer summation of finite things. The universe, in contrast, is "privately infinite," by which Cusa means that it is *unbounded* yet not actually infinite.[54] We can even say that the universe is "neither finite nor infinite," but by this Cusa only means that "it cannot be greater than it is."[55] Not being able to be greater than it is—and not being as great as God—it is finite; but *as it is,* it is privately infinite, since it is as great as it can possibly be as something physical. As physical, the universe is the "contraction" (*contractio*) of divine infinity: it is this infinity in a compressed state. But precisely such a "finite infinity"[56]—another coincidence of opposites—characterizes *infinite space.*

When Cusa remarks that "the world, or universe, is a contracted maximum" and "is, contractedly, that which all things are,"[57] he means that this world or universe (between which he does not distinguish) is a spatially maximal whole, even if it is not an *absolutely* maximal whole. As maximal, it is infinite; but as nonabsolute, it is finite: it is *this* world, a world that "sprang into existence by a simple emanation of the contracted maximum from the Absolute Maximum."[58] The finite infinity of the world, we might say, is the world put into its place: its "contracted infinity" is "infinitely lower than what is absolute, so that the infinite and eternal world [i.e., our world] falls disproportionally short of Absolute Infinity and Absolute Eternity."[59] But the distinctive privative infinity of this world remains unbounded, and in this format it contains, in contracted form, the very "Absolute Infinity" that it does not possess in itself without qualification.[60] The same special infinity of the cosmos is contained contractedly in the particular things of the world, and in this latter capacity it is irrevocably *spatial:* What else other than space could be the medium of universal contraction, with the result that "all things are in all things" in "a most wonderful union"?[61] If God is "in the one universe," the universe itself is "contractedly in all things."[62] Double *contractio* ensures at once the spatial infinity of the world *and* its failure to be divinely infinite. The world is unbounded yet undivine. Spatial infinity is secured only by the loss of divinization—just the reverse of what Bradwardine and other fourteenth-century theologians had held. *The infinitization of space requires its dedivinization.*

To be unbounded is to be without circumference. Cusa does not assert the lack of circumference dogmatically, or just to repeat his pseudo-Hermetic source. He argues that insofar as the earth is not a "fixed and immovable center"—it cannot be such a center, since fixity and immobility are always relative to the movement of something else—it cannot have a set boundary: if the world had a settled center in the earth (as Ptolemy notoriously held),[63] it would also have an equally settled perimeter. Moreover, it would also have a surrounding space: "It would be bounded in relation to something else, and beyond the world there would be both something else and space."[64] A boundary entails *something on the other side* of itself, and this something in turn requires "space" in which to be located. It is significant that Cusa uses *locus,* not *spatium,* in the phrase "and space" just cited. For the kind of space that is at stake in the situation is locatory, *not* infinite space. Locatory space is tantamount to "place" as this concept had been employed since Aristotle. It is a matter of a place for something—an "in which"—that lies beyond the boundary. But just such a place is lacking, indeed is superfluous, in a circumstance in which there is no effective boundary. To be infinite qua unbounded is to be placeless qua located. Between the full but nonspatial infinity of God and the essentially empty but precisely positional place of physical things lies the unbounded state, the spatial infinity, of the universe. Thanks to the articulation of this infinity, "a new spirit, the spirit of the Renaissance, breathes in the work of Cardinal Nicholas of Cusa."[65]

Bruno, deeply influenced by Cusa as he was, differed from him on at least two basic matters. For one thing, the infinity of the physical universe was for Bruno not less dignified or worthy than the infinity of God. As Paul Kristeller says, "Whereas Cusanus reserves true infinity for God alone, Bruno uses the relation between the universe and God as an argument for the infinity of the former."[66] Then again, Bruno extends spatial infinity from *this* world to *all* worlds, worlds that are themselves infinite in number. A third form of infinity, that of worlds in their innumerability, is thus added to the spatial and divine infinities distinguished by Cusa. The proposal of infinite worlds ensues from a principle of sufficient reason: "Insofar as there is a reason why some finite good, some limited perfection, should be, there is a still greater reason why an infinite good should be; for, while the finite good exists because its existence is suitable and reasonable, the infinite good exists with absolute necessity."[67] As Arthur Lovejoy puts it, it is "because of the necessity for the realization of the full Scale of Being that there must be an infinity of worlds to afford room for such a complete deployment of the possibles."[68] Crucial for the thesis of infinite worlds is thus a principle of plenitude, as is made explicit in Bruno's *On the Infinite Universe and Worlds*: "For just as it would be ill were this our space not filled, that is, were our world not to exist, then, since [particular] spaces are [otherwise] indistinguishable, it would be no less ill if the whole of space were not filled."[69] It would be ill, indeed, if the whole of space were not filled, for it then would be an utterly indistinct and purposeless void. For Bruno, however, things and the worlds they constitute do not fill in a preexisting void; they remove the need to presume the existence of any such emptiness, since their presence gives to space a distinctive, qualitative heterogeneity otherwise wholly lacking. The only space that exists is fully qualified, plenary space, described by Bruno as "not merely reasonable but inevitable."[70] The issue is not that of *horror vacui,* since nature does not rush to repair any momentary gaps but is always already full, never gappy or vacuous. As Bruno says explicitly, "Where there is no differentiation, there is no distinction of quality."[71] Worlds and the things they contain differentiate and fill up that which, without their distinguishing presence, would be a merely undifferentiated "undistinguishable inane" (in Locke's memorable phrase).

Bruno agrees with Cusa that the idea of a strictly bounded world lands us in the Stoic predicament of positing an empty extramundane space that has no other role than that of being occupied by some possible world. But God ensures that every possible world will become an actual one—"the possible and the actual [are] identical in God"[72]—and thus such space is otiose. Moreover, to believe that a given world occupies a preexisting empty space is to require a reason why it occupies *this* particular space rather than some other.

> For if we insist on a finite universe, we cannot escape the void. And let us now see whether there can be such a space in which is naught. In this infinite space is placed our universe (whether by chance, by necessity or by providence I do not now consider). I ask now whether this space which indeed containeth the world is better fitted to do so than is another space beyond?[73]

The answer is that there is no answer. There is no way to demonstrate convincingly that one stretch of characterless space is a better location for a world— or even for the universe—than another equally available but equally anodyne stretch.

Although he rejects any version of void—above all an external, unending void—Bruno continues to espouse the infinity of space. He does so without identifying this infinity with God. Infinite space is the space of the *universe,* a term that in careful moments Bruno distinguishes from *world:* "We see that the universe (*universo*) is of infinite size and the worlds (*mondi*) therein without number."[74] Rejecting the idea of a space *for* the world (such a space would be empty as well as qualityless), Bruno nonetheless requires a space shared fully by all worlds: such is the space proper of the universe. In this way, he avoids the earlier medieval choice between spaces *in, of,* and *between* worlds—all of which imply the existence, or at least the real possibility, of void. The space that matters most is not a space that is simply occupied, "taken over," by infinitely many worlds. It is, instead, a space that is *characterized* by these worlds: qualified so deeply that there is no latent or residual being beyond what discrete *cosmoi* bring to it, each in its own unique and diverse manner. Infinite space is not merely boundless; it is not just negative or privative; it has the positive character bestowed on it by the infinite worlds that make it up. "Infinite space is endowed with infinite quality," avers Bruno, "and therein is lauded the infinite act of existence, whereby the infinite First Cause is not considered deficient, nor is the infinite quality thereof in vain."[75]

The origin of such infinite space lies in God's own nature: God would be deficient if his creation were to be merely finite in form: "We insult the infinite cause when we say that it may be the cause of a finite effect."[76] We would also insult God if we thought that He was less than fully diligent: "Why should or how can we suppose the divine potency to be idle? Why should we say that the divine goodness, which is capable of communicating itself to an infinity of things and of pouring itself forth without limit, is niggardly?"[77] Even if we set aside God's superfetation of countless worlds and rely on a bland metaphysical principle such as "infinite perfection," which dictates that the universe is "far better presented in innumerable individuals than in those which are numbered and finite," we would have to posit a space capacious enough to accommodate these individuals (including whole worlds regarded as individuals). In short, "to contain these innumerable bodies there is needed an infinite space."[78] Space is needed to embrace and shelter—if not precisely to locate, or merely to underlie—the worlds that constitute the universe, the full *uni-versum,* of God's creation.

This last step is more radical than it may appear at first glance. It completely reverses our modernist assumption that space, above all infinite space, *comes first*—is literally a priori, whether cosmologically (as in Newton) or epistemically (as in Kant). On the contrary, asserts Bruno, infinite space *comes after* any creationist or metaphysical demand for infinite worlds. No wonder that Bruno is not concerned with infinity of *size,* that is, pure extension as such. (Nature is not, he exclaims, "endowed with infinite space [merely] for the exaltation of size or of corporeal extent.")[79] What matters is sufficient *room for worlds*—worlds without end. Rather than being sheer "ex-tension," *Aus-dehnung,* literally "drawn-out-ness," infinite space is roomful, which is to say that there is always just as much of it as is needed for the provision of a particular thing or, rather, a particular world-of-things: just this and not more. Room is not where you find it—that way lies preexisting space, and ultimately the void—but *where you need it.* As is most evident in architecture (and as had already been adumbrated by the Stoics), room is intrinsically accommodating. The wherewithal of universal space itself, it arises where worlds are to be set forth.

Just as room is a middle term between space and place, so the worlds that require room exist between the universe and bare things. It is a matter of middle terms—terms intrinsically plural. As the title of Bruno's 1584 treatise spells out, there is *one* "universe" but *many* "worlds": *De l'infinito universo et mondi.* Reinforcing this difference is the fact that whereas worlds and things are perceptible, *the* universe is not visible as such: plurality betokens perceptibility, oneness signifies invisibility. As Bruno puts it bluntly, "No corporeal sense can perceive the infinite."[80] Bodily sensation can take in physical things and the world-whole in which they are encompassed by earth and sky, but one cannot extrapolate from such sensations to the infinite space that is their setting.[81] On this point Bruno agrees with Cusa, who says that the sensory "progression does not continue unto the infinite."[82] For in the end the infinite universe and the finite worlds that comprise it are two kinds of things—or, as Leibniz might put it, two orders of things. Even if "all things are in all things," world and universe are not *in each other.* They are too radically different in nature and status for any such mutual insinuation. But the divergent twain does finally meet in the middle: the variant orders converge in the room that mediates between space and place.[83]

This suggests a new outcome of the Archytian conundrum. What will happen when the lonely figure reaches out from the world-edge is that *room will arise for the reaching:* just room enough for the actual motion and cubic extent of the arm or staff. Intrinsic to the infinity of universal space is its unstinting capacity to offer room—to make way for whatever is to appear in it. Bruno himself does not put it this way: unlike the Stoics, he has no technical term for "room." He merely cites Lucretius to the effect that *some space* is required beyond the edge, whether the motion of the arm succeeds or is blocked (for what does the blocking must itself be located outside the edge). He leaves undefined the exact status of this occasion-bound, roomful space, but his reasoning nonetheless requires it.

A further advantage to this interpretation of the ancient puzzle is that it allows us to grasp another meaning of the pseudo-Hermetic adage discussed earlier. If it is indeed the case that "the center of the universe is everywhere and the circumference nowhere," this may mean that no matter where we situate ourselves—even, *per impossibile,* on the edge of the world—we will be in a new center from which we move out, giving us the distinct impression that there is no inhibiting circumference. Construing the adage this way also allows us to reverse it, in keeping with Bruno's own famous formulation: "The circumference is everywhere and the center nowhere."[84] In other words, the edge is everywhere: we are always on the edge of things and of the world itself. The freedom of reaching out from successive centers is thereby counterpoised with the inhibition of being hemmed in by a series of circumferences. (Perhaps this is why Bruno insists that the infinite "has no outside and no beyond": every apparent move beyond is countered by a holding-in.) And if all this is so, we may draw the still more radical conclusion that the center and the circumference themselves coincide. They coincide not just for God (who, as Bradwardine had already insisted, is equally everywhere) but for anyone who strays into the room-creating circumstance in which place and space meet. For in this circumstance it does not matter whether we consider ourselves at the center or on the periphery; what matters is that we have the right room in which to live and move and have our being.

And the place of *place* in all this? The increasing obsession with infinite space from the thirteenth century onward had the predictable effect of putting place into the shadows. But place is not altogether lost from sight. We have seen the significant survival of the term *locus* in Cusa's lucubrations on extramundane space. Cardinal Cusanus also makes the striking statement that "no two places agree precisely in time and setting."[85] This claim is not just illustrative of Cusa's general rule that "equality between different things is *actually* impossible,"[86] but represents a strong assertion of the uniqueness of places, their unreducibility to interchangeable sites. If Heraclitus can speak of *idioi cosmoi,* "special worlds," then we are all the more justified in talking of special places—places in their idiosyncrasy. Bruno, who rarely speaks explicitly of place per se, would support this line of thought. A place is not only

finite—Thomas Digges's contemporary discourse of "infinite place"[87] would
be oxymoronic for Bruno—but it is *uniquely* finite, thanks to the dimensional
specifications that particular entities possess. In one passage, Bruno insists
that every body exists "in relation to other particular bodies, according to the
mode of [their] capacity—because [they are] above, below, innermost, right,
left, and according to all local differences."[88] The phrase "all local differences" is telling: not only is it applicable to places, but it is borrowed from
the structure of places themselves (a structure aptly described by precisely
such terms as "above," "right," etc.). Indeed, places may even be the most
dimensionally specific of all mundane entities—or, in an alternative nomenclature, the most thoroughly "explicative" of entities. If Being as such is
"complicatively one," places (and the worlds they inhabit) are explicatively
many.[89] As explicative, places unfold, distend, extend what is enfolded within
the invisible oneness of infinite space. But they do so, once more, only insofar
as there is adequate room in which to effect this explication in a uniquely
fitting manner.

From Bruno, therefore, we learn that *space makes room for place.* In saying
this, Bruno is building not only on Cusa but also on Epicurus (via Lucretius)
and, still farther back, on Plato (who proposed the first Western model of
room in the form of *chōra*). But he is also looking forward to the modern
preoccupation with infinite space: what Bruno says at the opening of his Fifth
Dialogue in *De la causa, principio, et uno* might well have been said by
Newton a century later: "the universe is, then, one, infinite, immobile."[90] In
looking backward and forward at once—in being what he himself calls "a link
of links"[91]—Bruno is a paradigmatic Renaissance thinker who is (in Lovejoy's words) "the principal representative of the doctrine of the decentralized,
infinite, and infinitely populous universe."[92] Given the heretical character of
all three strands of thought here singled out, it is not surprising that Giordano
Bruno became the first martyr of modern philosophy: he was burned at the
stake in the Campo dei Fiori, Rome, on February 16, 1600.

IV

> 'Tis all in peeces, all cohaerence gone;
> All just supply, and all Relation.
> —John Donne, "Anatomy of the World"

The year 1600 also marked the end of one of the most critical centuries in the
history of place and space. Thinkers of the sixteenth century attempted to
make a complete break with scholasticism—that is, with the very institution
that by the end of the thirteenth century had encouraged speculation concerning infinite space. (Bruno was not the only victim of the Inquisition: Cardano
was arrested in 1570, Campanella was imprisoned for more than thirty years

between 1592 and 1628, Telesio's works were proscribed in 1594, Patrizi's *Nova de universis philosophia* was condemned in 1594.)[93] Paradoxically, it was the very availability of Aristotle's writings in Greek—now accompanied by glosses from such commentators as Philoponus and Simplicius—that began the disengagement from scholastic thought. Closer attention to Aristotle's own words brought with it *both* a greater orthodoxy *and* a more critical stance.[94] At the same time, the enthusiasm for Plato and Neoplatonism, epitomized in the flourishing of the Florentine Academy in the second half of the previous century, spawned ingenious and imaginative approaches to the natural world.[95] A revival of interest in Epicurus, Lucretius, and the Stoics also had an important impact on new models of space and place in this rich and tumultuous period.

A sign of the times was the nearly universal rejection of space and place as categorial in status. No longer could "where" (Aristotle's *pou*) be considered one of the ten basic metaphysical categories, to be ranged alongside others such as "relation" or "quality." In particular, space and place could no longer be constricted to the Procrustean bed of "substance" and "accident," arguably the two most fundamental categories. It is striking to observe that every leading theorist of the natural world in the sixteenth century refused to assimilate space to the bivalent stranglehold of *substantia/accidens* that had dominated Western thinking for so many centuries. Bruno, Telesio, Campanella, Patrizi: all agreed that space has its own unique kind of being, its own status as a universal term in the analysis of natural entities. Patrizi put this point most tellingly in his condemned treatise.

> Granted that the [Aristotelian] categories serve well for worldly things [*in mundanis*]; Space is not among worldly things [*de mundanis*], it is other than the world [*mundus*]. It is the accident of no worldly thing [*mundanae*], whether body or not body, whether substance or accident—it is prior to them all. As all things come to be in it, so are they accidental to it; so that not only what are listed in the categories as accidents, but also what is there called substance, are for it accidents. Hence it must be philosophized about in a different way from the categories.[96]

For Patrizi, space is one of four elements—the other three being light, heat, and fluidity—but it is the *first* to be created.[97] Since space is infinite, God is here given credit for *actually creating something infinite*—not just, as so many scholastics of the fourteenth century had believed, *possibly* creating something infinite, or else something sheerly imaginary. Moreover, God is now held to create something to which He is Himself subject. Patrizi waxes positively Archytian at this point, virtually quoting the philosopher from Tarentum: "For all things, whether corporeal or incorporeal, if they are not somewhere, are nowhere; and if they are nowhere they do not even exist. If they do not exist they are nothing."[98] If God is to exist—albeit incorporeally—He must exist in the very space that He has brought forth to begin with, suggesting the image of the Uroboros: God biting His own (spatial) tail! This is not the divinization of space but the spatialization of the divine!

God is subject not just to space but to a particular property of infinite space, namely, its inherent three-dimensionality. Again in Patrizi's words:

> [Space] is not a body, because it displays no resistance, nor is it ever an object of, or subject to, vision, touch, or any other sense. On the other hand, it is not incorporeal, being three-dimensional. It has length, breadth, and depth—not just one, two or several of these dimensions, but all of them.[99]

Much like Philoponus, Patrizi points out that Aristotle's notion of place is two-dimensional only, lacking depth: "For what is [Aristotle's] *'locus'* other than Space, with length and breadth, even if in *locus* he himself foolishly overlooked depth (*profundum*), which is more properly *locus*?"[100] God's "profundity" here takes on literal sense. More portentous, the cubic character of "Space" (*spacium*) entails its essential emptiness, its status as vacuous in principle. Aristotle had assumed that dimensionality is inseparable from corporeality and thus that there can be no empty space, given that space is dimensional: for him, dimensions are not detachable from the physical substances of which they are essential attributes.[101] But if we can conceive of space in terms of dimensions that are *not* attributes of any substance whatever, that is, a *pure* "spatial extension" (again in Philoponus's phrase), then we have cognized an essentially empty space. Moreover, since dimensions themselves have no limit on their own magnitude, to commit oneself to three-dimensionality is to take a crucial step in the direction of infinite space.[102] It is also to move toward the closely related ideas of immobility, continuity, and homogeneity, which are articles of faith in seventeenth-century thought. For even if bodies move in it, the dimensional framework itself does not move; and dimensions are effectively the parameters only of that which is the *same* continuous materiality situated within their compass. Such a framework is essentially receptive of whatever is to be located in it; it yields to the *locatum* rather than resisting it and is penetrated by it as well as penetrating it.[103]

It does not matter that space is always *in fact* filled (as both Philoponus and Patrizi hold); what matters is that space is the kind of thing that can be *conceived* as endlessly empty in three dimensions.

> When [Space] is filled with a body, it is *locus;* without a body, it is a vacuum. And on this account this vacuum, like *locus,* must have the three common dimensions—length, width, and depth. And the vacuum itself is nothing else than three-dimensional Space [*spacium*].[104]

In other words, finite place becomes infinite space on two conditions: that it has three dimensions in fact (this condition is shared by place and space alike) and that it can be emptied of body in principle (only space is capable of this). In proposing this, Patrizi proves himself to be an exemplary Renaissance thinker indeed: by looking back a thousand years to Philoponus, he looks forward to Gassendi and Newton in the next one hundred years, since all three thinkers would assent to Patrizi's two conditions.

If infinite space is not actually empty, with what it is filled? This was a vexing question for the sixteenth century. Bruno, anxious to promote the plenary character of infinite space, had proposed that it was filled with ether. Patrizi, probably influenced by Proclus, prefers light because it is most like space itself. Both ether and light offer no resistance to the bodies that occupy them. But they introduce the perplexing prospect of an incorporeal body that fills space *before* discrete material bodies are located in it. As Patrizi says teasingly: space as filled with light is "an incorporeal body and a corporeal non-body." [105] Light is a *tertium quid* that mediates between space and place, nonbody and body, sharing properties of all four terms while offering something uniquely its own, namely, illumination.

Renaissance thinkers were especially prone to posit such mediational third terms, perhaps reflecting thereby their own liminal status between medieval and modern worlds. We have just considered another such term, room, of which there is, however, no explicit trace in Patrizi. [106] But Patrizi pursues another closely related and equally characteristic Renaissance strategy, that of combining contraries or dissimilars in unexpected ways. Where Cusa and Bruno had spoken of the identity between maximum and minimum, or between center and circumference, Patrizi maintains that extracosmic space is *both finite and infinite*. While the *locus* of the world is unequivocally finite— one world in one place—the *spacium* of what is beyond the world is finite insofar as it originates precisely at the perimeter of the world (which thus provides a lower bound) *and* infinite insofar as it goes on outward limitlessly into the universe (without any upper bound). [107] This is a variation, of course, on the Stoic model of a finite plenary world as the center of an infinite void, [108] and it makes evident Patrizi's somewhat compromising commitment to a single world in the vastness of space—compromising compared with Bruno's blatantly heretical idea of an infinity of worlds.

Compromise is a close cousin of confusion. One area of genuine confusion in Renaissance thinking sends us back to our primary theme: the relation between place and space. Despite the upsurge of interest in the actual (and not just imaginary) infinity of space that is manifest in Cusa, Bruno, and Patrizi, the vexing question of what this means for the conception of place in contrast with space remains unresolved. Any significant distinction of place from space is left unclarified, and a middle realm that somehow contains and combines both is assumed. This is a middle that is a muddle. Place and space are presumed to cohabit an undefined, or rather ill-defined, intermediate realm where each is the other's virtual likeness. This literal con-fusion is evident, for example, in Gianfrancesco Pico della Mirandola's statement that "place is space, vacant [*vacuum*] assuredly of any body, but still never existing as a vacuum alone of itself."[109] Here *spacium* and *locus* are simply equated, as if they were equivalent parts of an indiscriminate commixture. Once they are put together in the miasma of the middle realm, it does not matter in which direction an identity statement is formulated. If Gianfrancesco Pico can say that *place is space,* Tommaso Campanella will claim that *space is place:* space is "the place of all things that are sustained by the divinity."[110] Campanella's claim is only seemingly the contrary of Pico's. This is brought home by Campanella's further proposition that "there is no place and space outside place and space, just as there is no humanity outside man, nor linearity outside lines."[111] The indeterminacy of "place and space" is here reinforced by its reinscription in his version of the Archytian predicament: at the edge of the world, Campanella holds, there is neither place nor space beyond the place and space already realized within the world. Bruno, for his part, admits to the same indeterminacy in his own treatment of this continuing conundrum: "Certainly I think that one must reply . . . that if a person would stretch out his hand beyond the convex sphere of heaven, the hand would occupy no position in space, nor any place, and in consequence would not exist."[112] "No position in space, nor any place": it is a matter of indifference which term is thought to be at stake in the experimental situation. The point is not that there are no differences to be made between place and space but that such differences as exist are not recognized—they no longer count—in Bruno's and Campanella's repetition of the crucial circumstance first adumbrated by Archytas, then relayed by Aristotle and Lucretius. And if they do not matter here, why should they matter in more mundane situations?

There can be no more revealing contrast than that between the statements of Bruno, Campanella, and Pico—all of them composed in the sixteenth century—and a declaration of Pierre Gassendi's written in the middle of the next century: "Place," says Gassendi, "is nothing other than empty space."[113] The grammatical similarity between Gassendi's claim and those of Campanella and Pico—each bearing an "is" in an apparent identity statement—conceals the fact that Gassendi is not conflating, or even equating, the two terms. By adding the crucial qualifier "nothing other," he is saying that what had formerly been called "place" can now be *replaced* by "space." The clear implication is that space, and more particularly "empty space," encompasses and eclipses place—and thus undercuts its usefulness as a distinctive descriptive term. A muddle, a moment of uncertainty and of uneasy exchange, has given way to a new era of certainty in which space triumphs over place, in language as in concept. Patrizi—who stands precisely midway in history between Pico and Gassendi—already affirmed this triumph: "A vacuum is certainly prior to *locus,* and should be prior to it. But it is an [essential] attribute of Space [*spacium*] to be a vacuum, hence Space is prior to *locus* both in nature and in time." [114]

Even if the full ascendancy of space over place does not happen until the publication of Newton's *Mathematical Principles of Natural Philosophy* in the last part of the seventeenth century, the critical turning point in the debate between space and place occurs during the sixteenth century. Unlike preceding centuries—which in their complex continuity make it difficult to distinguish between a characteristically medieval and an early Renaissance theory of place and space [115]—the sixteenth century witnessed the slumbering specter of Space awakening defiantly. A powerful sense of something genuinely new was emerging, most dramatically in the uninhibited speculations of Cusa and Bruno, but insistently as well in the more cautious ruminations of Patrizi and the imaginative ideas of Campanella, who held that space is capable of feeling and sensing. [116] Campanella also believed that space seeks to expand at every opportunity. This intriguing idea anticipates Theodor Lipps's notion that "everything spatial expands," [117] a notion that is crucial to the experience of specifically modern architectural space. More important, however, Campanella's idea exemplifies the passion for the real (and not only the projected or supposed) infinity of space that had become pandemic by the end of the sixteenth century. Infinite space—and space, construed generously, is nothing if not infinite, as we have seen at successive reprises in this chapter—is space that expands endlessly, knows no term, has no limit, and finally engorges place in its massive maw. Even as dedivinized and thus as coextensive with the physical universe, the generality and openness of infinite space—in contrast with the enclosedness and particularity of finite place—have become virtually irresistible by the time we reach the threshold of the early modern era.

Part Three

The Supremacy of Space

Interim

Place is superior to things in place, so that being in place is being in something superior.
—Damascius, *In Aristotelis physicorum libros quinque posteriores commentaria*

No being exists or can exist unless it is related to space in some way.
—Isaac Newton, "De gravitatione et aequipondio fluidorum"

[In modern space] every place is equal to every other.
—Martin Heidegger, "The Age of the World Picture"

Descending from its position as a supreme term within Aristotle's protophenomenological physics, place barely survived discussion by the end of the seventeenth century. By the end of the eighteenth century, it vanished altogether from serious theoretical discourse in physics and philosophy. At that moment, we can say of place what Aristotle believes has to be said of time: "It either is not at all or [only] scarcely and dimly" (*Physics* 217b34). How this radical dissolution and disappearance of place occurred—how place ceded place fully to space in the course of just two centuries—is the subject of the next four chapters, which by their *via negativa* will set the stage for later developments, to be treated in Part IV. Extending from Bergson and Bachelard to Heidegger and Deleuze and Guattari, these later developments will vindicate the high esteem in which place was held in ancient philosophical accounts, but only against the backdrop of the decisive demise of interest in place under scrutiny here, in Part III. Integral to the genius of early modern

thinkers from Descartes to Leibniz is a disdain for the *genius loci:* indifference
to the specialness of place, above all its inherent "power." Where Aristotle
took for granted the power of place—a special noncausal power found in
its containing character, its qualitative differentiation, its heterogeneity as a
medium, and its anisotropy of direction—Western philosophers and scientists
of the seventeenth and eighteenth centuries assume that places are merely
momentary subdivisions of a universal space quantitatively determined in its
neutral homogeneity.[1] Places are at best convenient and expedient pockets in
the vast intact fabric of what Newton called "absolute space" in 1687. Even
the competing idea of "relative space," as articulated by Newton's archrival,
Leibniz, will leave little, if any, room for place.

I do not want to imply that the marginalization of place as a significant
concept arose exclusively during these first two centuries of modernity.
Rather, the change took place in an ever-lengthening shadow of preoccupation
with space, regarded as absolute and more particularly as infinite (and frequently both together). We have seen this preoccupation surface in ever more
manifest forms in late Hellenism and Neoplatonism, in medieval thought of
the thirteenth and fourteenth centuries, and in much Renaissance thought. It
occurred to an entire succession of thinkers, often of quite diverse back-
grounds, that the spatial world could not be contained, and thus could not
be conceived, as a matter of place alone. If place implies constriction and
delimitation, and if it is always tied to the specificities of a given locale (hence
its qualitative character), then some other factor must account for such things
as distance and extension, indeed anything sheerly quantitative that refuses to
be pinned down to place. Thus talk of "space" arose in the wake of Aristotle:
at first, hesitatingly and with a backward glance at Plato (in his employment
of *chōra* to designate a roominess that place as *topos* could not sustain); later
and more tellingly, in the invention of *spatium* (and its medieval variant *spacium*) as a way of distinguishing the properly spatial from the merely local
(*locus* taking over the delimited and delimiting role formerly assigned to *topos*). It was in exploring the extensiveness of space, its seemingly unde-
limitable outspread, its unendingness, that the coordinate but distinguishable
notions of spatial absoluteness and infinity began to seem irresistible.

This is not to say, however, that interest in place was simply set aside. This
interest continued apace—in the very face of the emerging fascination with
space. Thus Damascius, writing in the sixth century A.D., could still say un-
blushingly that "being in place is being in something superior."[2] Not that
place is superior to *space;* it is only superior to *what it contains:* "Place is
superior to things in place."[3] But place remains important enough to single
out and to praise for its own singular power, however limited in scope it may
be (its very power consists in its ability to be the limit for something else).
Only fifty years after Damascius made these claims, however, Philoponus vacillated between two formulations of the critical concept of extension: between
diastēma topikon and *diastēma cosmikon.* In the first formulation, we sense

the presiding presence of Aristotle: the "extension" is "of place." In the second
locution, the extension belongs to "the world." Where place is a correlate of
physical body—which has its own extension, *diastēma somatikon*—"world"
(*cosmos*) exceeds any body or group of bodies. World is poised between bodies and the universe, providing room to the former while stretching outward
toward the latter. But place is not here distinguished in any definite way from
space, whether cosmic or universal.[4]

The truth is that for many centuries place was lumped together with space,
compounded with it as it were. We have seen that Archytas's conundrum calls
for a specifically extracosmic space beyond the world-edge, and yet certain
medieval articulations of this conundrum continue to speak of *locus* rather
than of *spacium* in discussing this very perplexity. Even more blatant, leading
Renaissance thinkers remain capable of equating space with place and vice
versa. This is not simply confusion; it is the persistence of the ancient high
regard for place surviving through millennia of thought and riding piggyback
on the rising passion for space.

What makes the early modern epoch such a crucial moment is that by the
end of the epoch this high regard has vanished, with the result that the more
or less irenic cohabitation of place and space ceases to be a viable option.
Already by the middle of the seventeenth century William Gilbert can say
disdainfully that "place is nothing, does not exist, has no strength."[5] But it
has no strength (*vim*) and does not exist precisely because it has been denied
existence and power by those who prefer to locate strength in space. Place is
pushed into a puny position in the periphery.

Even then, the marginalization of place is not altogether victorious. Smat-
terings of place-talk survive at the very moment of Gilbert's condemnation:
Descartes and Locke still feel themselves bound to give some account of
place, however reluctantly. The hendiadys "place or space"—expressing an
indeterminate choice between two attractive options—is used by Descartes
and Leibniz alike. (Gassendi, adding to the confusion, even speaks of "region,
or space, or place"!)[6] But whereas Descartes intends the expression to refer
to two genuinely distinguishable notions when he uses it in the 1640s, Leibniz,
by 1715, means it in a quite different sense: now place is a mere aspect of
space, one way of regarding a paradigmatic spatial situation. The dissolution
of place, though radical and thorough, nevertheless takes almost a century of
concerted labor to accomplish. This labor is complete when the idea and term
"site"—*situs* in Leibniz's term—assumes a number of the tasks formerly assigned to "place," a word that (in its several European variants) drops out of
official eighteenth-century parlance about space.

Just as place, qua concept or word, does not disappear altogether as it
spirals downward in seventeenth-century discourse, so this same century does
not invent or discover space in its absoluteness and infinity. Thinkers of
the "century of Genius" give focus and point—*concentration*—to spatial
ultimacies intuited or inferred, or simply posited, during the preceding two

millennia, beginning with Anaximander's Boundless and the Atomists' Void. But by 1600 so much express attention has been paid to space that place comes to be regarded as something secondary, even effete and otiose, as Gilbert clearly implies. Place cannot but suffer from invidious comparison with the rising star of absolute/infinite space. The effect is that of a complemental series: the more of one, the less of the other. Cohabitation gives way to single occupancy as the era of space is definitively established—with place shorn of its prior primacy and put into an abeyance from which it will not recover for at least two hundred years.

One of the abiding ironies of the situation is that early modern thinkers, by insinuating a forced choice between place and space, and then between absolute and relative determinations of space itself, thrust apart what had been constructively and unproblematically combined in previous thinking. Plato's Receptacle is at once place-rich (i.e., full of regions and particular places, *chōrai* and *topoi*) and yet spacelike (*chōra* has no effective limit), absolute (i.e., all-encompassing, "omnirecipient") and yet relative (e.g., insofar as similar sensible qualities are drawn together *in relation to each other* in primal regions, pursuant to the principle that "like attracts like"). Even Aristotle's notion of *topos,* a comparatively minor item in the cosmology of the *Timaeus,* combines a certain absolutism—for example, in the idea of a *koinos topos,* the common place that is "the sum total of all places"—with a decided relativism (i.e., in the notion that places exert a differential influence on the bodies that occupy them, constituting a virtual "field of force").[7] Despite their dramatically different treatments, Plato and Aristotle both consider place as bringing together absolutist and relativist traits in ways that anticipate later notions of *space:* traits, however, that are kept rigidly separate in the post-Renaissance period. Similarly, Philoponus and Bruno espouse both absolutism and relativism in their conceptions of space. For Philoponus, every physical body "longs for a spatial extension not because of this extension, but because of its relation to the other bodies," yet these same bodies take up places in an absolute, fixed space of three dimensions: "It falls to the share of each body to occupy a definite part of the [spatial] extension."[8] For Bruno, "every determination of place must be relative," and yet every particular place is "a portion of space . . . beyond which infinite space extends."[9]

Only within the transcendental idiom provided by Kant at the end of the eighteenth century will there be an express effort to recombine the divergent directions of absolutism and relativism in one coherent framework. But a terrific price has to be paid for this act of recombination: space is no longer situated in the physical world but in the subjectivity of the human mind that formally shapes this world. Moreover, and as a direct reflection of this transcendental turn, any residual sense that place is importantly distinct from space will have vanished, with the result that place is given no attentive consideration, indeed is barely mentioned, in the *Critique of Pure Reason.*[10]

6

Modern Space as Absolute

Gassendi and Newton

I

> The universe is infinite, immobile, immutable.
> —Pierre Gassendi, *Animadversiones in decimum librum Diogenis Laertii*

> The celestial spaces are void of resistances.
> —Isaac Newton, *Philosophiae naturalis principia mathematica*

> I don't live in the infinite because in the infinite one is not at home.
> —Gaston Bachelard, *L'Intuition de l'instant*

To turn to the seventeenth century is to plunge into a turbulent world in which alchemy vied with physics, theology with philosophy, politics with religion, nations with each other, individuals with their anguished souls. No single treatment can do justice to this multifarious period of human history. We can, however, pick our way through it by attending to an assortment of figures who occupied themselves expressly with questions of place and space: Gassendi, Newton, Descartes, Locke, and Leibniz. Each of these thinkers—with the exception of Locke—was also a prominent scientist, and this double identity is no accident. To assess place and space in the first century of modernity is perforce to take into account scientific as well as philosophical thinking. Such double-barreled thinking does not just continue the ancient debate over void space—favored by Gassendi and Newton, reviled by Descartes and Locke—but also engages the renascent atomism evident in Bacon and Boyle as well as Gassendi and Newton. The much-derided mechanical view of nature so emblematic of the epoch raises issues of place and space, given that early modern mechanism has two ultimate terms: extension and motion.[1] These terms, through their mathematization by Galileo and Descartes, entail specific theses about space and place—to start with, their sheer quantifiability. Even on more particular issues such as the circularity of the heavens, of special

137

concern to Bacon and Kepler, implications for place/space loom large. The dramatic confrontation between the new science and Aristotelian physics proliferates, rather than represses, these implications. Pondering the putatively perfect circularity of the heavens—an article of faith for Aristotelians—Bacon had this to say:

> The human understanding is of its own nature prone to suppose the existence of more order and regularity in the world than it finds. And though there be many things in nature which are singular and unmatched, yet it devises for them conjugates and parallels and relatives which do not exist. Hence the fiction that all celestial bodies move in perfect circles.[2]

Everywhere we look in the seventeenth century, then, we find science and philosophy colluding on problems that bear on place and space alike. (We also find an increasing preoccupation with questions of time, but that is another story.)[3] What underlies the collusion, and makes the century coherent in the end, is the common premise of "simple location" in Whitehead's semitechnical sense of the term.[4] Simple location, says Whitehead in *Science and the Modern World,* "is the very foundation of the seventeenth-century scheme of nature."[5] It consists in the belief that any bit of matter "can be said to be *here* in space and *here* in time, or *here* in space-time, in a perfectly definite sense which does not require for its explanation any reference to other regions of space-time."[6] As an "absolute presupposition" in R. G. Collingwood's sense, simple location is sufficiently general and tenacious to support both absolutist and relativist paradigms of place or space.[7] For our purposes, we need only note that simple location entails the reduction of place to *position*—to a pinpointed spot in a massive matrix of relations—and the expansion of space to an *infinite universe* that makes this matrix possible. This becomes evident in another expression of the doctrine: "As soon as you have settled, however you do settle, what you mean by *a definite place* in space-time, you can adequately state the relation of a particular material body to space-time by saying that it is just there, *in that place;* and, so far as simple location is concerned, there is nothing more to be said on the subject."[8]

But in fact there is a great deal more to be said by anyone who, like Whitehead himself, objects to the doctrine as a disastrous legacy that deeply distorts living and lived experience, thereby committing what he calls "the fallacy of misplaced concreteness." This fallacy consists in "mistaking the abstract for the concrete."[9] In the case of simple location, this means taking abstracta such as "position" or "universe" as definitive designations of the concreta of place and field—hence as substitutable for these latter. As a result, place comes to be absorbed entirely into space: the concreteness of the former is wholly displaced into the abstractness of the latter. Despite Whitehead's use of the term in the above citation, place was denied any effective presence in an uncompromised spatial immensity. It is one thing to posit space as sheerly infinite—as did Bradwardine and Crescas and Bruno, Telesio and Campanella and Patrizi—but it is something else again to hold that such space is empty not only of things *but of place itself.* This latter claim is the specific accomplishment of seventeenth-century physics, which held that "place does not affect the nature of things, it has no bearing on their being at rest or being in motion." [10] According to the new physics, space is something self-sufficient and wholly independent of what is *in* space, including particular places; space is thus "an emancipated concept, divested of all inherent differentiations or forces." [11]

Such emancipation becomes evident in the work of Pierre Gassendi (1592–1633), a proponent of a revived Epicurean atomism who advocated the priority of space over matter and, in particular, the reality of the vacuum—a vacuum identical to "the abstract, homogeneous, infinite space of Euclidean geometry." [12] Here the fallacy of misplaced concreteness is writ large, in fact larger than any place or set of places can possibly contain! Regarded as an indispensable foundation of kinematics, this purely vacuous abstract space is at once absolutized and infinitized. Gassendi's espousal of such space emboldened Newton to make his own, still more decisive formulations later in the century. [13] Not only did Gassendi make important scientific advances—he was the first to proclaim that a moving body will continue in a rectilinear direction indefinitely, and he explicitly rejected the ancient model of impetus as the cause of motion [14]—but he made a fateful distinction between spatiality and corporeality in discussing the dimensions of length, width, and depth.

> Two sorts of dimensions are to be distinguished, of which the first may be called corporeal and the second spatial. For example, the length, width, and depth of some water contained in a vase would be corporeal; but the length, width, and depth that we would conceive as existing between the walls of the vase if the water and every other body were excluded from it would be spatial. [15]

For Aristotle, *all* dimensions are corporeal; they are attributes of actual physical bodies and thus exist in strict conformity to these bodies. [16] By positing an incorporeal dimensionality, Gassendi is in effect liberating space from matter, thereby repeating Philoponus's move of one thousand years earlier. Not only is space infinite and matter finite—this had been the conclusion of Crescas and Bruno—but space has a pure dimensionality independent of the concrete corporeal dimensionality of matter. Moreover (and here taking a step beyond Philoponus), Gassendi held that part of the purity of spatial dimensionality is its strict *measurability:* "Clearly, wherever it is possible to conceive some [purely spatial] interval, or distance, it is also possible to conceive a dimension because that interval, or distance, is of a determinate measure, or can be measured." [17] Measurability implies the sheer homogeneity of space, its strict regularity as isometric and isotropic (i.e., its homogeneity of measurement and direction, respectively). Gassendi is therefore maintaining not just that we can *think of* space independently of matter but that, when we do, space presents itself to us as having its own dimensionality and homogeneity. *And its own infinity:* as we realize when, pressing the evacuation of space to an extreme, we recognize that there is no effective limit to the void. For if we can imagine the sublunar sphere as empty, why can we not imagine every other celestial region as empty too? Thinking this way, we soon reach the Archytian world-cusp and all that lies beyond.[18]

Pure space has other attributes as well in the Gassendian worldview. As for Plato (and Bradwardine), it precedes creation; and it will subsist even after the universe is destroyed.[19] It is "boundless" (*immensa*) and thus constitutes a species of positive infinity. It is immobile and cannot change place.[20] Indeed, space is coextensive with the universe itself: "The totality of spaces corresponds to the totality of the universe."[21] Perhaps most important, space is sui generis: neither substance nor property, it (along with time) enjoys a unique mode of being that has to be added to Aristotle's list of basic categories, indeed, not only added, but shown to be supreme inasmuch as substances themselves are located *in* space and time. On this last point, Gassendi is positively Archytian: "There is no substance and no accident for which it is not appropriate to say that it exists somewhere, or in some place. . . . Even if the substance or the accident should perish, the place would continue nonetheless to abide."[22] And if place abides, then space is all the more triumphant. It and time are "real things, or actual entities," that "actually exist and do not depend upon the mind like a chimera."[23] As such, they serve as "conditions of natural bodies, or the things in the universe."[24] This bold claim looks far ahead to Kant, for whom space and time are also ultimate conditions for natural bodies (or at least for our experience of these bodies); it also looks immediately ahead to Newton, who is directly anticipated in Gassendi's conclusion that "space endures steadfastly and time flows on whether the mind thinks of them or not."[25]

Given this framework, it is not surprising that the role of place in relation to space is considerably problematized. Gassendi's attitude toward this role is highly ambivalent. On the one hand, he wants to preserve the concept and language of "place" in contrast with "space." He is convinced that we must be able to say that bodies *change place in space:* "Were anything whatever, or a part of the World, to change its place, the space in which it presently is would not move with it, but [would] remain unmoved while being abandoned [i.e., by what changes place]."[26] The immobility of space is the inverse complement of the mobility of place; place and motion are coimplicatory. Gassendi also wants to be able to say that God is *in every place* and not just in one place only—not even the Empyrean postulated by thinkers like Anselm and Campanus of Novara.[27] Hence "there is a kind of divine extension which does not exist in one place only, but in many, indeed, in all places."[28] The ubiquity of God calls for an indefinite plurality of receptive places in which God can dwell—and not just for an indifferent and planiform space.

On the other hand, despite these reasons for preserving the notion and term "place," Gassendi wishes to quantify place itself as fully as possible. In contrast with Aristotle's emphasis on the qualitative aspects of place (e.g., the directionality of up/down), Gassendi proposes that "place is a quantity, or some sort of extension, namely, the space or interval made up of the three dimensions length, breadth, and depth, in which it is possible to hold a body or through which a body may travel."[29] But precisely as quantified—as measurably dimensional in a noncorporeal manner—place becomes extremely difficult to distinguish from "space," a term that connotes an infinite and homogeneous medium. We have seen Gassendi say that "place is nothing other than empty space." He also says that "place is an interval, *or incorporeal space,* or incorporeal quantity."[30] Not surprisingly, Gassendi substitutes "space" for "place" in one and the same paragraph of the *Syntagma* without registering any sense of inconsistency: "It is therefore apparent that *place and time* do not depend upon bodies and are not corporeal accidents. . . . From this we conclude that *space and time* must be considered real things, or actual entities."[31] This nonchalant identification of "place" with "space" would not have been so momentous if space had been conceived differently by Gassendi—if, for example, it were to possess something like the diversity and inhomogeneity of Platonic *chōra.* Instead, the leveling-down of space to strict dimensionality and measurability, isotropism and isometrism, and homogeneity and immobility signifies that no vestige of the particularity of place, its peculiar qualities and special tropisms, remains within the monolithic space with which it is now increasingly identified. This is evident above all in Gassendi's admission that space, even if a perfectly "real thing" (i.e., in contrast with a fantasmatic or fictitious entity), nevertheless "cannot act or suffer anything to happen to it, but merely has the negative quality of allowing other things to occupy it or pass through it."[32] Such purified space is perfectly "passible" or penetrable by material bodies that occupy it, but it has no power of penetration on its own.

In other words, *the inherent dynamism of place, its power to act or simply to resist, has given way to the supineness of space regarded as an indefinitely passible, indeed a passive, medium.* What Plato and Aristotle (and even more markedly Iamblichus) had considered to be the capacity of place to influence direction and movement, generation and corruption—to effect physical change in general—yields to a conception of place as a merely quantified portion of an equiform and empty space: place has become a reduced residuum with no inherent ability to alter the course of things in the natural world. All that remains of place is its very name—and an empty name, a mere *flatus vocis,* at that.

II

The nominal survival of place is dramatized—and complicated—in Isaac Newton's *Philosophiae naturalis principia mathematica.* In this epoch-making work of 1687, Newton "incorporated Gassendi's theory of space into his great synthesis and placed it as the concept of absolute space in the front line of physics."[33] Given the manifest triumph of absolute space in Newton's masterwork, it is perhaps surprising to discover that place survives at all in this text, considered by Whitehead to be comparable to the *Timaeus* in its overall cosmological significance.[34] But in fact place is quite expressly present in the *Principia*—present not only in name but in several names: as "movable place" and "immovable place," "relative place" and even (most disconcertingly) "absolute place." This latter term seems oxymoronic, a confused combination of incompatible terms—in contrast with "absolute space," which appears to reflect a natural marriage of similars. But Newton is not being deliberately paradoxical, much less playful, when he asserts that absolute motion, that is, the motion with which he is most concerned in the *Principia,* is "the translation of a body from one absolute place into another."[35]

At first glance, the idea of absolute place might seem to be a mere recrudescence, at a metaphysicoscientific level, of Aristotle's notion of natural places as the terminal points of locomotion, that is, the "proper" lasting locales for determinate kinds of material things. But any such seeming "absolute" does not connote anything natural such as agency or power, much less appropriate settlement. Whether applied to space or place, time or motion, the term means for Newton at least five things, none of which implies the *dynamis* inherent in Aristotelian *topoi:* (1) immovability (this trait is lifted straight out of Gassendi); (2) having no relation to anything external (i.e., simple location); (3) remaining always selfsame, no matter what happens in its midst; (4) not needing any additional or supplementary reference system by which to situate what is located in the absolute sphere; (5) intelligible (i.e., versus "sensible").[36] In these various ways "absolute" stands contrasted with "relative," as in Newton's definition of "relative space" as

> some movable dimension or measure of the absolute spaces; which our senses
> determine by its position to bodies; and which is commonly taken for immovable space; such is the dimension of a subterraneous, an aerial, or celestial
> space, determined by its position in respect of the earth.[37]

Notice that here the very same places that in Aristotle's *Physics* are given an intrinsic attractive power (e.g., the atmosphere or the earth as pulling bodies "up" or "down" in accordance with their nature) are now regarded as merely relative in status—as having no more dynamism than a mathematical point, whose position is strictly relative to the arrangement of other surrounding points (as Aristotle himself would be the first to admit). Notice also that New-ton implies that relative space is not just "commonly taken" for "immovable [i.e., absolute] space," but *mistakenly* so taken. For a relative space is nothing but a "movable dimension or measure" of the absolute space that it occupies. More exactly, it is the "sensible measure" of that space, that is to say, its perceptible analogue but *not* its adequate representation: absolute space, being invisible, cannot be represented by *any* perceptible means.

It is just at this point that "place" enters Newton's discourse.

> But because the parts of [absolute] space cannot be seen, or distinguished from one another by our senses, therefore in their stead we use sensible measures of them. For from the positions and distances of things from any body considered as immovable, we define all places; and then with respect to such places, we estimate all motions, considering bodies as transferred from some of those places into others. And so, instead of absolute places and motions, we use rela-tive ones; and that without any inconvenience in common affairs.[38]

Relative places, like relative spaces, are matters of measurement; more pre-cisely, they are *means* of measurement: to be a "relative" place or space is to be in a perceptible (and thus measurable) arrangement with other places or spaces. More particularly, it is to be in an arrangement in which at least one other thing—whether place or body—is "considered as immovable" so as to allow for the determination of "positions and distances." And from such "sen-sible measures" as positions and distances, "we define *all places*" as well as all motions that are determined in relation to places (i.e., locomotions proper). Just as "relative" connotes the instrumentality and perceptibility of sensible measurement, so "place" means the result of such measurement. This way— the way of "convenience in common affairs"—lies an entire pragmatics of place that will be especially congenial to Locke.

We thus witness a first reduction of place: in its relative character, it is nothing but a means of measurement. But what of place in its *absolute* charac-ter? Surely, we protest, this is *not* reducible: Does not the very word "abso-lute" imply nonreducibility? Nonetheless, Newton recognizes at last three modes of reduction inherent in the very concept of absolute place—a triple reduction, in short. The first two modes of this reduction are at work in the following passage, which may represent the last official serious assessment of place in Western physics.

> Place is a part of space which a body takes up, and is according to the space, either absolute or relative. I say, *a part of space;* not the situation, nor the external surface of the body. For the places of equal solids are always equal; but their surfaces, by reason of their dissimilar figures, are often unequal. Positions properly have no quantity, nor are they so much the places themselves, as the properties of places. The motion of the whole is the same with the sum of the

motions of the parts; that is, the translation of the whole, out of its place, is the same thing with the sum of the translations of the parts out of their places; and therefore the place of the whole is the same as the sum of the places of the parts, and for that reason, it is internal, and *in the whole body.*[39]

In fateful anticipation of his eventual debate with Leibniz, Newton here rejects a relativist view that would restrict place to its mere "situation" as determined by "position," a term he refuses to limit to its quantitative determination (while also refusing to allow it to be the definition of place itself). At the same time, Newton denies the validity of the container model, which is dependent on "the external surface of the body" and which generates special paradoxes to which Crescas first pointed (e.g., on this model a full circle will occupy less of a place than a circle from which a pie-shaped piece has been cut out).[40] In lieu of container or situation—that is, of the ancient alternatives offered by Aristotle and Theophrastus, respectively—Newton does not propose any new model or view of place. Instead, he adopts a doubly reductive tactic. On the one hand, he *subsumes place under space* by making it (much in the manner of Bruno) "a part of space," that is, a mere portion of that which is always already there robustly and universally as an absolute given. As such, place has no being or identity apart from that of space itself, and is determined, indeed predetermined, by whatever attributes are ascribed properly to absolute space (e.g., the five attributes mentioned just above). On the other hand, Newton *collapses place into body:* the place of a body is none other than the totality of the places of the parts of that body and is thus "internal" to this body: "the place of the whole [body]" is nowhere other than "*in* the whole body." Thus body is not in place so much as place is in body.[41] Taken in one direction, place is dissipated in circumambient space; taken in another, it is compressed into the body for which it presumably offers the location. The two moves— both of which deny any autonomy to place—are specified in the first sentence of the citation given above: "Place is a part of space which a body takes up."

Given Newton's reductive nominalization of it, place amounts to the nearly tautologous fact that "any definite body occupies just *this* part of space and not another part of space."[42] Moreover, if it is generally true that "the place of the whole is the same as the sum of the places of the parts," then by transitivity the particular properties of given places can make no crucial difference in the constitution of the totality of places in the universe: which is to say, no crucial difference in the constitution of absolute space per se. As the merely constituent parts or indifferent portions of universal space, places have no integral, much less differential, being of their own. Nor do they have such being even when regarded as "absolute" in their own right. This becomes evident in another statement of Newton's, which mimicks Aristotle even as it departs from him and which introduces a final mode of reduction.

Wherefore, entire and absolute motions can be no otherwise determined than by immovable places; and for that reason I did before refer those absolute motions to immovable places, but relative ones to movable places. Now no other places are immovable but those that, from infinity to infinity, do all retain the same given position one to another; and upon this account must ever remain unmoved; and do thereby constitute immovable space.[43]

This remarkable passage seems to empower places—immovable, absolute places—by its claim that absolute motions can be determined only by reference to such places. In fact, all that Newton means is that absolute motion has to proceed between fixed points: points here designated by the nominal expression "immovable places." For, as he says expressly in the same Scholium from which this passage comes, "absolute motion is the translation of a body from one absolute place into another."[44] In *this* regard, relative places are no less important than absolute places, since "relative motion" is defined similarly as "the translation from one relative place into another."[45] But it remains that places, whether absolute or relative, are in no way responsible for the motion that takes place between them but only serve to demarcate and punctuate that motion.[46]

Moreover, even if it is true that places "constitute immovable space," they do so as neutral and undifferentiated parts, as continuous (and contiguous) segments of a homogeneous absolute space. And the fact that immovable, absolute places do this "from infinity to infinity" only clinches the case for the primacy of absolute space. For such places, albeit immovable, make no difference individually or collectively to the totality of space they co-occupy, and they certainly make no difference in terms of their relationship to each other. For this latter relationship is itself unchanging: "As the order of the parts of time is immutable, so also is the order of the parts of space."[47] If the order of the "parts of space," that is, absolute places, cannot be changed—if such parts or places always "retain the same given position one to another"— then nothing inherent or qualitative about these parts-as-places (or places-as-parts) will make any difference in the final picture, a picture in which absolute space is the sole survivor. In their very immovability and absoluteness, places are locked into a pattern of mutual relativity from which they are not allowed to escape. This not only constitutes a third and last reduction of any putative power they might possess but also attributes to them a paradoxical self-undermining status. Taken at their most absolute, places are most deeply relative to each other; they are relative in their absoluteness, absolute in their relativity. They are what they are not, and are not what they are.[48]

In Newton's "System of the World," then, places are put in an autodeconstructive position from which they cannot recover in the nature of the case. And if it is true (as Max Jammer avers) that "to Newton, absolute space is a

logical and ontological necessity,"[49] it is also true that absolute *place* is, logically and ontologically, a self-dissolving enterprise.

Dissolving into absolute space, a place of any sort becomes at best an
arbitrary subdivision of such space. When Newton claims that "times and
spaces are, as it were, the places as well of themselves as of all other things,"[50]
the qualifying phrase "as it were" (*tanquam*) is highly symptomatic of the
crisis of place occurring in the *Principia*. Given the dominance of spatial-
absolutist terms in Newton's thinking, he cannot say that places are *in fact*
"the places as well *of themselves* as of all other things." As the mere delineations of spatial regions, its specified stations, places have no standing of their
own: they cannot stand in themselves, of themselves, by themselves. They are
the mere minions of absolute space. They may be useful conceptually (i.e., as
ways of coming to finite terms with absolute space) and instrumentally (i.e.,
as means of measurement thanks to their perceptibility), but they have no
existence in themselves. They exist in name only.

Or, more exactly, *in text only*. Place's survival is not as a concept in physics
(or metaphysics) but as a bare literal term that proves indispensable at certain
pivotal moments of Newton's text. For example, the sentences immediately
following the citation analyzed in the preceding paragraph are quite saturated
with the language of "place."

> All things are *placed* in time as to order of succession; and in space as to order
> of situation. It is from their essence or nature that they are *places;* and that the
> primary *places of things* should be movable, is absurd. These are therefore the
> *absolute places;* and translations *out of those places,* are the only absolute
> motions.[51]

The repetition of explicitly placial terms in this passage does not signify a
sudden recognition of the importance of place in Newton's overall theorizing
but is, instead, symptomatic of the irrepressible role of place in *specifying* any
systematic thinking about space, above all absolute space. This sub-rosa return
of the reduced is all the more revealing for its marginality in the official
"definitions" and "axioms" of the *Principia*. Newton has spontaneous recourse to the idiom of place precisely when he sets forth a doctrine that is
place-limiting and (finally) place-banishing. Thus to say that "all things" are
"placed" in time and in space; that such things, temporal and spatial alike,
"*are*" places "from their essence or nature"; and that there exist "primary
places of things," that is, absolute places, "out of [which] . . . absolute motions" arise—all this is to claim far more *in the text* than can be admitted *in
the theory*. But the textual claim does show that to think of how things relate
to space and time, to consider things in their essential being, and to ponder
the nature of motion involve invoking place at every step. The fact that such
invocation occurs en passant and marginally serves only to heighten the
stakes, reminding us that the power of place (in this case, a power to specify

space) is considerable indeed—much more considerable in any case than is allowed for, or anticipated, in the "Newtonian Revolution" as Newton himself promulgated it and as his legion of true believers understood it.[52]

Leaving autodeconstruction and subtext aside, let us return for a last look at the main line of Newton's official thought. Concerning this thought, Koyré has written that Newton's commitment to absolute space is "indeed the necessary and inevitable consequence of the 'bursting of the sphere', the 'breaking of the circle', the geometrization of space, [and] of the discovery or assertion of the law of inertia as the first and foremost law or axiom of motion."[53] The geometrizing effected in the *Principia* (already undertaken by Galileo earlier in the seventeenth century)[54] is a far cry from that projected in the *Timaeus*. In Plato's text, the infusion of normalizing stereometric shapes served only to give to sensible bodies a formal regularity they would otherwise lack in the lap of inchaote *chōra;* but even after their geometrization, these same bodies remained located in discrete *topoi* set within the irregular, idiolocal regions provided by the Receptacle: no dissolution of place into space occurs here, not even in the final stages of creation. From the opening pages of the *Principia,* on the other hand, places are conceived as mere parts of space; and the geometrizing of space that occurs there belongs properly to mechanics, that is, to laws governing material bodies at rest or in motion. Instead of the bestowal of distinctive shapes, the aim of Newtonian geometrization is measurement: "Therefore geometry is founded in mechanical practice," says Newton, and is "nothing but that part of universal mechanics which accurately proposes and demonstrates the art of measuring."[55] But the basis of measuring is precisely the regularity, the homogeneity, of the space to be measured. In this way, too, the triumph of space over place is assured, given that implacement, moving into place or simply staying in place, asks merely to be experienced or perceived, not to be measured (and this is so even if place as relative may be used as a means of measurement).

In the end, place plays only one major role in Newton's cosmology—and that a tenuous one. As absolute, it occupies and structures the void *before* any occupation by bodies or forces. A corollary of Newton's commitment to absolute space is an acceptance of a strict universal void. Not only is it the case that "the celestial spaces are void of resistance" (for they lack even the material ether found in the sublunar realm), but there are vacua in the sublunar realm itself: "If all the solid particles of all bodies are of the same density and cannot be rarified without pores, then a void space, or vacuum, must be granted [to exist between them]."[56] But Newton does not simply equate vacuum or void with *empty space.* Speaking of the void, he says that "*something* is there, because spaces are there, although nothing more than that."[57] This something, I would contend, is precisely *absolute place,* here cryptically referred to as "spaces" by Newton. As a commentator remarks, "The point seems to be that even without bodies in it space is not a void since there is something *in* space, namely parts of space."[58] What else can these "parts of space" be but absolute places? Such places, despite their radically reduced status, are at least the proper contents of the void that is absolute space. They are the first citizens of such space—even if their own ultimate standing is no more than segmental.

But this promising direction—literally so, since the proposal just cited is contained in an unpublished essay on gravitation written while Newton was still a student—is in the end submerged in something else: Newton's massive monotheism. For another response to the question as to what fills the void is theological: God.[59] To say that this response is "theological" does not do justice to its seriousness in Newton's eyes. Although his theological ideas are barely discernible in the first edition of the *Principia*, he added a General Scholium to the second edition of 1713. In this Scholium, Newton singled out eternity and infinity as the two most important attributes of God: "His duration reaches from eternity to eternity; his presence from infinity to infinity."[60] Newton is careful not to claim that God merely *possesses* eternity and infinity: "He is not eternity and infinity, but eternal and infinite; he is not duration or space, but he endures and is present. He endures forever, and is everywhere present; and, by existing always and everywhere, he constitutes duration and space."[61] Leaving eternity and duration aside, it is evident that if God is Himself infinite, He is "everywhere present" in the infinite physical universe—and is thus indissociable from this universe, penetrating it all the way through at every level and at every putative place. Conversely, everything in the universe penetrates Him in turn: "Bodies find no resistance from the omnipresence of God."[62] In making such claims, Newton is not just saying that God needs infinite space in which to deploy Himself (though he certainly does: "If ever space had not existed, God at that time would have been nowhere").[63] Nor is he claiming only that God and space are coextensive—equal infinities, as it were. The point is still stronger: God *is* space; He "constitutes" it through and through; space is thus "an emanent effect of God."[64] Rather than being self-subsistent, space depends on God, whose very substance is bestowed on space: "He is omnipresent not *virtually* only but also *substantially*."[65] Indeed, it is God's substance that makes space both absolute and infinite: What else, implies Newton, could bestow such powerful parameters on space? After their dissociation in Patrizi and Gassendi, space and substance rejoin—in God.

Newton's celebrated claim that space is "God's sensorium" is at once misleading and clarifying. It is misleading if it is taken—as Leibniz took it—to mean that space is some kind of super *organ* possessed by God, for then space would be only an attribute of God and not an intrinsic part of His being. Newton, aware of the ambiguity, added a crucial qualifying phrase in his *Optics* (1706): "Does it not appear from Phaenomena that there is a Being incorporeal, living, intelligent, omnipresent, who in infinite Space, *as it were* in his Sensorium, sees the things themselves, intimately and thoroughly perceives them, and comprehends them wholly by their immediate presence to himself [?]"[66] Newton's claim is clarifying in that it allows us to realize that God's omnipresence in physical space is analogous to the way our own sensory systems permit us to be fully present to a given field of perception, fully immersed in it if not at one with it. What is perceptual intimacy for us is cosmological-ontological intimacy for God: intrinsic to God's being is His very sensing of the infinite spatial universe.

God's infinity, then, rejoins the infinity of space, with which it is ultimately one: "The quantity of the existence of God [is] eternal, in relation to duration, and infinite in relation to the space in which he is present."[67] When Newton dutifully repeats an Archytian argument for the unendingness of the physical universe—"We cannot imagine any limit anywhere without at the same time imagining that there is space beyond it"[68]—he assumes that the same is true of God, who is as boundless as the space with which He is comprement. But the parity of God and space in regard to a shared infinity leaves unresolved the question, how exactly is God *in* space, the very space He constitutes and senses? This question takes us back to place—at least to begin with. In an "avertissement au lecteur" that Newton intended to accompany the publication of Samuel Clarke's letters to Leibniz, we read that "the Hebrews called God *makom* or *place* and the Apostle tells us that he is not far from any of us for in him we live and move and have our being, putting *place* by a figure for him that is in all place."[69] As God is a place for us, He is in all places here below. Similarly, in a manuscript entitled "Of the Day of Judgment and World to Come," Newton says that "God is alike in all places, he is substantially omnipresent, and as much present in the lowest Hell as in the highest heaven."[70] The cosmologic at work here is that God is not just present but *completely present* in each place, that is, the doctrine of the whole-in-each-part, or "Holenmerism" in Henry More's term.

The crucial issue is this: Does such a doctrine, or indeed any talk of God's location "in all places," represent a genuine revalorization of place? Does any of this return us to place from infinite space? In contrast with the ancient marriage between immanence and place (a marriage marked by the preposition "in" to which Aristotle first drew systematic attention), is Newton bestowing on place a validity in his theology that is refused (with one possible exception) in his physics? I think not. On the one hand, Holenmerism involves intractable problems of the sort signaled by More himself: If all of God is present in one part, will anything be left over for other parts? How can He be altogether present both in a thing *and* in a part of that same thing?[71] On the other hand, the language of "in all places" is tantamount to "everywhere" or "ubiquity"—both of which words Newton uses interchangeably with the phrase in question—and, as a result, the specificity of place, its irremediable particularity, is once again dissolved in space. Recourse to place in Newton's theological thinking is in the end only a convenient cover for his deeper commitment to absolute, infinite space. For God is not just *a* place but, if a place at all, so comprehensive a place, so much a matter of all possible and actual places, as to be equivalent to the endless space that God shares with the universe at large. Better, then, to call God by what is His true nonempty name in Newtonian physics: "absolute space."[72]

This leaves us with one last unanswered question: If God possesses (or, rather, *is*) "boundless extent,"[73] does this not mean that He is an extended entity, that is, an entity having actual physical dimensions? Is His *immensitas* finally a material immensity and not only a spiritual one? Newton, who comes perilously close to this heretical position, steps back from it adroitly: for him, God remains (in the phrase of the General Scholium) "a spiritual being"[74] who is not materially voluminous in three dimensions.

Henry More, Newton's friend and fellow scholar at Cambridge, does not hesitate to take the leap. For More, even spiritual beings are extended, and this includes God Himself. Thus God is equivalent to space not merely because both are infinite but because both are *infinitely extended albeit incorporeal substances.* God and space are alike extended beings: we can say of each that it is something "Infinite Immovable Extended."[75] More's argument is straightforward: if extension can exist apart from matter, then it can inhere in what is not matter, that is, spirit; by the same token, infinite extension inheres in infinite spirit, that is, God. Thus God is unendingly extended in space just as space is unendingly extended in Him.[76] This is to take a bold step beyond fourteenth-century theology: not only is space divinized but God is spatialized. God is in the world as its infinite spatial setting. As More puts it in a letter to Descartes,

> It seems, indeed, that God is an extended thing (*res*), as well as the Angel; and in general everything that subsists by itself [is extended], so that it appears that extension is enclosed by the same limits as the absolute essence of things, which however can vary according to the variety of these very essences. As for myself, I believe it to be clear that God is extended in His manner just because He is omnipresent and occupies intimately the whole machine of the world as well as its singular particles.[77]

More here draws a conclusion in 1655—Spinoza will draw it, too, some twenty years later—that is radical indeed: God Himself is "an extended thing," thus present in the physical world, not just as a divine Person but as the very space of which this world is part.[78] To posit such a God existing in such a way is in the end, however, only a final dramatic step in a long march, which, beginning with Anaximander and the Atomists, continuing in Strato and Epicurus, taking flight in Crescas and Oresme, ends in Newton's assertion of an absolute, infinite space at once independent of matter and dissolvent of place.

Modern Space as Extensive

Descartes

I

All places are full of bodies.

Nothing has an enduring place, except insofar
as its place is determined in our minds.
—René Descartes, *Principles of Philosophy*

Henry More, who had enormous influence on Isaac Newton (the latter's idea
of "absolute space" is, arguably, a tidied-up version of More's "Infinite Immovable Extended"), found in René Descartes a much more recalcitrant
thinker. Beneath the *politesse* of their correspondence in the last year of Descartes's life, one detects an abyss of difference opening up. They differ not
just because More is a spiritualist and Descartes a materialist but, more crucial, because of their variant views on extension—which, by the middle of the
seventeenth century, had become the key to the nature of space. It is revealing
that already in Descartes's first letter of response to More the question of
whether God is an extended entity comes to the fore immediately. More had
said in his opening letter that "God, or an angel, or any other self-subsistent
thing is extended," and to this Descartes confesses his utter skepticism: "The
alleged extension of God cannot be the subject of the true properties which
we perceive very distinctly in all space."[1] Why not? In his rebuttal of More,
rather than rely on reason or understanding as to God's intrinsic nature—as
he does in the case of God's infinity—Descartes calls on *imagination:* "God
is not imaginable nor distinguishable into shaped and measurable parts."[2] To
think of God is certainly to conceive of a substance, but it is not to imagine
an *extended* substance. For the latter is an entity that has definitely shaped and
measurable parts, parts that exist separately from each other: *partes extra partes.* The parts exist separately precisely insofar as two or more of them cannot
occupy the same *place.*

Commonly when people say that something is extended they mean that it is
imaginable . . . and that it has various parts of definite size and shape, each of

which is non-identical with the others. These parts can be distinguished in the imagination: some can be imagined as transferred *to the place of others,* but no two can be imagined simultaneously *in one and the same place.* Nothing of this kind can be said about God or about our mind; they cannot be imagined, but only grasped by the intellect; neither of them can be distinguished into parts, and certainly not into parts which have definite sizes and shapes [and thus occupy equally definite places].[3]

In contrast, we *can* conceive that God or angels or the human mind "can all be at the same time in one and the same place."[4] In this case "place" (*locus*) is a receptive scene of conjunction between nonextended entities (hence Newton is quite justified in saying that God exists "in all *places*"), but it is a divisive scene of exclusivity and disjunction when it comes to extended things—things that cannot share the same place in any strict sense. We witness thus an exemplary case of simple location: to say that two or more extended things cannot occupy the same place is tantamount to saying that each of them is simply located in space.

But Descartes is not here interested in exploring the character of place per se; he invokes it merely as a test for what it means to exist in space: "Everyone imagines *in space*—even imaginary or empty space—various parts of determinate size and shape, some of which can be transferred in imagination to the place of others, but no two of which can be conceived as compenetrating each other at the same time in one and the same place, since it is contradictory for this to happen without any piece *of space* being removed."[5] The "in" and the "of" in this statement indicate the encompassingness of space vis-à-vis place—a sign of formal superiority to which we shall return below. What matters most to Descartes at this point is his resolute rejection of any form of spiritual extension: "so we clearly conclude that no incorporeal substances are in any strict sense extended."[6] What, then, *is* extended? Descartes's answer is straightforward: "Whatever is extended is a genuine body."[7] It follows forthwith that since incorporeal substances cannot fill space—having no extension proper, they cannot be simply located there, contrary to what More had asserted—only corporeal substances, or bodies, can do so. And they do so densely and without remainder, for Descartes is convinced that "there can be no completely empty space . . . there can be no space without body."[8] The Philoponean notion of a pure spatial extension, powerfully if only tacitly at work in the thought of More and Newton alike (and expressly active in Gassendi), is here rejected in favor of an extension that is bodily only. It is this extension—and this alone—that characterizes space. But what, then, is space?

The foundation of Cartesian physics and metaphysics lies in an insistent identification of space with *matter,* that is, with physical bodies possessing magnitude and shape. In making this move, Descartes at once distinguishes himself from Gassendi and Newton as recrudescent atomists *and* from that long line of anti-atomists stretching from Damascius and Simplicius through Bruno and More who sought to absolutize space at the expense of matter (whether by recourse to an intelligible void or to an all-pervasive God). In this respect, Descartes aligns himself with Plato and Aristotle in their concerted rejection of the Democritean void and in their common effort to make matter somehow coextensive with space.[9] In other respects, however, Descartes looks forward to Locke and especially to Leibniz in terms of a radical relativizing of space. But in taking up this latter direction, Descartes ironically will come to much the same conclusion as did his own absolutist critics, Gassendi and Newton: place has no independent status apart from that of the universal space to which it belongs. But this is to get ahead of the story—a story whose most revealing chapter remains that which treats extension, to which we must now return.

Extension (*extensio*) is the core concept in Descartes's view of space. Not only is it the common essence of matter and space, it determines the nature of quantity and dimension—and thus of all measurement of distance as well.[10] In his early work, *Rules for the Direction of the Mind* (1628), Descartes writes that "by extension we understand whatever has length, breadth, and depth, not inquiring whether it be a real body or merely space."[11] Putting it this way might make it appear—as it certainly did appear to Philoponus—that extension is something that can exist apart from that which is extended (*extensum*). But to think this would be in error; by entertaining "corporeal images" (i.e., images of physical bodies), we ascertain immediately that "there is no difference in the conception of the two,"[12] that is, of *extensio* and *extensum.* For we are unable to imagine any body that is not extended, or any extension that is not bodily. This means in turn that we cannot regard extension as an empty field or mere set of dimensions that comes to be occupied, fully or in part, by physical bodies—as Newton assumes to be the case. Extension and extended things are inseparable.[13] Not only is it the case that every material body is extended—this would be granted by all theoreticians of space, even by Pythagoras—but, contra More, every instance of extension is a material body. Not only does matter occupy space, but space *is* matter. As Descartes writes to the Marquess of Newcastle in October 1645, "We have the same idea of matter as we have of space."[14] To Mersenne he makes it clear that the idea of matter is analytically contained in the idea of space, thanks precisely to extension as their shared definition or essence: "something which has length and breadth and depth."[15]

Descartes is willing to concede to common sense that there must be *some* basis for distinguishing between matter and space, even if the two never exist apart from each other. For instance, if a given body *moves* through space, it is evident that one stretch of space occupied by that body is not identical with a second stretch occupied afterward by that same body.[16] But beyond the revealing case of motion, there is the fact that we can *conceive* matter and space as different from each other. Just as imagining exhibits their indissociability *in concreto* (as we have just seen in Descartes's response to More), so conceiving them points to their dissociability in thought. If the difference between matter and space is strictly unimaginable—cannot be put into an actual image—it is not *unthinkable*. As Descartes points out in his *Principles of Philosophy* (1644), we can *think* of the difference by means of a distinction between individual and generic unity.

> The difference consists in the fact that, in the body, we consider its extension as if it were an individual thing, and think that it is always changed whenever the body changes. However, we attribute a generic unity to the extension of the space, so that when the body which fills the space has been changed, the extension of the space itself is not considered to have been changed but to remain one and the same.[17]

Plausible as this difference is, it remains abstract, that is, a conceptual difference, since in (physical and metaphysical) fact the extension of a body and the extension of the space it occupies are identical. There is no room in the Cartesian worldview for the idea of an extension that is nonmaterial: in other words, an extendedness that might belong to mind or spirit or God but not to matter.[18]

It is instructive to notice that to reinforce the purely conceptual distinction between matter and space Descartes invokes a celebrated thought experiment that once more calls on imagination: if we remove all such properties as hardness, color, cold, heat, and so on, we invariably find left over "something extended in length, breadth, and depth."[19] By whatever route we take—whether by experience or in imagination, and whether we focus on matter or space (insofar as these are distinguishable at all in our understanding)—we always arrive at extension as a sheer unprescindable residuum. And extension is necessarily the extension *of something;* as an attribute and not something merely free-floating, extension must inhere in substance, and this substance can be nothing other than material substance or "body."[20] It is extension, therefore, that, as the common bond between matter and space, holds together the Cartesian world-picture, keeping it coherent and unified in the face of every divisive tendency. The spatial world is to be grasped as a plenary, seamless realm of *res extensae*—of material things whose very nature consists in their extension.

Three crucial corollaries follow from the equation of matter and space.

(i) *The world, though not strictly infinite in extension, is indefinitely extended.* In Descartes's view, God alone deserves the appellation "infinite," even though the world is boundaryless and thus indefinitely large. As he writes to More, "The reason I say that the world is indeterminately, or indefinitely, great is that I can discover no

bounds in it; but I would not dare to call it infinite, because I see that
God is greater than the world, not in extension (for I have often said
I do not think He is strictly speaking extended) but in perfection."[21]
Here the conception of an infinitely extended God is decisively rejected and is replaced with the idea of an indefinitely extended physical world, an idea that is much more akin to Anaximander's Boundless than to the Stoic model of a finite world suspended in infinite
space. Descartes argues for the indefinite removability of spatial
limits in a manner now familiar to us.

> It conflicts with my conception, or, what is the same, I think it involves
> a contradiction, that the world should be finite or bounded; because I
> cannot but conceive a space beyond whatever bounds you assign to the
> world; and on my view such a space is a genuine body. . . . When you
> imagine a sword going through the boundary of the world, you show that
> you too do not consider the world as finite; because in reality you con-
> ceive every place the sword reaches as a part of the world.[22]

In other words, extended matter constitutes a continuum with no determinate, much less final, limits.[23]

(ii)   *No vacuum or void can possibly exist.* Just as God's infinity entailed
infinite void space for fourteenth-century theologians, so the world's
indefinite extension requires a gapless *filled* space in Descartes's
eyes. As Koyré points out, Descartes rejects the idea of void even
more vehemently than does Aristotle.[24] Not only is any void—including any microvoid[25]—debarred by the notion of Nature as an
extensive continuum subject to *mathesis universalis* but the very idea
of void is a contradiction in terms if it is indeed true that matter and
space are the same thing. For every time there is (thought of) space,
there will be (thought of) matter that fills it.[26] To illustrate his conviction concretely, Descartes resorts to two kinds of evidence. On
the one hand, in his treatise *Le Monde* he cites contemporary experiments that show the imperfection of efforts to create a perfect vacuum in the laboratory: "All those spaces that people think to be
empty, and where we feel only air, are at least as full, and as full of
the same matter, as those where we sense other bodies."[27] On the
other hand, Descartes relies on a wholly nonempirical thought experiment to show the strictly contradictory character of a void: "If you
make the supposition that God removes all the air in a room without
putting any other body in its place, you will have to suppose *eo ipso*
that the walls of the room touch each other; otherwise you will be
thinking a self-contradictory thought."[28] A strict void would collapse
upon itself, abolishing its own boundaries. It would be a metaphysical nonentity, "nothing but a chimera" that cancels itself out.[29]

A void can be no part of Nature if Nature exists only as extended; for as extended, Nature will be entirely filled with material substance: a plenum.[30] The crux of the matter is matter itself. For the denial of void follows strictly on the im-matterment of extension. Descartes makes this clear in a letter to Chanut: "There cannot be any completely empty space, that is, space containing no matter, *because* we cannot conceive such a space without conceiving in it these three dimensions and consequently matter."[31] Thus even if it is true that Descartes's identification of space and matter was (in Koyré's word) "premature,"[32] once this identification has been made—once matter is entailed by the very notion of extension—there is no conceptual (much less physical!) room for a void. The growing commitment to a void that we have seen emerging, or perhaps more accurately reemerging, in the thousand-year trajectory between Philoponus and Newton is here placed sharply into question. In Descartes's acerbic assessment, the void is so much a matter of nothing that there is always something else—some matter (and just the right amount of matter)—to take its place.

(iii)   *Place is a subordinate feature of matter and space.* The notion of place was already implied when reference was made earlier to the idea of the generic unity of extension. This unity stays the same after a given body has been taken out of it: "When a stone has been removed from *the space or place in which it was* . . . we judge that the extension of the place in which the stone was remains and is the same, although the stone's place may now be occupied by wood, or water, or air, or any other body."[33] To put it this way, however, is not yet to give to place any distinctive status vis-à-vis space (with which it is revealingly coupled in the equivocal expression "space or place"). Its standing is either entirely purely conceptual in character—that is, dependent on the merely reflective distinction between generic and individual unity—or else it is simply identified with empty space, that is to say, with something that is in itself an outright *contradictio in adiecto.*

Nor can we infer the independent identity of place from such a seemingly straightforward assertion as that "extension occupies place."[34] Where Plato or Aristotle might have found in this last proposition an affirmation of their view that place *precedes* the bodies that occupy it—being as it were prefigured or preinscribed in the natural world—Descartes interprets his own pronouncement as meaning that "a subject occupies place *owing to the fact that it [the subject] is extended.*"[35] Rather than place preexisting what comes to occupy it, it is the extendedness of the occupying subject or object (i.e., a particular body) that is determinative of the place-of-occupation.

II

> When a body leaves a place, it always enters
> into the place of some other body, and so on to
> the last body, which at the same instant occupies
> the place vacated by the first.
>
> —René Descartes, *The World*

Nevertheless, Descartes does not claim in the manner of Bruno or Newton that place is merely a portion, a "part," of occupied space. Instead of subsuming place immediately into space, he lingers over the corpus delicti long enough to make an intriguing distinction between *internal* and *external* place: "We sometimes consider the place of a thing as its internal place [as if it were in the thing placed]; and sometimes as its external place [as if it were outside this thing]."[36] Let us consider more closely this ingenious and instructive distinction.

Internal place is equivalent to the *volume* taken up by a given material body and is thus determined by that body's size ("magnitude") and shape ("figure")—that is, by two basic modes of extension. As "simple natures," these modes are eminently measurable and are also subject to geometric specification. In contrast with the circumstance set forth in the *Timaeus* (where size and shape are grafted *onto* preformed and profuse sensible qualities), in the *Principles of Philosophy* size and shape belong inherently to material bodies and to their internal place—indeed, to both at once. This co-belongingness follows from the fact that magnitude and figure are aspects of the very same extension shared by a body and its own internal place.[37] Yet if this is so, internal place becomes indistinguishable from the matter that constitutes a given body; and if it is indistinguishable from this matter, it is also indistinguishable from its *space* (given the premise that the nature of matter = the nature of space). Hence Descartes can state nonchalantly, "internal place is exactly the same as space."[38] But to say this is to leave us with no effective distinction between place and space.

What then of *external place*? External place is place as it is determined by the relationship between a given body and *other* bodies; if internal place concerns mainly size and shape, external place is a matter of "situation among other bodies."[39] Where Aristotle had dismissed as an adequate model of place anything merely "relative to position" (*Physics* 208b24), Descartes takes the idea of relative position seriously, picking up a strand of thought left dangling by Theophrastus and Damascius, Aquinas and Ockham. That external place or situation adds something essential to any full consideration of place is evident in Descartes's claim that when we are forced to distinguish between "place" and "space," place will ordinarily refer to the situation of something vis-à-vis something else and space to its magnitude and shape. External place is at play in the circumstance where one thing "takes the place of another," even though it does not possess exactly the same volume—and thus not the same internal place.[40] The idea of external place thereby returns us to that generic unity of space that allows us to distinguish, at least in thought, between extension and things extended, space and bodies-in-space, or (mathematically speaking) the system of coordinates and that which it locates. For it is in terms of such unity that we can say that body B has taken the place of body A—that is, that B now occupies the position previously occupied by A.[41] Similarly, we say that the place itself changes if its situation vis-à-vis other places alters, even if its size and shape are unchanged.

Have we at last found a way to distinguish place from space within the Cartesian world system? If so, we could validate other claims made from within this system, for example, in the *Meditations,* where Descartes remarks as if it were self-evident that "by body I understand all that can be terminated by a certain figure [and] that can be comprised in a certain place, and so fill a certain space."[42] At stake in such a passage as this is not just the observation that place is to be distinguished from space on the basis of the inherent figure and volume of a given body but also the fact—albeit unremarked here—that the position of this body is determined by its relation to other positions in space. By thus invoking external place, one can build a case for place as having a certain standing of its own. It would have this standing at the very meridian point in seventeenth-century thought when, on almost every other front (in philosophy as in physics), place is surrendering its ground to space.

Even if it is true that external place is little more than a relationship between a group of bodies each with its own internal place, this does not mean that external place is merely the sum of a given set of plenary things, much less that it is Internal Place writ large (i.e., absolute space). Unlike internal place, external place is strictly relational in its composition and is not a function of such inherent modes of extension as magnitude or figure. It possesses a special power to "specify" and even to "determine" the generic unity of any given stretch of space.[43]

It would appear, then, that Descartes is on the verge of discovering an intrinsic property of place, one that in no way depends on the factor of containment (which is essentially linked with volume as a cubic unit of continuous magnitude). Such a discovery might seem all the more likely in view of the fact that Descartes comes close to identifying "place" and "external place" in the *Principles of Philosophy,* in many respects his most advanced philosophical text. As if conceding that the idea of "internal place" is analytically equivalent to space qua matter, he asserts there that " 'place' and 'space' differ, because *'place' designates situation more specifically than extension or shape* [i.e., magnitude and figure, the criteria of internal place]; and, on the other hand, we think more specifically of the latter [i.e., extension or shape] when we speak of space."[44] In short, "when we say that a thing is in a certain place, we understand only that it is in a certain situation in relation to other things."[45]

Fertile as this new direction of thinking is—we shall spend much of the next chapter exploring it more thoroughly—Descartes draws back from its full implications. In the end, he undermines the space-determinative power that he has just imputed to external place. This happens in two ways. (1) The ability of external place to determine and specify space depends on the presence of *motionless* bodies in relation to which a given external place is defined.[46] For it is only in relation to unmoving bodies that a given body can be said to be *situated* in a given place. Thus, in Descartes's own example, a person seated steadily in the stern of a ship at sea keeps the same place in regard to the other parts of the ship (which are stable in relation to the stern and to each other but in motion as belonging to the ship), whereas the same person in the same ship will be continually changing his or her place so far as the shoreline is concerned (since the ship is continually changing its position vis-à-vis a particular reference point on the shore). Ultimately, such a person has an altogether constant position only in relation to "certain supposedly motionless points in the heavens,"[47] that is, the putatively fixed stars. But if the latter are not in fact fixed in *their* position *and* if we cannot find anything fixed beyond them (and Descartes believes that we shall not be able to do so),[48] then an indispensable basis for determining external place will be lacking: without motionless bodies of *some* kind as ultimate relational referents, there can be no such place in the end. Without these referents, as Descartes says himself, "we shall conclude that nothing has an enduring [fixed and determinate] place, except insofar as its place is determined in our minds."[49] Given the exclusivity of *res extensa* and *res cogitans,* to be "determined in our minds" cannot count as being determined in space but only as determined by fallible representations of space.

(2) Nor will it do to invoke, in a move reminiscent of Aristotle, the inner surface of the surrounding body as an explanation of the power of external place. The title of section 16 of Part II of the *Principles* announces confidently that "external space is correctly taken to be the surface of the surrounding body."[50] But the discussion in this section soon reveals that since the surface in question must be a "common surface" *between* the surrounding and the surrounded terms, it has to be defined in terms of size and shape, *not* in terms of situation.[51] But if this is so, external place qua surface is in effect reduced to internal place, which depends precisely (and only) on size and shape, that is, the primary determinants of continuous magnitude. And this is in turn to reduce place of any kind to space as the universal system of coordination and

measurement, given that internal place is identical with space. Once again, "Internal place is exactly the same as space."[52] Further, Descartes is driven to observe (in critique of Aristotle) that a surrounding surface, even if perfectly matching the surrrounded object, could change with regard to its material content and yet the place would remain the same (assuming the object stayed in the same position vis-à-vis other objects)—as occurs when a boat is surrounded at different moments by different currents of water.[53] Thus the determining feature of external place can no more be the surface that surrounds a given such place than it can be the size and shape of the occupant of that place.

Therefore, on neither of the two grounds adduced by Descartes—neither in terms of a relationship to motionless objects nor in terms of its surface properties—does external place possess anything like an immanent power of determining, or even specifying, space as a homogeneous field of coordination. As if to clinch the matter, external place is finally held to be subservient to the very bodies it serves to collocate in a particular situation. Even of external place we must say that "a subject occupies place owing to the fact that it is extended." For there is no occupation of place, internal or external, by materially unextended entities: this is the point of the polemic with Henry More. And it is extended entities, that is, material bodies, that determine place, whether as internal (via magnitude and shape) or external (via position). These bodies are denizens or, more exactly, units, of extended and measurable space—which is therefore the final term, possessing the ultimate power.

In internal and external place alike, then, what ultimately matters is matter itself, the sheer extendedness of material bodies, whether this extendedness exists "in the thing placed" or is "outside this thing." In particular, relations between extended bodies—relations that constitute external place per se— have no separate status, no epistemological or metaphysical weight, apart from the very bodies they serve to situate. It is such bodies, and thus the space they occupy, that is determinative of place of every kind. This is what Descartes himself indicates when he writes that "the names 'place' or 'space' do not signify *a thing different from the body which is said to be in the place;* but only designate its size, shape, and situation among bodies."[54] In other words, every significant place-predicate—"size," "shape," "situation"— proves to be a body-predicate. Not only does this reductive move undermine any perduring distinction between external and internal place (for the predicates peculiar to each kind of place have the same standing insofar as they are mere modes of bodily extension); it also subverts the very idea of place as something inherently distinct from space, something with a differential and unreducible definition. For all its local interest, place is finally only a simple location in universal space, and as such is only a contingent and transitional phase in the production of a genuine *mathesis universalis.*

A striking symptom of this subversion of place into matter/space presents itself when, only a few pages later in the *Principles of Philosophy,* a discussion of movement opens with the observation, again reminiscent of Aristotle, that movement in "the ordinary sense" is "the action by which some body travels from one place to another." [55] But by the end of Descartes's discussion of movement we are told that the "transference" realized by movement "is effected from the vicinity of those bodies contiguous to it into the vicinity of others, *and not from one place to another.*" [56] Here the very notion of "place," despite Descartes's concerted attention to it, is superseded by the undefined, albeit suggestive, term "vicinity." Yet, unlike "region" in Plato or Aristotle, vicinity cannot be considered as *place:* at least not in Cartesian physics or metaphysics, since vicinity counts neither as internal place nor as external place, the only kinds of place recognized by Descartes. "Vicinity" oscillates in a conceptual and semantic limbo. If place itself "can be understood in several ways, depending on our conception," [57] the same is surely true of vicinity, but we are not informed as to its polyvalent connotations or their relation to the core senses of place, much less as to the monovalent significance of space.

In this telling way, place, subordinated first to space (whose univocal sense as extended in three dimensions is just what assures its postulated equivalence to matter), is subordinated a second time to vicinity—about whose exact meaning, however, we are given no determinate clue. The fate of place, merging with the vicissitudes of space, is left dangling. Its final status in Cartesian philosophy is literally ambi-guous. As internal *and* external, it is divided against itself, lacking the integrity of a single phenomenon, despite Descartes's desire for constructing a universal physics. In the end, there is no such single thing as "place," while there *is* preeminently a single universal "space" (whose own fate is tied precisely to the *thing,* i.e., the exemplar of unambiguous entityhood). It is as if Descartes's strategy were to bifurcate place into two forms, one of which is indistinguishable from space and the other merely "external"—which is to say, superficial compared to the depth, the third dimension, which only internal place qua space provides. Divide and conquer! With the result that space is the preestablished victor in any competition between place and space.

Place for Descartes is not nothing; unlike the void, it is not a mere chimera, something sheerly imaginary. (To say that we imagine the extensionality of space is not to say that space is imaginary—just the reverse!) Place is a hybrid entity: as volumetric, it is like a thing; as situational, it is unthinglike and purely relational. Just as Descartes claims in the *Meditations* that human beings exist in an uneasy intermediate state between nothingness and God (or, in a more Pascalian mode, between dread and delight), so place hangs in the balance between space and matter. Ambiguous and evanescent, the existence of place is heteronomous—defined in strict accordance with, and thus parasitic on, the rigorous realm of *res extensa.*

Modern Space as Relative

Locke and Leibniz

> Our Idea of Place is nothing else, but such a relative
> Position of any thing.
> > —John Locke, *An Essay Concerning Human*
> > *Understanding*

> Men fancy places, traces, and spaces, though these
> things consist only in the truth of relations and not
> at all in any absolute reality.
> > —Gottfried Wilhelm Leibniz, Fifth Paper in
> > Reply to Clarke

> All our knowledge, both of time and place, is essen-
> tially relative.
> > —James Clerk Maxwell, *Matter and Motion*

I

We have just witnessed a revealing vacillation—by no means the first we
have encountered—between an absolutist and a relativist conception of space:
between the view that space is one vast (and usually empty) arena and the
alternative view that it consists entirely in relations between things. Descartes,
in attempting to do justice to both conceptions by his distinction between
internal and external place, ends by doing justice to neither. His compromise
is as unsatisfying as were earlier middle-ground solutions to the problem of
the void (e.g., the idea of the world as a finite plenary presence surrounded
by an infinite vacuum). All such compromises, after all, only hold together
provisionally what is already available as a definite choice. Where Gassendi
and Newton made outright decisions to regard space (and, a fortiori, place) as

absolute, Descartes clings both to absolutism in his notion of space as internal place and to relativism in his description of external place. Only with regard to the void is he unhesitatingly decisive, vehemently rejecting voidness in favor of an infinitely divisible and nonlacunary material plenum. In this regard he is to be joined by Gottfried Wilhelm Leibniz, who also argues for a comparably dense plenum, albeit on very different grounds. But it will take the single-mindedness of Leibniz to espouse, in a wholly uncompromising way, the idea that space and place alike are altogether relative in their constitution.

Leibniz is anticipated in this last respect by John Locke, whose *Essay Concerning Human Understanding* appeared in 1690, almost half a century after the publication of Descartes's *Principles of Philosophy* and twenty-five years before the Leibniz–Clarke correspondence took place. Locke's treatment of place and space begins with a concerted critique of Descartes, especially the latter's effort to make corporeality and spatiality strictly equivalent. *"Space is not body,"* underlines Locke in the *Essay,* "because it includes not the Idea of Solidity in it."[1] Solidity—the resistance or impenetrability of a physical body—cannot be reduced to Extension, which "includes no Solidity, nor resistance to the Motion of *Body."*[2] Space is as distinct from Solidity as Thought from Extension. Hoisting Descartes on the petard of his own criterion of conceivability, Locke declares that "there is no necessary connexion between *Space* and *Solidity,* since we can conceive one without the other."[3] And if solidity—that is, the primary predicate of "matter"—has no conceptual or intrinsic tie to space, space itself is free to be the occasion of occupation by virtually anything, including *nothing.* We arrive thus at what Locke likes to call "pure Space," that is, space that has no preordained constituency.[4]

On the Lockean account, the simple idea of such empty, open space has three modifications, three "simple modes": "capacity" or sheer volume; "figure," or the relation between the extremities of a body; and "distance," which is the space between two or more bodies.[5] Distance is the crucial dimension so far as place is concerned. It is said to be "Space considered barely in length between any two Beings, without considering any thing else between them."[6] Descartes's emphasis on the volumetric—an emphasis that enabled him to assimilate space to matter, both possessing a common tridimensional axiality—gives way in Locke to a stress on the unidimensional factor of distance or length. For he holds this factor to be determinative of place (as also of time).[7] As distance is a modification of space, place is in turn a modification of distance. It is indeed a very particular modification, leading Locke to formulate one of the most structurally specific theories of place we have yet encountered.

> As in simple Space, we consider the relation of Distance between any two Bodies, or Points; so in our *Idea* of *Place,* we consider the relation of Distance betwixt any thing, and any two or more Points, which are considered, as keeping

the same distance one with another, and so considered as at rest; for when we find any thing at the same distance now, which it was Yesterday from any two or more Points, which have not since changed their distance one with another, and with which we then compared it, we say that it hath kept the same *Place:* But if it hath sensibly altered its distance with either of these Points, we say it hath changed its Place.[8]

Here is a much more convincing articulation of external place than Descartes had given of this notion; and it is coupled with the claim that what Descartes would have considered internal place is incoherent: "The word Place, has sometimes a more confused Sense, and stands for that Space, which any Body takes up."[9] Since the space-of-occupation is precisely equivalent to the space-of-solidity—that is, simply reflects the capacity and figure possessed by any given body—for Locke no separate consideration of internal place is called for.

What defines place as something separate from the space taken up by a body is the relations of that body with other entities. As the theory cited above makes clear, these relations are relations of distance or, more exactly, of *double distance.* For the place of something is determined, first, by its distance relative to something else—in particular, to at least two determinate "Points"—and, second, by the stable relationship of these points to each other.[10] What Descartes had designated as "motionless" objects in his discussion of external place qua "situation"—objects that proved problematic on closer inspection—Locke carefully describes as "*considered* at rest": that is, not moving *in relation to each other* during the determination and duration of a given place's sameness-of-position in relation to them. The *stabilitas loci* comes not from the mere distance between two things but from the distance between one thing (i.e., the thing-in-place) and an internally (albeit momentarily) unchanging dyad of two things. As Locke's example of "a Company of Chess-men" kept on a chessboard on a moving ship shows, the internally stable referential items can themselves be moving (e.g., over the sea) so long as they are not moving in relation to each other. The places of the chessmen vis-à-vis each other, as well as the place of the chessboard on the ship, remain the same, so long as the relationship of those parts of the ship that serve as points of reference is not affected by the ship's motion.[11]

Place, then, is a "Modification of Distance."[12] Moreover, it is a modification that is entirely *a matter of convention.* Beyond his insistence on distance as such, Locke's second innovation is his insistence that place, far from being "natural" or given (an assumption made alike by Plato and Descartes, Aristotle and Newton), is created by human beings for their own practical purposes. Indeed, the two innovations are closely related. For it is precisely because place is a function of distance—the determination of distance itself being a characteristically human preoccupation—that place is conventional in status.

Place, says Locke, is "made by Men, for their common use, that by it they might be able to design the particular Position of Things."[13] What matters about place, as made for "common use," cannot be only its containership or fit, much less any peculiar qualities it may possess. What matters will be determined by criteria of utility and performance.[14]

The conventionalism of Locke's celebrated philosophy of language and property[15] thus finds its counterpart in his philosophy of place. Place is what human beings create when (for largely utilitarian motives) they set about determining the distance between the positions of things. The determination of distance is tantamount to its measurement.[16] It follows that what Husserl designates the "mathematization of nature" in the thinking of Galileo and Descartes holds true for Locke as well.[17] Moreover, just as Descartes and Galileo both removed such merely "secondary qualities" as color and texture and temperature from place, so Locke also discounts such qualities, given that none of them can be converted into calculable distances.[18] It becomes evident that with Locke's conception of place as distance-determined, as with the phoronomic physics of Galileo and the analytical geometry of Descartes, the decisive steps have been taken toward that fateful reduction of place to "site" that will become the pervasive destiny of place in the eighteenth and nineteenth centuries. Place is no longer a genuine *measurant,* a measuring force, but something merely *measured.*[19]

For present purposes, we need only underline Locke's commitment to a strict relativism of place. "Our Idea of Place," he proclaims, "is nothing else, but such a relative Position of any thing."[20] The exclusionary force of the "nothing else, but" in this sentence is as striking as Locke's corresponding conception of motion as "nothing but change of distance between any two things."[21] Just as place per se is no longer invoked in this view of motion— the ancient paradigm of *loco*motion here being replaced by the paradigmatic role of distance in motion and place alike—so place is no longer anything that exists apart from "Space considered barely in length." If Gassendi and Newton dissolved place into absolute space by making the former a mere "portion" of the latter, Locke submerges place in space as something merely relative, a matter of distance alone. Yet what Locke finally says of place might well have been said by his otherwise divergent absolutist colleagues: it is "but a particular limited Consideration"[22] of the idea of space. For if place is a "Modification of Distance," and if "each different distance is a different Modification of Space,"[23] it ensues that place is nothing but a modification of space. Place as determined by measurable distance can be nothing other than a mode, and at that a particularly delimited mode, of space.

When Locke considers "Space" *separately from* "Place," he finds in Space something serenely stable and unchanging—indeed, something close to absolute. As in the cases of Philoponus, Descartes, and Newton (or, for that matter, Einstein), place-relativism comes paired with a space-absolutism. In Locke's case, the argument for absolutism is buried in his discussion of extension, which he ultimately distinguishes from an "expansion" that belongs to space alone.

> To avoid Confusion in Discourses concerning this Matter, it were possibly to be wished that the Name *Extension* were applied only to Matter, or the distance of the Extremities of particular Bodies, and the Term *Expansion* to Space in general, with or without solid Matter possessing it, so as to say *Space is expanded,* and *Body extended.*[24]

"Space in general" is a matter, once again, of "pure space," that is, space regarded as empty and unsolid. On the one hand, a commitment to such space leads Locke to espouse the genuine possibility of the void, which "signifies Space without Body."[25] On the other hand, it tempts him to descriptions of space that sound suspiciously Newtonian, as when he writes that "the Parts of pure Space are inseparable one from the other; so that the Continuity cannot be separated, neither really, nor mentally."[26] The same Parts are also said to be "immovable,"[27] and are thus directly reminiscent of those "absolute places" that are said in the *Mathematical Principles of Natural Philosophy* to be "parts" of "absolute space" and yet to be fixedly relative to each other.

Not only does Locke, premier theorist of place as relative, advocate the absoluteness of space; he also supports its infinity. "The Idea of Immensity," for example, is held to be not just legitimate but inevitable as soon as we begin to combine distances without any limit.[28] Even more to the point, the very *idea* of space is one of an unending, infinite expanse (hence the equation between Space and Expansion): in such an unlimited expanse, "the Mind finds no variety, no marks,"[29] that is to say, no sets of stable referential points by which it might begin to become a scene of well-situated places. Two arguments for spatial infinity are offered. First, Locke offers a vivid rewriting of the predicament of the person at the world-edge: "if there he spread his Fingers, there would still be *Space* between them without *Body.*"[30] Where Descartes had used his own version of this Archytian thought experiment to argue for the spatial indefiniteness of the universe, Locke infers instead its infinity. Second, Locke shows that the universe can be situated in infinity in a meaningful way: though we do not have any coherent idea of the "Place of the Universe," we are nevertheless perfectly able to say, indeed we have to say, that the universe does *exist somewhere:* "For to say that the World is somewhere, means no more, than that it does exist; this though a Phrase, borrowed from Place, signifying only its Existence, not Location."[31] On the basis of these two belatedly Archytian considerations, Locke concludes that the World or the Universe "moves or stands still in the undistinguishable Inane of infinite Space."[32]

In contrast with Philoponus—who, it will be remembered, pleaded for the

absolutism of space but rejected its infinity—Locke, in agreement with Newton, affirms the infinity of space along with its absoluteness. The mutual rein-
forcement of these two ultimate traits is essential to the apotheosis of Space
as supreme, and it is all the more revealing that this position is taken not just
by a theorist and spiritualist such as Newton but by an empiricist such as
Locke who officially espouses an instrumentalist and relativist view of place.
Locke's insistence on the conventionalism of place, its reduction to measurable distance, far from being incompatible with the supremacy of space,
contributes to this supremacy *from below* as it were, thereby allowing the
supremacy of space to remain an unquestioned article of belief in late seventeenth-century thought.

II

If Gassendi and Newton, Descartes and Locke all managed in their distinctive
and diverse ways to dissolve place in space, it took the peculiar genius of
Leibniz to deliver the coup de grâce. In comparison with his contemporary
Locke—whose *Essay* inspired Leibniz to write an entire treatise in response [33]—Leibniz managed to deliver this finishing stroke without having to
take the extraordinary step of reducing place to distance. For Leibniz, distance, although figuring into space and place alike, has a restricted role to play
in any rigorously monadological system of thought. The restriction stems from
the fact that distance applies only to things extended in space—whereas monads, the ultimate metaphysical constituents of the universe, are not themselves spatially extended or related, a point to which we shall have to return.
Monads are certainly real and they possess "active force," [34] but they cannot
be adequately conceived in terms of distance from each other—especially if
it is true that distance is nothing but the "minimal path from one thing to
another." [35]

It is revealing that when Leibniz discusses distance, he often adds a phrase
in apposition that is symptomatic of his difference from Locke: "distance or
interval," "situation or distance." [36] It is the notion of "interval" and more
particularly "situation" (a term he probably borrowed from Descartes) rather
than distance per se that is for Leibniz determinative of place and space. For
it is the way that things are situated vis-à-vis one another—the way they possess their proper "site" or "position" (*situs*), reflecting and representing each
other—that properly conveys their spatial character, *not* their metric distance
from each other. Situation thus cannot be constituted solely from relations of
distance between materially extended entities. It also includes an entire set of
possible relations between such entities. This becomes clear in Leibniz's Fifth
Paper to Clarke. At the very point where Leibniz's discussion appears most
like Locke's in regard to the determination of particular places, a sudden shift
occurs.

When it happens that one of those coexistent things changes its relation to a multitude of others which do not change their relations among themselves, and that another thing, newly come, acquires the same relation to the others as the former had, we then say it is come *into the place* of the former. . . . And though many, or even all, the coexistent things should change according to certain known rules of direction and swiftness [here is Locke's admission of motion into the points of reference], yet one may always determine *the relation of situation which every coexistent acquires with respect to every other coexistent, and even that relation which any other coexistent would have to this, or which this would have to any other,* if it had not changed or if it had changed any otherwise.[37]

Instead of holding himself to a *given* circumstance of items in relation, Leibniz here posits an entire order of possible relations that includes not only "every other coexistent" in a given system but even "*any other* coexistent," that is, anything else that *might* coexist with a particular item (and it *with them:* the relations are always bilateral on this more capacious conception). The force of this "might" applies precisely to the order of what is sheerly possible; it bears on what would happen if that particular order were to be realized—which, in fact, may never occur.

Taken in its totality, the complete collocation of coexistent things is the order of space. If space is thereby conceived by Leibniz as an "order of coexistence"—in the official formula of his mature writings, a formula counterposed with time as the "order of succession"—this means that space is not only *relative* ("order" is an entirely relational term, referring as it does to the internal relations of the items belonging to that order) but also *ideal* in status. Indeed, the two characteristics of space go hand in hand: it is just because space is constituted by an *order* of relations—and not just by a de facto grouping of items at determinate distances from one another—that it is also ideal; and it is because it is ideal that it constitutes an order. No ideality exists without relational ordering, and vice versa. What is at stake in space (as in time) is an ideal nexus of entities, not the entities themselves or their merely empirical configurations. As Leibniz says expressly, space "can only be an ideal thing, containing a certain order, wherein the mind conceives the application of relations."[38]

Does this mean, as we might be tempted to think, that space for Leibniz can exist only in the mind of God—that it is, in Michel Serres's description, "the structure of the domain of possibles in the divine understanding"?[39] Is the ideality and order of space so pure that it can find its own proper site only in the rarefied realm of God? Is space God's space? If so—and Leibniz is never far from this view—God would have to be spatial, or would, at the very least, include space within His domain. Yet for Leibniz, God is not space, nor is space even a property of God. Strictly speaking, we cannot say either that God is in space (for He would then be subordinate to it) or that space is in

God (because its partitioned character would mean that God has parts: which He decidedly does not).[40] Leibniz's solution to this impasse is to claim that God exhibits "immensity" but not "infinity"; while infinity is a trait of physical extension, immensity, albeit metaphysically momentous, is not extended.[41]

But what is it to be extended? To understand Leibniz on extension is to gain deeper entry to his doctrine of place and space. This understanding must begin with Leibniz's critique of Descartes's idea of extension. Not only is it the case that "body and space are distinct,"[42] but, more pointedly, extension in the Cartesian sense is inadequate to define material substance. For one thing, if such extension *were* definitive, two bodies would be indistinguishable if each possessed the same *extensio*—an absurdity for Leibniz.[43] For another, extension construed as three-dimensional matter cannot account for what is true of material substance: "Neither motion or action nor resistance or passion can be derived from it."[44] More is at stake in matter than size or shape or position. This "more" is something that lacks extension in the Cartesian sense—"something like the soul, which was once called a form or species."[45] Leibniz sometimes suggests that this animating, elastic power (equivalent to "active force") could even replace "extension."[46] At other times, Leibniz emphasizes that extension is not a primitive term but analyzes into various components: to wit, plurality, continuity, and coexistence.[47] Most important is the fact that extension is an attribute of a "subject" that unfolds less *as extended*— as a discrete inert body—than *in extension,* that is, in a series of overlapping phases in which this same subject is stretched out in what Whitehead might call an "extensive continuum."[48] As Leibniz puts it in a crucial formulation,

> Extension [as conceived by Descartes] is nothing but an abstraction and demands something which is extended. It needs a subject. . . . In this subject it even presupposes something prior to it. It implies some quality, some attribute, some nature in the subject which is extended, which is expanded with the subject, which is continued. Extension is the diffusion of that quality or nature. For example, there is in milk an extension or diffusion of whiteness.[49]

What is extended, then, is not simply a body, much less its matter, but rather a quality in (or of) a body. This explains why extension, properly speaking, is not a substance but a "phenomenon," and why we never perceive extended things except as qualified in various concrete ways.[50]

Extension, thus reconsidered, brings us abruptly to place—and not to space, as it does for Descartes. For if it is true that "an extended being implies the idea of a continuous whole in which there is a plurality of things [i.e., parts] existing simultaneously,"[51] then this extensive continuum of simultaneous parts has to have its own place if it is to be considered as one continuous whole. Or, more exactly, the immanent and extended continuum of an entity taken as a single "whole-parts" (in Gilles Deleuze's phrase) *is* its own place, its locus. For the qualities of that entity diffuse themselves through its parts, which are themselves co–located in one place. And this place in turn is diffused through the qualities: quid pro quo! Thus Leibniz says that "extension would formally involve a diffusion of parts beyond parts, though that which is diffused will not be matter or corporeal substance formally but only exigently. That which is diffused formally will be locality or that which constitutes *situs.*"[52] In place of Descartes's model of material body as a separate entity exhibiting a relation of *partes extra partes,* Leibniz proposes a model of a continuous entity whose parts inhere in each other in a continuous series of overlapping members. Instead of this entity possessing either a strictly volumetric place constituted merely by size and shape or a positional place determined by objective relations with other entities—that is, "internal" and "external" place, respectively—the whole of the entity and its parts alike are located in a single place. But they are not in that place as in a simple location in Whitehead's sense. They are *diffusely* so located: thanks to the extension of certain qualities over or through the place in question, and in accordance with "a law of the continuation of the series of its own operations" that is itself implicit in status.[53] The repetition of the implicit law is tantamount to the literal ex-tension of the qualities, and both occur in the same place—a place not only *of* the extended being that is found there but that is itself extended *in* that entity and not separate from it.

As Leibniz puts it in his "Conversation of Philarète and Ariste," the resulting notion of extension is to be "referred" to "situation or locality"—that is to say, to place.[54] He adds,

> Thus the diffusion of place forms space, which would be the first ground (*prōton dektikon*) or the primary subject of extension, and by which it would also apply to other things in space. Thus extension, when it is an attribute of space, is the diffusion or continuation of situation or locality, just as the extension of a body is the diffusion of antitypy or materiality.[55]

Here the momentous step to space from place occurs. Far from the two concepts being altogether separate—indeed, *nothing* is altogether separate in the Leibnizian monadology—they cohere. Just as the diffusion of qualities results in the extension of a thing, so the diffusion of the place reaches at once back into the thing and outward into space. This latter diffusion, that is, of place into space, concerns extension in a new and enlarged sense. Now extension is not merely the attribute of a single thing but includes an entire set of things as they coexist among themselves in a single spatial scene. We have passed from the "ichnography" of extension to its "scenography."[56] In so doing, we are able to say not only that space is extended but also that space itself is the "first ground" or "primary subject" of extension in its augmented and maximally diffuse form. As such, space is the very substance of extension—rather than the reverse, as Descartes would have it.[57]

Thus Leibniz maintains continuity even in the apparently dichotomous case of place versus space—terms whose diremptive antagonism we have witnessed on numerous previous occasions in this book. In particular, extension, a divisive term in Descartes, ties thing, place, and space together. A bodily thing is extended through its qualities in(to) a given place, and the extension of place in turn results in space as the scene of coexisting things. Nevertheless, difference remains, including at least one difference" that is potentially disruptive. Where the extension of a given *thing* is manifestly qualitative, the extension of things *in space* is quantitative only; and the distinction between quality and quantity is not easily bridged. Leibniz's formulations in his late essay "Metaphysical Foundations of Mathematics" are instructive.

> Quantity or magnitude is that in things which can be known only through their simultaneous compresence—or by their simultaneous perception. . . . Quality, on the other hand, is what can be known in things when they are observed singly, without requiring any compresence.[58]

This passage shows clearly how quality is linked to the individual thing (hence to place) while quantity is tied to compresent collocations of things (thus to space).

The difficulty here at stake is not just that quality and quantity as modal expressions of place and space are difficult to reconcile with each other. It goes deeper. By assimilating space to quantity, Leibniz takes a crucial step toward the progressive objectification of space as a monolithic conception in relation to which place will perforce become increasingly insignificant, if never entirely irrelevant. We see this happening in a statement from the same essay I just cited: "Extension is magnitude of space."[59] By declaring extension a mere matter of magnitude, Leibniz veers dangerously close to the Cartesian conception of space as internal place, that is, as volume measured by the amount of extended material body occupying that place.

In point of fact, though, the quantification of space leads Leibniz instead to reduce space to "position." Position, as a matter of quantity alone, is a matter of external relations—of one spot in space vis-à-vis another spot (or set of spots). A position in space is literally *posited,* that is, singled out as just *this* location, a location that, having no intrinsic determination, derives its entire significance from its relation to other locations. (Hence it would count as "external place" in Cartesian lingo.) Position as thus quantified is therefore an exemplary case of simple location in Whitehead's sense of the term. Not surprisingly, then, Leibniz gives to position a quite abstract standing. Insofar as it is basic to space itself, position becomes what Deleuze calls a mere "abstract co-ordinate."[60] Thus the concreteness of place is displaced into the abstractness of space. It is therefore not surprising, either, that Leibniz links the very idea of space as "the order of co-existence" with quantity, and even

with distance as a mode of quantity: "such order also has its quantity," he
writes to Clarke, "there is in it that which goes before and that which follows;
there is distance or interval."[61]

What *is* surprising, however, is that Leibniz does not fall into the fallacy
of misplaced concreteness, as usually happens with those who are committed
to the doctrine of simple location. For in the end Leibniz is critical of his own
seemingly irresistible temptation to quantify space, especially insofar as it is
based on position as a unique paradigm. In a fragment entitled "On the Principle of Indiscernibles" Leibniz expressly subsumes position and quantity under
quality.

> [Quantity and position] seem to be produced by motion *per se,* and are usually
> conceived by people in this way. But when I considered the matter more accu-
> rately I saw that they are mere results, which do not constitute any intrinsic
> denomination *per se,* and so they are merely relations which demand a founda-
> tion derived from the category of quality, that is, from an intrinsic accidental
> denomination.[62]

In the same fragment, he also avers that "all things which are different must
be distinguished in some way, and in the case of real things *position alone is
not a sufficient means of distinction.*"[63] Although Leibniz is here expressly
concerned with whether position in space (or date in time, for that matter)
adequately individuates an entity—it decidedly does *not* in his view—his remark is telling. For it indicates that position, like anything sheerly quantitative, is finally only what he terms a "purely extrinsic denomination." Such a
denomination, which is equivalent to a predicate that is not seated in any
actual subject, is imaginary—as imaginary as is empty space.[64] Indeed, it *does
not exist.*

> A consideration which is of the greatest importance in all philosophy, and in
> theology itself, is this: that *there are no purely extrinsic denominations,* because
> of the interconnexion of things, and that it is not possible for two things to differ
> from one another in respect of place and time alone, but that it is always neces-
> sary that there shall be some other internal difference.[65]

Paradoxically, "the interconnexion of things" is better served by quality than
quantity, for quality alone possesses an *"intrinsic* accidental denomination."[66] Yet quality, as we have seen above, is tied to place—and vice versa.
Can place in its qualitative status save space from dissolving into position, the
epitome of the quantitative and thus of the merely extrinsic?

For a brief moment at least, this appears to be possible. In "On the Principle
of Indiscernibles," Leibniz makes the startling claim that "to be in a place
seems, abstractly at any rate, to imply nothing but position. But in actuality,

that which has a place must express place in itself."[67] On the one hand, place can be considered positional only if it is conceived abstractly, that is, as simple location. On the other hand, there is such a thing as "place in itself," that is, something inherent and perhaps even substantial. This is place as it subtends the extensional continuation of a quality and that flows back into the thing that bears this quality (or set of qualities). In this latter capacity, place is intimately and uniquely bound to *what* is in place. As Leibniz says elsewhere, "An entity *is in* [*inesse*] some locus, or is an *ingredient* of something, if, when we posit [the locus], we must also be understood, by this fact and immediately, without the necessity of any inference, to have posited the entity as well."[68] To posit the locus as a place in itself is to coposit that which is *in that place*. And vice versa: to posit a physical thing as a qualitative whole is to posit as well its locus, that is, that which makes it be *here* and not somewhere else. This is why it can be claimed that what is in a place *expresses* that place: it not only reflects the circumambient world from its point of view, but it reflects that point of view itself—that is to say, its bodily being in a particular place and thus the taking up of a viewpoint from that place. Such a point of view or perspective is far more than a mere position, for it entails a swarm of representations of the universe that encompasses the idiosyncratic world of the perceiving subject, including that subject's own body. Just as place is needed as a locational matrix for the generation of extension (no extension without place), so place itself requires a body (no place without a body). This body expresses "place in itself": its point of view is none other than the perspective that place brings with it. Thus although every intelligent subject or "monad" expresses the entire universe, it does so only as the universe is seen from that unique place that the body brings with it. The result is an ichnographic perception of the universe, in other words, a view traced from a singular place—in contrast with God's scenographic survey of all that belongs to the order of space: God, being bodiless, is also placeless, despite the fact that He is everywhere in space.[69]

Despite these suggestive thoughts, in the end Leibniz not only allows space to be conceived in terms of a nexus of abstractly coordinated positions but also succumbs to a view of place as parallel to position and even, finally, subordinate to it. In the very same paper in which he holds that whatever is in a place "must express place in itself," he also maintains that "in general, place, position, and quantity, such as number and proportion, are merely relations, and result from other things which by themselves either constitute or terminate a change."[70] Place is cast with position and quantity as "mere results" of genuine substantial change; all are "merely relations which demand a foundation"—a foundation in "intrinsic accidental denomination,"[71] that is, in quality. Despite its importance as the basis for the diffusion that results in extension and as what a body expresses first of all (i.e., before or, rather, *as* the point of view from which the body expresses everything else), place ends by being something consequent and relative. How can we explain this reductive result?

It can be explained only, I believe, by invoking the supremacy of space. When Leibniz attends to discrete monads as intelligent body-subjects, he is able to recognize the significance and uniqueness of place. But as soon as the scene changes—as soon as we must deal with space as the totality of coexistence—this recognition dims: place is dissolved, if not diffused, in the abstractness of the spatial system. The ichnographic language of "place" (*locus, lieu*) gives way to the scenographic semiology of "position" (*positio, situs*), as in the following representative passage.

> [Monads] nevertheless have a certain kind of position (*situs*) in extension, that is, they have a certain ordered relation of coexistence with others, through the machine which they control. I do not think that any finite substances exist apart from [a] body, or, therefore, that they lack a position or an·order relative to the other things coexisting in the universe.[72]

A "position in extension"? It is evident that we no longer have to do with a place *for* extension—in which an extended thing can exfoliate—but with a circumstance in which extension has *already* been established as sufficiently determinate not to need the room for further development that place provides. What *is* needed is only "a certain ordered relation" among monads that make up the universe as a single harmonic whole. To institute and maintain this relation, position suffices. It suffices both at the level of single substances and at the level of the totality of substances, that is, the "universe." At the first level, place is reduced to sheer "sameness of place," that is, identity of position in a larger structure of coordinated positions. Such a position is merely that of being an empty place-holder: *into* position X either A or B can move, and each will occupy the "same place" so long as A and B continue to be related to $C, E, F, G,$ and so on, in a constant way (on the assumption, too, that the latter's set of locations stays fixed). As Leibniz admits explicitly in the Fifth Paper to Clarke—where this analysis reaches its most complete formulation—"in order to explain what *place* is, I have been content to define what is the *same place*."[73] Sameness implies homogeneity, and thus any peculiarities of a place, any qualitative idosyncrasies, are submerged in an exclusive interest in what is invariant about that place.[74] Such invariancy is best designated by the term "position," that is, a simple location indifferent to its occupants: whether A or B is located at position X makes no difference whatsoever to X, and very little difference (only an "extrinsic" one) to A and B.

If "the same place" therefore signifies nothing but the invariancy and indifference of position, and if the order of coexistence among monads is nothing but a vast network of interpositionalities, it follows forthwith that place cannot retain any independent standing vis-à-vis space. Within the totality of space (and space is nothing but a totality), place is a bare positional pocket—a mere edge or corner of the spatial universe, a phase of its completion: "That which comprehends all those places is called *space . . . space* is that which results from places taken together."[75]

Place is lost in space for several presumably sufficient reasons. First, it is lost in the *abstractness* of space, in its ideality and sheer possibility: the order of coexistence is not a concrete pattern but an order to the second power, that is, "an order of situations."[76] Such an order is "*a whole of relations considered independently of things,* thus [a whole] of ideal relations."[77] Second, place is lost in the *infinity* of space: only an infinite universe is worthy of God's immensity and can express his omnipotence, and only such a universe can "comprehend" monads infinite in number.[78] Third, and most decisive, place is lost in the *relativity* of space, its constitution as a structured set of relations. The oceanic status of space consists in a sea of relations in which place as merely nonsubstantial cannot but be drowned. In commenting on his model of place as a matter of nothing but relations between the position of A and B and the "fixed existents" $C, E, F, G \ldots$, Leibniz remarks that "in order to have an idea of place, and consequently of space, *it is sufficient to consider these relations* and the rules of their changes, without needing to fancy any absolute reality out of the things whose situation we consider."[79] Although for others the infinity of space entails its absoluteness, for Leibniz the very opposite is the case. True spatial infinity consists in an innumerable multitude of relations between things, not in some unthinkably capacious cosmic volume. And if the number of "simple substances" (monads) is infinite, then a fortiori the possible relations between these substances will also be infinite.

What is most remarkable—and ultimately most disappointing—is that the deeply relative nature of space need not have led Leibniz to reduce place to position. A different construal of this same relativity could very well underline the unique powers and properties of place, its full dynamism. Leibniz himself sometimes engages in this alternative reading of space and place—a reading of space as a matrix of sympathetic bonding between monads that calls for place as its locational basis. In the *Monadology,* for example, citing Hippocrates's dictum "all things conspire" (*sympnoia panta*), Leibniz speaks of "this interconnection or accommodation of all created things to each other, and each to all the others."[80] He also claims that "every body is affected by everything that happens in the universe, to such an extent that he who sees all can read in each thing what happens everywhere."[81] Positions as sheerly quantitative and only formally relational are not capable of creating an interconnection of all things with each other; only places in their qualitative porosity can do so. Moreover, to read in any given *thing* what occurs everywhere else is perforce to include in this reading the *place* of that thing—which must also bear the traces of everything else. And if a thing expresses everything else, the place of that thing must do so as well. Leibniz implies as much when he says that

> although each created monad represents the whole universe, it more distinctly represents the body which is particularly affected by [the universe]. . . . And just as this body expresses the whole universe through the interconnection of all matter in the plenum, the soul also represents the whole universe by representing this body, which belongs to it in a particular way.[82]

If the body is able to express "the whole universe"—and thus to express the totality of the spatial relations in the universe—will this not also be equally true of the *place* of that same body? And if the body belongs to the soul "in a particular way," does not this body also belong to place in a quite particular way, a way that allows each to express the universe in a consonant manner? Is there not, then, a special niche for place after all—that of acting as the immediate arena, the particular locus, of universal expression? Is this not what "point of view" signifies—the irreplaceable place of perception and thus of expression? Leibniz gestures in this direction in an unedited fragment: "Monads do not have a place except through harmony, that is, through agreement with the phenomena of place, which [agreement] arises from no influx, but from the spontaneity of things."[83] The spontaneity of things, their becoming as substances, provides the phenomena of place with the occasion for becoming the setting of harmonious agreement, an agreement that must take place spatially as well as temporally. Place is therefore the hidden basis for what Leibniz calls the "sympathy" that binds all things together.[84] Position is incapable of providing any such basis. Indeed, as Leibniz puts it in a late letter to Des Bosses,

> Monads, in and of themselves, have no position with respect to one another, that is, no real position which extends beyond the order of phenomena. Each is, as it were, a separable world, and they agree among themselves through their phenomena, having no other intercourse or connection *per se*.[85]

In "the order of phenomena," position has a role—for example, in the determination of distance—but it is not able to provide genuine intermonadic connection. Only place, richly enough construed, can furnish significant metaphysical agreement between the otherwise isolated phenomena of individual monads.

Had Leibniz pursued his own promising lead, he might have concluded that place is what mediates between a monad and the larger spatial universe. Since monads "have no windows through which something can enter or leave,"[86] their access to other spatial worlds occurs through their souls' *representations* of what their bodies perceive. This is why Leibniz claims that the soul "represents the whole universe by representing [the] body"—the body with which that soul is allied in preestablished harmony. Thus the soul does not grasp what is happening "outside" directly, but only by recourse to bodily states that are themselves the expression or "mirror" (and not the direct apprehension) of the universe. In one crucial passage in the *Monadology,* Leibniz has this to say about the body in its indispensable mediating function: "Since every monad is a mirror of the universe in its way, and since the universe is regulated in a perfect order, there must also be an order *in the representing being,* that is, in the perceptions of the soul, and consequently, in the body in accordance with which the universe is represented therein." [87] Intimated if not stated in these words is the intriguing idea that between the order of coexistence that is space and the "order in the representing being" (an order that is itself twofold: belonging to the soul and to the body) there exists still another order, a *between of the between,* so to speak: this I take to be the *order of place.* If it is true that the monad's body and soul constitute a representing order and that space is a represented order, the place in which the body-cum-soul is situated must itself possess an intermediate order that links representing and represented orders to each other. The link between body and place is especially intimate here, above all insofar as "point of view" is at stake. To be (or have) a point of view is to be (or have) a *body-in-a-place.* This place must be sufficiently orderly for the body to make sense of how it is affected by the universe: if the body were nowhere, or in a chaotic somewhere, it could not effect the representing activity that is its primary task.

Place, then, is the inter-order between the external order of space and the internal order of the monad. As the ultimate monadological mediatrix (or matrix), place is the ordering of orders and is as such essential to the entire "order of phenomena" to which Leibniz refers in the letter to Des Bosses cited above. Not only do things get ordered in place, but representations of body and soul are also ordered there.[88] Indeed, space itself gets ordered in place. Rather than place being comprehended in space, on this interpretation space is included in place—in *its* unique ordering power.

Such is the surprising result to which Leibniz might have been led had he taken his own emphasis on universal consonance and monadological expression to its limit—a limit that would have to recognize the interstitial, essential role of place in the coordinating, the coordering, of the external spatial universe and the internal life of monads. Then place would be recognized as something even more than what is requisite for bodies' points of view and for the diffusion generating the extension of these same bodies. As the concrete setting for the enactment of space in a body, place would be the scene of the scene of space—the hinge around which scenography and ichnography pivot.

Despite this auspicious direction, adumbrated if not fully articulated within Leibniz's own thinking, place is finally subordinated to position, and both to space, at the time of his death in 1716, as the conclusive albeit incomplete correspondence with Clarke makes clear. Just as Leibniz etherealizes space

by modeling it as a formal nexus of ideal and possible relations, so he etherealizes place by restricting it to positional identity within that same nexus. Even
though place and space are distinguishable in thought, the abstractness of one
calls for the abstractness of the other, and in the end they rejoin each other in
theoretical equipoise. "The mind," writes Leibniz to Clarke, "not contented
with an agreement [i.e., in relations between things], looks for an identity, for
something that should be truly the same, and conceives it as being extrinsic
to the subject; and this is what we here call *place* and *space*."[89] Thus "place"
and "space" become literally interchangeable to the exact extent that they
share an abstractness and formality that fail to do justice to the informality of
intermonadic community—to its concrete consonance and sympathy. Place
and space come close to becoming "purely extrinsic denominations," being
external to the monad, which is the sole source of individuation thanks to its
unique internal totality of perceptions and appetitions.

At the very most, we can say that to be in space is to gain the *possibility*
of being in place in a robustly differential sense.[90] But at the very least—a
"least" that ends by being the controlling factor—to be in place and space is
to gain mere formal identity of position. Such positional identity is featureless:
without qualities of any kind, without force, and perhaps even without duration or extension.[91] To be in place and space (and time)[92] is to be outside the
very fact of being situated in them.

Place qua position, along with space and time, thus becomes exterocentric
to the situated subject, indeed to all the things for which it provides sameness
of situation. We might say that *such place does not provide place*—at least
not place in any sense that involves even minimal concrete features like size
and shape, boundary or surface. Instead, place provides *site:* where "site" as
situs is construed as "abstract space" and thus as something entirely extrinsic
to what is sited.[93] Descartes's positing of "external place"—the opening move
in the modernist conception of place as "something merely relative,"[94] a move
extended by Locke in his even more externalist conception of place as distance—here reaches its most extreme expression. Place has become so external and so relative that it is utterly indifferent to what occupies it; all that
matters is the constancy of situational *locus,* that is, the simple location that
place furnishes to whatever takes up position in it—while it, place as reduced
to position, falls free of any influence from this occupant, much less of any
influence on this occupant in turn. Even the notion of *occupation in* something
is in question; strictly speaking, we must now talk of *taking up position at,* as
we would say that a geometric figure takes up a position at a certain point on
a two-dimensional plane. In this circuitous way, we return to the ancient, and
specifically Aristotelian, partnership of *thesis* and *stigmē,* position and point.
For Leibniz, place taken in all its austerity becomes the kind of position whose
only adequate representation is a point.

In the circuitous corridors of Leibniz's monadological maze—the labyrinth of endless folds found in his work[95]—place, despite its diffusive and qualitative powers, ends by being evacuated and eviscerated from within itself, rendered a null-point in/at its own origin, and is finally sublimated into space. Place becomes external to itself as well as to all that it serves to situate. The description of place yields to the analysis of site—to *analysis situs,* in Leibniz's altogether apt name for the geometric discipline he invented.[96] In such site-analysis, the sharp tips of Marduk's arrows and the straight lines of the Demiurge's cosmic geometrizing transmute into the empty points, the "point-summits,"[97] of a formal geometrization of place. What Leibniz says of points can also be said of his notion of places qua positions: they are "that which has no extension, or whose parts lack distance, whose size may be neglected, or is unassignable."[98] A point, like a position, is "the *locus* of no other *locus.*"[99] Its identity is so strict that it excludes the *loci* of other points or positions—even if, at the scale of space, it must be situated in relation to them in a common ideal order.

It becomes increasingly evident that in Leibniz's rationalism—just as much as in Locke's empiricism—place is the victim of a progressively radical rarefication: replaced by position and even by point, place is at once positionalized and pointillized. Even if a monad has no "*real* position," no full-fledged extension in space, it does have a *point of view,* from which it mirrors the universe. This view-point, belonging properly to the body, is indeed concretely placed. But the concreteness and the implacement are overshadowed by Leibniz's avid tendency to impute positions and points to place and space—both to both—wherever possible.[100]

The fact that Leibniz offers a much more systematic interpretation of space as relational than had any previous thinker is in itself a remarkable accomplishment, not least of all because of the forceful critique of Newton that this interpretation makes possible.[101] Even if salutary for space, Leibniz's achievement proved to be disastrous for place—disastrous for its survival as a viable concept in its own right, as we shall soon see. No less than in the case of Newton, and no less either than in any of the other seventeenth-century figures we have examined, place in Leibniz's nimble hands is shorn of the autonomy and power to which Archytas was the first, and perhaps still the most cogent, witness in the West.

Modern Space as Site and Point

I

> When we say that a thing is in a given place, all
> we mean is that it occupies such a position rela-
> tive to other things.
> —René Descartes, *Principles of Philosophy*

> The silence of these eternal spaces terrifies me.
> (Le silence éternel de ces espaces infinis
> m'effraie.)
> —Blaise Pascal, *Pensées*

Leibniz displayed a special alertness to the metaphor of *organism*—its dynamical aspects, its animating force, its inherent vitalism. Far from being something merely mechanistic, the organic body of the monad—which we have
seen to be intimately tied to place—is a "living being" or "divine machine."[1]
Since every monad is in effect a world filled with monads at increasingly
minuscule levels, organicity extends to everything in the end: "There is a
world of creatures, living beings, animals, entelechies, souls, in the smallest
particle of matter."[2] Hence every bit of matter can be compared to a pond
filled with fish or a garden replete with plants—provided that we imagine that
each part of each fish or flower is itself a pond or garden in turn, and so on,
ad infinitum.[3] The double infinity of the universe, at once infinitely large and
infinitely small, is held together by an all-pervasive organic bonding of each
part to every other part, where "every other" signifies not just a formal relation
of substitutability or a physical relation of distance but a comprehensive and
enlivening order of nature. As Collingwood remarks, "Leibniz's nature is a
vast organism whose parts are lesser organisms, permeated by life and growth
and effort, and forming a continuous scale from almost unmitigated mechanism at one end to the highest conscious developments of mental life at the
other."[4]

Leibniz's doctrine of panorganicism—which, viewed differently, can be considered a form of panpsychism—offers a viable alternative to the Cartesian choice between Matter and Mind as two entirely separate forms of substance, by pointing to a middle region in which the material and the mental are inextricably intertangled: a region of animate matter in which place, so long as it is not reduced to point or position, might regain its own animation, its own *dynamis*. "I do not think that we can consider souls as being in points," remarks Leibniz; instead, "they are in a place through a connection."[5] In its role as mediatrix and carried to a biological limit, place would become something like a "bioregion" or "ecological niche"—as it might be called in more recent nomenclature.[6] Whitehead, directly inspired by the example of Leibniz, set forth an entire philosophy of organism in which place is finally liberated from the restrictive bonds of simple location.[7]

Auspicious as is Leibniz's thinking in this respect, and leaping over two centuries to distinctively twentieth-century sensibilities as it does, its immediate sequel was much less encouraging. Another fold in the vast fabric of this thinking—for example, the reductive tendency to regard monads as "incorporeal automata," God as the "architect of the machine of the universe,"[8] and more especially place as analytically equivalent to position or point—triumphed less in his own writings (where a delicate but continual equipoise is established between mechanism and purpose, the perspective of God and of other monads, and place and position or point themselves) than, more fatefully, in the ensuing course of eighteenth-century thought. The strand of "*almost* unmitigated mechanism" in his own thought—in which mechanism is never entirely unrelieved by considerations of soul, final causality, life, and "grace" (i.e., by what Deleuze calls "the second floor")[9]—becomes unmitigated materialist mechanism in the remainder of this century, which Thomas Carlyle called the age of "Victorious Analysis." The philosophy of organism so pervasive in the *Monadology* and elsewhere was set aside in an obsessive concern with a philosophy and physics of matter understood as altogether unalive and unperceptive. Philosophers and physicists seized on a single fold—or, better, fault line—in the Leibnizian corpus to carry out their reductive scientistic schemes.

Collingwood and Whitehead, despite having ultimately quite different interests and aims, concur on this assessment of the neoclassical, post-Leibnizian era in Europe. For this era, as Collingwood says scathingly, the world is "a world of dead matter, infinite in extent and permeated by movement throughout, but utterly devoid of ultimate qualitative differences and moved by uniform and purely quantitative forces."[10] It is a world, adds Whitehead, in which "nature is a dull affair, soundless, scentless, colourless; merely the hurrying of material, endlessly, meaninglessly."[11] The rich significance bestowed on the world by qualitative sensuousness and, more largely, by life and lifelike forms is ignored in favor of the quantitatively determined forces and motions that are held to control and rule nature. The research program to

study these forces and motions—a program first devised by Galileo and Descartes and Pascal, Huygens and Boyle and Newton—is pursued with unrelenting vigor in the next century.[12] Obsession with this pursuit left no place in
"the remainder of things" for the "concrete realities" that prevail in everyday
experience.[13]

Nor was there a place in that same remainder for the concrete reality of
place itself, which after the death of Leibniz became ever more closely confined to mere position. Apart from the complex (and often surreptitious) influence of Leibniz, and even apart from the hegemony of natural science in the
eighteenth century, we must ask ourselves just how this confinement occurred.

II

> For what you speak of as several places are only
> parts of the same boundless space related to one
> another by a fixed position.
> —Immanuel Kant, *Inaugural Dissertation*
> (1770)

We have seen the initial primacy of place posited by Archytas and Aristotle
(and, to a lesser degree, by Plato and various Neoplatonists) give way to an
increasing preoccupation with the supremacy of space in certain later Neoplatonists, many medieval theologians, several Renaissance cosmologists, and a
number of seventeenth-century philosophers and physicists. But the very triumph of space over place brought with it an unanticipated outcome. No
sooner was the supremacy of space installed by the end of the seventeenth
century than a different trend developed: namely, the absorption of place into
position. This development was in many ways the opposite of what had happened in the preceding millennium, since instead of being subsumed into
something more encompassing, place was now shrunken into something much
more limited. It is clear that the groundwork for this countermove—place
disappearing into the term on its left in the series *position/place/space*—was
established by Locke and Leibniz in the resolutely relationalist part of their
thinking. For if it is true that space is determined entirely by relations, then
what matters most is not the size or shape of space, its capacity or volume,
but the exact positions of the items related to each other in a given spatial
nexus. The relations are altogether determined by these positions, and this is
true whether the relations themselves are construed in terms of objective distance (as in Locke) or of subjective expression (as in Leibniz): either way,
what counts is the internal relationship between the positions of terms, not the
character or quality of the space in which the terms and their positions inhere.
Where Descartes had still accorded explicit priority to volume by his identification of space with internal place, Locke and Leibniz explored external place

in terms of its positional determination, thereby bringing out the full potential of an important but mostly neglected term in the *Principles of Philosophy*.[14] Fifty years after the publication of Descartes's text in 1644, both place and space were being collapsed into their common denominator, position. By the opening of the eighteenth century, space was increasingly regarded as nothing but a set of mutually related positions, and a given place was just one of these positions taken in the splendid isolation of punctiform selfsameness.

The primacy of position is thus inscribed in the very theory of space as "something merely relative" and of place as identity of position within a particular group of spatial relations. If Locke cleared the way for this primacy, Leibniz endowed it with systematic dignity and continuing recognition. When Whitehead declares that "the eighteenth century continued the work of clearance [begun in the seventeenth century], with ruthless efficiency,"[15] he could be taken as referring to the clearing away of place to make room for position as the very basis for the supremacy of space in its relative nature.

Positional primacy manifested itself in diverse forms in eighteenth-century life and culture. The rise of neoclassicism in art and literature reflected a new concern with the precise position of objects in the scenes in which they were set, and the dominant royalist and aristocratic politics of the period also had much to do with "knowing one's place" in society, that is, acknowledging one's exact position in the social hierarchy. In physics, the motion of material things was conceived entirely in terms of changes relative to fixed positions.[16] Perhaps most revealingly, in architecture a whole manner of building flourished around what I shall call "site." By this term I here mean the leveled-down, emptied-out, planiform residuum of place and space eviscerated of their actual and virtual powers and forced to fit the requirements of institutions that demand certain very particular forms of building. Site is thus a specific form of "striated space," defined by Gilles Deleuze and Félix Guattari as "the relative global: it is limited *in its parts,* which are assigned constant directions, are oriented *in relation to one another,* divisible by boundaries, and can interlink."[17] Striated space in the form of site is the predictable result of Leibniz's new discipline of *analysis situs*. If space and place are both utterly relational, a sheer *order* of coexisting points, then they do not retain any of the inherent properties ascribed to them by ancient and early modern philosophers: properties of encompassing, holding, sustaining, gathering, situating ("situation" for Leibniz does not really *situate;* it merely *positions* in a nexus of relations). This loss in turn means a loss not only of the concrete particularity of place but also of the abstract absoluteness of infinite space—and the dissolution of both in the positional relativity of sites.

The triumph of site is the great theme of Michel Foucault's examination of eighteenth-century disciplinary and institutional space. At the beginning of *The Birth of the Clinic,* Foucault speaks of "the flat surface of perpetual simultaneity" that characterizes medical perception and practice in the century of

Enlightenment.[18] This surface, traversed by the gaze of the examining physician, is at once homogeneous and segmented: homogeneous as the sheer display of a given medical syndrome and segmented as located in (or projected onto) the observed body of a patient. The first is a matter of the abstract "configuration" of knowledge, the second of the "localization" of that same knowledge. Foucault's very terms of description are suggestive remnants of space and place, respectively.[19] But they are no more than echoes of a previous discourse now overtaken by the discourse of site, for what now matters is the site, the exact location, of a disease in a particular part of the afflicted body: "the nidus of infection."

In *Discipline and Punish,* Foucault extends this site analysis—no longer medical alone but fully historical and political—to entire institutional settings, including the architecture of these settings. The homogeneous and planiform surface of simultaneity (notice the presence of the Leibnizian criterion of co-existence in this notion) now characterizes the entire structure of prisons, hospitals, factories, barracks, reformatories, asylums, and so on. Both in architectural plan and in disciplinary régime, each of these institutions combines seriality with carcerality: in their built reality, each is in effect a line of cells, a set of segmented but contiguous and isomorphic positions within the site of the institution itself. The result is a "space of domination" in which surveillance becomes the privileged form of action and in which space and place alike (assuming these terms are still distinguishable) are *fixed:* "It is a segmented, immobile, frozen space. Each individual is fixed in his place."[20] Which is to say, *set in a position* in which "each individual is constantly located."[21] The mention of "constantly located" brings home the point that what was a matter of simple location in seventeenth-century physics and philosophy has become the fixed location of the "disciplinary individual," of "calculable man," in the course of the eighteenth century.[22] The act of "elementary location or *partitioning*" is tantamount to the suppression of dynamic (i.e., organic) place and space in the life of the individual person—not to mention that person's time, now strictly regulated by chronometric means in the workplace.[23] "The rule of *functional sites*" has taken over space, time, and place in a veritable "laboratory of power" whose aim is to bring about a constant "location of bodies in space."[24] Thanks to the micropractices of disciplinary power, such bodies become "docile bodies" in Foucault's telling term—bodies that exist only in sites and as a function of sites.[25] The fate of such bodies is to be incarcerated—positioned—in buildings. Bodies and buildings alike have become site-specific. Everything exists in a well-defined, indeed an overdetermined, position in "the analytical arrangement of space."[26]

The Panopticon is a paradigm of analytically arranged space, a veritable laboratory of sited power. The idea of constructing a Panopticon was proposed by Jeremy Bentham in a series of letters written from Russia in 1787, and he pursued it in vain with the British government until it was quashed by the king in 1803. Taken literally, "Panopticon" signifies "a place of sight" for "everything."[27] But what a strange place this is! In the Panopticon, there can be no hidden places, for the building is designed in such a way as to put every prisoner—or workman, madman, or schoolboy—on full view to the warden, who is located in a central inspector's lodge that has direct visual access to every cell in the structure. The cells are contiguous subdivisions of a continuous ring that encircles the lodge. The Panopticon's "inspective force" (in Bentham's own phrase) consists in the fact that the warden can observe anyone at any time, while not being visible himself (he is hidden behind screens and curtains): he is *seeing without being seen.*[28] The aim is not to realize constant inspection as such but to induce in the inmates the sense that they may be under scrutiny at any given moment. As Bentham puts it, "the persons to be inspected should always feel themselves as if under inspection, at least as standing a great chance of being so."[29] The "axial visibility" of each inmate to the warden's gaze is made possible by the ingenious character of the proposed construction, which combines "the *apparent omnipresence* of the inspector" (i.e., in the central chamber) with "the extreme facility of his *real presence.*"[30] As a "transparent building" that brings "vicinity to the public eye,"[31] the Panopticon is ultimately open to *everyone's* scrutiny—not just that of the appointed inspector, his family, friends, and servants but also that of the visiting supervisor, indeed anyone who wishes to come and look. It is thus a site for the application, intensification, and extension of power by society as a whole—power that extends knowledge by bringing behaviors of various sorts (e.g., aberrant, pedagogical, laboring, etc.) into unoccluded view.[32]

But our interest in the Panopticon is less as a scene for what Foucault likes to call "knowledge/power" than as a built *place.* Does such a building count as a genuine place, for example, a place of habitation, or is it in fact something else? Is a place with no hiding space still a place? Although Bentham uses the language of "place" liberally in his descriptions—in such phrases as "a place of safe custody" and "a place of labour"—he admits that only the inspector's lodge is "a complete and constant habitation."[33] Every other part of this building is *a place for being seen.* The very locution of "place for" connotes an instrumentalism or functionalism that converts place into site. If "place" always retains an aspect of particularity—of being just *this* place to inhabit—"site" must be grasped in terms of "a generalizable model of functioning."[34]

III

It is thus not surprising to find that the Panopticon is an indefinitely transferable architectural structure whose basic plan can serve not just for maximum security prisons but also for hospitals and schools, factories and poorhouses. The very fact that the Panopticon is "a simple idea in architecture" means that it is applicable virtually *anywhere.*[35] But to be replicable in any given place is to eviscerate place itself of any adherent power, any intrinsic qualities of its own. It is to convert the concrete specificity of a particular place into the "generalized function"[36] of being a site—which is no less efficacious, however, for being generalized and functionalized in endless replication. This replication is precisely what happened in the wake of Bentham's failure to find acceptance for his project in England. The "central-inspection principle" caught on elsewhere, notably in America.[37] Its "imaginary intensity"[38] proved to be difficult to resist. The reason for this, I suspect, is that the way had been prepared in Eurocentric culture during the seventeenth and eighteenth centuries—prepared precisely by the supersession of place by site in the writings of philosophers and physicists of this formative period.

Among the consequences of the theory, if not the fact, of infinite space having been pursued with scientific rigor (as well as religious fervor) in the previous century, two are of paramount importance: first, the gradual erasure of place-talk and place-thought among philosophers and physicists as well as architects; second, a temptation to retreat into Cartesian interiority. The two are, of course, closely related, as Hannah Arendt implies when she speaks of a "twofold flight from the earth into the universe and from the world into the self."[39] Nonetheless, rather than emphasize the two extremes of infinite space and infinitesimal self—as if these two directions were merely equal but opposite directions—I would put it another way. The decreasing availability of place as a personal and philosophical, architectural and physical Archimedean point that anchors much of experience and thought induced Descartes to seek the self-certifying certainty of the *cogito* and Newton to seek the world-certified certainty of a mathematically specified cosmic space and time. One absolute, entirely internal, rejoined the other absolute, wholly external, making common cause for certainty in the face of the abyss of no-place.

Site's defining features of homogeneity, planiformity, monolinearity, and seriality acted to paper over the abyss; they conspired to act as tranquilizing forces in the generation of a "flat surface of perpetual simultaneity." But these same traits can hardly hide the fact that site is an antidote to place, its very antithesis, its *pharmakon*—the remedy that is its destruction. If infinite space can still be considered as place taken to the limit (i.e., as the place of the universe as a whole, which is why Newton, concerned with just such a superplace, cannot dispense with the language of "absolute place"), site is no longer placelike in any respect. Site is the very undoing of place, its dismantling into punctiform positions. These positions are predelineated and precise, but they are also precarious: precarious because relative to *other* positions, which are in turn dependent on still other positions, in unending regress. (In the Panopticon, the jailers are observed by the warden, who is in turn observed by the supervisor; finally, everyone is subject to inspection.)

Site is anti-place hovering precariously over the abyss of no-place.

IV

> A science of all these possible kinds of space
> would undoubtedly be the highest enterprise
> which a finite understanding could undertake in
> the field of geometry.
> —Immanuel Kant, "Thoughts on the True
> Estimation of Living Forces"
>
> There is only one space.
> —Immanuel Kant, *Opus Postumum*

It is only fitting to end this part of the book with a brief look at Immanuel
Kant, who more than anyone else at once epitomizes and problematizes modern reflection about space as this emerges in the immediate wake of seventeenth-century thought. Kant delivers the final blow to place—more decisively
so than does Leibniz and his numerous progeny in the Age of Enlightenment.
But Kant also suggests a way to resurrect the importance of place on different
grounds (grounds to be considered only at the beginning of the next part). As
with so many thinkers already discussed, but now even more fatefully, Kant
looks forward and backward simultaneously—backward to the previous century (especially to Descartes, Newton, and Leibniz) and forward to twentieth-
century views (above all, to phenomenological approaches to place). What are
we to make of this most Janusian of thinkers, in whom so many antithetical
viewpoints converge?

The evolution of Kant's thinking about space and place is revealing. In his
very first publication, "Thoughts on the True Estimation of Living Forces," we
find the twenty-three-year-old student of Christian Wolff dutifully following
Leibniz—up to a certain critical point. Kant begins by agreeing with Leibniz
that matter is not merely extended but contains an "active force" (*vis activa*)
that belongs to matter "prior to its extension."[40] Such a force is the basis for
that "diffusion" which for Leibniz underlies the serial generation of extension
while being at one with place as the locus of the diffusion itself. Kant expresses this extensional generation thus:

> It is easily proved that there would be no space and no extension, if substances
> had no force whereby they can act outside themselves. For without a force of
> this kind there is no connection [between substances], without this connection
> no order, and without this order no space.[41]

Having said this in harmony with "Herr von Leibniz," Kant immediately afterward poses a question that he considers Leibniz to have answered only in a
circular fashion: What is the origin of the three-dimensionality of space? It

will not do to say, as does Leibniz in his *Theodicy,* that the origin is to be found in the fact that we can draw three lines at right angles to a given point *in space*—for then "space" is presumed to be such as to allow this triune crossing, that is, to be already, albeit implicitly, three-dimensional, which is to beg the question.[42] Rejecting an alternative explanation in terms of the powers of numbers, Kant opts for Newton's law of gravitation as more likely to lie at the origin of the three dimensions.[43] More important than this explanation itself (it hardly seems convincing: Kant himself will search elsewhere in later writings) is the conclusion that God could have chosen a different law as the basis for dimensionality and that had He done so, other kinds of space would have arisen: the world would then possess "an extension with other properties and dimensions."[44] Moreover, these other properties and dimensions would constitute alternative spaces that belong properly to other worlds than our own—a prospect denied by Leibniz in his conviction that God chose *this* world alone, with its unique spatiality, for perfectly sufficient reasons.[45]

In this essay, written in 1747 at the meridian point of the eighteenth century, Kant invokes "position" in two telling ways. First, the soul possesses "position in space," since without such a position it would not have sufficient stability to be influenced by extended substances (i.e., in perception) nor could it influence them in turn (i.e., in action).[46] Just *how* the soul has this position is not discussed; what matters most for our purposes, however, is that position suffices for the soul's connection with space: place is not mentioned. Second, the very idea of position "itself refers us to the mutual actions of substances."[47] Even if it is true that the interaction of substances can occur only in terms of determinate positions assumed by these substances, position itself is secondary to the dynamic interplay of forces of attraction and repulsion. But if position is thus ancillary to active force—a mere locatory marker of its effects—place is a fortiori superfluous, given that its power to locate with precision is far less considerable than that of position. In both instances, then, Kant implicitly asks, why call for place when bare position will do?[48]

The instrumental albeit delimited status of position is reaffirmed in the opening pages of Kant's 1768 essay "Concerning the Ultimate Ground of the Differentiation of Regions in Space." On the first page of this essay—to which we shall have occasion to return—Kant argues that positions belong properly to discrete bodies taken in isolation and that the proper destiny of positions is to refer us first to the "regions" to which they belong and, from thence, to "space." Remarking that Leibniz's projected *analysis situs* never materialized sufficiently to enlighten us as to the exact geometric nature of space, Kant observes that

> the positions of the parts of space in reference to each other presuppose the region in which they are ordered in such a relation. In the most abstract sense of the term, region does not consist of the [mere] reference of one thing in space

to another—that is really the concept of position—but in the relation of the system of these positions to the absolute space of the universe. In the case of any extended thing, the position of its parts relative to each other can be adequately known by reference to the thing itself. The region, however, in which this order of parts is orientated, refers to the space outside the thing. To be specific: it refers not to places in the space—for that would be the same thing as regarding the position of the parts of the thing in question in an external relation—but rather to universal space as a unity, of which every extension must be regarded as a part.[49]

This remarkable passage effectively ties position strictly to the parts of a given extended object and to an "order" or "system" such objects constitute when taken together. Thus far, Kant does not differ from Leibniz: space as an order of positions is relative, and is thus "the [mere] reference of one thing in space to another." But when the system of positions ordered in relation to each other is situated in turn—if we2z ask the further question, where is the system itself located?—we have to do with a *region*, which consists "in the relation of the system of these positions to the absolute space of the universe." Here what counts is not relation as such but the situation of being encompassed in "universal space *as a unity*." A region is, as it were, midway between a purely relational and an absolutist conception of space and is their common ground, their go-between. In this way, Newton is invoked even as Leibniz is affirmed, and the compatibility of absolutist and relativist models of space (a compatibility already adumbrated in these two predecessors) is once again indicated. But for present purposes the crucial step here taken by Kant is that whereby positions, though declared indispensable for grasping the location of parts of objects and for the relation of objects ("things") to each other, are absorbed into regions—which are themselves absorbed into absolute space. Indispensable in one respect, positions are dispensable in other respects, that is, precisely when they cannot be reduced to the sheer relationality of Cartesian "external place" or what Kant calls simply "external relation."

We should not be entirely surprised, then, to discover that in the period of his Critical philosophy that succeeded on the 1768 essay Kant makes very little use of "position" (*Lage*)—and almost no use whatsoever of "place" (*Ort*). What remains to characterize and constitute "space" (*Raum*)? The simple answer is "point" (*Punkt*). If place tends to be reduced to position by Leibniz—and to point only by implication—place is outright reduced to point by Kant. This reduction becomes evident in Kant's *Metaphysical Foundations of Natural Science* (1786), published just a century after Newton wrote the *Mathematical Principles of Natural Philosophy*. In the *Metaphysical Foundations,* both absolute and relative models of space are embraced, though only insofar as both models contribute to the newfound transcendental view that space "belongs merely to the subjective form of our sensible intuition of things or relations."[50] In the first section of this neglected work—which

applies the lessons of the *Critique of Pure Reason* (1781) to physics—Kant
announces without hesitation that "the place of every body is a point."[51] No
more straightforward reduction of place to point can be imagined. The body
in question is a *movable* body, and the perspective under which its place is
nothing but a point is said to be *phoronomic*. "In phoronomy," asserts Kant,
"I consider matter itself only as a point."[52] Phoronomy, as Kant discusses it
in the *Opus Postumum,* "merely treats of motion without considering force
(from which the motion arises)."[53] When force is set aside, matter remains—
matter regarded as acting through a bare point or set of points. Yet even in the
"dynamical" consideration of matter that takes force into account, the point
remains the critical term: "The action of the moving force that is exercised by
one point upon every other one external to it is in inverse proportion to the
space in which the same quantity of moving force has had to diffuse itself
in order to act directly upon this other point at the determinate distance."[54]
Kant disdainfully refers to "the common explication of motion as change of
place"—an explication first set forth by Aristotle, as we know—and strives to
undermine this ancient understanding of motion by the tart remark that "only
of a movable, i.e., physical, point can one say: motion is always a change of
place."[55] The motion that counts is not change of place but relocation of point.

Kant's focus on point represents the last step in the progression—or, more
accurately, the regression—that manifests itself in the century and a half after
the publication of Descartes's *Principles of Philosophy.* Reflecting the general
dissolution of place in space, this stepwise series has consisted in two basic
moves: first, the replacement of place by *position,* a move initiated by Descartes, continued and completed by Locke and Leibniz, and still tempting to
Kant in his early writings; second, the shrinkage of position itself into point.
The last step, initiated by Leibniz and completed by Kant in the *Metaphysical
Foundations of Natural Science,* is the most extreme. A position remains a
relational term, for there is no position save in a nexus of other terms with
which it is bound up: the chessboard in the ship's cabin, the ship in relation
to the shore, the shore in relation to the earth; *A* and *B* in position *X* in relation
to *C, E, F, G,* and so on. (A site is in effect a position that has become a
constructed, a "posited" reality.) Reduced in comparison with place—which
retains aspects of perceptual depth, ichnography, habitability, memorability,
and historicity: all of which position lacks—position is more complex than
point. For a point brings with it no inherent nexus or scheme of relations; it is
an isolated entity (if it is an entity at all, a question much debated among the
ancients). It is the point *of a body*—a body itself taken in isolation from other
bodies. As such, it is the ultimate form of simple location, given that there is
nothing simpler than a point in geometric or perceptual space. (This is doubtless why we speak of "pinpointing" something, i.e., giving to it the most
precise locus possible in a neutral field of particulars.)

In the end, we should not be surprised by the double move from place to position and from position to point. Not only does each move embody—the second more than the first—the continuing stranglehold of simple location, each also instantiates Leibniz's revealing remark to Clarke that "the mind, not contented with an agreement, looks for an identity, for something that should be truly the same, and conceives it as being extrinsic to the subject."[56] Nothing more strictly identical, more fully selfsame, can be imagined than a simple point; nor is there anything more external to the body or substance, the "subject," that bears or contains it. If position is the abstracted essence of perspective or "point of view" (a Leibnizian notion that, taken in its bodily reality, is perfectly concrete), point is the abstraction of position itself: its highly compressed minimal unit, that is, what is posited as "simply there." A position, shorn of its actual relations with *other* positions (it can never be shorn, as Leibniz would insist, of its ideal or possible relations to them), shrinks to a point or is at least punctiform. The ultimate *positio,* the most extremely condensed position, is the *punctum:* at the heart of everything thetic is to be found something stigmatic. The *stigmē* is therefore at a double remove from *topos;* its abstractness signifies a doubly misplaced concreteness. No wonder Aristotle had to reject point as a model for place.

Kant is a modern thinker *in extremis.* In thinking about place, he goes to two extremes, extremes that finally touch each other in a shared abstractness. As we have just seen, in his metaphysics of physics (i.e., in the text entitled *Metaphysische Anfangsgründe der Naturwissenschaft*) the pertinent extremity is that of the point, conceived both as the *terminus ab quo* and as the *terminus ad quem* of motion. In the *Critique of Pure Reason* (already adumbrated, however, in the *Inaugural Dissertation* of 1770, "On the Form and Principles of the Sensible and Intelligible World"), the extremity at issue is no longer the point but *space.* It is as if Kant, having gone to one end of a series in stressing the pure point, now goes to the other far end by emphasizing sheer space. Place, situated in the precise middle of this series and flanked by position and region, is eclipsed twice in this double extremism:

Point—Position—Place—Region—Space

From the transcendental perspective that underlies Kant's metaphysics of physical nature, space is no less abstract than point. Not only is it abstract as absolute or infinite, capacious or immense, scenographic and volumetric (all of these previous descriptions still apply, even if they are not thematized by Kant), it is now also abstract as the form of "*outer* sense," that is, what structures the external world in a way that is "extrinsic to the subject." Such is the lesson of the "Refutation of Idealism," a section added to the *Critique of Pure Reason* in 1787, immediately following the publication of the *Metaphysical Foundations of Natural Science.* In the "Refutation," Kant makes it clear that human consciousness itself depends on the well-ordered world of outer sense and in particular on its "permanence," that is, its capacity to *remain the same* even as perceptions of it vary over time.[57] Perduring substances in the spatial

192 The Supremacy of Space

world thus literally satisfy the Leibnizian criterion of "something that should be truly the same." But now the sameness is provided not in a compressed point or a determinate position but in an entire environment of stably situated objects surrounding the knowing subject and external to it.

Beyond its externality, space is twice again abstract, given that it is also the *form* of *pure* sensible intuition. On the one hand, space (like time) is "the mere form in which something can be an object of empirical intuition for our sense."[58] As such a form or "mode," space is something "subjective" and "receptive," and thus "a formal *a priori* condition for perceiving what is given to the senses as a whole."[59] In this transcendental perspective, both motion and force are located *in* space (and time) as in a formal matrix belonging to the cognizing subject: "The moving forces, attraction and repulsion, are *in it.*"[60] Also in space are positions and locations, since the sensible manifold as a whole "contains the positions, the locations, and the moving forces for outer and inner perceptions."[61] In its formality, space is the organizer of these diverse contents: "the mere form of the coordination of the manifold."[62] Indeed, space *is* "nothing but the form of all appearances of outer sense."[63] On the other hand, the intuition at stake in space is *pure,* that is to say, nonempirical because "prior to the perception of an object."[64] Its purity means that space (again, like time) is not the sensible object or content of intuition—not "a *given* manifold for perception"[65]—but the very act of intuition itself.

> Space and time are not objects of a given (empirical) intuition, *for, in that case, they would be something existent which affected our sense;* they are, rather, intuitions themselves—*not a dabile but a cogitabile*—the mere form in which something can be an object of empirical intution for our sense.[66]

Kant concludes that "space concerns only the pure form of intuition."[67] Thanks to its formality and purity—which together compose its transcendental ideality—space becomes the scene for the intuition of matter and force, position and location, and even the points that subtend all of the four terms just mentioned. As such a scene—a scene that is at the same time empirically real—space is as necessary as *chōra,* as totalized as Absolute Space, and as endless as Infinite Space.[68] Nevertheless, despite its enormous expansiveness, space is securely located *in the finite human subject* as part of the cognitive equipment of the knower, thus belonging to "the subjective constitution of [the] mind."[69] *Space belongs to mind*—not to God's mind (as Newton insisted) but to the human mind. The outer sense "has its seat in the subject only."[70] This radical subjectivism of stance notwithstanding, space includes points, locations, positions, matter, forces—and places! Just as much as place disappears in seventeenth-century physics and philosophy, so it vanishes again in the mind of the epistemic subject as conceived by Kant in the last decades of the eighteenth century:

> In order that certain sensations be referred to something outside me (that is, to something in another region of space from that in which I find myself), and similarly in order that I may be able to represent them as outside and alongside one another, and accordingly as not only different but as *in different places,* the representation of space must be presupposed.[71]

It is revealing that only a few lines later the term "places" is replaced by "spaces," which are in turn merely "parts" of the one universal space that is provided by the pure form of intuition: "We can represent to ourselves only one space; and if we speak of diverse spaces, we mean thereby only parts of one and the same unique space."[72] Places are not just phenomena—this status is properly reserved for *spaces*—but *epi*phenomena in the literal sense: ethereal appearances that sit *upon* the sturdier backs of particular spaces. They are no longer "well-founded phenomena," in Leibniz's phrase. They have become what Kant calls "mere appearances" (*blosse Erscheinungen*) situated *within* the one infinite space. Whereas for Aristotle sensible things are located squarely in places, for Kant places themselves are located in space as parts *of it:* "These parts [e.g., particular places] cannot precede the one all-embracing space, as being, as it were, constituents out of which it can be composed; on the contrary, they can be thought only as *in* it."[73] The "in" is still at stake, but the cosmical-real *in* of Aristotelian physics has given way to the transcendental-ideal *in* of Kant's metaphysics of nature—with the result that places are lost, irretrievably, in space.

Such is modern space, early and late. I say modern *space,* not modern *spaces.* Kant's own definitive judgment is that "there is only one space."[74] Modern space is ultimately one: "universal space as a unity," "one and the same unique space," is at stake throughout. Whether such space is cosmical or subjective in status does not matter in the final analysis. All that matters is that, whether located outside the human subject or within, space *stays the same:* absolute and infinite, homogeneous and unitary, regular and striated, isotropic and isometric. Such space is not only all-embracing but also all-consuming, remaining unappeased in its insatiable appetite for ingesting places, along with the positions and points to which places themselves get reduced in the course of the two centuries that compose the modern era. In this regard, Kant's claim for the transcendental ideality of space tells us nothing we have not already learned from the pre-Critical thinkers scrutinized in the last several chapters: Descartes and Gassendi and Newton, Locke and Leibniz and Kant himself in his early years. All presume and promote the supremacy of space; none hesitates to submerge places (properly plural) into space (only singular)—even if in so doing they must pay special heed to such crucial intermediaries as matter and force, distance and motion, extension and region, position and point, all of which contribute in distinctive ways to the apotheosis of Space.

Part Four

The Reappearance
of Place

Transition

> [Aristotle] therefore desired that space, prematurely liberated by Leucippus and Democritus, be led back to bodies in such a way that place was substituted for space and the inclusion of finite things in finite things for the infinite theater of movement. This artifice allowed him to bury space in bodies.
> —Henri Bergson, "L'Idée de Lieu chez Aristote"

Where have all the places gone? In the long wide wake of Aristotle, the answer has become increasingly evident: submerged in space. Aristotle's ingenious effort to "bury space in bodies"—to foreclose it in the tightly fitting places tailored for physical bodies as their most intimately containing surface structures—was foredoomed. The yawning emptiness of the void, the "gap" (*chaos*) lampooned by Aristophanes and first examined systematically by the Atomists, proved irresistible to Aristotle's successors, beginning with Strato in the third century B.C. Eight hundred years later, Philoponus launched an outright attack on place's putative power, above all the idea that the world comes equipped with preestablished "natural" places such as the "up" and the "down." Philoponus conceived of space as "pure dimensionality void of all corporeality,"[1] a formula that continues to haunt the early modern period. Once space is dissociated from the particular bodies that occupy it, it is bound to be emptied of the peculiarities and properties that these same bodies (beginning with their outer surfaces) lend to the places they inhabit—or that they take away from places by internalization or reflection. The inward partitioning of space, its incarceration in bodies-in-places, gives way to space as "the infinite theater of movement": an essentially empty theater.

Indeed, in Parts II and III we have witnessed the revenge of the void, its forcible reentry into philosophical and scientific discourse. No longer "prematurely liberated," it came to possess an enormously reinvigorated status in the two millennia after Aristotle's death in the early fourth century B.C. For Philoponus in particular, it had sufficient "force" (in his own word) to become the very name of space itself: "space and the void are essentially the same thing."[2] This Philoponean equation had a powerfully alleviating effect on all those who concerned themselves thereafter with space. Throughout the Middle Ages and especially the Renaissance—when Philoponus, rediscovered in the original Greek, was very much a person to contend with—his bold equation served to inspire thinkers preoccupied with the infinity of the universe, despite the continuing allegiance to Aristotle's finitism and plenarism on the part of other thinkers. The strongest challenge to the Philoponean equation, however, came not from the Aristotelians but from Descartes's counterequation of space and matter.

Nevertheless, we must not assume that the Philoponean move "Contra Aristotelem" reinstated anything like a strict void or utter vacuum. Philoponus emptied space of body, but he did not rid it of structure. By characterizing the void as *dimensional,* he gave assurance that it is not merely boundless or chaotic, thereby obviating any metaphysical anxiety one might feel in the face of something utterly inchoate. Philoponus even allowed that space is always de facto filled—"it is never without body"[3]—so long as one appreciates the fact that one can *think* it as "extension empty of body."[4] This latter formula is repeated almost verbatim by Kant, who affirms that "we can never represent to ourselves the absence of space, though we can quite well think it as empty of objects."[5] Others who shared Philoponus's vision felt free to give various contents to the void, such as light or ether,[6] or to designate it the "Empyrean." But what matters is less the exact character (or even the fact) of the content of the void than the void*like* character of space, however space itself is conceived. As vacuous, even if not a perfect vacuum, space lacks those specific attributes or qualities that would tie it to place as the specific setting of material bodies. But its very dimensionality allows space to be conceived in accordance with a multitude of alternative models, including those of Descartes and Kant. In making extension the essence of matter and space alike, Descartes, despite his effort to contest the void, is in effect continuing Philoponus's stress on the cubic or volumetric character of space in general, a character inherent in both space and void. Kant's early effort to derive dimensionality from the mathematics at work in the universal law of gravitation likewise exhibits the conviction that the structure of space is at one with the structure of the physical universe: he shares with Descartes a commitment to a *mathesis universalis.*

Nevertheless, in the very midst of the growing preoccupation with the void that stretches from the ancient Atomists to Philoponus and thence to Bradwardine and Newton, there is a countervailing current of commitment to the unreducibility of natural or "proper" places in the cosmos. This faith is evident in

Iamblichus and Damascius, in Crescas and Cusanus, and even in Bruno—all of whom regarded place as a distinctive form of cosmic being not to be dissolved in the dark abysm of empty, infinite space. These thinkers would not subscribe to Philoponus's sarcastic judgment that "to say place has power is ridiculous." They concur instead with Aristotle that place "has some power," however overshadowed this power may be in the emerging vision of an infinite universe. For them, place still serves important locatory purposes—a given body must, after all, be located *somewhere* in the infinity of space, occupying *some* locale within its capacious embrace—and it still bears qualities that no other entity or medium exhibits so completely: qualities of directionality, fit, density, contiguity, and interstice.

Despite such signs of remaining respect, by the seventeenth century place is largely discredited, hidden deeply in the folds of the all-comprehensive fabric of space. This occurs in the work of absolutists such as Gassendi and Newton as well as of relativists such as Locke and Leibniz, the last-named the master of intricate baroque folds. Despite their pitched battle over the ultimate nature of space itself, each of these figures would assent, albeit with certain reservations, to William Gilbert's stern judgment at midcentury: "There can be no place whatsoever in nature."[7]

With Gilbert's statement, a quite paradoxical point is reached: the void, denied outright by Aristotle, inherits by default the force that the Stagirite has attributed to place itself. It is as if this force, left orphaned in the wake of the war between absolutism and relativism, had returned to its own grandparent, the void. For in Gilbert's claim, the ancient idea of no-place recrudesces. To infer no-place from the spatial void—whether the void is dematerialized (as in the Philoponean tradition) or rematerialized (as by Descartes)—is tantamount to holding that there is no place at all, *no space for place,* in the order of things. Not only has place been deprived of its inherent force or power, it has lost any standing of its own in the cosmos. The cosmos itself, formerly a matrix of places, has yielded to the spatial (and temporal) imperialism of the *universum* (literally, the whole "turned into one"). In an infinite spatial universe, there is truly *no place in space* because place itself has been evacuated of its inherent qualities; it has undergone a virtual *kenosis* of its own content, emptied in the face of the Void of Space. Henceforth, place is nothing more than pure position, or bare point, simply located on one of the *XYZ* axes that delineate the dimensionality of space as construed in Cartesian analytical geometry. What Philoponus projected in speculation, seventeenth-century and eighteenth-century thinkers carry out with conviction and gusto.

Yet the manifest triumph of Space need not mean the demise of Place. Recall that the apparent no-place of mythical notions of chaos contained *in nuce* certain placelike attributes, often in the guise of specifically material or regional properties. A comparable persistence of placiality characterized the Platonic Receptacle, in which at least three kinds or levels of implacement are discernible. Aristotle rejected the notion of no-place as void or vacuum even more vehemently than did Plato, and in this way he "substituted" (in Bergson's word) the plenitude of place for the emptiness of space. Even the Atomists against whom he railed, however, adhered to notions of "position" and "interval" as belonging to any complete catalog of the material universe; atomic particles possess quite precise locations in the void and are allowed to cluster together in configurations not unlike those that occur spontaneously in the various "regions" of the Receptacle. The same covert respect for a place-like situating power even in the most unlikely of circumstances is found in those Stoic and medieval views (e.g., in Chrysippus and Crescas) that posit a finite material world suspended in an infinite void: once again the idea of a strict no-place-at-all is deconstructed by the necessity that material bodies be *implaced* in the void. At every point in this extraordinary story, the specter of a sheer placeless void is complicated by the explicit or implicit affirmation of place as anchoring and orienting a cosmos that otherwise would be drearily empty or devastatingly disorderly.

But in the uncompromising scientific thinking of Newton an actual physical universal void is posited in which there is no significant complication by place or placelike properties. Newtonian space is literally "absolute," for it is finally absolved of the specialness of place, even of those bare traces of place that we find still clinging defiantly to the theories of Aquinas and Oresme and, in early modern times, of Gassendi and Descartes. Place disappears in "the undistinguishable Inane of infinite Space," becoming the "nothing" dictated by Gilbert's simple but severe Latin: *locus nihil est.* And this is so even though the language of "absolute place" continues to be employed in Newton's *Principia:* in the end, such a place is merely a predelineated part, an integral portion, of absolute space.

We have also seen that it does not take absolute space as such—the modernist heir apparent to ancient notions of the void, as well as to burgeoning fourteenth-century ideas of infinite space—to push place off the cosmographic map. The concertedly relativist conceptions of Locke and Leibniz are no more accommodating to the peculiarities of place, and end by effecting their own acidic act of dissolution. By reducing place to distance or to identity of position, these early modern philosophers manage to delimit and deny place in their own quite effective ways, with Kant going to a further extreme in his reduction of place to point. Although all three modern thinkers differ on the status of the void, they agree with absolutists as diverse as Gassendi, More, and Newton that space is continuous and infinite, homogeneous and isotropic. And everyone concurs—even Leibniz, albeit fitfully—that what characterizes space in its entirety is its pure extensionality.

The ultimate reason for the apotheosis of space as sheerly extensional is that by the end of the seventeenth century place has been disempowered, deprived of its own dynamism. It has become at best an inert "part" (Newton), a mere "modification" (Locke), of a superintendent and universal Space. And space itself, serenely void of place, retains dimensionality alone as an abiding structure of its own extensiveness. All one can do with dimensions of height, breadth, and depth is to fill and measure them, or at least to measure *with* them, that is, to determine distances between particular points located in a neutral field. In this measuring game, by which Nature is mathematized down to its secondary qualities, place can figure only as a subdominant variation: as distance in regard to fixed reference points, or as punctiform position in relation to a formal nexus of other equally pointillistic positions. The grid of analytical geometry becomes the gridlock of physical space itself. Thrust into the limbo of a purely passive space regarded as impassive but not impassable, place is rendered vacuous (of) itself, freeing the field for the building of sites—themselves evacuated of any significant content.

If place somehow survives in this august and austere kingdom of space, it is only as a determinate, indeed an overdetermined, entity. The metric virtues first discerned in spatial relations—virtues premised on their continuity and selfsameness over time—come to be applied to place by an all too predictable transference. The quantification of space undertaken by Gassendi appears as the calculability of place in Descartes and Locke and Leibniz. But to make place calculable is to transform it into site. Cartographic representation is a case in point: the seventeenth century also witnessed the creation of metrically precise maps of the earth construed as a global scene for sites of discovery and exploitation.

How could it be otherwise, if place is conceived as a mere phase of space, as absolutists and relativists both hold to be the case? Given the increasing interchangeability of terms in phrases such as "space *and* place" and "space *or* place," place and space alike will find their most exact description as site-specification within a uniformly distributed plane of determination. The triumph of space over place is the triumph of space in its endless extensiveness, its coordinated and dimensional spread-outness, over the intensive magnitude and qualitative multiplicity of concrete places.

Yet site does not situate. Space on the modernist conception ends by failing to locate things or events in any sense other than that of pinpointing positions on a planiform geometric or cartographic grid. Place, on the other hand, situates, and it does so richly and diversely. It locates things in regions whose most complete expression is neither geometric nor cartographic. And if this is indeed the case, we are impelled to ask, how can we restore to place something like the interest and respect it enjoyed in mythic accounts, in early Greek and late Hellenistic and Neoplatonic philosophy, in long stretches of medieval thought—not to mention its abiding recognition in non-Western cultures? How, faced with the hegemony of Space, can we rediscover the special non-metric properties and unsited virtues of Place?

10

By Way of Body

Kant, Whitehead, Husserl, Merleau-Ponty

Even our judgments about the cosmic regions are subordinated to the concept we have of regions in general, insofar as they are determined in relation to the sides of the body.
—Immanuel Kant, "Concerning the Ultimate Ground of the Differentiation of Directions in Space"

Far from my body's being for me no more than a fragment of space, there would be no space at all for me if I had no body.
—Maurice Merleau-Ponty, *Phenomenology of Perception*

I

The body, the alterations of which are *my* alterations—this body is *my* body; and the place of that body is at the same time *my place.*
—Immanuel Kant, "Dreams of a Spirit-Seer Elucidated by Dreams of Metaphysics"

The most effective way to appreciate the importance of place again is not to approach it as a total phenomenon, to compare its virtues en bloc to those of space in a single systematic treatment. Such a totalizing treatment would lead to nothing but vacant generalities. What is needed is a new and quite particular *way into* place, a means of reconnecting with it in its very idiosyncrasy. Given the crushing monolith of space in the modern era, the best return to place is through what Freud calls a "narrow defile"[1]—not, however, the defile of dream (which is what Freud had in mind) but that of *body*. Place rediscovered by means of body? This will strike the skeptical reader as a most unlikely possibility. Yet in the end the most propitious clues are often those that are least obvious and that hang, like loose threads, from the mysterious mass to be explored. The *Leitfaden,* the guiding thread, needs to be at once easily accessible and, in its very looseness, followed with facility into the least crevice, the darkest corner, of a problematic phenomenon.[2] Such a thread is provided by the body in the case of place.

If we are surprised at this clue, it is only because one of the main agendas of philosophical modernity is the subordination of all discrete phenomena to *mind.* The "new way of ideas" introduced by Descartes and thinkers of the next century had for its most immediate effect the subsumption of every sensible appearance (indeed, *all* appearances, including those belonging to states of mind) under a representation whose status is unremittingly mental. For any appearance whatsoever to be apprehended it must assume the format of a representation ("idea," "apperception," *Vorstellung,* etc.), and the sum total of representations is considered to make up Mind itself. This panrepresentationalism takes in not only every particular phenomenon—every substance and every quality, primary or secondary—but also the universe (Kant speaks of "status repraesentatus universi" in "Thoughts on the True Estimation of Living Forces") and even space and time themselves, which on Kant's assessment we *represent to ourselves,* along with their contents. Thus we reach the paradoxical point noted at the end of the last chapter: space, the very basis of the perception of a permanent external world, is itself based on mind. Or, rather, *in* mind: for there exists, as Kant says expressly, "*in the mind* an outer intuition which precedes the objects themselves, and *in which* the concept of these objects can be determined *a priori.*"[3] Even when it concerns space, that is, *outer* sense, Kant's transcendentalism is first and foremost a mentalism in the form of a pure intuitionism.

Thus it comes as something of a shock to learn that it is Kant himself who proposes an alternative route to place that circumvents mind and representation alike, and all the more shocking given that place is part of the very world of appearances whose status is held to be representational. The new way of ideas is undercut—or at least suspended—as recourse is taken to what had been almost entirely neglected by the subjective idealists of the previous century and a half: the living human body.[4] Instead of misplaced concreteness, there is a return to the concrete basis of mental representations themselves— whose abstracted sensuous content calls for a corporeal foundation. Place demands such a foundation even more insistently. The qualitative character of place had been recognized by Leibniz even as his concern for precise positionality acted to quantify place into site. The more we reflect on place, however, the more we recognize it to be something not merely characterizable but actually experienced in qualitative terms. These terms, for example, color, texture, and depth, are known to us only in and by the body that enters and occupies a given place. Site may be bodiless—it entails a disembodied overview, a survey—but there can be no being-in-place except by being in a densely qualified place in concrete embodiment. Indeed, how can one be *in* a place except *through* one's own body? This question had been left in abeyance ever since Aristotle first observed that what counts as right versus left in a given circumstance depends on our bodily position.[5] But position is not yet place, and it took the genius of Immanuel Kant, paying close attention to "the first data of our experience,"[6] to discern that between body and place there is a special bond.

At first, this bond seems something not only exiguous but contingent: don't bodiless angels or a disincarnate God occupy places? Even the head of a pin is a place, albeit an extremely limited one (it is an instance of place-as-point). In his remarkable dissertation, "On the Form and Principles of the Sensible and the Intelligible World," Kant maintains that disembodied beings such as angels or God (or the human soul for that matter) possess only a "derivative" or "virtual" presence and are exempted from the genuinely "local presence"— from occupying the *place*—that is "the universal condition of externally, namely spatially, sensible things."[7] On the other hand, Kant insists that sensible things *must* occupy particular places: we cannot perceive them, much less know them, except in such places. If bodiless beings are unimplaced, sensible bodies (i.e., bodies perceivable by our own bodies) are inherently implaced entities.

At this preliminary point, Kant invokes the Archytian axiom that has guided so many other Western thinkers from before the time of Plato. According to Kant, however, the ancient axiom, if taken literally, commits the fallacy of "subreption," that is, the mistaken belief that the intelligible and sensible worlds are coextensive. What Kant designates "the subreptic axiom of the first class" is almost a direct transcription of the Archytian view that to be is to be in place: "*Whatever is, is somewhere and somewhen.*"[8] But God and other intelligible entities exist and yet lack any strict implacement: they are not somewhere in particular. Only material substances, sensible bodies, have place in the proper sense: they *are*, and they are *somewhere*. This claim goes both ways: on the one hand, to have a place is necessarily to exist, that is, to exist as a sensible body;[9] on the other hand, to exist as a sensible body is to have a place. Thus Kant in effect adds a crucial rider to Archytas's axiom: namely, to be—*to be sensible*—is to be in place.

But Kant also calls for something not present at all in Archytas, or in his many successors: the body. The body is the missing "third thing" between a sensible something and its particular somewhere. It is as if Kant were adhering to Plato's admonition in the *Timaeus:* "Two things alone cannot be satisfactorily united without a third; for there must be some bond between them drawing them together." [10]

Kant discovered the bond between body and place in his search for an "ultimate ground of the differentiation of regions in space"—to cite the title of that diminutive but pivotal essay of 1768 to which allusion has already been made at the end of the last chapter. In the six pathbreaking pages of this essay Kant shows that the body's role in the implacement of things in regions is that of providing these things with a directionality they would lack when considered merely as occupying positions relative to each other. Without the implementation of this role, material entities would be *unoriented,* lacking the definite directionality of "right" and "left," "up" and "down," "front" and "back." These paired terms, taken together, describe the three dimensions of space: the dimensionality of space follows from the directionality of the body. Giving up his earlier effort to deduce spatial dimensions from the laws of motion that obtain for all physical bodies, Kant proposes a distinctively *corporeal deduction:* it is only because our own bodies are experienced as *already* bifurcated into paired sides and parts (e.g., right and left hands, chest and back, head and feet) that we can perceive sensible objects as placed and oriented in regions that rejoin and reflect our own bodily bifurcations. Things are not oriented in and by themselves; they require our intervention to *become* oriented. Nor are they oriented by a purely mental operation: the a priori of orientation belongs to the body, not to the mind.

It is precisely orientation that is lacking in Leibniz's *analysis situs,* which restricts itself to the congruence that obtains between equal magnitudes and similar shapes. Unlike mathematical analysis, which has to do with the exact *equation* of magnitudes, *analysis situs* concerns itself with "the specifically spatial qualities of space." [11] But Kant demonstrates the existence of a set of phenomena that, though genuinely spatial, cannot be analyzed in terms of the two kinds of congruence singled out by Leibniz. These phenomena are termed "incongruent counterparts," and include such things as mirror images, right and left hands, and spherical triangles that have a common base and are otherwise equal in area and angles. Even though each of the two members of these dyads is exactly equal to the other member in terms of magnitude and shape— the two parameters of *analysis situs*—they cannot be substituted one for another, as you notice when you try to fit a glove for the right hand onto your left hand, or when you look into a mirror and see your features reversed from one side to the other. [12] Therefore, Leibniz's new geometry of space—which we have seen to be fateful for the determination of spatiality qua site in the eighteenth century and beyond—fails to account for an important part of the perceptual world, which includes the twining of plants, the turning of screws, and the twisting of snail shells. Many things come to us as having an inherent directedness that cannot be explained in terms of equality of magnitude or similarity of form.

Incongruent counterparts—termed "enantiomorphs" by contemporary to-pologists—are the exception that break an old rule and establish a new one.[13] The rule broken is precisely the one that regulates the relational model of space: incongruent counterparts have exactly the same internal spatial rela-tions between their constituent parts (e.g., the fingers of the right hand relate to each other just as do the fingers of the left hand) and yet remain nontrans-posable. The rule proved, according to Kant, is the absolute nature of space: the differences that obtain in the case of incongruent counterparts "relate ex-clusively to *absolute* and *original* space, for it is only in virtue of absolute and original space that the relation of physical things to each other is possible."[14] Yet Kant himself admits that the relation to absolute space that is the sought-for "ground" of directionality "cannot itself be immediately perceived,"[15] even though all of the "differentiations" pertinent to incongruent counterparts *can* be perceived. Nor is it at all clear why incongruent counterparts—and, more generally, the directionality they imply—require *absolute* space as a necessary condition. A lacuna opens in the text, and the mere invocation of the Newtonian paradigm remains unconvincing: as if the only choice were the familiar one between space as absolute and space as relative. There is a miss-ing ground in Kant's argument so far.

What supplies the missing ground and fills the lacuna is the human body. Only as ourselves composed of incongruent counterparts *in our own body* are we able to understand analogous counterparts in external perception and, more momentously, to grasp the spatial world as oriented in certain directions. But this means that the true basis of directionality is not absolute space but our own oriented/orienting body regarded as (in Merleau-Ponty's phrase) "the ab-solute source."[16]

The same corporeal ground is at stake in place. Kant intimates this when he writes in the *Prolegomena to Any Future Metaphysics* (1783) that "when two things are exactly alike in all points that can be cognized in each by itself (i.e., in all respecting quantity or quality), it must follow that *one can in all cases and relations be put in the place of the other,* without this substitution occasioning the least cognizable difference."[17] A *congruent* counterpart must be able to occupy the *same place*—not in Leibniz's purely positional interpre-tation of sameness-of-place but in a new model wherein places include direc-tionality as a constituent feature. That this is so is due once more to the con-crete contribution of the body. For there is an intimate and indissociable bond between the body and the places it inhabits. If incongruent counterparts can be understood only by allusion to our own self-directive body—"only by the relation to our right and left hands,"[18] as Kant puts it tersely in the *Prolego-*

mena—then the *implacement* of counterparts (the same implacement in the case of congruency, a different one in instances of incongruency) depends on the character and structure of this same body.

It is doubtless true that the essay of 1768 exhibits the "essentially subjectivist nature [of orientation]," [19] and thus foreshadows the emphasis on the transcendental subject in the later Critical philosophy of Kant. But in interpreting the human subject as a distinctively *bodily* subject and not as a mental or intuitive subject, the early essay offers a unique access to the understanding of *place*—and not just of "space" construed as something universal that stems from the knowing subject. Let me indicate how this is so in five steps.

(1) "Positions" are strictly relational and attach to parts of bodies or to parts of space—in contrast with "regions," which are always oriented in one way or another. When I say that I am going to "western Massachusetts," I refer to a region that cannot be exhaustively analyzed on a purely positional basis. It is somewhere I am going *with my moving body* and somewhere whose westerly orientation is not purely positional but a matter of a cardinal *direction.* I would have no concrete sense of direction—and the world no directedness—unless I had a lived body that possesses its own directionality. "West" is not determined merely by its relation to "east" or "north" or "south" but, more important, by such nonrelative things as the lay of the land, the trajectory of the sun, the direction of the winds—and my own body as situated *where I am* and as headed to *where I am going.* We need not subscribe to Kant's extreme view that a region consists in "the relation of the system of [a particular set of] positions to the absolute space of the universe" [20] to embrace the insight that a region, unlike space *simpliciter* on a sheerly relativist model, involves a manifest directedness—and thus a body that is already itself directional.

(2) The regions that matter most in our immediate perceptual experience are those that divide naturally into up/down, front/back, and right/left. Each of these dyads is to be imagined as a surface (or plane) that intersects with the surfaces or planes formed by the other two dyads. But we would have no acquaintance with such basic regions—basic to what we call "the three dimensions"—unless they were related to something immanent in our experience, namely, our own bodily state as receptive to the perception of such planes.

> Because of the three dimensions, physical space can be thought of as having three planes, which all intersect each other at right angles. Concerning the things which exist outside ourselves: it is only in so far as they stand in relation to ourselves that we have any cognition of them by means of the senses at all. It is, therefore, not surprising that the ultimate ground, on the basis of which we form our concept of directions in space, derives from the relation of these intersecting planes to our bodies. The plane upon which the length of our body

stands vertically is called, with respect to ourselves, horizontal. The horizontal plane gives rise to the difference between the regions which we designate by the terms *above* and *below.*[21]

Especially striking here is Kant's contention that we cannot know things that are at once sensible and external to us except "in so far as they stand *in relation to ourselves.*" This shows Kant taking his celebrated "Copernican turn" long before it is worked out in mentalistic terms in the *Critique of Pure Reason.* The turn is really a return—a return to ourselves as bodily beings. Starting from the very same disembódied point where Descartes ends— namely, the point of intersection of the *XYZ* axes of analytical geometry— Kant goes on to root this trisection in our body as the source of regional directedness. What Philoponus posited as *non*bodily (i.e., "spatial" versus "corporeal" extension) is shown to have a bodily basis. The body is the pivot around which the three dimensions of spatial extension arrange themselves and from which they ultimately proceed.

(3) The return at issue is not only to ourselves as bodies but, more particularly, to "the *sides* of our bodies." Moving ever closer to the narrow defile of the crucial clue, Kant specifies that it is only the body as structured into two sides that renders it so powerful an orientational force: "Even our judgments relating to the cosmic regions are, in so far as they are determined *in relation to the sides of our body,* subject to the concept which we have of regions in general."[22] Without such "regions in general"—by which Kant means such things as "the heavens" and more particularly "the stars"—there would be only "the positions of objects relative to each other."[23] But without the two-sided body as a guiding thread there would be no discerning of concrete "cosmic regions" to start with. Kant makes the telling point, which has been corroborated by contemporary geographers, that to read a star chart (or any map) we must orient the chart or map in relation to the right and left hands that hold it if we are to be able to use it for the purpose of getting oriented in space.[24]

(4) *All oriented places* in our experience depend for their intelligibility on the bilaterality of the human body.

> The same thing holds true of geographical [knowledge] and, indeed, of our most ordinary knowledge of the position of places. Such knowledge would be of no use to us unless we could also orientate the things thus ordered, along with the entire system of their reciprocal positions, by referring them to the sides of our bodies.[25]

In other words, "the position of places" (*die Lage der Örter*)—that is to say, any coherent clustering of places in a given cosmic region—depends for its directedness on its relation to our own double-sided body. Because of the body's dual, right/left insinuation into the place-world, our knowledge of the pattern of this world is rendered "ordinary," that is to say, unreflective, spontaneous, and reliable.[26] Positions depend on regions, but regions and the places they situate depend on bodies for their orientedness. To be a bilateral bodily being is to be the basis of orientation in particular places, that is, places that (along with the sensible things in them) are themselves ordered in regard to "cosmic regions." This means that the ordering of regions—and thus of the places located in them—is due to the ordering already operative in our directed and directive bodies. From and with such bodies we not only enter places and their regions, we constitute the very directedness that makes them distinctively configured—a directedness not restricted to that which is at work in congruent or incongruent counterparts but that is found in all known or knowable places and regions, none of which is neutral with regard to direction and orientation. In the essay "What Does It Mean to Orient Oneself in Thought?" (1786) Kant gives the example of getting situated in an unfamiliar room in which you have arrived blindfolded: you could not gain orientation in this room except in relation to a continuing sense of the difference between the right and left sides of your body. Only by reference to these sides can you know which way you are turning—and which way you have already turned. Since you can count on this differential reference, you will become oriented fairly soon in the room—as well as in the larger region to which the room itself belongs (e.g., by remembering how you have come to this place by bodily motions that have their own directionality).[27]

(5) A final step represents a twist on the body's bilaterality, namely, that the body's two-sidedness is not strictly symmetrical. If it were perfectly symmetrical, I would risk *dis*orientation, since I could not then "tell right from left." In fact, the distinction between right- and left-handedness involves a number of discrepancies, both in the detailed infrastructure of a given body and in the frequent dominance of the right hand over the left in terms of power and skill. This skewed symmetry underlies the uneven directional distributions that we find in many ordinary phenomena such as the whorling of hair growth on the crown of the head or the curling of hop plants around poles.[28] Most important, the directedness of places and regions—and of the things situated in them—stems ultimately from the asymmetrical bilaterality of the very body that is responsible for their orientedness. To say that something is "to the left of" something else—or even merely that it is "over there"—is to draw on the indispensable orienting powers of our nonequilateral bodies. To perceive things as oriented in places and regions (and these as oriented themselves) presumes the pregiven fact that our bodies are already situated with regard to right versus left directionality.

My earlier discussion of Kant had put place in the middle of an implicit series of terms:

Point—Position—Place—Region—Space

Kant's own perspicacious observations allow us to modify the series in such a way that body now becomes the critical middle term, the mediatrix between place and region, position and space:

Position—Place—*Body*—Region—Space

As Derrida might put it, the body is "the lever of intervention"[29] in the constitution of places and regions as directed in various ways. Without the body's
lopsidedly two-sided ingressions into particular regions and places, space
would be merely a neutral, absolute block or else a tangled skein of pure
relations built up from pure positions. But as we in fact experience the spatial
world, this world is composed of oriented places nested in diversely directed
regions. For this, we have the body to thank. And for bringing all this to
our attention, we have Kant himself to thank. In his tiny text of 1768 he
demonstrates—for the first time ever in Western thought—that *the most intimate as well as the most consequential inroad to place is through the body.*
Moving through the exiguous defile teased open by Kant, we can begin to
glimpse once again the full vistas, as well as the detailed virtues, of place.

II

> In the first place, the presented locus is defined
> by some systematic relation to the human body.
> —A. N. Whitehead, *Process and Reality*

> Every particular actual thing lays upon the uni-
> verse the obligation of conforming to it. . . . We
> conform to our bodily organs and to the vague
> world which lies beyond them.
> —A. N. Whitehead, *Symbolism,
> Its Meaning and Effect*

Kant demonstrates a quite special (and thus all the more convincing) way in
which the human body shapes and supports the particularity of place—at once
symbolizing this particularity and making it possible—and, by this very exhibition, he forestalls the reduction of place to site: if space is always already
regionalized by reference to the body, any given place within space will resist
being leveled down into site. Yet this brilliant burst of insight was short-lived.
Kant himself did not appear to put any considerable stock in it. Although he
makes fleeting reference to incongruent counterparts in several later writings,
they are not taken up in his systematic lecture series entitled *Anthropology
from a Pragmatic Point of View* (1798), where they would surely seem to
deserve mention. His immediate successors in German *Naturphilosophie,* being much more inclined to speculation than was Kant himself, simply passed
over the phenomenon in silence. Indeed, they neglected to pay any careful
attention at all to how the body relates to space. A growing preoccupation
with questions of becoming and genesis—with diachrony in many domains,
from the biological to the historical and the psychological—meant that thinkers of the nineteenth century were not concerted in their pursuit of the time-

less, or in any case synchronous, relations and properties of space. By the late 1880s Bergson was able to formulate his powerful polemic against the putatively pernicious "spatialization" of time. Tracing the modern degradation of time's durational depth—its profoundly heterogeneous and qualitative character—to an ongoing obsession with spatiality, Bergson attempted to promote time at the expense of space (and, thus, mutatis mutandis, of place). But this move, representative as it was of the nineteenth century's insistent temporocentrism and eloquent though it remains, only served to perpetuate the very view it was so trenchantly combating. For Bergson assumed that there was no intellectually respectable alternative manner in which to regard the nature of space as other than homogeneous and quantitative. Not only did he thereby overlook Plato's insistence on the inhomogeneity of space in the *Timaeus,* he failed to avail himself of Kant's ingenious insight into the intrinsic incongruousness of space and thus its essential heterogeneity, its "qualitative multiplicity" (to use Bergson's own phrase).[30]

Among the first persons to contest nineteenth-century complacency regarding the supposedly inferior and limited status of space was Alfred North Whitehead, who was expressly inspired by the *Timaeus* and who felt acutely the inadequacy of Bergson's critique of spatialization.[31] In *Science and the Modern World* (1925), Whitehead set forth a telling critique of seventeenth-century views of space (and of time) as a prelude to his own more constructive notions as fully formulated in *Process and Reality* (1929). As we have seen at several reprises, in his considered view the "fundamental assumption" of the seventeenth century was *simple location,* the view that "whatever is in space is *simpliciter* in some definite portion of space" and is nothing but a bit of matter without "any essential reference of the relations of that bit of matter to other regions of space and to other durations of time." Altogether absent from space conceived as "the locus of simple locations" is anything like Kant's notion of "reference (*Beziehung*) to the sides of our body."[32] Instead, in simple location every material body (including the human body) is considered to exist in strict isolation from every other body. Not just Newton and Gassendi and Descartes but even Locke and Leibniz—despite being primary theorists of the relational view—stand indicted as complicitous in the promulgation of simple location. For Locke and Leibniz alike, once a given location has been determined by a set of relations, no *further* set of relations needs to be posited—with the result that the location has been rendered simple, despite its relational character.[33]

The notion of place, insofar as it survives at all in absolutist or relativist theories of space, also falls prey to simple location: "As soon as you have settled, however you do settle, what you mean by *a definite place* in space-time, you can adequately state the relation of a particular material body to space-time by saying that it is just there, *in that place;* and, so far as simple location is concerned, there is nothing more to be said on the subject."[34] What

I have been calling "site" is place as seen through the reducing glass of simple location. Perhaps just because of this danger, Whitehead, not unlike Kant, prefers to speak of "region" rather than of "place."[35] But the exact choice of term does not matter. What matters is that an important sector of what Kant calls "original space"[36] has been subjected to conceptual shrinkage. As a result, the seventeenth-century conception of place is no longer true, or even adequate, to the human experience of ordinary places. As Whitehead says scathingly, "Among the primary elements of nature as apprehended in our immediate experience, there is *no element whatever* which possesses this character of simple location."[37] Among these elements is place, which is never simply located.

We are back, then, to the "fallacy of misplaced concreteness," the error of "mistaking the abstract for the concrete."[38] In committing the fallacy (which is distinctly reminiscent of subreption in Kant's sense) we are not just abstracting from experience—something that we have to do in any case and that can be perfectly "constructive"[39]—but, more crucially, we are replacing concrete experiential items *with their own abstracta*. Thus we "arrive at abstractions which are the simply-located bits of matter,"[40] while forgetting what they are abstractions *of* or *from*, including the places in which they inhere. When Whitehead says that "insofar as the excluded things are important in your experience, your [modern] modes of thought are not fitted to deal with them,"[41] he doubtless would put places in the set of "excluded things." In any case, it is clear that the abstraction "site" is not suited to deal with "place" inasmuch as the latter is conceptually buried beneath the former; in adverting to site instead of to place, "you have abstracted from the remainder of things."[42]

Place is not the only disinherited member of the remainder of things. Belonging to the same act of abstraction are those "secondary qualities" that Galileo and Descartes and Locke had attempted to subjectify by banishing them from the quantifiable world of mass and motion, distance and size, inertia and gravity. Detached from material objects because of the ways in which their precise appearance depends on the current physiological condition of the perceiver, these concrete qualities were denied full status in the natural world. Their fate was thus the same as that of place, with which secondary qualities are in any case closely allied: the particularity of a given place is very much due to the special color, texture, luminosity, and so on, of that place. When both the sensory qualia *and* the places they qualify are eliminated from the official agenda of the material world, we have a sparse remainder indeed, the virtual death of nature.[43] In becoming a mere series of sites for matter in motion, nature becomes placeless as well as qualityless; and *it is both precisely insofar as it is also bodiless.*

Just as there is no longer any place in the seventeenth-century scheme for secondary qualities, so there is no place for the animate organism—for the body as "the most intimately relevant part of the antecedent settled world."[44] It follows that if place and secondary qualities are to regain renewed recognition, we must undertake a new appreciation of the agency of the human body in enlivening and shaping the entire perceptual domain.

> We have to admit that the body is the organism whose states regulate our cognisance of the world. The unity of the perceptual field therefore must be a unity of bodily experience.[45]

It is true that similar remarks had led thinkers from Descartes to Berkeley to instill secondary qualities within the perceiver, on whose physiology their appearance depends. But they did so by invoking an objective body, itself just one more merely material object.[46] A different view of the body is called for, and Whitehead's description of it makes place central to its formulation.

> You are *in a certain place* perceiving things. Your perception takes place where you are, and is entirely dependent on how your body is functioning. But this functioning of the body *in one place,* exhibits for your cognisance an aspect of the distant environment, fading away into the general knowledge that there are things beyond. If this cognisance conveys knowledge of a transcendent world, it must be because the event which is the bodily life unifies in itself aspects of the universe.[47]

If we are to accord to secondary qualities a status in the circumambient world instead of ensconcing them in the physiology of the perceiving subject and his or her objective body, we must realize that the perceiver's body is not a mere mechanism for registering sensations but an active participant in the scene of perception. This scene is a place-scene, a scene of place—a scene punctuated by particular places. For if the active body "unifies in itself aspects of the universe," it must do so *from a certain place.* What other philosophers (most notably Leibniz and Nietzsche) would ascribe to the "perspective" of the perceiver, Whitehead attributes to the organic body-as-implaced. Such implacement belies simple location since it takes us out of ourselves and into the universe at large.

> In being aware of the bodily experience, we must thereby be aware of aspects of the whole spatio-temporal world as mirrored within the bodily life. . . . My theory involves the entire abandonment of the notion that simple location is the primary way in which things are involved in space-time. In a certain sense, *everything is everywhere at all times. For every location involves an aspect of itself in every other location.*[48]

If such deeply ramifying nonsimple location is to be possible, it must be on the basis of our body that we find ourselves in place (and find our way there as well). Far from being an isolated bit of matter, this body is itself a "total event."[49] It possesses a unique efficacy that allows it to reach out to all places from within its own implacement: thus to effect the "prehensive unification" of these surrounding places as well as to be their "objectification" (not in a reifying but in a "conforming" manner).[50]

Still we must ask: Just why is *the body* so important in all this? What is found in our own self-moving bodies that is not found in other actual entities, some of which are also organic? It is not enough to assert that to feel our own body functioning is to experience "the most primitive perception" or to have "a feeling of the world in the past."[51] Nor will it do to claim that "the body is that portion of the world where, in causal perception, there is some distinct separation of regions."[52] What needs to be accounted for is not the separation of regions but their togetherness by means of shared orientations, the merging of just those things kept apart in the doctrine of simple location—beginning with body and place themselves.

Just as the animate body allows for ordinary material objects to come into our ken in the first place, so it also embeds these objects' secondary qualities in prehensions that inform us about the world and not about the mind alone.[53] Bodily prehensions involve the "repetition" of the circumambient world in such a way as not to abstract from them but to conform to them.[54] "It is by reason of the body, with its miracle of order," observes Whitehead, "that the treasures of the past environment are poured into the living occasion."[55] They are poured into the living occasion in the quite particular conformations of places and regions.

Critical to the body's prehension of places is its "withness." More than any other single factor, withness is responsible for the body's unique contribution to our experience of the world in general and of places in particular: "We see the contemporary chair, but we see it *with* our eyes; and we touch the contemporary chair, but we touch it *with* our hands."[56] If it is true that "we feel *with* our body,"[57] then it is by means of the same bodily with-structure that we experience not only "the contemporary chair" (in relation to which our own eyes and hands belong to "the almost immediate past")[58] but also the place of that chair as well as our own place—and both as belonging to the same oriented regional nexus.[59] Place, then, arises *within the withness* essential to the body's primitive prehensions and repetitions of its environing world. Just as we are always with a body, so, being bodily, we are always within a place as well. Thanks to our body, we are in that place and part of it.

In contrast to Newton's view that "nature is merely, and completely, *there,* externally designed and obedient,"[60] on the Whiteheadian model the body is the arena in which the here and the there conjoin inextricably: "In this case, there is a dual reference, to the seat *here,* and to some objectified region *there.*"[61] The body, or more exactly *my own body,* is unique in bringing together here and there in a manner that resists the allure of simple location, according to which the "here" is merely the pinpointed position of my body regarded as an indifferent thing and the "there" the equally pinpointed spot of the contemporary object opposite me. Instead, the "there" *ingresses* into the "here," and vice versa.[62] Such ingression is made possible by my body as the pivotal member of a perceptual scene.

> If green be the sense-object [I perceive], green is not simply at A where it is being perceived [i.e., "here"], nor is it simply at B where it is perceived as located [i.e., "there"], but it is present at A with the mode of location in B.[63]

What Whitehead calls "modal location" is the implacing power of body itself, its ongoing ability to determine "location elsewhere" in terms of its own inherent prehensive unification and efficacious objectification—a unification and objectification that includes its own placial ambience.[64] It follows that the "reference" of the there (of perceived objects) to the here (of the perceiving body) is more than merely indicative. It is adumbrative and inclusive; and it operates precisely through place as a common milieu, a *koinos topos,* in which objects and body, there and here, are all situated in what Whitehead calls "the obvious solidarity of the world."[65]

But place could not play this intermediating and consolidating role if it were not for our access to it through and by—that is to say, *with*—our own animate and intimate body. The privilege of this body is to be at once a pivot and a prism of its immediate environs. No wonder that Whitehead can proclaim that "other sections of the universe are to be interpreted in accordance with what we know of the human body."[66] Among these "sections" are *places.* Not only is our own body moved into places as it situates and resituates itself over time; place itself qua "presented locus" is related essentially, and not just casually or contingently, to the action of our body.[67]

In maintaining this, Whitehead puts into a generalized, lawlike form what Kant had shown to be true in a particular instance. The reference of regions to the bilaterality of the human body is a singular, albeit quite exemplary, case of a more general reference—a "systematic relation"[68]—of place to body. For Kant and Whitehead alike, the human body constitutes the "ultimate ground of the differentiation of regions in space." Ground rather than remainder, subject rather than substance, ongoing prehensive activity rather than momentary passive registrant, this body takes us into place and keeps us there.

III

My body—in particular, say, the bodily part "hand"—moves in space; [but] the activity of holding sway, "kinesthesis," which is embodied

together with the body's movement, is not itself
in space as a spatial movement.
—Edmund Husserl, *The Crisis of European
Sciences and Transcendental
Phenomenology*

Is its place in the totality of space actually a
place for it?
—Edmund Husserl, "Foundational
Investigations of the Phenomenological
Origin of the Spatiality of Nature"

It has been said that one can philosophize for or against Kant but not without
him. Of the three post-Kantian philosophers under consideration in this chapter—Whitehead, Husserl, and Merleau-Ponty—Whitehead is furthest from an
active engagement with Kant. His attitude toward Kant is unremittingly critical, and his critique (if fully spelled out) would doubtless assert that Kant's
mature view of space and time as pure a priori forms of intuition exhibits
the fallacy of misplaced concreteness—flagrantly so.[69] Nevertheless, the two
thinkers would both agree that there is an internal tie between the body of the
organism and the places inhabited by that organism in the natural environment. That this convergence of conviction is largely fortuitous—there is no
evidence that Whitehead knew of Kant's essay of 1768—does not render it
any less significant: indeed, it is all the more impressive that two such major
thinkers, neither of whom is known for paying special heed to the human
body, should have uncovered the body/place linkage independently of each
other.

But we cannot claim the same contingent convergence in the case of Husserl, who thinks and writes with a constant wary eye on Kant. To begin with,
Kant considered a central part of his philosophical project in his early years to
be what he called "phenomenology in general."[70] Even apart from the striking
employment of the name "Phänomenologie," which Kant appears to have borrowed from the physicist J. H. Lambert, the essay under scrutiny in Section I
above is phenomenological in its concreteness of description and in its concern with "the first data of our knowledge." More important, Husserl, the
founder of phenomenology as a philosophical enterprise, takes over the term
"transcendental" from Kant, as we can see from the title of his last great work,
The Crisis of European Sciences and Transcendental Phenomenolgy. Husserl
considered himself to belong to a tradition of transcendentalism. For this tradition—which originates with Descartes—the ground of knowledge is to be
found in the domain of the "I-myself, with all of my actual and possible knowing life and, ultimately, my concrete life in general."[71]

Despite the fact that Kant gave to this tradition its most systematic form as a "rigorous science," he was only "on the *way.*"[72] He did not attain the goal, at least insofar as he did not grasp the need for a foundation in something other than pure mind: his "unexpressed 'presupposition,' " as Husserl puts it, is "the surrounding world of life," that is, what Husserl calls technically the "life-world (*Lebenswelt*)."[73] To neglect the life-world is to neglect the role of the "lived body (*Leib*)," which is conceived by Husserl as essential to the experience of the life-world. On his view, "in a quite particular way the living body is constantly in the perceptual field quite immediately, with a completely unique ontic meaning."[74] The "quite particular way" in which the lived body is in the perceptual field is that of "holding-sway (*walten*)," whereby the lived body engages with the sensuous aspects of things in such a way as to dovetail with them in an ongoing participation.[75] To all of this, especially to "the kinesthetically functioning living body (*Leiblichkeit*),"[76] Kant is held to be purblind. A truly transcendental phenomenology needs to return to the life-world, and thus to the lived-living body that animates it. It *also* needs to return to place, although the path to place is arduous in Husserl's phenomenology: it has to pass through the exacting gates of space and time before its own right of way is recognized.

Husserl's celebrated lectures of 1904–1905 on internal time-consciousness constantly allude to spatial structures as illuminatingly parallel to the structures of temporal experience. For example, retention and protention as "horizons" of the now are explicitly tied to spatial horizons.[77] Immediately following his forays into the constitution of time, Husserl began undertaking inquiries into space.[78] Thus it would be incorrect to include Husserl in the select company of those who, from Augustine to Bergson and James, accord primacy to time over space, nor did he fall fully into the temporocentrism that was so characteristic of the previous century. His own persuasion was that "spatiotemporal configuration" is in principle "prior to space and time themselves insofar as these are understood as identical persistent forms."[79] The deepest level of human experience, which Husserl calls "the primary world,"[80] is as spatial as it is temporal, and it behooves the phenomenologist to explore the spatiality of human experience as well as its temporality—indeed, the two together.

Even in his first investigations into spatiality, Husserl was struck by what he termed "the privileged position" of the human body.[81] Although in one respect this body is merely one more physical thing (*Körper*), in another respect (as a *Leib,* a lived body), it is something extraordinary: "the bearer of the I" and the locus of sensations felt by this I.[82] It is also extraordinary insofar as it is always experienced as "here" wherever and whenever I move.[83] This means that the body as lived presents itself as "the persisting point to which all spatial relations appear to be connected."[84] Among these relations are those of right and left, before and behind, above and below: Husserl here rejoins Kant's intuition that the three basic dimensions are rooted in the body.[85]

For Husserl, however, the body is the basis not only of the three dimensions but also of the more massive fact that "everything that appears belongs to its [i.e., the lived body's] environs."[86] Everything I encounter gives itself as arranged *around* the body with which I perceive. Thanks to my body, I am at the center of things: the "I-myself" is a bodily self that forms an *Ichzentrum*, an "I-center," of all my experiences.[87] In this critical centering capacity, my body is to be conceived as a "null-body" (*Nullkörper*) in relation to which everything in my immediate environs is given a location. Husserl adverts to the geometric idea of the null or zero point in a deliberate if ironic borrowing from Descartes. Just as the zero point in analytical geometry (i.e., the point where the *X, Y,* and *Z* axes coincide) is posited as stationary and invariant, so my body as *Nullpunkt* has the peculiar property of seeming always to be unmoving in relation to the surrounding world. "Everything in the world can run before me," writes Husserl in lectures of 1907, "but not my own body."[88] My body seems to stay put not only when things move around me but *even when it is itself moving.* Or, as Husserl puts it paradoxically, "the body moves, [yet] without 'getting farther away.' "[89] It never gets any farther away *from itself*—just as it cannot fling part of itself away.[90] It is stationary in regard to itself, just as it is stable in relation to everything perceived around it. The true *stabilitas loci* is found not in God, the sun, or perduring landmarks but *in myself:* I, or more exactly my body-self, am "the always persisting point of relation"[91] for all that appears in my perceptual experience. Kant had argued that the body is the source of orientation, but he did not take the further step of showing that it is such a source only inasmuch as it is the stable center of the entire perceptual field, which pivots around it.

What does my body, so situated, have to do with space and, in particular, *place*? In Husserl's first forays into the subject, space is regarded as something strictly objective. There is not yet the notion of a *lived* space that would correspond to the lived body, even though there is already a claim that this body, as centered and centering, is essential for the perception of objective space. Between this active body and the settled space it perceives there is a lack of communication. Husserl attempts to address this lack by positing between lived body and objective space a *Sehraum,* that is, a purely visual space. Visual (and also tactile) space is conceived by Husserl as constituting a discrete field with a "pre-empirical extension"[92] that possesses its own kinds of points, lines, boundaries, and depth. Each such field has its own "system of places" (*Ortssystem*) and is in effect the matrix of places that bear qualities as their distinguishing marks.[93] Nevertheless, place is here conceived mainly as simple location—as is indicated by the fact that Husserl uses *Ort* (place) and *Lage* (position) interchangeably.[94] As such, the "manifold of places" provided by a given field is "something absolutely invariable" and "always given"[95]—not something genuinely *lived* which changes in keeping with my experience of it.

Despite this shortcoming, Husserl also gestures toward a very different view of place. He does so in a consideration of kinesthesia, that is, the inner experience of the moving or resting body as it feels itself moving or pausing at a given moment. In the course of this discussion (a discussion he will pursue for the rest of his life) Husserl claims that even the invariably given manifold of places is "never given without a K [i.e., a kinesthetic sensation], nor is any K experienced without the whole manifold of places [being] fulfilled in a changing fashion."[96] A kinesthetic sensation acts to "motivate" a particular perception in that *if* I move my body in a certain way, *then* things will appear differently—including the places in which they appear.[97] Put more directly: the way I feel my own body being/moving in a place will have a great deal to do with the way I experience that place itself. And if kinesthetic self-awareness is itself the basic form that awareness of my body takes (whether this corporeal consciousness be visual or tactile),[98] then it will constitute a privileged entry into place as I actually experience it. Feeling my body means feeling how it is to occupy the place it is in. As Husserl puts it, "The place is realized through kinesthesia, in which the character (*das Was*) of the place is optimally experienced."[99] Such a place cannot be a mere site; it is a complex qualitative whole that answers to my kinesthetic experience of it.

Since Husserl has no concept of lived place as such, he resorts to various substitutes: not only "visual space" (*Sehraum*) but also the concrete "appearance" (*Apparenz*) of objective space, and above all "the near-sphere" (*Nahsphäre*). The last-named is of special interest. Thanks to my kinesthesias, I have access to a near-sphere that is a major part of my "core-world" (*Kernwelt*).[100] In and through—and around—this circle of nearness, places are constellated as nearby areas in/to which I can move. The near-sphere includes the approachability implied in the "I can" of kinesthetic awareness.[101] My own near-sphere is in effect the proximal place or places in which I *am* or to which I *can go* (my far-sphere, in contrast, contains places to which I do not have immediate access).

The importance of the near-sphere is not just that it fills the gap between body and place—I am *in place in the near-sphere* for the most part—but also that it is a crucial basis for the constitution of objective space, a constitution that does not arise from the whole cloth of pure intuition but from concrete things with which the lived body forms a natural alliance. Husserl writes that "in nearness (*in der Nähe*), in the relationship between uniform intuitive kinesthesias and [various] aspects belonging to them, spatiality is effectively constituted."[102] Spatiality is constituted as objective insofar as its composition results from the concatenation of places available to me in my near-sphere and thus accessible to my kinesthetic awareness within that sphere. What we call "space" (in the wake of its ascendency in the seventeenth century) is not just the "correlate"—as Ulrich Claesges, commenting on Husserl, calls it[103]—of my kinesthetically felt near-sphere but its very "expansion."

"The apperceptive expansion (*Erweiterung*) of the near-sphere (the primordial core-sphere)," says Husserl, "is realized in a homogeneous infinite open world of space."[104] This amounts to saying that the emptying and amalgamation of particular places, each of which is felt kinesthetically by the lived body, becomes in short order the planiform, absolute space of Newton. But that is possible only to the extent that places themselves depend on the lived body as the I-center or null-point, the "absolute here," of any given perceptual field. *Absolute space is dependent on the absolute here.* Here is the transcendental turn in a corporeal format! What is posited by Newton as itself bodiless (and certainly as having no crucial connection with the human body) cannot be constituted, much less apprehended, except by a body that in its essential mobility is always just *here*—here where I am in place.

Absolute space became an indispensable ingredient in early modern physics even though it is foreign to the lived body from which space of any kind, however abstract, takes its rise. As Husserl writes graphically in a fragment of 1914/1915, "External space (*der Ausserraum*) is homogeneous, even though it presents itself as oriented in various ways. . . . *But the lived body and its bodily space break the homogeneity asunder.*"[105] I take the term "bodily space" (*Leibesraum*) to be the conceptual equivalent of lived place—that is, of that particular place that the lived body experiences at any given moment. This very experience is animating: absolute or external space, deadened and flattened as homogeneous, is disrupted, made animate or lively (*leibhaftig*) just insofar as it provides the place of the lived body itself.[106] The lived body deconstitutes the very space it has constituted to start with.

It is but a short step from *Leibesraum* to *Lebenswelt,* the central concept in Husserl's late text, *The Crisis of European Sciences and Transcendental Phenomenology.* In the *Crisis,* Husserl offers a trenchant critique of seventeenth-century philosophy and science—a critique having many affinities with that found in Whitehead's *Science and the Modern World.* Much as Whitehead had despaired over the abstractive tendency of early modern philosophy and physics, so Husserl indicates the way in which Galileo and other thinkers of his time placed a "garb of ideas" (*Ideenkleid*) over the concrete life-world that they were scientifically scrutinizing. As Husserl puts it,

> In geometrical and natural-scientific mathematization, in the open infinity of possible experiences, we measure the life-world—the world constantly given to us as actual in our concrete world-life—for a well-fitting garb of ideas, that of the so-called objectively scientific truths.[107]

By imposing a theoretical garb of ideas on the life-world, what fits one's own method is confused with the ultimate nature of the world—on the assumption that this nature is, "in its 'true being-in-itself', *mathematical.*"[108] But Husserl admonishes us that in fact "we have no prospect of discovering nature's own axiomatic system as one whose axioms are apodictically self-evident [i.e., as in mathematics]."[109] To posit such a system is to force the life-world onto a Procrustean bed of alien concepts.

As a direct consequence of the imperfect fit between the garb of scientific-theoretical ideas and the life-world, there is a considerable unredeemed remainder of unmathematized and even unmathematizable material that does not attain representation in the symbols of mathematics or the formulas of physics—at least not in their modern formats. Husserl traces the origins of the seventeenth-century passion for mathematizing nature to the ancient art of measurement as it first emerged in the practical activity of surveying land. In such surveying, the identification and tracing of certain basic shapes and their subsequent normalization led to the creation of a plane geometry of ideal shapes such as we find paradigmatically in Euclidean geometry.[110] It is just here, at this inaugural moment, that place figures, though precisely as *what is being surpassed.*

> This art [of measuring] involves a great deal, of which the actual measuring is only the concluding part: on the one hand, for the bodily shapes of rivers, mountains, buildings, etc., which as a rule lack strictly determining concepts and names, it must create such concepts—first for their "forms" (in terms of pictured similarity), and then for their magnitudes and relations of magnitude, and also for the determinations of position, through the measurement of distances and angles related to known places and directions which are presupposed as being fixed.[111]

Place figures in this passage twice over. First, it provides the initial (albeit only tacit) *setting* for the "rivers, mountains, buildings, etc.," whose "bodily shapes" will be given "concepts and names." In this role, place is the indeterminate—or, better, predeterminate—scene of surveying, that is, the ground for more precise acts of identification and reidentification. Second, place serves as a basis for delineating *positions,* thanks to the fact that "known places" are "presupposed as being fixed." Not the shapefulness of places and their contents but their determinability as purely positional is here at stake.

Places (and in particular the places of landscape) are thus doubly presumed—as the reservoir of settings and as the basis of positions. Important as this double presumption is, the literally aboriginal status of place is soon suspended as survey gives way to plane geometry. Geometry of a specifically Euclidean cast, though building on practices of surveying, comes to dominate and "guide" these practices.[112] Two thousand years later, by the end of the Italian Renaissance, things have reached a point at which nature is mathematized across the board. For Galileo, "the whole concrete world must turn out to be a mathematizable and objective world."[113] In agreement with Whitehead, Husserl emphasizes that to mathematize the concrete world considerable efforts of abstraction are required: "All this pure mathematics [of Galilean

physics] has to do with bodies and the bodily world only through an abstraction, i.e., it has to do only with abstract shapes within space-time."[114] In other
words, it overlooks the concrete shapes of place as lived. But just as essential
to the new situation is something not stressed by Whitehead: *idealization.*
First and most thoroughly idealized are shapes considered as perfect limit-
forms such as circles, triangles, and so on. Yet this protoidealization (which
had already been undertaken by Euclid) is supplemented by a further idealization of the "sensory plena" that fill up daily experience in the life-world:
concrete qualities of smells, colors, sounds, and so on. This secondary idealization is a matter of mathematizing the various sensory plena, and to achieve
it one has to engage in "the performance of co-idealization of the sensible
plena belonging to the [formal] shapes."[115] In this way, early modern physics
came to posit nature as a universal causal framework within which forms and
qualities are both idealized.[116]

Husserl uncovers three distinct difficulties with this ambitious research
program—a program that ended with the radical subjectification of secondary
qualities as well as the virtual demise of any significant role for place.[117]

(1) It is one thing to treat *shapes* geometrically and quite another to re-
     gard specific sensory *qualities* in this abstractive-idealizing way. Such
     qualities "*cannot,* in their own gradations, be *directly* treated as are
     the shapes themselves."[118] Only an indirect mathematization of these
     qualities is possible.[119] This means in turn that their measurement will
     never be entirely exact and that the best to be hoped for is a correlation
     with precise shape measurement (hence Husserl's notion of "*co*-ideal-
     ization"). Galileo and his successors hold that there is "only *one ge-
     ometry,* i.e., one of shapes without having a second [geometry] for
     plena,"[120] even though any given physical entity will have both for-
     mal *and* sensory qualities, and thus should call for quite different
     geometries.

(2) It is an unproven assumption that there is a single universal causality
     underlying an absolute, objective spatiotemporality. The latter, which
     is not to be confused with the more directly experiential "spatiotempo-
     ral configuration" mentioned earlier, is a pure postulate of Galilean
     physics. Beneath such supreme and supervenient causality there is
     "the spatiotemporality of this pure life-world," whose distinguishing
     mark is what Husserl calls the life-world's "invariant general
     style."[121] The causality that is actually experienced by the perceiving
     organism forms part of this overall style and does not belong to the
     idealized-mathematized garb of ideas impressed on it.

(3) Missing from the seventeenth-century world-picture is any sense of
     the critical distinction between "lived body" (*Leib*) and "physical
     body" (*Körper*), a distinction we have seen to be a basic phenomeno-

logical given for Husserl. For Galileo, *all* bodies are regarded as merely physical bodies subject to laws of inertia and momentum. But this is to overlook the singular status of the lived body in the physical world and, still more seriously, its constitutive role in the life-world of human existence.

Just as Whitehead's philosophy of organism attempts to do justice to experience at the level of a bodily causal efficacy uncaptured by scientific description, so the organic body singled out by Husserl opens onto that "primary world" that is not amenable to direct mathematization.

> It is in this world that we ourselves live, in accord with our bodily [*leiblich*], personal way of being. But here we find nothing of geometrical idealities, no geometrical space or mathematical time with all their shapes.[122]

What then do we find at the level of the lived body? Where Whitehead points to visceral feelings as the *proprium* of "bodily efficacy,"[123] Husserl is more impressed by the "holding-sway" (*Walten*) at stake in kinesthesias as these are experienced by the lived body.

> All such holding-sway occurs in modes of "movement," but the "I move" in holding-sway (I move my hands, touching or pushing something) is not in itself [merely] the spatial movement of a physical body, which as such could be perceived by everyone. My body—in particular, say, the bodily part "hand"—moves in space; [but] the activity of holding sway, "kinesthesis," which is embodied together with the body's movement, is not itself in space as a spatial movement but is only indirectly co-localized in that movement.[124]

The hand returns: not this time as an incongruent counterpart but as an articulation of bodily holding-sway. Where Kant had invoked the hand as evidence of the "reference" that particular regions make to the bilateral human body, Husserl stresses the way this body *as lived* subtends space itself. For the lived body is not itself *in* space as a physical object exists in space. It moves *through* space as "indirectly co-localized in that movement." It resists direct localization—in effect, simple location—as much as secondary qualities resist direct idealization. Precisely as lived, the hand subsists on the near side of that objective position in space that Euclidean geometry pairs with the determination of formal shapes. As such, it reachs into and helps define the near-sphere and its co-localized "close things."[125] The hand, and the body to which it belongs, is less a cynosure of regions in space than it is the kinesthetically felt inroad into the near-sphere of the animate organism.

But how do we move in space by the holding-sway of the lived body? *Through the traversal of places*—of the particular places we move into and out of and across. In *The Crisis of European Sciences,* however, there is no

concerted discussion of place, much less of lived place. Instead, there is talk
of "the particular kinesthetic situation" and of the "situation in which bodies
appear, i.e., that of the field of perception."[126] We must ask, however: What
can such a situation (*Situation*) be but a form of lived place—place as it is felt
from within kinesthetically and place as an arena in which perceived bodies
appear from without? Husserl here brings us to the very verge of lived place
yet leaves us dangling. We sense that a crucial clue is still missing: something
that would show *in concreto* just how lived body and lived place link up with
each other.

The clue is provided by an altogether mundane experience: *walking*. As the
Romans liked to say, *Solvitur ambulando!* (Solve it by walking.) In a fragment
of 1931, "The World of the Living Present and the Constitution of the Surrounding World External to the Organism," Husserl singles out the experience
of walking as illuminating the mystery of how I build up a coherent core-
world out of the fragmentary appearances that, taken in isolated groupings,
would be merely kaleidoscopic. The core-world contains both the near-sphere
of familiar and accessible appearances and the far-sphere of unfamiliar and
unknown things. The disparate appearances of both spheres are brought together in one unified spatiotemporal "ensemble" (*zusammen*) every time I take
up the simple basic action of walking.[127] But this does not happen by a simple
survey of these appearances—as is implied on the earlier model of a *Sehraum*
that one would constitute merely by looking around: for this, as for basic
orientation, one might just as well be stationary.

What walking introduces is the fact that I must first of all unify *myself*
before I unify my environs. I cannot walk at all if I am utterly disjoint; to
walk is to draw my body together, at least provisionally; and to do so is to
constitute myself as one coherent organism.

> [In walking] my organism constitutes itself: by means of its relation to itself as
> an animate organism it is also constituted as moveable, along with the "I stretch
> out my arm," the "I move my eyes," along with spatially rolling my eyes in
> their sockets, etc. The kinesthetic activities and the spatial movements stay in
> union by means of association.[128]

Walking brings home to me that I am a "total organism, articulated into [par-
ticular] organs."[129] Not only the hand, then, but all organs or functional parts
of my body execute the actions of my entire body as *Total Organ* in accordance with the intentions and interests of what Husserl calls "the functioning
ego."[130] The unity of these body parts is supplied precisely by the kinesthetic
feelings systematically associated with the actual movements of the body as
it walks. As human beings experience themselves walking, there is a "kinesthetic flow localized in the hands, the eyes, the parts of the body, and [all of
these] as parallels to the outer spatial movements of these parts."[131]

The first kinesthetic activity, then, is to unify one's own moving body. Only as so unified can this same body begin to undertake the other activities by which it brings about a unified core-world; organic self-unification is the condition of the unification of the surrounding world. This latter unification proceeds in two primary ways. First, there is a "constitutive interconnection" between my already flowing bodily kinesthesias and the appearances of "things given as close and distant."[132] The appearances of things initially distant alter as they come into my near-sphere, but I know this alteration *with my body*. Whitehead's witness of the body is specified by Husserl as a characteristically kinesthetic awareness of the changing appearances of things perceived as "without" by means of continually correlated bodily sensations felt from within. The model is that of two planes in parallel. Second, there is the orientation effected by the moving body: here the model is decisively radial. For my body remains a center of orientation, even when I am walking.

> If walking begins, all worldly things there for me continue to appear to me to be oriented about my phenomenally stationary, resting organism. That is, they are oriented with respect to here and there, right and left, etc., whereby a firm zero of orientation persists, so to speak, as absolute here.[133]

Husserl agrees with Kant that the orientation of things around me depends on my body; but Husserl locates the source of such orientation not in the body's two-sidedness but in its "exceptional position"[134] as an "absolute here," by which Husserl means not just that I am literally *here*, at some precise spot in space—as if the "here" were only a pure point, interchangeable in principle with any other point: this way lies Hegel's abstract conception of the Here as a shifter, a deictic universal. To be absolutely here means that *with my body* I am *in this place:* the very place my body stands or sits or walks in. To be here in this way is absolute in that it is not dependent on any "theres"—in other words, on any other places that are merely part of an order of coexistent things; this would be to reduce my body's place to a bare position. Yet I am not here in splendid isolation, as in the case of simple location. My here-body relates to other (human or nonhuman) bodies without being a function of these relations themselves. It extends into my near-sphere and beyond, into the far-sphere of my circumambient core-world. The absoluteness of my stance resists dissolution in a nexus of sites even—and especially—as it affirms the uniqueness of the place I am in. It may not always be the case that "to be here is delightful,"[135] but Husserl is saying that it is certainly the case that my being-here is the absolute product of my body and my immediate place, the two together in an indissoluble composition. Walking is paradigmatic of this very com-position, since when I walk I am at once actually moving and yet experience myself as "a stable null-object."[136] In walking, I oscillate between the modes of "keeping still" and "keeping-in-operation."[137]

The result of this bivalent ambulatory action is twofold: the constitution of
stable things in my environment and the constitution of stable places for these
things. The two consequences of walking are closely connected. On one and
the same page of the 1931 manuscript Husserl maintains that, on the one hand,
walking establishes "oriented things" *as* "identical things" and that, on the
other, walking constitutes a "fixed system of places (*feste Ortssystem*)."[138] At
the opening of this essay, place had been described in purely objective terms:
"In accord with the particular circumstances, each particular is experienced in
a particular way as 'objectively' changed or not, as retaining the same place
(*Ort*) and spatial extension or as moving in it."[139] The invocation of "spatial
extension" (*raümliche Ausdehnung*) in close conjunction with place shows
that place is here construed as little more than position, as is confirmed by an
emphasis a few pages later on "the one position" at which an appearing thing
is located.[140] But by the end of the essay, place has become something else—
or at least it is on its way to being something else. Thanks to his close analysis
of walking, Husserl now accords to place an implicit dynamism it had at first
lacked. It has become, in short, lived place.

Lived place is present in the form of what Husserl calls a "steady system
of places."[141] Beyond the place of the body—the "body-place" as I have
called it—there is never just *one* place. In the clarified core-world we always
encounter a group of places, the various places of the things we perceive in
that field. Together, these places constitute a settled set. Without such a set,
things would be free-floating, flying off in all directions as it were. The *Ortssystem* is settled by dint of anchoring and locating perceptual things. But the
steady system in turn depends on an engagement with these things, for example, by walking through the primary world that holds them. We animate not
only the things but also their proper places. It is the lived body that makes
places live as the "basis-places" for the things we perceive.[142] A placeless
world is as unthinkable as a bodiless self, and it is because our selves have
such effective bodies—effective in orientation and in the coordination of
kinestheses with appearances—that the world is so placeful and thus so receptive to the things that inhabit it.

The lived body not only activates places but needs them in turn; it finds
them as well as founds them. How can this be? For the straightforward reason
that our own body is not only a *Leib* (lived body) but also (still) a *Körper*
(physical body). As a physical thing, our body is a thing among things, thus
requiring a "continuum of places"[143] in which to be located. For the body as
a *moved* thing, there is never not a place in the core-world. Indeed, despite its
considerable constitutive power, the lived body is something *also physical*
that calls for a preexisting place-world: it is aware of this necessity most
acutely when it is walking. For in walking my body must have *some place(s)
to go*. The human body as *Leib* may well coordinate and orient things in
regions, but it must itself be coordinated and oriented in the world in which it

walks. It is the *system* of places, preconstituted, that is responsible for each successive field of preoriented places. Hence it can be said that "every [body] has its place."[144]

My body, then, is *a body*—a sheerly physical entity—as well as a source of intentionality and projects, correlations and orientations (i.e., the lived body as transcendental in status). When I walk, I know myself to be a body with weight and force and volume, and as such I fit into a stable system of places that already populate the surrounding world: my stability as a massive thing is matched by the *stabilitas loci* of the place-world that awaits my movements. Body and place are still intimately allied, but now the glove is on the other hand: a quite incongruous hand. The transcendental turn is not the only way to get to the place-world in phenomenological investigations. We can also get there from the realist perspective of the material body's necessities. The defile to place through body is a two-way path, at once realist and transcendental.

Taking the realist direction at this point, Husserl is emboldened to ask the very unKantian question: "Is not space *already* a system of places (not just a system of orientation, orientation-space)?"[145] In this decisive suspension of the transcendental turn—a suspension all the more remarkable in that it is taken by the same philosopher who claimed to continue, indeed to culminate, the transcendental tradition itself—my body can even be said to be an extended thing. Descartes is reembraced from the other side of the transcendental divide. Husserl writes: "I can come to any place and be in it; thus my organism is also a thing, a *res extensa*, etc., movable."[146]

The two directions, realist and transcendental, despite their deep disparity, can be reconciled through the common term of *rest*. At stake in walking is not only motion, "keeping moving" (*In-gang-halten*), but also rest, "keeping still" (*Stillhalten*). Indeed, when I walk, rest is even prior to motion: "The 'I rest' precedes constitutively the 'I move myself.' "[147] Husserl points to such resting states as "the special stillness of standing, of sitting, of 'not-moving-myself-forward.' "[148] The overall primacy of rest—which reaches an acme in the case of the earth, which is experienced as resting *without* moving[149]—bespeaks Husserl's desire to find an ultimate stability in the transcendental landscape to which he is otherwise so fully committed. By considering rest as "something decisive and absolute,"[150] he establishes an Archimedean point to which all change must be related. Thus Husserl claims that "every re-alteration has its sense of rest; thus the constitution of 'rest' must found that of 'alteration.' "[151] What this means in effect is that motion (i.e, a form of alteration), including the motion of walking, is unthinkable without rest. The activity of the lived body—best exemplified in walking—is rooted in rest considered not as the absence of motion but as its terminal (or initial) state. At the most profound level, this body is "a basis without mobility."[152]

Indeed, for Husserl "the rigid body is the normal body,"[153] and the very idea of the "absolute here" is best exemplified by the body taken at rest. Rest

also affects the character of lived place. Just as we cannot walk without starting and stopping—and pausing—so the places around us, for all their enlivening by the *Leib,* are also reliably stationary: all places are resting places.
"We have a surrounding space as a system of places," says Husserl in another
essay of the same period, "i.e., as a system of *possible terminations* of motions
of bodies."[154] No wonder that Husserl can speak of the "steady system of
places with stable distances, stable configurations, [and] arrangements of resting things."[155] What the absolute here is for the lived body, the steady system
is for lived places. In both cases, stabilization is achieved—a stabilization that
is as much *given* as it is *constituted.* The transcendental thesis is true to the
extent that bodies animate places, endowing them with a directedness they
would not otherwise possess; but the realist doctrine is upheld by the fact that
places possess a steadiness that underlies this animation and makes it possible—and on which the body qua physical depends for its own implacement
and movement.

In walking, we move into a near-sphere of our own choosing, if not of our
own making. In this sphere, we encounter places as much as we enliven them.
The result is a place-world that is the correlate of the ambulatory body—a
world constituted by the very same body that depends on it for its own ongoing localization. Wallace Stevens is right to say that "I am the world in which
I walk."[156] But it is equally true that I walk in a world I am *not:* a world that
I, absolutely here, discover as already *there.* The here and the there, body and
space, realism and transcendentalism all meet finally—or rather, to begin
with—in place.

IV

> Spatial existence . . . is the primary condition of
> all living perception.
> —Maurice Merleau-Ponty, *Phenomenology*
> *of Perception*

> The originating locality, even in what concerns
> the "things" or the "direction" of a movement
> of things, is not identifiable in objective space.
> —Maurice Merleau-Ponty, *The Visible and*
> *the Invisible*

Franz Brentano, Husserl's mentor, was explicitly concerned with the difference between place and space. But in his investigations into this difference—
investigations he pursued until the very end of his career—we find no acknowledgment of the lived body's role in the constitution of place as distinc-

tively different from space. Thus, even as he proclaims in a statement dictated in 1915 that "it is undeniable that the determination of place is something positive," he speaks at the same time of bodies as merely "impenetrable" and as "physically and chemically multifariously specified."[157] Brentano's preoccupation with the intentionality of consciousness (in contrast with the materiality of objects) blocked his recognition of the lived body in relation to place. It was left to Husserl to grasp this significance and to bear it out in numerous writings, most of which were left unpublished at his death.

What exists in a scattered and mainly exploratory format in Husserl becomes focused and perspicuous in Merleau-Ponty. In his *Phenomenology of Perception* (1945), Merleau-Ponty pursued the thesis that it is primarily through our lived body that we have access to what both he and Husserl call the "primary world."[158] Indeed, without such a body there would be no world at all for us: "The [lived] body is our general medium for having a world."[159] Here skeptics will ask: How can the lived body, the body as felt and experienced by the human subject, assume such responsibility?

The lived body can take on such importance precisely because it possesses its own corporeal intentionality, not to be confused with the intentionality of mind.[160] Where the latter was for Brentano the exclusive mark by which to distinguish psychical from physical phenomena, the former contests the very psychical/physical distinction itself.[161] Corporeal intentionality replaces any rigid dichotomy of body and mind by an "intentional arc" binding us to the life-world we inhabit.[162] Thanks to this arc, which is rooted in the deepest and subtlest recesses of the lived body, we are provided with a reliable and persisting "anchorage" in the world.[163] So massive and yet sensitive is bodily intentionality that, thanks to its agency, there is at all times "a certain gearing of my body to the world"—a gearing that is "the origin of space."[164]

The origin of space! No longer is this origin sought in the world-building ambitions of a creator-god, much less in the pure mind of an austere transcendental subject. The origin is found straightforwardly in the body of the individual subject. Or, more exactly, it is found in the *movement* of that body. For space to arise, our body as geared into it cannot remain static; it must be in motion. Much as Husserl had given to kinesthesia in general (and to walking in particular) a constitutive role in the origin of space and place alike, so Merleau-Ponty regards bodily movement as "productive of space."[165] For Merleau-Ponty, it is not the objective displacement of one's own body that is spatiogenetic but, rather, the very *experience* of such movement: "Our bodily experience of movement is not a particular case of knowledge; it provides us with a way of access to the world and the object, with a 'praktognosia' which has to be recognized as original and perhaps as primary."[166] Such experience of our own body's movement is "pre-objective"—a key word that also applies to the world we come to know through this very same experience.

Just as we had to trace back the origin of the positing of space to the pre-objective situation or locality of the subject fastening himself on to his environment, so we shall have to rediscover, beneath the objective idea of movement, a pre-objective experience from which it borrows its significance.[167]

Crediting Kant with being the first to acknowledge explicitly that locating objects in space calls for the motility of the body—albeit for Kant a body not yet recognized as lived[168]—Merleau-Ponty takes up the example of the geometer. The latter does not merely project abstract figures into an equally abstract space but "knows the relationships with which he is concerned only by describing them, at least potentially, with his body. *The subject of geometry is a motor subject.*"[169] With this claim, we uncover the bodily basis of the abstracting and idealizing operations of Euclidean geometry to which Husserl had pointed in *The Crisis of European Sciences.* The lived body, in short, is the veritable demiurge of geometry and thus, by extension, of any physics that (in the manner of Galileo) presumes and builds on geometry regarded as an axiomatic body of knowledge.

For Merleau-Ponty, the lived body is the origin of "spatializing" as well as "spatialized" space; it makes the crucial difference, in the end it *is* the difference, between space as expansive and opening-up (*l'espace spatialisant*) and space as something fixed and closed-in (*l'espace spatialisé*).[170] The lived body does the spatializing that eventuates via various formal operations in the spatialized world of geometry (and physics). Its empowering force, most completely manifested in bodily movement, is what lends to space a "universal power"[171] to connect things that would otherwise be consigned to isolated positions in the indifferent vacua of homogeneous space. Galileo's apothegm "It moves!" (archly inverted by Husserl: "the earth does not move")[172] is superseded by Merleau-Ponty's operative dictum "I move." The movement of the earth, Galileo's prized premise, cedes place to the movement of the lived body—a body that Husserl (precisely in opposition to Galilean physics) had considered to be "phenomenally stationary," that is, unmoving in its very movement, resting in its own place.

It follows that space as experienced by our bodies is neither a collection of points nor a conglomeration of sheer relations; nor is it to be conceived as a matter of containment, for example, by an etheral medium or by contiguity with the inner surface of a strict surrounder.[173] None of these traditional notions of space adequately addresses two of its essential features: its expressiveness and its orientedness. The lived-moving body underlies both features. Just as the body continually exhibits "expressive movement"[174]—is never not expressive, not even when it is engaged in the most abstruse geometric operation—so the space in which it moves becomes an expressive space, having its own physiognomy and moods, its affectivity and style. Likewise, the same mobile body is continually orienting us in the particular space in which we find ourselves: where "orientation" signifies nothing as definite as cardinal directions but something closer to a sense of fit and of knowing one's way around. Taken together, expressive movement and bodily orientation result in *inhabitation.*

> We must therefore avoid saying that our body is *in* space, or *in* time. It *inhabits* space and time.... I am not in space and time; nor do I conceive space and time; I belong to them, my body combines with them and includes them. The scope of this inclusion is the measure of that of my existence.[175]

In this passage, the Aristotelian "in" of containment gives way to the very different Merleau-Pontian "in" of inhabitation. Kant is also contested: if I am not merely in space, neither is space *in me* (e.g., as a form of intuition). Rather than objective or subjective containment, it is a question of the active in-dwelling of space by means of my lived body construed as "the subject of space."[176]

If my lived body is the subject, indeed the very source, of expressive and oriented space, this fact will have important implications for the understanding of *place* and in particular "lived place" as I have come to call it in the course of this chapter. One immediate implication is that place cannot be reduced to sheer position in objective space. The distinction between what Merleau-Ponty calls "spatiality of situation" and "spatiality of position" means that place as experienced by the lived body cannot be simply positional, a matter of a literal *thesis.*[177] Thus bodily movement cannot be understood as "a mere change of place in objective space":[178] this is to limit place to strict sameness-of-place in the manner of Leibniz. It also ensues that we cannot reduce place to its ideational representation, tempting as it is to make this reduction in the manner of Descartes and Locke.

> Knowledge of where something is can be understood in a number of ways. Traditional psychology has no concept to cover these varieties of consciousness of place because consciousness of place is always, for such psychology, a positional consciousness, a representation, *Vor-stellung,* because as such it gives us place as a determination of the objective world and because such a representation either is or is not, but, if it is, it yields the object to us quite unambiguously.[179]

Place, precisely because it is not merely positional and often has indeterminate boundaries, presents itself to us as an ambiguous phenomenon—as ambiguous as is the lived body by means of which it is experienced and known. Just as we may say of the lived body that it "is not where it is, nor what it is,"[180] so we must also allow that place is neither *just where it is* nor *just what it is:* only concerning the simple location of a site can we say these things. Hence place is not the content of a definite representation. Any such mistaken view reflects that "prejudice about the [objective] world"[181] that the lived body belies in its forthright movements. Not being the content of definite representations—whether ideas or images—place is not determinate in character.

This means in turn that place has a *virtual* dimension overlooked in previous accounts. A place I inhabit by my body is not merely some spot of space to which I bring myself as to a fixed locus—a locus that merely awaits my arrival. Husserl's emphasis on a constant *Ortssystem* is here challenged by an appeal to the idea of place as an ambiguous scene of things-to-be-done rather than of items-already-established. A place is somewhere I *might* come to; and when I do come to it, it is not just a matter of fitting into it. I come into a place as providing an indefinite horizon of my *possible* action.

> What counts for the orientation of the spectacle [around me] is not my body as it in fact is, as a thing in objective space, but as a system of possible actions, a virtual body with its phenomenal "place" defined by its task and situation. My body is wherever there is something to be done.[182]

As this statement indicates, closely linked with the virtual is the notion of the *phenomenal*. Just as the "phenomenal field" is posited early in *Phenomenology of Perception* as an alternative to empiricist and intellectualist models of the perceptual world, so the phenomenal body is invoked later on, with the result that "the whole operation takes place in the domain of the phenomenal."[183] This whole operation includes the virtual movement of the lived body into (and out of) places of possible action as well as the various ways in which this body is itself a place.[184] Place as phenomenal may be regarded as a generalized description of Husserl's notion that we experience place and space as kinesthetically felt situations—in contrast with site, which is not felt by our lived body and thus lacks phenomenal presence.

But the phenomenality of my body-in-place is not limited to what kinesthetic feelings deliver. The lived body not only feels but *knows* the places to which it is so intimately attached.

> As far as bodily space is concerned, it is clear that there is a knowledge of place which is reducible to a sort of co-existence with that place, and which is not simply nothing, even though it cannot be conveyed in the form of an [objective] description or even pointed out without a word being spoken.[185]

What kind of knowledge is this? It is knowledge by acquaintance in the form of *familiarity*. Precisely because my body is a "means of ingress into a familiar setting,"[186] it possesses knowledge of places by direct (and continuing) acquaintance with them. In this connection, Merleau-Ponty stresses the "customary" body, a body that is "the matrix of habitual action."[187] By virtue of this aspect of the lived body, I can be said to know, at a preobjective and yet fully efficacious level, the places that populate my ongoing experience. A place is my *familiaris* (literally, a "familiar spirit"). As I know my way around my own house, so I know my way around all the familiar places of my "habitat": habitual body memory (which underlies an entire set of accustomed and skillful actions) combines with awareness of place to bring about a circumstance in which "being is synonymous with being situated."[188]

In thus proposing a praktognosia of place, Merleau-Ponty is claiming not only that the body provides a privileged point of access to place, or just that the body has unique powers vis-à-vis place. He is claiming that *the places we inhabit are known by the bodies we live.* Moreover, *we cannot be implaced without being embodied.* Conversely, *to be embodied is to be capable of implacement.* Not only do we discover ever new places by means of bodily movement; we find ourselves in the midst of places we already know thanks to the intimate link between their abiding familiarity and our own corporeal habituality.

Just as Whitehead challenges us to rethink place as something other than simple location, so Merleau-Ponty (following the lead of Husserl) invites us to reconsider the lived body as something other than a mere instance of *res extensa,* to the point that (unlike Husserl) he is unwilling to regard the physical body as essentially involved in implacement. As both customary and virtual in its action—hence as actively incorporating the past and constructively projecting the future—*le corps vécu* is held to be phenomenal in every sense of this altogether appropriate word. And yet Merleau-Ponty is not attributing to the body the kind of sheer autonomy imputed to the mind in the subjective idealism of Berkeley or in Kant's transcendental idealism. Thanks to his espousal of a specifically corporeal intentionality, Merleau-Ponty assures us that every activity of the body is closely attuned with its circumambient world: indeed, my lived body is said to be "the potentiality of [responding to] this or that region of the world."[189] It is, once more, a matter of our "anchorage in the world"—a mooring in a world not simply homogeneous and isotropic but regionalized in advance into a series of familiar settings. These settings are *none other than lived places:* places regarded not as the mere subdivisions of an absolute space or as a function of relationships between coexistents but as loci of intimacy and particularity, endowed with porous boundaries and open orientations. They are experienced and known through customary bodily actions. Although his view of place is less robustly realist than Husserl's—there is no equivalent in his writings to a steady system of preconstituted places—he nevertheless retains a firm commitment to the advance givenness of the preobjective place-world, a world we inhabit by means of our habituated/habituating bodies.

Two closely related questions can be raised concerning Merleau-Ponty's elevation of the lived body to such prominence in the experience and determination of place. First, does not this prominence accord undue weight to a "subjective" factor in the specification of place? Second, is the body truly indispensable in this specification? Can we not determine place in terms of other equally intrinsic features that make no reference whatsoever to the lived body?

In answering the first question, we must notice that kinesthesia, taken by both Merleau-Ponty and Husserl to be the most concrete form in which the "lived" aspect of the body arises for us, need not imply anything subjective, that is, inward and personal. To feel our body feeling its surroundings is not to be caught in "the circuit of selfness" (Sartre) but to engage ourselves openly and vigorously with these surroundings. As Whitehead has emphasized, feeling is a quite efficacious way of "prehending" the world: "All actual entities in the actual world, relatively to a given actual entity as 'subject', are necessarily 'felt' by that subject, though in general vaguely."[190] Kinesthetic feelings, far from being merely subjective in content or origin, are precisely what are fatefully "objectified" for the subject, thereby constituting the most precious evidence of the way the world, and most particularly the place-world, gives itself to us.[191]

Furthermore, as an actively *orienting* force, indeed as the very center of orientation, the lived body escapes self-enclosure. To orient, after all, is to orient *to*—to something *other than* that which does the orienting itself. This is evident both in ordinary circumstances of orientation (i.e., in a new city we are visiting for the first time) and in experiments discussed by Merleau-Ponty. In the Wertheimer experiment, subjects become oriented to a room as reflected in an oblique mirror that presents the interior of the room as tilted 45 degrees to one side. A moment of confusion and hesitation gives way to a successful adjustment to the room-as-slanted. The experiment thus "serves to show how the visual field can impose an orientation which is not that of the body."[192] Far from this circumstance being exceptional, it demonstrates that *all* orientation involves a gearing into a "spatial level" that is not embedded in one's body proper but in the surrounding world. This level constitutes a perceptual ground or, more exactly, "a general setting in which my body can co-exist with the world."[193] We may presume that this setting is in turn made up of particular places, each of which contributes to the basic level of a given situation. Whatever my body's constructive contributions to these places, their *level* (though not the places themselves) must be taken as something given, even as "preestablished."[194] When it comes to orientation, then, I am not the captive of a scene I have myself projected. As Merleau-Ponty puts it strikingly: "I already live in the landscape."[195] The same holds for my experience of depth, and for my sense of up and down, far and near, great and small.[196] The crucial clues for all of these arise from my environs, not from my lived body taken in isolation from its surroundings. Thinking in this direction, Merleau-Ponty delimits his own transcendental tendencies.

Does this mean that, in keeping with the second question, my body is dispensable in constitution of the place-world? So it might seem—and all the more so if we consider that place is sometimes specified by such extrabodily things as a season (e.g., a snowbound glade) or even by a technological entity (e.g., an automated lighthouse whose light sweeps out an arc in the night). In *Being and Time* Heidegger argues that a primary sense of place is established by various relations of instrumentality such as the "in-order-to" *(um-zu)* or the "whither" *(wohin)* of efficient use.[197] Examples such as these might lead us to suppose that far from being indispensable to place, the lived body is only contingently connected with it and might even be eliminated altogether from its constitution and purview.

But such a supposition is quite unwarranted. Even if it need not be literally present in every case, the human body is an at least implicit or tacit presence in all the places that fall within its ken. This presence is evident in the very instrumental relations singled out by Heidegger: if a hammer (in his own example) exhibits the in-order-to relation of pounding in a nail to hang a painting, what other than a *hand* of a human body is likely to effect the action of hammering? Not only is it the case—as Heidegger observes elsewhere— that "all the work of [our] hands is rooted in thinking"[198] but instrumental action of almost every kind requires a handed human body. This handedness has everything to do with how we experience the configuration of a given place, including a place-under-construction. In noninstrumental settings as well, the body remains a constitutive force. A snowbound glade could not constitute a full-fledged *place* unless I could at least tacitly, by imputation, feel myself to be there bodily—not entirely unlike Wallace Stevens's Snow-man who, "nothing himself, beholds / nothing that is not there, and the nothing that is."[199] Similarly, the lonely lighthouse is a place only insofar as I can, by proxy, as it were, imagine *someone's* body (not necessarily my own) inhab-iting it. In order to effect such imputations, I need to call on my virtual body, which is capable of inhabiting even the most remote and seemingly vacuous place. So long as something is a "possible habitat" for a possible body, it can count as a place.[200]

Somewhere where *no possible* human bodily presence could be found, ei-ther in fact or by imaginative projection, is not a place to begin with. Only a site can exist without such presence (indeed, a site *thrives* on the absence of body). To banish lived body from a place is to threaten to turn that place, the animated correlate of the lived body, into a de-animated site as unlived as it is unlivable.

The tie, the knot, between body and place is so thickly Gordian that it cannot be neatly severed at any one point. Merleau-Ponty teaches us not just that the human body is never without a place or that place is never without (its own actual or virtual) body; he also shows that the lived body is itself a place. Its very movement, instead of effecting a mere change of position, *constitutes place,* brings it into being. No demiurge need be enjoined to create such a place; nor need any formal geometry be imposed on space in order to generate it. *The body itself is place-productive,* bringing forth places from its expressive and orientational movements, its literally kinetic dynamism.

It is at once ironic and fitting that Merleau-Ponty's final reflections on place, as set forth in *The Visible and the Invisible,* concern human handedness: not now in the context of instrumental relations but in regard to that massive integumentation with the world that Merleau-Ponty came to call "flesh" (*la chair*). Flesh is exemplified in the unique manner in which one hand touches the other, including the fact that we can see and feel them touching; in and through this touching, we experience particular things—and thus the places they occupy.

> A veritable touching of the touch, when my right hand touches my left hand while it is palpating the things, where the "touching subject" passes over to the rank of the touched, descends into the things, such that the touch is formed in the midst of the world and as it were in the things.[201]

After nearly two hundred years, we have returned to a full recognition of the importance of the two-handedness of human beings. Yet what a different recognition this is! For Kant, who inaugurated our discussion of body and place, spatial regions refer to the bilaterality of our bodies: the vector is from outside and around us *in* and *toward* us. For Merleau-Ponty, the bilaterality of the touched–touching relationship sends us back *out* and *into* the environs around us, placing us "in the midst of the world and as it were in the things." We are thrust back out into the world precisely because the lived body is "a dimensional this" at one with the dimensionality of the spatial world as a whole.[202] Moreover, the role of conscious apprehension—crucial in Kant's conception—comes into question on Merleau-Ponty's assessment: "For my two hands to open upon one sole world, it does not suffice that they be given to one sole *consciousness*."[203] They are given instead to one sole *flesh*—a flesh that is ultimately the flesh of the world, with the result that my lived body can be considered as "the universal thing."[204]

There is a further difference between Kant and Merleau-Ponty: where the body for Kant is irremediably bifurcated into incongruent counterparts in matters of space and place, for Merleau-Ponty the hands are "the hands of *one same body,* . . . making of my hands one sole organ of experience, as it makes of my two eyes the channels of one sole Cyclopean vision."[205] Merleau-Ponty admits that this unification of dual parts is "a difficult relation to conceive."[206] But in a working note of November 1959 he conceives of it in this way:

> Consider the right, the left: these are not simply contents within a relational spatiality (i.e., *positive*): they are not *parts* of space (Kant's reasoning is valid here: the whole is primary), they are total parts, cuts in an encompassing, topological space—Consider the *two,* the *pair,* this is not *two acts, two syntheses,* it is a fragmentation of being, it is a possibility for separation (two eyes, two ears:

the possibility for *discrimination,* for the use of the diacritical), it is the advent of difference (on the ground of *resemblance* therefore, on the ground of the *homou ēn panta* [all things alike]).[207]

In his early recourse to bodily bilaterality, Kant not only moved the existing debate between absolutist and relativist conceptions of space onto a new level by showing that neither conception, taken by itself, is adequate for understanding curious pairings such as the right and left hands.[208] Husserl followed forth by picking out walking—an activity of right and left *legs*—as a paradigmatic path to the phenomenological understanding of place. Merleau-Ponty, less impressed with bodily bilaterality as such, points both to the singleness of the body to which right and left hands (and feet) belong and to the phenomenon of the "cut," the "separation," the diacritical "difference" between right and left. Viewed in terms of this disparity, incongruent counterparts are not just a spatial anomaly giving rise to a conceptual puzzle; their very in-congruency gestures toward a notion of place as deriving from difference, from "the possibility for *discrimination*"—from "a relation of real opposition."[209] Phrased differently, the unassimilability of right and left hands, their "functional asymmetry,"[210] has everything to do with the anisotropy of place, its oddities and idiosyncrasies.

Lived place thrives—is first felt and recognized—in the differentiated and disruptive corners, the "cuts," of my bodily being-in-the-world. This is why the child's experience of place is so poignantly remembered: in childhood we are plunged willy-nilly into a diverse (and sometimes frightening) array of places, for example, the places of "Combray" in the case of the young Marcel Proust. The extraordinary sensitivity of the child's lived body opens onto and takes in a highly expressive place-world that reflects the discriminative and complex character of the particular places that compose this world. It is from a somatocentric perspective, then, that we can best appreciate the differential character of the place-world and that we can grasp the sameness of space as something secondary or derived.

The sameness of abstract, objective space is essentially twofold: isotropic and homogeneous. Peculiarities of the lived body underlie and precede both of these characteristics. Handedness—or footedness, armedness, kneedness, and so on—undoes any illusion that space is simply monistic in its constitution or neutral in its tropism. Space comes to us always already contorted, twisted in the asymmetrical double helices of right versus left, here versus there, front versus back, near versus far, and so forth. These contortions begin in the bodily experience of place, which is where we first encounter them and where they have the most lasting effects. The sheer fact of having or being a lived body, possessing the peculiar mass of flesh we call our "own"— having an *Eigenleib,* an *Ichleib*—is enough to upset any a priori assumption that space is homogeneous, ever-the-same everywhere, *homou ēn panta.*

Merleau-Ponty helps us to realize that space is ever different from place to place, and from body to body: and one because of the other. For my flesh is finely meshed with the world's flesh—and thus with the places presented and sedimented within the world: a place-world in which I can live and move and have my being. If flesh is indeed a deep-lying "ground of resemblance" that makes both planiform space and diversiform place possible, this pervasive ground is at once concretized and exemplified in the double interleaving of body with place and place with body.

V

> Phenomenology is a philosophy for which the world is always "already there" before reflection begins—as an inalienable presence; and all its efforts are concentrated upon reachieving a direct and primitive contact with the world, and endowing that contact with a philosophical status.
>
> —Maurice Merleau-Ponty, *Phenomenology of Perception*

Merleau-Ponty culminates a late modern effort to reclaim the particularity of place from the universality of space by recourse to bodily empowerment. This effort began with Kant's prescient recognition of the orienting prowess of the two-sided body in situating us vis-à-vis "regions in space." It was extended in Whitehead's cogent critique of simple location and in his emphasis on the visceral body in coming to know what he also called "regions." It continued apace in Husserl's strikingly similar critique of the mathematization of nature and in his attempt to discover the kinesthetic foundations of bodily being-in-place. In bringing this microtradition to completion, Merleau-Ponty accorded full scope to the role of the lived body—above all, to its actively expressive movements, its orienting capacity, and its inhabitational powers. Other phenomenologically oriented writers have explored the further significance of lived space, but none has done so with such nuanced attention as Merleau-Ponty paid to the way the lived body gears into places in their felt intimacy.[211] Thanks to all four thinkers, place—which we have seen to be so deeply submerged in space as barely to survive discussion after the death of Leibniz—comes to be of genuine philosophical interest again. Its revival as a topic of focused philosophical concern may not have brought it to the pitch of concern that it enjoyed in ancient philosophy and in Hellenistic, Neoplatonic, and medieval times, but we have nevertheless witnessed in this chapter a turning that begins to reverse its almost complete neglect for nearly two centuries. This turn, moreover, is not just a return, since the exact form of the revival, that is,

the close association of place with the human body as felt and lived, is virtually unprecedented. (I say "virtually" because we must not forget that in the
Enuma Elish place is fabricated out of Tiamat's slain body! And on the far
side of our trajectory, Leibniz at least suspected the close imbrication of body
and place.) The change wrought is closer to a literal conversion—a *turning* of
place *with* body, the intertwining of each with the other.

I have attributed this conversion in the assessment of place to the recognition of what is at first glance a quite innocent, even a seemingly trivial, fact:
that we get into place, move and stay there, *with our bodies*. But the fact is
neither innocent nor trivial; it is momentous in its consequences. It is also
massively obvious, despite being massively overlooked in previous treatments
of place and space. For there is no getting around the fact that it is by our
bodies that we belong to the place-world. Think only of where you are *right
now:* the room you are in is accessible and familiar to you by virtue of the
perceptual and orientational powers of your body. Without these powers, you
would feel yourself so much out of place (if not actually displaced) that you
would not know what to do, much less where to go. You would not have come
to the room in the first place, nor could you settle there comfortably to observe
or think, nor could you eventually leave. However tacit its role may be, your
body is the very vehicle of implacement, and is sine qua non for being-in-
place.

If this is true, and so manifestly true, it is all the more amazing that the
body's role in matters of place was neglected for so long by philosophers—
and, by the same token, all the more important that this role was finally picked
out. It is not accidental, however, that such an act of recognition arose in the
period of later modernity, that is, when the formative and meaning-giving
capacities of the human subject were finally becoming acknowledged. At first,
these capacities were thought to be mainly mental: this is the high road of
transcendentalism, from Descartes on the *cogito* through Kant on the transcendental aesthetic and Husserl on the transcendental ego. Slowly but surely,
though, the subject's constitutive powers were also seen to be corporeal. The
dead body of *res extensa* ceded place to the live/lived body of the *Lebenswelt*.
What was a happy and isolated discovery for Kant became thematic for phe-
nomenologists—who themselves make a virtue of attending to the obvious,
the taken-for-granted, in human experience. But it is confirmatory of the
rightness of this recognition that Kant and Whitehead, coming from such very
different philosophical premises, both underlined the ingredience of the body
in matters of implacement. The low road of the body-subject in early modern
philosophy thus proved to be a privileged highway to place by late modernity.

Despite the obviousness of the body/place link, its belated acknowledgment has meant that my own treatment of this link has proceeded in paradoxes, for example, the combination of the obvious with the important. A
paradox throughout (one that started as a rhetorical flourish) has been the

realization that the narrow defile of the body is not so narrow after all: not only does the body open onto new vistas of Place (thus regaining its capital status), but the defile itself has proven to have its own width. It has shown itself to be much more complex than might be imagined—requiring even for its minimal description the collective talents of four of the subtlest thinkers of the modern era. Doubtless the most striking instance of this paradox of the constricted-cum-broad was Kant's uncovering of the enormous consequences entailed by a tiny and almost literally invisible detail, that of right versus left hands regarded as enantiomorphic.[212] This detail is a matter of indifference on a Leibnizian model of space as purely relational and an unexplained puzzle for Newtonian absolute space (despite Kant's appeal to this latter). Yet reflection on the odd fact of incongruency helped Kant to break the gridlock of absolutist versus relativist theories of space, and it ushered in a novel way of understanding how place is irreducible to space. Less dramatically but just as persuasively, Husserl drew crucial conclusions about place and space by attending to the ordinary activity of walking, and Merleau-Ponty grasped the dynamism of the lived body in its most habitual activities.

A phenomenon closely related to this last paradoxical point is the need to combine an appreciation of the whole body (i.e., the "organism") with an equal appreciation of its various parts, the bodily "organs." Both Husserl and Merleau-Ponty stress the global character of kinesthetic sensations—which reflect the entire *kinēsis* of our lived body, all of its changes and motions at a given moment. Similarly, Whitehead insists on the deep relevance of our total visceral sensibility for apprehending how we are placed in given situations. Kant considers the inherent directionality of the entire body in guiding its insertion into environing regions. At the same time, the pertinence of body parts is also emphasized by Kant: not only hands and feet but, by implication, any bivalently structured portion of the body. Indeed, if it is true that not just the actual but the *virtual* body is at stake in place—as Merleau-Ponty claims—then the imaginative projection of any and all parts of the body will become place-specific and place-specifying. Generally, we may say that if it is by the whole body that we inhabit *place* as such, it is by parts of this body that we gain access to particular *places,* become oriented there, and manage to find egress.

The whole body constitutes a genuinely corporeal transcendental subject, a "body-subject" (in Bruce Wilshire's apt term). Yet we have seen that the transcendental status of the human subject, far from being an unquestioned and pure realm of constitution, often comes coupled with the realist ontology of the larger place-world to which this subject cannot help but belong. Both Husserl and Merleau-Ponty refuse Kant's program whereby the real is merely empirical or else inaccessibly noumenal. Their concern is with the intricate dialectic between what is pregiven in places in the form of groupings (systematic or not) that are *already* present to us and what is contributed by our lived bodies, for example, the orientedness and expressivity of places. This dialectic is one of sedimentation and reactivation—to employ terms from Husserl's *Crisis of European Sciences* that are taken up again by Merleau-Ponty.[213] For the world of places is densely sedimented in its familiarity and historicity and its very materiality while, at the same time, it is animated and reanimated by the presence of the lived body in its midst. In the end, *both* factors—one realist in signification, the other idealist or transcendental—are required for a full determination of what it means to be bodily in a place.[214]

If the body/place nexus allows us to conjoin realism with transcendentalism—itself a deeply paradoxical combination—it also permits us to see that the bond between body and place is further paradoxical in being at once subjective and objective and, more especially, private and public. We have noted Whitehead's conviction that the body is "the most intimately relevant part of the antecedently settled world." The intimacy bespeaks not just subjectivity but radical privacy, which is expressed by the self-ascribing phrase "my body." Privacy is not to be confused with personal inwardness. Merleau-Ponty makes it clear that the body-subject is *pre*personal and anonymous: there is "another subject beneath me, for whom a world exists before I am, and who marks out my place in [that world]."[215] The deepest level of subjectivity is still place-bound.

The same is true of the widest plane of the public world—which, as Arendt has argued, is dependent (in the West) on the notion of the agora or forum.[216] The anonymous subjectivity of the lived body is continually confronted and connected with the intersubjectivity at stake in public places. It is striking that Husserl's prolonged ruminations on place and space as bodily experienced are increasingly linked with a phenomenology of *intersubjectivity*.[217] The "regions" on which both Kant and Whitehead focus are not without their social implications, whether in the form of the public activities situated with reference to cardinal directions (e.g., ceremonies, journeys, etc.) or in the form of the "corpuscular societies"[218] that structure all matter, including that constituting the human body itself. The "flesh of the world," to which Merleau-Ponty's analysis of the flesh of the lived body leads him, is also replete with social significance.[219] In all of these instances, the lived body—which is perhaps what human beings take to be the most self-enclosed and intimate thing they experience—shows itself to be continually conjoined with place, however impersonal and public in status it may be in given instances. The conjunction itself, however, is made possible precisely because the body is already social and public in its formation and destiny—as Foucault would insist—while places for their part are idiosyncratic in their constitution and appearance. Just as sedimentation and reactivation are both bodily and placial, so the public and the private realms realize themselves in body and place alike.

The various thinkers under discussion in this chapter have taught us that the narrow defile of body is broad indeed—broad, above all, when it leads to place (and place back to it). No matter how diminutive its actual size, to be a body in a place is not to be a constricted presence there. It is, on the contrary, to become enlarged and enlivened in that place, as in the Japanese art of origami, in which paper flowers exfoliate in water. The absolute here of the body opens onto the absolute there of place, thanks to the coordination of bodily kinesthesias with the perceptual appearances of things, an orientatedness shared by both body and place, and a corporeal virtuality that knows few limits. By the same token, the extent of place is less broad than we presume when place is taken to be merely a portion of space. Place has an intensity and intimacy familiar to the lived bodies that inhabit it—for example, in the infrastructure of directed regions and the proximity of near-spheres—and it is enclosed in boundaries that are also significantly intimate, as we sense whenever we find ourselves ensconced in a house or walking in a dense forest. Just as a place is animated by the lived bodies that are in it, a lived place animates these same bodies as they become implaced there.

All of the paradoxes I have been tracing reflect the ambiguous circumstance whereby bodies and places are as inseparable as they are distinguishable. The same paradoxes cease to be problematic and become distinctly promising, however, when we accept the fateful complicity of body and place themselves, and attempt to understand their mutual intertwining in ways that do justice to their differences while respecting their commonality. In their pioneering pursuit of this invaluable enterprise, Kant and Whitehead, Husserl and Merleau-Ponty have made essential and lasting contributions. In so doing, they have managed to stem the tide of indifference that has engulfed place—engulfed it in Time as well as in Space, the dominant cosmic parameters in the modern period. By regarding the body as the crucial clue, they have begun to retrieve the importance of place for Western thought.

11

Proceeding to Place by Indirection

Heidegger

> I do not want to be absolutely dogmatic by asserting
> that one cannot conceive Being except on the basis
> of time. Perhaps someday a new possibility will be
> discovered.
>> —Martin Heidegger, *Logik: Die Frage nach der*
>> *Wahrheit*

> The bare space is still veiled over. Space has been
> split up into places.
>> —Martin Heidegger, *Sein und Zeit*, Section 22

> Unless we go back to the world, space cannot be
> conceived.
>> —Martin Heidegger, *Sein und Zeit*, Section 24

What, on Freud's view, dreams provide for an understanding of the unconscious mind—a *via regia,* a "royal road"—the body has provided for place,
which by the end of the nineteenth century had come to be as repressed as
the libidinal contents of the unconscious mind. Nevertheless, promising and
productive as bodily inroads into place have shown themselves to be, they do
not exhaust the modes of effective reentry to the place-world. In this chapter
we shall consider the contributions of someone who neglected the role of the
body in implacement but who managed to find other means of access to place
as a subject of renewed philosophical importance. Indeed, it could even be
claimed that it was precisely by his deliberate refusal to invoke the body—
along with consciousness, its incongruent counterpart—that Heidegger made
his own way to place.[1] Heidegger's way back to place is a middle way, a *via*

media between body and mind, both of which are set aside in order to concentrate on what happens *between* them. In exploring this open between—this between of the Open—Heidegger was drawn into detours that, despite their digressive character, allowed him to glimpse aspects of place overlooked by other thinkers, ancient as well as modern. This is so in spite of the fact that these same detours are described in a vocabulary that is highly idiosyncratic and that, at least at first glance, seems to make little connection with previous descriptions of place.

Heidegger came to a full acknowledgment of the power of place only belatedly. In earlier phases of his thought, place was important not for its own sake but because of its usefulness in such disparate contexts as the work world, the work of art, and politics. Even when Heidegger abandoned an instrumental interpretation of place in his middle period, he still did not single out place as such. Yet in later writings place (along with region and other related terms) emerged as an increasing preoccupation. Heidegger himself underlined this slow but decisive augmentation of place in his evolving thought when, in a seminar at Le Thor in 1969, he maintained that his thinking had traversed three periods, each with its own leading theme: Meaning, Truth, and Place.

Heidegger gets back into place, then, not as "the first of all things" to be considered (as certain ancient thinkers had assumed), or in reactive flight before infinite space (a flight taken by many modern thinkers), but by indirection: by traveling through diverse "forest paths" (*Holzwege*), as he liked to put it. To begin with, he returns to place not through but despite the body's involvement in placiality: as if place could be reached *around* and *outside* the body itself. Still more tellingly, he returns to place despite his own obsession with inaugurating a postmetaphysical era in philosophy—an era in which one might well imagine place to be a dispensable item, given its preeminent position in classical metaphysical thinking from Plato through Philoponus, and continuing into the Middle Ages. Yet just as place emerges in the Cartesian abyss between consciousness and body, so it rises, Phoenixlike, from the ashes of metaphysical thought as deconstructed by Heidegger. Thanks to such features as gathering and nearness, place becomes for him the very scene of Being's disclosure and of the openness of the Open in which truth is unconcealed. In the end, place figures as the setting for the postmetaphysical event of Appropriation (*Ereignis*).

I

Still another mode of indirection is found in the fact that Heidegger takes place seriously despite his early emphasis on the primacy of *temporality*. *Being and Time* and other texts of the 1920s (most notably, *The History of the Concept of Time*) insist on temporality as uniquely capable of unifying the

care-structure of Dasein, or human being—temporality is said to be "the ontological meaning of care"—and the same writings point to the various modes
of ecstatic temporality essential to Dasein's authentic being-in-the-world. In
short, "temporality is constitutive for Dasein's Being."[2] Moreover, time is
said to be "the horizon of Being."[3] No such sweeping claims are made for
space, much less for place—neither of which is accorded the honor of being
fully authentic modes of being, much less disclosive of Being. How, then,
can Heidegger's unabashed temporocentrism accord any significant room for
place?

The curious fact is that this room is accorded, and even abundantly so, in
the very same book in which temporality or "primordial time" (*ursprüngliche
Zeit*) is held to be "the central problematic of all ontology."[4] I refer not just
to the revealing way that Heidegger, at certain critical moments, invokes features of place to describe temporality itself, for example, when he describes
its ecstatical character as "the primordial *'outside-of-itself'* in and for
itself."[5] Nor am I thinking only of his admittedly failed effort in section 70
of *Being and Time* to derive spatiality from temporality—a failure to which
we shall return. I have in mind early parts of this same pathbreaking text that
expressly take up questions of place and space.

Take, to start with, Heidegger's "preliminary sketch" of "Being-in-the-
World in General as the Basic State of Dasein." Admonishing the reader that
being-in-the-world is an essentially "unitary phenomenon," Heidegger analyzes the character of "being-in" (*In-Sein*) as an *existentiale* of Dasein. As
such, it is contrasted with mere "being in something" (*Sein in . . .*) or "insideness" (*Inwendigkeit*), which amounts to a situation of sheer containment:
"By this [latter] 'in' we mean the relationship of Being which two entities
extended 'in' space have to each other with regard to their location in that
space."[6] Such a strict container model is, of course, ultimately derivative from
Aristotle—to whom Heidegger is here making barely veiled reference, as he
also does in speaking of a totalized "world-space" (*Weltraum*) that contains
all less capacious containers. Essential to the container model is a "definite
location-relationship" between two determinate "present-at-hand" (*vorhanden*) entities, both of which are considered only with regard to their "categorial" characteristics.[7] Dasein's own being-in, however, cannot be reduced to
anything like this: "One cannot think of it as the Being-present-at-hand of
some corporeal Thing (such as a human body) 'in' an entity which is present-
at-hand."[8] Disregarding the clue that this "human body" (*Menschleib*) presents, Heidegger identifies the truly existential character of being-in in terms
of Dasein's proclivity for inhabiting and dwelling.

'In' is derived from "*innan*"—"to reside," "*habitare*," "to dwell." 'An' signifies
"I am accustomed," "I am familiar with," "I look after something." . . . The
expression '*bin*' is connected with '*bei*', and so '*ich bin*' ['I am'] means in its

turn "I reside" or "dwell alongside" the world, as that which is familiar to me in such and such a way. "Being" [*Sein*], as the infinitive of '*ich bin*' (that is to say, when it is understood as an *existentiale*), signifies "to reside alongside . . . ," "to be familiar with . . ." *'Being-in' is thus the formal existential expression for the Being of Dasein, which has Being-in-the-world as its essential state.*[9]

Dasein's way of being-in consists in dwelling or residing, that is, being "alongside" *(bei)* the world as if it were at home there. No wonder that Heidegger considers such residing to contain echoes of taking care (as in *colo:* "I take care") and cherishing (as in *diligo:* "I cherish").[10] Each of these expressions bears on place, especially on home-place, conjuring up a dense and suggestive sense of implacement as in-dwelling on which Heidegger will elaborate in later writings.

In *Being and Time,* however, Heidegger draws back from this early honorific assessment of dwelling by remarking that, despite the existential promise of residing alongside the world caringly, "Dasein's facticity is such that its Being-in-the-world has always dispersed itself or even split itself up into definite ways of Being-in."[11] "Dispersed" (*zerstreut*) is a strong word; it can also mean "distracted," "dissipated," or "driven away"; echoes of "destruction" (*Zerstörung*) are not far away. Heidegger's point is that Dasein is ineluctably drawn into the sticky morass of "concern" (*Besorgen*), especially its degraded modes. As a result, Dasein's "existential spatiality" is, from the beginning, a distracted involvement in the affairs of the everyday world.[12] In recognition of this concernful absorption, Heidegger proceeds to an analysis of place (and region) that has little to do with caring and cherishing and everything to do with instrumental values—in effect picking up where John Locke left off in 1690. But Heidegger's approach is not merely reductive: it eschews, for example, Locke's emphasis on the relativity of position as essential to place. In fact, Heidegger gives a nuanced account of what we might call the *practicality of place,* its intimate infrastructure as experienced by those who spend their workaday lives there. As such, Heidegger's assessment points to place in its middle course: neither sheer location in world-space nor dwelling in depth, but place-as-pragmatic—as the realm of worked-on things.

Place-as-pragmatic is treated in the third chapter of division 1 ("Preparatory Fundamental Analysis of Dasein") of *Being and Time.* The first part of this chapter ("The Worldhood of the World") is entitled "Analysis of Environmentality and Worldhood in General" and describes Dasein's complex "dealings" (*Umgang*) with "ready-to-hand" (*zuhanden*) entities that make up the world of work as constituted by basic instrumental actions, signs and references, and involvement and significance. It is a matter of "dealings *in* the world and *with* entities within-the-world."[13] The result of such dealings is that Dasein understands the world, albeit prethematically, as the vast *wherein (das*

Worin) of its multiple practical activities—a wherein with which Dasein always finds itself "primordially familiar."[14] The "wherein" is a matrix of instrumental involvements structured by such pragmatic relations as the "in-which," the "in-order-to," and the supervalent "for-the-sake-of-which" through which Dasein lets ready-to-hand entities be involved in a context of significance. All of these relations come together in the where*in*—an "in" that yields the "where" of familiarity and orientation and that makes up the worldhood of the practical world in which Dasein finds and assigns itself.[15]

Not surprisingly, Heidegger claims that the Cartesian conception of the world as *res extensa* fails to account for any such *Worin,* including its pragmatic structures. Why is this so? Not because Descartes has no notion of place or space (we know that he has both, in fact) but because place and space, like everything else in the Cartesian world-picture, are posited exclusively as present-at-hand. Descartes's equation of matter with space amounts to identifying strictly extended substance with volumetric space, with the result that no empty room is left—certainly no room for a void, but also no room for the "leeway" (*Spielraum*) that Heidegger finds essential to concernful being-in-the-world.[16] Just as Aristotle's model of place is limited by its tightness of fit, so Descartes's model of place and space is such that matter is contained so tightly that the world cannot "come before us" as "authentically ready-to-hand."[17] Both models err by restricting the Being of the world to the present-at-hand, which is the leading instance of that purely categorial "determinate presence" (*Anwesenheit*) from which, on Heidegger's reading, Western philosophy has suffered since at least Plato.[18]

To escape Aristotle as well as Descartes, Heidegger proposes in the next part that we think of human implacement quite differently, that is, in terms of "The Aroundness of the Environment and Dasein's Spatiality"—where "aroundness" (*das Umhafte*) and "environment" (*Umwelt*) seem slyly to allude, via the prefix *um-* (i.e., "around"), to Aristotle's surrounder (*periechon*).[19] But what a different kind of surrounding! In the first of three sections of this crucial part, Heidegger seizes on "closeness" (*die Nähe*) as the most salient characteristic of the spatiality of the ready-to-hand in its familiarity. "Every entity that is 'to hand,' " Heidegger announces, "has a different closeness, which is not to be ascertained by measuring distances."[20] Where Locke had insisted precisely on "distance" in his discussion of place, Heidegger sees closeness as determined by two nonmetric matters: Dasein's "circumspective concern" (*umsichtiges Besorgen*) and its "directionality" (*Ausrichtung*). Circumspective concern takes account of what is happening in the immediate environs of the ready-to-hand—in what Husserl would have called the "near-sphere"—while directionality provides orientation to what lies within this close arena: for example, it locates equipment somewhere in particular. Heidegger expressly rejects the idea that this "belonging somewhere"

(*Hingehörigkeit*) is a question of bare "position" (*Stelle*). Instead, when closeness is realized by the conjoining of circumspective concern with directionality, *place results.*

> Equipment has its *place* (*Platz*), or else it "lies around"; this must be distin-
> guished in principle from just occurring at random in some spatial position.
> When equipment for something or other has its place, this place defines itself as
> the place of this equipment—as one place out of a whole totality of places
> (*Platzganzheit*) directionally lined up with each other and belonging to the con-
> text of equipment that is environmentally ready-to-hand. Such a place and such
> a multiplicity of places are not to be interpreted as the "where" of some random
> Being-present-at-hand of Things.[21]

To be *somewhere*—and not just to be simply located at a pinpointed position
in world-space—is to be in some particular place, with its own distinctive
"there" (*Da*) and "yonder" (*Dort*) specifying its directedness. Place, then, is
indispensable as the basis for the locatedness of the ready-to-hand.

But place in turn is unthinkable apart from *region.* In making this move,
Heidegger revisits a sequence we have observed in the case of Kant: position—place—region. As in Kant, region assumes a certain primacy in relation
to place. (Only, however, a *certain* primacy; in the end, we shall see how for
Heidegger place and region are of coordinate significance.) But while for Kant
a region's distinction is merely that it is more encompassing than a given
place—hence Kant's stress on "cosmic regions"—according to Heidegger a
region offers more than increased room. It provides the very condition of
possibility for the implacement of the ready-to-hand. This means that a given
instrument is located in relation to an ultimate "whither" (*das Wohin*) that
gives to a region its own *whereabouts*—as *Gegend,* the word Heidegger uses
for "region," can also be translated. For the appropriate whither includes factors of practical purpose (i.e., the "for-the-sake-of which"), movement (i.e., in
terms of "hither" and "thither"), range (*Umkreis*), and the totality of a given
group of places.[22] Even more significant, a region affords the aroundness
primarily at stake in Dasein's spatiality: "The regional orientation of the multiplicity of places belonging to the ready-to-hand goes to make up the
aroundness—the 'round-about-us' (*das Um-uns-herum*)—of those entities
which we encounter as closest environmentally."[23] The paradox is that this
regional surroundingness, in which we are always already immersed by virtue
of a prior involvement, is usually unremarked by the human subject, since it
shares the character of "inconspicuous familiarity" possessed by so many
ready-to-hand things: just as we become aware of these latter mainly at moments of breakdown, so we gain consciousness of a region primarily when we
cannot find something in its usual place.[24] More generally, it is by means of
places that we are aware of a region, leading Heidegger to claim that regions
"always are ready-to-hand already *in individual places.*"[25] Even though re-

gion is the broader and more encompassing term, a given region is available primarily through the places it harbors—places that act thus as its "indicators" (*Anzeigen*). Such indication contains an element of exhibition. Heidegger's most convincing example is that of the rooms of a house: by their placement in the house, they and their arrangement indicate—betoken and display—the "sunny side" and "shady side" of the house, that is, two of its most important regions.[26]

To illustrate this immanent regionality of Dasein, Heidegger proceeds to discuss right and left as "directions of orientation" (*Richtungen*). Dasein does not project such directions onto a neutral and undirected ground, that is, a featureless "space." The world presents itself as already oriented in various specific ways that link up with Dasein's own basic directionality.[27] Heidegger diverges from Kant at just this point. Citing the example of orienting oneself in a dark room, Heidegger does not implicate the body as an explanatory factor. Instead, "I necessarily orient myself both in and from my being already alongside (*bei*) a world which is 'familiar.'"[28] To be "already alongside a world" is tantamount to having already discovered myself in a region of that world. If Dasein's directionality is "essentially co-determined by being-in-the-world,"[29] this is as much as to say that Dasein is directed both *in* a region and *by* a region—often, though not necessarily, the same region. (I am directed by the same region when I find my way in a darkened room, but by a different region when I am traveling from one set of places to another.)

In the end, orientation is a conjoint production, requiring both familiarity with a region and Dasein's directional powers. As such, it is a paradigm of the delicate balance Heidegger wishes to strike in general between the contribution of the human subject and the pregivenness of its surroundings. The very idea of *being/in-the-world* already points to this balance: only Dasein can *be* somewhere, but where it is, is *in the world,* a world it has not created by its own efforts: a public, shared world.[30] Yet Dasein does make a decisive difference in the way being-in-the-world comes to be shaped. Human beings are responsible for letting things be involved with each other in equipmental groupings, for construing the ready-to-hand in terms of signs that refer, and for understanding the basic "significance" (*Bedeutsamkeit*) possessed by an equipmental context. Yet, by the same token, "to free a totality of involvements is, equiprimordially, to let something be involved *at a region.*"[31] Region, like world, is something Dasein is already *alongside* and finds itself *in* as already there. Just as it is true that "as being-in-the-world, Dasein has already discovered a 'world' at any time,"[32] so Dasein has already found itself in a region. This region is precisely "its own discovered region," and we witness in this very phrase the delicate balance in question. The region is "discovered" and is to this extent given, yet it is discovered as "its own" and is to this degree something for which it is responsible.

The search for an equipoise between what is given and what is shaped is nowhere more evident than in Heidegger's discussion of place and region. At the beginning of section 24, he says the following two distinct things in the course of a single paragraph:

(1) "By a 'region' we have understood the 'whither' to which an equipment-context ready-to-hand might possibly belong, when that context is of such a sort that it can be encountered as directionally de-severed—that is, as having been placed (*platzierter*)."

(2) "*With* anything encountered as ready-to-hand there is always an involvement in (*bei*) a region. To the totality of involvements which makes up the Being of the ready-to-hand within-the-world, there belongs a spatial involvement which has the character of a region. By reason of such an involvement, the ready-to-hand becomes something which we can come across and ascertain as having form and direction."[33]

Statement (1) argues that we could not even "encounter" (*begegnen*) the ready-to-hand as a coherent equipmental context (*Zeug-zusammenhang*) unless that context had been "directionally de-severed" (i.e., made close) by an individual Dasein, whereas statement (2) emphasizes involvement (*Be-wandtnis*) in an already constituted public region in which we "come across" items ready-to-hand. This contrast, far from being a contradiction, is another articulation of the balance to which I have just pointed above. What is remarkable about this new expression of the balance is that *an implicit idealism is now associated with place and an implicit realism with region.* For place is regarded as the result of Dasein's directional de-severing, that is, its oriented bringing-close. This is what is indicated by the past participial phrase "*having been* placed."[34] Place is not something we come across as something we *are simply in;* it is what we precipitate by the conjoint action of directing and de-severing—thus something to which our direct intervention gives rise. There is no place without this intervention.[35]

Region, by contrast, is too massively public to be the mere product of any individual Dasein's constitutive activity; to invoke a later term of Heidegger's: it has too much "gathering" power. Hence it is something that Dasein is already alongside and that provides for ready-to-hand things a matrix of "spatial involvement." It is "*by reason of* (*auf deren Grunde*) such an involvement" that the ready-to-hand "becomes something which we can *come across.*" In later editions of *Being and Time,* Heidegger significantly substituted *vorfindlich* (literally, "as found before") for *erfindlich* ("as discovered," but also "as invented") as the German for what is here translated as "come across"; with this alteration, he stressed the *found* character of the ready-to-hand within a region, a character that contrasts with Dasein's *founding* inventiveness. The involvement provided by a given or found region exceeds what an individual Dasein can itself constitute—as do the "form and direction" possessed by the ready-to-hand things harbored in that same region. Dasein can only "ascertain" these two properties as they are pregiven by the region in question.[36]

In this complex and circuitous way *Being and Time* ascribes to place and region a curious parity. *Places,* even if less in the limelight of Heidegger's analysis than are regions, are essential to being-in-the-world in two ways. On the one hand, ready-to-hand things do not truly *belong somewhere* until they have undergone the implacement that an individual Dasein's directionality and de-severance (*Ent-fernung:* removal-of-distance) bring with them: places are essentially places for such things.[37] On the other hand, as we saw earlier, places are also indispensable to being-in-the-world as the foci of appearance for regions, which present themselves "in individual places." In this capacity, places become the "indicators" of regions even as they are eclipsed by them: we need particular places to guide us into regions and to situate us there. In contrast, *regions* are essential to being-in-the-world as the pregiven publicly shared parts of any environing world. Without their encompassing and dense presence, we would have nothing to de-sever and nothing in which to be directed. Moreover, we would have no "whereabouts" for the very places we have *already* constituted—or any range and sense of aroundness in the environment. There would not even be an equipmental context—thus no basis for "freeing entities for a totality of involvements."[38]

A placeless world would amount to an unremitting realism of regions; a regionless world would entail an unrelieved idealism of places. Without places, being-in-the-world would be merely diffuse and disjointed—overt and public and yet shapeless. Without regions, being-in-the-world would be much more congealed and punctate than it is—and overwhelmingly idiosyncratic, merely a function of the interests of individual Daseins. With both places and regions, being-in-the-world and the world itself become as coherent as they can be and mainly are (even if they remain uncanny in their depths). At the very least, places and regions provide a practicable basis for the everyday demands and relations in which human beings are ineluctably entangled. To recognize them as coeval necessities is essential to understanding what it means to be in a world to begin with.

What, then, about *space*? Are we ready to unveil it at last? Heidegger's final step in "The Aroundness of the Environment and Dasein's Spatiality" is to suggest how space emerges from the complicated composition of places and regions just described. If "position" is the shrunken residue of place, "space" is the belated and dilated legacy of region: it is what region *becomes* in the realm of the present-at-hand.[39] Position and space are at opposite ends of the spectrum of present-at-hand interpretations of Dasein's spatiality, but precisely for this reason they are inextricably conjoined: space is "the pure 'wherein' (*Worin*) in which positions are ordered by measurement and the

situations of things are determined."[40] But Heidegger's interest is less in space
as a fully determinate end product of *vorhanden* thinking than in the ontological genealogy of space: how it arises in Dasein's world.

Space does not derive directly from place. Particular places (and there are
only particular places) obscure space: they are too condensed and focused,
and have too little aroundness or range, to embrace space. Regarding regions,
however, we have "that on the basis of which space is discovered beforehand
in Dasein."[41] In part, the ground for this discovery of space is found in the
involvement we have seen to be essential to the constitution of a region—an
involvement with the ready-to-hand that establishes its whereabouts, its
whither. But underlying involvement itself is a basic action so far neglected
in the discussion of region: "making room" (*einräumen*). This is an *existentiale* of Dasein and consists in the various ways in which Dasein arranges and
moves ready-to-hand things so as to create a sense of greater spaciousness:
for example, in arranging furniture or in building a house. Making room in
such ways is equivalent in turn to "giving space" (*Raum-geben*), but it is
crucial to realize that space arises in no direct or immediate fashion from such
room-making. Instead, the basic action of making room is that of "freeing the
ready-to-hand *for its spatiality.*"[42] Space emerges from spatiality for which
room has been made for a totality of involvements, but it does so only inasmuch as regional spatiality itself is inconspicuously present—with the result
that "space itself becomes accessible for cognition."[43] There can be no such
homogeneous medium as space unless room has been made (and thus spatiality opened up) within a given region of the ready-to-hand.

In this way, *room* reenters the history of place—after more than a millennium of neglect. As it did for Plato and the Stoics, Cusanus and Bruno, room
mediates between space and place. Heidegger's contribution to this history is
to make room such a mediatrix expressly by virtue of the ingrediency of region, whose amplitude and dynamism make possible the generation of place
and space alike. For the effect of region is the creation of the very spatiality
(*Räumlichkeit:* literally, "roomliness") from which place is precipitated and
space discerned.

Having set forth this general schema, Heidegger proceeds to draw three
conclusions. First, "space" is not located in the human subject—as Kant
would have us believe. For this subject is not mental (and thus worldless) but
spatial (hence in-the-world). This means that space is always already *in the
world,* however veiled its presence may be there: if space is indeed a priori, it
has this status only insofar as it inheres in the spatiality of regions.[44] Second,
an entire genealogy of space now becomes possible, one that would begin
with the thematizing of the circumspective spatiality at stake in concrete activities such as surveying and building, proceed to the disinterested looking that
corresponds to the present-at-hand and that finds expression precisely in
Kant's model of space as a form of intuition, and end in the construction

and contemplation of a sheerly homogeneous space (including its geometrical representation in *analysis situs*).[45] What matters here is not the correctness of the sequence—which Heidegger himself amends elsewhere[46]—but the general thesis that pure space is a belated by-product of a long evolutionary-epistemological history whose starting point is every Dasein's primordial implacement in a circumspectively available regionality. Third, the last stage of this history of space brings its own stark consequences: the three-dimensionality of space arises from the present-at-hand neutralization of the spatiality of the ready-to-hand; places are reduced to bare positions; and the world, losing its environing character (i.e., its own "worldliness"), becomes Nature.[47]

Despite these strong contentions, Heidegger feels compelled to add that "space in itself, so far as it embraces the sheer possibilities of the pure spatial Being of something, remains proximally still concealed."[48] Here Heidegger issues a promissory note on which he will manage to make good only in the late essay, "Time and Being" (1962):

> The interpretation of the Being of space has hitherto been a matter of perplexity, not so much because we have been insufficiently acquainted with the content of space itself as a thing, as because the possibilities of Being in general have not been in principle transparent, and an interpretation of them in terms of ontological concepts has been lacking. If we are to understand the ontological problem of space, it is of decisive importance that the question of Being must be liberated from the narrowness of those concepts of Being which merely chance to be available and which are for the most part rather rough; and the problematic of the Being of space (with regard to that phenomenon itself and various phenomenal spatialities) must be turned in such a direction as to clarify the possibilities of Being in general.[49]

This pronouncement does not merely open up a vista of future work to be done. It also amounts, albeit unintentionally, to a self-critique. For it is Heidegger himself who has confined space—and place and region as well—to "narrow" and "rather rough" concepts of Being, that is, *Zuhandensein* and *Vorhandensein*. Moreover, he has analyzed all three phenomena entirely in terms of the actualities of the everyday world (plus the theoretical world in the case of the present-at-hand). This leaves us wondering if these phenomena are adequately conceived as ready-to-hand or present-at-hand—or even as based in human being at all. Heidegger says significantly that space itself "need not have the kind of Being characteristic of something which is itself spatially ready-to-hand or present-at-hand."[50] But if *space* has other possible kinds of Being, why not also region and place? For example, place and region could be seen as deeply pertinent to such basic phenomena of Being-in as falling and thrownness, state of mind and understanding. These latter components of the "existential constitution of the 'there,' " none of which is ready-to-hand or present-at-hand, all call for a placial and regional analysis—as do also the constituents of Being-with and Being-one's-Self. Such an analysis would expand the meaningful range of place and region. Short of this, the dogmatic restriction of *Platz* and *Gegend* to the instrumental world and of *Raum* to the scientific world closes down on their full scope within the existential analytic of Dasein.

This is not to deny the invaluable contribution made by *Being and Time* to an understanding of place and region from the standpoint of Dasein's engagement in "instrumental complexes" (in Sartre's term). No one else, not even Locke, has given a comparably nuanced account of what terms such as "place" and "region" mean in the context of the everyday practical world. Yet even if this is Dasein's primary world, it is not the only world in which human beings engage, as Heidegger himself is aware. In section 12 of *Being and Time* he points to possibilities of dwelling that are not merely instrumental in character. The later analysis of the uncanny continues to explore the home-world and its loss in the form of Dasein's ineluctable being "not-at-home" (*un-heim-lich*) in the world.[51] For the uncanny is not only *nothing* (nothing substantial in the manner of the *zuhanden* or *vorhanden*) but *nowhere:* it represents the radical absence of *any* particular place or region, indeed even a definite "here" or "yonder."[52] Anxious at the prospect of such atopia, Dasein "turns thither towards entities within-the-world by absorbing itself in them."[53] But in this defensive and reactive flight from the nowhere and the nothing Dasein is ultimately fleeing not anxiety or the uncanny as such but that which grounds both: namely, the *world* (and thus its own being-in-the-world).[54]

More is at stake here than an alternative, noninstrumental sense of the world. Anxiety is an ontological, not a psychological, state and hence "discloses, primordially and directly, the world as world."[55] The world *as world* is something Dasein evades systematically not just because the world is located nowhere in particular and is ontically unsolid but more especially because it is an abyss of possibilities that threatens Dasein's self-certainties: "Anxiety discloses Dasein *as being-possible.*"[56]

Could it be that when Heidegger posed to himself the question, "Might space have been determined otherwise?" he experienced angst of a distinctly philosophical sort? For he then had to confront the immensely threatening possibilities opened up by "the ontological problem of space." Anxious at these possibilities—which exceed any "narrow" or "rough" categories—was he not moved to flee into his own analysis of the familiar embrace of the ready-to-hand and the present-at-hand? In short, did he not shrink back from the uncanny vision of radically *other* possible modes of space?

This direction of interpretation seems supported by several symptomatic statements in the text itself of *Being and Time.* First, in the long passage just cited above Heidegger refers to the fact that "the possibilities of Being in general have not been in principle transparent." To explore these basic ontological possibilities is to entertain *new* possibilities of being spatial: possibilities that transcend, and thus threaten, the delimited possibilities at stake in practical and theoretical contexts. Second, Heidegger says expressly (in the final paragraph of section 24) that "unless we go back to the world, space cannot be conceived" and that "spatiality is not discoverable at all except on the basis of the world."[57] For space belongs properly *to the world,* just as spatiality belongs to *being-in-the-world.* But the world is precisely that which makes us anxious if we face it *as world*—and all the more anxious if we experience it as the source of indefinite possibilities for our being-in-the-world. As if to reinforce the likelihood of the anxiety that would ensue if one were to pursue "the problematic of the Being of space," Heidegger adds that "space becomes accessible only if the environment is deprived of its worldhood."[58] But to deprive the environment—the reliable *Umwelt*—of its worldhood is to deprive it of the inhabitational bedrock on which Dasein counts as a creature who cares, cherishes, and dwells.[59]

The bedrock hangs over an abyss of sheer possibilities of space—and of space as pure possibility, indeed of the very possibility of pure space. No wonder, dangling thus, Dasein feels intensely anxious and not-at-home, and flees into the comforting and tranquilizing embrace of everyday dealings and gossipy talk as well as the reflective reassurances of sheer theory. Yet what is glimpsed in the moment of anxiety, Dasein's abyssal *Unheimlichkeit,* remains "the more primordial phenomenon."[60]

"Anxiety," Heidegger adds in an aside, "can arise in the most innocuous situations."[61] Has it perhaps arisen in the innocuous situation of speculating about space as something to be understood on the ground of new possibilities of Being? Has Heidegger glimpsed these possibilities and shrunken back from the anxiety they occasion? Has he fled in the face of the ontologically uncanny—the not-at-home of sheer possibility—into the arms of the actual at-home of the instrumental and theoretical realms? Does not his stress on familiarity, as well as on closeness and involvement, directionality and de-severance, and even on exact observation, bespeak a "turn thither" toward the canny, the known, the palpable, and the predictable? Is this not what is signi-fied by the confinement of place and region to the ready-to-hand and of space to the present-at-hand?

Only once does Heidegger explicitly relate the notion of the uncanny to his own earlier analysis of Dasein's spatiality. Discussing the "nowhere" that is the antithesis of the "belonging somewhere" that obtains for items placed in regions, he says revealingly: " 'Nowhere', however, does not signify nothing: *this is where any region lies,* and there too lies any disclosedness of the world for essentially spatial Being-in."[62] This is a most remarkable admission. A region, the quintessence of locatory reliability and of ontic security, is *itself located nowhere.* A trap door to the void suddenly springs open—in the very middle of the proscenium of the properly situated. Heidegger cannot close the door he has opened himself. "That which threatens cannot bring itself close from a definite direction within what is close by; it is already 'there', and yet nowhere; it is so close that it is oppressive and stifles one's breath, and yet it is nowhere."[63] The ontological emptiness under an ontically reassuring region is too close for comfort. As a result, *Being and Time* moves into retreat. Regions return to their proper stations, and places to their own regions. The drama continues as if the door to the demonic underworld had never sprung open.

II

> With Dasein's spatiality, existential-temporal
> analysis seems to come to a limit.
> —*Being and Time,* section 70

The drama of *Being and Time* is finally the melodrama of time's triumph. Very soon after he treats anxiety, Heidegger retreats from any further serious consideration of space, region, and place. Division 2, "Dasein and Temporality," occupies, both in fact and in substance, the remainder of the published text. In this section of the book, Heidegger argues that Dasein's potentialities for being-a-whole and its being-toward-death are most fully realized in the anticipatory resoluteness whose adequate analysis is exclusively temporal. Temporality is proclaimed to provide "the meaning of authentic care,"[64] and the entire existential analytic of Dasein is repeated with a view to the primacy of temporality. This primacy is such that it rules over the instrumental and theoretical worlds—and, most significant for us, over the spatiality of Dasein.

Thus we reach section 70 of *Being and Time,* a section boldly entitled "The Temporality of the Spatiality that Is Characteristic of Dasein." Intrinsic to the hegemony of temporality is its ability to account for spatiality—to "embrace" it by existentially "founding" it.[65] To talk of embracing and founding spatiality is to make a final effort to attain ontological reassurance in the face of the anxiety occasioned by the radical possibilities of space, as well as by the existential demands of place and region. But does Heidegger succeed in this concerted attempt to subject spatiality to temporality? I think not—and Heidegger himself, on further reflection, thought not. In his late essay "Time and Being," he makes a rare gesture of retraction, as brief as it is definitive: "The attempt in *Being and Time,* section 70, to derive human spatiality from temporality is untenable."[66] Yet Heidegger does not tell us how this untenability occurs.

The attempted derivation is at once too dogmatic and too loosely reasoned to be tenable. For example, Heidegger announces sternly that "Dasein's specific spatiality must be grounded in temporality"[67]—yet never demonstrates any grounds for this "must" other than his own temporocentrist preoccupation.

Archytas argued coherently, if compactly, for his claim that "one has to grant priority to place."[68] Heidegger provides no argument whatsoever for an equally imperialist claim. Instead, he merely repeats the primary thesis of division 2: "Temporality is the meaning of the Being of care."[69] When he adds that "Dasein's constitution and its way to be are possible ontologically only on the basis of temporality,"[70] he does not notice the circularity of this statement: as a creature of care, whose very meaning is temporal in character, Dasein cannot but be founded on temporality. More generally, the possibilities of space (and thus of spatiality as well) that are still at stake at the end of the third chapter of division I cannot be assumed to be dependent on those of time, much less of temporality, without a specific deduction of this dependency. Instead of any such deduction—which Heidegger explicitly refuses to undertake[71]—we are treated to several paragraphs of casual remarks aimed at showing that what had been presented as an entirely spatial matter in sections 22 through 24 has an underlying temporal dynamic. Thus we now read that "the self-directive discovery of a region is grounded in an ecstatically retentive awaiting of the 'hither' and 'thither' that are possible" and that "both bringing-close and the estimating and measurement of distances within that which has been de-severed and is present-at-hand within-the-world, are grounded in a making-present belonging to the unity of that temporality in which directionality too becomes possible."[72] But it is not at all clear what the analysis of the hither and thither gains by being described as "an ecstatically retentive awaiting," much less how these two modes of the regional whither are *grounded* in such temporality. Nor is any comparable grounding in "making-present" evident in the case of bringing-close, de-severing, and directionality: indeed, insofar as place is precipitated by these actions, the "having-been" of the past would seem to be a more appropriate temporal tag.

Heidegger admits in this section that "the function of temporality as the foundation for Dasein's spatiality will be indicated [only] briefly."[73] Nevertheless, unpersuasive analyses of the sort just reported are less revealing of Heidegger's failure to derive spatiality from temporality than is another quite curious feature of this flawed part of the text. This is the fact that the only truly cogent passages are those that add new insights into *spatiality* without any allusion to temporality. It is only in section 70, for example, that we are told that "Dasein *takes space in*."[74] Space is not projected by Dasein, nor is Dasein simply located in space. Instead, Dasein internalizes space and makes something of it. What is made of it is precisely room and leeway. These latter two notions, only sketched in the discussions of division I, are now suggestively embedded in the following observation:

> In existing, [Dasein] has already made room for its own leeway. It determines its own location (*Ort*) in such a manner that it comes back from the space it has made room for to the "place" which it has reserved.[75]

Dasein takes space in only so as to "break into space" more freely.[76] Such an *Einbruch* into space is accomplished by making room for leeway: clearing the space for diverse engagements. From such spatial latitude, Dasein comes back (*zurückkommt*) to place. Not only is Dasein here accorded a place of its own— its own existential *Ort,* rather than a mere ready-to-hand *Platz*—but such a place is seen to entail a more capacious room whose intrinsic leeway, instead of taking us away from place, permits a more decisive insertion into place itself.[77]

Beyond implications for place per se (about which nothing more is said in *Being and Time*), the passage I have just cited delineates a basic movement of Dasein's spatializing that was only implicit in sections 22 through 24: a move-ment *from* a more expansive environment or public world *back to* a more confined corner of this same environment. Rather than room having to be built up by the accretion or summation of smaller spaces, it is the staging arena for more precise and delimited operations in particular places. Heidegger applies this from/back-to schema to region as well as to place: "Out of the region that has been discovered beforehand, concern comes back de-severantly to that which is closest."[78] Here Heidegger supplements his previous emphasis on being already located in a pregiven region with the idea that Dasein's con-cernful dealings always return *from the region of ready-to-hand involvements to the more immediate ambit of its own actions.* The back-to is ultimately back to Dasein.

As a direct consequence, in section 70 Dasein assumes a proportionately larger role in the constitution of place and region than it had antecedently: "To Dasein's *making room for itself* belongs the self-directive discovery of something like a region. . . . Concernful being-in-the-world is directional— *self-directive.*"[79] This is to give to Dasein a more ample constitutive role: as "self-directive" (*sich ausrichtend*), it is responsible not only for the precipita-tion of place but also for the making of room (and its leeway) and for the discovery of region. Dasein is also, as we have just seen, responsible for de-termining its own location and for the taking in of space (and thus as well for breaking into space). All of this reflects Heidegger's increasing absorption in questions of Dasein's authenticity—and thus its temporality (*Zeitlichkeit*), which, despite its ecstatic, outgoing movements, concerns the self (in contrast with *Zeit* and *Temporalität,* both of which bear on what exceeds the confines of Dasein's being-in-the-world). But it also reflects Heidegger's apprecia-tion of the way the human self can make a decisive difference in the experi-ence and fate of spatiality as such, thereby illustrating that "Dasein itself is spatial."[80]

Despite these additions and advances, *Being and Time* exhibits, at the level of explicit intention, an overall effort to delimit Dasein's spatializing powers by subordinating them to the putatively greater dynamics (or, better, ecstatics) of temporality. In performing this subordination, the book embodies a form of flight—a shrinking back before the spatial structures of Dasein, as if these structures occasioned a special philosophical anxiety in Heidegger himself during the period of its composition. Will this philosopher be able to overcome, or at least to suspend, this anxiety in subsequent writings so as to confront the undelimited possibilities of space and spatiality, region and place? Will he be able to turn *toward* these possibilities rather than turn away from them?

III

> In the vicinity (*Nähe*) of the [art] work, we are suddenly somewhere else than we usually tend to be.
> —Martin Heidegger, "The Origin of the Work of Art"

It is a matter of *turning* in any case—of what Heidegger himself designated as "the Turning" (*die Kehre*) that occurred in the years following the publication of *Being and Time*. This turning, I shall argue, is very much a (re)turning to Place and associated notions—as much a turning in their direction as toward Being and Language. The importance of the later notion of "the Clearing" (*die Lichtung*), for example, cannot be grasped without an appreciation of the centrality of place in Heidegger's mature thinking; the Clearing is an open place in which Being or Language (indeed, Being-as-Language) appears. Nor can Heidegger's understanding of building and dwelling, of things, of the fourfold, and of the "topology of Being" be understood without continual allusion to place. But this is to get ahead of the story by several decades.

The idea of the Turning arises in a lecture course of the summer of 1928, "The Metaphysical Foundations of Logic." Here we find the first public mention of *die Kehre,* regarded as an essential turning to "metontology," which treats "beings as a whole" in new ways. One of these ways is a heightened sensitivity to the presence of multiplicity—in beings, in Being, and in Dasein. "Multiplicity belongs to Being itself," we are told, and "the intrinsic possibility of multiplication ... is present in every Dasein."[81] Where in *Being and Time* the emphasis had been on being-in-the-world as a "unitary phenomenon"—unitary thanks to being-in as dwelling, the care-structure, and above all temporality—and Dasein's "dispersion" was regarded as a "deficient mode," in the lecture course of 1928 (his last given while at the University of Marburg) Heidegger places the stress on a radical "dissemination" that is the reflection of Dasein's essential multiplicity of modes of being-in-the-world: "In its metaphysically neutral concept, Dasein's essence already contains a primordial *bestrewal* (*Streuung*), which is in a quite definite respect a *dissemination* (*Zerstreuung*)."[82] No longer is it only a matter of Dasein's having "always dispersed itself or even split itself up into definite ways of Being-in," it is one of an *in*definite number of ways of being lost in the world, deeply and even permanently distracted there.

In *The Metaphysical Foundations of Logic,* Heidegger proceeds to sketch a number of these forms of ineluctable lostness: for example, turning away from beckoning beings so as to turn to still others, historicity (in which Dasein "stretches itself along" in time), and being-with-one-another. But the most arresting instances of Dasein's dissemination are three others: "being dispersed in a body," "being disunited in a particular sexuality," and "factical dissemination [in] spatiality."[83] This triad of disseminated terms is striking: body, sexuality, spatiality. Of these, *body*—which we know to be systematically ignored in *Being and Time*—is regarded as the most important. For "embodiment" is said to be an "organizing factor" for *all* of Dasein's multiplicity, including sexuality and spatiality.[84] This is easiest to see in the case of sexuality, where the human body organizes and performs sexual differences: hence Heidegger's use of *Zwiespältig,* literally "two-fold." But he leaves unexplored the relation between embodiment and spatiality—the very relation we have seen to be of such crucial significance for Kant and Whitehead, Husserl and Merleau-Ponty. One hint, however, bears on this relation: "The transcendental dissemination proper to the metaphysical essence of neutral Dasein, as the binding possibility of each factical existential dispersion and division, is based on a primordial feature of Dasein, that of *thrownness.*"[85] To be thrown into the world is to be placed there *in* a body and *by* a body. How else could we experience the adversity and shock of thrownness except in bodily terms—terms that are in turn the basis for the "moods" that arise from the same action? Moreover, the thrownness is *into* the world, and precisely into the world as a scene of the multiple: "This thrown dissemination *into a multiplicity* is to be understood metaphysically."[86] How else can such a multiplicity—which, adds Heidegger, is the presupposition for Dasein to let itself "be governed by beings which it is not"[87]—exist but in *spatial* terms? If the transcendental condition of dissemination is bodily thrownness, the transcendental condition of multiplicity is spatiality. For only in the spread-outness of spatiality can Dasein disseminate itself into the multiplicity of "beings which it is not." The manyness and otherness of these beings—their being outside Dasein and their being next to each other—require a laid-out spatiality that answers to, even as it connects deeply with, the bestrewed bodiliness of Dasein.[88]

A "Supplement" that was not read during the lecture course of 1928 adds one further thought—a thought that looks far ahead into the later depths of the Turning.

The human being is a creature of distance! And only by way of the real primordial distance that the human in his transcendence establishes toward all beings does the true nearness to things begin to grow in him. And only the capacity to hear into the distance summons forth the awakening of the answer of those humans who should be near.[89]

Evident in this statement is the conviction that both distance (*Ferne*) and near-ness (*Nähe*)—confined to a categorial status in *Being and Time*—call for a very different understanding that exceeds the circumspective concern of Da-sein. For the nearness and distance now at stake are not matters of measure-ment, or even of the concrete action of bringing-close. They concern "all beings" and "things" that surpass the practical as well as the theoretical realm and can be reached only by a radical "transcendence" that overcomes, how-ever imperfectly and momentarily, Dasein's scatteredness. One suspects that Heidegger has here begun to unveil two of the neglected possibilities of space to which he had pointed so fleetingly at the end of section 24 of *Being and Time:* space, too, is radically multiple.

Heidegger suspends his pursuit of space and spatiality until 1935, when these topics (including place) return with a vengeance. They return in two texts, one of which is highly conflicted vis-à-vis these same topics and the other warmly welcoming, both testifying to Heidegger's still unresolved am-bivalence toward matters spatial.

The first text is the lecture course, "An Introduction to Metaphysics," deliv-ered at the University of Freiburg in the summer of 1935. So far as matters of space and place are concerned, there are clearly two strains in this text as it was finally published in 1953. The first of these gives to Dasein a distinctive place of its own.

> Dasein should be understood, within the question of Being, as *the* place (*Stätte*) which Being requires in order to disclose itself. Dasein is the place of openness, the there. . . . Hence we say that Dasein's being is in the strict sense of the word "being-there" (*Da-sein*). The perspective for the opening of Being must be grounded originally in the essence of being-there as such a place for the disclosure of Being.[90]

Here Heidegger—belatedly—underlines the placial significance of his coin-age, "Dasein." The priority accorded to the "yonder" over the "here" in *Being and Time* is transformed into the general thesis that Dasein, as a creature who continually transcends itself, is always already there in the very place it stakes out. But an important shift of emphasis has occurred since the text of 1927: there, we discerned a basic movement back from the open room or leeway provided by regions to place; now, the action is *from* Dasein *into* the open place of its "there." In both cases, however, Dasein is in its own place, whether we say that it "determines its own location" or that it is "the place of open-ness" itself. To be Dasein is to be there-in-its-place. Reinforcing this line of thought is Heidegger's claim that the there-place, as we might call this new sense of place qua *Stätte,* is most characteristically a *polis.* Rejecting the usual translation of this term as "city-state," Heidegger insists that *polis* in its proper meaning is "the place, the there, wherein and as which historical being-there is. The *polis* is the historical place (*Geschichtsstätte*), the there *in* which, *out* of which, and *for* which history happens."[91] Indeed, every significant place is a "place and scene of history," whether it is occupied by priests, poets, thinkers, elders, or the military.[92] Each of these types of figure sees to it that the "world-building" that is "history in the authentic sense"[93] goes on in the *polis,* and each does so only insofar as *limits* are respected—limits that do not confine but allow for the most effective building-up of world within the place of the *polis.*

> What thus comes up and becomes intrinsically stable (*ständig*) encounters, freely and spontaneously, the necessity of its limit, *peras.* This limit is not something that comes to beings from outside. Still less is it a deficiency in the sense of a harmful restriction. No, the hold that governs itself from out of the limit, the having-itself, wherein the enduring holds itself, is the Being of beings; it is what first makes a being into a being as differentiated from a non-being. . . . Limit and end are that wherewith a being begins to *be.*[94]

As Heidegger will say fifteen years later, the limit is "not that at which something stops but, as the Greeks recognized, that from which something *begins its presencing.*"[95] For Heidegger, the limit (*Grenze*) is not the present-at-hand perimeter of Aristotle's surrounder; nor is it anything merely ready-to-hand such as the wall of a workshop.[96] Within a limit, room is made—and thus place. To lack limit is to lack place, and conversely: not to be in place is to be unlimited. A limit is a positive power within which place is made. Invoking Aristotle against himself, we may say that if place "has some power," this is due in large measure to its very limit. The estate of place, its *real* estate, is a power of the limit, and is realized in the *polis* as "the place of history" by the actions of poets and statesmen, warriors and priests, activists and thinkers.[97]

This is a promising direction of thought, but it comes paired with a second direction that acts to undermine it both from without and from within. *From without:* not the delimited *polis* but the undelimited *geo-polis* menaces at the margins of *An Introduction to Metaphysics.* I refer to a notorious passage in which Germany is depicted as "situated in the center"—the geographic center between America and Russia, both of which exhibit "the same dreary technological frenzy, the same unrestricted organization of the average person."[98] "Caught in a pincers," Germany is "the nation with the most neighbors and hence the most endangered."[99] As "the most metaphysical of nations," Germany has a duty to "move itself and thereby the history of the West beyond the center of their future 'happening' and into the primordial realm of the powers of Being. If the great decision regarding Europe is not to bring annihilation, that decision must be made in terms of new spiritual energies unfolding

historically from out of the center."[100] Here the literalizing of place into geopolitical position occurs without hesitation, as does the evocation of the
"metaphysical" and the "spiritual" with which such literalizing is closely allied.[101] The *polis* as the power-place of bounded actions has become the un-
bound space of geopolitical, metaphysical, and spiritual powers. In this latter
space, the specter of Nazism looms unmistakably large: room, all too much
room, has been cleared for Hitler's burgeoning effort to reterritorialize
Europe.

From within: returning to the theme of *das Unheimliche* in 1935, Heidegger
now finds in the not-at-home something other than the nowhere and the nothing that are the sources of ontological anxiety. Commenting on Sophocles's
line that "there is much that is strange, but nothing that surpasses man in
strangeness," Heidegger links the strange with the uncanny—the latter construed as what "casts us out of the 'homely', i.e., the customary, familiar,
secure."[102] Heidegger adds this telling remark:

> Man is the strangest of all, not only because he passes his life amid the strange
> . . . but because he departs from his customary, familiar limits, because he is the
> violent one, who, tending toward the strange in the sense of the overpowering,
> surpasses the limit of the familiar (*das Heimische*).[103]

Far from being a matter of critique or regret, the violence of human beings is
seen as symptomatic of adventuresome, creative action: "The violent one, the
creative man, who sets forth into the un-said, who breaks into the un-thought,
compels the unhappened to happen and makes the unseen appear—this violent
one stands at all times in venture."[104] A barely veiled allusion to Hitler (or
perhaps to Heidegger himself), these words signify that the violence of the
creative person involves the breaking of boundaries: such a person "departs
from his customary, familiar limits" and "surpasses the limit of the familiar."
But if that is the case, this person also breaks with place—breaks away from
place and breaks place itself. This is tantamount to leaving the *polis* and to
destroying it as a "place of history." Heidegger does not hesitate to draw this
consequence, contrary as it is to his earlier praise of the place of the *polis* as
a scene of constructive activity.

> [There is something] political, i.e., at the place of history, provided there be (for
> example) poets *alone,* but then really poets, priests *alone,* but then really priests,
> rulers *alone,* but then really rulers. *Be,* but this means: as violent men to use
> power, to become pre-eminent in historical being as creators, as men of action.
> Pre-eminent in the historical place, they become at the same time *apolis,* without
> city and place, lonely, strange *(unheimliche),* without issue amid beings as a
> whole, at the same time without statute and limit, without structure and order,
> because they themselves *as* creators must first create all this.[105]

This is a self-deconstructing passage indeed, since it claims both that the creative-violent ones are "pre-eminent *in* the historical place"—that is, the *polis*—*and* that, as "without statute and limit," the same figures are *apolis,* without effective implacement in history. The creative action undoes its own basis: the limit. By becoming undelimited, it ceases to have a place in which to *be* creative. It is revealing that in this very context, Heidegger reinvokes dispersion, now in a *third* sense: a matter neither of regrettable distraction nor of Dasein's disseminative multiplicity, *Zerstreuung* is now a predictable and acceptable consequence of being a violent creator.

> In venturing to master Being, [the violent one] must risk the assault of non-being, *mē kalon,* he must risk dispersion, instability, disorder, mischief. The higher the summit of historical Dasein, the deeper will be the abyss, the more abrupt the fall into the unhistorical, which merely thrashes around in issueless and placeless confusion.[106]

This passage, too, is autodeconstructive. For the violent one is not only dispersed in attaining the heights of "historical Dasein" but someone who in scaling these same heights falls into the "unhistorical" and flails about in "issueless and placeless confusion." Heidegger has just said expressly that the creator is "without issue" (*ohne Ausweg*), and he has also just argued that to be creative is to fall outside the *polis* and thus outside place and history alike. To be "issueless and placeless" is not only a *risk* of being creative; it is an outcome of it that undermines, "disperses," creative action—which needs both place and limit, indeed, place-as-limit. Inspired by his allegiance to a Nazi ideology of violence, Heidegger himself, the creative thinker, has here fallen into the "confusion" he condemns.

An Introduction to Metaphysics, despite its tame title, shows itself to be a mare's nest of conflicted thinking; the essay thinks against itself. It is revealing not just of Heidegger's ambivalent attitude toward contemporary politics (its infamous elided passage, praising Nazism, is only the most egregious symptom of this attitude) but of his equally complicated posture toward place. Ultimately, the two are conjoined: they are *one* con-fusion. For it begins to be evident that Heidegger's simultaneous draw to and repulsion from Hitler has everything to do with his skewed and self-dismantling pronouncements about place.[107] The political here determines both place and *polis*. Indeed, the priority of the political is what is mainly operative in the second strand of thought in this polemical and tortured text—a strand that, deconstructing itself from within as well as discrediting itself from without, acts to shadow, and perhaps even to undo, the constructive and promising work of the first strand (i.e., that which weaves together place and *polis*). In the end, the two strands act against each other; cross-stitched into the text, they unravel it as a whole, turning a putatively seamless work into an unseamly document.

The theme of "conflict" and especially of *polemos* as "original struggle" (*ursprünglicher Kampf*) is present throughout *Einführung in der Metaphysik*.[108] The same theme carries over into another text of 1935, "The Origin of the Work of Art," delivered as an invited lecture in Freiburg in the fall of that same year. This time, however, Heidegger manages to weave a much more coherent fabric out of oppositional threads and to present a view of place at once novel and self-sustaining. For place is now the scene of conflict between earth and world in the work of art—and of the delicate resolution of this conflict.

Why, to begin with, is place sought in the work of art? Is this not a most unlikely setting? What could be more peaceable—less conflictual—than art? Nietzsche said that "we possess *art* lest we perish *of the truth.*"[109] But Heidegger considers truth to reside in art—and precisely in a "primal conflict" (*Urstreit*) that has little, if anything, to do with pleasure or peace: "Truth is the primal conflict in which, always in some particular way, the Open is won."[110] The Open (*das Offene*) is the polemical arena, "the space of conflict" (*Streitraum*), between actions of clearing and concealing. Truth is conceived as the openness of the Open, and its emergence from untruth brings with it "the leeway of openness" (*die Spielraum der der Offenheit*). Such leeway makes possible the institution of places, which arise *within* its cleared ambience: "Only the openness of beings," says Heidegger, "first affords the possibility of a somewhere (*Irgendwo*) and a place (*Stätte*) filled by present beings."[111]

For Heidegger, the primary question to ask about art is not "what is it?" but "where does a work [of art] belong?"[112] The what-is question—the *ti esti* of Aristotle—leads to a false essentialism, to mere definitions and formal features. The question as to *where* leads us straight to the work of art itself: to where it exists as a scene of primal conflict and unconcealment. Such a scene embodies the leeway of openness, taken as tantamount to "the lighting-clearing of the There" (*die Lichtung des Da*).[113] The There now at issue is no longer that of Dasein alone as being-there; it belongs primarily to the work of art as something that *stands there*—that takes its stand somewhere, in a particular place. The work's where-being consists in its there-standing. An exemplary case of such *Dastehen* is a Greek temple, which "simply stands there in the middle of [its] rock-cleft valley."[114] It stands there in its truth: "Truth happens in the temple's standing where it is (*im Dastehen*)."[115] But how does truth happen there, in that there-place?

It happens in a more concrete conflict than that between clearing and concealing—the *Urstreit* of truth proper. The conflict at stake in the work's whereness is that between earth and world: "The temple-work, standing there, opens up a world and at the same time sets this world back again on earth, which itself only thus emerges as native ground."[116] The place of the work—not to be confused with a workplace (that way lies craft, not art)—is a scene of struggle between two dimensions or levels, a struggle unremitting and unirenic: "World and earth are always intrinsically and essentially in conflict, belligerent by nature."[117] The conflictual (*streitig*) character of the earth/world relation stems from the deep differences between earth and world themselves—differences that have their own placial and spatial determinations. Thus "world" is characterized by expansiveness (*Weite*) and by the "broad paths" (*weiten Bahnen*) of an entire people and their destiny. The work "sets up" (*aufstellt*) the world in and as the Open, and it does so by *making room for spaciousness.*

> By the opening of a world, all things gain their lingering and hastening, their remoteness and nearness, their scope and limits. In a world's worlding is gathered that spaciousness (*Geräumigkeit*) out of which the protective grace of the gods is granted or withheld. . . . A work, by being a work, makes room for that spaciousness. "To make room for" (*einräumen*) means here especially to liberate the Open and to establish it in its structure. . . . The work as work sets up a world. The work holds open the Open of the world.[118]

The action of *einräumen*—a word we have met before—reappears as the basis for the spaciousness of world, its "roominess" (i.e., the literal sense of *Geräumigkeit*). Only *from within* this capacious openness can the more particular spatial modalities of near and far and the temporal modalities of hastening and lingering arise—and not the other way around (as in the ready-to-hand *Platz,* for which Dasein's bringing-close is the primary operation). It is as if the world of the work *clears the way* for the more particular activities instigated by individual human beings.

And the earth? It, too, is characterized in primarily spatial terms. It "juts through" (*durchragt*) the world, and its basic action is that of "setting forth" (*herstellen*): "In setting up a world, the work sets forth the earth."[119] But the forward motion of jutting and setting forth is counterbalanced by an equal but opposite motion of *setting back* (*zurückstellen*)—a setting back of the work into its own materiality that amounts to an action of grounding. Such setting-back in setting-forth results in the earth's self-concealment: "To set forth the earth means to bring it into the Open as the self-secluding."[120] This last point is crucial: even if "the earth is *essentially* self-secluding,"[121] it does not simply withdraw from openness. It comes *into* the Open *as* self-secluding (*sich verschliessende*). In this way, "the work lets the earth be an earth."[122]

The conflict of earth and world is therefore a scene of internecine spatial struggle. The world makes room for a spaciousness that includes the setting-forth of earth in its very self-seclusion. Locked into strife as they are, the two antagonists are also partners. If it were not for world, there would not be sufficient breadth and scope for earth to appear: thanks to the expansiveness of the world, instead of being merely "closed up," the earth comes forth as itself "openly cleared."[123] If it were not for earth, there would not be sufficient reserve and resistance to serve as "native ground" in which world could appear: rather than being free-floating and indecisive, it sets itself up decisively *on* the earth. But intrinsic to the interspatiality of the scene is the fact that the opponents bring each other into their own: self-seclusion is not fully itself, nor is earth truly grounding and sheltering, *until* it arises in the midst of world, and the world displays its broad-rangingness only as profiled against the adversity and constrictedness of earth. Even though there is no full reconciliation in the conflict of earth and world, there is a mutual solicitation of each by the other: "In essential striving (*Streit*) the opponents raise each other into the self-assertion of their natures."[124]

Thanks to this reciprocal influence, the antagonism is not merely polemical, nor is it only violent. In striking contrast to what he maintained in *An Introduction to Metaphysics,* Heidegger now says unequivocally that "earth is that whence the arising brings back and shelters everything that arises *without violation.*"[125] As world is expanding, earth is sheltering. Much as they are agitated, they do not violate each other; within their very strife, they attain repose: "The repose of the work that rests in itself thus has its presencing in the intimacy of striving."[126]

Such repose has a specifically spatial expression, for the intimacy at stake in the work occurs as a "common cleft" (*Umriss*) in which both earth and world participate and in which the otherwise divisive "rift" (*Riss*) between them becomes a bond of connection.[127] Just here place reenters the scene explicitly: "As the earth takes the rift back into itself, the rift is first set forth into the Open and thus *placed,* that is, set, within that which towers up into the Open as self-secluding and sheltering."[128] Further, placement in the common cleft arises in the form of a *figure,* a shape or *Gestalt.* In the artwork, figure is not an intact and preexisting form imposed on bare matter; it is the condensed emblem of the conflict between earth and world—a conflict that reaches repose in a shared fissure. This fissure, fragile and insignificant as it may seem, makes possible not just the figure of the work but the very place where truth resides.

> The strife that is brought into the rift and thus set back into the earth and thus fixed in place is *figure, shape, Gestalt.* Createdness of the work means: truth's being fixed in place in the figure. Figure is the structure in whose shape the rift composes and submits itself. This composed rift is the fitting or joining of the shining of truth. What is here called figure, *Gestalt,* is always to be thought in terms of the particular placing (*Stellen*) and framing or framework (*Ge-Stell*) as which the work occurs when it sets itself up and sets itself forth.[129]

With this conclusive pronouncement, we have come full circle: truth's primal conflict of clearing and concealing in the Open occurs as the belligerency between earth and world in the artwork. The precarious repose ensuing from this struggle is condensed in the common cleavage traced between earth and world. *In* this cleavage, *as* this cleavage, is found the figure that fixes truth in

place—ties it down to a created work's own disclosed openness. The openness
of the Open that is truth itself is realized in the discrete somewhere of an
implaced figure. Where a work of art belongs is found in the same place as
where its truth resides: "in the fixing in place of truth in the figure."[130]

To be "fixed in place" (*festgestellt*) is not to be boundaryless, to bleed
indefinitely into infinite space. Heidegger stresses that the work of art is always framed. To be "*festgestellt*" entails having a "Ge-Stell," a frame or
framework. But the frame of an artwork is tantamount to its boundary: *Ge-
Stell* means "the gathering of the bringing-forth, of the letting-come-forth-
here into the rift-design as bounding outline (*peras*)."[131] But where "limit" in
An Introduction to Metaphysics existed only in order to be trespassed and set
aside, "boundary" (as *Grenze* can also be translated) is acknowledged and
honored as such in "The Origin of the Work of Art." For "the boundary in the
Greek sense [i.e., *peras*] does not block off; rather, being itself brought forth,
it first brings to its radiance what is present."[132] Rather than violation, what
is at stake in the boundary of an artwork is its "radiance" (*Scheinen*): not only
does such radiance underlie the beauty of the work, it is the basis of the
lighting that makes its Open into a clearing (*Lichtung*) for truth. If a work's
boundary "sets free into the unconcealed,"[133] this is due to its radiance, its
uncontainability within arbitrary or confined borders. To be fixed in place in
the work is to be set within a boundary or frame that, far from merely enclosing, opens up by its radiance into the openness of the Open. A work of art
radiates through its boundary by giving "guiding measure" in the case of the
worldhood of the work, and by "setting bounds" in terms of its earthly character.[134]

Where does a work of art belong? Heidegger's answer is "within the realm
that is opened up by itself."[135] This "realm" (*Bereich*) is a complex place. It
is composed of earth and world—taken in their conflict and in their repose. It
is riven by an internal cleavage while exposing itself, standing there, in the
Open. But it is not so open as to be unbounded. The work of art is *bound to
be in place:* place that, though framed, is not a mere position or site. The
place of the work is certainly not a *Stelle* (position), perhaps not even an *Ort*
(location).[136] It is a *Stätte,* with all that this latter term implies of the continuous and settled—even of home. "Home," like "boundary," is revalorized in
the essay of 1935; rather than something to be transcended in the creative
violence that is *apolis,* it is inscribed in the work itself, especially in its earth-
dimension. As "native ground" (*heimatliche Grund*), the earth subtends the
world and provides for it something like a home-place: "Upon the earth and
in it, historical man grounds his dwelling in the world."[137]

With this last statement, we have returned to the theme of dwelling (*Wohnen*) with which Heidegger's first considerations of place began in *Being and
Time*—and around which his very last considerations will circle. This time,
however, the concern with dwelling or residing is not displaced by an analysis

of the instrumental world. For in *Der Ursprung des Kunstwerkes* Heidegger expressly sets the work of art aside from anything merely workly. Not only is the work of art incomprehensible in terms of craft alone, it is not of the order of the ready-to-hand.[138] Instead of using up material in order to attain practical goals, the work allows its material element, its earth, to come into its own; more generally, the work possesses a "self-sufficient presence" lacking in an item of equipment.[139] A work of art may *reveal* what is essential about the *zuhanden*—for example, the "reliability" inherent in peasants' shoes as painted by van Gogh—but it cannot itself be considered as something to employ or manipulate. The focus in *Being and Time* on realms of practical involvement and theoretical assessment gives way in "The Origin of the Work of Art" to an interest in a realm that is neither practical nor theoretical. Nor is it "aesthetic" in any usual sense of the word. It is the realm in which truth happens in the Open—an Open that is nowhere else but "*in* the work."[140] That is to say: *in the place* afforded by the concrete configuration of earth and world.

IV

> We take the region itself as that which comes to meet us.
>
> —Martin Heidegger, "Conversation on a Country Path"

Missing from Heidegger's writings of the 1930s is any significant treatment of *region,* arguably the most important spatial term in *Being and Time.* Given the intimate tie between region and the ready-to-hand in the latter text (to be ready-to-hand is to be located in a region; to be in a region is to be something ready-to-hand), it is perhaps not surprising that there is no room for it in the geopolitical vistas of *An Introduction to Metaphysics* or even in the otherwise receptive Open of "The Origin of the Work of Art." In contrast, place does survive, albeit in the form of *Stätte* instead of *Platz* and thus as no longer dependent on Dasein's de-severing and directing actions. Indeed, *severing* is now very much at stake—the separating inherent in violent action, which repudiates nearness for the sake of distant goals—while *indirection* is more critical than direction: if there is any directedness in the artwork, it stems from truth's need to be manifest and not from the pursuit of Dasein's determinate interests. During the time of Heidegger's Turning, the immanent teleology of equipmental regions—as guided by their absorptive whitherness—is regarded disdainfully as a matter merely of the workplace, of craft and the workaday world, and as such irrelevant to the overarching creative aims of art and politics. No wonder, then, that regions go underground in Heidegger's texts of this crucial middle period.

But the Turning was to take a further twist in the decade after 1935. In a reconstructed trilogue that originally took place in 1944–1945, Heidegger returned to the topic of region—this time, however, without any mention of place. "Conversation on a Country Path" (first published in 1959) conveys a conversation not just between a "Scholar," a "Scientist," and a "Teacher" but, more particularly, between Heidegger and himself: for the primary task is how to think the Open (*das Offene*) in regional terms. The Open, the most encompassing term of analysis in "The Origin of the Work of Art," is encompassed in turn by the very notion notably neglected in that epochal essay. Early in the conversation, the delimited model of horizon—at work in all representational thinking of objects as merely set over against us (*Gegen/stände*)—is encased in openness as its condition of possibility: "What is evident about the horizon, then, is that it is but the side facing us of an Open that surrounds us; an openness that is filled with views of the appearances of what to our re-presenting are [mere] objects." [141] If it is the case that the horizon is merely an aspect of the Open, how then are we to construe the Open itself? The Teacher responds: "It strikes me as something like a *region,* an enchanted region where everything belonging there returns to that in which it rests." [142] Rest is not unlike the repose at stake in "Origin," yet it is not the result of a conflictual genesis. For the return is to what *remains* the case: an abiding somewhere. Where? *In a region,* whose gathering power is such that it effects the abiding of rest: "The region gathers, just as if nothing were happening, each to each and each to all into an abiding, while resting in itself." [143]

At this critical moment in the conversation, the static noun form "region" (*Gegend*) is superseded by two other forms, the active gerund *Gegnen* (regioning) and the older noun form *Gegnet* (that-which-regions). If it is to be more encompassing than the Open, region itself has to be diversified. The task becomes not to delineate regions regarded as settled domains but to capture the action of regioning whereby that-which-regions is constituted. The action of regioning is at least twofold. On the one hand, if a region "rests in itself," it nevertheless does not remain *static;* it changes and moves. In fact, it retains what *moves toward us:* "A region holds what comes forward to meet us." [144] Instead of standing over against us in the manner of represented objects, regions bring themselves and their contents toward us as concerned parties. In *Being and Time,* regions are structured by interrelations of the ready-to-hand and of Dasein's involvement in them; in "Conversation on a Country Path," regions *involve us.* On the other hand, the action of regions is that of *gathering* or *sheltering* in the broadest sense—so broad that it includes the prototypes of space (qua "expanse") and time (qua "abiding").

Teacher: Regioning is a gathering and re-sheltering for an expanded resting in an abiding. *Scholar:* So the region itself is at once an expanse and an abiding. It abides into the expanse of resting. It expands into the abiding of what has freely turned toward itself. *Teacher:* That-which-regions is an abiding expanse which, gathering all, opens itself, so that in it the Open is halted and held, letting everything merge in its own resting.[145]

The Teacher's remark reinforces the intimate tie between *Gegnet* and *Offene.* The Scientist tightens this tie into a virtual identity: "The Open itself is that-which-regions. . . . That-which-regions is the opening of the Open."[146] The near-equivalence is accomplished by the invocation of a concept common to both: "waiting" (*Warten*). Just as the Open is not sought (much less represented in images or words) but *awaited,* so that-which-regions is not discovered (much less created): as it comes toward us, we have no choice but to *let it come* and to *receive it.* Hence the Teacher adds: "Waiting means: to release oneself into the Open of that-which-regions."[147] To wait is not to "wait for" (*warten auf*); it is to let regioning occur *in* the Open or, more exactly, *as* the Open. For "insofar as waiting relates to the Open and the Open is that-which-regions, we can say that waiting is a relation to that-which-regions."[148]

The plot is thickening—in and around that-which-regions. So polymorphous is the power of that-which-regions that the multifarious possibilities initially located by Heidegger in an indeterminate pure "space"—from which he had first backed away—seem to have been relocated in the new notion of *Gegnet.* That-which-regions is extremely embracing. It includes not only material things but also immaterial thoughts.[149] It also allows us to glimpse a new vision of nearness and distance—a vision that carries forward the abortive "Supplement" to the *Metaphysical Foundations of Logic.* For thinking (*Denken:* philosophical thinking oriented to Being) can be considered the "coming-into-the nearness of distance."[150] Such "nearness" (*Nähe*), the same word employed in the "Supplement," is not metrically determined proximity, nor is it even the result of bringing-close. It belongs, along with distance, to that-which-regions, which comes toward us and presents itself as near or far. Not only are nearness and distance "nothing outside that-which-regions"[151] but that-which-regions manifests itself primarily in these two closely related ways.

> *Scientist:* Then that-which-regions itself would be nearing and distancing.
> *Scholar:* That-which-regions itself would be the nearness of distance, and the distance of nearness.[152]

To be in a region is to be "moving-into-nearness"—as Heidegger translates Heraclitus's fragment consisting in a single word: *anchibasie.*[153] But, by the same token, you do not *step into* a region as something determinate or external. You are already there within it. All that remains to do is to release yourself to it as that to which you already belong and are appropriated—in relation to which you are *already near.* It is a matter, therefore, of "letting-yourself-into-nearness."[154]

V

> May world in its worlding be the nearest of all
> nearing that nears, as it brings the truth of Being
> near to man's essence.
> —Martin Heidegger, "The Turning"

A preoccupation with the nature of nearness spans the entirety of Heidegger's work. In *Being and Time* Dasein is characterized as having "an essential tendency towards closeness."[155] Dasein is continually bringing-close, but such bringing is exclusively a matter of putting into readiness and having to hand—and placing what has been thus procured into a convenient region (or, more likely, realizing that it was already located in that region). In a marginal note made in his own copy of *Being and Time,* Heidegger queries his earlier idea of bringing-close: "How much and why? Being as constant presence [here] has priority, making present."[156] Given this puzzlement, it is not surprising that Heidegger avoids the topic of nearness almost entirely for over a decade: nearness, along with the notion of region with which it is so closely affiliated, falls into oblivion. We can certainly enter into the vicinity (*in der Nähe*) of the work of art and the *polis,* but nearness as such does not belong in any important way to the public realms of art or politics. Only in the *apolis* of the country path, far from the art world, do nearness and region come to concern Heidegger once more—the two topics being inseparably intertwined in the Open they conjointly make possible.

At a still later period, from 1950 onward, a final turn in this development is taken. Nearness becomes even more crucial than region, and offers a way back to place as well. Mindful of the complexity of Heidegger's last writings, I shall give only the briefest of indications as to how this happens, pointing out how nearness leads Heidegger to a renewed concern with dwelling and thence to a revised vision of place.

In "The Thing" (first delivered in 1950) Heidegger restates a point already adumbrated in *Being and Time:* "All distances in time and space are shrinking," yet this technological fact "brings no nearness."[157] For "short distance is not in itself nearness. Nor is great distance remoteness."[158] A series of dromocentric paradoxes follows forthwith. Both distance *and* nearness are abolished in the era of technology—distance as objectively measurable, nearness as immeasurable. In this era everything is "equally far and equally near" or, just as tellingly, "neither far nor near."[159] Also paradoxical is the fact—not now a mere technological fact—that we cannot encounter nearness directly, but only by attending to *what* is near, namely, "things."[160] A celebrated discussion of what constitutes a *thing* (and not a mere object) ensues, including an emphasis on the gerundial character of "thinging" (*dingen*) that rejoins the basic action of regioning. Most important for our purposes is Heidegger's claim that "thinging is the nearing of world."[161] Nearing (*Nähern:* translated as "bringing close" in *Being and Time*) is no longer bringing useful things of equipment into an everyday, practical context—as if things were preconstituted entities. For without nearness, there would be no things: "In the default of nearness, the thing remains annihilated."[162] Nearing *is* the thinging of things.[163]

To be a thing, then, is not just to *be near,* for example, close to Dasein or to other things. More than mere proximity is at stake. What matters is to *bring near,* to draw close (to) what is otherwise far or remote. This is what a thing does in the case of the fourfold (*das Geviert*) composed of earth and sky, mortals and gods.

> The thing things. In thinging, it stays earth and sky, divinities and mortals. Staying, the thing brings the four, in their remoteness, near to one another. This bringing-near is nearing. Nearing is the presencing of nearness. Nearness brings near—draws nigh to one another—the far and, indeed, *as* the far. Nearness preserves farness. Preserving farness, nearness presences nearness in nearing that farness.[164]

Preserving (*wahren*) and staying (*verweilen*) are ways that a thing in its nearing holds the fourfold close to one another—so close that the members of the fourfold constitute "the simple onehood of world."[165] The more successful the nearing operation, the more the one world of the fourfold is realized and the less is nearing itself in evidence. As nearing accomplishes its work of rendering thing into world, it vanishes from view, yet is ever more ingredient: "Bringing near in this way, nearness conceals its own self and remains, in its own way, nearest of all."[166]

"The Thing" circles back to *Being and Time* by returning not only to the topic of nearness but to what it brings forth: *world.* The earlier principle that "unless we go back to the world, space cannot be conceived"[167] is still valid. Now, however, the operation by which world itself is realized is found in the nearing accomplished by things. And the same operation is responsible for the revival of another notion already prominent in the master text of 1927: *dwelling.* For dwelling or inhabiting is residing in the nearness of things: "As we preserve the thing qua thing we *inhabit nearness.*"[168] On the basis of this insight, Heidegger wrote "Building Dwelling Thinking" (1951), in which the topic of dwelling is at stake throughout. Proclaiming that "the fundamental character" (*Grundzug*) of dwelling is "sparing and preserving" (*Schonen*), he observes that such sparing is tetradic with respect to the differential destinies of earth, sky, gods, and mortals. At the same time, dwelling is "always a staying with things."[169] "Staying with" (*Aufenthalt bei*) carries forward the earlier theme of "residing alongside" (*Sein bei*) the world and being "absorbed" there—in short, an *existentiale* of Dasein's Being-in that was said to "call for still closer interpretation."[170] This interpretation is now provided, almost twenty-five years later: one is absorbed in the world, residing there, by *staying with things*. But this is tantamount to saying that one dwells in the world by letting things be, releasing them, in their nearness.[171] Dwelling is accomplished in the nearing of things (though not, significantly, in literally keeping things close) as these things bring the fourfold into one common world and maintain it there.

In claiming this, Heidegger is led back to *place*. For the members of the fourfold reside not just anywhere in the world in which they exist but *somewhere in particular*. This "somewhere" is their place or "seat," their *Stätte*, in a thing. But a thing in turn has its own "location," its *Ort*. This is easiest to see in the case of a built or constructed thing such as a bridge.

> To be sure, the bridge is a thing of its own kind; for it gathers the fourfold in such a way that it allows a *seat (Stätte)* for it. But only something *that is itself a location (Ort)* can make space for a seat. The location is not already there before the bridge is. Before the bridge stands, there are of course many positions (*Stellen*) along the stream that can be occupied by something. One of them proves to be a location, and does so *because of the bridge*. By this seat are determined the localities (*Plätze*) and ways by which a space is provided for.[172]

This remarkable passage reinscribes terms now familiar to us—most notably, *Stätte* and *Platz*—as well as the basic action of making room (*einräumen:* here translated as "make space" and "provide for"). But this is done in a way that constitutes a new composition, indeed a new vision, of place. For "place" is in effect the whole here depicted. It is nothing preexisting—as "positions" are in world-space—but arises *with the bridge regarded as a thing*. When it does arise, place shows itself to be locatory in two ways: locatory *of* the bridge-thing and locatory *for* the fourfold. In the first action, it is "itself a location," an *Ort;* in the second, it makes room for a "seat," a *Stätte*, for the fourfold, admitting and installing it.[173] The first operation transforms what would otherwise be a mere spot or position, a "simple location," into a full-fledged location. The second operation "allows" or "grants" (*verstattet*) a seat by way of opening up sufficient room for the fourfold to reside in the bridge. When both operations are effected, place results.

On the far side of such implacement is found *space;* on the near side, *localities*. Heidegger's mature model permits both space and locality to be spun off from place as its *eschata*, its extremities. Space, as Heidegger adds, is "in essence that for which room has been made (*das Eingeräumte*)" by being "granted" and "joined," that is, "gathered," by the thing as a location.[174] It is also something bounded: a space is "cleared and free, namely within a boundary, Greek *peras*."[175] A space is the result of location's double efficacy, its ability to clear out as well as to close in, to be locatory for as well as of.

Hence spaces are brought forth from locations, not the other way around: "Spaces receive their being from locations and not from 'space.' "[176] Similarly, localities are "determined" by the same dual action: "The space allowed by the bridge contains many localities variously near or far from the bridge."[177] When considered reductively, these localities become "bare positions" (*blosse Stellen*) at a determinate "distance" (*Abstand*) from each other. Although we take them for granted, positions and distance alike are late by-products of the process of implacement, its offcasts or outcasts, as it were. Intervals, dimensions, extension, mathematical manifolds, and so on, are even more belated by-products of the same process—as is the idea of a single universal "space." Regarding the latter, Heidegger has this to say:

> The space provided for in [a] mathematical manner may be called "space," the "one" space as such. But in this sense "the" space, "space," *contains no spaces and no localities*. We never find in it any locations, that is, things of the kind the bridge is. As against that, however, in the spaces provided for by locations there is always space as interval, and in this interval in turn there is space as pure extension.[178]

This passage makes it clear that the relationship between place and space is not reciprocal. To begin with, space is something from which everything placial—any location or locality—has been eliminated. But to begin with place—that is, with things-as-locations—is to start with something that contains space *in potentia*. There is no return to place from space, but from place space is (eventually) generated. It is a one-way street. Heidegger here reaffirms his claim in *Being and Time* that "space is still *one* of the things that is constitutive for the world."[179] As something generated by implacement—generated along with other things—it is only one of the pieces of the world's furniture. In addition and along the way, "various phenomenal spatialities" (again in the words of the 1927 text) are spun off: intervals and positions, dimensions and distances, extensions and analytic-algebraic relations, mathematical manifolds, and so forth. The mere fact that these products of spatialization are increasingly universal in scope does not prove, as Heidegger adds, that they *ground* the particular places that they attempt to measure in terms of determinate magnitudes.[180] If there is a ground, it lies in place and not in space.

Place, then, is no mere "part" or "portion" of space—as Locke and Newton, Descartes and Gassendi had insisted. On the contrary: space is part of place, belonging to its gradual ontogenesis and implicit in it. In tracing out the historical vicissitudes of this ontogenesis, my own account in this book has exhibited much the same derivation of space from place. In particular, it has shown that the idea of a universal space was a deferred and slowly evolving notion that took at least two millennia to emerge from the matrix of implacement in which it began. What is demonstrable diachronically in the history of philosophy is also true of the individual's own experience. "Space" is nascent within the "spaces" that are the very places of that experience: "Spaces, and with them space as such—'space'—are always provided for already within the stay of mortals."[181]

If this is indeed the case, then mortals, including Heidegger himself, have nothing to fear from the abstract infinity of space, or from its indefinitely many possibilities: not if spatial infinity itself is something generated and not given. The task is not to deal with infinite space, which is after all our own creation or conception, but to "persist through" places, to "go through" and to "stand in them."[182] When we do these things (which we do precisely by staying *with things*), we find that the relevant parameters are not measurable intervals or exact dimensions—neither *diastēmata* nor *diastēseis*—but *degrees of nearness.* Much as Kant distinguished between "extensive" and "intensive" magnitude (the latter, which is appropriate for sensations, is a matter of degree), so we must discern the difference between being merely *at* a locus or position, in other words, proximate *to* it, and being *near* a thing. To be near a thing is to share in its location—a nonsimple location composed of thing and mortal, who come together there in dwelling and staying. The bridge over which mortals move is "variously near or far" to or from the "many places" along its banks; but it is only *approximately so:* a matter of more or less. The tree on the east bank is *over there;* the landscape beyond is *all around;* the next bridge is *somewhere down the river.*

It follows that the nearness/farness of such locations is engaged by thought as well as by hand or foot.

> If all of us now think, from where we are right here, of the old bridge in Heidelberg, this thinking toward that location is not a mere experience inside the persons present here; rather, it belongs to the nature of our thinking *of* that bridge that *in itself* thinking gets through, persists through, the distance to that location.[183]

Not only is this statement a rejection of any representationalist theory of space—whereby spaces and places are the mere contents of consciousness—but it contests the primacy of the absolute here of the implaced person. Not the somatocentric pinpointed here but the diffuse there is the operative factor in my engagement in the place-world.[184] And I am engaged by things in their comparative nearness/remoteness (an indefinite dyad whose terms refuse monovalent definition). "We always go through spaces," adds Heidegger, "in such a way that we already experience them by staying constantly with near and remote locations and things."[185] Such staying, which is tantamount to dwelling, can be with the most "distant" as well as the closest things. In saying this, we return to the paradoxes of nearness with which this last phase of Heidegger's thinking began.

VI

> Since time as well as Being can only be thought
> from Appropriation as the gifts of Appropria-
> tion, the relation of space to Appropriation must
> also be considered in an analogous way.
> —Martin Heidegger, "Time and Being"

Another strand of this late turning occurs in Heidegger's important essay
"Time and Being" (1962). Nearness is now extended to temporal as well as
spatial matters. Heidegger asks of time what he had earlier asked of the artwork: "But *where* is time? Is time at all and *does it have a place*?"[186] Instead
of attempting to show the temporality of spatiality—it is in this essay that
Heidegger admits to the failure of such an attempt in *Being and Time,* section
70—the question now bears on the implacement of time, its becoming-place
as it were. A simple observation is made: "The present understood in terms of
the now is not at all identical with the present in the sense in which the guests
are present."[187] The guests are present not just in the same time but in the
same space—or, better, "time-space," a term Heidegger adapts to his own
purposes in the wake of Einstein. What matters is not the term but the fact
that time becomes present to human beings in specifically placial and spatial
ways. "Presence means: the constant abiding that approaches man, reaches
him, and is extended to him."[188] "Abiding" is a temporal mode; "reaching"
and "extending" are spatial forms. As in "Conversation on a Country Path," a
broadening and loosening of basic notions reflect Heidegger's growing preoccupation with intensive magnitudes. "Dimensionality," for example, is now
conceived as "a reaching out that opens up" rather than "the area of possible
measurement."[189] Heidegger also stresses that more crucial than the three
modes of time—past, present, and future—is their "interplay" (*Zuspiel*), a
spatially charged word that recalls "leeway" (*Spielraum*). Such interplay is
time's "true extending" (*Reichen*), the way it effloresces, its "fourth dimension."[190] We could say that interplay is a matter of *outreach*. But it is also a
circumstance of *inreach:* which is to say, of nearness.

Nearness returns for a last time—to gather time as well as space into its
midst. It does so precisely in terms of place. The action of "nearing nearness"
(*nähernde Nähe*) anneals time from within and is the very basis of its dimensionality: it is "the first, original, literally incipient extending in which the
unity of true time consists."[191] Thanks to nearness, an entire "realm" (*Bereich*)
of temporal interplay arises. As "prespatial," this realm cannot be given a
precise location (*Ort*); but it remains placial: if it is not an *Ort*, it is an
Ortschaft, a locale, a settled place (e.g., a town).[192] As a result, "true time" can
be considered "the nearness of presencing out of present, past, and future—the
nearness that unifies time's threefold opening extending."[193] Thus nearness is

a placial mode of presencing that gathers time together in its threefoldness: the converse of section 70 of *Being and Time,* wherein temporality in its tripleness is held to ground space.

But Heidegger cautions that such presencing (*Anwesen*) is not the same thing as simple presence (*Anwesenheit*); nearness withholds as much as it gives: "This nearing of nearness keeps open the approach coming from the future by withholding the present in the approach."[194] The same is true of the past and the present itself, which are held apart from each other and from the future. But *where* are they held apart? They are held apart *in their very nearness:* which is to say, *in place.* The three temporal modalities come close to each other only by respecting their remoteness from one another in one and the same place. It is in place, then, that "nearing nearness has the character of denial and withholding. . . . The giving that gives time is determined by denying and withholding nearness."[195] Indeed, this may be generalized: the withholding inherent in the nearness of place is an instance of a "withdrawal" (*Entzug*) that characterizes all giving. Such withdrawal extends beyond time to Being, which is not merely "sent" (*geschickt*) but *withdrawn* in the sending itself: "To giving as sending there belongs keeping back."[196]

This complex pattern is found even in *Ereignis,* the "event of Appropriation" into which Being and time are both assimilated. For this Appropriation is at the same time an Expropriation, an *Enteignis.*

Insofar as the destiny [i.e., the sending: *Geshick*] of Being lies in the extending of time, and time, together with Being, lies in Appropriation, Appropriating makes manifest its peculiar property, [i.e.] that Appropriation withdraws what is most fully its own from boundless unconcealment. Thought in terms of Appropriating, this means: in that sense it expropriates itself of itself. Expropriation belongs to Appropriation itself. By this expropriation, Appropriation does not abandon itself—rather, it preserves what is its own.[197]

The *proprius* root of "Appropriation" and "Expropriation" (via the *eigen-* buried in *Ereignis* and *Enteignis*) signifies *own* and *peculiar* (or *particular*), both of which imply what is *near* in the sense of what is in the vicinity, what is around (*peri-* "around," is an etymon of *proprius*). Descartes's effort to describe place in terms of "vicinity" in his *Principles of Philosophy*—which we saw to be an idle but suggestive gesture—is here at least partly redeemed.

Even at the farthest limit of Heidegger's postmetaphysical thought, then, we find nearness as an active ingredient. This is not wholly unexpected, given that space, like time or Being, is said expressly to be a "gift of Appropriation"—something given in its very withdrawal.[198] As an *event,* moreover, Appropriation is ineluctably spatiotemporal: to be an event is to exist in space and time alike. Or more exactly: it is to exist in place. For an event is something that *takes place,* that calls for and constitutes place at the origin—indeed, *as* the origin—of time and space. But to be at/as the origin of both is to

be back to/in place. This is above all true of space: "We can admittedly succeed in this [i.e., the task of considering space as a gift of *Ereignis*] only when
we have previously gained insight into the origin of space in the properties
peculiar to place and have thought them adequately."[199] From the event of
place the gift of space proceeds. The generation of space as outward, as extended, even as infinite, is possible only from within the bounded nearness,
the withheld intimacy, the spatiotemporal Appropriation of place.

VII

> Three terms, which carry each other forward
> even as they mark the stages of the path of [my]
> thought: Meaning—Truth—Place.
> —Martin Heidegger, remark at the Thor
> Seminar (September 6, 1969)

In the vast array of Heidegger's later writings on place-pertinent topics, one
clearly discernible intention stands out. This is an effort to specify more exactly and fully what "the openness of the Open" means. This term, central to
the discussion in "The Origin of the Work of Art," had taken over from
"being-in-the-world" the role of what Heidegger also calls "the clearing" (*die
Lichtung*): the role of a space freed up so that singular events can occur in its
midst, including *Ereignis* as an ultimate Event. From *Being and Time* onward,
the clearing/opening is consistently conceived as an activity that "makes
room" (*einräumt*) for something more particular to take place. Or, rather, to
have place within its free ambience. The ambience itself provides "leeway"—
Spielraum or, in a later locution, *Zeit-Spiel-Raum*, "free scope"—within which
things in the richest sense can have a home. The leeway must be "thrown
open" (as the past participle of *einräumen* may also be translated) by connecting with a "there" or "yonder" *back from which* a place for things may be
established or enjoyed.

If there is one coherent paradigm that characterizes Heidegger's multifarious pronouncements on space and place, early and late, it is that which posits
a basic movement *from* a cleared open out there *to* a given locus over here.
As Heidegger puts it in "Building Dwelling Thinking": "I am never here only,
as this encapsulated body; rather, I am *there,* that is, I already pervade the
room, and only thus can I go through it."[200] The operative adverb here is
"through," for to go through (*durchgehen*) or pervade (*durchstehen*) a room
presumes that the room itself is already sufficiently cleared for my passage: it
is cleared as *there* for my moving or stationary body *here.* Such an active
back/to/through structure contrasts with the static "in" at stake in Aristotle's
container model of place—where what counts is being strictly surrounded on
all sides, just being *in* something, with no openness and no clearing before or

after. For Heidegger, a place may provide "shelter" (e.g., for the fourfold) without being a tight container.[201] In fact, it *cannot* be such a container, since the primary effect of place is to create room and not to enclose or delimit it. In so doing, place brings about the openness of the Open.

The philosophical advantage of the Open, indeed its virtual ineluctability within Heidegger's developing thought, is evident. It shifts the responsibility for room-clearing away from Dasein's individuated directionality and de-severance, that is, its own personal way of making room and giving clearance. The opening of the Open is the disclosure of an impersonal truth—thus of an equally impersonal Being. Dasein can enter the Open, witness it, and even contribute to it (e.g., in art and politics). But human being cannot create the Open, which at once precedes and outlasts any individual Dasein or any col-lectivity of Daseins. "Being-in" and "residing"—early themes in *Being and Time*—already point toward this nonhumanocentric horizon, but they are soon buried under the description of Dasein's literally instrumental role in particu-lar places and regions. As soon as this early protopragmatism is set aside and confined to mere handicraft in the case of art, the way is cleared for the Open to be thought not just as the scene for the disclosedness of truth (this, too, is implicit in *Being and Time*) but as the scene for a new conception of place and region, now liberated from their strictly ready-to-hand status.

The Open is not Heidegger's last word—far from it. Its advantage ends by being its own disadvantage. It *names* what thinking about place requires in the wake of Aristotle, Descartes, and Heidegger's own first phase. It gives conceptual *Spielraum* to place itself, inviting fresh approaches in its midst. But, by the same token, its very clearedness, its lack of definition and de-limitation, becomes a liability once one attempts to spell out what a new look at place might entail. No wonder, then, that Heidegger began to ponder the nature of "limit" and "boundary" in the 1930s: the Open, taken to its limit (that is to say, to its *lack* of limit), openly threatens to be boundaryless, to go on forever in the manner of endless space![202] So that there will be no possible confusion between the Open and infinite space, new and more precise names have to be sought. A first step in this direction, for example, occurs late in "The Origin of the Work of Art" with the positing of an internal cut or rift (*Riss*) in the work, a common cleavage around which earth and world are configured and set in place. Along with the strife itself between earth and world, this cut ensures that the work as a clearing or Open is not a simple whole: it is, in Sartre's phrase, a "de-totalized totality."

But more than internal complication or detotalization is called for. As we have seen, Heidegger next seizes on the idea of *gathering* in his discussion of "region" in "Conversation on a Country Path." Gathering (*versammeln*) is an action that draws things together within a bounded space. To avoid any sense that such space is preestablished (as the Open still seems to imply), Heidegger gerundizes "region" as he had done earlier in the case of "world" (and will do still later with "thing," "time," "space," and "event of Appropriation"). A gathered and gathering region does not stand there as something entitative and pregiven; it regionalizes itself—not entirely unlike the thrashing action of *chōra,* an action that directly precipitates regions. Nevertheless, Heidegger does not rest satisfied: although the action of gathering is retained in later writings (just as the Open still makes an occasional reappearance), it is not specific enough to account for what is particular about place. Gathering can be the collecting of virtually anything, and that-which-regions and regioning are similarly afflicted with generality. Hence Heidegger's turn to the idea of a *thing,* that is, something not merely self-sufficient but so condensed and intense as to be a gathering-place for the fourfold of earth and sky, gods and mortals. These latter become "world-regions"[203] that cluster in the place of the thing—a thing that, itself located, affords locus or "seat" to these cosmic regions.

To cluster items together is to draw them near to each other. "Nearness" is thus a natural next step to take in this progression of thought. Like the Open itself, but in precisely the opposite direction, it names what Heidegger seeks: the closeness, the intimacy, of things as they are gathered, and themselves actively gather, *in a particular place.* To be in a place is to be near to whatever else is in that place, and preeminently the things that are co–located there. Places holding things are in turn assembled in regions, drawing nigh to each other in a protoaction of regionalized nearing that achieves more than mere proximity. What more? In a word: *dwelling.* For dwelling is always "dwelling in nearness."[204] But in the late essay devoted to the topic of dwelling, Heidegger says surprisingly little about dwelling itself. Instead, he tells us a great deal about building and, in particular, how a built thing such as a bridge gathers an entire landscape about itself.[205] He also describes the complex structure of place that is pertinent to this scene: the bridge is at once a location in the landscape and a seat for the fourfold, giving rise to localities nearby and, ultimately, positions in a world-space. In this way room is made not just for tools, and for dwelling, but for space itself: "Space is in essence that for which room has been made, that which is let into its bounds."[206] Not only the Open but space is cleared by places.

Nearness assumes an increasingly important role in Heidegger's very late writings. It is a notion that refuses to be sublated and that, of all place-specific terms, is pursued most insistently. The extent of the pursuit is indicated by its verbal proliferation: not only is it rendered an active gerund (*nähernd; nahebringend*), even its noun form becomes prolific in the form of "the near" (*die Nähe*), "nearhood" (*Nahheit*), and "nighness" (*Nahnis*).[207] Why this extraordinary focus on nearness? Partly because nearness, not being a matter of distance qua interval, is precisely what cannot be measured by space and time taken as objectively parametric in nature.[208] But more crucially for our purposes, nearness brings with it the right level of specificity for thinking about place. With nearness, the Open is not enclosed from without, nor is it fissured from within or gathered as a region or located as a thing; it is specified—but as what? As *neighborhood.* As set forth in "The Nature of Language" (1957–1958), neighborhood is what nearness "brings about."[209] No more than there is a preexisting region is there anything like a neighborhood given in advance. Neighborhood is induced by the nearness of the things or people who coinhabit a place in common: "Neighborhood means: dwelling in nearness."[210] But to dwell near to someone or something has two special features: it is a reciprocal relation (if I am a neighbor to you, you are the same to me) and it entails a face-to-face encounter.

> A neighbor, as the word itself [i.e., *Nachbar*] tells us, is someone who dwells near to and with someone else. . . . Neighborhood, then, is a relation resulting from the fact that the one settles face to face with the other.[211]

In the nearness of neighborhood, place is pinned down and particularized, made intimate. How much more intimate can any experience be than a face-to-face encounter? Place is the scene of this encounter. It is what makes concretely possible the interinvolvement of neighbors. Perhaps we should speak more exactly of the *interplace* of neighborhood, that is, the betweenness that place offers among otherwise disparate items. The "multifarious between" that Heidegger attributes to "world" in *Hebel der Hausfreund* (1957) belongs as well to place.[212] Moreover, if "nearness manifests itself as the motion in which the world's regions face each other,"[213] place is in turn the intermediate matrix of this mundane motion. What Heidegger says of space might better be said of place: "Throwing open, admitting and releasing—they all belong together in the Same."[214] In its action of "admitting and releasing" (*zulässend-entlassend*), place makes neighborhood possible as the same settled scene. For place, much more than space, affords room in the form of locality and location, thereby giving to neighborhood a sustained basis in nearness. The nearing of nearness occurs as the interplacement of neighbors in face-to-face relations.

Despite the manifest importance of nearness and neighborhood in his late thinking, Heidegger takes up the relation of place and space for a final time without recourse to these concepts, drawing instead on terms more familiar from earlier writings. In "Art and Space," the last major text he composed (1969), Heidegger explores the role of space, and more particularly place, in the plastic arts, especially sculpture. Eschewing any reliance on space as "objective" or "cosmic," he proclaims that the action of "clearing space" (*Räumen*) amounts to a "releasing of places" (*Freigabe der Orte*).[215] Such clearing is a "making room" (*Einräumen*) that, by allowing and setting up an Open, lets things appear and human dwelling occur—and in so doing, gives "guarantee" (*Gewährnis*) to places. Just here, late as the moment is, Heidegger asks for the first time: "Still, what is place?"[216] His answer is remarkably apt and economic: "Place opens a region (*Gegend*) by every time gathering things into their belonging together."[217] Region or, rather, "that-which-regions" (*Gegnet*) is that "free expanse" (*freie Weite*) by means of which the Open lets things attain their own rest. But, as we have learned from "Building Dwelling Thinking," things are themselves places and do not just belong to a place, much less merely occupy positions in an empty homogeneous space. The things sheltered in the regional Open are tantamount to the places of that Open. This line of thought allows Heidegger to draw a crucial conclusion, one already tacitly at work in *Being and Time* yet never articulated as such in that work: "Place is not found in pre-given space construed as physical-technological space. Space unfolds only from the free reign (*Walten*) enjoyed by the places of a region."[218] Even the empty spaces in a building or piece of sculpture count as places, and, more generally, the plastic arts represent "the embodiment of places."[219] These places open up "regions of possible human dwelling and of the possible lingering of things that approach and surround human beings."[220]

The theme of *possibility*—in particular, possible ways to dwell in space—resounds here. It rejoins a passage from "The Nature of Language" that bears on the fact that a neighborhood, like a thing, is itself a place, a "seat" (*Stätte*) for reiterable possibilities of future implacement.

> The neighborhood of which we have spoken is the seat (*Stätte*) that gives us room (*verstattet*) to experience how matters stand. . . . Anything that gives us room and allows us to do something gives us a possibility, that is, it gives that which enables us. "Possibility" so understood, means something else and something more than mere opportunity.[221]

From two directions, then, we return at the end to that vista of sheer spatial possibility from which Heidegger had at first shrunk back in *Being and Time*. Thirty years later, Heidegger is willing to do what he could not bring himself to do earlier, namely, to "embrace the sheer possibilities of the pure spatial Being of something."[222] He can do so inasmuch as he has discovered that this possibilizing spatial Being resides in *place*—or, more exactly, in the regions that places institute in the course of generating something like space.

Rediscovering the importance of place in this way is like finding a conceptual neighborhood where one can feel at home: where one can dwell face-to-face in the nearness, even the uncanniness, of sheer possibility. The neighborhood of nearness as set forth in "The Nature of Language" brings home and specifies the place for dwelling first adumbrated in section 12 of *Being and Time*. In that premonitory section, Heidegger had remarked that Being-in of a merely *vorhanden* sort disallows the mutual touching that characterizes genuine residing and that renders things "encounterable."[223] In the text of the late

1950s, encounterability is described in terms of a face-to-face meeting in the
nearness of a neighborhood, for example, the "country" of a region.[224] The
continuity is more than merely striking: it makes good on a promissory note
first issued in Heidegger's early masterwork, and then neglected out of a preoccupation with time and temporality. For Heidegger now pursues that "new
possibility" of which he had already spoken in his lectures on *Logic* in 1925–
1926: another way of conceiving Being apart from "the basis of time."[225]

In his continual turning (and returning) to matters of place in the aftermath
of *Being and Time,* Heidegger at last succeeds in liberating himself from "the
narrowness of those concepts of Being which merely chance to be available
and which are for the most part rather rough."[226] He has even liberated himself from the narrowness of his own concepts of time and temporality that
acted to occlude his vision of an alternative route to Being—a vision via place
(and thus also via the Open, region, things, and nearness). The circuitous and
digressive character of Heidegger's path over more than four decades should
not blind us to the fact that he ends by giving the most suggestive and sustained treatment of place in this century.

It is remarkable enough that Heidegger managed to do justice to place in
the face of his own temporocentrism. What Bergson did for duration, Heidegger does for place—despite the primacy he accords to temporality. And it is
all the more remarkable that Heidegger accomplishes this even though he
rarely addresses place itself as a thematic topic. To recognize the ingredience
of place in Being, to see it as the very setting of the event of Appropriation,
does not call for turning place into a trim topic of apophantic discourse. It is
to acknowledge instead the special value of pursuing, even through the most
sinuous corridors, a "topology of Being."[227]

12

Giving a Face to Place in the Present

Bachelard, Foucault, Deleuze and Guattari, Derrida, Irigaray

I

> Everything takes form, even in infinity.
> —Gaston Bachelard, *The Poetics of Space*

> Space is everywhere open. . . . We are in this place.
> —Jean-Luc Nancy, *The Inoperative Community*

In tracing out Heidegger's thinking about place and "various phenomenal spatialities" such as region and neighborhood, we have pursued place into some of its more arcane corners and subtler surfaces. We have learned much about the panoply of meanings that place can exhibit as well as the range of roles it can assume in widely divergent contexts. If the effect is kaleidoscopic—leading us to savor place's "free scope," its *Zeit-Spiel-Raum*—it has allowed us to recognize, indeed to re-recognize, the power of place. Earlier encomia of place (articulated at the moment of its dawning recognition in the West) tend to be terse, as we see in Archytas's fragmentary utterances and Aristotle's condensed lecture notes; or else, at the opposite extreme, they are effusive and panegyrical, as in Iamblichus's and Proclus's dithyrambs. Heidegger chooses a middle path. For him, place is intriguing and valuable, indeed often indispensable, yet not something to be adulated as such. It does not take on the consistently highlighted status of Being or Being-in-the-world, of Truth or Language, the Fourfold or the event of Appropriation. Yet it never becomes merely parasitic on these major terms, nor is it just their by-product or offspring; it retains its own features and fate, its own local being.

The fact remains, however, that in the course of Heidegger's drawn-out engagement with place, the phenomenon itself all too often slips from view. No ground itself, place goes underground, becoming part of Heidegger's complex polylogue with other thinkers and other concepts. The result, if not the intent, is that of interment. Place is caught in the coiling corridors of Heidegger's labyrinthine lifework.

Emerging from these corridors, we are led to ask, is it not time to *face place*—to confront it, take off its veil, and see its full face? Is it not time to face up to place? Or even to give it a new face, so that we can at last find *it*, and thus our own ineluctably implaced selves, once again?

In and around (and sometimes distinctly athwart) the long shadow cast by Heidegger's imposing work, there are significant signs of a renewed and rising interest in place on the part of philosophically minded authors who think independently of the thinker of Being. The signs are provided by such figures as, in France, Bachelard, Braudel, Foucault, Deleuze and Guattari, Derrida, Lefebvre, Irigaray, and Nancy; in Germany, Benjamin and Arendt and M. A. C. Otto; and in North America, Relph, Tuan, Entrikin, Soja, Sack, Berry, Snyder, Stegner, Eisenman, Tschumi, and Walter. Each of these figures has succeeded in fashioning a fresh face for place.

Common to all of these rediscoverers of the importance of place is a conviction that place itself is no fixed thing: it has no steadfast essence. Where Heidegger still sought something resembling essential traits of place (e.g., gathering, nearing, regioning, thinging), none of the authors I have just named is tempted to undertake anything like a definitive, much less an eidetic, search for the formal structure of place. Instead, each tries to find place *at work*, part of something ongoing and dynamic, ingredient *in something else:* in the course of history (Braudel, Foucault), in the natural world (Berry, Snyder), in the political realm (Nancy, Lefebvre), in gender relations and sexual difference (Irigaray), in the productions of poetic imagination (Bachelard, Otto), in geographic experience and reality (Foucault, Tuan, Soja, Relph, Entrekin), in the sociology of the *polis* and the city (Benjamin, Arendt, Walter), in nomadism (Deleuze and Guattari), in architecture (Derrida, Eisenman, Tschumi), in religion (Irigaray, Nancy). To read this bare list of names and topics is to become aware of a far-flung and loosely knit family resemblance of changing and contingent traits. This suggests that there is no singular, much less ideal, Place behind so many different (or at least differential) masks. To this extent, the recent history of place may seem all the more hidden, since there is no official story to be told, only a series of significant incidents to be recounted. But in this episodic history, "everything takes form, even in infinity." Or rather: *everything takes face* in a diverse yet intense immersion in the subject of place.

The fate of place in Western thought has already called for an expansive account in this book, and I do not want to prolong it unduly. This last chapter, accordingly, will contain mere sketches of several only of the most promising and evocative contemporary directions, limiting itself to those with an expressly philosophical orientation. Not claiming to be exhaustive of the whole picture in the present, these vignettes are meant to serve as signposts for further exploration. But they do single out ways in which to revalorize place in our own lives, to *give point to place.* The figures to be treated in brief successive sections of this chapter—Bachelard, Foucault, Deleuze and Guattari, Derrida, and Irigaray—will help us to acknowledge and appreciate more fully the many faces of the places that are to be found with and in and around us.

II

> Psyche is extended; [but] knows nothing about it.
>
> —Sigmund Freud, note of August 22, 1938
>
> We do not change place, we change our nature.
> —Gaston Bachelard, *The Poetics of Space*

Gaston Bachelard offers a first refacing of place—in and through the image, more specifically, the poetic image. In Bachelard's writings on the poetic imagination (pursued from the late 1930s until the early 1960s), the issue of implacement arises from a continuing concern with understanding how poetic images are situated in the human psyche. As Bachelard says in *La terre et les rêveries de la volonté* (1948), "If one puts images in their true place in psychic activity—before thoughts (*pensées*)—one cannot help but recognize that the first image of immensity is a terrestrial image."[1] To put images "in their true place" (*à leur vraie place*) is to find for them a proper locus in the mind or, more exactly, the soul.[2] Aristotle had claimed that the soul is "the place of forms," but to be the place of *images* is to be a very different place than Aristotle had in mind: it is to be receptive and absorptive of images in a manner that has little if anything to do with precise positioning in hierarchical stratification (the most characteristic way in which concepts are located in the rational soul on Aristotle's account). Metaphors of the pigeonhole and the ladder give way to the spider's web or the beehive as we begin to appreciate what is at stake in poetic imagery: intense efflorescence. The very model of place as a surface—another insistent Aristotelian theme—has to be reassessed: what matters in the psychical implacement of images is not how they are contained *by* a surface (as if their fate were to be strictly surrounded) but how they appear *at* a surface, that of the soul itself: "The poetic image," writes Bachelard in *The Poetics of Space,* "is a sudden salience on the surface of the psyche."[3] If images are indeed efflorescent phenomena, then the place in which they appear must be capable of reflecting or "reverberating" with them, not altogether unlike the Receptacle in the *Timaeus:* the psyche, like the Receptacle, must be comparatively characterless in order to resonate with the images that flash across its surface.[4] The psychic surface must send forth the images it receives; it must give place to them by fulgurating with them, shining with their momentary presence. The sense of place that counts here is not that of place as it contains and perdures but as it lights up with the sudden spark of a single striking image, like a shooting star in the dark abysm of night.

At stake in this basic nisus of Bachelard's work is a major issue: the spatiality or, better, the placiality of the psyche. In proposing that the soul provides place for images, Bachelard is contesting not only Aristotle but Descartes as well. Contra Aristotle, he is holding that there is a valid sense of place for nonsensible items; place can be nonphysical and yet still count fully as place. In the ancient world, only Plotinus and his successors had dared to posit a strictly nonsensible form of place, that is, "intelligible place." (The analogue in *space* to intelligible place is, as we have seen, the infinite imaginary space that medieval theologians took to be equivalent to God.) In late modernity, Bachelard endorses another significant exception to the sense-bound Aristotelian schema: psychic place. But to affirm the soul as a place or set of places is also to fly in the face of Descartes, for whom the soul has no extension of any kind. It is evident to Bachelard, however, that poetic images flare up *somewhere,* and the place in which they do so is psychical in nature. This is not to maintain that psychic place is three-dimensional, much less that it is essentially empty. Here thinking against both Descartes and Philoponus, Bachelard argues that the extension of soul has its own properties and parameters, among them, a special kind of insideness and its own modalities of surface and depth (whereby, for example, a poetic image may "touch the depths before it stirs the surface").[5]

The more we think in this last direction, the closer we come to Freud, who also proposes psychic depth and interiority and who, at the very end of his life, proclaimed the unconscious to be extended.[6] Bachelard is aware of the parallel course he is on with Freud—and with Jung as well. A relation of congenial competition with psychoanalysis is palpable from *The Psychoanalysis of Fire* (1938) to *The Poetics of Space* (1957), the two books that frame Bachelard's thinking about poetic imagery and the psyche. What is an exceptional comment in Freud, or an equally exceptional dream in Jung,[7] becomes for Bachelard a region of research that deserves its own name: "topoanalysis." In topoanalysis, descriptive psychology, depth psychology, psychoanalysis, and phenomenology all come together in a common enterprise, one that can be defined as "the systematic psychological study of the localities of our intimate lives."[8] Less a method than an attitude, topoanalysis focuses on the placial properties of certain images, for instance the house: "On whatever horizon we examine it, the house image would appear to have become the topography of our intimate being."[9]

A direct corollary of topoanalysis is this: *taken seriously, topoanalysis undermines temporocentrism.* The more we attend to the *topoi* of psychic life, the more we realize that this life—contrary to what Kant and Bergson, James and Husserl contend—is not merely a function of its durational flow. Space, rather than time, is the form of "inner sense." When we look within ourselves in the classical gesture of Saint Augustine, we do not find a sheer sequence of moments, much less "absolute flux" (Husserl); instead, "all we know is a series of fixations in the spaces of the stability of being—a being who does not want to melt away and who, even in the past, when he sets out in search of things past, wants time to 'suspend' its flight." [10] What introspection discloses are "motionless" memories—all the more "solid" for being "better spatialized." [11] To come to terms with the inner life, it is not enough to constitute a biography or autobiography in narrative terms; one must also, and more crucially, do a topoanalysis of the places one has inhabited or experienced. "For a knowledge of intimacy, localization in the spaces of our intimacy is more urgent than determination of dates." [12] Not only more urgent but more *true,* for the temporal recounting of a life gives only "a sort of external history, for external use, to be communicated to others." [13] In this way Bachelard turns the tables on time: rather than being more universal than space (as Kant had held) or descriptive of the deep self (as Bergson maintained), time is absorbed into psychic spatiality: "In its countless alveoli space contains compressed time." [14] Indeed, when we immerse ourselves in psychical depth and interiority we find that "here space is everything" and that the unconscious, far from being the seat of pure duration or repressed memories, simply "abides." [15] The further we pursue the inherent placiality of the unconscious, the less imperative become the demands of time—whether at the level of conscious narration or of unconscious ideation. To affirm psychical placefulness is to reformulate the Archytian axiom: to be psychical is to be in place.

Thus far, then, Bachelard argues for the psyche or soul as a placial receptacle for images, above all, poetic images. At the same time, images offer location to their own contents, whether these contents be cognitive, emotive, linguistic, or (again) imaginational. Scintillating on the surface of the psyche, while also proceeding from the depths, particular images act to implace such contents by offering them imaginal aegis, a home for their continued prospering. Bachelard calls this specifically imaginal sense of place "felicitous space"; in contrast with the "indifferent space" of the surveyor, this is "the space we love," that is, "eulogized space." [16] It fosters a veritable "topophilia" on the part of those who savor this imagistic implacement—above all, dedicated readers of poetry. A love for images goes hand in hand with topoanalysis: "topoanalysis bears the stamp of a topophilia." [17]

We are reminded of Heidegger's call for a "topology of Being." This call was issued out of Heidegger's concern to discover "the poetizing character of thinking"—a character that, along with space, is said to be "still veiled over." [18] Moreover, just as space was said in *Being and Time* to be "split up into places," [19] so poetic images are for Bachelard split into the places they offer for their own content. Heidegger would not agree that poetry and

philosophy come together in the *image*—a term of which he was deeply skeptical—but he would concur that the true task of the conjoint venture of poetizing and philosophizing is to lay bare a topology, a *logos* (account) of the *topoi*
(places) into which poetizing thinking fits and where Being finds its own
proper place (*Ortschaft*).[20] What Bachelard calls "topoanalysis" Heidegger
terms *Erörterung,* "im-placing" or "placing through." In the final phase of his
career, Bachelard seeks philosophically inspired poetic images as much as
does Heidegger in his later writings. In the end, however, despite a shared
passion for regarding poetry as a set of privileged *topoi,* the two thinkers part
company. The topology that matters most for Bachelard is not that which
bears on Being but, instead, on "our [own] intimate being."[21] And the radical
transcendence of Heideggerian ontotopology—wherein Being is considered
"the *transcendens* pure and simple"[22]—cannot be reconciled with the psychical immanence of Bachelardian topoanalysis.

Topoanalysis, presupposing the psyche as the seat of all significant images,
seeks the detailed description of particular images. Such images shelter contents that arrange themselves into systematic themes, for example, earth, water, air, fire—which, taken together, constitute Bachelard's own distinctive
fourfold. An imagistic-psychical *topic* is thus inherently *thematic.* It is not
merely formal or structural; the content or theme of a given topic informs it
from within. Moreover, there is in principle no limit to the number of topically
arranged themes and subthemes that are subject to topoanalysis. Yet certain
themes are undoubtedly privileged, most notably, that of the house, to which
the first two chapters of *The Poetics of Space* are devoted. For the house—
especially when it is also a home—contains "la topographie de notre être
intime."[23] If Heidegger considered the *world* to be "the house in which mortals dwell,"[24] Bachelard will say the same of the *image (and memory) of the
house,* which constitutes its own poetic place-world, inhabited by the reader
of poetry and the topoanalyst alike. Attention to the subtle structures of the
imagined/remembered house, its imaginal topography, will give us a concrete
sense of the scope and limits of topoanalysis.

The house is a paradoxical entity. As a home, it is "our first universe" and
our "first world."[25] As such, it precedes our sense of a more capacious and
unending universe. Bachelard scolds philosophers who posit the universe as
existing before, and independently of, the house qua home. They claim to
"know the universe before they know the house," whereas in fact what human
beings know first—and never forget—are "the intimate values of inside
space."[26] Such space is not set apart from the house/home but is at one with
it, and is not yet geometrical.[27] Size is irrelevant: a simple hut has more, not
less, oneiric potential than a mansion. What matters is the degree of intimacy
and intensity of our experience there; when these are acutely felt, the very
distinction between universe and world—which we cannot help but make
once we undertake a concerted cosmology—becomes otiose. For the "dy-

namic rivalry between house and universe" is already resolved at the primitive level of the inhabited house. At this level, a world embraces both, a world that depends as much on image as on fact: "When the image is new, the world is new."[28]

Thus, rather than claim that the world is a house—a cosmological claim— topoanalysis tries to convince us that *the house is a world*. It is a place-world, a world of places. Here, Bachelard rejoins Heidegger's early description of the "sunny" and "shady" sides of the house as locales (*Plätze*) that orient the division and arrangement of a house into rooms (*Räume*).[29] But topoanalysis deepens this description by exploring the intimacy of a house *room by room,* that is to say, place by place. The exploration is not architectural, much less geometrical; it is a matter of rooms as dreamed, imagined, remembered—and *read:* "It therefore makes sense from the standpoint of a philosophy of litera- ture and poetry to say that we 'write a room', 'read a room', or 'read a house.' "[30] When topoanalysis is guided by poetry in particular, it elicits in the reader an entire "oneiric house, a house of dream-memory."[31] Such a house is based on bodily habits inherited from one's original home, but a poem extends these habits by delineating the layout of rooms.

> Over and beyond our memories, the house we were born in is physically in- scribed in us. It is a group of organic habits. . . . We are the diagram of the functions of inhabiting that particular house, and all the other houses are but variations on a fundamental theme. . . . The house, the bedroom, the garret in which we were alone, furnishes the framework for an interminable dream, one that poetry alone, through the creation of a poetic work, could succeed in achieving completely.[32]

Poets and topoanalysts both recognize the privileged status of the body in getting us back into place—in particular, our childhood home. They also af- firm that the house we reenter by means of images or words is itself bodylike: "The house acquires the physical and moral energy of a human body. It braces itself to receive the downpour, it girds its loins."[33] An imagined or remem- bered room within such a body-house " 'clings' to its inhabitant and becomes the cell of a body with its walls close together."[34] To return to an inhabited room, whether in fact or in fantasy, is to return to an organic part of a house that is itself experienced as a megabody, with windows for eyes and a front door for mouth.[35]

No more than the members of a human body are disarticulated parts are the rooms of a house wholly separate from each other. Each room has its own character—as we can see from the difference between a bedroom and a study, or a parlor and a closet, especially as these are described by poets—and yet rooms concatenate, say, as the rooms of a given "floor," or of a "wing" of a house. Perhaps the most important concatenation is that which clusters around the implicit vertical axis of many Western houses—an axis that runs between basement and attic. These two extremities of the house could not be more different in their oneiric values. The attic is "the rational zone of intellectualized projects," whereas the basement is the domain of the unconscious: "The unconscious cannot be civilized. It takes a candle when it goes to the cellar."[36] In the one, light is the order of the day; in the other, lack of illumination induces a permanent night: "In the attic, the day's experiences can always efface the fears of night. In the cellar, darkness prevails."[37] Supporting this diurnal/noctural disparity is the inherent directionality of attic and cellar: one imagines or remembers oneself going *up* to the former and *down* to the latter.[38]

The house, then, is "one of the greatest powers of integration for the thoughts, memories, and dreams of mankind."[39] For our purposes, it is exemplary on two basic counts. On the one hand, a topoanalysis of the house demonstrates that psychic places are not merely diffuse or formless. To the contrary: they possess their own precision. Topo*logy* honors its own etymon as "structure," "system," "word." The imagined/remembered house may not be physically substantial or even extant, but it is highly structured and knows its own limits: "In the oneiric house, topoanalysis only knows how to count to three or four."[40] Imaginary space, far from being arbitrary or chaotic, is consistent, specific, and finely wrought—once again, not unlike the unconscious as investigated by Freud or Jung.[41] On the other hand, the house exhibits "the being of within,"[42] that is, the interiority experienced in inhabited houses, especially when this inhabitation is a matter of memorably contented dwelling, of being-well and of well-being. Then "the values of inhabited space"[43] become evident—values that transcend anything that Euclidean geometry can capture.

At stake here is nothing less than a new understanding of the "in," a preposition that has haunted the pages of this book since at least its third chapter. This "in" is antipodal to the *en* of Aristotle's *Physics*—that nonpsychical interiority that results from being strictly surrounded on all sides. Precisely in its distance from Aristotle's *en,* Bachelard's "in" is closer to Heidegger's notion of Being-in as "residing alongside" (*Sein bei*). Yet this latter feature remains a largely empty and formal function of Dasein's being-in-the-world. Even Heidegger's later emphasis on dwelling in "Building Dwelling Thinking" lacks concreteness and specificity. Although we are told that dwelling is "the basic character of Being in keeping with which mortals exist,"[44] just *how* this basic character manifests itself is not shown, and the reader is left with such generalities as "the way in which you are and I am, the manner in which we humans *are* on the earth, is *Buan,* dwelling."[45] As already noted, we learn a lot more about building and the fourfold than about dwelling in the essay of 1951. *The Poetics of Space,* appearing six years later, has much more to say about the specificities of human dwelling—about its "countless diversified nuances."[46] The point of topoanalysis (in this respect, closely resembling phenomenology) is to pursue a given *topos* into its most minute particulars. In

the case of dwelling, this means probing such microtopics as chests and draw-
ers and closets, corners and nests and shells—to each of which densely descriptive pages are devoted in *La poétique de l'espace.*

In Bachelard's concrete topoanalysis—which traces the "drama of intimate
geometry"[47]—four concrete traits of the *in* of inhabitation stand out.

(1) The "in" paired with "out" in dwelling cannot be reduced to the here/
there, which Bachelard considers "the unfortunate adverbs of place."[48] Where
the here closes in tightly—for example, to the locus of the body as an absolute
"null-point" (Husserl)—the "in" ingredient in inhabitation is a fluid focus, one
that is in constant communication with the "out": for instance, by means of
doors and windows, whereby the outside world becomes part of the being of
within (and vice versa: *through* these apertures in the house we are in continual contact with the surrounding world). There is "an osmosis between intimate and undetermined space."[49] Thanks to this osmotic, two-way flow,
dwelling is in-dwelling in such a way that we also find ourselves *out in* the
ambience of that which we inhabit.

(2) Contributing to the continuity between inside and outside is the comparative *lack of limit* that inhabitation brings with it. A home may be one's
"castle," and yet in the world of felicitous space it need not be a fortress set
apart from the wider world. On the contrary! Oscar V. Milosz, cited approv-
ingly by Bachelard, writes, "Away with boundaries, those enemies of horizons! Let genuine distance appear!"[50] But, to be topoanalytically precise, we
should again distinguish between *limits* and *boundaries.* A room in our home
is not experienced as a limit, that is, a geometrically determined border or
perimeter. To inhabit such a room is for *it to be in us,* and for us to be in an
entire house and world *through it.*[51] But, by the same token, a room may also
be experienced as having a boundary, that is, as something with shape and
force. We experience this in the case of doorways that are genuine thresholds.
Bachelard cites Porphry: "A threshold is a sacred thing."[52] A threshold is
something we pass over, and as such it contains a felt difference between
being inside and outside—sometimes a difference that is "painful on both
sides."[53] Indeed, to be in an intimately inhabited room is not merely to tolerate
but to *require* boundaries.[54] It is only the "lazy certainties" of a "reinforced
geometrism," superimposed on our experience of inhabitation, that demands
limits instead.[55]

(3) To be un(de)limited albeit bounded is to enjoy the conditions for *concentration.* To dwell in a house is to feel oneself to be *in the center* of things
without, however, necessarily being literally *at the center.* The difference is
that between a strictly geometric centeredness and an inhabitational being-
centered-in that is as thick as it is porous. Concentration, like inhabitation
itself, is two-way. Just as I am in the dwelling that is also in me, so I feel
centered by being within the dwelling in which I reside—orienting myself by
what is around me—while I am also *centering* insofar as I give direction to

things and rooms in that same dwelling. In this twofold way, I realize "the valorization of center, of concentrated solitude."[56] Not only myself but nonhuman things become concentrated in the intimate sphere: "Every object invested with intimate space becomes the center of all space."[57] Such centeredness of self and thing is a gift of dwelling, something gained in the inhabitation of houses. Yet the gift and the gain do not require literal residing. Images suffice: "They give us back areas of being, houses in which the human being's certainty of being is concentrated, and we have the impression that, by living in such images as these, in images that are as stabilizing as these are, we could start a new life."[58] Concentration is a major means of stabilization. Thus the house in which I live a concentrated life is a genuine "restingplace," and as such it is as "motionless" as the memories of my dwelling there will be (no wonder, then, that domiciles *house memories*).[59]

(4) The previous three traits of in-habitation come together in the phenomenon of "intimate immensity." To be in a house, indeed to be in its most secluded nook, is not only to feel oneself to be protected from a hostile outer world; it is also to experience oneself in a larger world *in miniature.* For the miniature is "*vast* in its way."[60] Instead of feeling confined to the nook, I find in this miniplace a burgeoning world that exceeds both nook and house as literal entities. Not only the house, then, but even the most minute part of it is capable of containing a world—of *being a world* and not just being-in-a-world. To be a world, or even just to be "world conscious,"[61] requires more than participating in an analogy between the microcosm of the room one is in and the macrocosm of the universe that exceeds this room. More than parallelism is at play in intimate immensity. To feel such immensity is to feel *infinity in intimacy,* a universe in a grain of sand—one's own grain, on one's own beach. I feel at one with the universe not because I am extended out into it, or can merely project myself there, but because I experience its full extent *from within* my discrete place in the house. Felt from the very being of within, the most redoubtable being of without comes easily within one's compass. Limits fade and concentration occurs as I connect the tiny and the enormous in a single stroke.

Thanks to intimate immensity, I also connect place with space. The beguiling and bedeviling dichotomy between these terms—the one a paradigm of the finite, the other always tending to the infinite—is overcome, and without delay! In intimate immensity *I enter space from place itself.* I come to the immense *from within* rather than on the basis of exteriority, that is, of *partes extra partes.* Place is no longer just a delimited part or portion of space. Space is now wholly immanent in place rather than the reverse. Even the "absolute elsewhere" is not located in absolute space but *in a particular place.* Infinite space, the most alien of prospects for Pascal, can thus be "the friend of being."[62] Such a radical reversal—difficult to imagine in the exclusionary terms of early modern physics and metaphysics—becomes perfectly possible in a psychical spatiality that is sufficiently porous to find poetic expression. The reversal is possible because the in/out dyad has lost its divisive and diremptive character. To be *in the out*—and to feel *the out in*—is to be in a situation in which clarity and distinctness no longer rule. In this situation, we enter "the entire space-time of ambiguous being."[63] Such being is at once *virtual* (i.e., not simply real) and *general* (i.e., not strictly universal).[64]

By virtue of the double reversal effected by intimate immensity the very difference between place and space is suspended. The circumstance is such that "intimate space loses its clarity, while exterior space loses its void."[65] In this important pronouncement, "intimate space" is equivalent to place—rendered less than fully clear and distinct by its immanent immensity—while "exterior space" is tantamount to infinite space, at once full and compressed into intimacy. Place and space shed their usual differentia: the clarity and distinctness of the near and small in the one case, the emptiness of the far and enormous in the other. They coalesce in a common *intensity:* "Immensity in the intimate domain is intensity, an intensity of being, the intensity of a being evolving in a vast perspective of intimate immensity."[66] At the same time, place and space have both gained *density* in the richly ambiguous sphere of inhabitation to which Bachelard's imaginal psychography points us.

I have taken the house—the leading topic of *The Poetics of Space*—to be exemplary of two basic vectors in Bachelard's later work: the intricacy of psychical topography and the inner structure of inhabitation. If to be exemplary is to be highly instructive, it is also not to be the only case in point. In fact, Bachelard's writings teem with instances of both tendencies, as if to suggest that poetic-psychical implacement is proliferative by its very nature. Each of the four material elements yields a multitiered schematization of considerable subtlety, as do reverie and even the history of science.[67] Everywhere one looks, one sees a profusion of imaginal *topoi*. Similarly, inhabitation is by no means restricted to the house or home, archetypal as these are; inhabiting occurs in the repose of earth, in the stillness of water, indeed wherever possibilities of dwelling—by imaginative infusion if not by bodily habitude—arise. As Bachelard writes in *The Poetics of Reverie,*

> Dreaming before the fire or before water, one knows a sort of stable reverie. Fire and water have a power of oneiric integration. Then the images have roots. In following them, we adhere to the world; we take root in the world. . . . In the still waters, the world rests. Before still water, the dreamer adheres to the repose of the world. . . . The soul is at home everywhere in a universe which reposes on the pond.[68]

Indeed, the well-being of reposeful residing is at home in all the places, actual or virtual, in which imagining and remembering flourish in felicitous space.

In such space—or, rather, in its constituent and concatenated places—the two vectors of topography and inhabitation converge in the reverberation of particular images as these resonate in the soul of the reader of poetry or in ordinary experiences of remembering and reverie. A "felicitous amplitude"[69] of connotations induces a condensed cosmos at once all-encompassing (i.e., immense) and yet snugly fitting (i.e., intimate). In this psychical paradise, entire fields of images are proffered by houses or material elements—and by many other elementary things. Such imaginal fields, being multilocular, furnish numerous resting places for possible experiences of in-dwelling.[70] In these fields, there is always *plenty of place* in which to dwell—in imagination, memory, and the poetry that combines both. For each topic has its own locus, each theme its own content; the topic and theme rejoin in forming configurations possessing boundaries apposite for genuine in-habitation. Without the purchase provided by such imaginal configurations, one could not talk meaningfully of dwelling *in* them. "The imagination of matter"—the subtitle of Bachelard's *Water and Dreams*—is an imagination of something substantial enough to reside in, albeit only in the fulgurating afterlife of an image. Material imagination puts us in touch not with ephemera but with what is dense and intense enough for inhabitation, real or imagined. Topoanalysis explores the intimate in-dwelling that ensues.[71]

III

> Space is not the setting (real or logical) in which
> things are arranged, but the means whereby the
> positing of things becomes possible.
> —Maurice Merleau-Ponty, *Phenomenology*
> *of Perception*

Since Bachelard's death (in 1962, the same year in which Heidegger delivered his last important public lecture, "Time and Being"), new directions have been sought—and new faces found—for place. Despite the welcome vistas opened up by the psychical poetics of imagined matter, thinkers about place have shared a growing conviction that an approach such as Bachelard's neglects certain concrete aspects of place that call out for close attention in the second half of the twentieth century. To consider the sexual, social, political, and historical aspects of space is to acknowledge what Bachelard termed "the diverse coefficients of reality" and, in particular, the "coefficient of adversity."[72] To overlook such coefficients is to engage in a dangerously delimited enterprise—an enterprise privileging "subdued" and "non-thetic" being, as Merleau-Ponty characterized Bachelard's preoccupation with the material elements.[73] It is to pursue topoanalysis in one extreme fashion, that whereby the psyche is wholly absorbed in musing on images and their placial properties. Bachelard himself did not hesitate to admit that "any doctrine of the imaginary is necessarily a philosophy of excess."[74] If this is indeed so, it is time to move to quite different extremities and to assess disparate modes of excess.

The movements to be traced in this and subsequent sections proceed in each case from what is comparatively subdued to what is comparatively adverse. The *terra infirma* of Psyche—where all is ambiguous and diaphanous—cedes place to the *terra firma* of Soma, this latter signifying not only the lived body but all that possesses robust historical and physical thinghood. The softness of the psychic realm hardens as we enter into new forms of topoanalysis, now directed at resistant, sturdy Secondness—to employ Peirce's term for rugged actualities that oppose, even as they define, basic human projects. Thus we shall journey from the obscure byways of *la vie intime* into the exposed highways of public life: the privilege of musing and dreaming ahistorically and apolitically will yield to rigorous historical research, political action, and other forms of engaged activity. As a consequence, the intensity and density associated with intimate immensity will give way to a model of place in which the distended and open, the laid out and the laid bare, will figure prominently—which is not, however, to return to the Heideggerian Open, much less to Cartesian extension! The comparative stability at stake in the gentle psychodrama of reverie—the *stabilitas loci* that underlies both the motionlessness of memories and the permanence of dwelling—will be sacrificed for what (though adverse) is changing and mobile, for what (though durational) exists in transition rather than in stasis, and for what (though seemingly self-evident) cannot be assumed or imagined to be the case.

It is a matter, in short, of moving into a scene "of other spaces"—the title of a lecture given by Michel Foucault in 1967. These other spaces will give rise to *other places,* as Foucault says expressly: "We might imagine a sort of systematic description—I do not say a science because the term is too galvanized now—that would, in a given society, take as its object the study, analysis, description, and 'reading' (as some like to say nowadays) of these different spaces, of these other places."[75] Not just topoanalysis, then, but a distinctive *heterotopoanalysis* is called for in this movement outward and onward, a movement for which Foucault will be our guide in this section. In the lecture in question, he set the stage for his own later discussions of eighteenth-century spatiality (treated earlier in this book) by proposing that "space itself has a history."[76] This seemingly innocent proposition is in fact of considerable significance. If it is true that there is a genuine genealogy of space—and, mutatis mutandis, of place—then we cannot maintain that place or space is simply one kind of thing, to be discovered and described once and for all. Not only is space not absolute and place not permanent, but the conception of each is subject to the most extensive historical vicissitudes. The extremity we now enter is that of the historicity of our subject: a challenging prospect indeed.

At stake here is not just accuracy of description. Foucault's own hasty sketch in "Of Other Spaces" is highly problematic, for instance, his claim that medieval space is simply "the space of implacement" or that Galileo merely substituted infinite space for place.[77] We have seen that matters are in fact much more complicated than this: just as the medieval period was already fascinated with spatial infinity, so the seventeenth century was still pondering the vicissitudes of place. But what is most important is Foucault's claim that fundamental ideas of place and space vary widely from era to era—and from society to society. There are no constants in this conjoint history; "space" and "place" are as variable as time is usually taken to be: ever-altering, never the same. This should not surprise us: after all, this entire book has been devoted to tracing out the shifting and often concealed "history of place." We have witnessed Heidegger's brief foray into this history in his essay "Building Dwelling Thinking." But Foucault is the first to formulate fully the genealogical thesis: space and place are historical entities, subject to the vagaries of time. (Also, and especially, *of power,* as Foucault insists; preferred spatial modalities in architecture, social organization, police surveillance, etc., are expressions of specific distributions of power: "Once knowledge can be analyzed in terms of region, domain, implantation, displacement, transposition, one is able to capture the process by which knowledge functions as a form of power and disseminates the effects of power."[78] But the proposal that "knowledge is power" does not alter the historicist thesis; taking this thesis to be true, it gives to it an explicitly political interpretation.)

In keeping with his genealogical approach, Foucault offers an arresting reading of twentieth-century notions of space and place. We live, he suggests, "in the epoch of space"—an epoch in which time, the dominant concern of the nineteenth century, has been absorbed into space: "I believe that the anxiety of our era has to do fundamentally with space, no doubt a great deal more than with time. Time probably appears to us only as one of the various distributive operations that are possible for the elements that are spread out in space."[79] Time is swallowed by space—space not now in the form of abiding memories (also ingestive of time on Bachelard's account of such memories) but the exterior and public space at stake in networks of simultaneous interconnection, for example, in cybernetic or electronic matrices of communication. Foucault's description of this situation is revealing.

> The present epoch will perhaps be above all the epoch of space. We are in the epoch of simultaneity: we are in the epoch of juxtaposition, the epoch of the near and far, of the side-by-side, of the dispersed. We are at a moment, I believe, when our experience of the world is less that of a long life developing through time than that of a network that connects points and intersections with its own skein.[80]

Remarkable here is the concatenation of simultaneity with the near and the far, that is, of a primary predicate of space with a basic property of place. This is tantamount to a juxtaposition of Leibniz with Heidegger. In this implicit competition, Leibniz wins out, since the prevailing criterion is "juxtaposition" or "the side-by-side"—to which the near cannot be reduced.[81] Moreover, Leibniz emerges victorious precisely in terms of his own master signifiers, "site" and "relation."

> Today site has been substituted for extension, which had itself replaced implace-ment. A site is defined by relations of proximity between points or elements: formally, we can describe these relations as series, trees, or grids. . . . Our epoch is one in which space takes for us the form of relations among sites.[82]

The ever-lengthening shadow of *analysis situs* serves to warn us that the historicity of space and place alike is not a merely momentary matter: continuity as well as change characterizes their epochal manifestations. In the case of the purely positional or relational model of space or place construed as site, we witness something that, born in the era of Descartes and brought to full expression by Leibniz, still remains in force today.

This is not to say that the contemporary experience of place or space is entirely dominated by site. Foucault himself admits that, despite the "theoretical desanctification of space" that was carried out in the seventeenth and eighteenth centuries, there is a refractory survival of "the hidden presence of the sacred" in certain unquestioned spatial oppositions: private space versus public space, family space versus social space, leisure space versus work space.[83] Indeed, he cites Bachelard's "monumental work" as an indication of the survival of "a space thoroughly imbued with qualities and perhaps thoroughly fantasmatic as well."[84] Acknowledging that Bachelard's descriptions of these qualities are "fundamental for reflection in our time," he nevertheless regards such descriptions as having to do only with "internal space."[85] In fact, the external space in which we live at this point in history is at once nonqualitative and heterogeneous: neither Bachelard's richly qualitative imaginary plenum nor early modern models of homogeneous and (usually) void space does justice to what we now experience: "We do not live inside a void that could be colored with diverse shades of light, we live inside a set of relations that delineates sites which are irreducible to one another and absolutely not superimposable on one another."[86]

Examples of such sites include railroads, restaurants, beaches, and houses (described by Foucault as "closed or semi-closed sites of rest"): in each case, we have to do with a set of relations that condenses or mimicks the totality of historical and social circumstances in which it is stationed. Foucault does not, however, linger on these instances. Precisely because he might agree with Bachelard that the house is a compressed and miniaturized world thanks to its intimate immensity, it fails to exhibit what is of most interest to Foucault: "The curious property of being in relation with all other sites, but in such a way as to call into question, neutralize, or invert the set of relations that they happen to designate, mirror, or reflect."[87] He recognizes two exemplary cases in point: utopias and heterotopias. Whereas utopias are "sites with no real place" and represent a perfected (and thus radically transformed) state of society, heterotopias are real places that contest and reverse sites within a given society.[88] These "countersites" include cemeteries and gardens, as well as places of crisis (e.g., menstruation huts, boarding schools) and places of punishment or treatment (e.g., hospitals or prisons, thus including panoptica). Each of these heterotopias is at once "absolutely different" from the surrounding places they reflect—and yet at the same time actually locatable in geographic reality. Indeed, their locatability is intrinsic to their considerable power as peripheral entities: to come in from a position "outside of all [other, ordinary] places"[89] is effective only if what ingresses has a certain determinacy of shape and locus. This is not a matter of simple, but of *effective,* location. To make a difference in the social fabric, a heterotopia must possess a focus for the application of force. This focus is found in the marginal location of the heterotopia itself: from this location, force can be exerted more effectively than if it stemmed from the center of the circumstance. The systematic study of such noncentral sites, "heterotopology," names Foucault's main arena of research during the last fifteen years of his life.[90] In this regard, his concerted search for *des espaces autres* punctuating the historical and political order of things (and challenging that order itself) could not depart more dramatically or drastically from Bachelard's involuted topoanalysis of the places of a receptive reverie.

Despite the promise of heterotopology—and its brilliant attainments in such books as *The Birth of the Clinic, Discipline and Punish,* and *The History of Sexuality*—it harbors three problems. First, Foucault nowhere makes a clear, much less a rigorous, distinction between such basic terms as "place," "space," "location," and "site." As a consequence, these terms are often run together or interchanged indifferently. Thus, as we have seen, heterotopology is said to study "these different spaces, these other places." To this we are tempted to respond: Which does it study—spaces or places? Still more problematically, a "heterotopia is capable of juxtaposing in a single place several spaces, several sites that are in themselves incompatible."[91] The terms may not be incompatible, but Foucault has set space, place, and site side by side in this sentence, whose incongruity bears comparison with the passage from Borges's "Chinese Encyclopaedia" of which Foucault himself was so fond: "(a) belonging to the Emperor, (b) embalmed, (c) tame, (d) sucking pigs, (e) sirens." Just as Borges's sentence lacks, on Foucault's own analysis, a "common locus" in which to situate such heterogeneous items, so his own juxaposition of space and place, location and site lacks a coherent ground of connection—and thus of differentiation.[92]

Second, despite his formidable critical prowess (as applied to the diversities of unacknowledged power), Foucault offers no critique of the idea of "site" by which he so often characterizes the twentieth-century experience of space. The Leibnizian heritage of this term is ignored, with the result that Foucault appears to acquiesce in the very phenomenon that, from the perspective of power/knowledge, is loaded with the most repressive and sinister implications. An acceptance of the status quo in matters of space and place—an unwillingness to question the idea of "site" beyond merely invoking the conceptually parasitic notion of "countersite"—skirts dangerously close to a retrograde slide toward the status quo ante. Leibniz finally prevails in the very face of Foucault's brilliant analysis of the Panopticon as a paradigm of eighteenth-century sited space.

Third, Foucault subtly undercuts his own historicist thesis—his single most valuable contribution to the analysis of space and place—by suggesting that heterotopology is a discipline with universalist aspirations. The "first principle" of heterotopology—that "there is probably not a single culture in the world that fails to constitute heterotopias"—stands in tension with the "second principle": "A society, as its history unfolds, can make an existing heterotopia function in a very different fashion."[93] But if historical difference is truly radical, will there not come a point (or perhaps there has already been such a point) when there are not only very different heterotopias but *no heterotopia at all* in a given society? Does not the historicist thesis undermine the universalist claim? To these questions no adequate answer is forthcoming from the unfinished torso of Foucault's work.

IV

> Nothing completely coincides, and everything intermingles or crosses over.
>
> Here the absolute is local, precisely because place is not delimited.
>
> —Deleuze and Guattari,
> *A Thousand Plateaus*

A Thousand Plateaus (1980), the monumental work of Gilles Deleuze and Félix Guattari, explores the vast vista opened up in the wake of *Anti-Oedipus,* the preceding volume in the authors' series entitled *Capitalism and Schizophrenia.* True to its title, *A Thousand Plateaus* (no narrow defile here!) discusses a plethora of topics, both in their historical particularity and in their abiding philosophical and political significance. Especially pertinent for our purposes is chapter 12, "1227: Treatise on Nomadology:—The War Machine." In this chapter, the authors explore a society that, like the heterotopias sketched by Foucault, proves to be at once delimited in its form of appearance (its most complete form occurred precisely in 1227 on the steppes of central

Asia) and yet transcultural in its implications (i.e., affording a model for similar situations elsewhere). The crucial "other space" for Deleuze and Guattari is that belonging to nomads who exist on the fringe of settled civilizations. From this margin, raids and other incursions are made into the fixed and fortified strongholds ruled by kings and members of priestly castes: the "state apparatus." Acting in bands and packs (much as in guerrilla warfare), this metamorphic war machine infiltrates and upsets the royal state from the outside; it is thus a "pure form of exteriority."[94] The authors detect the working of this extramural invasion not just in the case of ancient city-states but in other, analogous circumstances, for example, in the history of science, where an official state-sanctioned science such as mathematics or physics is continually challenged by a "nomad" or "minor" science such as metallurgy or hydraulics. The static character of the *state*—a word stemming from *stare*, "to stand"—is contested by the fluid, metamorphic nature of amateur, bootstrapping science. The latter's protean actions are *heteros*, "other," to the established sites of "royal science." The inherent legalism of state science, its logocentric obsession, exhibits itself in a search for mathematical constants and eidetic forms, and in a preference for hylomorphic schemata (i.e., in which form is imposed on matter). In contrast, offbeat and unofficial sciences are concerned with "material-forces" rather than with matter-form per se; they seek vague essences as well as "singularities in matter" and "individuations through events or haecceities."[95] The *Compars* of the immured state, its closed-in and regularized spatiality, is starkly etched against the *Dispars* of the bricoleur's home laboratory—which, like a transitory nomadic camp, is set up with materials ready at hand in a casually arranged workplace that lacks fortified walls.

So far, then, two plateaus have been sketched—or, more specifically, a securely buttressed high-standing mesa and an outlying and surrounding plain. The landscape terms of this primary contrast are neither accidental nor merely rhetorical. They reflect the extreme sensitivity of Deleuze and Guattari to issues of concrete implacement, that is, their conviction that *where something is situated* has everything to do with *how it is structured.* Only in the imperialist perspective of a royal science such as that of Newtonian physics does implacement supposedly become a matter of indifference: the law of gravity is presumed to be universal and to operate between any two bodies found anywhere in the physical universe. Gravitational forces are schematized in parallel laminar lines that are determinable metrically. But in the very different perspective of a nomad science such as the hydraulics of flood control—or even, more expansively, of sea power—the role of place is pervasive and not to be ignored. Here the material forces move not in perfectly straight lines in a gridlike space but in spiral and vortical motions in concrete places, for example, in the coursing of floodwater and in storms at sea. How water moves is a direct reflection of *where it is:* it makes a difference whether water is on dry

land or on the high seas. If the geometry of gravitation is still Euclidean (typified in its postulate of parallel lines that never meet), that of hydraulic motion
is vectorial, projective, and most especially topological—thus a function of
the place it is in. *Gravitas* induces an exact science of weights and measures,
hence of the precise parameters of invariant declinations that are the same
anywhere on earth. In contrast, *celeritas,* that is, comparative swiftness, calls
for an "anexact" science of approximation that takes account of just where a
motion occurs, that is, of its varying inclination and direction.[96]

All of these contrasts point to a major distinction that is of particular import
in an emerging philosophy of place: that between *smooth* and *striated* space,
to which Deleuze and Guattari devote a separate chapter in *A Thousand Plateaus.* This distinction stems from the composer Pierre Boulez, who contrasts
"striated" musical forms that are ordered by fixed schemata (e.g., the octave)
and "smooth" forms that allow for considerable irregularity (e.g., non-octave-
based scales). In the first case, we have to do with a space that is "counted in
order to be occupied," whereas in the second case space is "occupied without
being counted."[97] Counting is not merely a matter of numbering but, more
generally, of assigning determinate values. In striated space, there is sufficient
homogeneity of surface so that distinct (and thus numerable) points can be
specified and thus counted; motion in such space is always from point to point,
hence from one countable simple location to another: such is the legacy of the
seventeenth-century effort to evacuate space of any qualitative properties so
that, properly neutralized, it can be assigned definite values, mathematical and
otherwise. It is a matter, in short, of sheer extension—which lends itself to
centration (i.e., as the point of intersection of the *XYZ* axes in analytical geometry) as well as to universalization (i.e., held to obtain *every*where). Precisely
as homogeneous and planiform (arranging itself in flat, parallel planes), such
space is subject to linear striation by precise paths and is projected as seen
from a fixed point of view—as in monofocal perspective—thereby allowing
for the perfect reproduction of its contents indifferently *any*where. Smooth
space, by contrast, is heterogeneous and filled with "qualitative multiplicities"
(in Bergson's term) that resist exact centration or reproduction, and all the
more so universalization. In such space we are always immersed in a particular palpable and nonplaniform field on which we cannot take an external point
of view (even though, paradoxically, to be in that field is to engage in "outside
thought" vis-à-vis royal science). As Deleuze and Guattari put it,

> Smooth space is precisely the space of the smallest deviation: therefore it has
> no homogeneity, except between infinitely proximate points, and the linking of
> proximities is effected independently of any determined path. It is a space of
> contact, of small tactile or manual actions of contact, rather than a visual space
> like Euclid's striated space. Smooth space is a field without [parallel] conduits
> or channels. A field, a heterogeneous smooth space, is wedded to a very particu-
> lar type of multiplicity: nonmetric, acentered, rhizomatic multiplicities that

occupy space without "counting" it and "can be explored only by legwork." They do not meet the visual condition of being observable from a point in space external to them; an example of this is the system of sounds or even of colors, as opposed to Euclidean space.[98]

Smooth space provides room for *vagabondage,* for wandering and drifting between regions instead of moving straight ahead between fixed points. Here one moves not only in accordance with cardinal directions or geometrically determined vectors but in a "polyvocality of directions"—directions that are as much heard as seen, and in any case not merely posited as exigencies of theory.[99] On the high sea, or in the windswept desert, one *listens to* direction, *feels it,* as much as one sees it (sometimes, as in an Arctic storm, one cannot discern directional markers of any kind, and yet a native to the region *knows* how to get to places). In these circumstances, when everyone is in effect a nomad, one must engage in "an extraordinarily fine topology that relies not on points or objects but rather on haecceities, on sets of relations (winds, undulations of snow or sand, the song of the sand or the creaking of ice, the tactile qualities of both)."[100] One finds one's bearing *where one is,* that is, in the very place, the local absolute one occupies—without counting. "The nomad, nomad space, is localized and not delimited."[101]

As deeply localized, nomad space always occurs *as a place—in this place.* But as undelimited, it is a special kind of place. It is a place that is not just *here,* in a pinpointed spot of space, but in a "nonlimited locality."[102] For the place at stake in nomad space is intrinsically vast. It is immense without being either infinite or intimate. Neither Newton nor Bachelard—who together constitute the extremities of modern thinking about space, one championing the infinite, the other the intimate—sanctions such space. For in its nondelimitation, nomad space is no more a purely dimensional, empty physical infinity than it is a condensed plenary presence within the psyche. Belonging neither to Physis nor to Psyche, nomad space is "exterior" without being extended, and "pure" without being imaginary. Its vastness cannot be measured by any metrics of extension. As Descartes would say—for quite different reasons—its extension is *indefinite.* This is why a characteristic nomadic space is an entire *region*—a steppe, a desert, a sea—that, despite its enormity, is not a strictly measurable space with definite borders.[103] To inhabit such a region is not merely to be *at* a place in it, much less at a point *in* it (there are no points in nomad space).[104] Nor is it to be at the *center* of the vastness: centration is more properly to be found in Husserl's absolute here of the body, or else in the global absolute of religion (e.g., a sacred place as the center of the cosmos).[105] Instead, the nomad is spread throughout the whole region he or she inhabits, as much there as here, always on the way *between* the places of this region: "The life of the nomad is the intermezzo."[106] It is a life on the lam. It is not—as Heidegger would have it in his concerted flight from Husserl's absolute here—that the nomad is always there *rather than* here. He or she is here/there *and* there/here, in between here and there, this place and that place, distributed between them, as it were.[107]

Smooth space, nomad space, therefore points to what we might call *place-as-region*. If Bachelard could argue that time is compressed into space, and Heidegger that space and place are in principle the same (either because space is already "split up into places" or because space "receives its being from places"),[108] Deleuze and Guattari maintain in effect that region and place converge. A region is not the mere totalization of places, as if places were assigned or allocated to *parts* of a region. The region itself is a place. When I— I as nomad—live and move on the steppe, I exist *through* the whole region, here/there in all of it, not just in part of it. Localization undeniably exists: at any given moment, I am *somewhere* and not drifting *nowhere* (as nonnomads who have never lived on the desert or steppe, or been at sea, doubtless fear). But my being somewhere is not restricted to being in a single locality: the ship is always moving on, the caravan continues, the dog team careens over the ice. I am distended everywhere in the region; I am potentially *any place* in it. The region is the place I am in. Thus the absolute has become the local, rather than the reverse. For *place itself is everywhere*—everywhere in, indeed *as,* the region. "Here the absolute is local, precisely because place is not delimited."[109] This dual conundrum is the crux.

In this paradoxical situation, more important than locality (qua unit) is the "local operation" (the action), whereby I make my way through the localities that punctuate a region, modifying them along the way.

> For the nomad . . . locality is not delimited; the absolute, then, does not appear at a particular place but becomes a nonlimited locality; the coupling of the place and the absolute is achieved not in a centered, oriented globalization or universalization but in an infinite succession of local operations.[110]

Local operations are the very basis of the constitution and experience of smooth space, and they consist for the most part of relays whereby one moves little by little across a landscape or seascape, aided by beasts of burden, ships, and other slow-moving vehicles. If the migrant is someone who goes from point to point in a journey, the nomad proceeds by "relays along a trajectory."[111] Relays involve skilled motions of catching up and carrying on, all in close proximity to the ground or sea on which one moves. In such nomadic or smooth space one moves not only efficiently but intensely. For smooth space is a matter of "intense *Spatium* instead of *Extensio*."[112] We experience such intense spatiality above all when we "voyage in place," that is, literally do not move our bodies yet still manage to get somewhere. Bedouins crouch in a stationary position on galloping horses, and in this immobile mobility they do not move in relation to the region that they nevertheless traverse.[113]

Such a voyage in such a place/region is measured neither in terms of quantity of distance or motion or time nor in terms of its psychical resonance; its intensity is not intimate but belongs to the very vastness of the region in which the journey is made.[114]

If Bachelard undermines Cartesian dualism by the idea of intimate immensity, he does so only by collapsing space into the cozy places of the psyche. Deleuze and Guattari undercut the same dualism by the idea of *immersion in a region*. The directionality of the undermining is now reversed: not from exteriority to interiority but the other way around. The "being of within" yields to a being of *without*. Immersion in nomadic smooth space is immersion in something more vast than any psyche can provide, more vast not just in literal physical extent but as an adumbrated, unending (yet not infinite!) *Spatium*. One is immersed in something seemingly endless—the Unlimited. The desert or the sea, disappearing over the horizon, is limitless in the arc of its vanishing.[115]

Immersion in smooth space is at once body based and landscape oriented. We witness this double basis of immersion in the role of *directions* in nomadic space. To move in such space is not to follow a set course between fixed points: the points of origin and destination (assuming there are such) are invisible, and the path one takes/makes is immediately erased by the shifting sands or sea or winds. In inclement weather and at night, even the horizon ceases to be visible. As a consequence, one must continually find one's way by determining the appropriate direction. The local operations of relay must be oriented by the discovery (and often the continual rediscovery) of direction; otherwise, these operations would be in vain. It follows that "smooth space is directional rather than dimensional or metric."[116] As we have learned both from Philoponus and from Descartes, dimensionality belongs to *Extensio*. Directionality, in contrast, adheres to intense *Spatium*. What makes the situation intense is precisely the way in which the lived body, being next to the earth or water, orients itself by noticing landmarks or seamarks that stake out the region one is in. As we have learned from Kant, orientation in "cosmic regions" requires a bilateral body that can interpret these environing markers as lying to the right or left—or above or below, front or back—of where one is now located. It is not a matter of estimating the correct *distance* to the marker but of orienting one's bilateral body *to* or *by* the marker, aligning oneself with its implicit vector. The sense of direction that results thus arises from a peculiar but potent synthesis of the body and the salient objects of its encircling landscape. (This synthesis is such that even if the local clues are missing in immediate perception, one can still detect or remember one's way.)

Deleuze and Guattari, while ignoring the body's bilaterality, nevertheless suggest a significant new link between body and place, one that is specific to being in smooth space. Since such space is never a matter of point of view or distance in any metric sense—even landmarks become proximal presences—it must be experienced by actions at "close range," for example, by "legwork," by walking, hearing, and more generally by various haptic modalities. Each of these local operations establishes contiguity with the ground one is on, whether land or sea. Everything is experienced in relation to this ground, which is felt fully with the aesthesiological and kinesthetic body. On the ground, "there is no intermediary distance, or all distance is intermediary." [117] What is most crucial is not—as in classical, representationalist theories of perception—*what* one perceives but *how* one negotiates one's bodily ingression in the immediate vicinity.

> The first aspect of the haptic, smooth space of close vision is that its orientations, landmarks, and linkages are in continuous variation; it operates step by step. Examples are the desert, steppe, ice, and sea, local spaces of pure connection. Contrary to what is sometimes said, one never sees from a distance in a space of this kind, nor does one see it from a distance; one is never "in front of," any more than one is "in" (one is "on" . . .).[118]

The *on* of smooth space replaces the *in* of container space, the *at* of the point, and even the *with* of sedentary dwelling. For dwelling is here accomplished in traveling. One does not move *to* a dwelling but *dwells by moving,* that is, by transition from place to place within (or, again, *as*) a region. There is thus an "absolute of passage" that is identical with the local absolute: "There exists a nomadic absolute, as a local integration moving from part to part and constituting smooth space in an infinite succession of linkages and changes in direction." [119] The "local integration" is effected by the moving body, which is the bearer of an unhoused inhabitation, the very vehicle of a space without conduits or settled sites. The result is a peculiar but important form of dwelling that breaks with the paradigm of the settled, to which Heidegger and Bachelard still cling. Nor is it a matter of the unhomely, the literally *unheimlich,* within the home; the nomad is perfectly at home on the desert or steppe: nothing is uncanny there. Instead, it is a matter of a continual deterritorialization of the land, converting it into the absolute ground of an ongoing journey. "With the nomad," write Deleuze and Guattari, "it is deterritorialization that constitutes the relation to the earth, to such a degree that the nomad reterritorializes on deterritorialization itself." [120]

In contrast with "the open smooth space in which the body moves" [121]—moves precisely by not moving!—striated space freezes movement and disembodies location, leaving no places for dwelling. Rather than the "amorphous" character of smooth space, it possesses determinate properties, above all lines that designate analytical-geometrical position and gravitational force.[122] Such striations connect visible points within a delimited and closed surface. This surface becomes increasingly homogeneous the more it is striated.[123] As uniform, it is subject to the exact measurement of distance and to the optics of point of view. Indeed, striated space comes to be dominated by "the requirements of long-distance vision: constancy of orientation, invariance of distance through an interchange of inertial points of reference . . . [and] constitution of a central perspective."[124] Even the "immersion in an ambient milieu" that we have seen to be indispensable to smooth space is reduced to a set of positions on a grid or map. Everywhere, the effort is to bring the Unlimited into limits—whether the Unlimited is the ocean, the desert, or the earth itself. This encompassing Whole is brought to order, an imposed order of interlineation and segmentation between fixed positions. The result is a space of sites rather than a region of places.[125]

As this circumstance of forcible reduction indicates, smooth and striated spaces are not entirely independent of one another. Not only are smooth spaces typically bordered by striated ones, but the two interact in manifold ways: "Smooth space is constantly being translated, transversed into a striated space; striated space is constantly being reversed, returned to a smooth space."[126] The most convincing single instance of this is found in the fate of world oceans. At first smooth spaces par excellence, these vast nomadic spaces become progressively striated with latitude and longitude lines in the fifteenth century; but in the course of time, "the sea reimparts a kind of smooth space" thanks to the nuclear submarine and other members of a "fleet in being" that moves independently of cartographic striations.[127] While it is true that smooth space is more powerfully deterritorializing than striated space, this does not mean that it always wins out—or that it is always allied with constructive and salutary forces. Deleuze and Guattari insist that their own unabashed preference for smooth space, especially when regarded as a heterotopic basis of resistance and revolution, does not entail an unconditional endorsement of such space. "Never believe," they admonish, "that a smooth space will suffice to save us."[128] As between nomadic and sedentary space, we cannot simply choose; it is a matter of "not better, just different."[129] There is even a certain final parity between the two. The distributing and journeying of the one complement the allocating and settling of the other: "The smooth is a *nomos*, whereas the striated always has a *logos*."[130] The fact that "all becoming occurs in smooth space" cannot conceal the equally important fact that "all progress is made by and in striated space."[131] The ethical and political advantages of emphasizing smooth space should not blind us to the necessity of striation— including the striation of smooth space itself. The relative global and the local absolute, despite their deep disparities, belong together. They constitute a dyad of striated and smooth that, in matters of place and space, is as indispensable as Plato's metaphysical dyad of the limited and unlimited, the odd and the even, the same and the different.

V

> We appear to ourselves only through an experience of spacing which is already marked by architecture.
>
> It gives a place to them all.
> —Jacques Derrida, "Point de Folie"

> Thus, architecture faces a difficult task: to dislocate that which it locates. This is the paradox of architecture.
> —Peter Eisenman, "Blue Line Text"

> Architecture's [ultimate] importance resides in its ability to accelerate society's transformation through a careful agencing of spaces and events.
> —Bernard Tschumi, *Event-Cities*

To rethink space as place—and not the reverse, as in the early modern era—is the urgent task of everyone under consideration in this final chapter. The task is realized in diverse ways. Bachelard proceeds by a concerted revalorization of *res cogitans* as *mens imaginans*. Where thinking substance is a paradigm of spacelessness for Descartes, imagining mind for Bachelard exemplifies a new placefulness, no longer beholden to physical space but acting on its own quasi-autonomous psychical terms. In the imaginal psyche there is no room for anything but places . . . and more places. Similarly, albeit on entirely different terrain, Foucault rethinks modern space in terms of heterotopic places that contest the hegemony of dominant social and political structures. Deleuze and Guattari, allies of Foucault in many respects, likewise reconceive space as heterogeneous place: striated space gives way to smooth space, which yields open-ended, nomadic, nonsegmentary places (whether in amateur experimentation or transitory settlement).

In their insistence on becoming and movement, however, the authors of *A Thousand Plateaus* overlook the placial potential of *settled dwelling*—of what I have elsewhere called "built places." Instructive as is nomadic circulation in the smooth spaces of deserts and steppes, it represents only part of the full range of human habitation. We have already encountered several different forms of dwelling: the stringently controlled and internally transparent Panopticon (an exemplary institution of state power), the centrally situated buildings of cities in relation to which heterotopic "other spaces" act as antisites, the remembered or imagined childhood homes whose cozy nooks inspire adult reveries—not to mention Heidegger's dual emphasis on dwelling as Being-in and as thing-based. But we have not yet addressed the more straightforward case of architecture: How do built places convert space into place? This we shall now do by reference to the work of Jacques Derrida.

Derrida on built place? The very idea seems anomalous given Derrida's celebrated preoccupation with textuality and, above all, with intertextuality—matters seemingly far from place, especially built place. If there is any sense of place at stake in this preoccupation, it appears to be the unbuilt labyrinth of intertextuality from which there is no effective exit. Or more aptly: the Tower of Babel, which Derrida compares to "the text's spinal column."[132] But the affinity between building and writing goes deeper than this. Derrida has admitted, in an autobiographical aside, that writing for him is a special form of spatial configurating: "I have the feeling that when I . . . write, when I build certain texts, the law for me, or the rule, has to do with the spacing of the text. What interests me is not really the content but some distribution in the space, the way what I write is shaped, spatially shaped."[133] As a writer, Derrida shapes groups of words, making a composition that, though not literally architectural, meets architecture midway in the notion of *constructing*. This care for typographical construction is most conspicuously evident in a text such as *Glas,* with its double and triple columns making up a complex composition of vertical banding. It also follows—in keeping with Derrida's dictum that "there is nothing outside the text"—that "building is the writing of a text."[134] Just as texts are built, so buildings are written.

On Derrida's reading, texts of every kind are made up of written traces, which require for their very generation and maintenance a place of composition and construction. Even the formidable idea of "protowriting" (*archi-écriture*) calls for a place in which to appear—and to disappear, thanks to the self-effacing action of the prototraces (*archi-traces*) that arise in that place. A very special kind of place, that of the text, is therefore posited by Derrida. Already at stake for him, as it was for Aristotle, is the question of the "where." But Derrida seeks to suspend the question of the "what" with which Aristotle was ultimately more concerned. If the *what* is a metaphysical issue, the *where* is a matter of physics—or of text. How can we deny the physical or textual fact that traces, above all written traces, must appear/disappear *somewhere*? The textual somewhere is conceived by Derrida as a "scene of writing" (*scène de l'écriture*), itself taken to be an exemplary instance of the "field of beings" (*champ de l'étant*). This field-scene is instituted by writing *before* it becomes a "field of presence" (*champ de présence*), that is, before it becomes a set of positions determined by the what or essence, the *ti esti* or *eidos,* of its occupants.[135] Such a scene also precedes space and time: it is "not [any] more *in* time than *in* space."[136] It follows that the repression of writing—for example, by the putative primacy of speech—brings with it a claim as to the priority of time (as inner) and space (as infinite).[137] In its unrepressed state, however, writing constitutes a scene that undermines the primacy of space and time by its basic action of "spacing" (*espacement*), that is, by its own "tracing" (*tracement*). Space and time stem from such a writing-scene, not it from them—thanks to the fact that tracing qua writing requires a "specific zone" that refuses the general status of an origin or a *telos*.[138] I would propose that this zone is none other than *place*, differently thought and differently written.

Even if Derrida rarely employs the word "place" (*lieu, place*) as such in his grammatological writings, the very idea of grammatology (stemming from *grammē*, line, written stroke, visible mark) entails a notion of place of and for writing: *of it* as integral to its presentation, *for it* as a setting for its production. The operative premise of grammatology would then be: no tracing, thus no writing, without placing. To make a written mark of any kind—whether doubly articulated and noniconic as in alphabetic writing or singly articulated and iconographic as in the case of Neolithic petroglyphs—is to require a surface of inscription, *somewhere to write*. This somewhere need not be literally physical, for example, a page or a screen; it can be psychical, as in the case of the Freudian unconscious, wherein Derrida detects an arena of psychographic inscription, a region of encrypted signs.[139]

. In the grammatological perspective, then, place is the condition of possibility for writing—a condition that does not demand the actual physical instantiation of writing. Derrida refuses to reduce prototraces to empirical traces: the former are bodylike yet not material, not entirely unlike Syrianus's oxymoronic notion of "immaterial bodies."[140] Protowriting (*archi-écriture*) creates the textual somewhere for the appearance and registration of literal material marks. To posit place as a sine qua non for writing is to give new force and scope to topoanalysis: not only does poetry yield to such analysis, as Bachelard had emphasized; *all* writing, prosaic or poetic, is seen to be subtended by place as a precondition. Indeed, Derrida would maintain that poetically conveyed imaginal places presuppose textual place, the written scene of marks from which all literature arises. And if this is true, grammatology is inseparable from topoanalysis (and the reverse, as Derrida would insist).

The primacy of tracing entails the primacy of spacing. Spacing itself occurs as the continual provision of places—mainly, places of/for writing. After the publication of *Of Grammatology* in 1967, however, Derrida became increasingly sensitive to the fact that *espacement* is not delimited in its operation to the production of written traces, that is, to the generation of texts and intertexts. The web (*trame*) woven by the action of spacing eventuates in other quite significant webworks: film, painting, dance; politics, economics, religion; and, perhaps most notably, architecture. In a series of interviews and essays dating from the middle 1980s, Derrida has singled out *archi-tecture* in much the same spirit in which he had formerly engaged *archi-écriture*. This is hardly surprising, given that "-tecture" and "textual" are, along with "texture," linguistic cousins in the *text*-family of words—a family held together by the common metaphor of weaving, itself a fundamental form of creative spacing in human experience. Hence Derrida speaks of the "architect-weaver" who acts by "twining the threads of a chain."[141] Nor is it surprising that Derrida brings architecture and writing together expressly when he says that architecture is "a writing of space, a mode of spacing which makes a place for the event."[142]

If Foucault found in the institutional architecture of the eighteenth century the most telling exemplification of disciplinary space—hence of "site"—Derrida discovers in contemporary architecture the basis for another kind of spacing. Where Foucault writes of "other spaces," Derrida speaks of "other spacing."[143] Foucault's phrase alludes to a fully institutionalized architecture; "other spacing," in contrast, points to the very process by which the event of building arises in the first place, thus to the constructional event (not to be confused with physical construction as such) that precedes fully fashioned houses, schools, bridges, and so on, as well as to the eventual experience of a given built place. Nevertheless, Derrida's critique of institutional architecture—that is, construction that unreflectively pursues the built equivalents of metaphysical determinants such as origin and telos, utility and beauty[144]—leads him to a renewed appreciation of heterotopic space. An example of such (literally other) space is the *Folies* of the Parc de la Villette in Paris, a project whose chief architect is Bernard Tschumi. Derrida is as fascinated as is Foucault with the prospect of a genuinely alternative place created in the very midst of urban space. Parks, it will be recalled, constitute exemplary instances of heterotopias in Foucault's sense of the term. As a consultant to the Villette project—he was asked by Tschumi to design (with Peter Eisenman) a small park within the larger Parc—Derrida was able to ponder the deconstructive significance of a heterotopic place both in design and in writing. Derrida's response to Tschumi's invitation was perhaps too ambitious, as we can see from this statement: "Here's my idea: design *chōra,* the impossible place: design it."[145] Too ambitious insofar as *chōra* is precisely what *cannot* be designed: the Demiurge *imposes* design only as borrowed from *another* order, that of the Forms; he does not try to shape *chōra* from within and on its own terms.[146]

In the end, the Villette park proved to be a very difficult place to design—difficult at least from the standpoint of Derrida's collaboration, a collaboration that led to misunderstandings and is so far without concrete issue. (Archytas, in contrast, was a successful city planner!) Still, in the course of his association with the project, Derrida had the opportunity to ponder the meaning of this postmodern heterotopia in ways that proved to be productive and suggestive.

One of these ways—and one that is profoundly pertinent to place—is the idea of architecture as *event*. Rejecting the paradigm of architecture as "the trial of the monumental moment" (where the monument connotes something stubbornly closed in on itself in accordance with a fixed *archē* and *telos*),

Derrida proposes that a building is more of a happening than a thing. It is a happening not just in the sense of the event of construction—significant and necessary as this is—but in that, even as already constructed, it *continues to occur,* to be "the imminence of that which happens now."[147] Derrida's stress on the "now"—*maintenant,* a veritable leitmotiv of his writings on architecture—should not lead us to think that the event of architecture is a purely temporal affair. "Maintenant" also means (and can be translated as) "maintaining"—that is to say, persisting in space and time alike, being *held-in-hand* there (as the root sense of "main-tenant" signifies, though not in any ready-to-hand sense).[148] Nonetheless, as we have seen in the case of the trace, space and time do not have the last word; the last, or rather the first, word belongs to place. For the event of architecture is its very *taking place:* it brings forth "figures that are promised as events: so that they will take place."[149] But in the case of architecture an event is not only something that takes place (*a lieu*); it also *gives place* (*donne lieu*), gives room for things to happen. We are reminded of Heidegger's emphasis on *Räumen* (clearing space), *Einräumen* (making room), and *Raumgeben* (giving space). Similarly, "spacing," a term that persists throughout Derrida's writings, implies the clearing of space for events to happen: spacing is giving them room in which to occur. *Such room is room for place.* "Room," a word of very specific architectural significance, has also served in philosophical discourse to mediate between place qua *topos* and place qua *chōra,* and more generally between place and space. Remembering this mediating role, let us say that *to give room in architecture is to give place to building.* Such room-giving is at stake when Derrida says that architecture is "a mode of spacing that makes a place for the event." Such a place (*place* in French) is not a mere locus *in which* events arise. Derrida is as critical as Heidegger of any vestige of the Aristotelian *en* of containment: "If Tschumi's work indeed describes an architecture of the event, it is not only in that it constructs places (*lieux*) *in which* something should happen. . . . This is not what is essential."[150]

What is essential—without being an essence—is that room be made (and thus given) for the "eventmental dimension" to happen: a dimension that consists in such things as "sequence, open seriality, narrativity, the cinematic, dramaturgy, choreography."[151] Each of these instances of the eventmental calls for a place of its own, for example, a line, a screen, a page, a blueprint, a stage, a wall. In his plans for redesigning bridges in Lausanne, Tschumi includes a semitransparent glass wall onto which electronically generated images will be presented, thereby creating an "electrotecture" (see fig. 1).

A structure such as this is not just a location of events but a place for these events: a place-to-happen that constitutes a veritable "scenography of passage."[152] Passage connotes movement between places; but it also means a place *through which* to pass. Passage, like event itself, has "temporal" as well as "spatial" properties. The same is true of the closely related idea of

Figure 1.   Lausanne Metropont Bridge Project: the "electrotecture" beam

happening—another way of considering the architectural event. As Derrida
puts it in one of his "Fifty-Two Aphorisms for a Foreword": "To say of architecture that it is not [e.g., not monumental] is perhaps to understand that it
happens. It gives place to itself without returning to it, there is the event."[153]
Architecture, then, does not occupy a place but provides place—place to itself
first of all—and in so doing occurs as an event that "there is." In simplest
terms, "It happens." As happen*ing,* architecture is a matter of time; as happen-
stance, it is consolidated in a discrete space. Both aspects are at work in every
event, which is to say *every place,* of architecture.

   Where we live and in particular our home-place is something abiding
enough to maintain our own actions or thought, though not permanent in the
manner of a monument. In standing in my home, I stand *here* and yet feel
surrounded (sheltered, challenged, drawn out, etc.) by the building's boundaries over *there.* A person in this situation is not simply in time or simply in
space but experiences an event in all its engaging and unpredictable power. In
Derrida's words, "this outside engages us in the very thing we are," and we
find ourselves subjected to architecture rather than being the controlling subject that plans or owns, uses or enjoys it; in short, architecture "comprehends
us."[154] Just as there is no magisterial subject, there is no master builder (i.e.,
the original meaning of "archi/tect"). There is only the "there is"—the event
of the subject who experiences the event of the building.

If we are comprehended or engaged by a building we occupy—by its eventmental place of passage—we are also *spaced out* in it. Such is the literal sense of "e-spacement" as well as the clear connotation of "é-vénement" (i.e., "coming out"). Rather than being closed *in*—as both Aristotle and Heidegger insist, despite all their divergences—architectural event-making is outward-bound, something "expansive" in Locke's word. It may not be true that "everything spatial expands," [155] but architectural place is expansive par excellence. And if architecture "spaces itself out in what is not itself," then Derrida suggests that we ought to speak of a "transarchitecture." [156] Transarchitecture is neither expressive (this way lies effusive rococo or romantic buildings) nor merely impassive (as in many buildings in the international style). Instead, transarchitectural practice such as is found in the Parc de la Villette "s'explique avec l'événement"; [157] that is to say, it *folds out* (*ex-plicare*) in forming the event, refusing to remain confined to any simple location by expanding outward in accordance with the event it embodies. So conceived, a building *spaces itself out in place.* Not because place is what a building is *in,* that is, its bare locus, but because place is what a building expands *into:* what it becomes (and is always still becoming). This expansion is not into indefinite, much less into infinite, space. It is into the ambience of the building: thus beyond its own immediate "proto-place" and into the surrounding "com-place." But conversely it is also, and just as much, a motion from resistant "counter-places" in the environs inward—toward the here of the in-dwelling subject.[158] This is a subject, moreover, who "receives from this other spacing the invention of its gestures." [159] The subject in question is therefore no more self-enclosed than is the built structure in which that same subject is found. The subject spaces out in the very building that, in the course of its own *espacement,* "makes a place for the event." In so doing, building and subject alike let that event take place; they bring it to implacement, find place for it.

Architectural spacing-out is a matter of alleviation—lightening the load of physical matter and the equally weighty matter of the historicity of architectural styles. It is a question of loosening up "duration, hardness, the monumental [and] the hyletics of tradition." [160] Deconstruction in architecture proceeds precisely by such degravitational spacing-out, which takes three basic forms: movement, dislocation, and the point. Let us look at each of these in turn.

(1) *Movement.* A building designed in a deconstructive mode keeps us kinetic in the very midst of a place that, by its sheer durability and stability, might tempt us to stay put. "Movement" is here more than walking, which too often sticks to a preestablished path. Aimless divagation of the body is a more appropriate form of movement in (and between) buildings designed in the spirit of transarchitecture. What matters in such drifting is "opportunity for chance, formal invention, combinatory transformation, wandering." [161]

(2) *Dislocation.* The result of such aleatory moving is a continual dislocation from fixed circumstances. No simple location exists here, but also no simple displacement. For place is now to be found in the restless dislocation

of passing between identifiable places and in the process disidentifying these places themselves. Tschumi's *Folies,* for example, "put into operation a general dislocation; they draw into it everything that, until now (*maintenant*), seems to have given architecture meaning."[162] Derrida singles out the importance of *de-* and *dis-* words in Tschumi's vocabulary: "destabilization," "deconstruction," "dehiscence," "dissociation," "disruption," "disjunction."[163] One is reminded of Heidegger's emphasis on the *Un-fug,* the "disjoint," in his essay "Anaximander's Saying."[164] But where Heidegger—and Derrida himself, commenting on this same essay—maintains the disjoint as a philosophical concept, an architect such as Tschumi tries to instill a "disjunctive force" in the constructed work itself. As Tschumi writes, "At La Villette, it is a matter of forming, of acting out dissociation. . . . This is not without difficulty. Putting dissociation into form necessitates that the support structure (the Park, the institution) be structured as a reassembling system."[165] To design dissociation is to pursue spacing-out to its architectural limit, as occurs at La Villette: a series of disconnected buildings whose various uses are left up to the choice of those who pass through them.

(3) *Point.* Tschumi also says, "The red point of the *Folies* is the focus of this dissociated space."[166] Why the *point*? Isn't this, the slenderest of geometrical entities, a most unlikely thing to emphasize in architecture, an enterprise whose constructional units tend to be bulky and massive? But for Tschumi a point is critical in any project of architectural disaggregation. A point is the antithesis of the monument, and deconstructive architecture is resolutely anti-monumental. A point is also the spatial equivalent of the aphorism in philosophy: hence Derrida's decision to entitle a foreword to a collaborative volume of architects and philosophers "Fifty-Two Aphorisms for a Foreword." A point, like an aphorism, undoes the pretentions of the systematic and the total—that is, the *Gesamtwerk,* whether in architecture or in philosophy (and philosophy, as architectonic in its aspirations, is ineluctably allied with architecture in its penchant for monumentalizing). For both Derrida and Tschumi, a point is the most effective deconstructive agency in the realm of space; it is the deconstruction of space as an indifferent, homogeneous medium. "Each point," writes Derrida, "is a breaking point: it interrupts, absolutely, the continuity of the text or the grid."[167] As Derrida already averred in *"Ousia and Grammē"* (an essay exactly contemporary with the *Grammatology*), a point is that most paradoxical of geometric entities: at once open and closed, it both concentrates (on itself) and binds together (other points, ultimately entire lines).[168]

Despite what we might think, a point is not atomic: Aristotle already held, as we have seen, that it is both divisible and indivisible. Nor does a point imply a void (as does an atom). Instead, a point, especially as it is realized in architectural space, is abyssal or "groundless" (*sans fond*) without being merely suspended in a vacuum like an isolated physical particle.[169] In this respect, a point is again like an aphorism: monadic, concentrating in itself an entire point of view (though a view that is ultimately sightless).[170] Thanks to its concentrated nature, a point takes everything in—while being at the same time the ultimate unit of spacing-out that refers to nothing else. As such, it is (in Derrida's words) "the point of transaction with the [very] architecture which it, in turn, deconstructs or divides."[171] Moreover, far from being inimical to place (as if threatening to dissolve it, as Aristotle had presumed), the point can be the very basis of a new sense of place. Derrida and Tschumi would agree that the point is ineffective as a container—hence it cannot be the ultimate unit of place if place is to be regarded as a surrounding surface—but *for this very reason,* that is, its anticapacitative and nonenclosive status, it is promising for an architecture of disjunction and disruption. Neither containing nor contained, the point is the opening move in transarchitecture, a singular source of its deconstructive power. For the point is the ultimate explosion of permanent presence.

As architecture goes from movement to dislocation to the point, the effect of *espacement* is ever more disruptive—and yet ever more significant for *emplacement.* To go out in space in these descriptive ways is to come back to place: a new sense of place that has more to do with motion than stability, dislocation than location, point than containing surface. The place that results is alleviated, decondensed, and desedimented by the very building that makes it into an event. It is a "place without place," as Derrida puts it in a letter to Eisenman.[172] A place apart, as it were: apart from space and time in their traditional guises. Apart, too, from any bare locus—as defined by position and constituted as site. It is a question of a place that thrives from the disaggregation of space by a deconstructive movement of ap/point/ment.

We return, then, from diaphanous space to appointed place by way of buildings rather than by bodies. Yet this return has profound implications for the human body. As in the case of the "docile bodies" on which Foucault focused, the lived body is profoundly affected by its architectural setting, whatever form this may take. As Eisenman states, "Both the body and the gaze are implicated by the interiority of architecture."[173] No wonder: they are caught up in this interiority, housed there, and thus reflect its structures. And, conversely, a building bears "the signature of the body"[174] in its own design and construction and use; it is usually intended, after all, to be inhabited by bodies that dwell or work therein.

Nevertheless, the place to which we come back in architectural spacing-out is not only, and certainly not necessarily, a steady place of inhabitation, a fixed dwelling. Deconstructive, transarchitectural building in particular effects a destabilization and pointillization of place very much at odds with the fixed location and extended space of those dwelling places or workplaces that are constructed on (all too aptly named) "building sites." In deconstructive projects, such stable sites become what I have called "anti-sites." Or as Eisenman archly puts it, "By treating the [building] site not simply as presence but as both a palimpsest and a quarry, containing traces of both memory and immanence, the site can be thought of as *non-static*."[175] Nonetheless, just as to dislocate is not to displace, to pointillize is not to pulverize. Place remains— in and through its very difference from the paradigmatic site-spaces of most houses and temples, schools and prisons, including many of those constructed in the last two centuries in Eurocentric culture.

Indeed, one of the most fateful consequences of a deconstructive architecture is its critique of habitation in the usual Western and, more specifically, Heideggerian senses. Habitation may well be one of the "invariants" of Western architecture—along with sensitivity to the sacred, recognition of beauty and harmony, and realization of ethicopolitical ends—and its centrality to building arises historically from the Greek emphasis on values of the *oikos*, the household.[176] Heidegger, from *Being and Time* onward, reaffirms these same values as inherent in dwelling (*Wohnen*), even if he also complicates them by his recourse to *Unheimlichkeit* and to *Heimatlosigkeit*. But Derrida discerns in such values, even as thus complicated, the shadow of an un-self-critical metaphysics of presence, an overestimation of the value of nearness and proximity. Accordingly, he wonders if there is "an architecture that wouldn't be simply subordinated to those values of habitation, dwelling, sheltering the presence of gods and human beings."[177] He asks still more radically: "Is it possible to undertake a work [i.e., an architectural work] without fitting it out to be habitable?"[178] Just as there is "no habitat for the aphorism,"[179] so it would follow—by the continuing parallel between aphorism and architecture—that habitation, rather than being the foremost aim of architecture, could be subordinated to other aims that have little if anything to do with dwelling. For example, Tschumi's extraordinary design for a new airport at Kansai, Japan, certainly includes hotels (i.e., temporary dwelling places), but it also involves an effort (in Tschumi's own words) to "enlarge the airport into an event, a spectacle, a new city of interchange and exchange, of business commerce, and culture—a twenty-four-hour-a-day continuous invention. . . . People would fly to Kansai International because it is the place to be."[180] Tschumi's plan (fig. 2) gives some idea of what is here projected. Much the same complex multilevel event holds for Tschumi's design for the Kyoto train station (fig. 3).[181]

Does this mean that architects should strive to build uninhabitable structures? Or that deconstruction is tantamount to destruction, to the reduction of buildings to ruins or to tottering structures? Certainly not: Eisenman himself is perhaps best known for eccentrically designed yet quite livable houses. Yet it does mean that habitation ought not to be regarded as an exclusive or even primary aim but as assimilable to other aims, thereby eventuating in axiologically as well as structurally heterogeneous buildings, buildings with several levels of meaning (several "bands" in Tschumi's term). It is not a matter of dismissing a traditional value such as habitation but first of deconstructing it

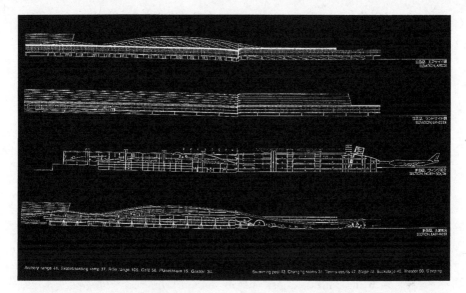

Figure 2. Kansai International Airport: elevations and sections, showing cafe, garden, rifle range, skateboarding ramp, swimming pool, etc.

and then *reincorporating* it within new architectural works. Hence Derrida's exhortation to contemporary architects: "You have to construct, so to speak, a new space and a new form, to shape a new way of building in which those [traditional] motifs or values [e.g., of habitation] are reinscribed, having meanwhile lost their external hegemony." [182] Given the problematic status of

Figure 3. Kyoto Railway Station and Convention Center: elevation and section, including wedding chapel, athletic club, historical museum, gourmet market, etc.

"space" in Western thought, it would be better to say that it is a matter of constructing *a new place* with a new form—a new way of building not just at or on a place but *building place itself,* building it anew and otherwise.

In the end, Derrida, in dialogue with Eisenman and Tschumi, effects a double deconstruction of the "in" at stake in built places: the "in" of *in*habitation and that of the body *in* buildings. In both deconstructive moves, we witness an effort to escape the confinement and containment implicit in the Western valorization of abiding residence (itself a form of the metaphysics of presence) within built structures taken as totalizing and totalized units for living. The escape is made by way of spacing-out in its various forms—where "out," however, is not merely the other member of the binary pair "in/out."[183] The "out" also implies the *trans-*, as in transition, translation, transference, transgression—though *not* of transcendence, which implies an ideal place beyond current actualities. (Tschumi speaks of "transprogramming" in his recent work.)[184]

The aim, finally, is to *go toward place* in all its disjointed imperfection and disrupted unrealization: to go toward it precisely as something in the very process of being built (and just as likely unbuilt). In architecture, place is a "detotalized totality" (Sartre), that is, no kind of *thing.* It is so desubstantialized as not even to be projectable in advance.[185] It is a matter of place without place—the atopic in topos. Such place, relieved of the burden of metaphysical (if not physical) presence, is in the advance position: in advance over space and time. At the same time, it is at one with the event for which it is the place.

Yet place as such is not given—not in architecture, or in any other human enterprise. Place *is not;* place *is to be:* if not entirely projectable, it is at least promised; it is to be found, if not completely constructed. The last of Derrida's "Fifty-Two Aphorisms" reads as follows:

> Maintaining, despite the temptations, despite the possible reappropriation, the chance of the aphorism, is to keep within the interruption, without the interruption, the promise of giving place, if it is necessary/if it is missing (*s'il le faut*). But it is never given.[186]

The ambiguity of the "it" in the last sentence is instructive: Does it refer to "aphorism," "interruption," "giving place"? Probably all of these, along with a term whose lack of mention should not obscure its undeniable importance: "event." Architecture is a making of place by the very promise of giving place—even if place per se, the place of place, will never be given as such. Atopia is ingredient in every topos. A built place, however monumental it may aspire to be, is not given; it does not even exist. Such a place is less the product of architecture—if this word entails an enterprise delimited by site-bound institutional rules—than of an "anarchitecture."[187]

A built place is an event, the taking place of place in the very excess of spacing-out. No wonder that "it gives place to itself without returning to it, there is the event." In Tschumi's words, it is a matter of "a mode of spacing that gives its place to events."[188] Or we can say with Philipe Sollers:

CHANCE

WILL HAVE TAKEN PLACE

BUT THE PLACE

fuses with beyond

outside the interest

indicated as far as it is concerned

in general

according to such-and-such obliquity by such-and-such

declivity.[189]

VI

> We must, therefore, reconsider the whole question of our conception of place, both in order to move on to another age of difference (each age of thought corresponds to a particular time of meditation on difference), and in order to construct an ethics of the passions. . . . How can we mark this limit of a place, of place in general, if not through sexual difference?
> —Luce Irigaray, "Sexual Difference"

> Woman is still the place, the whole of the place in which she cannot take possession of herself as such.
> —Luce Irigaray, *Speculum of the Other Woman*

> Fluidity is the fundamental condition.
> —G. F. Leibniz, *New Essays on Human Understanding*

It is time to put a final face on place—or, rather, to find a face that has been almost entirely obscured in the long history of the subject. This is the bivalent face of gender as it bears on the fate of place. Place and gender? Place as sexually specific? Sexual identity as place-bound? These issues have not only been undiscussed; they have never even been raised in traditional Western thinking. From at least Aristotle onward, it has been assumed that sexual difference makes no difference when it comes to matters of place and space. Indeed, one suspects that by conceiving place in exclusively physicalistic terms and by locating it unequivocally in the natural realm, Aristotle was aiming to expunge any trace of the gendered treatments of place that were still prominent in Hesiod (whose phrase "broad-breasted Earth" is cited with barely concealed contempt by Aristotle at the beginning of his discussion of place in his *Physics*) and in Plato (for whom *chōra* qua Receptacle is as undeniably "feminine" as the Demiurge is forthrightly "masculine"). Beyond Plato and Hesiod lay the collective memory of Tiamat's defeat by Marduk, a saga still seething in Mediterranean minds when ancient Greek philosophy first arose in the sixth century B.C.

To take up the question of gender and place at the very end of this book is not, then, to enter into something altogether new; it is to come full circle. It is to come back to an ancient conviction that sexual identity does make a difference in how place is conceived and experienced by human beings (and doubtless by other animals as well). This conviction bears on something combative and violent—an issue of literal "gender trouble," as the Mesopotamian myth presumes. But to reengage such a conviction does not mean regressing to chaos, in the manner of Hesiod: "Foremost of all things Chaos came to be." Sexual difference may take human beings into the abyss, but it is not only, much less necessarily, a *mise en abyme*. Even the nothingness that yawns in the "primal Gap" posited by Aristophanes has a certain shape. It was Aristophanes, after all, who speculated that the two sexes were originally conjoined in one well-rounded conjugal being that was subsequently, and to ill effect, split apart. Freud, speculating on the origins of bisexuality in human beings, alludes to this protomyth of Aristophanes. As does Luce Irigaray: "According to that story, man and woman were once joined together in such a way that they rolled around, locked in embrace. Then they were split apart, but endlessly each seeks to find the lost half and embrace it once more."[190]

Irigaray, the last author on place to be considered in this book, takes us back to primal origins. She does so by taking us back to body, thus following the Ariadnean thread trailing through the labyrinthine defile occupied by other figures concerned with the relationship between body and place. But unlike these others, she takes us back to a resolutely sexed (as well as sexual) body. None of the thinkers treated in chapter 10 deigned to consider questions of sexual specificity. Bachelard points to a distinctly gendered reverie—that exhibiting *anima* in Jung's sense—but evades its corporeal connotations.

Deleuze and Guattari discuss the "becoming-woman" of the modern subject, yet their discussion of this notion is as disembodied as is Bachelard's elegy to anima-inspired poetic reverie.[191] Only Irigaray explores the pertinence of sexual difference *in the body* of man and of woman as this difference relates to place. She does so, moreover, in the form of a commentary on Aristotle's *Physics*, book 4, chapters 2 through 5: the very text that launched two millennia of debate about place and space in Western philosophy! Thus in taking up the challenge of Irigaray, we return not just to body but to a canonical text that in effect deprived body-in-place of any trace of sexually specific meaning. For Aristotle, to be properly in place, to be in place proper (*autos topos*), is not to possess any such meaning, which he would consider philosophically irrelevant. For Irigaray, there is no being in place except for a being who is already differentiated in accordance with bodily specificity—and deeply saturated with sexual history. Moreover, just as Aristotle denied to place any intrinsic political or religious significance (place has such significance only on loan as it were, e.g., from the *polis* or from the First Mover), so Irigaray will attempt to restore both kinds of significance to place—but only insofar as place is understood as something sexually significant to begin with.

To begin with: there are bodies and there are places. Or rather: there are bodies-*as*-places. For example, the mother's body as a place for the prenatal child. Here is a place for something "solid," that is, the child's growing body. Such a body-place is not only organically based and regulated; it is highly valorized by virtually all societies, given the prized status of childbearing. Much less valorized (and presumably less necessary from an adaptive point of view) is a woman's body as a place for pleasure—for *jouissance* qua female orgasm. Such a pleasure-place is a cause for doubt, if not consternation, from an Aristotelian standpoint: for the fluid contents of orgasm, bodily juices, spill out from their organic container. In orgasm (both male and female) the body-container fails of its proper purpose. Here, indeed, "fluidity is the fundamental condition."[192] Woman's pleasure in particular "is meant to 'resemble' the flow (*épanchement*) of whatever is in the place that she is when she contains, contains herself. 'Wine', perhaps, that man might spill out in the sexual act? Elixir of ambrosia, and of place itself."[193]

Irigaray takes Aristotle's metaphor of place-as-vessel seriously—more seriously (though less literally) than the Master of Those Who Know. Not only can the body-as-vessel be moved from one place to another, but even when not moving it is in effect *a place of place*. Ironizing on Aristotle's concern about an infinite regress of place—a cognitive nightmare first propounded by Archytas and Zeno—Irigaray affirms the fact that not only is a woman in a place (e.g., a home) but "place, in her, is in place, not only as organs [within her], but as vessel or receptacle. It is place twice over: as mother and as woman."[194] The further irony is that men would like to deny any significant implacement to women, social and political as well as organic and erotic, by positing "a female *placelesness*."[195] Woman, though doubly implaced, is herself deprived of any "proper place." Nevertheless, woman *is* a place, insists Irigaray.

> As for woman, she is place. Does she have to locate herself in bigger and bigger places? But also to find, situate, in herself, the place that she is. If she is unable to constitute, within herself, the place that she is, she passes ceaselessly through the child in order to return to herself. And this captures the other [i.e., the child] in her interiority. For this not to occur, she has to assume the passage between *the infinitely large* and *the infinitely small*.[196]

But to negotiate the passage between the infinitely large and the infinitely small—the problematic terms of Zeno's paradoxes and of Kant's antinomies—is to deal with place as a middle ground between extremes: the "passage from one place to another, for her, remains the problem of place as such, always within the context of the mobility of her constitution."[197] Rather than just being the first or last place for a single kind of other (viz., a man), she is also a place in relation to a child, her own mother, or God. Ultimately, she becomes the place she is only *across* or *through* (*à travers*) many others: "I go on a quest through an indefinite number of bodies, through nature, through God, for the body that once served as place for me."[198] The possibility of salvation by place glimmers just where dispersion into many places looms large: woman can be "scattered into *x* number of places that are never gathered together into anything she knows of herself."[199]

Yet the female body becomes the intensely extensive place it is not only through interaction with other places but also through her own being and agency. For her body is already a place insofar as it is itself an envelope containing a receptacle.

> She is able to move within place as place. Within the availability of place. Given that her issue is how to trace the limits of place herself so as to be able to situate herself therein and welcome the other there. If she is to be able to contain, to envelope, she must have her own envelope. Not only her clothing and ornaments of seduction, but her skin. And her skin must contain a receptacle.[200]

Like the Platonic Receptacle—like *chōra*—woman-as-place is a moving force. But, unlike *chōra,* she is this as a double envelope, at once enveloping (i.e., by the skin of her entire body) and enveloped (in her vagina and womb). Thus she has both "extension without" (her body as an envelope of flesh) and "extension within" (by virtue of her genitalia and internal organs). Without this dual extendedness, she would be abyssal and lead others into an abyss.[201] *With* it, she is anything but extended in a Cartesian sense, where everything is external to everything else: *partes extra partes*. Nor is she "purely exterior" in the manner of the "outside thought" of Deleuze and Guattari's nomad space.

Her body-place is a matter, instead, of *partes intra partes,* of parts that envelop other parts—both a woman's own body-parts and those of others (her child in gestation, her lover in intercourse). Sexual desire reflects this involution, in the form of a double enclosure: "If desire is to subsist, a double place is necessary, a double envelope."[202]

Put otherwise: a feminine body-as-place is *doubly engaging:* it engages *itself* by its anatomical invagination (i.e., its interior parts inside its own skin), and thanks to its active receptivity it engages *others* (children, lovers, mother, God). For a woman's body, doubleness is the truth of the matter, and for this body Aristotle's dictum remains pertinent: "The minimum number, strictly speaking, is two."[203] If it were not for the pregiven twoness of the female body's own place, its other engagements could not take place. It would not only be less than fully engaged; it would not be engaging at all, not even with itself.[204]

Whereas Aristotle's model of envelopment as strict containment entails an enclosedness with no exit, however, Irigaray's paradigm leads in just the opposite direction: to a porous body-place that exhibits "the openness of the open" (Heidegger's phrase as taken over by Irigaray).[205] It is a question of something not just contingently but *in principle* open: "Woman, insofar as she is a container, is never a closed (*fermée*) one. Place is never closed (*clos*). The boundaries [of her body] touch against one another while still remaining open."[206] Contrary to Aristotle's exclusionary physics, to be doubly enveloped is to be doubly open: open to oneself within oneself and open to the other outside oneself. But the other is also within: as in the internal *imago* of the mother, in pregnancy, or again in sexual intercourse. These internalizations of the other (some of which occur in males as well) would not be possible unless the woman's body were open to begin with. Or more exactly: half-open or "slightly open" (*entrouverte*). For an Aristotelian container to be even partly porous is disastrous, since the contents would then flow out and lose their place. Containment in any rigorous sense is an all-or-nothing affair. The same is true of Spinoza's definition of God as a *causa sui* whose essence envelops existence strictly and totally: not to be enveloped in this way is not to exist—not with the necessity that belongs to God. It follows from this definition that woman "does not *have to exist* as woman because, as woman, her envelope is always slightly open."[207] Woman fails the test of Godhead—not surprisingly, given that God is defined by men for men[208]—just as she fails to be a proper container precisely because her body is the wrong kind of envelope: it is not a strict surrounder. No wonder. As "holey space,"[209] this body gapes open instead of holding tightly in. Woman's body has an oxymoronic structure: it is an open/enclosure.

No wonder again: woman's body, unlike God's or that of a physical thing, is an organic body. This mere fact makes all the difference. For a body whose primary property is extension in anything like a Cartesian sense—including infinite extension in the case of Spinoza's (or More's) God—has no internal hollows. The same is true for the physical thing ensconced in an Aristotelian container: even when this thing is water or air, it is conceived as something massively and uniformly there, a single sensible substance without gaps. Just as a solid inorganic physical body is without interior passages, so its envelope is without holes. Both are closed in on themselves, unperforated: two continuous magnitudes, one containing and the other contained. By the same token, as inorganic, both are intrinsically unchanging and unmoving. Spinoza's God is as static as place on Aristotle's official definition: "the first unchangeable limit of that which surrounds."[210]

Irigaray proposes the female body as the scandalous exception that proves the rule: it is a paradigm of place and yet is neither unperforated nor stationary. Quite to the contrary, it is always (at least slightly) open and always (to some degree) moving. This is precisely what we witness in the case of *lips:* facial or genital lips never stop moving and never stop opening. They touch each other continually, not only in sexual activity but in *every* activity. As such, they *perform place;* they act it out and, by the same token, act it *in.* Lips connect inside and outside as a common threshold wherein what is within the body meets what is without: palpably and not only visually.[211] Crucial to lips is their mucous character—that is, wet in such a way as to facilitate ingestion, yet not entirely aqueous; viscous rather than hard-edged, self-moving rather than merely moved; self-placing rather than placed by something else. A body equipped with lips is as essentially twofold as a body equipped with arms, legs, and hands. The latter three pairs, on which Kant focused in his essay of 1768, traffic with the surrounding world, whereas lips mediate the transactions between that world and the world within. On Irigaray's reading, lips are quasi-organs, not passive parts. Their vibrant being calls into question any such notion as that of "the body without organs" (Deleuze and Guattari). Lips are congruous and contiguous counterparts situated at critical *limina* of the organic body; they are that body's indefinite but determinative dyads.[212]

A general thesis emerges from Irigaray's densely suggestive writing. The thesis, stated more abstractly than Irigaray herself ever in fact states it, is that *(the sexually differentiated) body and (its) place are so intimately linked as to be virtually interchangeable.* The point is not just that there is no place without body, or vice versa, but that body itself *is* place and that place is as body-bound as the body itself is sexually specific.[213] If Deleuze and Guattari wish to conflate place and region (thereby enlarging the scope of place), Irigaray just as intentionally conflates place and body—thereby extending the range of place in a different direction. The effect is to burst the bounds of place when these bounds are determined by the limits of inorganic, sexually undifferentiated body; it is to make place something elastic and alive—an interactive and engaging envelope—that reflects the enveloped body in its dynamic and developmental being. As a result, both place and body lose the inelastic and rigid moorings to which they are consigned in straitened physical and metaphysical models, for example, those of *res extensa* or God as First Mover. Liberated from these moorings, each takes on properties of the other: place becomes porous (and not just closed) and body becomes surrounding (and not just surrounded). Both become entities in movement, and they move together.

But Irigaray herself would not rest content with such sweeping statements—adumbrations of which can already be detected in Husserl's notion of the intimate relation between the lived body and its life-world. Her concern is to interpret any such propositions in ways that are at once feminist, political, and religious. For her, the body that matters most in place—the body that is pure movable matter[214]—is the female body. Thanks to this body and its repressed history, implacement is as potently political as it is inherently religious in its consequences. For example, it has special political significance insofar as the female body, whether as mother or as lover, all too often becomes a place *for man*—for his exclusive inhabitation and exploitation—rather than a place enjoyed by woman *for itself* and *on its own terms.* In *Elemental Passions* Irigaray asks her fictitious male lover: "But what am I for you, other than that place from which you subsist? Your subsistence. Or substance."[215] In "Place, Interval" she presses the point home: precisely as an inviting and sheltering double sheath, woman's body becomes for man "the first and unique place,"[216] that which is at his disposition without his offering to woman a place of his own, or even any appreciation of the different kinds of place the two sexes embody: places that are strictly unexchangeable.[217] Man may supply space—for example, the global space of geographic exploration—but he fails to provide place. Not offering place, indeed being empty of place himself, man desperately seeks place elsewhere: in woman. "The masculine is attracted to the maternal-feminine *as place.*"[218] Why? Because the female body seems to offer aegis, promising to satisfy man's "need for solidity," for "a rock-solid home."[219] Whether as a place for conception or for sexual adventure or merely for consolation, woman's enveloping/enveloped body becomes a microcosmic dwelling place, "the only place where he can live."[220] This is to reduce place to a site of exploitation or pleasure or commiseration, a home-place, without allowing woman to assume (a) place for herself. She has become place *as such,* at once physical and metaphysical—without the opportunity to be a sexually specific body/locus that is neither mere "thing" nor exalted essence.[221] To be place as such is to lack a place of one's own.

> The maternal-feminine remains the *place separated from "its" own place,* deprived of "its" place. She is or ceaselessly becomes the place of the other who cannot separate himself from it. Without her knowing or willing it, she is then threatening because of what she lacks: a "proper" place.[222]

A man is nourished and protected in woman as home-place, but in so doing he "forgets the other *and* his own becoming"; his continual Odyssean search for lost domesticity "prevents him from finding either the other or himself."[223] Precisely because Western man has built "a world that is largely uninhabitable,"[224] he is all the more obsessed with turning woman into a habitable home-body—with disastrous consequences for both sexes and for the world at large. At the same time, he evades the specificity of his *own* body, the way it might become a place distinctively different from the place proffered by woman's body. Fleeing into mind and space, he delegates to woman the entire responsibility for body and place.

What, then, is to be done? To raise a question with political edges is to call for an answer with political implications. Irigaray's answer is that men and women ought to constitute and cultivate places that are reflective of their differential sexual identity: "If any meeting is to be possible between man and woman, each must be a place, as appropriate to and for the other, and toward which he or she may move."[225] Such differential implacement should happen not just in architectural terms but also in the two realms men and women share most fully: "perception" and "conception," that is, the way they sense and think about things. Still more basically, it ought to happen in the form of the capacity of each sex to "receive the self and envelope the self."[226] Between men and women there has to be reciprocal (albeit asymmetrical) transport: "mutual enveloping in movement,"[227] a movement by which each sex affords the other both freedom and necessity. But this can occur, once more, only in differentiated placing of each in relation to the other, "which would mean that, at each phase, there were two places interdetermining each other, fitted one in the other."[228] For this interplacement to be possible, however, "the concept of the masculine would have to cease to envelope that of the feminine, since the feminine has no necessity if it exists uniquely for the masculine."[229] Instead, what is truly unique—woman's doubly enfolded body—must be respected for what it is: a place of pleasure and of possible procreation that is not defined by man or destined for his use. Then the female body will be seen as itself a cause: as a place with its own causal efficacy rather than a place that is merely an effect.[230] It will be a place for man and woman to *be* rather than for man alone to *have*. Instead of woman being forced to find a place in the generic "he"—to make a place for herself there, on its terms—man might come to find his place in the "she," an en-gendered place no longer defined exclusively in pangeneric masculine ways.

Irigaray is not so naive as to believe that the relations between the sexes—in particular, relations between the kinds of places each represents for the other—can be ameliorated in any direct or simple way. The situation is too complicated for easy solutions. Appeals to reciprocity and respect, for example, miss the mark: these presume a homogeneous ethical/political space. What is at stake is place, its asymmetries and idiosyncrasies and incongruities, and how its characteristic configurations bear on ethical and political issues. Rather than formal relations of reciprocity—in which all parties can remain indifferent to each other as persons—concrete relations of intimacy and near-ness (i.e., of "vicinity") are of greater pertinence.[231] Above all, it is necessary to recognize that at this historical moment men cannot simply give over *their* places to women (to do so would be only to reinforce an already overbearing patriarchalism) while women, for their part, must cultivate their own places for themselves and for each other. These places ought to reflect their bodily habitudes and interests, that is, their lived specificities, as closely as possible. The same holds true for men, who must attempt to constitute places in the light of their quite different organic structures and corporeal propensities. If this were to be done by both sexes, the places that result would more ade-quately reflect the diverse sexual orientations and gender identities of those who shape them and live in them.

Dimensions other than the political, in particular religious ones, are also at stake in Irigaray's discourse about body/place. Indeed, Irigaray maintains that "the opening in the envelopes between men and women should always be mediated by God."[232] This is not as radical—or as reactionary—a thought as it may at first appear. Not if God, too, is a place: God is "*that which is its own place for itself,* that which turns itself inside out and thus constitutes a dwell-ing (for) itself."[233] Otherwise said: God is an ultimate envelope, an entity that envelopes himself/herself (and everything else) and *for this reason* is self-caused, *causa sui.* Irigaray, however, does not remain satisfied with a purely theological term such as "God." For her, a privileged pathway to religious as well as to interpersonal life is to be found in the unique configuration of the female body, which is spiritual and transcendent *in its very corporeality.* Thanks to its place-affording erotism, woman's body both receives God and moves toward God: "Nothing [is] more spiritual, in this regard, than female sexuality."[234] Female sexuality is spiritual insofar as it creates "a place of transcendence for the sensible."[235] Irigaray takes the term "spiritual" in a quite elemental sense, that is, as an alchemical sublimation of the intimate materiality of the female body qua place: "This place, the production of inti-macy, is in some manner a transmutation of earth into heaven, here and now."[236] Intimacy is no more closed off than the body that experiences and subtends it. It is implicated with divine infinity, not with physical immensity. And if sexual desire reaches toward the infinite, it does so only by a double movement back toward the material matrix of this body and, simultaneously, on toward God construed as "another container."[237] The sexual act is thus the "most divine of acts."[238]

The paradox is that it is precisely because the feminine body is enclosed twice over that it is capable of extending its own sensuality toward God. This presumes in turn that God is no longer conceived abstractly but considered *as a body,* albeit a superbody, that *becomes.*[239] At the same time, suggests Iri-garay, woman is Godlike by virtue of her self-transcending immanence: "She would be cause for herself—and in a less contingent manner than man—if she enveloped herself, or re-enveloped herself, in that envelope that she is able to 'provide.' "[240] Only woman can provide this envelope because only she has a body, and thus a place, that can envelope itself in itself. Twice enclosed—and twice implaced—woman moves (in) and connects (with) the religious realm.

Nevertheless, despite the uniqueness of woman's body-as-place, and despite man's exploitation of woman as "a place of attraction,"[241] Irigaray holds out hope of a time-to-come when a more nuanced, that is, a more place-sensitive and body-specific, relationship between men and women will be possible—a time, too, when openness to a different religious receptivity and sensibility will emerge. She ends her commentary on Aristotle's *Physics* with a series of questions that are as disturbing as they are promising.

> Does man become place in order to receive and because he has received female *jouissance*? How? Does woman become place because she has received male *jouissance*? How? How does one make the transition here from physics to meta-physics? From the physical receptacle for the penis to the enveloping of a receptacle that is less tangible or visible, but which *makes place*?[242]

How, indeed, unless by *making room for place* in the lives of men and women alike—place in the body and as the body, place between bodies, place receptive to the divine? Such lives would not abandon such room-for-place on behalf of a totality whose name is "Space" or "Time," much less on behalf of God "Himself." Instead, (gender-neutral, undifferentiated) space would become (bodily-sexually specific) place.

"The search for creation" will occur in the only place where it can be pursued: in the reengendered bodies of those who envelop themselves and each other in an embrace of mutual recognition and satisfaction while maintaining and respecting sexual difference, however fluid this difference may be.[243] From within this embrace, the creative enmeshment of body and place—and thus of woman and man, parent and child, self and God—can begin to take its rise.

Postface: Places Rediscovered

These places, spread out everywhere, yield up and
orient new spaces.
—Jean-Luc Nancy, *The Inoperative Community*

I

Irigaray's challenging reading of Aristotle's *Physics* reanimates an ancient
(and very recent) question: How are body and place related? A first answer,
given by Aristotle himself, posits a rigid material body in place by virtue of
its sheer contiguity with the inner surface of what immediately surrounds it—
a strictly physical intimacy that works by close containment. This containment
acts in effect to cap and control the vagrant and violent movements of elemental qualities and powers as depicted in Plato's *Timaeus,* a cosmogonic tale in
which the tumult of *chōra* gives way to the order of determinate *topoi.*
Whether this yielding already yields what is essential to the *non*determinate
places of dynamic bodies—especially female bodies—is Irigaray's challenge
to Plato and Aristotle alike.[1] Even if this challenge remains unresolved, one
thing is certain: the delimitation of body by place is a characteristic Greek
obsession and can also be found in the Stoics, various Hellenistic thinkers, the
Neoplatonists—and is still visible in Descartes's idea of "internal place" with
its strict confinement to the exact size and shape of the implaced body.

But what if "body" is not merely inert physical body but something organic
and ever-changing? Aristotle, aware of the complications that the growth of
living bodies poses for his conception of place (most notably, that the place
of a burgeoning thing must change with every micron of growth), chooses his
exemplary cases from the nonliving world of earth, water, and air. But he can
barely conceal his anxiety: "Just as every body is in a place, so in every place

331

there is a body; so what shall we say about things that increase in size?"[2] What shall we say indeed?

It is only with extreme belatedness in the history of philosophy that Aristotle's searching question begins to be addressed adequately. Starting with Kant and continuing in Husserl and Whitehead and Merleau-Ponty, place is considered with regard to living organisms and, in particular, the lived human body. Not only does this put us in a better position to account for the specifically human experience of place; it opens up fresh vistas on place itself—allowing us to grasp its scope as well as its limits—while eliciting a renewed interest in the specificities of implacement, which had become submerged under the twin modern obsessions with infinite Space and chronometric Time. The seemingly contracted locus of the lived body, which is always just *here,* has proved to be an effective basis for what has become an expansive vision of what place is all about, even when it is located over *there* and far away. Irigaray and, to a lesser extent, Foucault and Deleuze and Guattari have continued to enrich the same vision. In the case of Irigaray, what appears at first to be a limited point of view shows itself to have remarkable range; the gendered/sexed body opens onto "greater and greater envelopes, vaster and vaster horizons"[3] that include the vexed relations between the sexes as well as the divine dimension. The sexual specificity of the body is something continually being surpassed—"débordé," in Irigaray's own term—toward encompassing ethical, political, social, and religious matrices. Much as Kant had demonstrated that the mere difference between the right and left hands has everything to do with our insertion into surrounding cosmic regions, so the body in its equally binary sexual differentiations leads into whole interpersonal and extrapersonal worlds. The sexually specific body, despite (or, rather, because of) its specificity, affords a spacious view of place that is drawn out to the boundary of the known universe and beyond. The fate of place is at once clarified and complicated by the folds of the en-gendered lived body in which place itself is enveloped and which its actions envelop in turn. The postmodern (re)turn to body effected by Irigaray deepens and extends the late modern insights of Kant and other more immediate predecessors such as Husserl and Merleau-Ponty—and in so doing dissolves the rigidity and constriction inherent in Aristotle's inaugural, and still powerfully tempting, model of physical bodies snugly invested in their tightly fitting surrounders.

II

Letting the body take the lead in this way allows us to grasp more clearly a pattern implicit in the philosophical history of place. The pattern is a tendency toward increasing inclusiveness and thus away from the exclusiveness endemic in Aristotle's effort to confine place to the status of a mere containing surface. Such exclusiveness entails literal exclusion—exclusion of abstract parameters such as extension and dimension, as well as of concrete sensible qualities such as those belonging to the female as a distinct sex. Already in the fourth century B.C., Aristotle was skeptical of inclusive notions of place or space such as Anaximander's *to apeiron* and Plato's *chōra,* both of which Aristotle attempts to compress into his own concept of *hulē,* "matter." Since matter in turn is held to be inessential to place, the latter is in effect reduced to an immaterial membrane encircling those things that are strictly physical. Place is literally marginalized: it becomes the closest static surface coextensive with the edges of a physical thing, that is, what is (at) its very margins.

This early marginalization of place proved to have enormous repercussions in the history of philosophy and science. It set the stage for the gradual and forceful encroachment of space upon place—ending in the virtual disappearance of the latter into the former. But this disappearance only occurred after there had been a prolonged round of brilliant efforts to save place from premature extinction in the putatively universal medium supplied by space. These efforts took the form of making place itself ever more inclusive. Theophrastus, Aristotle's immediate successor in the Lyceum, argued for a quasi-organic model of place as relationality that looks forward to Whitehead and Irigaray as well as to Locke and Leibniz. In the ancient Academy, Strato proposed that place is a matter of sheer volume, presaging the idea of an "absolute place" that is still alive in Newton and even (with important modifications) in Einstein. The Stoics insisted that the cosmos in which the earth is located is a finite and self-maintaining place—even if a place set in turn within the infinity of the extracosmic realm. Although ancient Atomists from Democritus and Leucippus to Epicurus and Lucretius posited a limitless void, they also allowed leeway for the unique places of particular configurations of atoms in motion. Even more striking were Neoplatonic attempts to open up place from within, whether as "intelligible place" (Plotinus), as divine "light" (Proclus), or as having special powers of "gathering" and "sustaining" (Iamblichus).

But the effort to safeguard room for place by making it ever more inclusive could not withstand a rising temptation to accord primacy to space. Philoponus, as we have seen, is pivotal in this regard: although he officially denied infinite space, his concern with dimension (*diastasis*) led him to conceive of an extension (*diastēma*) empty in principle even though always full in fact. Consequently, boundary (*peras*), on whose dynamic character Iamblichus had insisted, became otiose: nothing can effectively limit pure dimensionality. The paradox is that, by making place all-inclusive, Philoponus sounded the death knell for place itself. To be *all*-inclusive by virtue of possessing unlimited dimensions—in short, to be coextensive with the universe—is a prerogative reserved for God alone (a conclusion congenial to a Christian believer such as Philoponus). Fourteenth-century theologians did not hesitate to identify God's immensity with the unending (even if imaginary) extent of the universe, but no sooner had they done so than the very term "place" (*locus*) was disempowered and "space" (*spacium*) adopted in its stead: a space limitless in its range and not at all "intense" as in the interpretation of Deleuze and Guattari. From here it is but a short step to the Renaissance preoccupation with the outright physical infinity of the universe and thence to the Cartesian idea of space as indefinite "extension" (*extensio*)—within which place can be, at best, only a subordinate part, a volumetric entity. A half century after Descartes's death, place has become lost in the inane of infinite space—banished to being no more than a mere "portion," a "particular limited consideration," within that endless empty maw.

In the era that stretches from Aristotle to Newton, then, place lost out to space. It lost out precisely because the project to salvage place by extending its scope—a project undertaken by Aristotle's commentators and critics, all of whom agreed that the conception of place in the *Physics* was too delimited to bear the load that being-in-place entails—led, contrary to the most earnest intentions, to the loss of place itself, its dissipation in the undelimited void of open space. A first attempt to preserve the power of place thus came to grief. By the end of the era, place had become the faceless minion of space. Having lost its uniqueness (i.e., as *this* particular place) as well as its boundedness (i.e., as precisely this place and *not another*), it merged with space in the generation of the infinity of the universe from an unlimited set of simple locations. The only trace of place remaining after it had been incorporated into space occurred in the form of *site,* which in Leibniz's deft hands became the dominant spatial module of the modern age, affecting and infecting every aspect of modern life: architecture and medicine, schools and prisons, not to mention philosophical thought itself. The neoclassicism and Enlightenment of the eighteenth century reflected the dominance of site-space construed as the "relative global."[4] The ensuing exhaustion of qualitative spatiality—of placial properties that evade the parameters of distance and position, indeed of sheer relation—set the stage for the triumph of temporocentrism in the nineteenth century.

Yet, in spite of the rise of the global absolutes of Space and Time, the demise of interest in place was still not complete. The most striking case in point is provided by Kant, the apostle of Enlightenment and the advocate of the transcendental ideality of space and time. As we know, Kant argued that in its orientational powers the two-sided body constitutes a place in space: as Irigaray would later say, thanks to this body "place would twist and turn on itself."[5] Such convoluted, body-specific place, ensconced in cosmic regions, has its own peculiarities (i.e., as structured by incongruent counterparts) and powers (e.g., of giving or finding direction). Recapturing place in this seemingly innocent and exiguous corner of the universe—precisely in the margins of mainstream thought—the body was poised for a philosophical comeback. The comeback was deferred for a century and a half, during which time the idea of place as body-based lay dormant; but a persuasive revival of this idea

occurred in Husserlian and Merleau-Pontian phenomenology and in Whiteheadian ontology.

Even though the importance of place is rediscovered in the narrow defile
of the lived body, this rediscovery does not represent a return to place in its
exclusiveness. On the contrary: place is once again appreciated in terms of its
inherent inclusiveness. But the inclusive is no longer sought in the dimensionality of purely physical or metaphysical immensity, much less in infinity. Nor
is it even confined to the body. Bachelard discerns an "intimate immensity"
in the nonmaterial realm of the psyche. He lays bare an impressive array of
placial phenomena that reside in the interiority of psychic life—in "the being
of within." As we have seen, the equivalent of Bachelardian topoanalysis has
been pursued in other domains as well, perhaps most saliently in Foucault's
examination of heterotopias, which extend the reach of place outward and
sideward—onto the very fringes of society—as well as inward and downward,
into the incarcerated cells of repressive Western institutions. Whichever way
we choose to go, there is an expansion of the range of place beyond its role
as strict container or simple locator or (more generally) as site-specific. As
arenas of resistance, or merely of difference, heterotopic places are both reem-
powered and reempowering—as we witness in Derrida's conception of a deconstructive architecture of place-as-event, featuring built places as nonstatic
anti-sites.[6] Such double reempowerment is also discernible in Irigaray's (and
other feminists') conviction that the female body is a place of otherness *within*
society—hence its potential for changing the social order were it to become
demarginalized.[7]

An equally promising resource for the revalorization of place is found in
Heidegger's expansive views of place as dwelling, nearness, and the event of
Appropriation. Furthermore, the "multifarious between" envisioned by Heidegger's evolving discussion of place serves to underscore the inclusiveness
of implacement once it is grasped as the opening of the Open, the very Clearing that makes room for the manifestation of Being and the fourfold. What
could be more inclusive, ontologically considered, than place regarded as the
epiphanic scene of the veiling/unveiling of Truth?

Heidegger's early emphasis on region, which bears fruit in his eventual
focus on "that-which-regions" and "regioning," is explored further in Deleuze
and Guattari's model of nomad space. This latter, the epitome of "smooth
space," is distinctly regional in character: so much so that the two French
thinkers distend place to the point where it coincides with region, taken to be
equivalent to an "undelimited locality" that can be considered as a "local
absolute." In line with this distention and yet not entirely unlike Hellenistic
and medieval thinkers, Irigaray suggests that there is no reason to stop even
at the region if it is true that "the elements fill the universe,"[8] thereby putting any definitive difference between finite place and infinite universe into
question. Given that the material elements are found equally everywhere,

"the universe is [to be] conceived as a closed vessel, the receptacle for all the elements."⁹ Here Aristotle is turned on his head and Plato put back on his feet: place as enclosure is affirmed, but only insofar as the elements that make up place inhabit and suffuse the universe as a whole, now considered as a gigantic sievelike vessel—which, though entirely enveloped, leaks throughout.

In this circuitous manner, the vision of quantum theory (a most decidedly un-Aristotelian kind of physics) is reaffirmed: the universe is unending yet finite. To be *somewhere* in the universe—to be at a particular *place in it*—is to be *everywhere through* the same universe: efficacious throughout and thus omni-located. Whitehead doubtless had quantum theory (as well as Leibniz) in mind when he wrote that "everything is everywhere at all times."¹⁰ Or let us say, *every place is everywhere*—everywhere thanks to an unforecloseable causal efficacy, and thanks to the fact that a single place is capable of reflecting the whole universe of space. A place is the *event* of this reflection. As such an event, place accomplishes what is begun in body: it possesses an inclusiveness that does not exclude anything but reaches out to everything, that is, to all constructed as well as natural things. Whitehead remarks that "in being aware of the bodily experience, we must thereby be aware of aspects of the whole spatio-temporal world as mirrored within the bodily life."¹¹ But the mirroring power of place is even more extensive than that of body; as bodies expand into places, so places exfoliate through (built and given) things into (social and natural) regions, and regions expand in turn into worlds. From body and thing and region we come to world, but we do so only insofar as the event of place is active throughout.

We come, in short, to a world in places—a place-world that subsists in the many particular places that reflect it, much as the many waves of a sunlit sea reflect the circumambient light, each in its own manner. Places extend to world without end. If, as Irigaray says, "there is always more place, more places, unless they are immediately appropriated,"¹² this is only true inasmuch as each unappropriated place (i.e., each place not subjugated to site), despite its boundaries (indeed, on account of their very openness), ingresses into the world in its entirety and draws that world back into itself. Such is the elemental, the eventmental power of place. Thanks to this power, place is to be recognized as an undelimited, detotalized expansiveness, resonating regionally throughout the unknown as well as the known universe.

III

With this vision of place, it seems that we have returned to the thesis of place's primacy. The ancient Archytian axiom appears vindicated: to be is (still, or once again) to be in place. But to reaffirm the importance of place we need not posit its privileged status in the manner of Aristotle, for whom place is "prior to all things." It is not a matter of a new foundationalism—with Place in an invulnerable supreme position formerly assigned to God or Thought or Being. Nor is it even a question of the victory of Place over Space and Time, tempting as it may be to think in these competitive terms. Instead, it is a matter of realizing that the significance of place has been reasserted on a very different basis from that which it enjoyed in the ancient world, where its primacy was physical, metaphysical, and cosmological (physical and metaphysical in Aristotle; metaphysical and cosmological in Plato, Neoplatonism, and Hellenistic philosophy). The new bases of any putative primacy of place are themselves multiple: bodily certainly, but also psychical, nomadological, architectural, institutional, and sexual. Since there is no single basis of the primacy of place, there is no monolithic foundation on which this primacy could be built. What is at stake is a polyvalent primacy—an equiprimordiality of primary terms.

Is this, then, to intimate a multifoundationalism? Not so. On the one hand, place as newly emergent calls for recognizing the rhizomatic structure of implacement and the many ways in which place figures in human and nonhuman settings. Not mere multiplicity but radical heterogeneity of place is at play. On the other hand, place is not entitative—as a foundation has to be—but eventmental, something in process, something unconfinable to a thing. Or to a simple location. Place is all over the place, not just here or there, but everywhere. Its primacy consists in its omnilocality, its continual inclusion in ever more expansive envelopments. Which means that there is no simple origin or telos of place: no definitive beginning or ending of the matter. The primacy of place is not that of *the* place, much less of *this* place or *a* place (not even a very special place)—all these locutions imply place-as-simple-presence—but that of being an event capable of implacing things in many complex manners and to many complex effects. It is an issue of being in place differently, experiencing its eventfulness otherwise. Otherwise than traditional physicists or metaphysicians, cosmologists or ethicists, would have foretold in ancient, medieval, and modern periods of Western history. But not otherwise than certain native peoples, many artists, and some postmodern thinkers know and have attempted to set forth.

IV

The prominence of place in early Greek thought having been subdued by the growing preoccupation with space in late Hellenistic and medieval philosophy, the very idea of place came to inhabit the underworld of the modern cultural and philosophical unconscious. We have seen how this has happened—in considerable detail. But *why* did it happen? Why when place is all around us—there for everyone to see, right under our physical feet and before our conceptual eyes? Why when place serves as an abiding framework for all

that we experience in space and time? Why in the face of its very obviousness
and supportiveness was there such a flight to space? Why did its history become so hidden? We can only suppose that infinite space was not just a source
of existential anguish à la Pascal; it must also have offered a special form of
comfort, a reassuring presence. Can one not dissolve one's samsaric sorrows
in the endless ethereality of empty space? Such space, after all, offers an
infinite amount of *Lebensraum:* if *this* world is unsatisfactory, then numberless others are in the offing. Doubtless this open-ended prospect of world after
world is what appealed to Bruno—and threatened the ecclesiastical hierarchy
of his day. At the same time, infinite space suggests the possibility of unlimited control: such space is not only measurable and predictable (hence mathematizable) but altogether "passable." Like the metaphysical dove invoked
by Kant at the beginning of the *Critique of Pure Reason,* one imagines oneself
cleaving the air of infinite space freely and without hindrance.[13]

No wonder Western thinkers were drawn to this vista—a vista that included
infinite time as well. In invidious contrast with this freewheeling vista, place
presents itself in its stubborn, indeed its rebarbative, particularity. One has no
choice but to deal with what is *in place,* or *at place:* that is, what is *at stake
there.* Regarding the particular place one is already in, one cannot speculate,
much less levitate or miraculate, freely; one has to cope with the exacting
demands of being just there, with all its finite historicity and special qualities.
(In this regard, place is more closely allied with nonchronometric time: the
time of urgency and deadline, the time that delimits rather than extends. Just
as lived time seems ever to be running out, to be "closing time," so place
always possesses its delimiting boundaries.) Perhaps in earlier eras people
were more able and willing to deal with the complexities, or more exactly the
perplexities, of place; "since Copernicus," as Nietzsche said, "man has been
running from the center into X."[14] If place is centered and finite (e.g., as
home-place, sacred place, birth-place, place of burial), space is infinite and
decentered. This is not to say, however, that place is always and only centered—far from it!

In the modern era, dromocentrism has replaced lococentrism. Modern humans have eagerly embraced a space that is less suggestive of infinite settled
extension than of *speed*—if not the speed of light, the speed of their own
frenzied movements through space in imagined or real flights.[15] No wonder
that the slow legwork of being in a place may seem parochial, or merely
irritating, in contrast with the grandomania occasioned by an ecstatic outlook
onto cosmic or "universal" space: an outlook first attained in the Archytian
conundrum of standing at the edge of the known world. To subjectify such
space in the manner of Kant is not to lose the seductive power of this universality; on the contrary, it is to guarantee it within the knowing subject, who
does not have to voyage any farther than his or her own epistemophiliacal
mind to savor the serenity, the unlimited traversibility, of infinite space—its

allure as an open domain for "space travel" of every imaginable sort. Entranced by this prospect, who could resist the temptation to obliterate place in the infinite sky of space, or else to bury it in the nether regions of modernist thinking?

V

If place is indeed to come (back) into its own, it must appear in distinctly different forms than those examined in the earlier parts of this book. In fact, the shape of place, its very face, has changed dramatically from the time of Archytas and Aristotle. So much so that we may have difficulty recognizing place *as place* as it comes out of the concealment in which it has been kept for over two millennia. It certainly no longer appears as a mere container: hence Heidegger's immediate, unequivocal rejection of the container model early in *Being and Time* and his transformation of this model's closed-in, present-at-hand structure into that of the Open, a regionalized neighborhood that is more an event than an entity. Hence, too, Derrida's denial that place as such, that is, place as literal thing or as essence, is ever simply *presented:* for him, too, place is an event, a matter of *taking place.* By the same token, Irigaray transfigures the model of containment into the image of half-open and partially touching lips: the hard shell of the containing surface becomes the soft sheath of erotic engagement. Place remains something that surrounds, but no longer as an airtight, immobile, diaphanous limit. It is the event of envelopment itself.

Place, thus disinterred, is rising in ever-proliferating guises: not just as imaginary *topoi* in Bachelard, as *heterotopoi* in Foucault, as the scene of written-in traces and spaced-out buildings in Derrida, or as discrete "localities" (Heidegger, Deleuze and Guattari), but also as social-political "enclaves" in Lyotard and "sense of place" in Stegner.[16] It appears as well in the recent concern with the pertinence of "local knowledge" on the part of anthropologists and other social scientists; and it surfaces in the current efflorescence of "cultural geography." Never having vanished into Space (or Time) altogether, place is abounding: this is so even when it is called by various names, and itself names different events and experiences. The newly grasped inclusiveness of place subtends this profusion and makes it possible.

Despite the seduction of endless space (and the allure of serial time), place is beginning to escape from its entombment in the cultural and philosophical underworld of the modern West. Not yet wholly above ground, it is there to be seen or at least glimpsed, in this locale or that, here and there, now and then, wherever, somewhere. "The material, local presence," writes Jean-Luc Nancy, is "here or there, *selfsame with somewhere.*"[17] He adds that "all presence is that of a body,"[18] whether of a god or a human being or another animal. For Nancy, place calls for recognition in our own time out of a renewed respect for the body's presence beneath and through it: implacement entails embodiment, and vice versa. More than any other single factor—more even than the psyche or society, architecture or politics—the organic body links the diverse appearances of place: it renders them all incarnate, part of the history of the body itself. And if this is so, it calls for a postmodern revision of Archytas's premodern dictum, a brief but fateful supplement: to be is to be in place—*bodily.* Or let us say: *at least bodily,* though also (as I have emphasized just above) in many other ways as well.

If space did not yet exist as a concept distinct from place in Aristotle's worldview, and if place became increasingly lost in space after the demise of the classical era, in the twentieth century we stand witness to a third peripeteia: *space is now becoming absorbed into place,* in the form of the "spaces" (*not* "space") of which Heidegger speaks in "Building Dwelling Thinking," in the "smooth spaces" of *A Thousand Plateaus,* and in the "open spaces" of Nancy's "Divine Places." "Space has been split up into places": this simple sentence from *Being and Time* has proven prophetic in the seven decades since it was first written. In a dramatic reversal of previous priorities, space is being reassimilated into place, made part of its substance and structure. As a result of this reversal, spacing not only eventuates in placing but is seen to *require it to begin with.* The empty, metric dimensionality of sheer spatial extension no longer exercises, much less dominates, the philosophical mind; dimensions have become concrete and cling to place or region: height counts as "up on the ceiling" or "in the sky."[19] At the level of the lived body, dimensionality has become one with directionality—as we see saliently in the experience of lived depth.[20] As is also said in *Being and Time,* "all 'wheres' are discovered and circumspectively interpreted as we go our ways in everyday dealings; they are not ascertained and catalogued by the observational measurements of space."[21]

The "where" is *back in place,* once again and finally. Painting, as one case in point, is no longer being done exclusively from a removed point of view, that is, "the view from nowhere" that obtains for homogeneous monofocal space. Painters are acknowledging that they paint *up close,* in the near sphere of full bodily engagement with the subject matter: "A painting is done at close range, even if it is seen from a distance."[22] Nor is divinity, to cite another instance, conceived as a matter of aloof and elevated immensity but as concrete dwelling in believers' bodies and in "divine places" that are no longer explicitly ceremonial in any established or monumental way.

The term "divine places" is that of Nancy, who, like Irigaray, extends his consideration of place to the religious sphere. Unlike Irigaray, however, Nancy believes that human beings now live in a time of complete "destitution," in which both God and gods are radically absent: "the divine has deserted the temples."[23] Even if it can be claimed after Nietzsche (and as has been known in a number of non-Western religions for a very long time) that human beings have assumed "the place of the god, this place is empty: it is a place that exists in place of the god. Particular places have taken the place of God and the gods: this is precisely what makes them divine. Despite their ineradicable emptiness (i.e., with regard to belief and ritual), such places are where the power is, for they generate novel spaces. Spaces come from places, not the other way around. Nancy here joins the company of those who maintain the priority of place over space—a priority regained, however, only in (and as) *many places,* places in the indefinite plural.

Divine places are in Nancy's view the most instructive instance of this exhumation and revalorization of place. The divine, previously considered coextensive with infinite space and its most privileged inhabitant, is now *spaced-out into places,* the very places we inhabit in daily life. If there is no longer any proper place for God or the gods, that leaves them homeless and ourselves destitute. Nevertheless, this very situation "opens something up, outside of all places, it makes a spacing-out."[24] The event of "spacing-out" (a term we have met in discussing Derrida) occurs outside of all historically and institutionally sanctioned places, but it is not made *in no place,* for example, in a void. No-place is not to be found even in this devastated scene—any more than it was found in the precreationist states of chaos or nonbeing we examined at the beginning of this book. After divine intervention as well as before it, place abides.

> Divine places, without gods, with no god, are spread out everywhere around us, open and offered to our coming, to our going or to our presence, given up or promised to our visitation, to frequentation by those who are not men either, but who are there, in these places: ourselves, alone, out to meet that which we are not, and which the gods for their part have never been . . . other tracks, other ways, other places for all who are there.[25]

Nancy thus concurs with Irigaray's auspicious assertion that "there is always more place, more places, unless they are immediately appropriated." There are more places than we can keep track of, or visit, much less own or exploit. Only when appropriated (or, more precisely, expropriated) do places become closed-in and closed-down sites—which, failing to be genuinely spaced-out, are spread thin in a technological landscape consisting merely of positions and distances, bare locations and barren relations. Such a wasted (and wasteful) site-scene lacks region and is destitute of depth.

Yet places abound even in this blasted, desolate wasteland. Here, too, places are "spread out"[26]—a locution that eerily echoes "ex-tension," while departing decisively from the early modern legacy of *res extensa.* To spread out in places is to leave (behind) the extensiveness of homogeneous infinite space and to inhabit a new kind of space, one that is heterogeneous and open, genuinely spaced-out. If such space is "everywhere open,"[27] it is open pre-

cisely *in places,* for it is in them alone that space attains poignancy and plenitude, along with that qualitative diversity and ample discernibility that signal
the implacement of space itself. And if "it is granted to us to see the limitless
openness of that space,"[28] we shall see it most surely in the undelimited localities of our concrete bodily movements, that is to say, in our most engaged
experiences of being-in-place—in many different ways and in many different
places.

Notes

Preface: Disappearing Places

1. Immanuel Kant, *Critique of Pure Reason,* trans. N. K. Smith (New York: Humanities, 1965), A34B50, p. 77.

2. See *Getting Back into Place: Toward a Renewed Understanding of the Place-World* (Bloomington: Indiana University Press, 1993).

3. See Paul Virilio, *Speed and Politics,* trans. M. Polizzotti (New York: Semiotext[e], 1986), passim.

4. On this interactive aspect of technology, see Joshua Meyrowitz, *No Sense of Place: The Impact of Electronic Media on Social Behavior* (Oxford: Oxford University Press, 1985). This not to deny that the open networking of television or e-mail, a networking that is potentially endless and numberless, is more akin to *space.* It is almost as if the ancient dialectic of place and space is being replayed within the domain of technology itself! Moreover, the dromocentrism to which electronic technologies contribute so massively is itself not without placial significance: when life becomes sufficiently accelerated, we find ourselves more, not less, appreciative of the places we are so rapidly passing through. Every race, after all, is a race between *someplace* we start and *someplace* we end.

5. See Victor Turner, *The Ritual Process: Structure and Anti-Structure* (Chicago: Aldine, 1969), chaps. 3 and 4. Jean-Luc Nancy, however, would disagree: "*In place of* community there is [now] no *place,* no site, no temple or altar for community. Exposure takes place everywhere, in all places, for it is the exposure of all and of each, in his solitude, to not being alone" (*The Inoperative Community,* trans. M. Holland [Minneapolis: University of Minnesota Press, 1991], 143; his italics). I shall return to Nancy's position briefly at the end of this book.

6. See Hannah Arendt, *The Human Condition* (Chicago: University of Chicago Press, 1958), passim.

7. See John Rawls, *A Theory of Justice* (Cambridge: Harvard University Press,

343

1971), esp. sec. 22, "The Circumstances of Justice." The "objective circumstances" of justice include the fact (cited first of all) that "many individuals coexist together at the same time *on a definite geographical territory*" (p. 126; my italics). This is so, even though in the "original position" posited by Rawls a "veil of ignorance" is presumed with respect to the "specific contingencies which put men at odds" (p. 136) and which thwart their obligation to "evaluate principles solely on the basis of general considerations" (ibid., 136–137).

8. Martin Heidegger, *Being and Time,* trans. J. Macquarrie and E. Robinson (New York: Harper, 1962), 138.

Chapter One: Avoiding the Void

1. Friedrich Nietzsche, *The Genealogy of Morals,* trans. F. Golffing, in *The Birth of Tragedy and The Genealogy of Morals* (New York: Doubleday Anchor, 1956), 299.

2. Whereas the idea of "nonplace"—that is, something merely not a place—does not expunge the possibility of other place-related items such as regions, "no-place" (as I shall abbreviate "no-place-at-all") connotes the radical absence of place of any kind, including cosmic regions. Thus no-place is tantamount to what I shall call "utter void" or "strict void" or "absolute void."

3. The full statement is "Know that the world is uncreated, as time itself is, without beginning and end" (cited from the *Mahapurana,* in *Primal Myths: Creating the World,* ed. Barbara C. Sproul [New York: Harper & Row, 1979], 17, 193).

4. A. K. Coomaraswamy and M. F. Noble, *Myths of the Hindus and Buddhists* (New York: Dover, 1967), 392–395. Chaos (to be considered at greater length in Section II below) figures prominently in the Hindu cosmogony: at the close of each *kalpa,* or Day of Brahma, the three worlds are resolved into chaos (*pralaya*), and at the end of one hundred Brahama years, "all planes and all beings . . . are resolved into chaos (*maha-pralaya,* 'great chaos'), enduring for another hundred Brahama-years" (ibid., 393). Notice that in certain traditions creation may be admitted but the role of a creator god is barred. In Taoism, for example, creation is regarded as the spontaneous product of the interaction between heaven and earth: "Creation is the spontaneous work of heaven and earth, repeating itself regularly in every year, or in every revolution of time or the *Tao,* the order of the universe" (De Groot, *The Religion of the Chinese,* cited by F. M. Cornford, *From Religion to Philosophy* [New York: Harper, 1957], 99). Much as in Hesiod's *Theogony,* creation proceeds from a primal separation *without* a distinct creator. At the extreme, both creation and creator are denied. The Jain myth cited just above adds the following lines: "Some foolish men declare that Creator made the world. The doctrine that the world was created is ill-advised, [and] should be rejected" (*Mahapurana,* 192). In these words, we find a conception of the world as self-sustaining and self-evolving—as needing neither a special moment of creation nor a special creator to bring it into being.

5. The original statement of Archytas (as reported by Simplicius) is in part: "all existing things are either in place or not without place" (cited and translated in S. Sambursky, ed., (*The Concept of Place in Late Neoplatonism* [Jerusalem: Israel Academy of Sciences and Humanities, 1982], 37).

6. I say "spiritual" since certain cosmogenetic accounts concern an entirely nonmaterial evolution of the universe. I have in mind the Gnostic notion of the bringing forth of ten spiritual eons by the process of *Barbelo* (the second principle) out of God as the

first principle. Each of these eons is considered to be "at once places, extents of time, and abstractions" (Bentley Layton, *The Gnostic Scriptures* [New York: Doubleday, 1987], 14). The place in question is that of a stage on the journey of creation, a complex journey that only later leads to the creation of a material world.

7. I make a similar point in *Getting Back into Place: Toward a Renewed Understanding of the Place-World* (Bloomington: Indiana University Press, 1993), chap. 1, where a much briefer account is given of the role of place in doctrines of creation (as well as a discussion of God-as-place). As I shall try to demonstrate below, the converse also holds: *topogenesis is cosmogenesis* insofar as a close scrutiny of the role of place in the emergence of the cosmos reveals much about the nature and structure of the cosmos itself. To be sensitive to place is to learn deeply about the created world.

8. Mircea Eliade, *The Sacred and the Profane: The Nature of Religion,* trans. W. R. Trask (New York: Harcourt Brace Jovanovich, 1959), 34; his italics.

9. Ibid., 47. This sentence is in italics in the text.

10. "Out of nothing nothing can be made." Lucretius, however, doubts whether *any* force can create *anything* in this situation: *"Nothing can ever be created [even] by divine power out of nothing"* (*The Nature of Things,* trans. R. D. Latham, in *Theories of the Universe,* ed. M. K. Munitz [New York: Free Press, 1957], 43; italics in the original).

11. Marcel Griaule, *Conversations with Ogotemmêli: An Introduction to Dogon Religious Ideas* (Oxford: Oxford University Press, 1965), 73. See also pp. 28–29, 49, 65, 67. I owe this reference to Henry Tylbor.

12. This is the paraphrase of Robert Graves in *The Greek Myths* (Baltimore: Penguin, 1955), I:27. The Pelasgians were Paleolithic peoples who invaded Greece from Palestine in the middle of the fourth millennium B.C.

13. "The very word 'chaos', derived from the Greek root *cha-* (*chaskein, chainein*), implies, as 'yawning', 'gaping', an idea of terror and fright" (Max Jammer, *Concepts of Space: The History of Theories of Space in Physics,* 2d ed. [Cambridge, Mass.: Harvard University Press, 1970], 9). Also note that there is an ancient etymological link between *chaos* (chaos) and *chōra* (space). Both have the same root sense of "separation," "opening," "hollow." On this point, see F. M. Cornford, *Principium Sapientiae* (New York: Harper & Row, 1965), n. 10.

14. This is the translation of *Theogony* 116–134 in G. S. Kirk, J. E. Raven, and M. Schofield, *The Presocratic Philosophers* (Cambridge: Cambridge University Press, 1983), 35. Note that "Erebos" designates the "place of darkness" between Gaia and Hades.

15. See Cornford, *Principium Sapientiae,* 198–203; Kirk, Raven, and Schofield, *Presocratic Philosophers,* 43–45. The latter authors point to further striking parallels not only in the Egyptian Book of the Dead and a Hurrian-Hittite epic but also in the Maori myth of the separation of Rangi (sky) from Papa (earth).

16. P. Diamandopoulos, "Chaos and Cosmos," in *The Encyclopedia of Philosophy,* ed. P. Edwards (New York: Macmilllan, 1967), I:80. Indeed, the *Theogony* represents a radical revision of most other Ionian cosmogonies, which concur that "in the beginning there is a primal Unity, a state of indistinction or fusion in which factors that will later become distinct are merged together" (Cornford, *Principium Sapientiae,* 190). On this paradigm, as manifest, e.g., in Anaximander's notion of the Boundless (*to apeiron*), separation *follows* such Unity.

17. John Burnet, *Early Greek Philosophy* (New York: Meridian, 1958), 7.

18. Aristotle, *Physics* 208b31–32; Hardie and Gaye translation; my italics. "Space" translates *chōra* and "place" *topos*.

19. As Cornford observes, "In the modern mind the word Chaos has come to be associated with a primitive disorder in which, as the Ionian pluralists said, 'all things were together'. This is not the sense of the word in sixth- and fifth-century Greek" (*Principium Sapientiae,* 194). See also Kirk, Raven, and Schofield, *Presocratic Philosophers,* 36–37, on the same point. There is a striking parallel between chaos and Merleau-Ponty's idea of "flesh": both are easily construable as disordered and primitive, yet both are sources of emerging structure by way of differentiation. (Cf. M. Merleau-Ponty, *The Visible and the Invisible,* trans. A. Lingis [Evanston: Northwestern University Press, 1968], 248–251, 273–274. See also Merleau-Ponty's remarks on the nonamorphous, shaped character of the abyss as an "opening out" in the introduction to *Signs,* trans. R. McCleary [Evanston: Northwestern University Press, 1964], 21).

20. Kirk, Raven, and Schofield, *Presocratic Philosophers,* 39.

21. Ibid., 38; their italics. They are commenting on Cornford's earlier interpretation in *Principium Sapientiae,* p. 195: Hesiod's "cosmogony begins with the coming into being of a yawning gap between heaven and earth . . . and the first thing that happened was that they were 'separated from one another.' "

22. This is the phrase of Kirk, Raven, and Schofield, *Presocratic Philosophers,* p. 36.

23. Aristophanes, *The Birds,* line 693.

24. Not only the *Theogony* but also a number of other similar cosmogonies reveal this trait: "The feature common to all these systems is the attempt to get behind the Gap, and to put Kronos or Zeus in the first place" (Burnet, *Early Greek Philosophy,* 7). As for Eros, Cornford comments that he steps into the Gap as "a transparent personification of the mutual attraction [between earth and sky] which is to reunite them" (*Principium Sapientiae,* 195).

25. On obtrusions (*Aufdrängenen*), see Edmund Husserl, *Experience and Judgment,* trans. J. S. Churchill and K. Ameriks (Evanston: Northwestern University Press, 1973), 77 ff.

26. Cited from D. A. Mackensie, *Myths of China and Japan* (London: Allen & Unwin, 1923), 261.

27. "First there was the great cosmic egg. Inside the egg was Chaos, and floating in Chaos was P'an Ku, the Undeveloped, the divine Embryo. And P'an Ku burst out of the egg" (ibid., 260). In a still earlier Taoist text, Chaos is the source of the primary separation.

In the beginning there was chaos. Out of it came pure light and built the sky. The heavy dimness, however, moved and formed the earth from itself. Sky and earth brought forth the ten thousand creations . . . and all of them take the sky and earth as their mode. The roots of Yang and Yin—the male and female principle—also began in sky and earth." (Cited by Charles Long, *Alpha: Myths of Creation* [New York: Braziller, 1963], 126)

28. Rik Pinxten, Ingrid van Dooren, and Frank Harvey, *Anthropology of Space: Explorations into the Natural Philosophy and Semantics of the Navajo* (Philadelphia: University of Pennsylvania Press, 1983), 9, 14. For a more complete account of the Navajo creation myth, see Leland C. Wyman, *Blessingway* (Tucson: University of Arizona Press, 1970), and Gladys A. Reichard, *Navajo Religion: A Study of Symbolism*

(New York: Pantheon, 1950), 2 vols. On the Celtic view, see John Rhys, *Lectures on the Origin and Growth of Religion as Illustrated by Celtic Heathendum* (London: Williams and Norgate, 1862), 669. For ancient Japanese beliefs on the matter, see W. G. Aston, trans., *The Nihongi* (London: Allen & Unwin, 1956).

29. "In the beginning there were only mists. There was no world then, only the white, yellow, blue, black, silver, and red mists floating in the air. The mists came together and laid on top of each other, like intercourse" (Stanley Fishler, *In the Beginning: A Navajo Creation Myth,* Utah University Anthropological Paper no. 13 [Salt Lake City, 1953], 9). This declaration comes close to identifying the moment of chaos with the moment of separation: if the mists can lie on *top* of each other, they are already distinguishably—if vaguely!—different.

30. Pinxten, van Dooren, and Harvey, *Anthropology of Space,* 10. Pinxten's native consultants insisted that "there is air between both at any particular place" (ibid., 12). Spindles are posited as holding Heaven apart from Earth.

31. Indeed, it may be speculated that dawn is the original model for the horizon line, since the dawn delineates the opening between sky and earth and makes their difference more distinctly felt. Cassirer remarks that "in the creation legends of nearly all peoples and religions the process of creation merges with the dawning of light" (Ernst Cassirer, *Mythical Thought,* vol. 2 of *The Philosophy of Symbolic Forms,* trans. R. Manheim [New Haven: Yale University Press, 1955], 96). Dawn, it might be added, is a genuinely spatiotemporal notion: it occurs at the *beginning* of the day but *between* earth and sky.

32. From the Ainu creation myth as retold by Maria Leach in *The Beginning* (New York: Funk and Wagnalls, 1956), 205.

33. I take the term "basis body" from Husserl's late manuscript, "Foundational Investigations of the Phenomenological Origin of the Spatiality of Nature," trans. F. Kersten, in P. McCormick and F. Elliston, eds., *Husserl: Shorter Writings* [South Bend: University of Notre Dame Press, 1981], 223 ff.).

34. Genesis 1:1–2 in the *Holy Bible: Revised Standard Version* (New York: Nelson, 1953), 1. Subsequent references in the text will be to the recognized subdivisions of this edition.

35. Aristotle, *Physics* 220a27. This same line can also be translated: "The least number, without qualification, is the two" (Hussey translation).

36. *Physics* 200b21 (Hussey translation). The full statement is "there cannot be change (*kinēsis*) without place and void and time . . . because they are common to everything and universal."

37. Job 38:4–12; as translated in the *Revised Standard Version,* p. 557. A closely related passage occurs in Proverbs 8:27–30: "When he established the heavens . . . when he drew a circle on the face of the deep . . . when he assigned to the sea its limit . . . when he marked out the foundations of the earth" (ibid., 669).

38. On the question of geometry's origin in the art of surveying and on the proto-geometer's construction of basic "limit-shapes," see Edmund Husserl, "The Origin of Geometry," in *The Crisis of European Sciences and Transcendental Phenomenology,* trans. D. Carr (Evanston: Northwestern University Press, 1970), 353–378.

39. Cited in Sproul, *Primal Myths,* 17.

40. Elsewhere, cosmic emptiness is recognized as a *second* state of the universe situated between the first beginning and the plenitude of creation proper. Thus we read

in the *Huai-Nan Tzu,* a Chinese text of the Han dynasty, that "before heaven and earth had taken form all was vague and amorphous. Therefore it was called the Great Beginning. *The Great Beginning produced emptiness and emptiness produced the universe.* The universe produced material-force which had limits" (cited from the *Huai-nan Tzu* 3:1a in Sproul, *Primal Myths,* 206; my italics). For an illuminating discussion of emptiness in an epistemological context, see C. W. Huntington, Jr., with Geshé Namgyal Wangchem, *The Emptiness of Emptiness: An Introduction to Early Indian Madhyamika* (Honolulu: University of Hawaii Press, 1989).

41. On these underworlds and their "place of emergence," see Aileen O'Bryan, *The Diné: Myths of the Navajo Indians* (Washington, D.C.: U.S. Bureau of American Ethnology, Bulletin 163, 1956), 1–3.

42. "in [that] place he created; the brick-mold he built; the city he built; living creature(s) he placed therein" (from Alexander Heidel, *The Babylonian Genesis* [Chicago: University of Chicago Press, 1942], 52).

43. Cited from "A Maori Cosmogony," trans. Hare Hongi, *Journal of the Polynesian Society* 16, no. 63 (September 1907):113 (Wellington: Polynesian Society).

44. Cited from F. H. Cushing, "Outlines of Zuni Creation Myths," in *Thirteenth Annual Report of the U.S. Bureau of American Ethnology* (Washington, D.C.: Smithsonian Institution, 1891–1892), 379.

45. It is curious to reflect that the word "anxiety" is rooted in ideas of narrowness and constriction—whereas we have been confronting circumstances in which the very *lack* of enclosure induces the anxiety of placelessness. (Pathologically speaking, the difference is that between claustrophobia and agoraphobia.) It appears that we encounter here an instance of what Freud has termed "the antithetical meaning of primal words." (See the essay of this title in *Standard Edition of the Complete Psychological Works* (London: Hogarth, 1954–1975), 11:155–161.)

46. Cited from the Book of the Dead (ca. 2000–1500 B.C.), in C. Doria and H. Lenowitz, eds. *Origins: Creation Texts from the Ancient Mediterranean* (New York: Doubleday Anchor, 1976), 87. For other conceptions of primeval water, see Sproul, *Primal Myths,* 183–186, 188, 256.

47. *Physics* 208b25–26 (Hardie and Gaye translation).

48. "He existed, Taaroa was his name. In the immensity [space] / There was no earth, there was no sky / There was no sea, there was no man" (cited in E. S. Craighill Handy, *Polynesian Religion* (Honolulu: Bishop Museum Press, 1927), 11. And the Tuamotuan people open their epic story of creation with the words: "It is said that Kiho dwelt in the Void" (Frank J. Stimson, *Tuamotuan Religion* [Honolulu: Bishop Museum Press, 1933], 12).

49. Cited from Sproul, *Primal Myths,* 17. The Hopi myth thus reenacts the kenotic self-emptying of many Gnostic texts.

50. Stimson, *Tuamotuan Religion,* 12.

51. Ibid., 12–13. The primacy of Night here rejoins Hesiod's similar stress: "From Night [was born] Bright Sky [*Aither*] and Day, whom Night conceived and bore in loving union with Erebus" (from the *Theogony*).

52. From M. E. Opler, *Myths and Tales of the Jicarilla Apache Indians* (New York: Stechert, 1938), 1; cited in Sproul, *Primal Myths,* 263. The two sentences here cited may also be construed as specifying contemporaneous states; but if so, they are all the more susceptible to toporeversal.

53. Chuang Tzu, *Basic Writings,* trans. B. Watson (New York: Columbia University Press, 1964), 38.

54. Adrian Recinos, *Popul Vuh: The Sacred Book of the Ancient Quiché Maya,* trans. D. Goetz and S. G. Morley (Norman: University of Oklahoma Press, 1950), 81.

55. R. E. Hume, ed. and trans., *The Thirteen Principal Upanishads* (London: Oxford University Press, 1971), 214.

56. For the assessment of space in terms of *vorhanden* and *zuhanden* properties, see M. Heidegger, *Being and Time,* secs. 12, 22–24. I have treated Heidegger's ideas in my essay "Heidegger In and Out of Place," *Duquesne Studies in Philosophy* (Silverman Phenomenology Center, Duquesne University, 1990), 62–97.

57. *Physics* 222b6 (Hardie and Gaye translation). Hussey translates: "time will not give out, for it is always at a beginning."

Chapter Two: Mastering the Matrix

1. The convergence of *bará* with the Greek *temnein,* "to cut, sever, mark off," and German *Ort* (one of whose original meanings is also "tip of an arrow") is especially striking—and all the more so since *Ort* means "place" and *temnein* is a source (via *temenos,* "precinct") of Latin *templum,* that is, a primal built place. Suggested here is the idea that to be a place is to be *cut out of* concrete materials ("timber" also derives from *temnein*) from within a circumambient "space."

2. These are the first two stanzas of the *Enuma Elish* in the translation of N. K. Sandars, *Poems of Heaven and Hell from Ancient Mesopotamia* (Baltimore: Penguin, 1971), 73. I have also consulted Alexander Heidel's more scholarly version in *The Babylonian Genesis: The Story of Creation,* 2d ed. (Chicago: University of Chicago Press, 1963). Unless otherwise indicated, however, further citations from the *Enuma Elish* will be from Sandars's translation. I wish to thank Catherine Keller for bringing to my attention the link between Tehom and Tiamat.

3. It should be noted, however, that the *Enuma Elish* may well have influenced the *Theogony.* For an argument to this effect, see F. M. Cornford, *Principium Sapientiae* (New York: Harper, 1965), chap. 15.

4. *Enuma Elish,* 73.

5. Ibid., 82, 85.

6. Ibid., 74.

7. Ibid., 75.

8. Ibid., 75.

9. On memorialization, see my *Remembering: A Phenomenological Study* (Bloomington: Indiana University Press, 1987), chap. 10. For Freud's theory of the murder of the primal fat'.er, followed by propitiatory memorialization of the father in the form of shrines and sacrifices of a totem animal, see his *Totem and Taboo* (*Standard Edition of the Complete Psychological Works* [London: Hogarth, 1958], esp. pt. 4). See also René Girard, *La Violence et le sacré* (Paris: Grasset, 1972). It is pertinent that the origin of the word "matter" is affine with the Indo-European root **dem-* or **dom-,* a root signifying "to build," which also gives rise to the Latin *domus,* "house." Marduk's role in the *Enuma Elish* is that of the archetypal builder in an epic that forms part of an entire series of Sumerian texts in which building is the prototypical activity.

On this constructional proclivity—especially in contrast with, say, Australian aboriginal myths of origin in which building does not figure at all—see Jonathan Z. Smith,
To Take Place: Toward Theory in Ritual (Chicago: University of Chicago Press, 1987),
chaps. 1, 2. Smith writes, "*Enuma Elish,* the best known cosmogonic text from the
ancient Near East, is dominated by building. . . . It is, essentially, a narrative of the
creation of the holy city of Babylon" (p. 19).

10. *Enuma Elish,* 75.

11. Ibid., 87. On the original meaning of "Tiamat" and "Apsu," see N. K. Sandars's
introduction to her translation of the *Enuma Elish,* pp. 24 ff.

12. *Enuma Elish,* 90.

13. In the end, Ea figures as the architect for Marduk as master builder: "Let Ea be
his architect and draw the excellent plan" (*Enuma Elish,* 96), as Marduk's triumphant
lieutenants proclaim after his victory over Tiamat.

14. *Enuma Elish,* 91.

15. Paul Ricoeur, *The Symbolism of Evil,* trans. E. Buchanon (Boston: Beacon
Press, 1967), 179. See also pp. 182–183: "Marduk personifies the identity of creation
and destruction. . . . Violence is inscribed in the origin of things."

16. "Marduk" means "sun-child" or "son-of-the-sun" in Semitic; and the title
"Lord of the Land" or "Lord of the World" is bestowed on him in the "Hymn of Fifty
Names" with which the *Enuma Elish* closes.

17. *Enuma Elish,* 92. Heidel translates the last clause as: "He split her open like a
mussel into two [parts]; half of her he *set in place,* and formed the sky [therewith] as
a roof; he fixed the crossbar [and] posted guards; he commanded them not to let her
waters escape" (*Babylonian Genesis,* 42; my italics). I have traced out the close links
between building and body in *Getting Back into Place: Toward a Renewed Understanding of the Place-World* (Bloomington: Indiana University Press, 1993), chap. 3.

18. Thus to Ricoeur's claim that in the *Enuma Elish* "cosmology completes theogony. . . . [W]hat there is to *say* about the world is the result of the *genesis* of the divine"
(*Symbolism of Evil,* 177; his italics), we need to add that the genesis itself of the divine
is from a primordial state of elemental regions: theogony completes cosmogony.

19. *Enuma Elish,* 92. (Enlil is an ancient Sumerian god of the universal air.) Note
that in Heidel's translation the first sentence runs: "He crossed the heavens and examined the regions" (*Babylonian Genesis,* 43).

20. *Enuma Elish,* 99.

21. Ibid., 92.

22. "He gave the moon the lustre of a jewel, he gave him all the night, to mark off
days, to watch by night each month the circle of a waxing and waning light. . . . He
took the sun and set him to complete the cycle from this one to the next New Year"
(ibid., 93).

23. Ibid., 93. At p. 92, Nebiru, or "zenith," the central band of the heavens (as well
as Marduk's astral name), is set up as an ultimate ground of orientation from on high.
Cardinal directions help to assure that "the foundations are firm in every direction" (p.
107). Such directions are themselves placelike: see my *Getting Back into Place,* chaps.
3–4, and Yi-Fu Tuan, *Space and Place* (Minneapolis: University of Minnesota Press,
1976), chaps. 6–7.

24. *Enuma Elish,* 93–94.

25. Cf. ibid., 94–96, 98–99. Babylon is said to be "the home of the gods" (p. 96),

but it is also the residence of ordinary mortals: the gods reside in the temples of Parakku (the Tower of Babel) and of Esagila (the temple of heaven). The early appearance of temples is striking in view of the connections discussed in the first note to this chapter.

26. Ibid., 97. The gods confirm Marduk's creation of man at p. 101: "He created man a living thing to labour for ever, and gods go free." ("Man" here signifies the human person, female as well as male.)

27. For example, Marduk boasts, "I, not you [Ea], will decide the world's nature, the things to come. My decrees shall never be altered, never annulled, but my creation endures to the ends of the world" (ibid., 82). By mentioning "decrees," Marduk points to the power of the *word,* a theme reinforced in other passages: cf. ibid., 86, 88, 107. But Marduk's creation, unlike that of Yahweh, is not *by the word.*

28. *Enuma Elish,* 110.

29. Ibid., 107.

30. Ibid., 110.

31. From Sandars's introduction to *Poems of Heaven and Hell from Ancient Mesopotamia,* p. 61.

32. Ibid., 61; my italics. Cf. Jonathan Z. Smith's similarly dubious claim: "in many respects it is improper to term this text a cosmogony" (*To Take Place,* 19).

33. *Enuma Elish,* 102.

34. Ibid., 95.

35. Marduk says to the assembled gods: "In the former time you inhabited the void above the abyss, but I have made Earth as the mirror of Heaven" (ibid., 95). Tiamat is referred to as "Chaos" at p. 106 ("he carried off Chaos meshed in his snare") and p. 107 ("[Marduk] came as king to confront Chaos"). For an interpretation of Tiamat as Chaos, see Susan Niditch, *Chaos to Cosmos: Studies in Biblical Patterns of Creation* (Chico, Calif.: Scholars Press, 1985), passim.

36. "When Tiamat heard him her wits scattered, she was possessed and shrieked aloud, her legs shook from the crotch down, she gabbled spells, muttered maledictions" (*Enuma Elish,* 90).

37. Ricoeur, *Symbolism of Evil,* 180. Notice, once more, the close link between separation and the creation of place, as is suggested in the ancient link between *chōrizein* (to separate) and *chōra* (space, place).

38. On the confrontation of Tiamat and Marduk as representatives of gender differences—and as raising basic questions of special pertinence to feminist concerns—see the remarkable discussion of Catherine Keller, *From a Broken Web: Separation, Sexism, and Self* (Boston: Beacon Press, 1986), 74–78, 81–83, 88–90, 106–107, 115–118. It is striking how, viewing Tiamat as the primal stuff of creation, Keller makes this interpretation (which agrees with my own) the basis for a feminist critique of the creationist model set forth in the *Enuma Elish:* "The separative [male] ego feels creative chaos as regressive disorder, and depth as an atmosphere of death. . . . Dead, she now functions as the facelessly inhuman, the *prima materia,* the defaced stuff, upon which his transcendent andromorphism enacts its new creation" (p. 78). There is considerable truth in this gender-sensitive reading of the *Enuma Elish.* Yet I find myself wondering: Is Tiamat truly to be understood as chaos, or even as disorder?

39. For further discussion of matrices, especially in their formal versus material formats, see my *Remembering,* 293–299.

40. Sandars, introduction to *Poems of Heaven and Hell from Ancient Mesopotamia*, 16.

41. See *Enuma Elish*, 95.

42. Mircea Eliade, *The Sacred and the Profane: The Nature of Religion*, trans. W. Trask (New York: Harper & Row, 1959), 77; his italics.

43. *Timaeus* 52a. Almost always, I shall employ Cornford's translation in *Plato's Cosmology: The Timaeus of Plato Translated with a Running Commentary* (New York: Liberal Arts Press, 1957). Subsequent references in the text will employ its Stephanus numbers.

44. I cite the celebrated phrase from *Timaeus* 37d; my italics. Cornford's translation is: "an everlasting image moving according to number."

45. Plato, *Timaeus* 49a; see also 52d.

46. For this appellation, see *Timaeus* 50d, 51a. In the opening paragraph of this section, I put "male" and "female" in double quotes to indicate that Plato *imputes* these attributes to the Demiurge and to the Receptacle, respectively, without offering an express argument for the attribution itself. I return to the question of gender implications of *chōra* in my discussion of Irigaray in the last chapter of this book.

47. *Timaeus* 50b–c; my italics. The Greek for matrix is here *ekmageion*, which connotes a modifiable lump or mass in which impressions are made. See also Plato, *Theatetus* 191c.

48. On the interpretation of the Receptacle as mirrorlike, see Cornford's commentary in *Plato's Cosmology*, pp. 184–185, 194, 200.

49. Aristotle claims precisely this at *Physics* 214a12 ff. In the end, however, the Atomists' *kenon* is not a strict void. For one thing, it is characterized as consisting in "intervals" (*diastēmata*) whose determinacy, albeit negative, is incompatible with a complete void. For another, the atoms themselves are held to cluster together into vortices, thus configurating the space they occupy. It is more coherent to consider the Atomists' use of *kenon* as space, especially empty space, and even to regard it as the first philosophical designation of a neutral, open, and unbounded space. See Keimpe Algra, *Concepts of Space in Greek Thought* (Leiden: Brill, 1995), 38–52. On the Atomists' view of space, see also C. Bailey, "Matter and the Void According to Leucippus," in M. J. Capek, ed., *The Concepts of Space and Time: Their Structure and Their Development* (Dordrecht: Reidel, 1976), 17–19, as well as Cornford's account of ancient Atomism in his "The Invention of Space," in *Essays in Honor of Gilbert Murray* (London: Allen & Unwin, 1936), 215–235. Cornford argues that Plato rejects both the "internal void" of an enclosed but gappy universe and the "external void" of unending space beyond the known world. I provide a more complete discussion of ancient Atomism at the beginning of chapter 4.

50. On these interstices, see *Timaeus* 58a–c; and Cornford's commentary at *Plato's Cosmology*, p. 200.

51. Duhem's interpretation is here dubious: "According to Plato, then, there is, outside of the limited, spherical world, a necessarily unlimited space, where this Universe is located. Since nothing exists in this space, it is empty" (Pierre Duhem, "Plato's Theory of Space," excerpted in Capek, *Concepts of Space and Time*, 22; on the same page, Duhem grants that there is no void internal to the Receptacle). But the space of the "Universe" is none other than that of the Receptacle, which is decidedly *not* empty. As Cornford says, "Space has a shape of its own, being coextensive with the spherical

universe, outside which there is neither body nor void" (*Plato's Cosmology,* 188; see also p. 200). In other words, the nothing (the "outside which") is not to be confused with the void.

52. *Timaeus* 52b. "*Hedra*" connotes "seat," "residence," "place of dwelling."

53. Cornford, *Plato's Cosmology,* 181; his italics. Cornford adds: the Receptacle "is simply the place 'in which' the qualities appear" (*Plato's Cosmology,* 187). Plato uses the phrase *to en hō* at *Timaeus* 49e: "Only in speaking of that *in which* all of them are always coming to be, making their appearance and again vanishing out of it, may we use the words 'this' or 'that.' "

54. *Timaeus* 52d–53a; my italics. The early part of this passage makes it clear that the reason for speaking of "the Receptacle" is that it *receives* the characters that, once received, come to *qualify* it; but there is no inherent qualification to begin with. As Derrida comments, "*Chōra* cannot receive *for itself,* thus it cannot *receive,* it only lets itself borrow the properties (of that) which it receives" (Jacques Derrida, "*Chōra,*" in *Poikilia: Festschrift pour J.-P. Vernant* [Paris: Ecole des Hautes Etudes, 1987], 271; his italics; a modified form of this essay has appeared in English under the title, "Khōra," trans. I. McLeod, in J. Derrida, *On the Name,* ed. T. Dutoit [Stanford: Stanford University Press, 1995], 89–127).

55. On the metaphor of winnowing, see *Timaeus* 52e–53a; and Cornford's explication in *Plato's Cosmology,* pp. 201–202. In winnowing grain, places are not preestablished—the winnowing basket is an open expanse—but they are *created by the very action of winnowing.* This is just what happens in the case of the Receptacle, whose violent motion makes regions for the material qualities and places for the primary bodies.

56. Derrida's remarks are again apt: the Receptacle " 'is' nothing other than the sum or the process of that which comes to be inscribed 'onto' it, regarding its subject, precisely its subject, but it is not the *subject* or the *present support* of all [this]" ("*Chōra,*" 273; his italics). In short, it is not a *substance* that possesses properties that belong properly to it.

57. " '*Chōra*' is 'room' that is filled, not vacant space (*kenon*). . . . 'Place' would, indeed, be a less misleading translation of *chōra* than 'Space', because 'place' does not suggest an infinite extent of vacancy lying beyond the finite sphere of the universe" (*Plato's Cosmology,* 200 n; "infinite extent" here makes reference to the "external void"). Then one wonders why Cornford did not employ "place" in his otherwise excellent translation of the *Timaeus.* Heidegger remarks that the Greeks "experienced the spatial on the basis [of] *chōra,* which signifies . . . that which is occupied by what stands there. The place belongs to the thing itself. Each of all the various things has its place. That which becomes is placed in this local 'space' and emerges from it" (Martin Heidegger, *An Introduction to Metaphysics,* trans. R. Manheim [New Haven: Yale University Press, 1959], 66). For a careful and somewhat skeptical reading, see Algra, *Concepts of Space,* esp. p. 38: "the terms *chōra* and *topos* could in a number of contexts be used interchangeably, both in ordinary Greek and in their first philosophical applications." Even then, however, *topos* tends to denote "relative location" and *chōra* always signifies a larger extension than *topos* (e.g., as in Plato's *Laws* 760c: "The places [*topoi*] of the country [*chōra*]"). And Algra admits that "at least Plato and Aristotle may be charitably credited with such a conceptual distinction [i.e., place : space :: *topos* : *chōra*]" (p. 32). See also Luc Brisson, *Le Même et l'autre dans la structure*

ontologique du Timée de Platon: Un commentaire systématique du Timée de Platon
(Nanterre: Lettres et sciences humaines, 1974), 213: "*chōra* and *topos* [as employed
in the *Timaeus*] oscillate between identity and difference."

58. I take the terms "clear space for" and "leeway" from Heidegger's discussions
of *einräumen* and *Spielraum* in *Being and Time,* "The Origin of the Work of Art" and
"Time and Being." For further discussion, see chapter 11.

59. The distinctness of *topos* and *chōra* appears in this passage: "anything that is
must needs be in some place (*topos*) and occupy some room (*chōra*)" (*Timaeus* 32b).
A representative passage in which both *chōra* and *topos* occur alongside each other in
accordance with the distinction just made is found at *Timaeus* 57c: "In the course of
suffering this treatment, [the created 'primary' bodies] are all interchanging their regions (*chōrai*). For while the main masses of the several kinds are stationed apart, each
in its own place (*topos idios*), owing to the motion of the Recipient, the portions which
at any time are becoming unlike themselves and like other kinds are borne by the
shaking towards the place (*topos*) of those others to which they become like."

60. For this designation, see *Timaeus* 52a. The Greek term translated as "everlasting" is *aiōnios,* which is usually translated as "eternal." But Cornford opts for "everlasting" (usually designated by *aidios*) in view of the fact that the abiding duration of
celestial movement is perduring, not eternal in any strict sense. See his comments in
Plato's Cosmology, p. 98 n.

61. "The cosmology of Plato as expressed in the *Timaeus,* in reverting to the tech-
nique of myth, represents, on the whole, a fateful step backward in the history of
the subject" (Milton K. Munitz, *Space, Time, and Creation: Philosophical Aspects of
Scientific Cosmology* [New York: Dover, 1981], 15). Ironically, Munitz considers the
Timaeus to be a failure vis-à-vis "the promising and prophetic ideas of the atomistic
materialists" (ibid.), that is to say, vis-à-vis Plato's opponents in this same dialogue.
For a very different view, compare Whitehead's opinion that the *Timaeus* is one of the
two greatest postmythical cosmologies in the West (the other is Newton's *Principia*):
Process and Reality, ed. D. Griffin and D. Sherburne (New York: Free Press, 1978),
93. Whitehead adds that "the space-time of modern mathematical physics, conceived
in abstraction from the particular mathematical formulae which apply to the happenings in it, is almost exactly Plato's Receptacle" (*Adventures of Ideas* [New York: Mentor, 1960], 154). Derrida offers a third interpretation: the *Timaeus,* precisely in its
discussion of *chōra,* refuses to be classified either as *muthos* or as *logos,* and puts this
very choice itself in question: "Does such a discourse belong to myth? Does one do
justice to the thought of *chōra* by continuing to rely on the alternative *logos/muthos*?
What if this thought *also* calls for a third genre of discourse? . . . How to think that
which, exceeding the regularity of *logos,* its law, its natural or legitimate genealogy,
still does not belong, *stricto sensu,* to *muthos*?" ("*Chōra,*" 266; his italics).

62. Derrida, "*Chōra,*" 272–273.

63. See Edmund Husserl, *Ideas,* I, sec. 76.

64. *Timaeus* 58b–c.

65. Ibid., 52e. Cornford remarks that "we can now see, in fact, why the four kinds
have not permanently come to rest, in separate regions, each as a homogeneous mass
in which no change could occur" (*Plato's Cosmology,* 245). At a micro-level, the
changes occur as the breakup of particles of the four elements and, in particular, of the

triangular surfaces of these particles as they jostle one another in continual contact. On this development, see *Timaeus* 57d–58c.

66. As Whitehead observes, the Receptacle is at most "the matrix *for* all begetting," the "*foster*-mother of all becoming" (*Adventures of Ideas*, 154; my italics). I emphasize the words that indicate the need for qualification. Even if the Receptacle is not literally a begetter, it remains a matrix and thus, as Brisson shows, part of a continuous series that extends from nourishment (*trophos*) and nurse (*tithēnē*) and mother (*mētēr*) to *chōra* and *topos*—with the Receptacle in the middle position. Cf. Brisson, *Timée de Platon*, 214–215.

67. Thus I agree with Cornford that "there is no archetype of Space" (*Plato's Cosmology*, 193); but it does not follow that Space "exists in its own right as surely as does the Form" (ibid.). On my reading, Space exists only as providing locus for phenomenal appearances and material things. To be such a bare locatory "this," is not nothing, however, as Cornford admits: "The Receptacle is the *only* factor in the bodily [realm] that may be called 'this', because it has permanent being and its nature does not change" (ibid., 181; my italics).

68. "This, indeed, is that which we look upon as in a dream" (52b). The analogy is not surprising insofar as a dream is itself a hybrid entity, combining the fantastic with the merely sensible in a "dream scene" that is the oneiric equivalent of place. See also 51b: the Receptacle partakes "in some very puzzling way of the intelligible and [is] very hard to apprehend." On the theme of the "bastard" character of the *hupodochē*, cf. Duhem, in Capek, *Concepts of Space and Time*, 22, where the hybridization at issue is said to be that of *noēsis* and *aisthēsis*.

69. "Such local movement, which for a changing being is the beginning of its existence at a certain place followed by its subsequent disappearance from the same place, presupposes a place that persists while this movement is taking place" (Duhem, in Capek, *Concepts of Space and Time*, 21). Brisson elaborates: "*chōra* presents itself in its spatial aspect as that without which no movement would be possible" (*Timée de Platon*, 212).

70. Cornford goes so far as to claim that "chaos, if it never existed before cosmos, must stand for some element that is now and always present in the working of the universe" (*Plato's Cosmology*, 37; see also pp. 203–207 for further discussion).

71. *Plato's Cosmology*, 223. Compare Whitehead's remark in *Adventures of Ideas*, p. 152: Plato "expressly denies omnipotence to his Supreme Craftsman. The influence of the entertainment of ideas is always persuasive, and can produce only such order as is [materially] possible."

72. On this theme, essentially a treatment of the perfectly circular motion of the World Soul, see *Timaeus* 33b–41a.

73. Cornford, *Plato's Cosmology*, 210.

74. Ibid.

75. M. Merleau-Ponty, "Eye and Mind," in *The Primacy of Perception*, ed. James Edie (Evanston: Northwestern University Press, 1964), 185.

76. *Timaeus* 53c; my italics. "Body" here means "primary body," that is, the configuration of sensuous quality with a regular solid shape (e.g., cube, pyramid, octahedron, icosahedron).

77. I refer to Cornford's extended discussion in *Plato's Cosmology*, pp. 210–239.

78. The Greek *dēmios* ("belonging to the people") appears to derive from the same *dem-* stem that, as pointed out in a previous note, is the ultimate etymon of Indo-European words connoting "building," "house," "domestic," etc. The "demi" of Demiurge is thus not to be construed as "half" (the latter *demi* derives from the Latin *dimidium*).

79. Thus it also does not matter that Plato here privileges the plane triangle as a minimal unit. Elsewhere, at *Laws* 894a, he indicates that the ultimate geometric *archai* resolve into "indivisible lines." In Pythagorean mathematics, by which Plato was so deeply influenced, there is a rigorous progression from numbers to points to lines to surfaces to solid figures and finally to sensible bodies. (On this point, see Cornford, *Plato's Cosmology*, 212 n 3, with special reference to an article by A. T. Nicol, "Indivisible Lines.") But in the context of the *Timaeus*, whose ultimate cosmological units are the four primary bodies, it is understandable that the triangles constituting their surfaces should be given a privileged position.

80. See Eliade, *The Sacred and the Profane*, chap. 1 ("Sacred Space and Making the World Sacred").

81. For Heidegger, the modern, that is, Cartesian, sense of invisible, homogeneous "extension" derives from *chōra*: "Might *chōra* not mean: that which abstracts itself from every particular, that which withdraws, and in such a way precisely admits and 'makes place' for something else?" (*An Introduction to Metaphysics*, 66).

82. Brisson, *Timée de Platon*, 212.

83. This transformation occurs thanks to the sharing of the same triangular units: see *Timaeus* 56c–57c.

84. Albert Rivaud, *Timée, Critias*, vol. 10 of *Platon*, ed. and trans. A. Rivaud (Paris: Alcan, 1925), 80; cited by Cornford, *Plato's Cosmology*, 229. See also Rivaud's *Le problème du devenir et la notion de la matière* (Paris: Alcan, 1906), 303–315.

85. This is Cornford's word at *Plato's Cosmology*, p. 229. Cornford's interpretation of the *Timaeus*, to which I am deeply indebted, vacillates between this hierarchical reading and the more measured view that is expressed in a passage I have cited before: "The Demiurge introduces as much order and proportion as Necessity allows" (ibid., 223).

86. Whitehead, *Adventures of Ideas*, 125. On the opposition of Immanence and Imposition, see ibid., p. 138.

87. From the "Homeric Allegories" of Heraclitos the Grammarian, ca. 30 B.C.–ca. A.D. 14; cited in C. Doria and H. Lenowitz, eds., *Origins: Creation Texts from the Ancient Mediterranean* (New York: Doubleday Anchor, 1976), 155.

88. Ibid.

89. Derrida's formulation of undecidability, on which I here rely, is as follows: "neither/nor, that is, *simultaneously* either *or*" (Jacques Derrida, *Positions*, trans. A. Bass [Chicago: University of Chicago Press, 1981], 43; his italics).

90. "A Ritual for the Purification of a Temple," cited from F. Thureau-Dangin, *Rituels accadiens*, in Doria and Lenowitz, *Origins*, 81.

91. The first phrase is from the second stanza of the *Enuma Elish*, the second from "A Ritual for the Purification of a Temple," third stanza.

92. For further discussion of the survival of Tiamat in the Old Testament, see Alfred Jeremias, *Das Alte Testament im Lichte des Alten Orients* (Leipzig: Hinrichs, 1916), 36 ff.

93. Another, related conundrum whose solution is likewise an affirmation of the two alternatives as neither/nor and both/and concerns Plato's (literally) ambiguous position with regard to the question as to whether the Receptacle is to be conceived as matter or space. It is the former insofar as it is an in-which (*en hoi*) for sensible qualities and an out-of-which (*ex hou*) for phenomenal bodies; it is the latter as an in-which for phenomenal bodies in motion: i.e., a locatory space for these bodies. For a perspicuous treatment of this amphiboly, see Algra, *Concepts of Space,* 76–120.

94. From the second century A.D. fragments of the *Orphic Argonautica* as cited in Doria and Lenowitz, *Origins,* 122.

95. From an Indian myth of creation in the *Baiga;* cited in *Beginnings: Creation Myths of the World,* ed. P. Farmer (New York: Atheneum, 1979), 15. The at least implicit presence of such primal water is felt even in the *Timaeus. Hupodechomai,* the verb from which *hupodochē* (Receptacle) derives, means "to receive beneath the surface of the sea." (Other senses include "to welcome guests under the roof of one's home"; "to hearken"; to "undertake"; and "to become pregnant.")

96. "When Yahweh of the gods was making earth and skies / not even a wild bush existed on earth / not even a wild grass had come up" (cited from the *Biblia Hebraica* in Doria and Lenowitz, *Origins,* 160).

97. In a previous note, I pointed to the difficult discernibility of *chōra* from *topos.* But we can also say that *chōra* is always already topogenetic. Such is what Brisson has in mind when he speaks of *chōra* as signifying "total implacement wherein phenomena subject to generation and corruption appear" (*Timée de Platon,* 212).

98. Archytas, as cited and translated in S. Sambursky, ed., *The Concept of Place in Late Neoplatonism* (Jerusalem: Israel Academy of Sciences and Humanities, 1982), 37.

99. John Milton, *Paradise Lost,* bk. 2, lines 891–898.

100. I have not thematized Night or Darkness in my own account, but it is crucial to many creation myths, especially those of the early Greeks, who often emphasize their importance. Milton is doubtless drawing on his classical education. For pertinent examples, see Doria and Lenowitz, *Origins,* 164–167.

101. Whitehead writes that "Milton, curiously enough [i.e., curiously for a contemporary of Newton], in his *Paradise Lost,* wavers between the *Timaeus* and the Semitic doctrine [of creation]" (*Process and Reality,* 95).

102. This is Walter Kaufman's translation of the final sentence of *The Genealogy of Morals*—a sentence I have cited before in Golffling's alternative translation.

103. "While Plato does not admit the void of the Atomists in his World, neither can one say that he admits what these philosophers call the plenum, that is, the indefinite, but rigid and impenetrable substance, from which they form bodies; in space, in the *chōra,* Plato admits no real bodies other than combinations of geometrical figures" (Duhem, in Capek, *Concepts of Space and Time,* 22–23).

104. It is due to this connective power that depth becomes of such central importance in the determination of place; for it is within depth that things are drawn together even as they are set apart: "This being simultaneously present in experiences which are nevertheless mutually exclusive, this implication of one in another, this contraction into one perceptual act of a whole possible process, constitute the originality of depth. It is the dimension in which things or elements of things envelop each other, whereas breadth and height are the dimensions in which they are juxtaposed"

(M. Merleau-Ponty, *Phenomenology of Perception,* trans. C. Smith [New York: Humanities, 1962], 264–265). This description of depth is reminiscent of Plato's description of the Receptacle. In the latter there is also contraction and mutual implication as "things or elements of things envelop each other."

105. These phrases occur at *Adventures of Ideas,* p. 190 and p. 138, respectively. The Receptacle is "Plato's doctrine of the medium of intercommunication" (p. 192). See also p. 154: "The community of the world, which is the matrix for all begetting, and whose *essence is process with retention of connectedness*—this community is what Plato terms the Receptacle" (my italics).

106. See *Remembering,* chap. 12, esp. pp. 292–295.

107. See S. Kierkegaard, *Concluding Unscientific Postscript,* trans. D. F. Swenson and W. Lowrie (Princeton: Princeton University Press, 1941), 107: "Existence separates, and holds the various moments of existence discretely apart." The citation from E. M. Forster is found in his novel *Howards End* (New York: Putnam, 1910), 22.

108. This is a Greek text by the Neoplatonist Damascius, ca. A.D. 500, which builds on an Iranian text of ca. third century A.D.; as cited in Doria and Lenowitz, *Origins,* 156.

Chapter Three: Place as Container

1. See Aristotle, *Categories* 2a1, 5a9–14. Interest in the "where" is not restricted to physicists and metaphysicians. Robert Graves remarks that " 'where?' is the question that should always weigh most heavily with poets who are burdened with the single poetic theme of life and death" (*The White Goddess* [New York: Farrar, Straus & Giroux, 1966], 251). Even cartoon characters care about place: Linus says, "Sometimes I lie awake at night, and I ask 'Why am I here?'—Then a voice says 'Where are you?'—'Here' I say. . . . 'Where is "here" '? says the voice" (*Peanuts,* Charles Schulz, summer 1993).

2. See *De Caelo* 279a11–18 and *Physics* 212b8–18, respectively.

3. As Aquinas puts it in his commentary on Aristotle's *Physics:* "After the Philosopher in Book III has treated motion and the infinite . . . in Book IV he intends to treat those things which pertain to motion extrinsically. First he treats those things [i.e., place and void] which belong to motion extrinsically as measures of the mobile body. Secondly . . . he treats time which is the measure of motion itself" (St. Thomas Aquinas, *Commentary on Aristotle's Physics,* trans. R. Blackwell, R. Spath, and W. Thirlkel [New Haven: Yale University Press, 1963], 189). The infinite, it should be noted, belongs to motion *intrinsically* insofar as it belongs to the genus of the continuous. We shall return later in this chapter to Aristotle's treatment of time. As for the void, suffice it to say that Aristotle rejects it no less vehemently than had Plato in the *Timaeus;* but, unlike Plato, he does so by a series of carefully constructed arguments: see *Physics,* bk. 4, chaps. 6–9.

4. *Physics* 208a31–32. (Unless otherwise noted, I shall cite the translation of Edward Hussey in *Aristotle's Physics, Books III and IV* [Oxford: Clarendon Press, 1983]. Most of the subsequent references to passages from *Physics,* book 4, will be placed in parentheses in the main text.)

5. According to Aristotle, all determination of rest and motion is to be made in terms of place, which is in this respect their common limit. See Pierre Duhem, *Le*

système du monde (Paris: Hermann, 1913), I:200: "Place is the fixed term which allows us to judge of a body's rest or its movement."

6. *Physics* 208a29–31. Plato's main formulations of this argument are found at *Timaeus* 52b and at *Parmenides* 145e. Zeno maintains that "everything that exists is somewhere," and Gorgias follows suit by remarking that "the unlimited is not somewhere." (I cite Zeno and Gorgias from F. M. Cornford, *Plato's Cosmology* [New York: Liberal Arts Press, 1957], p. 192 n. and p. 195, respectively.) Whitehead says that "everything is positively somewhere in actuality" (*Process and Reality,* ed. D. R. Griffin and D. W. Sherburne [New York: Free Press, 1978], 40; see also pp. 46, 59, and 231 for comparable formulations of the same "ontological principle"). This coherent tradition of reaffirming the Archytian axiom of the primacy of place depends on the *Physics* as an essential moment of relay and reformulation.

7. Both statements are at *Physics* 208b34–209a1. In this case, I cite the translation of Hardie and Gaye (as reprinted in J. Barnes, ed., *The Complete Works of Aristotle* [Princeton: Princeton University Press, 1984], 355). Hussey translates as follows: "If such a thing is true, then the power of place will be a remarkable one, and prior to all things, since that, without which no other thing is, but which itself is without the others, must be first."

8. If Platonic *chōra* survives in any form at all, it is as "intelligible matter" (*hulē noētē*). On this possibility, see Hussey's comments in the notes to his translation in *Aristotle's Physics,* p. 184. In general, we can say that the Receptacle in Plato plays the *role* of Aristotelian matter, especially intelligible matter—even if it remains true, as I have stressed, that the Receptacle is not itself composed *of* or *from* matter (e.g., in the form of material qualities) in the account given in the *Timaeus.*

9. W. D. Ross, ed. and trans., *Aristotle's Physics* (Oxford: Oxford University Press, 1936), 54. Ross implies that *chōra* is reduced in Aristotle to a mere designation of *megethos:* avoiding direct discussion of *chōra,* Aristotle "says much about *megethos;* he accepts it as a familiar attribute of material things" (ibid.).

10. Real as such issues may be, they are in the end Aristotle's own issues and arise from his conception of prime matter as the substratum for contrarieties. As Hussey comments, "This is yet another case of Aristotle's criticisms of previous thinkers being made in Aristotelian terms and using Aristotelian assumptions. Plato is not so much misrepresented [by Aristotle] as automatically excluded from serious consideration because his ontology is different" (*Aristotle's Physics,* xxxii). Aristotle's other substantive critique concerns Plato's effort to make triangular shape the indivisible constituent of physical bodies; according to Aristotle, this overlooks both the irreducibility of body to *any* shape and the resolvability of shape itself into line and point. (For another expression of this critique, see *De Caelo* 299a6–11, in consultation with H. H. Joachim's commentary in his *Aristotle on Coming-to-Be and Passing-Away* [Oxford: Clarendon Press, 1922], 73–74.) For a thorough discussion of Aristotle's critique of Plato—a discussion that by and large validates this critique—see Keimpe Algra, *Concepts of Space in Greek Thought* (Leiden: Brill, 1995), 110–117.

11. Aristotle's *Physics* is "the hidden and thus never sufficiently comprehended basic book of occidental philosophy." (Martin Heidegger, "Vom Wesen und Begriff der *Physis:* Aristotelis' Physik B, I," first given as a lecture course in 1939, reprinted in M. Heidegger, *Wegmarken* [Frankfurt: Klostermann, 1967], 312.)

12. *Physics* 208a28–29; my italics. The other two questions to be pursued are

"whether it is or not" and "what it is" (ibid.) These latter are more properly metaphysical questions, but for Aristotle they are best answered by a painstaking descriptive analysis.

13. On the history of the word "phenomenology," see Herbert Spiegelberg, *The Phenomenological Movement: A Historical Introduction* (The Hague: Nijhof, 1960), I:11–23. It is clear in any case that Aristotle's physics is not to be judged by contemporary, or even by Newtonian, standards—in relation to which it will be viewed as having certain shortcomings. For a discussion of two of these shortcomings in the light of modern physics, see Hussey, *Aristotle's Physics*, x. In a broader historical perspective, the impact of the Aristotelian conception of place has been considerable. As Max Jammer asserts, "Aristotle's theory of places is of greatest pertinence not only because of its important implications for physics, but also because it was the most decisive stage for the further development of space theories" (Jammer, *Concepts of Space: The History of Theories of Space in Physics*, 2d ed. [Cambridge, Mass.: Harvard University Press, 1970], 17).

14. *Physics* 208b12–22. It becomes apparent that of the six dimensions here set out, "above" and "below" are in effect *primus inter pares*. See, for example, ibid., 212a21–29, where the upward is associated with the extreme outer limit of the celestial system and the downward with its center in the earth, thereby giving to these two dimensions a definite priority in relation to the known universe. In this instance, cosmology takes precedence over phenomenology. (See also *Categories* 6a11–18; and Duhem's commentary in *Le système du monde*, I:205–208.) Also note that the orientation of the other four dimensions is more immediately dependent on bodily position. For further discussion, see my *Getting Back into Place: Toward a Renewed Understanding of the Place-World* (Bloomington: Indiana University Press, 1993), chap. 4.

15. *Physics* 210a14–24. In the same spirit, Aristotle pursues the different senses of "part" in *Metaphysics* bk. 5, chap. 25, and of "have" in *Categories*, chap. 15: "have" and "in" are closely and, in certain respects, conversely related.

16. Hussey argues that this last sense is meant by Aristotle to be construed as "chronologically the first use, and probably epistemologically [also]" (*Aristotle's Physics*, 109). To assert phenomenological priority is in no way incompatible with this claim—indeed, such priority is strengthened by it.

17. On this point, see *Physics* 211a23 ff. Hussey remarks that "because place is a bounding limit, it is 'together with' (*hama*) the object and so extends just as far as the object does" (*Aristotle's Physics*, 118). But it must be added that, however inseparably continuous they may be, the outer surface of the object and the bounding surface of the place remain distinguishable. They do not form a "common surface" in Descartes's strict sense of the term (see *Principles of Philosophy*, pt. 2, sec. 15).

18. *Physics* 211a25–27; Hussey's italics. Aristotle adds: "If the *whole* air were our place, a thing would not in every case be equal to its place, but it *is* thought to be equal; this kind of place is the primary place in which it is" (211a25–28; Hussey's emphasis).

19. *Physics* 209b1; see also 210b34–35. On place in its "primary" (*prōtos*) form, see ibid., 211a28.

20. On this interpretation of the phrase *ho pas potamos*, see Duhem, *Le système du monde*, I:200, where Simplicius (who in turn relies on Alexander of Aphrodisias)

is cited in his work *In Aristotelis Physicorum libros commentaria,* bk. 4, chap. 4. I shall return to this ambiguity in the last section of this chapter.

21. This is W. D. Ross's alternative translation of *Physics* 212a20–21 (*Aristotle's Physics,* 56).

22. "Because place is a limit, it is a surface and therefore 'circumscribes' rather than 'receives' the object" (Hussey, *Aristotle's Physics,* 118). But my colleague Walter Watson has pointed out to me the misleadingness of Hussey's use of "circum*scribes.*"

23. The heavens "are not, as a whole, somewhere or in some place, since no body surrounds them. . . . The upper part moves in a circle, but the whole is not anywhere" (*Physics* 212b8–9, 14–15).

24. Indeed, more than one paradox. Another is found in the fact that the outermost sphere of the heavens must be at once at rest (since it serves as the ultimate place for all that it contains) and moving (as we can see by direct observation of the changing positions of the planets). Duhem addresses this paradox in *Le système du monde,* I:202–205, claiming that it is resolvable. Ross, by contrast, regards it as strictly unresolvable: cf. *Aristotle's Physics,* 58. For Ross, this paradox is only part of a still more general problem: "The condition that the place of a thing must be no larger than the thing itself [i.e., on the first notion of place as a strict container], proves incompatible with the requirement that the place of a thing must be at rest [i.e., the second notion]" (*Aristotle's Physics,* 57). For to find a place at rest, one must often go beyond that which immediately contains a given thing—as occurs precisely in the instance of the celestial system itself: "It is only a remote or larger place constituted by the celestial system that is necessarily (on Aristotle's view) exempt from translation" (ibid.). But the celestial system *does* "translate"; that is, it moves in a circular or rotational manner. Fortunately, we need not enter into this debate, which became concerted and protracted following Aristotle's death in 323 B.C. (For a systematic survey of this aftermath, see Duhem, *Le système du monde,* chaps. 5, 6; and Aquinas, *Commentary on Aristotle's Physics,* 214–216. For a lucid statement of the paradox and problem at stake, see Henri Bergson's thesis of 1889, "L'Idée de Lieu chez Aristote," *Les Études Bergsoniennes* (1949), 2:84–87, esp. the statement on p. 86: "A body possesses a place [*lieu*] on the condition of being at a remove [*éloigné*] from this place.")

25. Eugène Minkowski, *Lived Time: Phenomenological and Psychopathological Studies,* trans. N. Metzel (Evanston: Northwestern University Press, 1970), 277 ff.

26. As Sambursky remarks: "Aristotle occasionally had recourse to mathematics in order to explain certain physical facts, for instance in his discussion of motion. But on the whole, mathematics, and geometry in particular, was to him nothing more than perceptible things seen in abstraction from their perceptible qualities. . . . It never occurred to Aristotle that mathematical elements, for instance geometrical shapes, could be used as symbols to describe physical realities. This was precisely what Plato did in the *Timaeus* and what is at the bottom of Aristotle's objections to his theory, not only where they are of a principal nature but also where they refer to technical details" (Shmuel Sambursky, *The Physical World of Late Antiquity* [London: Routledge, Kegan & Paul, 1962], 32–33). On the notion of mathematics as "idealizing abstraction" on Aristotle's view, see Stefan Körner, *The Philosophy of Mathematics* (London: Hutchinson, 1960), 18–21.

27. *Physics* 226b21–22. For a discussion of *hama* as it relates to space and time

alike—and in their interaction—see Jacques Derrida, *"Ousia* and *Grammē,"* in *Margins of Philosophy,* trans. A. Bass (Chicago: University of Chicago Press, 1982), 53–57.

28. This matching of limit on the part of the container and the contained, their contiguity of surface, may represent the only remaining valid sense of space (*chōra*) on the Aristotelian paradigm: where "space" implies something distinguishable from "place" qua *topos* and that, by the same token, is not reducible to extensive magnitude (*megethos*). But if so, Aristotle himself fails to acknowledge such a sense of space as such.

29. *Physics* 209a7–13; my italics. The first phrase of this citation contains one of the very rare mentions of place *and* space: *topos* and *chōra* taken together in a virtual hendiadys. Aquinas comments on this passage as follows: "There cannot be any difference between a point and the place of a point. For since place does not exceed that which is located in place, the place of a point can only be something indivisible. But two indivisible quantities, like two points joined together, are only one. Therefore for the same reason the place of a surface will not be other than the surface, nor will the place of a body be other than the body" (*Commentary,* 193). Aquinas makes it clear that the statement cited above is part of a series of "six probable arguments [which] are given to show that place does not exist" (ibid.) and that Aristotle's eventual answer to this argument occurs at 212b24–28, where Aristotle maintains that a point, not being a changeable body, does not have a place to begin with. (The same holds for surfaces "and other limits.")

30. *De Caelo* 299b9. In the *Timaeus,* however, the surface is preferred to the line, for the possibility of three dimensions depends on having a surface. On this point, see Cornford, *Plato's Cosmology,* 212–213 n 4.

31. This is Euclid's classical definition in *The Thirteen Books of Euclid's Elements,* 2d ed., ed. Thomas Heath (Cambridge: Cambridge University Press, 1926), I:153; my italics.

32. *Parmenides* 138a3–7; Cornford translation. Hussey remarks that Aristotle's "implied argument [at *Physics* 209a7–13] may be that the place of a point would have to be without extension, like the point itself, and therefore itself a point; but two distinct points cannot coincide" (*Aristotle's Physics,* 102).

33. Hussey supports Aristotle's denial of point as a place between *locations* (which points possess) and *places* (which points do not possess). The explanation for Aristotle's rejection of places for points "is simply that, while the argument does yield locations of points, for there to be places there must be not only locations but *surrounding* locations" (*Aristotle's Physics,* 121; his italics). Yet this explanation falls through if points can be said to be themselves fully surrounded. H. A. Wolfson remarks similarly that for Aristotle "there can be no place unless one body is contained by another body, for it is only then that there is a surrounding, equal, and separate limit" (H. A. Wolfson, *Crescas' Critique of Aristotle: Problems of Aristotle's Physics in Jewish and Arabic Philosophy* [Cambridge, Mass.: Harvard University Press, 1929], 44). I shall return to the question of location qua *position* below.

34. Max Simon, as cited by Thomas Heath, *The Thirteen Books of Euclid's Elements,* I:157–158; my italics.

35. For a detailed discussion of such cases, see Proclus, *A Commentary on the First*

Book of Euclid's Elements, ed. and trans. Glen R. Morrow (Princeton, N.J.: Princeton University Press, 1970), 73–74.

36. Indeed, Proclus himself admits that, although the point is "everywhere indivisible and distinguished by its simplicity from divisible things," as it "descends in the scale of being, even the point takes on the character distinctive of divisibles" (ibid., 75–76).

37. *Posterior Analytics* 87a36–37. Alternately, "a point is a unit having position" (*De Anima* 409a5). See also *Metaphysics* 1016b31: "That which has not position [is] a unit, that which has position a point."

38. See Proclus, *Commentary,* 78: "The unit [i.e., the number one] is without position, since it is immaterial and outside all extension and place; but the point has position because it occurs in the bosom of imagination and is therefore enmattered." It needs to be noted that Aristotle is not wholly consistent when it comes to the question of whether numbers have position. At *Physics* 208b24–25 he says that "mathematical objects . . . are not in place, but still have right and left according to their position relatively to us."

39. Cf. F. E. Peters, *Greek Philosophical Terms* (New York: New York University Press, 1967), 196; and Hussey, *Aristotle's Physics,* 101. A still later sense of *thesis* is "positing judgment" (e.g., as in Husserl's notion of "the thesis of the natural standpoint").

40. "The dots which stand for the [Pythagorean] pebbles are regularly called 'boundary stones' (*horoi, termini,* 'terms'). . . . It must have struck [the Pythagoreans] that 'fields' could be compared as well as numbers" (John Burnet, *Early Greek Philosophy* [New York: Meridian, 1958], 109).

41. Proclus, *Commentary,* 73. For an account of Proclus's conception of place in contrast with the point, see Duhem, *Le système du monde,* I:338–342.

42. Place, says Aristotle without hesitation, "has three dimensions, length, breadth, and depth, by which every body is bounded" (209a4–5). I have discussed the role of depth in the constitution of place in *Getting Back into Place,* pp. 67–70, 268–270.

43. On the importance of surfaces in the perception of depth, see J. J. Gibson, *The Perception of the Visual World* (Boston: Houghton Mifflin, 1950); and my essay, " 'The Element of Voluminousness': Depth and Place Reexamined," in *Merleau-Ponty Vivant,* ed. M. C. Dillon (Albany: SUNY Press, 1991), 1–30.

44. *Metaphysics* 1085a12. The deep and the shallow is a species of the Great and the Small taken as ultimate generative principles.

45. If we hold (as Aristotle himself holds) that even a line is not composed of a series of contiguous points, the ability of points to constitute depth will be still more seriously compromised: "Nothing that is continuous can be composed of indivisibles: e.g., a line cannot be composed of points, the line being continuous and the point indivisible" (*Categories* 5a1–5; cf. *Physics* 215b19 and the commentary by Heath, *The Thirteen Books of Euclid's Elements,* 155–156, as well as Proclus, *Commentary,* 79 ff.)

46. It may, however, be said to *merge* with another point, as when a smaller dot comes to be incorporated into a larger dot.

47. See Euclid, *Elements,* bk. 1, definitions 3, 6. In the above discussion, I am not distinguishing between "containing" and "surrounding."

48. Simon, cited by Heath, *The Thirteen Books of Euclid's Elements,* 157; my italics.

49. Indeed, shapes can be considered types of limit: a shape, says Plato, is "the limit of a solid" (*Meno* 76a).

50. Proclus, *Commentary,* 71.

51. Ibid., 75.

52. Aquinas, *Commentary on Aristotle's Physics,* 214; my italics.

53. Proclus, *Commentary,* 109.

54. Martin Heidegger, "Building Dwelling Thinking," in *Poetry, Language, Thought,* trans. A. Hofstadter (New York: Harper & Row, 1971), 154; his italics. Heidegger, however, relates "boundary" (*die Grenze*) to *peras* and not to *horos* despite his simultaneous allusion to *horismos:* "A space (*ein Raum*) is something that has been made room for, something that is cleared and free, namely within a boundary, Greek *peras*. . . . That is why the concept is that of *horismos,* that is, the horizon, the boundary (*die Grenze*)" (ibid.).

55. It is significant that *horos* signifies not only "boundary" or "boundary marker" but "landmark" (e.g., as found in monumental stones): a landmark not only delimits in the manner of a property line but is something visible from many directions; it is a cynosure of attention and in this very respect a source of "active presencing." Still other forms of such presencing are included in the scope of *horos,* which can also mean a rule or standard and even the definition of a word. (For indications of the rich semantic range of this term, I am indebted to Eric Casey.)

56. *Physics* 219b16–22. G. E. L. Owen contends that this passage contradicts Aristotle's insistence that the point has no place. On the one hand, "since a point cannot lie within a boundary, it cannot strictly have (or be used to mark) a location." On the other hand, passages such as that just cited "commit him to denying this." (Both claims are made in "Aristotle: Method, Physics, and Cosmology," in G. E. L. Owen, *Logic, Science, and Dialectic: Collected Papers in Greek Philosophy* [Ithaca: Cornell University Press, 1986], 155.) But is not Aristotle merely analogizing moving things to points, and then only in respect of their selfsameness over time and between places? Owen himself goes on to remark that the above passage "*correlates* the moving object with points in time and space" (ibid., 161; my italics). Surely such correlation does not commit Aristotle to what is for him the unacceptable position that points *have* places. We need only conclude, I think, that points are immensely useful in elucidating certain natural phenomena that present themselves as pointlike: not only moving objects but sources of light, the joints of an animal, and the location of the earth as at the center of the universe. (Owen discusses these examples and others at p. 162. See also his cogent argument in another essay that Aristotle's critique of point-as-place is in effect a sophisticated version of Plato's proof at *Parmenides,* 138a2–b6—perhaps ultimately derived from Zeno—that the indivisible One is placeless: see Owens's essay "Tithenai ta phainomena," in ibid., p. 245.)

57. "A point had been defined by the Pythagoreans as 'a monad having position'; Plato apparently objected to this definition and [yet] substituted no other, for according to Aristotle, he regarded the genus of points as being a 'geometrical fiction' [*Metaphysics* 992a20]" (Thomas Heath, *A History of Greek Mathematics* [Oxford: Clarendon Press, 1921], I:293).

58. Proclus, *Commentary,* 72.

59. "Aristotle points out that even indivisible lines must have extremities . . . while the definition of a point as 'the extremity of a line' [Plato] is unscientific" (Heath, *History of Greek Mathematics,* I:293).

60. Proclus, *Commentary,* 72. A comparison of the Proclean point and the Platonic *chōra* inevitably suggests itself: both are generative sources, matrices, and "feminine." (On the femininity of the point, see ibid., p. 81.)

61. Ibid., 73.

62. G. W. F. Hegel, *Encyclopedia of the Philosophical Sciences,* trans. W. Wallace (Oxford: Oxford University Press, 1971), sec. 256. Somewhere between Proclus and Hegel falls John Berger's claim: "In death it is scale that falls apart; just as, at conception, a point fuses with the universe to create scale" (*End of Faces, My Heart, Brief as Photos* [London: Writers & Readers, 1984], 53).

63. Derrida, "*Ousia* and *Grammē,*" 41–42. Derrida adds: "As the first determination and first negation of space, the point spatializes or *spaces* itself. It negates itself by itself in its relation to itself, that is, to another point" (p. 42; his italics).

64. See G. W. F. Hegel, *Philosophy of Nature,* trans. M. J. Petrie (London: Allen & Unwin, 1970), I: secs. 260–261, where place as "the posited identity of space and time" is said to be "the concrete [i.e., fully actualized] point." The *abstract* point is the first determination of space and thus precedes time and place.

65. I am thinking of such passages as this (cited before in chap. II): "He split [her carcass] apart like a cockle-shell; with the upper half he constructed the arc of sky, he pulled down the bar and set a watch on the waters, so they should never escape." Could the 'bar' invoked in this passage presage the line as that which the point first generates in the early Greek conception—and perhaps also the "horizon line" of the *horismos*? (The three passages from the *Enuma Elish* that I have cited in this paragraph come from the translation of N. K. Sandars in *Poems of Heaven and Hell from Ancient Mesopotamia* [Baltimore: Penguin, 1971].)

66. Thus *stiktos* means "punctured" or "spotted"; and *stizein* (the root of "stigma") signifies "to mark or brand with a pointed instrument" (e.g., to tattoo) as well as "to beat black and blue" (shades of Marduk once more!).

67. Not long after Aristotle's death, Euclid substituted *sēmeion* for *stigmē* in his *Elements.* Proclus only occasionally reverts to the earlier term. (For Proclus's use of these terms, see Proclus, *Commentary,* pp. 78–79, as well as Heath, *The Thirteen Books of Euclid's Elements,* I:156.) Ferdinand de Saussure reminds us that *sēmeion* signifies primarily "sign," for example, as mark, token, omen, signal, seal, or watchword. (Ferdinand de Saussure, *Course in General Linguistics,* trans. W. Baskin [New York: McGraw-Hill, 1966], 16: "I shall call [this new science] *semiology* (from the Greek *sēmeion* 'sign')" [his italics]. One of the extended senses of *sēmeion* not mentioned by de Saussure is precisely that of limit or boundary.) It is not, however, as if *sēmeion* and *stigmē* are unrelated: two of the meanings of *sēmainō* include to mark (as by a milestone) and to *stamp* with an insignia. In essence, the sting is taken out of the point after Aristotle, whose delimitation of it allows—paradoxically—for its enormously expanded role in the hands of Proclus: no longer a sticking point, its immanent power is unlimited in the created world, where it assumes "the premier rank in the All."

68. "Now the before and after [i.e., the primary structure of time] is in place primarily. . . . But since the before and after is in magnitude, it must also be in change, by analogy with what there is there [in magnitude]. But in time, too, the before and

after is present, because the one always follows the other of them" (*Physics* 219a14–
20). Aristotle here suggests a veritable ontogenesis of time from place, passing through
change and magnitude. As he puts it succinctly: "Change follows magnitude, and time
follows change" (220b25–27; see also 219b15–16). Change and magnitude, time and
place are all continuous, divisible quantities; but their destinies are differential. From
place as "root-basis" (in Husserl's term) the other three quantities spread out rhizomati-
cally—*rhiza* signifies "root"—first as magnitude-in-place, then as change-of-magnitude
(which qua motion implicates place in the case of locomotion), and finally as time that
calibrates changing-moving magnitude.

69. But it should be noted that Aristotle was the *first* philosopher to link place and
void: "There is no evidence that [void] had ever before him been brought into relation
with place" (Friedrich Solmsen, *Aristotle's System of the Physical World* [Ithaca: Cornell University Press, 1960], 140).

70. On void as "extension between tangible bodies," see *Physics* 211b14–28,
213a27–213b1, 214a6. Hussey comments on Aristotle's general strategy in discussing
the concept of void among his predecessors: "He consistently assumes that a theory of
void must be a theory of *space*, i.e, of pure 'unsupported' extension, which when
invaded by a body remains to be occupied by that body (rather than retreating before
it or being extinguished by it)" (*Aristotle's Physics*, xxxv; his italics). For a detailed
discussion of empty interval and pure extension as a mistaken conception of place, see
Henry Mendell, "Topoi on Topos: The Development of Aristotle's Concept of Place,"
Phronesis 32 (1987):222 ff.

71. *Physics* 214a25. It is noteworthy that this argument, too, stems from ordinary
belief: some "think that the void is responsible for change in the sense of being that in
which change occurs—this would be the sort of thing that some people say place is"
(214a24–26).

72. *Physics* 214b16–17; translator's italics. Being empty of medium or resistance,
the void cannot account for differential flows or speeds through it: see 215a35–215b14.
The same holds for directedness. In common critique of Aristotle, Avempace and Crescas argue that the "original time of motion" is unaffected by the fact of occurring in a
void: see Wolfson, *Crescas' Critique of Aristotle*, 57–58.

73. Motion is unexplained on the idea of void for two reasons: first, "if there is
void it is not possible for anything to move" (214b30–31), since movement requires
differential direction (see 214b32–34); second, the void lacks the crucial difference of
up versus down on which *any* natural motion is dependent: "In as much as it is void,
the above will be no different from the below" (215a8–9). Rest, on the other hand, is
rendered moot as well: "No one will say why something moved [in a void] will come
to rest somewhere; why should it do so here rather than there?" (215a18–20). For
Crescas's defense of the void as a condition, if not a cause, of motion and rest, see
Wolfson, *Crescas' Critique of Aristotle*, 54–55. Crescas here looks simultaneously
backward to the Atomists and forward to Newton—for both of whom a void is a
necessary basis of motion and rest.

74. On the Anaximinean notion of condensation and rarefaction, see all of chapter
9 of book 4, where Aristotle maintains that his notion of matter, regarded as potential,
accounts fully for these twin processes. By the same token, displacement is impossible
in a void: see *Physics*, 216a23–216b3.

75. Hussey, *Aristotle's Physics*, 128. Hussey adds: "There is a tacit use of the

principle that a permanent feature of the universe cannot be completely idle in explanation" (ibid.). Bergson agrees: "In fact, empty space, were it to exist, would produce
nothing. Now what produces nothing is in Aristotle's eyes deprived of any existence"
("L'Idée de Lieu chez Aristote," 98). Needless to say, what holds for the void also
holds for the vacuum. (The latter notion is hinted at in such statements as "that is void,
in which there is nothing heavy or light" [214a12–13] or "that which is not full of
body perceptible by touch" [214a7–8]. These statements look forward to the seventeenth-century preoccupation with creating a perfect vacuum, that is, a finite space
empty of any particular material substance. Even Aristotle's general notion of a "separated void" comes close to the vacuum, especially when it is defined in Hussey's terms
as "a receptive extension actually free of body" [*Aristotle's Physics,* 128]. But we must
acknowledge that, even if places are not voids, they nonetheless may be momentarily
vacuous, that is, when the bodies that determine their volume are taken away.)

76. On this association, see Proclus, *Commentary,* definition 1, esp. p. 72: the point
"secretly possesses the nature of the Unlimited and strives to be everywhere in the
things that it bounds."

77. Concerning the actual versus potential void, Aristotle says definitively: "It is
manifest that there is neither a distinct void, whether without qualification or in the
rare, nor potentially a void" (217b20–23; where "rare" refers to the void as a rarified
whole). As for universal placement, he says: "Not everything that is, is in a place, but
[only] changeable body" (212b27–28). The "only," supplied by the translator, is cryp-
tic, given that the entire physical world is composed of changeable bodies—and of
nothing but such bodies.

78. Freud's statement occurs in "Three Essays on the Theory of Sexuality," *Standard Edition of the Complete Psychological Works* (London: Hogarth, 1953), 7:222.
Concerning reimplacement, Aristotle says: "That place is, seems to be clear from re[im]
placement [*antimetastaseōs*]: where there is now water, there air in turn is, when the
water goes out as if from a vessel, and at some other time some other body occupies this
same place" (208b1–4). A place is something, then, that calls for continual occupation.

79. "Tout est plein dans le monde d'Aristote" (Bergson, "L'Idée de Lieu chez Aristote," 95).

80. See *Categories* 5a9–14 and *Physics* 211b14–28. A thorough discussion of this
change in view—first noted by Pacius in 1580—is presented in Mendell, "Topoi on
Topos," 206–231. Mendell argues that the static, volumetric analysis of the *Categories*
cannot account for the fate of place in physical change—except via the idea of reimplacement—and that Aristotle was thus led to the more "dynamic" view of the *Physics,*
according to which place is a function of the holding action of the inner surface of the
container. But this container, as we have seen, is definitive of place only insofar as it
can be regarded as itself unmoving and hence as static in its own right. Here we
witness a difficulty that continually afflicts a container model of place, constituting
thereby a virtual antinomy: place must be at once dynamic (to account for change on
the part of the occupant) and static (to validate the requirement of sameness-of-loca-
tion). As Duhem states the problem: "In order to determine the nature of place, Aristotle imposed on this nature two conditions which his *Physics* renders irreconcilable:
on the one hand, he wanted that place envelope and circumscribe the implaced body,
as is required by the usual sense of the words "place," "lodging" [*lieu, logement*]. On
the other hand, he wanted place to be an immobile limit [*terme*] in whose absence one

could not judge that a body is moved by local movement, nor what this movement is" (Duhem, *Le système du monde,* I:204). Aristotle's vacillation between two distinctly different models in the *Categories* and in the *Physics* may not reflect so much a failure to attain an adequate model—much less conceptual confusion on his part—as an at least implicit recognition of this essentially unresolvable antinomy. For a recent assessment that regards the discrepancies between the *Categories* and the *Physics* as reflecting "a growing awareness of the problems inherent in the common sense notions of place and space," see Algra, *Concepts of Space in Greek Thought,* chap. 4, esp. pp. 121–153, 173–190.

81. "The place [of changeable body] is not the world but *a part of the world,* which is an extreme and in contact with changeable body" (*Physics* 212b18–20; my italics). I borrow the phrase "place tight" from Mendell, who writes that Aristotle's "container would be place tight by definition" ("Topoi on Topos," 224).

82. Solmsen remarks that "the notion of 'containing' . . . has meanings that fall outside a purely local relationship" (*Aristotle's System of the Physical World,* 133). One of these is precisely that of the part/whole relationship—that is, the first of the eight forms of "in" distinguished in *Physics,* bk. 4, chap. 3. Moreover, just as the part is *in* the whole, so the whole can be said to be *in* the part (i.e., the second sense distinguished at bk. 4, chap. 3). Either way, something more capacious than the immediate surrounder is at stake in such senses of containment.

83. "There is an obvious sense in which a place, as a local container, has the characteristic of being up or down. Places are up and down, not in virtue of being containers, but rather in virtue of the fact that they can be located in an absolute sense with respect to the (fixed, motionless) Earth and the outer sphere (*Physics* 212a20f.)" (Michael Bradie and Comer Duncan, "An Aristotelian Model of Space and Time," unpublished paper, 1985, p. 4). Aristotle's mature model thus accounts for the movement of a sensible body from one confined place to another, but it coexists uneasily with the view that all natural bodies gravitate toward the earth as a fixed center. Notice, however, that the requirement of an absolute or global space is not equivalent to a demand for *infinite* space. On the contrary: "The idea of the absolute center and the finiteness of the universe are interdependent: overthrow one, no matter which, and you inevitably overthrow the other" (S. Sambursky, *The Physical World of the Greeks,* trans. M. Dagut [Princeton: Princeton University Press, 1987], 208; see also p. 100: "only a finite body can have a center"). Aristotle's cosmology does not require that the *earth* exist at the center—though this happens to be the case—but that some such entity exist there. (When Aristotle makes this latter concession in *De Caelo,* it is notable that he conceives of such an absolute location as pointlike: *De Caelo* 271a4–5 [see also 285b8–11 and 287b4–14]. Point and place merge once more—now, however, only in the most extreme cosmic context!) On this entire question, see G. E. L. Owen, "Aristotelian Mechanics," in *Logic, Science, and Dialectic,* 315–333; and Solmsen, *Aristotle's System of the Physical World,* 292–303, as well as Liba Taub, *Ptolemy's Universe: The Natural Philosophical and Ethical Foundations of Ptolemy's Astronomy* (Chicago and LaSalle: Open Court, 1993), 74 ff.

84. This question is judiciously treated by Richard Sorabji in *Matter, Space, and Motion: Theories in Antiquity and Their Sequel* (Ithaca: Cornell University Press, 1988), 188–192. Sorabji takes seriously a recent suggestion of Myles Burnyeat to the effect that the vessel's place is the lasting *rim* of a hypothetical hole in the river regarded as one massive geographical entity. (See Myles Burnyeat, "The Skeptic in His

Place and Time," in *Philosophy in History,* ed. R. Rorty, J. B. Schneewind, and Quentin Skinner [Cambridge: Cambridge University Press, 1984], n 15.) But Burnyeat's solution has difficulty in accounting for the place of a *moving* boat that has successively *new rims:* how can such mobility of perimeters be reconciled with the requirement of the immobility of place?

85. For further difficulties, consult Sorabji, *Matter, Space, and Motion,* 192–201; Algra, *Concepts of Space in Greek Thought,* chap. 5; as well as Victor Goldsmidt, "La théorie aristotélienne du lieu," in *Mélanges de philosophie grecque offerts à Mgr. Diés* (Paris: Vrin, 1956), esp. pp. 110–119.

86. The theme of Aristotelian place as something systematically submerged surfaced during a graduate seminar on the phenomenology and physics of space I taught with Patrick Heelan at Stony Brook in the fall semester of 1990. See also Heelan's book, *Space-Perception and the Philosophy of Science* (Berkeley: University of California Press, 1983), esp. chap. 4, "Hyperbolic Space: The Model." It is revealing that Heelan now prefers to call such space "Aristotelian *space.*" His entire discussion in the book just cited is an invaluable treatment of non-Euclidean spaces in a format that is formally rigorous while being sensitive to the specificities of the experience of such spaces.

87. "Aristotle is in no way a geometer; he is above all an observer. What he considers as real is first of all that which observation reveals to him; this essential character of all of the peripatetic philosophy is shown most perfectly in the theory of place and movement which the Stagirite proposes" (Duhem, *Le système du monde,* I:189). G. E. L. Owen, however, offers a dissenting view: "This is not to say (and it does not commit Aristotle to supposing) that in the *Physics* proper the analyses either start from or are closely controlled by our inspections of the world" ("Tithenai ta phainomena," 244). On this issue, I side with Duhem: surely the cogency of Aristotle's treatment of place, movement, void, and time in the *Physics* stems precisely from his close attention to mundane phenomena. For further support of the Duhemian view, see J. Morsink, "The Mandate of Topics I, Z," *Apeiron* 16 (1982):102–128.

88. *De Caelo* 268a7.

89. See Heidegger, *Being and Time,* trans. J. Macquarrie and E. Robinson (New York: Harper, 1962), esp. sec. 83, where Aristotle is taken to task for considering the "succession of nows" (*Jetztfolge*) in a merely *vorhanden,* "present-at-hand" way. (Concerning Heidegger's claim, see Derrida, "*Ousia* and *Grammē,*" and my essay "Derrida's Deconstruction of Heidegger's Views on Temporality: The Language of Space and Time," in *Phenomenology of Temporality: Time and Language* [Pittsburgh: Silverman Phenomenology Center, 1987], 89–113. For Bergson's critique of time's spatialization, see *Time and Free Will,* trans. F. L. Pogson (New York: Harper, 1960), esp. chap. 2, pp. 91–106. *Time and Free Will* was written nearly simultaneously with "The Idea of Place in Aristotle," and it is tempting to speculate that Bergson applied to time as unspatialized *durée réelle* the sense of place as capacious and embracing—as distinctly *not* present-at-hand—which he had learned from Aristotle's inaugural treatment of the subject. If so, place plays for him the role of covert model for a renewed and postmetaphysical notion of *time:* by no means the only instance in which the power of place has surreptitiously influenced leading conceptions of time in the West.

90. Archytas, in S. Sambursky, ed., *The Concept of Place in Late Neoplatonism* (Jerusalem: Israel Academy of Sciences and Humanities, 1982), 37.

Interlude

1. On the reinvocation of Hesiod, this time as the first formulator of "cause" or first explanatory principle, see *Metaphysics,* bk. 1, chap. 4, where the same passage cited from the *Theogony* in *Physics,* bk. 4, chap. 1, is re-cited: "First of all things came chaos."

2. For Aristotle's examination of place in his own tetradic causal terms, see *Physics,* chaps. 1–4. Overall, Aristotle is skeptical as to the applicability of the four causes to place ("no one of the four kinds of explanation is present in it" [209a19–20], yet it can be plausibly argued that place serves as a final cause for motion. For this interpretation, see Richard Sorabji, *Matter, Space, and Motion: Theories in Antiquity and Their Sequel* (Ithaca: Cornell University Press, 1988), 186–187, as well as its critique by Keimpe Algra, *Concepts of Space in Greek Thought* (Leiden: Brill, 1995), 199–221.

3. In this paragraph I build on James Hillman's distinction of "world" vs. "universe" as set forth in his *Re-Visioning Psychology* (New York: Harper & Row, 1975) and in conversation, and on Erwin Straus's distinction of "sensing" vs. "perceiving" in his *Primary World of Senses,* trans. J. Needleman (Glencoe, Ill.: Free Press, 1963), 318–322.

Chapter Four: The Emergence of Space in Hellenistic and Neoplatonic Thought

1. For a detailed treatment of the Boundless, see Charles H. Kahn, *Anaximander and the Origins of Greek Cosmology* (New York: Columbia University Press, 1960), appendix 2. In this appendix, Kahn argues that *to apeiron* underlies, conceptually and historically, both the Atomistic void and the Platonic *chōra.* See also Paul Seligman, *The Apeiron of Anaximander: A Study in the Origin and Function of Metaphysical Ideas* (London: Athlone Press, 1962), passim.

2. This is the version of Diogenes Laertius as ascribed to Leucippus and as translated by David Furley in Furley's *The Greek Cosmologists* (Cambridge: Cambridge University Press, 1987), I:140. For further discussion of world formation according to the Atomists, see G. S. Kirk, J. E. Raven, and M. Schofield, *The Presocratic Philosophers* (Cambridge: Cambridge University Press, 1983), 416–421.

3. For an interpretation of the "great void" as the space between the earth and the stars, see Furley, *The Greek Cosmologists,* 141. Place is also entailed in the fact that each atom has not only a "shape" (*schēma*) but also an "arrangement" (*taxis*) and a "position" (*thesis*). These place-related factors are responsible for the "differences" (*diaphorai*) among clusters of atoms that, ultimately, make up physical things. On this last point, see Aristotle, *Metaphysics* 985b15–22 and *De Caelo* 801.

4. "Letter to Herodotus," in *The Philosophy of Epicurus,* ed. and trans. G. K. Strodach (Evanston: Northwestern University Press, 1963), 166. But Epicurus argued, against the early Atomists, that the *kinds* of atoms and their modes of combination are limited in number. Simplicius says that Democritus "calls space (*topos*) by these names—'the void' (*kenon*), 'nothing' (*ouden*) and 'the infinite' (*apeiron*)" (Simplicius, *De Caelo,* 242 18 ff., as translated in Kirk, Raven, and Schofield, *The Presocratic Philosophers,* 414).

5. On the porousness of Atomistic space—attributed to Leucippus—see Aristotle, *On Generation and Corruption* 325b10.

6. Epicurus gives the following argument for this twice-over infinity: "The totality of things is unlimited, because anything limited has an end point and this end point is seen against something else. But the totality, having no end point, has no limit and, having no limit, it must be infinite and without boundaries" ("Letter to Herodotus"). In this line of thought, the infinity of space is more persuasive than the infinity of things in space: why could there not be a finite number there? A. A. Long provides a reason: "A limited number of atoms in infinite empty space would not be sufficient to hold one another together; they could not form the plurality of compounds which we experience" (A. A. Long, *Hellenistic Philosophy: Stoics, Epicureans, Sceptics,* 2d ed. [London: Duckworth, 1986], 32). A consequence of this step, however, is that the compounds themselves are not infinite but only (as Epicurus explicitly avers) "indeterminate in number" ("Letter to Herodotus," 117).

7. On this point, see *On Generation and Corruption* 324b35 and the commentary of Cyril Bailey, *The Greek Atomists and Epicurus* (Oxford: Clarendon Press, 1928), 70–76. Epicurus says straightforwardly that "if what we call 'the void' or 'space' or 'impalpable being' were nonexistent, bodies would not have anywhere to exist, nor would they have a medium through which to move, as they manifestly do" ("Letter to Herodotus," 155–156).

8. Aristotle as cited by Simplicius's commentary on the *Physics* and given in Bailey, *The Greek Atomists and Epicurus,* 75. We shall return to the paradox of *existing without being* below.

9. Furley suggests that the primary difference between "Aristotelians" and "Atomists"—in his assessment, the two great opponents in ancient Greek cosmology—is to be found in the commitment to wholism (i.e., "giving priority in explanation to whole forms") versus explanation in terms of "component parts." (See his *Cosmic Problems: Essays on Greek and Roman Philosophy of Nature* [Cambridge: Cambridge University Press, 1989], 233.)

10. The phrase occurs in Epicurus's "Letter to Herodotus." Bailey, following Usener, says that "the missing words [i.e., *sōmata kai topos* in the basic sentence *alla mēn kai to pan esti* . . . can be supplied with certainty from other passages" (Bailey, *The Greek Atomists and Epicurus,* 279 n 1). But the certainty is less than absolute. Rist speaks of Usener's "probably false supplement [of] *topos*"—citing Lucretius's use of *inane* rather than *locus* in the corresponding passage in *De rerum natura* (J. M. Rist, *Epicurus: An Introduction* [Cambridge: Cambridge University Press, 1972], 56 n). Inwood concurs with Rist's skepticism (Brad Inwood, "The Origin of Epicurus' Concept of Void," *Classical Philology* 76 [1981]: 276 n 14). But Sedley remarks that "Usener's [interpolated phrase] *sōmata kai topos* has had an undeservedly bad press," pointing out that the same formula with *topos* occurs elsewhere in Epicurus. Sedley himself, however, admits that an equally good case can be made for Gassendi's preference for the phrase *sōmata kai kenon.* (See David Sedley, "Two Conceptions of Vacuum," *Phronesis* 27 [1982]: 192 n 18.) Gassendi's preference, coming as it did in the early seventeenth century, when space had gained evident superiority over place, could have been predicted.

11. As reported by Diogenes Laertius, *The Lives and Opinions of Eminent Philosophers,* bk. 10 ("Epicurus"), sec. 40.

12. Inwood, "The Origin of Epicurus' Concept of Void," 275. I have substituted "intangible substance" for "intangible nature." Inwood adds that "Epicurus' void as place corresponds to [the] primary place in Aristotle" (p. 281) and that "for both Aristotle and Epicurus, then, place is the boundary of the *periechon*—the surrounding body or *phusis,* respectively" (p. 282).

13. Inwood, "The Origin of Epicurus' Concept of Void," 276. It follows that the primary motivation for positing an *infinite* void is here obviated, despite the fact that "the problem of motion is what motivated the Atomists' theory of the infinite universe" (Furley, "The Greek Theory of the Infinite Universe," in *Cosmic Problems,* 12).

14. Furley, "Aristotle and the Atomist on Motion in a Void," in *Cosmic Problems,* 78.

15. Sedley, "Two Conceptions of Vacuum," 182. At ibid., we also read that "void *is* a space-filler." Sedley, drawing on a suggestion of Jonathan Barnes, proposes that we interpret the sentence "nonbeing exists (*to mē on einai)*" as parsing into: "nonbeing" = "that which is unreal"; while "exists" = "there is that which is unreal" (pp. 180–181).

16. Sedley refers to the Archytian axiom—without attribution to Archytas—when he speaks of "the plausible and widespread assumption that to exist is to occupy a place" ("Two Conceptions of Vacuum," 180). He draws the following consequence: "When a place is occupied by nothing, insofar as the occupant is nothing it does not exist, but insofar as it occupies a place it does exist" (p. 183).

17. Aristotle's effort to appropriate the void proper as "place" and his outright denial of vacuum has been treated above in chapter 3. Now, however, we can appreciate how much Aristotle misread the ancient Atomists—made them swerve in his own direction. Indeed, we can say that Aristotle systematically misconstrued the early Atomists by presuming that *their* void, especially as conceived by Democritus, is placelike: there is "no independent testimony for Democritus' alleged identification of void and place. Aristotle has thrust his own concept of place on Democritus for the purpose of attacking the existence of void" (Inwood, "The Origin of Epicurus' Concept of Void," 275 fn 5). See also Sedley's observation: "It suits [Aristotle] to treat void as place, because he has already defined place in such a way as to deprive it of independent existence, and he now seizes the opportunity to tar void with the same brush (especially *Physics* 214a16–22)" ("Two Conceptions of Vacuum," 179).

18. Sextus Empiricus, *Against the Professors,* bk. 10, chap. 2, in the translation of A. A. Long and D. N. Sedley, eds., *The Hellenistic Philosophers* (Cambridge: Cambridge University Press, 1987), I:28.

19. Long and Sedley, *The Hellenistic Philosophers,* I:30. The full sentence is: "By choosing instead space in the broadest sense—a notion which he is, arguably, the first ancient thinker to isolate—he ensures the permanence of his second element [i.e., the void]."

20. For this translation, see Long and Sedley, *The Hellenistic Philosophers,* I:30.

21. Long and Sedley, *The Hellenistic Philosophers,* I:30. With this step, we are on the way to Space. In Epicurus's proleptic vision we attain "the first clear recognition of geometrical space as a three-dimensional extension which persists whether or not it is occupied by body" (Sedley, "Two Conceptions of Vacuum," 188).

22. On the question of parts of atoms—their spatial *minima*—see David Furley, *Two Studies in the Greek Atomists* (Princeton: Princeton University Press, 1967), Study I ("Indivisible Magnitudes"), esp. chaps. 1, 8. It is of interest that Epicurus, countering

Aristotle's critique of partless atoms in Democritus and Leucippus, posits parts of atoms—not physical parts but measurable parts of their pure extension (e.g., edges of shapes). Concerning internal relations between the atoms of a given complex, all that we can say is that "compound bodies consist of atoms variously spaced out" (Sedley, "Two Conceptions of Vacuum," 191) and that space qua intangible substance "cannot be part of a compound object" (Long and Sedley, *The Hellenistic Philosophers*, 1:30). Finally, despite the stress on position (*thesis*), Epicurean space supplies this only problematically: *from where* does it come?

23. The Greek phrase is *amoiroi tou kenou*. It is cited by Simplicius in his commentary on Aristotle's *De Caelo* and quoted in turn by Bailey, *The Greek Atomists and Epicurus*, 79. Melissus, disciple of Parmenides, posited infinite space—but an infinite *full* space. It is the infinity *plus* the emptiness of space that is the expressly anti-Parmenidean thought of the first Atomists.

24. Lucretius, *De rerum natura*, bk. 1, lines 31–34, as translated in Long and Sedley, *The Hellenistic Philosophers*, 1:28. The phrase "so long as it exists" (*dum sit*) adds an Archytian rider.

25. The link between extension and space is especially telling. Thus Sorabji, in a discussion of early Greek theories that stressed three-dimensional extension, says revealingly that "they might indeed be called theories of *space*" (*Matter, Space, and Motion: Theories in Antiquity and Their Sequel* [Ithaca: Cornell University Press, 1988], 200; his italics).

26. I say "essentially," since the void is sometimes and in part occupied (precisely by atoms) and since a material body may be less than fully plenary, for example, if it contains empty interstices or vacua. I borrow the phrase "order of being" from Sedley: bodies and void for Epicurus are "the only two orders of being that are required to account for the universe" ("Two Conceptions of the Vacuum," 191).

27. It is striking that Simplicius contrasts Strato most particularly with the ancient Atomists, for whom space is undifferentiated and can exist *without* any bodies in it. See Simplicius, *Corollary on Place* (*Physics* 601.14–24).

28. Cited in David Furley, "Strato's Theory of the Void," in *Cosmic Problems*, 149. "Interval" here translates *diastēma*, while "middle" translates *metaxu*.

29. Cited from a fragment from Simplicius by Furley, "Strato's Theory of the Void," 151.

30. Furley cites the view from a fragment compiled by Wehrli that "the void is isometric with the cosmic body and is always filled with body" ("Strato's Theory of the Void," 152). It is difficult to square this mention of "cosmic body" with Furley's denial that Strato did not support any idea of infinite space: "There is no trace of the infinitely extended, centerless space of Atomist theory [in Strato]" (ibid., 159). My own hypothesis is that Strato took such space for granted, perhaps having been convinced of it by Epicurus—who may have suggested to him a resolution of the *horror vacui* that ensures the continual and immediate filling of microvoids in matter. (On this last point, see ibid., 156–158.)

31. On this complex of closely coordinated ideas, see Sorabji, *Matter, Space, and Motion*, 213–214.

32. Thus Sextus Empiricus (ca. A.D. 150–225), reporting on the Stoics, says, "They say *chōra* is an extension partly occupied by body and partly unoccupied" (cited in Algra, *Concepts of Space in Greek Thought*, 265).

33. "Fire occupies more space than an equivalent amount of any of the other elements which are then transmuted to it. Accordingly, when the world is all fire it must take up more room than when it is, as now, a mixture of the four elements; there must be room into which it can expand" (F. H. Sandbach, *Aristotle and the Stoics* [Cambridge: Cambridge Philological Society, 1985], 42).

34. Cited at Long and Sedley, *The Hellenistic Philosophers*, I:294.

35. *De Caelo* 279a13–14. Aristotle adds that "it is possible for body to come to be" in a void (ibid.). But as he has just shown in the same text that it is *impossible* for any bodies to occupy the void—*De Caelo* 278b21–279a7—it follows that *no body at all* can exist in the void. Put otherwise, void is "what can be occupied, but is not [in fact] occupied, by something that exists, i.e., something corporeal" (cited from a fragment attributed to Chrysippus by Sandbach, *Aristotle and the Stoics*, 43). As Hahm puts it, "Since there is never any body outside the cosmos, there can be no place and so no void [in Aristotle's sense], which is defined as place deprived of body" (David E. Hahm, *The Origins of Stoic Cosmology* [Columbus: Ohio State University Press, 1977], 103).

36. As Chrysippus said expressly: "The void is said to be infinite. For what is outside the world is like this, but place is finite since no body is infinite. Just as anything corporeal is finite, so the incorporeal is infinite" (as cited by Stobaeus, in Hahm, *The Origins of Stoic Cosmology*, 294). Notice that in making such a claim Chrysippus implies that if *per impossibile* there were to be a body in the void it would have to be infinite in extent—yet all bodies are finite.

37. Another argument is also invoked: a person situated at any presumptive boundary would always be able to reach out still further, thus pushing back the extension of space indefinitely. See Hahm, *The Origins of Stoic Cosmology*, 122. We shall return to this argument, which stems ultimately from Archytas, at the end of this chapter.

38. Sextus Empiricus, *Against the Professors*, cited in Long and Sedley, *The Hellenistic Philosophers*, I:294.

39. Cleomedes, cited in Long and Sedley, *The Hellenistic Philosophers*, I:294.

40. Stobaeus, cited in Long and Sedley, *The Hellenistic Philosophers*, I:294. Sextus Empiricus agrees with Stobaeus's assessment, and adds that "existent" (*on*) signifies physical body: "place is what is occupied by an existent and made equal to what occupies it (by 'existent' they now mean body)" (cited from *Against the Professors*, ibid.). For place to be occupied "by several things" raises the question of whether more than one thing can exist in a place: the "problem of interpenetration." Richard Sorabji traces the history of this problem—especially vexatious for the Stoics—in his *Matter, Space, and Motion*, chap. 6, "Can Two Bodies Be in the Same Place? Stoic Metaphysics and Chemistry."

41. On this transformation, see S. Sambursky, *Physics of the Stoics* (Princeton: Princeton University Press, 1975), 4.

42. Ibid., 7.

43. Hahm, *The Origins of Stoic Cosmology*, 125.

44. Sambursky, *Physics of the Stoics*, 1.

45. Stobaeus, cited in Long and Sedley, *The Hellenistic Philosophers*, I:294.

46. Hahm, *The Origins of Stoic Cosmology*, 105. Hahm adds: "Chrysippus views place and void as coordinate species of a third thing, 'that which is capable of being occupied by body' " (ibid.).

47. Thus Hahm comments that "the Stoics probably used the term 'room' to denote space which *combines place and void (i.e., the 'all')*" (ibid., 296; my italics).

48. Sextus Empiricus, cited in Long and Sedley, *The Hellenistic Philosophers,* I:268; my italics.

49. Ibid.; my italics.

50. "One must not conceive place as a mere limit (*peras*) in the way that we conceive the mathematical surfaces as limits of mathematical bodies, but as the physical boundaries (*horoi*) of physical bodies, and as the alive boundaries of ensouled living beings" (Iamblichus, as discussed by Simplicius in his *In Aristotelis categorias commentarium* and as translated by S. Sambursky in *The Concept of Place in Late Neoplatonism* [Jerusalem: Israel Academy of Science and Humanities, 1982], 47).

51. Syrianus, as reported by Simplicius in *In Aristotelis physicorum libros quattuor priores commentaria* and translated in Sambursky, *The Concept of Place in Late Neoplatonism,* 57–59. Syrianus says this in the very midst of a critique of the Stoics, especially their doctrine of material interpenetration.

52. Ibid., 57. I here give the slightly different translation of Sorabji in *Matter, Space, and Motion,* p. 207. A fuller statement is: "What devolves to each entity from the more universal place is separate from that which is in place and is not its principal [i.e., special] place. By having in view the common and broadly [conceived] place, they also deem place immobile" (ibid.).

53. Syrianus's phrase "broad, shared place" comes from *The Concept of Place in Late Neoplatonism,* p. 57 (again I use Sorabji's version of this text). Sambursky identifies such a broad place with "absolute space" at ibid., 56 n 4.

54. Plotinus, *Enneads,* II, 5, as translated in Sambursky, *The Concept of Place in Late Neoplatonism,* 39.

55. On these various kinds of place, see Iamblichus at ibid., p. 45. "Intrinsic place" translates *ho [topos] ousiōdēs tis.*

56. Sorabji, *Matter, Space, and Motion,* 206, with reference to this passage in Iamblichus: "Everything else should likewise be defined in accordance with the proper nature of each thing, such that the limits (*perata*) will be truly akin to whatever things they perfectly limit within themselves" (Iamblichus as cited by Simplicius in Sambursky, *The Concept of Place in Late Neoplatonism,* 47).

57. Iamblichus, as cited in Simplicius, *In Aristotelis physicorum libros quattuor priores commentaria* and translated in Sambursky, *The Concept of Place in Late Neoplatonism,* 47. See also the similar passage cited in Simplicius, *In Aristotelis categorias commentarium:* place is a "power sustaining and supporting bodies, raising up the falling ones and gathering together the scattered ones, filling them up as well as encompassing them from every side" (Sambursky, *The Concept of Place in Late Neoplatonism,* 43).

58. This last phrase occurs at ibid., p. 43. I am indebted to Sorabji's discussion of these various powers in *Matter, Space, and Motion,* p. 205.

59. Cited by Simplicius, *In Aristotelis physicorum libros quattuor priores commentaria,* and translated in Sambursky, *The Concept of Place in Late Neoplatonism,* 43. Urmson translates the same phrase as "of like nature with things in place" (Simplicius, *Corollaries on Place and Time,* trans. J. O. Urmson [London: Duckworth, 1992], 73).

60. Simplicius, in Sambursky, *The Concept of Place in Late Neoplatonism,* 43.

Urmson translates: "in no way cut off from their first emergence among beings, nor from being in its central sense" (*Corollaries on Place and Time*, 73).

61. Simplicius, *Corollaries on Place and Time*, 71. "Essence" here translates *ousia*. See Sorabji's remark: for Simplicius, "the essence and the place of a thing become hard to distinguish, even though they are not the same" (*Matter, Space, and Motion*, 210).

62. These statements of Iamblichus are found in Samburshy, *The Concept of Place in Late Neoplatonism*, p. 45. I have substituted "reality" for "existence." Place as cause is discussed at ibid., p. 43.

63. For Iamblichus, place both "has" and "is" power. See the passages cited by Sorabji, *Matter, Space, and Motion*, p. 205, where the phrase "a power that acts" is also quoted.

64. Iamblichus, cited in Samburshy, *The Concept of Place in Late Neoplatonism*, 45.

65. Ibid.

66. Such is Samburshy's interpretation of the following sentence of Iamblichus: "Bodies possess Being in place as encompassed by it and as preserving their own extension in the unextended nature" (ibid., 45; cf. n. 6).

67. Ibid.

68. Ibid. For other affirmations of Archytas, see also p. 45 and p. 49. It is evident that Archytas is taken to be the true ancestor of the Iamblichean view of the powers of places.

69. For arguments in favor of this interpretation, see Sorabji, *Matter, Space, and Motion*, 206.

70. Damascius, cited by Simplicius, *In Aristotelis physicorum libros quattuor priores commentaria* and translated by Sorabji in *Matter, Space, and Motion*, 206.

71. On different senses of measuring, see Martin Heidegger, "On the Nature of Language," in *On the Way to Language*, trans. P. D. Hertz (New York: Harper & Row, 1971), 102.

72. *Matter, Space, and Motion*, 206. Sorabji also notes that "insofar as it is an ideal unit of measurement rather than an instrument of measuring, place is even unextended" (ibid., 110).

73. Simplicius, *Corollaries on Place and Time*, 69.

74. Proclus, as recounted by Simplicius, *In Aristotelis physicorum libros quattuor priores commentaria*, and translated in Samburshy, *The Concept of Place in Late Neoplatonism*, 67. The "immaterial ones among those that move" refers to the celestial bodies. Proclus's clinching argument for the bodily character of the cosmic place is that if place is indeed exactly coextensive with what is in place, then there must be equality between two quantities *of the same kind of thing*, in this case bodily things. On this point, see Sorabji, *Matter, Space, and Motion*, 118.

75. Sorabji, *Matter, Space, and Motion*, 109, with reference to Simplicius, *In Aristotelis physicorum libros quattuor priores commentaria*, 615, 34. I have capitalized "world soul."

76. Proclus, cited by Simplicius, *In Aristotelis physicorum libros quattuor priores commentaria*, translated by Sorabji, *Matter, Space, and Motion*, 115. Sorabji points out that the verb *embibazein* is used by Plato for the way a soul is implanted in a vehicle. Proclus adds: "you will see the cosmos not moving as a whole, so that it may imitate

its place, but moving in respect of its parts, so that in this way it may be inferior to place" (ibid.). Duhem argues that the supracelestial sphere as "the light above the empyrean" anticipates modern ideas of an all-encompassing ether: see Pierre Duhem, *Le système du monde* (Paris: Hermann, 1913), I:341–342.

77. Proclus, as cited in *In Aristotelis physicorum libros quattuor priores commentaria,* and translated in Sambursky, *The Concept of Place in Late Neoplatonism,* 69. Note that "shape" is here equivalent to "mold" and that Damascius and Proclus converge on the idea that the ultimate place of the universe is moldlike.

78. Sorabji, *Matter, Space, and Motion,* 109–110.

79. Proclus, cited by Simplicius, *In Aristotelis physicorum libros quattuor priores commentaria,* and translated in Sambursky, *The Concept of Place in Late Neoplatonism,* 67. The same contrast obtains when the question of interpenetration is at stake: "The appeal to indivisibility lay at the root of Proclus' explanation of interpenetration: it is because place, or space, cannot be parted by a barrier that it goes right through it. There could not be a greater contrast with the earlier [Atomist] idea that the interpenetration of bodies is made possible by the infinite division of these bodies" (Sorabji, *Matter, Space, and Motion,* 117).

80. Proclus, as cited by Simplicius, *In Aristotelis physicorum libros quattuor priores commentaria,* and translated in Sambursky, *The Concept of Place in Late Neoplatonism,* 69: where the Greek suggests "light at the summit, the divine peak of the worlds" (ibid., 68 n 5). Bergson remarks on the importance of the qualitative dimension of place—even in Aristotle—by way of contrast with early modern conceptions: "Instead of an empty and unlimited space, [Aristotle describes] places which are not only limited by their size but also defined by their quality" ("L'Idée de Lieu chez Aristote," *Les Études Bergsoniennes* (1949), 2:100).

81. Syrianus, as cited and translated by Sorabji, *Matter, Space, and Motion,* 112.

82. Philoponus, *Corollaries on Place and Void,* trans. David Furley (London: Duckworth, 1991), 28.

83. Ibid., 39; my italics. I here translate *chōra* as "room" rather than as "space" (preferred by Furley).

84. Thus it follows that "if you think of bodily extension without matter, it will no longer be in place" (Philoponus, *Corollaries,* 66). The tight link between body and place is reinforced by the following further statement: "Body is in place qua body, and body is three-dimensional, and so it is in place in its three dimensions; but in that case it is necessary that its place be extended in three ways, in order to receive in its own three dimensions that which is itself three-dimensional" (ibid., 66–67). The similarity between bodily extension thus conceived and Cartesian *extensio* is striking.

85. "Of course, I do not mean that this extension either ever is or can be empty of all body. Not at all. But I do claim that it is something different, over and above the bodies that come to be in it, and empty by its own definition, although never without body" (ibid., 29–30). More briefly put: "Void can never exist in separation from body" (p. 41). See David Sedley's excellent discussion of the in fact/in principle occupation of spatial extension in his "Philoponus's Conception of Space," in *Philoponus and the Rejection of Aristotelian Science,* ed. R. Sorabji (London: Duckworth, 1987), 140–153.

86. "Neither will the body qua extension be in another extension: rather, qua bodily extension it will be in spatial extension" (Philoponus, *Corollaries,* 66). I have altered

Furley's awkward term "place-extension" to "spatial extension," which is used by
Sedley and Sambursky alike. Furley's term is, however, a literal transcription of the
Greek *diastēma topikon*. But the kind of place here at stake is precisely not the particular place that encompasses a body—that is, bodily extension proper (*diastēma
sōmaton*)—but a roomier place that is already on its way to infinite space.

87. Philoponus, *Corollaries*, 23, 65.

88. Ibid., 29. This phrase is equivalent to "bodiless in its own definition" (p. 28).
Philoponus argues explicitly against the idea of place as a body at ibid., 16–17. If it
were a body, then another body could not occupy it; and if, *per impossibile*, it *could*
occupy it, it would be divided—which is contrary to the indivisible nature of pure
spatial extension.

89. Ibid., 39, 28.

90. Sedley, "Philoponus's Conception of Space," 141; his italics. "Space" is here
equivalent to "spatial extension." Sedley shows that, though there is for Philoponus no
actual void, there is a real threat of vacuum, a "force of vacuum," that forces the
philosopher to take it seriously and make at least important *conceptual* room for it.
More than this: we cannot grasp space fully except through pondering the real possibility of vacuum: "Although space is ontologically prior to vacuum, in order of understanding it is not: the most effective way to get to the notion of space is *through* that
of vacuum" (ibid., 151; his italics).

91. Philoponus, *Corollaries*, 23. Even more pithily put: "Body does not coincide
with surface" (p. 72). A related argument is that motion is not possible among surfaces
alone: see ibid., 27. Even if to have three dimensions is not necessarily to *be* a body,
any body that is in place must be in an extension that is tri-dimensional. (On this last
point, see p. 21 and pp. 66–67.)

92. For this fourfold satisfaction, see ibid., 39.

93. Ibid., 30.

94. Both citations in this sentence are from ibid., 45. "Boundary" translates *peras*.

95. "For since it subsists as the place of bodies, [only] so much of its subsists as
can be occupied by the bodies of the cosmos, but it is coterminous with the boundaries
of these bodies" (ibid., 45). Put otherwise, "the surface of the outermost body"—that
is, of the whole cosmos—can be imagined as "coinciding with the [inner] boundary of
the void" (ibid., 46). But just because one can imagine that the outer surface of the
cosmos coincides with the inner surface of the void does not prove that one must
suppose that there is such a coincidence. One suspects that the coincidence itself is an
article of faith and that to support it Philoponus is driven to confuse imagining it to be
the case—which he admits is a contingent matter—and *having to suppose that it is the
case*.

96. Philoponus's argumentation is unconvincing, not just because of its stealthy
retreat to an Aristotelian criterion, but also because it seems to work only for an indefinite, not an infinite, number of bodies. We *can* imagine a boundary around a vast
heap of rocks that are projected, say, over the Himalayas, but can we imagine any such
boundary for an *actual infinity* of rocks? Philoponus's only effective response to this
objection is to say that success in this more limited *Gedankenexperiment* may enable
us, by analogical extension, to know what success in the more crucial experiment
would be like. (I am indebted to Janet B. Gyatso for discussion of this point.) Philoponus's theological motive is that he "cannot easily allow such an infinity, given his

Christian arguments against an infinity of past time for the history of the universe" (Sorabji, *Matter, Space, and Motion,* 141). Another motive for Philoponus's rejection of infinity may have been the *horror vacui* that is so evident in his physics. (On this point, see Sedley, "Philoponus's Conception of Space," 143 ff.)

97. Philoponus, *Corollaries,* 29.

98. Ibid., 44. This statement, which draws on the Aristotelian formula *echei tina dunamin,* is embedded in a critique of Aristotelian natural places, a critique that also seems to have an ulterior motive in Christian theology: "Hence light things move upwards, desiring not simply to be in contact with the surface of the container, but rather desiring the station which the Creator allotted to them. For then they have their being most fully, and then they achieve their perfection" (ibid., 44). On Philoponus's denial of power to place, see Sorabji, *Matter, Space, and Motion,* 211.

99. "Philoponus obviously rejects the conception of Iamblichus and his followers that place has a rank superior to that of the bodies in place and thus exerts a certain power on the encompassed bodies" (Sambursky, *The Concept of Place in Late Neoplatonism,* 224 n 10). For bodies now take the lead once again—as they had for Aristotle! "So it is not place," says Philoponus, "that has the power to move bodies to their proper places; it is *the bodies that have a desire to keep their own station*" (*Corollaries,* 44; my italics).

100. Concerning the belated but considerable legacy of Philoponus in the Renaissance, see Charles B. Schmitt, "Philoponus's Commentary on Aristotle's *Physics* in the Sixteenth Century," in Sorabji, *Philoponus and the Rejection of Aristotelian Science,* 210–229. Through Henry More, the influence of Philoponus may have reached Newton himself.

101. Philoponus, *Corollaries,* 44.

102. Theophrastus, cited in Simplicius, in *Corollaries on Place and Time,* 72. This view obtains for the entire cosmos, which is conceived as a single enormous organism by Theophrastus. It remains that Philoponus's agreement with Theophrastus is about natural places alone. Order and position are less crucial when it comes to nonnatural, noetic places: on this point, see Sorabji, *Matter, Space, and Motion,* 211.

103. On Philoponus as "a true upholder of Theophrastus," see Sorabji, *Matter, Space, and Motion,* 211–213.

104. Damascius as cited by Simplicius in *Corollaries on Place and Time,* 52.

105. As cited by Simplicius, *Corollaries on Place and Time,* 79.

106. *Corollaries on Place and Time,* 73.

107. Ibid., 73.

108. Cited by Simplicius in *Corollaries on Place and Time,* 36–37.

109. Simplicius: "The place also that exists together with bodies is extended with them" (ibid., 66).

110. Simplicius, *Corollaries on Place and Time,* 68. Simplicius also says: "place is extended through its participation in the object in place, just as the object in place is measured and located by means of place" (p. 67) and that "place is a pre-requisite as a measure of extension in position" (p. 65).

111. Ibid., 69.

112. Ibid., 66.

113. On this triple distinction, see ibid., 70–71. The unique place (*idios topos*) is the "essential place" to which reference was earlier made. Both it and the immediate

place cling to a particular extended thing and vanish when this thing vanishes. The shared place—"the common broadly conceived place" (p. 58)—is the arena in which the variant positions of an extended body are taken up successively. For discussion of this distinction, see Sorabji, *Matter, Space, and Motion*, 209–210.

114. Simplicius, *Corollaries on Place and Time*, 61.

115. Ibid., 61. This conclusion is reached after an analysis of harmony in music, where the issue of "good arrangement" is paramount.

116. "The transcendent measure . . . exceeds the object measured through its superiority in power and its unity of being" (ibid., 65). See also p. 70: place "has a certain transcendent character that encompasses everything in respect of place that body embraces corporeally."

117. Ibid., 64.

118. Ibid., 61.

119. Aristotle, *De Caelo* 279a12–13. As Sorabji comments, once Aristotle "rejects the obvious view that place is a three-dimensional extension he is left with the idea that a thing's place is the inner surface of its physical surroundings. This at once makes it impossible for place to be extracosmic, or infinite. For there cannot in this sense be a place of, or outside, the cosmos, since the cosmos has no physical surroundings. Nor yet can a surrounding surface have a more than finite diameter" (*Matter, Space, and Motion*, 138–139).

120. Hahm, *The Origins of Stoic Cosmology*, 106.

121. Ibid., 107.

122. Eudemus here gives the report, as stated by Simplicius, *In Aristotelis physicorum libros quattuor priores commentaria,* and translated by Sorabji, *Matter, Space, and Motion*, 125. I have substituted "staff" for "stick." Other versions of this same question—which had a considerable legacy in the ancient and medieval worlds—are cited by Sorabji at p. 126 and by Hahm, *The Origins of Stoic Cosmology*, 106.

123. Cited from Alexander of Aphrodisias, *Quaestiones* 3.12, and translated in Sorabji, *Matter, Space, and Motion*, 126. Alexander, perhaps Aristotle's primary defender of a finite universe in the Hellenistic world, also argues that one cannot argue from the limited character of the cosmos to anything *un*limited beyond it: Sorabji, *Matter, Space, and Motion*, 136–137. In the above statement Alexander overlooks the possibility that in merely stretching out one's arm, one creates a space by this very act: a space having the very volume of the arm. Such is John Buridan's point in his fourteenth-century *Questions on the Physics:* "Before you raise your arm outside this [last] sphere nothing would be there; but after your arm has been raised, a space would be there, namely the dimension of your arm" (cited by Edward Grant in his *Much Ado About Nothing: Theories of Space and Vacuum from the Middle Ages to the Scientific Revolution* [Cambridge: Cambridge University Press, 1981], 15). Buridan's premise is that "space is nothing but a dimension of body and your space [is] the dimension of your body" (cited at ibid.). Notice that on Buridan's analysis the space in question is not a separate void space external to the lonely figure on its edge but a space that is strictly internal to the arm of such a figure—that is, a space delimited by the outer dimension or shape of this arm.

124. Cited from Simplicius's commentary on Aristotle's *De Caelo* in Sorabji, *Matter, Space, and Motion*, 127. The phrase, "something, either empty or solid," refers to the clause in the original statement: "what is outside will be either body or place."

Chapter Five: The Ascent of Infinite Space

1. As Duhem remarks, "For Aristotle, no infinite magnitude exists in actuality, for the universe is limited. It cannot exist potentially either; however great a quantity is realized, there exists a limit that cannot be surpassed, for no quantity can exceed the boundaries of the world" (Pierre Duhem, *Medieval Cosmology: Theories of Infinity, Place, Time, Void, and the Plurality of Worlds,* ed. and trans. R. Ariew [Chicago: University of Chicago Press, 1985], 73. On the strict limitation of matter in the universe, see p. 77. All of part 1 of Duhem's text—which is drawn from volume 7 of his *Le système du monde* (1956)—is devoted to the question of the infinitely large and infinitely small.

2. Aristotle, *Physics* 212b8–9. See also 212b15: "The upper part moves in a circle, but the whole [of this part, i.e., the outer sphere] is not anywhere."

3. Cited by Duhem, *Medieval Cosmology,* p. 146, from Bacon's mid-thirteenth-century work, *Questiones supra librum Phisicorum a magistro dicto.*

4. Cited by Duhem, *Medieval Cosmology,* p. 154, from Aquinas's *In libros Physicorum Aristotelis expositio,* book 4, lectio 7.

5. Cited by Duhem, *Medieval Cosmology,* p. 154, from the same text of Aquinas cited above, note 4. Aquinas holds, however, to the view that the earth is in fact the immobile center of the cosmos: "that which is naturally immobile at the center is the earth" (cited at p. 153).

6. Cited in Duhem, *Medieval Cosmology,* p. 155, from Aquinas's *In libros Physicorum Aristotelis,* book 4, lectio 6; my italics. Duhem holds that Aquinas is drawing on Robert Grosseteste's distinction between "material" and "formal" place: "Materially, place is mobile; formally it is immobile" (cited in Duhem, *Medieval Cosmology,* 155, from Grosseteste's *Super octo libris Physicorum Aristotelis brevis et utilitis summa,* bk. 4).

7. Cited in Duhem, *Medieval Cosmology,* p. 161, from Giles's *In libros de Physico auditu Aristotelis commentaria accuratissime emendata,* bk. 4, lectio 7. Giles's premise is that "the position of the universe itself is absolutely immobile" (ibid.).

8. "It is because of the movement of heaven that all the parts of the earth tend toward the center" (cited in Duhem, *Medieval Cosmology,* p. 195, from Jandun's *Quaestiones de motibus animalium*).

9. Duhem, summing up Scotus's view; *Medieval Cosmology,* 186.

10. Aquinas also held that God can create an actual infinite magnitude *if*—and only if—such magnitude is possible in principle. On this in-principle possibility, which is not incompatible with Aquinas's conviction that God does not *in fact* create such a magnitude, see Duhem, *Medieval Cosmology,* pp. 12, 14–15. For the larger background of intellectual politics of the period, see Gordon Leff, *The Dissolution of the Medieval Outlook* (New York: Harper & Row, 1976). (I wish to thank Lee Miller for this last reference, and especially for a close reading of the original version of this chapter.)

11. "Made available to the Latin West in the late twelfth and early thirteenth centuries, this body of literature served as a repository of issues and opinions on place and space that was destined to generate nearly four centuries of discussion and debate" (Edward Grant, "Place and Space in Medieval Physical Thought," in *Motion and Time, Space and Matter: Interrelations in the History of Philosophy and Science,* ed. P. K. Machamer and R. G. Turnbull [Columbus: Ohio State University Press, 1976], 137).

It should be noted that the commentaries of Philoponus and Simplicius on Aristotle's *Physics,* though not fully translated into Latin until the sixteenth century, were paraphrased in some of the texts of Averroës. Moreover, Philoponus was an important influence on Avempace, whose work was in turn decisive for Averroës.

12. The full statement is: "If we must assign a date for the birth of modern science, we would, without doubt, choose the year 1277 when the bishop of Paris solemnly proclaimed that several worlds could exist, and that the whole of the heavens could, without contradiction, be moved with a rectilinear motion" (Duhem, *Études sur Léonarde de Vinci* [Paris: Hermann, 1906–1913], II:412). But Duhem also cautions that "the collapse of Peripatetic physics did not occur suddenly; the construction of modern physics was not accomplished on an empty terrain where nothing was standing. The passage from one to the other was made by a long series of partial transformations, each one pretending merely to retouch or to enlarge some part of the edifice without changing the whole" (*Medieval Cosmology,* 3). Duhem's claim as to inaugural significance of the 1277 Condemnations has proved controversial. It is denied outright by Alexandre Koyré. (See Koyré, "Le vide et l'espace infini au XIVe siècle," *Archives d'histoire doctrinale et littéraire du moyen age* 24 [1949]: 51.) A middle-range position is taken by Edward Grant in his *Physical Science in the Middle Ages* (Cambridge: Cambridge University Press, 1971), chap. 5. For a recent assessment, see David Lindberg, *The Beginnings of Western Science* (Chicago: University of Chicago Press, 1992), chaps. 10, 11, 12. Both Lindberg (p. 365) and Leff (*Dissolution of the Medieval Outlook,* 117) emphasize that contemporary developments in physics, taking place largely independently of debates in theology, also pointed to the infinity of space: for example, the Merton school as inspired by the work of Robert Grosseteste (1170–1253).

13. "Quod prima causa non posset plures mundos facere." I cite the translation of Edward Grant in his *Source Book in Medieval Science* (Cambridge, Mass.: Harvard University Press, 1974), 48.

14. From A. D. Menut and A. J. Denomy, eds., *Nicole Oresme: Le Livre du ciel et du monde* (Madison: University of Wisconsin Press, 1968), 172–174.

15. Ibid., 179. Others who explicitly endorsed the thesis of plural worlds in the wake of the Condemnations were Richard of Middleton at the end of the thirteenth century and William of Ockham in the fourteenth century. For further discussions, see Edward Grant, "The Condemnation of 1277, God's Absolute Power, and Physical Thought in the Late Middle Ages," *Viator* 10 (1979):220 ff. Even Aquinas, before the Condemnations, admitted that God could, if He wished, create other worlds, but that this would be neither economical nor for the best. Nor did Aquinas draw any implications for infinite space from this bare possibility—which he preferred to link with chance rather than with God's will. Cf. *Summa Theologica,* I, pt. 1, question 47, article 3.

16. "Quod Deus non possit movere caelum motu recto. Et ratio est, quia tunc relinqueret vacuum." Again I cite Grant's translation from the *Sourcebook,* p. 48, where Grant argues that *celum* signifies "world" and not just "heavens."

17. Translated by Edward Grant from Oresme's *Le Livre du ciel et du monde,* 370, in Grant's *Source Book,* 553 n 25.

18. From Clarke's Third Reply to Leibniz (1716), cited from *The Leibniz-Clarke*

Correspondence, ed. H. G. Alexander (New York: Philosophical Library, 1956), 32; my italics.

19. The very term "spatial extension" (*diastēma topikon*) connotes the existence of "absolute places" (in Newton's term) within the cosmos. As Grant remarks, "The place of successive occupants of the interior of a pitcher, for example, air and water, is a three-dimensional, incorporeal void, which is but part of an absolute, three-dimensional void space that not only contains the entire cosmos but is coterminous with it. . . . In Philoponus's cosmos, bodies move in an absolutely immobile, three-dimensional void space" (*Much Ado About Nothing,* 20). By making the incorporeal void coextensive with the cosmos—itself resolutely finite—Philoponus assures that this void is not undelimited.

20. Concerning Robert Holkot, see Grant, "The Condemnation of 1277," 224; concerning Richard of Middleton, see Duhem, *Medieval Cosmology,* 182 ff.

21. Menut and Denomy, *Nicole Oresme,* 178; my italics.

22. This is Grant's paraphrase in "The Condemnation of 1277," 215. On Buridan's own vacillation, see p. 128; my italics. Grant remarks that "contrary to the principles of Aristotelian natural philosophy, God could, if he wished, create worlds other than ours, move our world rectilinearly, create an accident without a subject, and do anything else contrary to those accepted principles. But once that concession was made, whether voluntarily or under the duress of possible excommunication, all were free to retain the traditional opinions, as indeed they usually did" (p. 216).

23. Grant, *Source Book,* 46. Grant adds: "Thus while it was naturally impossible for more than one world to exist, or for a vacuum to exist, God could achieve both of these effects if He so desired" (ibid.). Participants in the debate included Albert of Saxony (1316–1390) and John Buridan, both of whom argued that "no place is a vacuum" (Buridan) even if God could annihilate everything, or empty the sky, and thus create a vacuum. The issue of vacuum continued to exercise Galileo, who argued for minute interstitial vacua much in the manner of Marsilius of Inghen and Nicholas of Autrecourt at an earlier time. Pascal can be said to have delivered the coup de grâce by proving that "nature does nothing at all to avoid a vacuum"—given that atmospheric pressure explains physical phenomena formerly attributed to nature's supposed abhorrence of a vacuum (e.g., the extreme difficulty of separating two slabs of marble whose surfaces are contiguous with each other). This debate of several centuries' duration is documented in Grant, *Source Book,* pp. 324–332. See also D. Mahnke, *Unendliche Sphäre und Allmittelpunkt* (Halle: Niemeyer, 1937).

24. Menut and Denomy, *Nicole Oresme,* 179; my italics.

25. Ibid., 279. Oresme adds: "This explains why we say God is always and everywhere" (ibid.). God is in *place* as well as space only as an *a fortiori* deduction: if God is in all of space, then He must also be in the places that belong to such space.

26. Ibid. It remains an unanswered question as to whether infinite space itself is finally dimensional for Oresme; certainly it is so on the plane of imagination; but insofar as this space is real qua divinely inhabited, is it extended? Grant thinks not (he calls it "transcendent and nondimensional" in his *Source Book,* 553 n 26); but I think the issue is far from clear, since one can suppose that God brings with Him his own sort of dimensionality, however hypothetical or speculative it may be. Such, for example, is the view of Suarez (ca. 1548–1617), who wrote that "we cannot conceive the disposition

and immensity of the divine substance except by means of a certain extension, which, of necessity, we explain by means of a relation to bodies" (cited from Suarez's *Disputationes Metaphysicae,* 2:100, by Grant in *Much Ado About Nothing,* p. 154).

27. "No one during the Middle Ages came to believe that God had actually created a three-dimensional finite or infinite vacuum outside the world" (Grant, *Much Ado About Nothing,* 121). The matter was not a simple one. Grant shows that no less a thinker than Buridan vacillated between a position in which he allowed that God *might* create an "infinite, immobile, three-dimensional space" and another position in which such a creation would be "a threat to and limitation on God's absolute power" (ibid., 128). Thus Buridan "surely exhibited the dilemma that the creation of actual infinites posed to fourteenth century scholastics" (ibid.). Creative compromises were tried out by others. Thus Jean of Ripa proposed in the middle of the fourteenth century that whatever finite or infinite vacuum may exist, God's immensity "circumscribes" any such vacuum: God is not only *in every void,* but every void is *in Him.* (For further discussion, see ibid., pp. 129–134.)

28. From *Hermetica, the Ancient Greek and Latin Writings which Contain Religious or Philosophic Teachings Ascribed to Hermes Trismegistus,* ed. and trans. W. Scott (Oxford: Clarendon Press, 1924), I:318.

29. As translated by Grant in *Source Book,* 556–567.

30. Oresme, as Grant notes, believed in "a really existent extracosmic space. . . . Its reality is affirmed by reason and understanding alone" (*Much Ado About Nothing,* 120). Such cognitive reality is compatible with Oresme's characterization of the infinite void as "imagined," since, in comparison with anything reported by the senses, it is imaginary in status. But, ultimately, it is an object of intellect—just as Trismegistus had claimed. Similarly, for Bradwardine, God is "omnipresent in an imaginary infinite place void of everything but the deity" (Grant, *Physical Science in the Middle Ages,* 77), but this very place—i.e., this infinite space—becomes real by the very fact of God's ubiquitous presence in it.

31. Grant, *Much Ado About Nothing,* 142. The full statement is: "Bradwardine enunciated a new kind of void, one empty of everything except God and, because the latter is extensionless, perhaps also extensionless. Thus did Bradwardine affirm the actual existence of a 'spirit-filled', imaginary infinite void space."

32. From the *De causa Dei contra Pelagium* as translated in Grant, *Source Book,* p. 559; my italics. Grant comments elsewhere: "Though God is not present *in any particular place,* He is nevertheless present in *every particular place*" (*Much Ado About Nothing,* 136; my italics).

33. Grant, *Source Book,* 559.

34. Ibid. As Grant comments, "Obviously, place B can be rightly conceived as representing each and every place outside, or beyond, the world. Hence God is everywhere" (p. 556 n 11).

35. Grant, *Much Ado About Nothing,* 142.

36. Unlike the Stoics, however, Crescas allowed for multiple worlds. See H. A. Wolfson, *Crescas' Critique of Aristotle* (Cambridge, Mass.: Harvard University Press, 1929), passim, as well as Grant's treatment in *Much Ado About Nothing,* p. 22 f. Grant claims that "Crescas may have been the first scholar in Western Europe since Greek antiquity to have adopted unequivocally the existence of an infinite three-dimensional void space" (*Much Ado About Nothing* 332 n 20). Crescas here draws close to Philopo-

nus's insistence on the three-dimensionality of "spatial" or "cosmical" extension, but he takes a step further by insisting that "the three-dimensional vacuum extends infinitely beyond our world in every direction" (*Much Ado About Nothing,* 22).

37. *Much Ado About Nothing,* xii. Grant adds that "Isaac Newton operated within the same intellectual framework in the seventeenth century as did Thomas Bradwardine in the fourteenth."

38. Bradwardine, *De causa Dei contra Pelagium,* in Grant, *Source Book,* p. 560.

39. The term *situs imaginarius* is used by Bradwardine at ibid., p. 558.

40. This is Grant's descriptive phrase at *Much Ado About Nothing,* p. 142: "In view of the theological nature of Bradwardine's version of a God-filled infinite space surrounding our finite cosmos, it comes as no surprise to discover that those who adopted some form of his conception were ipso facto concerned with the *divinization of space* rather than with its geometrization or physicalization" (his italics).

41. Frances A. Yates, *Giordano Bruno and the Hermetic Tradition* (Chicago: University of Chicago Press, 1964), 1; my italics.

42. Indeed, the very *first* claim made by Koyré in this classic text acknowledges the Atomistic vintage of the idea of infinity yet immediately equivocates by asserting that the Atomists were never acceptable to the mainstream of Greek or medieval thinkers and that, in any case, it is "impossible to reduce the history of the infinitization of the universe to the rediscovery of the worldview of the Greek Atomists" (*From the Closed World to the Infinite Universe* [Baltimore: Johns Hopkins University Press, 1957], 5). This is certainly true, but Koyré neglects the immense intermediate history of rumination about the infinite that lies between the Atomists and Renaissance philosophers. In a buried footnote, Koyré admits the importance of "the history of the Platonic and Neoplatonic revival from the Florentine Academy to the Cambridge Platonists" (p. 277), yet does not treat Neoplatonists such as Iamblichus or Philoponus who were so critical to the growth of the idea of infinite space.

43. This text was edited by C. Baemker as *Das pseudo-hermetische Buch der XXIV Meister* in the series *Beiträge zur Geschichte der Philosophie und Theologie des Mittelalters* (Münster, 1928), vol. 25. (Cited in Koyré, *From the Closed World to the Infinite Universe,* 279 n 19.)

44. This expansion of the Latin formula "sphaera cuius centrum ubique, circumferentia nullibi" is found in Giordano Bruno's 1584 treatise, *Concerning the Cause, Principle, and One,* trans. S. Greenberg in S. Greenberg, *The Infinite in Giordano Bruno* (New York: King's Crown Press, 1950), 162. Bruno's own twist on the basic formula is that, in the end, the center and the circumference are *not* distinguishable—indeed, they are ultimately the same *under the aspect of infinity.*

45. "Drawing the (penultimate) conclusion from the relativity of the perception of space (direction) and motion, [Cusa] asserts that as the world-image of a given observer is determined by the place he occupies in the universe; and as none of these places can claim an absolutely privileged value (for instance, that of being the center of the universe), we have to admit the possible existence of different, equivalent world-images, [and] the relative—in the full sense of the word—character of each of them" (Koyré, *From the Closed World to the Infinite Universe,* 16, commenting on Cusa's *On Learned Ignorance,* I, ii, chap. 2).

46. Bruno, *Concerning the Cause, Principle, and One,* p. 162. In other words, there is no effective edge or limit inasmuch as an edge or limit implies that there is

something *beyond* or *outside* it; but there is nothing at all beyond or outside—not even the "beyond" or the "outside" as such! Not only can one not stretch one's arm or staff *into* nothing, one cannot climb to a position that could be designated *as the edge* from which such stretching has to take place (that is, if "stretching" is to retain its basic sense of reaching out from a determinate position).

47. I here allude to Bruno's 1584 book, *The Expulsion of the Triumphant Beast* (Spaccio de la Bestia Trionfante), translated into English by A. D. Imerti (New Brunswick: Rutgers University Press, 1964).

48. *Nicholas of Cusa on Learned Ignorance,* trans. J. Hopkins (Minneapolis: A. J. Banning, 1981), 52.

49. As Cusa puts it archly, "the possibility-of-being, or matter . . . is not actually extendable unto infinity" (ibid., 90). By the same token, nothing plural, however great in magnitude, can ever amount to *the* absolute maximum: "Absolute Oneness is free of all plurality" (p. 97; see also p. 91).

50. Ibid., 53; his italics.

51. "And just as there cannot be a greater, so for the same reason there cannot be a lesser, since it is all that which can be. But the Minimum is that than which there cannot be a lesser. And since the Maximum is also such [i.e., such that it cannot sustain a lesser], it is evident that the Minimum coincides with the Maximum" (ibid., 53).

52. Ibid., 53. Concerning incomprehensibility, Cusa has this to say: "Since the unqualifiedly and absolutely Maximum (than which there cannot be a greater) is greater than we can comprehend (because it is Infinite Truth), we attain unto it in no other way than incomprehensibly. For since it is not of the nature of those things which can be comparatively greater and lesser, it is beyond all that we can conceive" (ibid.).

53. On the oneness of the Maximum, see ibid., bk. 1, chap. 5; bk. 2, chap. 3; on its necessity, see bk. 1, chap. 6.

54. "Only the absolutely Maximum is negatively infinite. . . . But since the universe encompasses all the things which are not God, it cannot be negatively infinite, although it is unbounded and thus privately infinite . . . for it is not the case that anything actually greater than it, in relation to which it would be bounded, is positable" (ibid., 90).

55. Ibid., 90. See also p. 114: "Although the world is not infinite, it cannot be conceived as finite, because it lacks boundaries within which it is enclosed."

56. "Every created thing is, as it were, a finite infinity or a created god" (ibid., 93).

57. Ibid., 96.

58. Ibid., 97.

59. Ibid., 97.

60. The contraction of divine infinity in finite infinity is implied by Cusa's claim that "God, since He is immense, is neither in the sun nor in the moon, although *in them,* He is, *absolutely,* that which they are" (ibid., 97; my italics). The paradox, of course, lies in the fact that God, being maximally infinite, can exist *in* finite things. Cusa's answer is that He is in them by way of contraction: just as they are "enfolded" in Him, so He "unfolds" Himself in them: they are unfolded *from* Him. (On enfolding vs. unfolding, see bk. 2, chap. 6.)

61. Ibid., 99. Cusa's statement that "all things are in all things" should be compared with Whitehead's remark that "everything is everywhere at all times" (Alfred North

Whitehead, *Science and the Modern World* [New York: Cambridge: Cambridge University Press, 1926], 93).

62. *On Learned Ignorance,* 98.

63. Concerning Ptolemy's conception of the earth as located at the center of the universe—entailing a strictly locatory sense of place—see Liba C. Taub, *Ptolemy's Universe: The Natural Philosophical and Ethical Foundations of Ptolemy's Astronomy* (Chicago: Open Court, 1993).

64. *On Learned Ignorance,* 114. The first part of the argument is as follows: "If [the world] had a [fixed] center, it would also have a [fixed] circumference" (ibid.). The premise behind this argument is not merely geometrical; the ultimate premise is that in God, that is, in the Absolute Maximum, "the center of the world coincides with the circumference" (ibid.).

65. Koyré, *From the Closed World to the Infinite Universe,* 23. It is revealing that Koyré *also* describes Cusa as "the last great philosopher of the dying Middle Ages, who first rejected the medieval cosmos-conception and to whom, as often as not, is ascribed the merit, or the crime, of having asserted the infinity of the universe" (p. 6). Cusa, like Crescas, is clearly a liminal figure—a true turning point in the history of place/space.

66. Paul O. Kristeller, *Eight Philosophers of the Italian Renaissance* (Stanford: Stanford University Press, 1964), 136.

67. Cited from Bruno's *De l'infinito universo e mondi* by Arthur O. Lovejoy, *The Great Chain of Being: A Study of the History of an Idea* (New York: Harper & Row, 1960), 118.

68. Lovejoy, *Great Chain of Being,* 118–119. The term "Scale of Being" is Lovejoy's, but it is implied in Bruno's statement that "innumerable grades of perfection must, through corporeal modes, unfold the divine incorporeal perfection" (Bruno, *On the Infinite Universe and Worlds,* trans. D. W. Singer, in *Giordano Bruno: His Life and Thought* (New York: Greenwood, 1968), 257; I shall employ Singer's translation from here on).

69. Bruno, *On the Infinite Universe and Worlds,* 256.

70. Ibid., 255.

71. Ibid., 254. Bruno adds: "Where there is no differentiation there is no distinction of quality and perhaps there is even less of quality where there is naught whatsoever" (ibid.). Recall that Aristotle rejected the void on similar grounds: the lack of differentiation in a void disallows motion within it.

72. Lovejoy, commenting on Bruno, in *Great Chain of Being,* 117.

73. *On the Infinite Universe and Worlds,* 254.

74. Ibid., 256. Dorothea Singer remarks that "Bruno uses 'universo' for the infinite universe. . . . [He] uses 'mondo' not only for our terrestrial globe, but for the universe as apprehended by our senses, and as conceived by the Aristotelians" (*Giordano Bruno,* 231 n 2). In contrast, "as a rule, Nicholas [of Cusa] uses 'world' and 'universe' interchangeably" (Hopkins, *Nicholas of Cusa on Learned Ignorance,* 194 n 46).

75. *On the Infinite Universe and Worlds,* 258.

76. Cited from *De Immenso* (1586) by Lovejoy in *Great Chain of Being,* p. 117.

77. Cited from *On the Infinite Universe and Worlds* by Lovejoy in *Great Chain of Being,* p. 118.

78. Both statements are from *On the Infinite Universe and Worlds,* 257. See also Bruno's remark in the same text that "the immense and infinite universe is the composition that results from such a space and so many bodies comprised within that space" [cited by Arthur D. Imerti, in G. Bruno, *The Expulsion of the Triumphant Beast,* 51).

79. *On the Infinite Universe and Worlds,* 257.

80. Ibid., 250.

81. "Since then we have experience that sense-perception deceiveth us concerning the surface of this globe on which we live, much more should we hold suspect the impression it giveth us of a limit to the starry sphere" (ibid., 251).

82. Nicholas of Cusa, *On Learned Ignorance,* 89. See also *On the Infinite Universe and Worlds,* 55–56.

83. In all strictness, the twain is a quatrain in the larger picture of Bruno's philosophy. Just as there are two orders of the finite—things and worlds—so there are two orders of the infinite: that of the universe and of God. Where God's infinity is an "all-comprehensive totality"—it pervades not just the universe but every part of it—that of the universe is a noncomprehensive totality since it pervades the whole but is not found in the parts (i.e., particular things). On this distinction, which Cusa would be the first to dispute, see Bruno's *On the Infinite Universe and Worlds,* 261–262.

84. I cite Lovejoy's translation of both versions in *Great Chain of Being,* p. 120, from the Fifth Dialogue of *Concerning the Cause, Principle, and One.*

85. Cusa, *On Learned Ignorance,* 88.

86. Ibid.; his italics.

87. "The glorious court of ye great God, whose unsercheable [*sic*] works invisible we may partly by these his visible conjecture, to whose infinit [*sic*] power and maiesty such an infinit place surmounting all other both in quantity and quality only is conueient" (cited by Lovejoy, *Great Chain of Being,* p. 116, from Digges's 1576 text, *A Perfit Description of the Caelestiall Orbes*).

88. *Concerning the Cause, Principle, and One,* 164.

89. On complication vs. explication, see *Concerning the Cause, Principle, and One,* 165–168. The language of *complicatio* and *explicatio* is Cusan in origin. It continues in Leibniz—as is stressed in Gilles Deleuze's recent interpretation: *The Fold: Leibniz and the Baroque,* trans. T. Conley (Minneapolis: University of Minnesota Press, 1993).

90. *Concerning the Cause, Principle, and One,* 160. By "immobile," Bruno means that there is no local motion of the universe as a whole: the universe "does not move itself locally, because it has nothing outside of itself to which to transport itself—since it is itself all" (ibid.).

91. Bruno attaches this phrase to imagination in *On the Infinite Universe and Worlds,* p. 264.

92. Lovejoy, *Great Chain of Being,* 116.

93. For further discussion, see Alfonso Ingegno, "The New Philosophy of Nature," in *The Cambridge History of Renaissance Philosophy,* ed. C. B. Schmitt and Q. Skinner (Cambridge: Cambridge University Press, 1988), 253 ff. ("The Struggle with Authority").

94. Concerning the critical tendency, see Charles B. Schmitt, "Experimental Evidence for and Against a Void: The Sixteenth-Century Arguments," *Isis* 58 (1967): 352. But it was also true that "fifteenth- and sixteenth-century commentaries on the *libri*

naturales [i.e., Aristotle's philosophy of nature] were more faithful to the text and more intent on discerning, and usually defending, its original meaning" (William A. Wallace, "Traditional Natural Philosophy," in *Cambridge History of Renaissance Philosophy,* 203).

95. For an account of this development, see Ingegno, "The New Philosophy of Nature," 236–244. As Grant asserts, "Whether taken independently or as part of the Neoplatonic tradition, or even as the major link in the *pia philosophia,* that great chain of pagan and Christian philosophers and theologians stretching from Zoroaster to Ficino and beyond, Plato was the central figure in the powerful eclectic philosophies that were developed in opposition to the dominant Aristotelian natural philosophy and cosmology of medieval and early modern scholasticism" (*Much Ado About Nothing,* 183).

96. I cite Benjamin Brickman's translation of a portion of Patrizi's *Nova de universis philosophia* (1587): "On Physical Space, Francesco Patrizi," *Journal of the History of Ideas* 4 (1943): 240–241; as slightly modified by Grant, *Much Ado About Nothing,* 204. Grant points out that Telesio had maintained already in 1565 that space is unlike anything else and that even certain scholastic thinkers of the time agreed— though on different grounds. Indeed, John Buridan and Walter Burley had speculated in the fourteenth century that space could not be captured in the mold of substance/ accident, but they had presumed that this was true only of a supernaturally created space, not of ordinary physical space.

97. Here Patrizi differs from Bruno, who held that space is essentially uncreated, a primal given, not unlike Platonic *chōra* in this regard. For Bruno, space does not emanate from God or characterize Him.

98. "On Physical Space," 225. See also Patrizi's statement that space is "that which all other things required for their existence, and could not exist without, but which could itself exist without any other things, and needed none of them for its own existence" (ibid., 225).

99. Ibid., 241.

100. Ibid., 226.

101. For Aristotle, as A. C. Crombie remarks, "dimensions could not exist apart from bodies with dimensions; he conceived dimensions as quantitative attributes of bodies, and no attribute could exist apart from the substance in which it inhered" (A. C. Crombie, *Medieval and Early Modern Science.* Vol. 2: *Science in the Later Middle Ages and Early Modern Times* [New York: Anchor, 1959], 36).

102. Patrizi himself invokes the Archytian argument that there can be no effective limit to space once we place ourselves on its edge. See Patrizi, "On Physical Space," pp. 236–237, for this argument, as well as Grant's comment in *Much Ado About Nothing,* p. 386 n 131.

103. Bruno, here less presciently modern, had contended that space is "impenetrable" and that space is at once receptive *and* impenetrable (*impenetrabile*). On his view, only discontinuous magnitudes are penetrable, that is, accessible *between* the disconnected parts. Concerning this doctrine, consult Bruno's late treatise *De immenso et innumerabilibus* (1591). Nevertheless, both Bruno and Patrizi consider space to be infinite, homogeneous, continuous, and immobile—and thus both anticipate seventeenth-century models. The crucial difference is that Patrizi bases all such properties expressly on three-dimensionality: "With a tridimensionality that offers no resistance

to the reception of bodies and can indeed penetrate bodies by yielding to them, space could coexist simultaneously with bodies and serve as their absolutely immobile container. By making the assumption that [tridimensional] space simultaneously yields to and penetrates bodies, Patrizi clearly indicated that space is continuous, immobile, and homogeneous" (Grant, *Much Ado About Nothing*, 202).

104. Patrizi, "On Physical Space," 231. See also Patrizi's statement that "when, however, it is said that *locus* is different from the *locatum*, this is to be taken to mean that every *locatum* is a body, while *locus* is not a body, otherwise two bodies will interpenetrate. Hence, *locus*, not being a body, will of necessity be a Space (*spacium*) provided with three dimensions—length, breadth, and depth—with which it receives into itself and holds the length, breadth, and depth of the enclosed body" (ibid.). (*Spacium* is medieval Latin for classical Latin *spatium*.)

105. Ibid., 241. In the chapter "On Air" in his *Pancosmia*, Patrizi says that "among bodies space is the most incorporeal of all because it is the rarest" (cited in Grant, *Much Ado About Nothing*, 386 n 139). For further discussion of light in Patrizi, see John Henry, "Francesco Patrizi da Cherso's Concept of Space and Its Later Influence," *Annals of Science* 36 (1979): 556 ff.

106. I say "no explicit trace," since the following passage points to something akin to room as discussed in the pages just above: "Neither of these two kinds of Space [i.e., of the world and of the universe] is a body. Each is capable of receiving a body. Each gives way to a body. . . . Neither offers any resistance to bodies and each cedes and leaves a *locus* for bodies in motion" ("On Physical Space," 238). The idea of "leaving a *locus*" for bodies is closely akin to the notion of "making room" for them.

107. See "On Physical Space," 236–237, as well as Grant's discussion in *Much Ado About Nothing*, 201–202. Recall that for Bruno *cosmic* space, the space of *this* world, is also finite and infinite at once.

108. Patrizi also believes in minute interstitial vacua within the world. On these internal vacua, see Henry, *Francesco Patrizi*, 563–564. Medieval thinkers had also posited interstitial vacua: e.g., Nicholas of Autrecourt (see Grant, *Much Ado About Nothing*, 75).

109. Gianfrancesco Pico della Mirandola, *Ex vanitatis doctrinae gentium et veritatis Christianae disciplinae* (composed between 1502 and 1514), 6, chap. 4, p. 768, cited in C. B. Schmitt, *Gianfrancesco Pico della Mirandola (1469–1533) and His Critique of Aristotle* (The Hague: Nijhoff, 1967), 140–141. Gianfrancesco was the nephew of the more famous Giovanni Pico. The younger Pico was decisively influenced by Philoponus and by Crescas.

110. Tommaso Campanella, *Universalis philosophiae*, bk. 2, chap. 13, p. 288; cited in Grant, *Much Ado About Nothing*, 195.

111. Campanella, *Metafisica*, vol. 2, bk. 10, chap. 1, art. 5; cited in Grant, *Much Ado About Nothing*, 195.

112. Bruno, *On the Infinite Universe and Worlds*, 253. Bruno doubtless learned of the conundrum in reading Lucretius, *De rerum natura*—or perhaps Cicero, who treats it in his *De natura deorum*, I, 20, 54. A separate history of the fate of Archytas's provocative thought experiment could well be written.

113. "Locum nihil esse aliud, quam spatium hactenus descriptum" (the chapter title to Gassendi's discussion of *locus*) in his *Operia Omnia* (Lyon, 1658), III, 216. I owe the citation and the translation to Schmitt, *Gianfrancesco Pico della Mirandola*,

143. The nondistinction between place and space can also be seen in Bernardino Telesio's *De rerum natura* (composed between 1544 and 1553). For Telesio, perhaps the first Renaissance thinker to posit an infinite *homogeneous* space, "place" (*locus*) possesses the very character of receptivity that both Bruno and Patrizi attribute explicitly and exclusively to "space" (*spacium*)—a character that will survive, virtually unscathed, in Kant's idea that space is one of the two great forms of human sensible intuition regarded as "receptivity." Campanella, moreover, believed that the ultimate source of spatial structure, especially its three-dimensionality, is to be found in the mind: the mind (*mens*) "divides space [and makes] a line, a surface, and a depth, since it is in a metaphysical world of a higher order" (*Metafisica*, 2: 370; cited in Grant, *Much Ado About Nothing*, 196; see also Campanella's *Physiologia* [1592] for further discussion).

114. Patrizi, "On Physical Space," 239–240. Indeed, in another statement, cited in fuller form above from Patrizi's *Nova de Universis Philosophia*, even the vacuum is replaced by space: "The vacuum itself is nothing else than three-dimensional Space" (ibid., 231). Notice once more the stringently reductive language of "nothing else," thus enabling Patrizi to propose that the vacuum, the very archetype of space for many thinkers (including Patrizi himself on occasion), to be superseded by space, its own ectype!

115. Thus I would disagree with Wallace's claim that "the development of thought . . . from the onset of the thirteenth century to the mid-seventeenth may be likened more to a continuum than to a series of discrete jumps" ("Traditional Natural Philosophy," 202). There may well be a continuum from the thirteenth to the sixteenth century, but the sixteenth century is a genuine turning point, marking a paradigm shift in matters of place and space.

116. "Even in matter we find appetite and sense, so why not in space as well?" (cited from Campanella's *Del senso delle cose*, bk. 1, chap. 12, in Grant, *Much Ado*, 196, where Grant remarks that Campanella "endowed space with sense and feeling"). To point to what is special in the sixteenth-century grasp of space is not to deny the deep connections between sixteenth- and seventeenth-century speculation on space: Kepler was decisively influenced by Bruno, and Gassendi by Patrizi. On Kepler's explicit acknowledgment of Bruno's influence—as admitted expressly to Galileo—see Ingegno, "The New Philosophy of Nature," 261–262. On Patrizi's profound effect on Gassendi, see Grant, *Much Ado About Nothing*, 389 n 165: "Gassendi, in his posthumously published *Syntagma philosophicum* (Lyon, 1658), mentioned Telesio, Patrizi, Campanella, and Kenelm Digby. Of these authors, it was only Patrizi's spatial doctrine that was described by Gassendi."

117. Theodor Lipps, cited in Rudolf Arnheim, *The Dynamics of Architectural Form* (Berkeley: University of California Press, 1971), 86. Concerning Campanella's idea that space expands indefinitely, see Grant, *Much Ado About Nothing*, 196–198.

Interim

1. Alluding precisely to Aristotle, Bergson remarks on the importance of the qualitative dimension of place in contrast with early modern conceptions: "Instead of an empty and unlimited space, [Aristotle describes] places which are not only limited by their size but also defined by their quality" ("L'Idée de Lieu chez Aristote," *Les Études*

Notes to Pages 134–136

Bergsoniennes [1949], 2:100; this is a translation of Bergson's Latin dissertation of 1889, *"Quid Aristoteles de loco senserit"*).

2. Damascius, *Damascii diadochi dubitationes et solutiones de primis principiis,* ed. C. A. Ruelle (Paris, 1889); translated in S. Sambursky, ed., *The Concept of Place in Late Neoplatonism* (Jerusalem: Israel Academy of Sciences and Humanities, 1982), 95. "Place" here translates *topos.*

3. Ibid.

4. Recourse to "room" as a mediating term, however suggestive it may be, here only displaces the problem of how place and space are related to each other. The displacement is evident in Philoponus's claim that "the cosmic extension, which is the room (*chōra*) and the place (*topos*) of the universe, does not have in itself any differences" (from Philoponus, *In Aristotelis physicorum libros quinque posteriores commentaria,* 569, lines 13–15; as translated in Sambursky, *The Concept of Place in Late Neoplatonism,* 119). The bare juxtaposition of *chōra* and *topos,* the two equiprimordial terms of ancient discourse on place, is especially striking.

5. William Gilbert, *De mundo nostro sublunari philosophia nova* (Amsterdam, 1651), bk. 2, chap. 8, p. 144; cited in Max Jammer, *Concepts of Space: The History of Theories of Space in Physics* (Cambridge, Mass.: Harvard University Press, 1969), 90. The Latin is *locus nihil est, non existit, vim non habet.*

6. The full sentence is "It is no less necessary for matter always to have some form than for region, or space, or place to have some body" (Pierre Gassendi, *Syntagma philosophicum,* section on Physics, translated by C. B. Brush, *The Selected Works of Pierre Gassendi* [New York: Johnson, 1972], 386). But Gassendi also indulges in the more usual bivalent format when he compares "time, or duration" to "place, or space" (ibid., 395).

7. The phrase "sum total of all places" as a description of Aristotle's *koinos topos* is from Jammer, *Concepts of Space,* p. 22. Jammer remarks that "of great interest from our point of view is a passage in Aristotle's *Physics* [208b9–14] in which space is likened (using a modern expression) to a field of force" (p. 19). (In chapter 3 I have pointed to other relativist aspects of Aristotle's idea of place such as the relativity of certain aspects of place to the bodily position of the person in a place.) For further treatment of the modern relevance of Aristotle's model of space, see S. Sambursky, *The Physical World of the Greeks* (Princeton: Princeton University Press, 1987), 92 ff., esp. p. 96: "Aristotle's combination of geometry and matter to form his concept of place is not unlike the conception of space in the General Theory of Relativity." For a discussion of Aristotle as anticipating certain notions of early modern physics—e.g., motion and speed—see Edward Hussey, *Aristotle's Physics, Books III and IV* (Oxford: Clarendon Press, 1983), 176 ff.

8. Philoponus, *In Aristotelis physicorum libros quinque posteriores commentaria;* as translated in Sambursky, *The Concept of Place in Late Neoplatonism,* p. 119. Philoponus is driven to place-relativism in his rejection of the idea of preexisting natural places à la Aristotle: "Place does not have any power to make bodies move to their proper places. It is rather that the bodies seek to preserve their arrangement" (cited from *In Aristotelis physicorum libros quinque posteriores commentaria,* by Richard Sorabji, *Matter, Space, and Motion* [Ithaca: Cornell University Press, 1988], 213). But, while refusing the infinity of space, Philoponus affirms its ultimate absoluteness in the idea of a single volumetric whole of space, empty in principle but always filled in fact.

9. The first statement is taken from Harold Höffding, *A History of Modern Philosophy* (New York: Dover, 1955), 125: "Since the horizon [for Bruno] forms itself anew around every place occupied by the spectator as its central point, every determination of place must be relative." The second statement is from Bruno's dialogue *De l'infinito* as cited and translated in Paul Henri Michel, *The Cosmology of Giordano Bruno*, trans. R. E. W. Maddison (London: Methuen, 1973), 168. (The phrase "a portion of space" will recur in Newton's *Mathematical Principles of Natural Philosophy*.) Bruno suggests an interesting compromise: relativism belongs to place, whereas infinitism is true of space. Places, always plural, belong to particular worlds—they are how these worlds are articulated from within—whereas infinite space, strictly singular, is the ambience for all such worlds: "There is a single general space, a single vast immensity which we . . . declare to be infinite" (Bruno, *On the Infinite Universe and Worlds*, trans. D. W. Singer, in *Giordano Bruno* [New York: Schuman, 1950], 363).

10. The bare mention occurs in Kant's almost equally bare allusion to "motion" as "alteration of place": see Immanuel Kant, *Critique of Pure Reason*, trans. N. K. Smith (New York: St. Martin's Press, 1965), A 32 B 48, p. 76. Another side of Kant's attitude toward place, however, will emerge in the discussion at the beginning of chapter 8.

Chapter Six: Modern Space as Absolute

1. Concerning mechanism in the seventeenth century, Collingwood remarks that "instead of being an organism, the natural world is a machine: a machine in the literal and proper sense of the word, an arrangement of bodily parts designed and put together and set going for a definite purpose by an intelligent mind outside itself " (R. G. Collingwood, *The Idea of Nature* [Oxford: Oxford University Press, 1945], 5). The ultimacy of extension and motion is perhaps first proposed by Francis Bacon: as A. C. Crombie remarks, "Bacon was one of the earliest modern writers to propose the complete reduction of all events to matter and motion" (A. C. Crombie, *Medieval and Early Modern Science* [New York: Doubleday, 1959], 2:290). Boyle also adhered to this reduction—as, prototypically, did Descartes and Hobbes.

2. Francis Bacon, *Novum organum*, xlv; cited in M. H. Nicolson, *The Breaking of the Circle: Studies in the Effect of the "New Science" Upon Seventeenth-Century Poetry* (New York: Columbia University Press, 1960), 9. The circularity of the heavens is an emblematic instance of what Bacon calls an "Idol of the Tribe."

3. For my own version of this story, see *Getting Back into Place: Toward a Renewed Understanding of the Place-World* (Bloomington: Indiana University Press, 1993), chap. 1.

4. Another candidate for the ur-premise of the century is "local motion." Crombie, commenting on Descartes, makes this claim: "All natural phenomena could eventually, when sufficiently analyzed, be reduced to a single kind of change, local motion; and that conclusion became the most influential belief of seventeenth-century science" (Crombie, *Medieval and Early Modern Science*, 164). But it can be argued—and Whitehead would argue—that local motion is logically contained in the paradigm of simple location.

5. Alfred North Whitehead, *Science and the Modern World* (Cambridge: Cambridge University Press, 1926), 72. "Apart from [simple location]," adds Whitehead, "the scheme is incapable of expression" (ibid.).

6. Ibid., 62; his italics. Whitehead's own view is that "among the primary elements of nature as apprehended in our immediate experience, there is no element whatever which possesses this character of simple location" (ibid.).

7. "Curiously enough, this character of simple location holds whether we look on a region of space-time as determined absolutely or relatively" (ibid., 62). Thus the doctrine of simple location is "independent of the controversy between the absolutist and the relativist views of space or of time" (p. 72). Concerning "absolute presupposition," see R. G. Collingwood, *Essay on Metaphysics* (Oxford: Clarendon Press, 1940), chap. 1.

8. Whitehead, *Science and the Modern World*, 62; my italics.

9. Ibid., 64. Another formulation of the fallacy is as follows: "By a process of constructive abstraction we can arrive at abstractions which *are* the simply-located bits of material" (ibid., 72; my italics).

10. Max Jammer, *Concepts of Space: The History of Theories of Space in Physics*, 2d ed. (Cambridge, Mass.: Harvard University Press, 1969), 91, commenting on the doctrine of William Gilbert as contained in the latter's *De mundo nostro sublunari philosophia nova* (Amsterdam, 1651). Gilbert's work on magnetism had convinced him that an attractive force (i.e., gravity) passes through all material objects irrespective of the particular places they occupy at the time.

11. Jammer, *Concepts of Space*, 90.

12. Crombie, *Medieval and Early Modern Science*, 2:159. Whether infinite space was "geometrized" in the seventeenth century is itself a controversial question: Koyré assumed it was, but Grant expresses doubts: see Edward Grant, *Much Ado About Nothing* (Cambridge: Cambridge University Press, 1981), 232–234. On Gassendi's atomism, see M. J. Osler, "Baptizing Epicurean Atomism: Pierre Gassendi on the Immortality of the Soul," in V. Chappell, ed., *Grotius to Gassendi*, vol. 2 of *Essays on Early Modern Philosophers* (New York: Garland, 1992), 239–260; and especially L. S. Joy, *Gassendi the Atomist: Advocate of History in an Age of Science* (Cambridge: Cambridge University Press, 1987). Gassendi also shows the influence of the Stoics: see Grant, *Much Ado About Nothing*, 217, 213.

13. Jammer comments, "The independence, autonomy, and priority of space, all vigorously propounded by Gassendi, were a timely concession to the requirements of the new physics. . . . Gassendi's conception of space became the foundation, both of the atomistic theories of the seventeenth century with their discontinuous matter filling continuous space, on the small scale, and of celestial mechanics on the large scale" (*Concepts of Space*, 94). But joint credit for the explicitation of such space should also be given to Patrizi, who was a crucial influence on Gassendi: "Three-dimensional void space as described by Patrizi and Gassendi would eventually attract powerful supporters who would make it the absolute space of the new physics and cosmology" (Grant, *Much Ado About Nothing*, 221; see also p. 388 n 162, 163).

14. On these scientific achievements, see Crombie, *Medieval and Early Modern Science*, 2:159.

15. Pierre Gassendi, *Physics*, in his *Syntagma philosophicum*, as translated in *The Selected Works of Pierre Gassendi*, ed. C. B. Brush (New York: Johnson Reprint, 1972), 385. The obvious similarity between this statement of Gassendi's and Philoponus's position should not be altogether surprising, since the Greek commentaries of Philoponus were widely disseminated from the sixteenth century onward: see Charles

B. Schmitt, "Philoponus' Commentary on Aristotle's *Physics* in the Sixteenth Century," in *Philoponus and the Rejection of Aristotelian Science,* ed. R. Sorabji (Ithaca: Cornell University Press, 1987), 210–230.

16. In Gassendi's own words, "Aristotle denies that any other dimensions except the corporeal exist or that there exists any interval (*diastēma*) beyond the body's that is contained by the vase or in place" (Brush, *Selected Works,* 385).

17. Brush, *Selected Works,* 387.

18. Concerning Gassendi's invocation of the Archytian conundrum, see Grant, *Much Ado About Nothing,* 389 n 168. For Gassendi's cosmic thought experiments, see Brush, *Selected Works,* 383–385, 386, 387, and esp. p. 136: "Imagine that not only the earth, but also the entire universe was reduced to nothing, hence that these spaces were empty as they were before God created the world." The near-equation between "empty" and "nothing" in this last sentence is especially striking—as if to say that infinite space, the void, and nothingness are somehow equivalent.

19. On this heretical point, see Brush, *Selected Works,* 388. On p. 390 Gassendi says that space is "not one of those things that can be created."

20. On space's boundlessness and immobility, see Brush, *Selected Works,* 388.

21. Brush, *Selected Works,* 388.

22. Ibid., 384. Grant points out that Gassendi is not the first to declare space to be independent of substance/accident classification—both Patrizi and David Gorlaeus hold first honors—but he is certainly the most persuasive: see Grant, *Much Ado About Nothing,* 209–210.

23. Brush, *Selected Works,* 384–385. On p. 384 Gassendi says that place and time—that is, *space* and time—are "certain incorporeal natures of a different kind from those ordinarily called substances or accidents."

24. Ibid., 383. The subject of this sentence is "place and time," but it is entirely characteristic of Gassendi in the *Syntagma philosophicum,* his final summing-up, to regard "place" and "space" as interchangeable. The interchange often occurs from one sentence to the next. Thus, having just asserted that God exists "in every place," Gassendi adds immediately: "That God be *in space* is thought to be a characteristic external to His essence" (Gassendi, "The Reality of the Infinite Void According to Aristotle," trans. M. Capek and W. Emge, from the *Syntagma philosophicum* in M. Capek, ed., *The Concepts of Space and Time: Their Structure and Their Development* [Dordrecht: Reidel, 1976], 94; my italics).

25. Brush, *Selected Works,* 385. It follows that "even if there were no bodies, there would still remain both an unchanging place and an evolving time" (p. 384).

26. Gassendi, "The Reality of the Infinite Void According to Aristotle," 93.

27. On the Empyrean, see Duhem, *Le Système du monde: Histoire des doctrines cosmologiques de Platon à Copernic* (Paris: Hermann, 1913–1959), 7:197–200.

28. Gassendi, "The Reality of the Infinite Void According to Aristotle," 94.

29. Brush, *Selected Works,* 385.

30. Ibid., 385; my italics.

31. Ibid., 384; my italics.

32. Ibid., 389. It is this "negative quality" that allows Gassendi to claim that space is uncreated: it is beneath God's dignity to create things with negative proclivities of any kind. For further discussion, see Grant, *Much Ado About Nothing,* 210–212.

33. Jammer, *Concepts of Space,* 94. Chapter 4, "The Concept of Absolute Space,"

traces out the deep continuities between Newton and his philosophical and religious forebears.

34. The *Timaeus* and the Scholium of Newton's *Principia* are "the two great cosmological documents guiding Western thought" (A. N. Whitehead, *Process and Reality*, ed. D. W. Sherburne and D. R. Griffin [New York: Free Press, 1978], 94).

35. Isaac Newton, *Mathematical Principles of Natural Philosophy*, trans. A. Motte, ed. F. Cajori (Berkeley: University of California Press, 1962), 1:6. (This is from the "Scholium" added to the opening "Definitions.") I shall refer to Newton's text hereafter as *Principia*.

36. This last trait, though not named as such by Newton, follows from his claim that "in philosophical disquisitions, we ought to abstract from our senses, and consider things themselves, distinct from what are only sensible measures of them" (*Principia*, 8). Taken in conjunction with trait (2), this claim is tantamount to the fallacy of misplaced concreteness. As Whitehead says explicitly, "Readers [of the Scholium], and almost certainly Newton himself . . . fall into what I have elsewhere termed the 'fallacy of misplaced concreteness' " (*Process and Reality*, 93).

37. *Principia*, I, 6.

38. Ibid., I, 8.

39. Ibid., 6–7; his italics. This citation constitutes all of section 3 of the Scholium.

40. For a discussion of the paradox here mentioned, see Jammer, *Concepts of Space*, 76–78.

41. Newton seems to have been drawn to this radical thesis long before the *Principia* was concluded: "In a manuscript he never published, Newton argued that bodies might just be special regions of space, specially endowed with certain causal characteristics by God" (A. Koslow, "Ontological and Ideological Issues of the Classical Theory of Space and Time," in *Motion and Time, Space, and Matter: Interrelations in the History of Philosophy and Science*, ed. P. K. Machamer and R. G. Turnbull (Columbus: Ohio State University Press, 1976), 225). The text in question is "De Gravitatione et Aequipondio Fluidorum," probably written between 1664 and 1668. But the phrase "in the whole body," taken from the *Principia*, indicates that Newton still entertained, twenty years later, the same radical idea that (as Koyré puts it) "place—*locus*—is thus something which is *in* the bodies, and *in which* bodies are in their turn" (*From the Closed World to the Infinite Universe* [Baltimore: Johns Hopkins University Press, 1957], 163; his italics). Notice how such a claim reverses Aristotle's position, according to which bodies are in place to begin with and not vice versa.

42. Jammer, *Concepts of Space*, 110; his italics.

43. *Principia*, I, 9.

44. Ibid., I, 7.

45. Ibid.

46. Furthermore, as one recent commentator notes, "the existence of absolute motion or rest cannot be established merely from the existence of relative motion or rest" (Florian Cajori, "An Historical and Explanatory Appendix" to the *Principia*, II, 640). Relative motion or rest makes perceptible only what happens imperceptibly in absolute motion or rest. The same point applies for absolute versus relative place—or absolute versus relative space.

47. *Principia*, I, 8.

48. In the same early manuscript mentioned in an earlier footnote, Newton explic-

itly maintained a relational view of space: "He claimed that regions of space (and moments of time) are individuated solely by their relation to all other regions of space (or all other moments)" (Koslow, "Ontological and Ideological Issues," 225, with reference to "De Gravitatione et aequipondio fluidorum").

49. Jammer, *Concepts of Space,* 101.

50. *Principia,* I, 8.

51. Ibid.; my italics.

52. I take the phrase "Newtonian Revolution" from I. Bernard Cohen's *The Newtonian Revolution* (Cambridge: Cambridge University Press, 1980). It is striking that Cohen's excellent book, one of the most comprehensive studies of Newton to have appeared in any language, does not discuss the concept of place at all, not even in passing. Here, as in other comparable cases, the studious "second look" goes further in extirpating an ill-fitting notion from a theoretical corpus than does the author of that corpus himself. As we have seen in a number of instances, for example, that of Damascius and of Philoponus, ambivalence toward place persists tenaciously but revealingly in the first look, and more particularly in the actual text, of the founder of a given tradition.

53. Koyré, *From the Closed World to the Infinite Universe,* 169.

54. On Galileo's geometrizing, see Edward Husserl, "The Origin of Geometry," in *The Crisis of European Sciences and Transcendental Phenomenology,* trans. D. Carr (Evanston: Northwestern University Press, 1970), 353–378; and Alexandre Koyré, *Galilean Studies,* trans. J. Mepham (Atlantic Highlands, N.J.: Humanities Press, 1978), chaps. 1, 2, esp. p. 78: "Galileo's thorough-going geometrisation *transfers to space that which is valid for time*" (his italics).

55. *Principia,* I, xvii. Concerning the unit of geometry and mechanics in Newton, see Jammer, *Concepts of Space,* 96–97.

56. The first citation in this sentence is from "The System of the World," *Principia,* II, 497; the second is from ibid., p. 415. On the distinction between material and immaterial ether, see Grant, *Much Ado About Nothing,* 247. In the wake of Gassendi and Gilbert, Newton espouses an astringent atomism in which forces of inertia and gravity are located in material particles and not in the places they occupy. The evacuation of physical forces from space and their transference to mere particles have the effect of further disempowering the places that form the subdominant delineations of the parts of absolute space.

57. Cited from "De Gravitatione et aequipondio fluidorum," in Koslow, "Ontological and Ideological Issues," 233; his italics.

58. Koslow, "Ontological and Ideological Issues," 233; his italics.

59. To Newton's claim that "*something* is there because spaces are there, although nothing more than that," Edward Grant responds: " 'nothing more', that is, except God Himself " (*Much Ado About Nothing,* 243). If this is true, *God takes the place of (absolute) place itself! Deus sive Locus!*

60. *Principia,* II, 545. Newton's first description of God is more Anselmian: God is "a Being eternal, infinite, absolutely perfect" (ibid., 544).

61. *Principia,* II, 545.

62. Ibid.

63. Cited from "De Gravitatione et aequipondio fluidorum," in *Unpublished Scientific Papers of Isaac Newton, A Selection from the Portsmouth Collection in the*

398tes to Pages 148–150

University Library, Cambridge, ed. A. R. Hall and M. B. Hall (Cambridge: Cambridge University Press, 1962), 137. The Hall edition gives the complete text of the essay from which Koslow cites.

64. Space "is as it were an emanent effect of God, or a disposition of all being" ("De Gravitatione et aequipondio fluidorum," 132). "Emanent" signifies "flowing from" God as source.

65. *Principia,* II, 545; his italics.

66. Newton, *Opticks: Or a Treatise of the Reflections, Refractions, Inflections, and Colours of Light* (New York: Dover, 1952), 370; my italics. I have changed "Sensory" to "Sensorium." A few pages later, Newton adds that "the Organs of Sense are not for enabling the Soul to perceive the Species of Things in its Sensorium, but only for conveying them thither; and God has no need of such Organs, he being every where present to the Things themselves" (ibid., 403). On the history of the crucial qualifier *tanquam,* which Newton supposedly added as a rebuttal to critiques by Leibniz and others, see A. Koyré and I. B. Cohen, "The Case of the Missing *Tanquam:* Leibniz, Newton and Clarke," *Isis* 52 (1961): 555–566. Koyré and Cohen argue that a "sensorium," properly understood, is not an "organ" and thus that God may well possess a spatial sensorium after all.

67. "De Gravitatione et aequipondio fluidorum," 136. It is again striking how much of Newton's mature doctrine—even the theological import—is anticipated in this early essay: in the General Scholium of the *Principia* Newton will say that God "endures forever, and is everywhere present, and by existing always and everywhere (*semper et ubique*) He constitutes duration and space."

68. "De Gravitatione et aequipondio fluidorum," 133. Another, more medieval way to put the same Archytian point is that "there exists a greater extension than any we can imagine" (ibid., 134).

69. Cited in Frank Manuel, *The Religion of Isaac Newton* (Oxford: Clarendon Press, 1974), 35 n; his italics. I have replaced the Hebrew letters with "makom."

70. "Of the Day of Judgment and World to Come," cited in Manuel, *Religion of Isaac Newton,* 101. Newton complicates his case when he adds that "the enjoyment of his blessing may be various according to the variety of places, and according to this variety he is said to be more in one place [and] less in another" (ibid.). But this appears to contradict the notion that God is truly ubiquitous—a character that does not properly admit of degrees.

71. These are More's objections to Holenmerism as reported by Grant, *Much Ado About Nothing,* 223–235.

72. Koyré observes that in "De Gravitatione et aequipondio fluidorum," Newton equates space in general with "God's space." In the *Principia,* "he still thinks so; but he does not *say* so; he calls it instead absolute space" (A. Koyré, *Newtonian Studies* [Chicago: University of Chicago Press, 1968], 104; his italics).

73. The phrase "the boundless extent of God's existence with respect to his ubiquity and eternity" occurs in the same "avertissement" as that in which *makom* was cited just above: Manuel, *Religion of Isaac Newton,* 35 n. I should add that *makom* may never have meant a merely particular place but a supernal and supernatural place that was already, even in early Hebrew theology, on its way to infinite space. (On this last point, see Jammer, *Concepts of Space,* chap. 2, "Judaeo-Christian Ideas about Place.") It is also striking to notice how even as careful a commentator as Edward

Grant, when commenting on Newton's notion of God, slides quickly from "place" to "space" or vice versa within one and the same sentence: "As the place in which God is omnipresent, space must be eternal" (*Much Ado About Nothing*, 243); "infinite space may not be God's organ, but it is surely the place where He is dimensionally omnipresent, not figuratively but literally" (p. 246).

74. *Principia*, II, 544: "The word God usually signifies *Lord;* but every lord is not a God. It is the dominion of a spiritual being which constitutes a God."

75. Cited from More's *Enchiridium metaphysicum*, chap. 7, by Koyré, *From the Closed World to the Infinite Universe*, 151.

76. As Grant puts it pithily, "because there is only one infinite spirit, infinitely extended space must inhere in God Himself" (*Much Ado About Nothing*, 227). But the converse also holds: God must inhere in infinitely extended space—thanks to More's ultimate premise that "everything, whether corporeal or incorporeal, possesses extension" (ibid., 223). I have profited from Grant's entire discussion of More (pp. 221–228) as well as from Koyré's treatment in *From the Closed World to the Infinite Universe*, chaps. 5, 6.

77. Letter to Descartes of December 2, 1648; cited in Koyré, *From the Closed World to the Infinite Universe*, 111.

78. As Grant remarks, "If Newton conceived infinite, extended, void space as God's attribute, it surely follows that God is an extended being" (*Much Ado About Nothing*, 244). But only More was willing to commit himself *explicitly* to this thesis: he took "the incredibly bold and unheard-of-step" of claiming that "God must be a three-dimensional being" (ibid., 223). The step is unheard-of in Greek and medieval cosmologies—much as these systems of thought might have been tempted, by the rigor of cosmologic, to take this step themselves. Where the infinite universe that surrounds the closed material world is at once nondimensional and (qua unextended) imaginary in the thinking of Bradwardine—who tended to locate God precisely in this "imaginary infinite void" (*De causa Dei contra Pelagium*)—now God is at one with an infinite, extended, and real void that permeates the entire universe, including the known material world here below. It was in the Renaissance, as we have seen, that this momentous step first became fully possible: "From the introduction of the Greek concept of a separate, infinite, three-dimensional void space in the sixteenth century to Spinoza's *Ethics* in 1677, approximately 150 years, space had become indistinguishable from God Himself. Spinoza took the final step and conflated God, extension, matter, and space as one infinite, indivisible substance. One could go no further and few, if any, would go as far" (Grant, *Much Ado About Nothing*, 229). It should be noted, however, that Spinoza distinguished between the perceptible extension of ordinary material entities and the extension of God: only the latter is infinite and eternal and is an object of understanding, not of perception.

Chapter Seven: Modern Space as Extensive

1. Letter of February 5, 1649, as translated by A. Kenny, *Descartes: Philosophical Letters* (Oxford: Clarendon Press, 1970), 240.

2. Ibid., 240. For Descartes, the imagination, capable of entertaining corporeal things alone, is itself a corporeal faculty, one that is intrinsically allied with the body.

3. Ibid., 239; my italics.

4. Ibid., 239. In the case of God, Descartes also needs to be able to say that He is not just in one place but *everywhere*—and has effects everywhere without being extended in any strict sense. Hence Descartes's admission to More that "God's essence must be present everywhere for His power to be able to manifest itself everywhere; but I deny it is there in the manner of an extended thing" (letter of August 1649 to More). Elsewhere, Descartes develops the idea of a "power" exerted by God or angels *on* extended substance, without that power itself being based in any such substance: for example, in the letter of April 15, 1649, where Descartes says that "in God and angels and in our mind I conceive there to be no extension of substance, but only extension of power" (*Philosophical Letters,* 249, letter to More, April 15, 1649; see also pp. 239, 250). Newton, despite his extreme skepticism concerning Descartes's theology, will claim similarly that (in Koyré's words) "extension is a certain effect of God, *effectus emanitivus,* and also, or thus, a certain affection of every entity, that is of everything that is" (*Newtonian Studies* [Cambridge, Mass.: Harvard University Press, 1965], 86).

5. *Philosophical Letters,* 239–240; letter to More of February 5, 1649; my italics.

6. Ibid., 239. God is not extended in any *strict* sense, but can be considered as "extended in power," that is, in His effects on the properly extended world. In this regard, Descartes meets More halfway, given that the latter had claimed that "God, *in his own manner,* is extended" (letter to Descartes of December 11, 1648; my italics). But it remains that for Descartes incorporeal substances lack the very criteria—that is, *partes extra partes,* shapes, and exclusive location in place—that would render any agreement complete. Koyré, speaking on behalf of More, puts it this way: "Descartes was right in looking for substance to support extension. He was wrong in finding it in matter. The infinite, extended entity that embraces and pervades everything is indeed a substance. But it is not matter. It is Spirit; not *a* spirit, but *the* Spirit, that is, God" (Koyré, *From the Closed World to the Infinite Universe* [Baltimore: Johns Hopkins University Press, 1957], 147; his italics).

7. *Philosophical Letters,* 240 (letter to More of February 5, 1649).

8. Ibid., 240. According to Descartes, when we *think* that there is empty space—as we do in childhood, or as the Greek Atomists did—we are only imagining empty *places:* "All places in which we perceive nothing are void" (ibid., 240). Place is at once a criterion of exclusion in the realm of imagined space and an exemplar of false, or at least naive, imagining when we attempt to think of empty space.

9. Descartes's contempt for the ancient Atomists comes through in the same letter to More of February 5, 1649: "I [do] not hesitate to disagree with great men such as Epicurus, Democritus, and Lucretius, because I saw that they were guided by no solid reason, but only by the false prejudice with which we have all been imbued from our earliest years. . . . Since Epicurus, Democritus, and Lucretius never overcame this prejudice, I have no obligation to follow their authority" (*Philosophical Letters,* 240). For an extended comparison between Descartes and Newton—that most modern of Atomists—see Koyré, *Newtonian Studies,* chap. 3, "Newton and Descartes," esp. Appendix M, "Motion, Space, and Place."

10. In contrast with Aristotle (for whom dimension is in effect direction) Descartes defines dimension in a strictly quantitative way as "the mode and aspect according to which a subject is considered to be measurable" (*Rules for the Direction of the Mind,*

trans. E. S. Haldane and G. R. T. Ross in *The Philosophical Works of Descartes* [Cambridge: Cambridge University Press, 1973], 1:61). On the relationship between extension, quantity, and volume, see Descartes, *Principles of Philosophy*, trans. V. R. Miller and R. P. Miller (Dordrecht: Reidel, 1983), Part II, sec. 9. For an excellent discussion of Descartes's doctrine of extension, see Gerd Buchdahl, *Metaphysics and the Philosophy of Science: The Classical Origins, Descartes to Kant* (Oxford: Blackwell, 1969), 90–104. I owe this last reference to Patrick Heelan.

11. *Rules for the Direction of the Mind,* 57.

12. Ibid., 58. On "corporeal images," see p. 57. At p. 59, Descartes says that "it is both possible and necessary to use the imagination as an aid." On the particular use of imagination in this context, which we have already seen to be importantly at work in Descartes's answer to More, see Rule XIV: "that extension has to be brought before the mind exclusively by means of bare shapes depicted in the [corporeal] imagination" (N. K. Smith's translation of the second sentence in this rule: N. K. Smith, trans., *Descartes' Philosophical Writings* [London: Macmillan, 1952], 85; in italics in the text). On the role of imagination in Descartes's philosophy, see Véronique Fóti, "The Cartesian Imagination," *Philosophy and Phenomenological Research* 46 (1986): 631–642, and my *Imagining: A Phenomenological Study* (Bloomington: Indiana University Press, 1976), 222–223.

13. "By extension we do not here mean anything distinct and separable from the extended object itself" (*Rules for the Direction of the Mind,* 57). In other words, extension is equivalent to extended body, that is, to the magnitude of a body.

14. Descartes, *Philosophical Letters,* 184. For Newton's variant views on extension, see Koyré, *Newtonian Studies,* 83–93.

15. *Philosophical Letters,* 62 (letter of January 9, 1639).

16. Norman Kemp Smith puts it this way: "One part of space cannot be conceived as itself visiting another part of space; if motion is to be possible (and experience indubitably testifies to its occurrence), it must be motion of a something which, as *occupying* space, can occupy now one part of it and now another, i.e., as a something, a 'subject', which while always conforming to spatial requirements is yet, in respect of this capacity for motion, so far independent of them" (N. K. Smith, *New Studies in the Philosophy of Descartes: Descartes as Pioneer* [New York: Macmillan, 1966], 193; see also Buchdahl, *Metaphysics,* 96). Here we must ask: Is not a "part" of space itself a place? Does not motion point to the unrescindability of place as much as to the distinction between matter and space? At one point Descartes himself says that movement is "nothing other than *the action by which some body travels from one place to another*" (*Principles of Philosophy,* 50; his italics). But the problematic relationship between place and space in Descartes's thinking renders this statement—to which we shall return below—less than fully illuminating.

17. *Principles of Philosophy,* 43–44. N. K. Smith refers to Descartes's "admission that extension considered in and by itself is a mere abstraction and that qua existent it is indistinguishable from the extended" (*Descartes' Philosophical Writings,* 192). If this were not so, Descartes would be headed—as he is dangerously close to doing in the citation above from the *Principles*—toward a commitment to the Philoponean distinction between "spatial" and "bodily" extension.

18. Thus we circle back to the debate between Descartes and More. More's first letter to Descartes (December 11, 1648) says: "God, in his own manner, is extended

and spread out, and is therefore an extended thing. And yet He is not that body, or matter, which your mind—ingenious artist that it is—has so skillfully turned into globules and striated particles. Hence, the concept of *extended thing* is broader than that of *body*" (translated and cited in Capek, *The Concepts of Space and Time,* 85; his italics).

19. *Principles of Philosophy,* 44; *Meditations* I and II (i.e., the celebrated piece of wax). See More's critique of this thought experiment in the letter cited in note 18, above (p. 86 in Capek, *Concepts of Space and Time*). David Allison points out to me that while we can go from a piece of wax to extension as its unprescindable essence, we can't reverse the process. This indicates that Descartes's view of extension is more methodological than metaphysical: a matter of definition or assertion rather than an article of ontology. I am grateful to my colleague for this suggestion and for his close reading of the above pages.

20. Descartes is distinctly conservative on this point: not only are there no attributes that do not inhere in substances (see *Principles of Philosophy,* I, sect. 11), but space and time in their extensional nature are themselves attributes: Descartes refuses to follow Gassendi's radical thesis that space and time are neither attributes nor substances. But this leaves unclarified Descartes's own notion of substance.

21. *Philosophical Letters,* 250–252 (letter of April 15, 1649). See also the letter of February 12, 1649, p. 242: "God is the only thing I positively conceive as infinite. As to other things like the extension of the world and the number of parts into which matter is divisible, I confess I do not know whether they are absolutely infinite; I merely know that I can see no end to them, and so, looking at them from my own point of view, I call them indefinite."

22. Letter to More of April 15, 1649 (*Philosophical Letters,* 251–252). Notice that Descartes here argues from (mental) limitation to (physical) infinity. For alternative statements, see the letters to More of February 5, 1649, and to Chanut of June 6, 1647, and especially *Principles of Philosophy,* p. 49: "We understand that this world, or the universe of material substance, has no limits to its extension. For wherever we may imagine those limits to be, we are always able, not merely to imagine other indefinitely extended spaces beyond them; but also to clearly perceive that these are as we conceive them to be, and, consequently, that they contain an indefinitely extended material substance."

23. Whether Descartes can maintain the distinction between *infinite* and *indefinite* as it applies to material extension is moot. In the Fifth Meditation Descartes writes that extension is "that quantity which the philosophers commonly term continuous, the extension in length, breadth, and depth that is in this quantity, or rather in the quantified thing to which it is attributed." N. K. Smith, commenting on this passage, remarks that "as being thus continuous, extension has to be recognized as being *at once infinite in extent and infinitely divisible.* His treatment of time is very different; denying it to be continuous . . . he seeks to account for it in an atomistic manner" (*New Studies in the Philosophy of Descartes,* 193 n; my italics).

24. "The void . . . is rejected by Descartes in a manner even more radical than by Aristotle himself " (Koyré, *From the Closed World to the Infinite Universe,* 101). See also Koyré's *Newtonian Studies,* 164–169. On the other hand, despite his adamant refusal of the void, Descartes is amenable to the idea of an aboriginal chaos. His "Treatise on Light" entertains the situation in which God makes the universe "to be a chaos as confused and as embroiled as any poet can depict" (cited in Smith, *New*

Studies in the Philosophy of Descartes, 116). Nor is chaos a purely speculative notion: "It is only by way of the assumption of [an] initial chaos, as at least hypothetically possible, that the sufficiency of the laws of motion in accounting for one and all of nature's happenings can be demonstrated" (Smith, *New Studies in the Philosophy of Descartes*, 115).

25. For Descartes's rejection of microvoid space within matter, see *The World*, trans. M. S. Mahoney (New York: Abaris Books, 1979), 27, 35.

26. "The existence of a vacuum involves a contradiction, because we have the same idea of matter as we have of space. Because this idea represents a real thing to us, we would contradict ourselves, and assert the contrary of what we think, if we said that that space was void, that is, that something we conceive as a real thing is not real" (letter of October 1645 to the Marquess of Newcastle, *Philosophical Letters*, 184). Even if we can *think of* sheer magnitude as a set of proportions without thinking of a particular body, in imagination and perception the magnitude will always be that of a determinate body.

27. Descartes, *The World*, 27. The premises of this argument are that (i) "all bodies, both hard and liquid, are made from the same matter" (p. 25); (ii) all intervals are always entirely filled, even those between particles of air (cf. pp. 35, 37). Elsewhere, Descartes argues that we believe in empty space only because we think in purely relative terms: "because an urn is made to contain water, it is said to be empty when it is only filled with air" (*Principles of Philosophy*, 47). But no matter how empty something *seems* because its usually proper content is absent, it is never entirely empty in fact.

28. Letter to Mersenne, January 9, 1639 (*Philosophical Letters*, 62). For a more complete statement, see *Principles of Philosophy*, 47–48. Henry More responded to this line of thought by saying that it is precisely God who would hold the walls apart: "If God imparts motion to matter, which you had maintained, could He not press against the sides of the vessel and keep them from coming apart?" (cited in Capek, *Concepts of Space and Time*, 87).

29. The phrase "nothing but a chimera" comes from *The World*, p. 31.

30. For further specification of this plenum, see *Philosophical Letters*, pp. 62–63, where three kinds of bodies are distinguished as filling up the universe.

31. Letter of June 6, 1647 (*Philosophical Letters*, 221); my italics. (Notice that here Descartes denies that we can even *conceive* of a matterless space insofar as we cannot think of space without dimensions.) The argument is found again in *Principles of Philosophy*, p. 47, and is repeated in condensed form in the letter to More of February 5, 1649: "Since I believe that such real properties [as extension provides] can only exist in a real body, I dared to assert that there can be no completely empty space" (*Philosophical Letters*, 240). On the other hand, Descartes concedes that "what is commonly called empty space" is "real body *deprived of all its accidents*" (letter to More of August, 1649 [*Philosophical Letters*, 257]; my italics)—all, that is, except extension itself, which is undeprivable.

32. Koyré, *From the Closed World to the Infinite Universe*, 99: "By his premature identification of matter and space [Descartes] deprived himself of the means of giving a correct solution to the problems that seventeenth-century science had placed before him." Concerning this controversy, see also Jonathan Rée, *Descartes* (London: Lane, 1974), 55–57.

33. *Principles of Philosophy,* 44–45; my italics. Descartes adds that the place in question "may even be believed to be empty" (ibid.), where the emphasis falls on "believed."

34. *Rules for the Direction of the Mind,* 58: "My conception is entirely the same if I say *extension occupies place,* as when I say *that which is extended occupies place"* (his italics).

35. Ibid.; my italics.

36. *Principles of Philosophy,* 46. (Words in brackets are those added in the French version of the *Principles*—a version read and approved by Descartes himself.) Notice that the phrase "as if it [i.e., place] were in the thing placed" introduces the controversial idea, which we also noted in Newton, of place inhering *in the body* that is in that very place.

37. "For in fact," says Descartes in section 10 of the *Principles* (entitled "The Nature of Space or Internal Place"), "the extension in length, breadth, and depth which constitutes the space occupied by a body, is exactly the same as that which constitutes the body" (*Principles of Philosophy,* 43). Notice that in the very midst of a discussion of internal *place,* Descartes does not hesitate to speak of "the space occupied by a body" as if it were equivalent to such a place.

38. *Principles of Philosophy,* 46.

39. Ibid., 45.

40. On this point, see *Principles of Philosophy,* pp. 45–46, where Descartes again substitutes "space" for "internal place": "We frequently say that one thing takes the place of another although it is not of precisely the same size or shape; but then we are [implicitly] denying that it occupies the *same space* as the other did" (my italics).

41. Descartes complicates this point when he insists that the generic unity of an extension of space can "remain one and the same" only "as long as it remains of the same size and shape *and maintains the same situation among certain external bodies"* (*Principles of Philosophy,* 44; my italics; see also p. 45). This seems to argue that both internal and external place are essential to the generic unity of space. Would it not be more economical—and accurate—to attribute internal place to the particular unity of space and external place to its generic unity?

42. *Meditations on First Philosophy,* Second Meditation, as translated by J. Veitch (Buffalo: Prometheus Books, 1989), 80. Nevertheless, both place and space are defined in terms of figure and magnitude.

43. "Specify" occurs at *Principles of Philosophy,* p. 44; "determine" at p. 45.

44. *Principles of Philosophy,* 45–46; my italics.

45. Ibid., 46. The rest of this sentence, however, contains a crucial equivocation: "but when we add that it [a thing] fills that space, *or that place,* we understand also that it has the specific size and shape of that space" (ibid.; my italics). What can the phrase "or that place" signify except a regressive reduction of external place to internal place—and thus to space, with which internal place is identified?

46. "In order to determine that situation [i.e., entailed in external place] we must take into account some other bodies which we consider to be motionless: and, depending on which bodies we consider, we can say that the same thing simultaneously changes and does not change its place" (*Principles of Philosophy,* 45). We shall return to the question of fixed reference points in discussing Locke and Leibniz.

47. *Principles of Philosophy,* 45. These celestial points can be said to offer a guar-

antee, in the physical world, for the system of coordinates that underlies analytical geometry.

48. "One has no reason to believe," says Descartes, "that the Stars, rather than the Earth, are motionless" (*Principles of Philosophy,* 95). Descartes's denial of motion to the earth is probably a concession to the Inquisition. Strictly speaking, for him *all* heavenly bodies, including the earth, are in motion.

49. *Principles of Philosophy,* 95. In the earlier Haldane and Ross translation: "If at length we are persuaded that there are no points in the universe that are really immovable, as will presently be shown to be probable, we shall conclude that there is nothing that has a permanent place except in so far as it is fixed by our thought." This line of argument was first set forth—in criticism of Aristotle—by Philoponus (see Jammer, *Concepts of Space: The History of Theories of Space in Physics* [Cambridge, Mass.: Harvard University Press, 1969], 57).

50. *Principles of Philosophy,* 46. "External space" is here equivalent to external place.

51. "We understand by 'surface' the common surface, which is not a part of one body more than of the other, and which is thought to be always the same provided that it retains the same size and shape" (ibid.).

52. Ibid., 46.

53. By the same token, sameness of place is preserved if the vectors of surrounding elements cancel each other out: "If we suppose a boat to be driven in one direction by the flow of a river, and in the other by the wind, with perfectly equal force (so that it does not change its situation between the banks), anyone will easily believe that it remains in the same place although all its surrounding surfaces change" (ibid.). Descartes here picks up on an ancient tradition of critique, extending from Simplicius through Buridan, that points to the fragility of the criterion of the surrounding surface. For a lively account of this tradition—to which I have already referred in chapter 4— see Richard Sorabji, *Matter, Space, and Motion* (Ithaca: Cornell University Press, 1988), chap. 11.

54. *Principles of Philosophy,* 45; my italics.

55. Ibid., 50; in italics in the text. In the "proper sense," movement is defined as "the transference of one part of matter or of one body, from the vicinity of those bodies immediately contiguous to it and considered as at rest, into the vicinity of [some] others" (ibid., 51; in italics).

56. Ibid., 52; my italics.

57. Ibid. Henry More objected to the invocation of "vicinity" in an astute critique of Descartes's theory of motion: for an account of this critique, see Koyré, *From the Closed World to the Infinite Universe,* pp. 142–143.

Chapter Eight: Modern Space as Relative

1. John Locke, *An Essay Concerning Human Understanding,* ed. P. H. Nidditch (Oxford: Clarendon Press, 1975), 172. Italics his; Locke also italicizes "Idea." Solidity is defined in this way: "That which thus hinders the approach of two bodies, when they are moving one towards another, I call *Solidity*" (p. 123; his italics). Although Solidity is separately discussed in the *Essay,* it is critical to the understanding of Locke's views of place and space. Solidity, which is "inseparably inherent in Body"

(p. 123), already implies place: "The idea of *solidity* ... arises from the resistance which we find in Body to the entrance of any other Body *into the Place* it possesses, till it has left it" (pp. 122–123; my italics). Moreover, solidity is essential to space as well: solidity "is the *Idea* which belongs to Body, whereby we conceive it *to fill space*" (p. 123; my italics). It fills space in the specific manner of refusing penetration by other bodies: its inherent resistance "keeps other Bodies out of the space which it possesses" (p. 124). In the end, solidity is located between sheer "hardness" and "pure space," which unlike solidity "is capable neither of Resistance nor Motion" (p. 124).

2. Ibid., 172; his italics. Locke himself discerns two kinds of extension in a manner that recalls at once Newton and Philoponus: "the Extension of body" is "the cohesion or continuity of solid, separable, moveable Parts"; "the Extension of space" is "the continuity of unsolid, inseparable, and immoveable Parts" (ibid., 126). In the first three editions of the *Essay*, Locke similarly speaks of Extension as "belonging to Body only" and remarks that "space may, as is evident, be considered without [such bodily extension]" (cited in *An Essay Concerning Human Understanding*, ed. A. C. Fraser [New York: Dover, 1959], I:220 n 1). For this reason, Locke prefers to restrict, wherever possible, the term "Extension" to bodily extension, reserving the term "space" for spatial extension. It is of interest that at an earlier stage of his thinking, that is, 1677–1678, Locke maintains that "Space in itself seems to be nothing but *a capacity or possibility for extended beings, or bodies, to exist*. . . . In truth it is *really nothing,* and signifies no more but a bare possibility that Body may exist where now there is none . . . or if there be a necessity to suppose a being there, it must be God, whose being we thus suppose extended but not impenetrable" (cited from Locke's *Miscellaneous Papers [1677–78]* in the Fraser edition, p. 155 n 4; his italics). Strikingly, Locke here espouses, in the very year of the publication of Spinoza's *Ethics,* the idea that God is extended and fills all space—which is, moreover, said to be "infinite" (*Miscellaneous Papers,* 156). But, as I remark in note 32, below, this view is not maintained in any serious way in the *Essay.*

3. *Essay,* 177; his italics. It might be wondered how one can conceive of solidity without space—at least the minimal space in which the solidity in question occurs.

4. "Pure Space" occurs, for example, in the *Essay*, p. 173, where the equivalent phrase "simple Space" is also used. Pure space is tantamount to void or "vacuum," which Locke defines as "pure Space without Solidity" and as originating in "the Place [a moving body] deserted" (p. 124).

5. "Capacity" is the extent of something "considered in Length, Breadth, and Thickness" (*Essay,* 167). "Figure" is defined as "the Relation which the Parts of the Termination of Extension, or circumscribed Space, have amongst themselves" (p. 168). Notice how this definition makes figure or "shape" itself a *relational* property. Figures thus conceived are infinitely variable: see p. 169. Given his ambivalent attitude toward the term "extension," it is not surprising that Locke sometimes applies this term to "capacity" (e.g., at p. 167) and sometimes to what he calls "Matter it self, the distance of its coherent solid parts" (p. 179). It is not surprising that capacity in Locke's sense is most closely related to internal place in the Cartesian sense—and that both involve "extension" and "matter," albeit inconsistently in Locke's case.

6. *Essay,* 167.

7. "There is another sort of Distance, or Length, the *Idea* whereof we get not from the permanent parts of Space, but from the fleeting and perpetually perishing parts of

Succession" (*Essay*, 181). The "spatialization of time" here receives one of its most direct expressions.

8. *Essay*, 169; his italics. The inclusion of the factor of time in this statement reflects the common basis of place and time in distance.

9. Ibid., 171.

10. In his usual lucid way, Locke makes it clear that he does not mean literal points: "Vulgarly speaking in the common Notion of *Place,* we do not always exactly observe the distance from precise Points; but from larger Portions of sensible Objects, to which we consider the thing placed to bear Relation" (*Essay*, 169; his italics). If points per se are thus not necessary constituents of distance, "positions" *are* indispensable on Locke's conception: for in determining place by recourse to distance, we "design the particular Position of Things" (p. 170). It can be seen that Locke is thinking of the determination of place in terms of *triangulation:* place is a function of at least *three* positions, each of which could be considered the apex of a triangle. My colleague Marshall Spector suggests that we might regard such triangulation as a step toward the necessity of a three-dimensional coordinate system. In any case, it rejoins Plato's claim that the spatial world is ultimately structured by triangles! For an astute analysis of place-relativism as based on such triangulation of positions, see Andrew Newman, "A Metaphysical Introduction to a Relational Theory of Space," *Philosophical Quarterly* 39 (1989): 200–220.

11. For Locke's example, see the *Essay*, pp. 169–170. In this analysis, Locke appears to adapt Descartes's earlier example of a sailor seated in the stern of a ship (*Principles of Philosophy*, 45, 50).

12. *Essay*, 170.

13. Ibid.

14. The choice of sets of stable reference points—coordinate systems in effect—will be decided by "those adjacent things, which best serve to [one's] present Purpose, without considering other things, which to another Purpose would better *determine the Place* of the same thing" (*Essay*, 170; his italics).

15. Concerning the placial implications of Locke's analysis of property, I have benefited from discussions with James E. Donelan and especially from reading his unpublished paper, "Locke, Place, and Property."

16. Measurement is explicitly invoked at the beginning of Locke's discussion of space: "Men for the use, and by the custom of measuring, settle in their Minds the Ideas of certain stated lengths, such as are an Inch, Foot, Yard, Fathom, Mile, Diameter of the Earth, etc. which are so many distinct Ideas made up only of Space" (*Essay*, 167; Locke italicizes several of these words).

17. On the mathematization of nature, see Edmund Husserl, *The Crisis of European Science and Transcendental Phenomenology*, trans. D. Carr (Evanston: Northwestern University Press, 1970), Pt. 1, esp. sec. 9, "Galileo's Mathematization of Nature."

18. At one point, however, in a critique of Descartes's overemphasis on sight and touch as the origin of the idea of extension, Locke recommends that Cartesians take more seriously "their Ideas of Tastes and Smells . . . their Ideas of Hunger and Thirst, and several other Pains" (*Essay*, 178–179).

19. I take the term "measurant" from M. Merleau-Ponty, *The Visible and the Invisible*, trans. A. Lingis (Evanston: Norhwestern University Press, 1968), 103: "We have

with our body, our senses, our look, our power to understand speech and to speak, *measurants* for Being, dimensions to which we can refer it." See also p. 260, where the body is said to be a "universal measurant." But if this is true of the body, why not also of place? On the close imbrication of body and place, see my *Getting Back into Place: Toward a Renewed Understanding of the Place-World* (Bloomington: Indiana University Press, 1993), chaps. 3, 4.

20. *Essay*, 171. Locke capitalizes "Idea." Once again, the ship example is paradigmatic, this time of a sheer and seemingly interminable relativism of position: if we can say of the places of the chess pieces, of the chessboard, of the cabin in which the board is located, and of the ship itself that, given sufficiently stable reference points, "these things may be said properly to be in the *same Place,* in those respects [i.e., with regard to the reference points]," on the other hand, since "their distance from some other things, which in this matter we did not consider, being varied, they have undoubtedly *changed Place* in that respect" (*Essay*, p. 170; his italics). Thus one and the same spot in space—where "space" is regarded as an unchanging matrix—can be considered both as an unchanging *and* a changing place, depending on the choice of the referential system to which this spot is related. This is instrumentalism with a vengeance, leading at the limit to a destabilization of the entire place-world.

21. Ibid., 173.

22. Ibid., 171: "The *Idea* therefore of *Place,* we have by the same means, that we get the *Idea* of Space, (whereof this is but a particular limited Consideration), *viz.* by our Sight and Touch; by either of which we receive into our Minds the *Ideas* of Extension or Distance" (his italics).

23. Ibid., 167.

24. Ibid., 180; his italics.

25. Ibid., 177. Locke does not attempt to "prove the real existence of a *Vacuum,* but the *Idea* of it; which 'tis plain Men have, when they enquire and dispute, whether there be a *Vacuum* or no?" (p. 178; his italics).

26. Ibid., 172.

27. "The parts of pure *Space,* are immovable, which follows from their inseparability" (*Essay*, 173; his italics).

28. "This Power of repeating, or doubling any *Idea* we have of any distance, and adding it to the former as often as we will, without being ever able to come to any stop or stint, let us enlarge it as much as we will, is that, which gives us the *Idea* of *Immensity*" (*Essay*, 168; his italics).

29. *Essay*, 171.

30. Ibid., 176; his italics. The preceding part of this statement is as follows: "I would ask, Whether, if God placed a Man at the extremity of corporeal beings, he could not stretch his Hand beyond his Body? If he could, then he would put his Arm, where there was before *Space* without *Body*" (pp. 175–176; his italics).

31. Ibid., 171.

32. Ibid. "Inane," Latin for "empty space" or "void," is in italics. Locke, again in tandem with Newton, linked eternity and infinity: "I would fain meet with that thinking Man, that can, in his Thoughts, set any bounds to Space, more than he can to Duration; or by thinking, hope to arrive at the end of either: And therefore if his *Idea* of Eternity be infinite, so is his *Idea* of Immensity" (p. 176; his italics). I would disagree with Edward Grant's judgment that infinite space "is God's immensity" (*Much Ado About Nothing: Theories of Space and Vacuum from the Middle Ages to the Scientific Revolu-*

tion [Cambridge: Cambridge University Press, 1981], 406 n 329). In a passage to which Grant refers, Locke writes that "the boundless invariable Oceans of Duration and Expansion . . . comprehend in them all finite Beings, and in their full Extent, belong only to the Deity" (*Essay,* 200). But I do not think that Locke means this as a metaphysical, much less a cosmological, claim; it is a rhetorical flourish that says in effect: since we cannot know anything of this infinity, we can concede that it might as well belong to God.

33. I refer to Leibniz's *New Essays on Human Understanding* (1703–1705). For a comparative assessment of the two philosophers based on a close study of this text, see Nicholas Jolley, *Leibniz and Locke: A Study of the New Essays on Human Understanding* (Oxford: Clarendon Press, 1984).

34. Leibniz's first systematic statement of active force, also termed "primitive force," occurs in his *Specimen Dynamicum* (1695). In Leibniz's view, extension is merely a capacity for receiving motion, whereas active force as a "first entelechy" or "substantial form" of a body is the potentiality of motion itself. Even a nonmoving body possesses the passive force of what Leibniz calls "antitupia," or resistance, which is in effect that body's maintaining itself in the same place. Thus place figures into the minimal or passive end of the spectrum of effective force—a spectrum whose active end is found in motion, which (as in Locke) is no longer tied to place.

35. Leibniz, "Metaphysical Foundations of Mathematics" (ca. 1714), in *Philosophical Papers and Letters,* ed. L. Loemker (Chicago: University of Chicago Press, 1956), 2:1091. By "minimal path" Leibniz means a path in which "the intermediate stages are related in the simplest way to both extremes" (ibid.). (Path itself is defined in terms of place: "A *path* is the continuous and successive locus of a movable thing" [ibid., 1086; his italics].) Although a restricted notion, distance is nevertheless sine qua non in an extended universe. Hence in the *Monadology,* Leibniz remarks that the communication between bodies "extends to any distance whatever" (ibid., 1054).

36. Both phrases occur in Leibniz's Fifth Paper to Clarke as reprinted in *Philosophical Papers and Letters,* 2:1151, 1145.

37. Ibid., 1145–1146; my italics. Leibniz italicizes the word "place" in the first sentence.

38. Ibid., 1147. The famous formula occurs inter alia in "The Metaphysical Foundations of Mathematics," ibid., 1083: "Space is the order of coexisting things, or the order of existence for things which are simultaneous." Hidé Ishiguro stresses the ideality of relations on Leibniz's conception: for him, "relations are abstract entities made by abstraction out of things being 'in situation' with one another" (H. Ishiguro, "Leibniz's Theory of the Ideality of Relations," in H. Frankfurt, *Leibniz: A Collection of Critical Essays* [New York: Doubleday, 1972], 201). In thus positing the ideality of space, Leibniz anticipates Kant: "Space plays, with Leibniz, the role of the transcendental in Kant" (Michel Serres, *Le système de Leibniz et ses modèles mathématiques* [Paris: Presses Universitaires de France, 1968], 2:778). Serres adds that as for Kant space for Leibniz "conditions measurement, size, divisibility" (ibid.), and as such it determines both distance and figure. Space is thus "the a priori form of all worldhood" (Yvon Belaval, *Études leibniziennes* [Paris: Gallimard, 1976], 207). Leibniz himself says explicitly in his paper "First Truths" (ca. 1680–1684): "Space, time, extension, and motion are not things but *well-founded modes of our consideration*" (*Philosophical Papers and Letters,* 1:417; my italics).

39. Serres, *Le système de Leibniz,* 2:782.

40. For both points, see the Fifth Paper to Clarke, *Philosophical Papers and Letters,* 2:1149.

41. On the distinction between "immensity" and "infinity"—terms whose differences, as we have glimpsed, go back to the Middle Ages (though Locke, as we have just seen, does not distinguish them in any important way)—see *Philosophical Papers and Letters,* 2:1143, 1149.

42. "An Example of Demonstrations about the nature of Corporeal Things, Drawn from Phenomena," in *Philosophical Papers and Letters,* 1:222; his italics. Leibniz questions whether this distinction is merely a childhood prejudice as Descartes held (p. 223), and he argues for its truth by a simple thought experiment: when we perceive a body it is always in space, yet we can think of space without body. See p. 224, where this experiment is set forth with this conclusion: "Two things are diverse if one can be thought of without the other. Therefore space and body are diverse." It is of interest that in at least one passage Leibniz identifies "empty *place*" with pure extension: "The concept of an empty place and of extension alone is the same" (2:642).

43. This critique appears already in "First Truths," p. 416: given Cartesian *extensio* as definitive, "there could exist two corporeal substances perfectly similar to each other, which is absurd." It is absurd on the principle of sufficient reason, whereby there must be a definitive reason why one exemplar *rather than the other* exists.

44. "Critical Thoughts on the General Part of the *Principle* of Descartes," *Philosophical Papers and Letters,* 2:642. Elsewhere, Leibniz makes it clear that mobility requires resistance: "Extension is not sufficient to constitute matter or body, since they [i.e., the Cartesians] have to add mobility, which is a result of antitypy [i.e., impenetrability] or of resistance" ("Conversation of Philarète and Ariste," ibid., 2:1011).

45. "First Truths," 1:417. "For the substance of bodies," adds Leibniz, "there is required something which lacks extension; otherwise there would be no principle to account for the reality of the phenomena or for true unity" (ibid.).

46. Such a suggestion is made in a letter to De Volder dated March 24/April 3, 1699: "I believe that our thinking is completed and ended in the concept of force rather than in that of extension" (*Philosophical Papers and Letters,* 1:838).

47. "Nor do I think that extension can be conceived in itself, but I consider it an analyzable and relative concept, for it can be resolved into plurality, continuity, and coexistence or the existence of parts at one and the same time" (*Philosophical Papers and Letters,* 1:838). The plurality is of the coexisting parts of any thing; the continuity is that of the thing as a whole. See also the letter to De Volder of July 6, 1701: "In extension I think of many things together—on the one hand, continuity, which it has in common with time and motion, and, on the other, coexistence" (ibid., 85).

48. On the extensive continuum, see A. N. Whitehead, *Process and Reality,* ed. D. R. Griffin and D. W. Sherburne (New York: Free Press, 1979), 61–82, 97. Gilles Deleuze compares Whitehead's notion with Leibniz's in his recent study, *The Fold: Leibniz and the Baroque,* trans. T. Conley (Minneapolis: University of Minnesota Press, 1993), 76–78.

49. "Conversation of Philarète and Ariste," in *Philosophical Papers and Letters,* 2:1010. Another passage says: "There is required in extension, the notion of which is relative, a something which is extended or continued as whiteness is in milk. . . . [T]he repetition of this, whatever it may be, is extension" (ibid., 642). As Deleuze puts it,

"Extension exists when one element is stretched over the following ones, such that it is a whole, and the following elements are its parts. Such a connection of whole-parts forms an infinite series that has no last term nor limit (if one neglects the limits of our senses)" (*The Fold,* 77).

50. Extension, like motion and bodies themselves, "are not substances but true phenomena, like rainbows and parhelia" ("First Truths," in *Philosophical Papers and Letters,* 1:417). Further, "mere extension never appears to [people] without being invested with some color, or conatus, or resistance, or some other quality" ("An Example of Demonstrations About the Nature of Corporeal Things, Drawn from Phenomena," *Philosophical Papers and Letters,* 1:223). Nevertheless, extension remains an *attribute* of material things: "Duration and extension are attributes of things, but time and space are taken by us to be something outside of things and serve to measure them" (*Philosophical Papers and Letters,* 2:1011).

51. "Critical Thoughts on the General Part of the *Principles* of Descartes," *Philosophical Papers and Letters,* 1:642.

52. Letter to Des Bosses of February 5, 1712, *Philosophical Papers and Letters,* 2:977.

53. The phrase cited comes from a letter to Arnauld of March 23, 1690, *Philosophical Papers and Letters,* 2:599.

54. "I should always distinguish between the extended or extension, and the attribute to which being extended, or diffusion, a relative concept, is referred. This would be situation or locality" (*Philosophical Papers and Letters,* 2:1011).

55. *Philosophical Papers and Letters,* 2:1011.

56. On the ichnographic versus the scenographic, see a letter to Des Bosses in *G. W. Leibniz: Die Philosophischen Schriften,* ed. C. I. Gerhardt (Berlin, 1875–1890), 2:438: "For there are diverse scenographies according to the situation of the spectator, so that a geometrical ichnography is not the only mode of representation." "Ichnography" connotes the tracing of a ground plan, while "scenography" signifies a drawing in perspective, from a distance. I owe this reference (and several others as well in what follows) to Donald Rutherford of Emory University.

57. Loemker remarks that the term *prōton dektikon,* borrowed from Aristotle's *Physics* (bk. 7, chap. 4), is the "term which Leibniz commonly uses for substance in the last period of this thought" (*Philosophical Papers and Letters,* 2:1198 n 295).

58. "Metaphysical Foundations of Mathematics" (ca. 1714), *Philosophical Papers and Letters,* 2:1084; all in italics in the text.

59. Ibid.; in italics in the text.

60. "Space and time are not limits but abstract coordinates of all series, themselves [taken] in extension" (Deleuze, *The Fold,* 77).

61. Fifth Paper to Clarke (1716), in *Philosophical Papers and Letters,* 2:1151. Leibniz adds that "relative things have their quantity as well as absolute ones" (ibid.).

62. "On the Principle of Indiscernibles" (ca. 1696), in *Leibniz: Philosophical Writings,* ed. and trans. G. H. R. Parkinson (London: Dent, 1973), 133–134. This brief but remarkable essay was first published in L. Couturat, ed., *Opuscules et fragments inédits* (Paris: Presses Universitaires de France, 1903), 8–10.

63. "On the Principle of Indiscernibles," 133; my italics.

64. See the Fourth Letter to Clarke, in *Philosophical Letters and Papers,* 2:1118: "If space is a property or attribute, it must be the property of some substance. But what

substance will that bounded empty space be an affection or property of . . . ?" If empty space is not a property of any possible substance, it is imaginary in status.

65. "On the Principle of Indiscernibles," 133; my italics.

66. For this reason, only qualitative change is real change; all other change, including that of quantity, is merely "relative." Already, in his early "Dissertation on the Art of Combinations" (1666), Leibniz considered quality to be "something absolute" and imputed to quantity an entirely "relative" status: "An affection (or mode) of a being, moreover, is either something absolute, which is called *quality,* or something relative, and this latter is either the affection of a thing relative to its parts if it has any, that is, *quantity,* or that of one thing relative to another, *relation*" (*Philosophical Papers and Letters,* 1:122; his italics). Space, however, is indubitably a relation, and thus, by this logic, a mode of quantity—as is place, to the degree that it is constituted wholly by relations, a reduction to which we shall return.

67. "On the Principle of Indiscernibles," 133. Even distance is momentarily redeemed in this line of thought! "Distance and the degree of distance involves also a degree of expressing in the thing itself a remote thing, either of affecting it or of receiving an affection from it" (ibid.).

68. "Metaphysical Foundations of Mathematics," *Philosophical Papers and Letters,* 2:1085; his italics.

69. Leibniz writes to Lady Masham on June 30, 1704: "One must place the soul in the body, wherein there is located the point of view from which it at present represents the universe to itself " (cited in Donald Rutherford, *Leibniz and the Rational Order of Nature* [Cambridge: Cambridge University Press, 1995], chap. 7, "Modelling the Best of All Possible Worlds," n. 35). More fully stated: "Since every organic body is affected by the entire universe through relations which are determinate with respect to each part of the universe, it is not surprising that the soul, which represents to itself the rest in accordance with the relations of its body, is a kind of mirror of the universe, which represents the rest in accordance with (so to speak) its point of view" (ibid.).

70. "On the Principle of Indiscernibles," 133.

71. Ibid., 134. Although this last claim is expressly said to be true of quantity and position, the lumping of place with these latter surely makes it applicable to place as well. This is so despite Leibniz's further contention that the foundation in question is "derived from the category of quality" (ibid.). One suspects that "quality" is here the wild card: when it is allied with place as what is extended there, place is nonpositional; when it is construed as a "category," it is more foundational than place can ever be— and place, by default, is thrown together with such sheerly relative phenomena as position and quantity.

72. Cited by Rutherford, *Leibniz,* 413.

73. From the Fifth Paper to Clarke, in *Philosophical Papers and Letters,* 2:1148; his italics.

74. In a paper entitled "On Nature Itself" (1698), Leibniz remarks that "under the assumption of perfect uniformity in matter itself, one cannot in any way distinguish one place from another, or one bit of matter in the same place" (*Philosophical Essays,* trans. R. Ariew and D. Garber [Indianapolis: Hackett, 1989], 164). Even though Leibniz rejects the uniformity of matter, he ends by espousing the homogeneity of place— a curious and ironic result, given that place is far more of a paradigm of heterogeneity than is matter.

75. *Philosophical Papers and Letters,* 2:1146; his italics.

76. "I don't say that space is an order or situation which makes things capable of being situated . . . but an order of situations, or an order according to which situations are disposed, and that abstract space is that order of situations when they are conceived as being possible. Space is therefore something merely ideal" (Fifth Paper, 1163).

77. Serres, *Le système de Leibniz,* 2:781; his italics. Serres adds that "it is therefore very much an order of *possible* relations, of all possible relations" (ibid.; his italics). Despite his emphasis on space as pure possibility, Leibniz is as strenuously opposed to the vacuum as is Descartes: "Everything is a plenum in nature" (from the Fourth Letter to Clarke, as cited in *Philosophical Papers and Letters,* 2:1034). Leibniz's primary critique of the vacuum is that it has no effective reason for being: "The fiction of a material finite universe moving forward in an infinite empty space cannot be admitted. . . . Such an action would be without any design in it: it would be working without doing anything, *agendo nihil agere*" (ibid., 1141).

78. Leibniz writes to Des Bosses on September 20, 1712: "Why actually an infinity of monads? I reply that the mere possibility of an infinity is enough to establish this, since it is manifest how very rich are the works of God" (*Philosophical Papers and Letters,* 2:988). In the Fourth Paper to Clarke, sec. 9, Leibniz discusses infinite space in terms of "immensity" in such a way as to make it evident that about the existence of infinite space there can be no doubt: see p. 1118.

79. Fifth Paper, *Philosophical Papers and Letters,* 2:1146; his italics. By "absolute reality," Leibniz refers to his archrival Newton's conception of space. Despite his resolute rejection of any such spatial reality taken as a single substance, Leibniz is not entirely averse to the idea of absolute space. As an abstract coordinate system, space on Leibniz's view edges toward something absolute, since there can finally be only *one* "order of situations." Moreover, in regarding space as "unchanging," Leibniz edges perilously close to absolute space in its "immovability." ("Space is therefore something extended which . . . we cannot think of as changing" ["An Example of Demonstrations about the Nature of Corporeal Things, Drawn from Phenomena" (*Philosophical Papers and Letters,* 1:223–224)].) At one point Leibniz even applies "absolute" to place as if this were an unproblematic move: "That which is diffused formally will be locality or that which constitutes *situs;* it will be necessary to conceive this itself as something absolute" (letter to Des Bosses of February 5, 1712; *Philosophical Papers and Letters,* 2:977). But here "absolute" is construed literally as that which cannot be *further* dissolved. Finally, in "The Metaphysical Foundations of Mathematics," Leibniz says, without qualification, that "*absolute* space is the fullest locus, or the locus of all loci" (ibid., 2:1087; his italics). Despite these occasional forays into the realm of absolute space, Leibniz makes it clear in his exchange with Clarke that he must finally reject any form of absolute space or time in his mature monadology.

80. Both the clause cited and the citation from Hippocrates are from *The Monadology,* sec. 56, in *Philosophical Essays,* 220.

81. Ibid., sec. 61.

82. Ibid., sec. 62. "Expression" in Leibniz signifies less any representation per se, much less a mental image, than a *rule of relation between monads.* (I owe this interpretation to Donald Rutherford.)

83. Cited by Rutherford, *Leibniz,* n. 37.

84. On sympathy, see the letter to De Volder of April, 1702: "Any two things *A*

and *B* not only have in common that they are things or substances; they also have some kind of sympathy (*Philosophical Letters and Papers,* 2:858).

85. Letter of May 29, 1716, in *Philosophical Essays,* 201.

86. *Monadology,* sec. 7. As a result, "neither substance nor accident can enter a monad from without."

87. Ibid., sec. 63; my italics. For the mirror analogy, see *Monadology,* sec. 56: "Each simple substance is a perpetual, living mirror of the universe." Section 77 makes it clear that both soul and body operate as mirrors of the universe. For Leibniz, the soul is the "dominating monad" or "primitive entelechy" that is paired with a "primary matter" that has "passive power" to form the whole monad (letter to De Volder of June 20, 1703, *Philosophical Papers and Letters,* 2:864). Despite possessing primary matter, monads are not strictly speaking *extended.* This is why Leibniz says that they "have a situation (*situs*) in extension" or a "position in extension" (same letter, pp. 865, 866). This is tantamount to claiming that the soul is situated in the body, which is in turn situated in space; but only the latter situation is strictly positional, since the soul cannot possess a position in *its own body,* even though the latter is extended. Leibniz seems to acknowledge this anomalous circumstance in a text of 1691: "I agree that every body is extended and that there is no extension without body. Nonetheless, we must not confound the notions of place, space, or of pure extension with the notion of substance which, besides extension, includes resistance, that is to say, action and passivity" ("Whether the Essence of a Body Consists in Extension," *Journal des Savants,* June 18, 1691; cited in P. Wiener, ed., *Leibniz: Selections* [New York: Scribner's, 1951], 102). Soul is the source of "action" and body of "passivity"; even if the body itself is extended, the monad as a simple substance is composed of both soul and body and thus cannot itself be confused with "*pure* extension"—that is, with the order of space at large. But on my reading, it can be—indeed it must be—anchored in place.

88. The order of place as the basis for point of view is also sine qua non for the soul's representational activity. As Deleuze says, the soul concerns itself with "what remains in point of view, what occupies point of view, and without which point of view would not be" (Deleuze, *The Fold,* 22). On my reading, "that without which point of view would not be" is precisely place. I owe this reference and the discussion of this and related points to Irene Klaver.

89. Fifth Paper to Clarke, *Philosophical Papers and Letters,* 2:1147; his italics. On abstraction and place, Ishiguro remarks that "the concept of [the] place of an individual spatial locus . . . is obtained by abstraction from consideration of things having certain relational properties to each other" ("Leibniz's Theory," 201). So too the concept of space abstracts from the totality of these same properties; it is thus "an abstraction from the relational properties, or [from] the mutual connections of things" (Ishiguro, ibid.).

90. See this remark in the Third Paper to Clarke: "Space is nothing else but that order or relation [of bodies], and is nothing at all without bodies *but the possibility of placing them*" (*Philosophical Papers and Letters,* 2:1109; my italics).

91. "Duration and extension are attributes of things, but time and space are taken by us to be something outside of things and serve to measure them" ("Conversation of Philarète and Ariste," 2:1011). See also Loemker's remark (2:1192, sec. 214). If place *is* like force in its sheer functionality, it does not itself possess force: only substances have force.

92. "The case is the same with respect to time" ("Conversation of Philarète and Ariste," 2:1109). Such is Leibniz's characteristic ploy—a ploy of space-time parallelism—that is pursued at every available opportunity.

93. The phrase "abstract space" occurs in the Fifth Paper to Clarke, *Philosophical Papers and Letters,* 2:1163: "That abstract space is that order of situations when they are conceived as being possible." Site is defined officially as "a certain relationship of coexistence between a plurality of entities; it is known by going back to other coexisting things which serve as intermediaries, that is, which have a simpler relation of coexistence to the original entities" ("Metaphysical Foundations of Mathematics," *Philosophical Papers and Letters,* 2:1091). Site includes qualitative as well as quantitative relations: "Situs is a mode of coexistence. Therefore it involves not only quantity but also quality" (ibid., 1084; first sentence is in italics). But as purely relational, site favors quantity, whose close alliance with relation we have seen asserted in "On the Principle of Indiscernibles."

94. Third Paper to Clarke, *Philosophical Papers and Letters,* 2:1108.

95. Deleuze reminds us that the word "labyrinth" has fold in its origin via *labium,* "lip." He writes "the unit of matter, the smallest element of the labyrinth, is the fold" (*The Fold,* 6).

96. On *analysis situs,* see Leibniz's "Studies in a Geometry of Situation" (1679) as translated in *Philosophical Papers and Letters,* 1:381–396. In this text, Leibniz states that "many things easily become clear through a consideration of situation, which the algebraic calculus shows only with greater difficulty" (p. 390). Such a geometry focuses on similarities and congruences.

97. I take this term from Serres, *Le système de Leibniz,* for example, 2:781: "Space is a whole of point-summits of relations." Leibniz's fascination with points—his pointillism, as it were—answers to his equal fascination with *limits,* for example, in the notable instance of the differential calculus, which he devised contemporaneously with Newton.

98. "The Theory of Abstract Motion" (1671), in *Philosophical Papers and Letters,* 1:218.

99. "The Metaphysical Foundations of Mathematics," in *Philosophical Papers and Letters,* 2:1087.

100. But it must be stressed that Leibniz rejects geometrical points as ultimate atomic units: see Deleuze, *The Fold,* 6. On metaphysical versus mathematical points, see *Philosophical Papers and Letters,* 2:745–746. The former are "exact and real," while the latter are "exact but are nothing but modalities." Leibniz also discusses "physical points," that is, "when a corporeal substance is contracted" (ibid.). On point of view, the following statement in a letter to De Volder is characteristic: "It follows that each monad is a living mirror, or a mirror endowed with an internal action, and that it represents the universe according to its point of view" (ibid., 1035).

101. I have not focused on this critique, since it is set out so elegantly by Leibniz himself in his correspondence with Clarke, and is so often cited in standard accounts of the philosophy of space and time: for example, Max Jammer, *Concepts of Space: The History of Theories of Space in Physics* (Cambridge, Mass.: Harvard University Press, 1969), 113–120; Bas van Fraassen, *Introduction to the Philosophy of Time and Space* (New York: Columbia, 1985), 35–44, 108–114.

**Chapter Nine: Modern Space as Site
and Point**

1. "The body belonging to a monad which is its entelechy or soul constitutes what
may be called a *living being* with that entelechy; with a soul it constitutes an *animal.*
. . . So each organic body belonging to a living being is a kind of divine machine or
natural automaton infinitely surpassing all artificial automata" (*Monadology,* secs. 63–
64, as included in *Philosophical Papers and Letters,* ed. L. Loemker [Chicago: University of Chicago Press, 1956], 2:1055).

2. *Monadology,* sec. 66; in *Philosophical Papers and Letters,* 2:1056. Cf. the contemporaneous statement in the *Principles of Nature and Grace, Based on Reason:* "not
only is there life everywhere, joined to members or organs, but there are also infinite
degrees of it in the monads, some of which dominate more or less over others" (*Philosophical Papers and Letters,* 2:1035). Another way to put this is to say that "even in a
physical sense we are moving across outer material pleats to inner, animated, spontaneous folds" (Gilles Deleuze, *The Fold: Leibniz and the Baroque,* trans. D. Conley [Min-
neapolis: University of Minnesota Press, 1993], 13).

3. See *Monadology,* sec. 67, for this metaphor.

4. R. G. Collingwood, *The Idea of Nature* (Oxford: Oxford University Press,
1945), 110. I have omitted the final clause of this sentence: "with a constant drive or
nisus working upwards along the scale." This nisus is that of the domination of some
monads by others, and finally of all monads by God, who is the only strictly bodiless
being, though He still possesses His own fully comprehensive (i.e., scenographic)
point of view.

5. Cited from Leibniz without attribution by Deleuze, *The Fold,* p. 12.

6. For an extension of Leibniz in the direction of an ecologically sensitive feminism, see Carlyn Merchant, *The Death of Nature: Women, Ecology, and the Scientific
Revolution* [New York: Harper & Row, 1983), 275–290. Merchant singles out Leibniz
as the first modern thinker of organism and vitalism.

7. See Alfred North Whitehead, *Science and the Modern World* (Cambridge: Cambridge University Press, 1926), esp. chap. 4, "The Eighteenth Century." The new sense
of place is expressed thus by Whitehead: "There is a prehension, here *in this place,* of
things which have a reference to *other places.* . . . This unity of a prehension defines
itself as a here and a now, and the things so gathered into the grasped unit have
essential reference to other places and other times" (pp. 86–87; my italics). On the
influence of Leibniz on Whitehead's philosophy of organism, see pp. 81, 87, 91.
Deleuze says that "Whitehead is the successor, or *diadochos,*" of Leibniz (*The Fold,*
76). But Whitehead also gives credit to Locke—with whom we have seen Leibniz to
be paired in critical respects—in *Process and Reality,* ed. D. R. Griffin and D. W. Sherburne (New York: Free Press, 1978), xi, 54, 123, 128, 147.

8. "There is in [monads] a certain sufficiency (*autarkeia*) which makes them the
sources of their internal actions and, so to speak, incorporeal automata" (*Monadology,*
sec. 18, in *Philosophical Papers and Letters,* 2:1047). On God as the "architect of the
machine of the universe"—that is, the universe regarded as ruled by efficient causality—see ibid., sec. 87, p. 1060). The universe is also, however, a "moral kingdom" of
final causes that, despite its very different order, exists in a perfect harmony with the
"physical kingdom" of nature. Everywhere in Leibniz, the moderating role of the "also,

however," is to be found, thereby precluding one-sided readings of this philosopher, including his views on place and space. For discussion of this last point I am indebted to Robert Crease.

9. See Deleuze, *The Fold,* chaps. 1 and 8, esp. p. 13: "The soul itself is what constitutes the other floor or the inside up above, where there are no windows to allow entry or influence from without."

10. Collingwood, *The Idea of Nature,* 112. Collingwood's use of "quantitative" fits closely with my assessment of the fate of place when it was considered solely with regard to quantity. But Leibniz himself, as we have seen, endorses *both* a qualitative and a quantitative assessment of place.

11. Whitehead, *Science and the Modern World,* 69. Both Whitehead and Collingwood are speaking expressly of the seventeenth-century worldview—but it is precisely this worldview that becomes fully articulated in eighteenth-century philosophers and physicists. This is not to discount other, quite different directions in this new century, such as Vico's "New Science," the emerging importance of *Bildung,* and the increasing interest in imagination so evident in Kant's *Critique of Judgment* (1790) and the early romantic philosophers and poets. But all of these variant views arose in reaction to the very mechanism and scientism inherited so unquestioningly from the previous century. On the significance of *Bildung,* "the greatest idea of the eighteenth century," see Gadamer, *Truth and Method* (New York: Seabury, 1975), p. 10; concerning the "Romantic Reaction," see Whitehead's chapter of this title in *Science and the Modern World,* pp. 93–118.

12. The philosophes of the eighteenth century "applied the seventeenth-century group of scientific abstractions to the analysis of the unbounded universe. Their triumph, in respect to the circle of ideas mainly interesting to their contemporaries, was overwhelming. . . . The notion of the mechanical explanation of all the processes of nature finally hardened into a dogma of science" (Whitehead, *Science and the Modern World,* 74–75).

13. We recognize here another version of the fallacy of misplaced concreteness. Speaking of the view of lifeless nature that is the legacy of the seventeenth century to the West, Whitehead expostulates that "this conception of the universe is surely framed in terms of high abstractions, and the paradox [of the accomplishments of genius in such an arid philosophical atmosphere] only arises because we have mistaken [their] abstraction for concrete realities" (*Science and the Modern World,* 69). Whitehead is inclined to locate the source of the abstractness in the success of early modern mathematics: "The great characteristic of the mathematical mind is its capacity for dealing with abstractions" (p. 70). The abstraction is precisely from "the remainder of things" (p. 73). On the importance of what "remains over," see also E. Husserl, *Ideas: General Introduction to Pure Phenomenology* (New York: Macmillan, 1962), sec. 33.

14. I say "important but mostly neglected," since Descartes proleptically foresaw the collapse of place into position when he wrote that "the difference between the terms 'place' and 'space' is that the former designates more explicitly the position, as opposed to the size and shape that we are concentrating on when we talk of space" (*Principles of Philosophy,* sec. 14; in the translation of J. Cottingham, R. Stoothoff, and D. Murdoch, *The Philosophical Writings of Descartes* [Cambridge: Cambridge University Press, 1985], 1:229). In another version given by the same translators, "situation" is used instead of "position."

15. Whitehead, *Science and the Modern World,* 93. Whitehead is referring expressly to the clearing away of "the world of muddled thought" (ibid.) that was taken to be inherent in the scholasticism still surviving in the seventeenth century.

16. Thus Joseph Louis Lagrange's *Méchanique analytique* (1788) made mechanics a branch of "analysis" by attempting to "deduce equations of motion which are equally applicable whatever quantitative measurements have been made, *provided that they are adequate to fix positions*" (Whitehead, *Science and the Modern World,* 78; my italics). Earlier in the century, Pierre Louis Moreau de Maupertuis discussed the relationship between the energy intrinsic to motion and that intrinsic to position: see his 1736 essay, "Sur les lois de l'attraction," *Suite des Mémoires de mathématique et de physique, tirés des registres de l'Académie Royale des Sciences de l'année MDCCXXXXII* (Amsterdam: Pierre Mortier), 2:473–505.

17. Gilles Deleuze and Felix Guattari, *A Thousand Plateaus* (vol. 2 of *Capitalism and Schizophrenia*), trans. B. Massumi (Minneapolis: University of Minnesota Press, 1987), 382; my italics.

18. The phrase is from Michel Foucault, *The Birth of the Clinic: An Archeology of Medical Perception,* trans. A. Sheridan Smith (New York: Pantheon, 1973), 6.

19. The terms "configuration" and "localization" are discussed at *Birth of the Clinic,* pp. 3, 11.

20. Foucault, *Birth of the Clinic,* 195. The phrase "fixing in space" occurs at p. 231. On the "space of domination," see M. Foucault, *Discipline and Punish: The Birth of the Prison,* trans. A. Sheridan (New York: Pantheon, 1977), pp. 187 ff. On surveillance, see *Discipline and Punish,* pp. 170–177 ("Hierarchical Observation").

21. Foucault, *Discipline and Punish,* 197. The full statement is "This enclosed, segmented space, observed at every point, in which the individuals are inserted in a fixed place, in which the slightest movements are supervised, in which all events are recorded, in which an uninterrupted work of writing links the centre and periphery, in which power is exercised without division, according to a continuous hierarchical figure, in which each individual is constantly located, examined and distributed among the living beings, the sick and the dead—all these constitute a compact model of the disciplinary mechanism."

22. "Calculable man," that is, the subject of the newly emerging human sciences, appears at *Discipline and Punish,* p. 193. "Disciplinary individual" is found at p. 227.

23. On time regulation, see *Discipline and Punish,* p. 220, as well as the studies of E. P. Thompson concerning timetables in eighteenth-century England. The phrase "elementary location or *partitioning*" is at p. 143 (his italics).

24. The phrase "laboratory of power" occurs at *Discipline and Punish,* p. 204; "the rule of functional sites" is at p. 243 (his italics); and the last phrase in this sentence is at p. 205.

25. On docile bodies, see *Discipline and Punish,* pp. 135–169. On the entire topic of disciplinary space, see Thomas R. Flynn, "Foucault and the Spaces of History," *Monist* 74 (1991): 165–186.

26. *Discipline and Punish,* 203. It is tempting to imagine that to place/space/site correspond three kinds of architecture: thus "place" architecture might well emphasize enclosure and, more generally, domestic virtues; "space" buildings are monumental, on the order of the Imperial city or Nuremburg; and "site" constructions would

be typified by the eighteenth-century buildings singled out by Foucault as exemplary of empty, panvisional seriality. But it would be more accurate to say that we have to do here with three modes of ordering available to *all* building, such that it would be exceptional to exemplify one mode only. For the most part, *every* construction can be said to involve aspects of all three modes. A Greek temple is placelike, or place-creating, in its inclusion of closely bounded interior rooms; but it is spatial in the way that it connects with the larger landscape (e.g., with certain sanctified mountain formations, as Vincent Scully has shown), and it is even sited on the basis of the carefully calculated geometry by which it is positioned vis-à-vis other buildings in the same temple complex. Much the same can be said of the ordinary middle-class house: its ensconced interiority is set within a carefully carpentered frame, itself situated in turn on what is called (not accidentally) a "building site"; and all of this is positioned in that properly termed "spatial" expanse called a city, a county, or a region. Thus we ought to think of place, space, and site as three potential directions of *any* effort to construct habitable and enduring buildings. (I owe this clarification to a discussion with Tom Brockelman.)

27. This is Bentham's own etymology of the term. See *The Works of Jeremy Bentham,* ed. J. Bowring (Edinburgh: Tait, 1843), 11:97.

28. *The Works of Jeremy Bentham,* 4:44; his italics. The phrase "inspective force" occurs at p. 44.

29. Ibid., 44.

30. Ibid., 45; his italics. The phrase "axial visibility" is Foucault's at *Discipline and Punish,* p. 20. Such visibility is complemented by the "lateral visibility" of the prisoners to each other.

31. The last phrase is from *The Works of Jeremy Bentham,* 4:177; the word "vicin-ity" is in italics. The prior phrase is from *Discipline and Punish,* p. 207.

32. "Thanks to its mechanism of observation, [the Panopticon] gains in efficiency and in the ability to penetrate into men's behavior; knowledge follows the advances of power, discovering new objects of knowledge over all the surfaces on which power is exercised" (*Discipline and Punish,* 204).

33. *The Works of Jeremy Bentham,* 4:45. The phrases cited earlier in the sentence are from p. 46.

34. *Discipline and Punish,* 205. See also p. 205: such "functioning, abstracted from any obstacle, resistance, or friction, must be represented as a pure architectural and optical system."

35. The phrase "a simple idea in architecture" comes from *The Works of Jeremy Bentham,* 4:207. Foucault comments that "Bentham dreams of transforming [various disciplinary practices] into a network of mechanisms that would be *everywhere* and always alert, running through society without interruption in space or in time. The panoptic arrangement provides the formula for this generalization" (*Discipline and Punish,* 205; my italics).

36. *Discipline and Punish,* 207.

37. See plates 4–6 of *Discipline and Punish* for instances of American adaptations of Bentham's project: e.g., the penitentiary at Stateville.

38. *Discipline and Punish,* 205. The phase "central-inspection principle" occurs in *The Works of Jeremy Bentham,* p. 40.

39. Hannah Arendt, *The Human Condition* (Chicago: University of Chicago Press, 1958), 6. These are the two most characteristic directions of the early modern period in its alienating power.

40. Immanuel Kant, "Thoughts on the True Estimation of Living Forces, and Criticism of the Proofs Propounded by Herr von Leibniz and other Mechanists in their Treatment of this Controversial Subject, together with some Introductory Remarks Bearing upon Force in Bodies in General," as translated in J. Handyside, ed., *Kant's Inaugural Dissertation and Early Writings on Space* (Chicago: Open Court, 1929), 4: "Leibniz, to whom human reason owes so great a debt, has been the first to teach that in body there inheres a force which is essential to it, and which indeed belongs to it prior to its extension." The locus classicus of Leibniz's doctrine of *vis viva* is found in his "Specimen Dynamicum" (1695), as reprinted in *Philosophical Papers and Letters*, 2:711–738. For further thoughts on force, see Kant's 1763 essay "Enquiry Concerning the Clarity of the Principles of Natural Theology and Ethics," trans. G. B. Kerferd and D. E. Walford, *Kant: Selected Pre-Critical Writings and Correspondence with Beck* (Manchester: Manchester University Press, 1968), 18–20, where Kant argues that the impenetrability of extended substances, their "antitypy," is itself a force.

41. Kant, "Thoughts on the True Estimation of Living Forces," 10.

42. On Leibniz's attempted deduction, see his *Theodicy* (1714), sec. 351; Kant's critique of circularity is at "Thoughts on the True Estimation," p. 10.

43. "The threefold dimension seems to arise from the fact that substances in the existing world so act upon one another that the strength of the action holds inversely as the square of the distances [between them]" ("Thoughts on the True Estimation," 11). The exact relationship between distance, force, and dimension, however, is not clarified by Kant, even if his overall direction is evident: the mutual interaction of substances is the generative factor that underlies all spatial phenomena.

44. "Thoughts on the True Estimation," 12: "This law [of the inverse square of distances] is arbitrary, and . . . God could have chosen another, for instance the inverse threefold relation; and . . . from a different law an extension with other properties and dimensions would have risen."

45. For further discussion of the notion of a "solitary world" with a spatiality of its own, see Kant's 1755 essay, "A New Elucidation of the First Principles of Metaphysical Cognition," in *Theoretical Philosophy, 1755–1770*, trans. D. Walford and R. Meerbote (Cambridge: Cambridge University Press, 1992), 42. Such an isolated world would contain substances whose determinations of place, position, and space are unique to that world and without relation to ours.

46. "The soul, as having position in space, must be able to act outside itself" ("Thoughts on the True Estimation," 7). Later, Kant will describe this ability to act in space as the "orbit of activity." This orbit, while "in space," exceeds the actual space filled or occupied by a given substance. See Kant's 1755 "Physical Monadology," in *Theoretical Philosophy, 1755–1770*, pp. 58–59 (where the phrase "orbit of activity" is discussed) and his "Dreams of a Spirit-Seer Elucidated by Dreams of Metaphysics" (1766), where Kant distinguishes between "being active in" a space and "filling" it: *Theoretical Philosophy*, 310–312.

47. "Thoughts on the True Estimation," p. 7: "The concept of that which we entitle position, as we find upon analyzing it, itself refers us to the mutual actions of substances."

48. This is not to say that Kant never mentions place in his earliest writings. The "New Elucidation" singles out place (*locus*) along with position and space as the primary modes of "relations of substances" by means of "reciprocal determinations" and "external connections": see *Theoretical Philosophy,* Proposition XIII, pp. 40 ff. But such relations are decidedly secondary compared to substances and their inherent forces, and Kant presumes that a substance can exist that has *no place*: "If you posit a number of substances, you do not at the same time and as a result determine place, position, and space. . . . It follows that substances can exist in accordance with the law which specifies that *they are in no place*" (ibid., 42; his italics). In the "Physical Monadology," Kant makes it clear that space of any kind—thus including place and position as its determinations—is a creature of relations between substances: "Space is not a substance but a certain appearance of the external relation of substances" (ibid., 57). One recognizes in this last formulation a strong echo of Leibniz's famous formula for space as a *phaenomenon bene fundatum.* Kant also reinstates Leibniz's sheerly relational view of space, which "can be described only in terms of external relations" (p. 59) and which is thus entirely dependent on the "external presence" of existing substances (p. 58). The "internal determinations" of substances, on the other hand, "are not in space" (p. 58), leading to a dichotomy in this "physical monadology" that is never resolved—and that will still shadow Kant's later writings, where things in themselves are considered nonspatial in contrast with phenomena as always already spatialized. It should be noticed, finally, that place per se—as a phenomenon in its own right—receives no discussion of its own in either of these important essays of 1755.

49. Kant, "Concerning the Ultimate Ground of the Differentiation of Regions in Space," in *Theoretical Writings,* 365–366. I have changed "direction" to "region" in translating *Gegend.*

50. Kant, *Metaphysical Foundations of Natural Science,* trans. J. W. Ellington, in *Kant's Philosophy of Material Nature* (Indianapolis: Hackett, 1985), 24. The discussion of absolute and relative interpretations of space occurs at pp. 18–21, where we read that "relative space" is "the space in which motion is perceived," whereas "absolute space" is "that in which all motion must ultimately be thought." Thus relative space is regarded by Kant as essentially "movable" and absolute space as "absolutely immovable." (By "immovable" Kant does not mean unmovable *as an entity* (e.g., the universe) but as a *concept* of the absolute reality of space. I owe this clarification and others in this section to my colleague Jeffrey Edwards.

51. Ibid., 21. Similarly, in each physical body "there is only one point that constitutes its place" (ibid.).

52. Ibid., 30. *Phora* is Greek for "motion" (and, more specifically, "locomotion"), and thus phoronomy considers bodies with respect to their sheer movability, without regard to "dynamical" considerations of force. In so doing, it regards them as moving points transposed between points: "A body that is in motion is for a moment in every point of the line that it traverses" (*Metaphysical Foundations,* 25).

53. Kant, *Opus Postumum,* trans. E. Förster and M. Rosen (Cambridge: Cambridge University Press, 1993), 3. With this statement, we witness the radical change in Kant's treatment of force that has taken place in the more than fifty years that separate "Thoughts on the True Estimation of Living Forces" (where "active force" permeates all matter) from the *Opus Postumum.* It can be argued that the concept of "ether" developed in the latter text takes over much of the conceptual work of *vis viva* in the

former; but it does so only by invoking the important notion of "field," which has implications for place only barely suggested by Kant. Nevertheless, in the *Metaphysical Foundations of Natural Science,* Kant insists that he wants to consider matter apart from extension—an anti-Cartesian move he still shares with Leibniz. Thus he writes, "I wanted to determine the very concept of matter independently of the concept of extension and thus could consider matter as a point" (*Metaphysical Foundations,* 21). But the concept of space as merely a matter of external relations—so prominent in the early writings of 1755–1768—is now notably missing.

54. From "Metaphysical Foundations of Dynamics," chap. 2 of *Metaphysical Foundations,* p. 75. We witness here Kant's continuing fascination with the inverse square law. Notice the pairing of "point" with "space"—a linkage to which I shall return shortly. Kant's notion of "diffusion" does not possess the suggestive ambiguity found in Leibniz's employment of the same term.

55. Ibid., 21. Kant reminds the reader that "contrary to this [i.e., the common] explication, one might remember that internal motion, e.g., fermentation, is not included in it" (ibid.). In the common explication, a keg of beer is moved from one place to another; but the contents of the keg undergo a motion of development independent of change of place: "The motion *of a thing* is not identical with the motion *in this thing*" (ibid., 22; my italics).

56. Fifth Paper to Clarke, *Philosophical Papers and Letters,* 2:1147.

57. "All determination of time presupposes something *permanent* in perception. . . . [P]erception of this permanent is possible only through a *thing* outside me" (Kant, *Critique of Pure Reason,* trans. N. K. Smith [New York: Humanities Press, 1960], B 275, p. 245; his italics). Paradoxically, the invocation of the "permanent" (*Beharrlichkeit*) brings with it a reinstatement of spatial relativism: "Inner experience itself depends upon something permanent which is not in me, and consequently can only be in something outside me, to which I must regard myself as *standing in relation*" (ibid., B xl, pp. 35–36; my italics).

58. *Opus Postumum,* 160. The locus classicus for Kant's position is, of course, the Transcendental Aesthetic of the *Critique of Pure Reason.* But I find certain passages in the *Opus Postumum* to be more economical and apt, and will cite these along with more familiar sentences from the *Critique.*

59. *Opus Postumum.* Kant underlines "perceiving." On space as "a mode of intuition," see p. 159: "Space is not an object of intuition . . . but rather is itself a mode of intuition."

60. Ibid.; my italics. See also p. 159, where "moving forces in space" are represented as "something sensible" in formal intuition: "Attraction of bodies at a distance, and repulsion (in virtue of which they are bodies, that is, self-limiting matter) already lie *a priori* in the concept of the possibility of experience, as the unity of space and time."

61. Ibid., 159. See also p. 158: "One must first have an intuitive representation of the size of [a] space—its position and situation, as well as its shape—in order to be able to determine what exists in it." The capacious character of space is also indicated in this passage: space contains "locations in an intuition (extension), change of location (motion), and laws according to which this change is determined (moving forces)" (*Critique of Pure Reason* A 49 B 67, p. 87).

62. *Opus Postumum,* 160. Space and time are "only the formal element of the

composition (*complexus*) of possible objects of the perceptions of outer and inner sense" (ibid.).

63. *Critique of Pure Reason* A 26 B 42, p. 71.

64. Ibid., A 25 B 41, p. 70. Not surprisingly, purity involves an element of abstraction: pure intuition occurs "if we abstract from these objects [i.e., of sensibility]" (A 27 B 43, p. 72). In a passage such as this, we begin to suspect that misplaced concreteness is still very much at play in the late eighteenth century.

65. *Opus Postumum,* 160; his italics.

66. Ibid., 160; his italics. Said more succinctly: "Space and time are not objects of intuition but pure intuition itself " (p. 161).

67. *Critique of Pure Reason* A 29, p. 74. Strangely, this crystalline claim was excluded from the second edition. The compact phrase "pure form" stands surety for a priori, which in addition connotes the necessity and universality of spatial intuition: "An *a priori,* and not an empirical, intuition underlies all concepts of space" (A 25 B 39, p. 69).

68. On the absolute aspect of space, see *Critique of Pure Reason* A 23 B 38, p. 68: "The representation of space must be presupposed [i.e., in regard to any particular part of space]." Concerning spatial infinity, Kant says: "Space is a quantum, which must always be represented as part of a greater quantum—hence, as infinite, and *given* as such" (*Opus Postumum,* 171; his italics). Space is thus "represented as an infinite *given* magnitude" (*Critique of Pure Reason* A 25 B 39, p. 69; his italics). The First Antinomy also treats the infinity of space: see *Critique of Pure Reason* A 426 B 454–A 427 B 455, pp. 396–397. On the empirically real but transcendentally ideal status of space, see *Critique of Pure Reason* A 28 B44, pp. 72–73.

69. *Critique of Pure Reason* A 23 B38, p. 68. Kant's invocation of "mind" (*Gemüt*) guarantees the subjectivism of human knowing.

70. Ibid., A 25 B 41, p. 70. Kant also asks here the revealing question, "How, then, can there exist *in the mind* an *outer* intuition which precedes the objects themselves, and in which the concept of these objects can be determined *a priori?*" (ibid.; my italics). For Kant's denial that space and time are God's intuitions—Newton would say God's *sensoria*—see A 49 B 71, pp. 89–90.

71. *Critique of Pure Reason,* A 23 B 38, p. 68; my italics. Notice that "region" as well as "place" are here incorporated *into space.* We shall return to the status of region at the beginning of the next chapter.

72. Ibid., A 25 B 39, p. 69. Kant adds: "Space is essentially one; the manifold in it, and therefore the general concept of spaces, depends solely on [the introduction of] limitations" (ibid.). Similarly, "space comprehends all things that appear to us as external, but not all things in themselves" (ibid., A 27 B 43, p. 72). The mention of space as *comprehending* is reminiscent of Leibniz's claim that space is "that which comprehends all these places" (Fifth Paper to Clarke, *Philosophical Papers and Letters,* 2:1146), but in Kant's eyes Leibniz fails to distinguish between phenomena and things in themselves. By making space and time "confused" modes of representation, Leibniz presumes a continuum between intuitions and concepts that destroys the independent status of space and time as intuitive but *non*conceptual. The same confusion occurs in considering them as "well-founded phenomena"—yet not ultimately real substances. Concerning Kant's mature critique of Leibniz (and thus of his own earliest writings), see "The Amphiboly of Concepts of Reflection," *Critique of Pure Reason* A 260 B

316–A 289 B 346, pp. 276–296. For Kant's critique of Leibniz on space specifically, see Gerd Buchdahl, *Metaphysics and the Philosophy of Science: The Classical Origins, Descartes to Kant* (Oxford: Blackwell, 1969), 574–580.

73. *Critique of Pure Reason* A 25 B 39, p. 69; his italics. Reinforcing the point, Kant says that space, unlike a concept, contains "an infinite number of representations *within* itself " (A 25 B 40, p. 70; his italics).

74. *Opus Postumum,* 163. See p. 162: "There is only one space and one time. The absolute unity, which embraces everything, is likewise the infinity of this object, which is really subject, and which is intuiting and, at the same time, intuited." In the *Critique of Pure Reason* he says simply that "space is essentially one" (A 25 B 39, p. 69).

Transition

1. Philoponus, *In Aristotelis physicorum libros quinque posteriores commentaria,* ed. H. Vitelli (Berlin, 1888), 567; cited and translated in Max Jammer, *Concepts of Space: The History of Theories of Space in Physics,* 2d ed. (Cambridge, Mass.: Harvard University Press, 1970), 56.

2. This statement (cited by Jammer in *Concepts of Space*) has occasioned a recent commentator to remark that "Philoponus goes beyond the general run of Platonists in actually adopting 'void' as his *name* for space" (David Sedley, "Philoponus's Conception of Space," in *Philoponus and the Rejection of Aristotelian Science,* ed. R. Sorabji [Ithaca: Cornell University Press, 1987], 141; his italics). On the inherent "force" of the void, see Philoponus's claim that "perhaps this is the force of void—the fact that this kind of quantity [i.e., space] is never separated from substance" (cited from Philoponus's *In Physica* by Sedley at "Philoponus's Conception of Space," p. 144).

3. "The force of the void (vacuum) proves both that this extension exists and that it is never without body. . . . But [there is] extension, distinct from the contained body and empty by its own definition" (cited and translated by D. Furley from *Commentaria in Aristotelem Graeca* in Furley's "Summary of Philoponus' Corollaries on Place and Void," in Sorabji, *Philoponus and the Rejection of Aristotelian Science,* p. 133).

4. Cited from Furley, "Summary," p. 132.

5. *Critique of Pure Reason* A 24 B 38, p. 68.

6. On the ether, a notion already espoused by Aristotle, see E. A. Burtt, *The Metaphysical Foundations of Modern Science* (New York: Doubleday, 1932), 111 ff., 189 f., 264 ff. It is striking that Kant was obsessed with demonstrating in his last work (by a transcendental deduction) the existence and necessity of ether as a universal medium of "world-material" (*Welt-stoff*): see *Opus Postumum,* ed. E. Förster, trans. E. Förster and M. Rosen (Cambridge: Cambridge University Press, 1993), 62–99; Burkhard Tuschling, *Metaphysische und transzendentale Dynamik in Kants opus postumum* (Berlin: de Gruyter, 1971), and the forthcoming book of Jeffrey Edwards, *Force, Substance, and Physics: An Essay on Kant's Philosophy of Material Nature* (Cambridge: Cambridge University Press). If ether exists as a universal material medium—even as a transcendental field of matter itself—it would complicate the claim (cited just above) that we can think of space as "extension empty of body." If ether exists, then space may indeed be empty of individuated bodies, but it is not empty of matter: on the contrary, it is filled with a concrete material "stuff." Concerning light, its continuing

importance for the theory of space is evident from Proclus's speculations to those of Leibniz, who at one stage was inclined to make it into a universal solvent (see "On the Principle of Indiscernibles," in *Leibniz: Philosophical Writings,* ed. and trans. G. H. R. Parkinson [London: Dent, 1973]). Kant, for his part, writes that "the light, which plays between our eye and the celestial bodies, produces a mediate community between us and them, and thereby shows us that they coexist" (*Critique of Pure Reason,* trans. N. K. Smith [New York: Humanities Press, 1965], A 213 B 260, p. 235).

7. William Gilbert, *De mundo nostro sublunari philosophia nova* (Amsterdam, 1651), p. 144. In this statement Gilbert anticipates Leibniz's view that place has no proper force of its own.

Chapter Ten: By Way of Body

1. "When, after passing through a narrow defile (*engen Hohlweg*), we suddenly emerge upon a piece of high ground, where the path divides and the finest prospects open up on every side, we may pause for a moment" (Sigmund Freud, *The Interpretation of Dreams,* trans. J. Strachey [New York: Avon, 1965], 155). Where Freud pauses before the dual prospect of consciousness and the unconscious as ways of understanding dreams, we are here pausing between mind and body as primary pathways into the nature of place.

2. For Kant's use of *Leitfaden,* also translatable as "clue," see the *Critique of Pure Reason* A 76 B 102, sec. 3, "The Clue to the Discovery of all Pure Concepts of the Understanding."

3. *Critique of Pure Reason* A 25 B 41, p. 70; my italics. Concerning the problematic status of Kant's transcendental idealist doctrine of space, see Paul Guyer, *Kant and the Claims of Knowledge* (Cambridge: Cambridge University Press, 1987), chap. 16, "Transcendental Idealism and the Forms of Intuition."

4. I say "almost entirely neglected," since Berkeley makes bodily motion (along with touch and vision) intrinsic to the estimation of distance—which is itself a basic parameter of place: "What [one] sees only suggests to his understanding, that after having passed a certain distance, *to be measured by the motion of his body,* which is perceivable by touch, he shall come to perceive such and such tangible ideas which have been usually connected with such and such visible ideas" (George Berkeley, *An Essay Towards a New Theory of Vision* [London: Dent, 1934], 33).

5. "Relatively to us, they—above, below, right, left—are not always the same, but come to be in relation to our position (*thesis*), according as we turn ourselves about, which is why, often, right and left are the same, and above and below, and ahead and behind" (*Physics* 208b14–18; Hussey translation).

6. Kant, "Concerning the Ultimate Ground of the Differentiation of Regions in Space," trans. D. Walford, in *Kant: Selected Pre-Critical Writings and Correspondence with Beck,* ed. G. B. Kerferd and D. E. Walford (Manchester: Manchester University Press, 1968), 43. Hereafter referred to as "Concerning the Differentiation." (Elsewhere in this chapter, I shall follow the more recent translation of this same essay, by D. Walford and R. Meerbote, in *Kant: Theoretical Philosophy, 1755–1770* [Cambridge: Cambridge University Press, 1988]). The phrase "first data of experience" (*die ersten data unserer Erkenntnis*) is reminiscent of Husserl's search for the *Evidenz* of concrete experience.

7. These phrases are taken from section 27 and the note to section 30 in Kant's *Inaugural Dissertation* of 1770, as translated in *Kant: Theoretical Philosophy, 1755–1770*, pp. 410, 415–416. Kant has Henry More in mind when, in discussing the localization of numinous entities, he says sarcastically that "there come to be bandied about those idle questions about the places in the corporeal universe of immaterial substances" (ibid., 410). While Kant certainly does not believe that all entities are sensible—he wants to leave as much room for God or the soul as does More—he denies that supersensible things have any legitimate local presence. But Kant himself had held a position very close to More in an early essay, "Dreams of a Spirit-Seer Elucidated by Dreams of Metaphysics" (1766), translated in *Theoretical Philosophy*, esp. pp. 308–313. Thus Kant asks: "Where is the place (*Ort*) of this human soul in the world of bodies?" (p. 312). At p. 311 "spirit-natures" or "spirit-substances" are said to "occupy" (*einnehmen*) places, to be "present in space," yet not to "fill" (*erfüllen*) place or space as do material substances. Nevertheless, contra More, Kant does not consider spiritual substances to be genuinely "extended," for they lack shape of any determinate sort.

8. *Inaugural Dissertation*, in *Theoretical Philosophy*, 409; his italics. Kant is aware of the pervasive influence of this axiom; he calls it "the well-known popular axiom" that "*whatever exists, is somewhere*" (ibid., 408 n; his italics). The fallacy of subreption is formally defined as "the confusion of what belongs to the understanding with what is sensitive" (p. 408), and in its first form it prescribes that "the same sensitive [i.e., sensible] condition, under which alone the *intuition* of an object is possible, is a condition of the *possibility* itself of the object" (p. 409; his italics).

9. It is "true in the highest degree" that "*whatever is somewhere, exists*" (ibid., 408 n.; his italics).

10. *Timaeus* 31c (Cornford translation). Plato adds that "of all bonds the best is that which makes itself and the terms it connects a unity in the fullest sense" (ibid.). One could argue that it is precisely the body that connects things and places "in the fullest sense." Strangely enough, even though Plato would agree that both places (*topoi*) and regions (*chōrai*) are essentially oriented, he does not give to the body any active role in the constitution of such cosmic orientedness.

11. This is the phrase of Walford and Meerbote in their explication of the 1768 essay: see *Theoretical Philosophy*, p. lxix; "specifically spatial qualities" is in italics.

12. Kant's way of putting it is that the two counterparts "can be exactly equal and similar, and yet still be so different in themselves that the limits of the one cannot be the limits of the other" ("Concerning the Differentiation," 369).

13. On the notion of "enantiomorph," see Graham Nerlich, *The Shape of Space* (Cambridge: Cambridge University Press, 1976), esp. p. 29. After reviewing recent literature on enantiomorphs as well as Kant's own later vacillations, Nerlich concludes that "Kant's first ideas were almost entirely correct about the whole of the issue" (ibid., p. 30). A comprehensive treatment of Kant's views on enantiomorphs is found in J. V. Buroker, *Space and Incongruence: The Origins of Kant's Idealism* (Dordrecht: Reidel, 1981).

14. "Concerning the Differentiation," 371; his italics.

15. Ibid., 369. It is notable that Kant's move to absolute space in this essay is made in a dogmatic tone and without the detailed argumentation that he supplies for his discussions of position, region, and the body. Moreover, absolute space is said to be "a fundamental *concept*" (p. 43)—a view that he will recant only two years later in the

Inaugural Dissertation, where space and time are characterized as sensible *intuitions.* (As Kant says more clearly in the *Critique of Pure Reason,* "the original representation of space is an *a priori* intuition, not a concept" [A 25 B 40, p. 70].) It is striking that the very same incongruent counterparts that are here adduced as proof of the absoluteness of space are later invoked as proof of the transcendental ideality of space, for example, in the *Prolegomena to Any Future Metaphysics* (1783), sec. 13. For further discussion of the relation between incongruent counterparts and absolute space, see Peter Remnant, "Incongruous Counterparts and Absolute Space," *Mind* 62, no. 287 (1963): 393–399; and for the tracing out of Kant's changing interpretations of incongruent counterparts, consult N. K. Smith, *A Commentary on Kant's Critique of Pure Reason* (New York: Humanities Press, 1962), 161–166.

16. "I am the absolute source" (M. Merleau-Ponty, *The Phenomenology of Perception,* trans. C. Smith [New York: Humanities, 1962], ix). What Merleau-Ponty says of the pregiven surrounding world also obtains for incongruent counterparts: "My existence does not stem from my antecedents, from my physical and social environment; instead *it moves out toward them and sustains them*" (ibid.; my italics).

17. Kant, *Prolegomena to Any Future Metaphysics,* trans. E. B. Baxter (London: Bell, 1883), 32; my italics.

18. Ibid., 33.

19. Walford and Meerbote, résumé of the 1768 essay in *Theoretical Philosophy,* p. lxxx. See also pp. xliv, lxx. The authors add that "the importance of [the essay of 1768] for an understanding of the development of Kant's views on space and time, and therefore for an understanding of the emergence of the critical philosophy itself, can scarcely be exaggerated" (p. lxx). It is revealing that in the *Prolegomena,* Kant shows his own vacillation between a bodily and a mental interpretation of the subject when he writes that "the difference between similar and equal things which are not congruent (for instance, helices winding in opposite ways) cannot be made intelligible by any concept, but only by the relation to the right and the left hands, which *immediately refers to intuition*" (*Theoretical Philosophy,* p. 33; my italics). Here we are tempted to ask: Is not the relation to two-handedness sufficient? Why need we "immediately" refer two-handedness to "intuition," a mentalistic term that is part of the baggage of transcendental philosophy?

20. "Concerning the Differentiation," 365. Otherwise put, regions relate groups of positions to "universal space as a unity," and in so doing they "order" these groups or "systems," that is, orient them. (The phrase "universal space as a unity" is from p. 365; "universal absolute space" is mentioned at p. 369.) Once more, however, the invocation of absolute or universal space seems gratuitous: Why are regions (and not, say, places themselves, as for Newton) implicated so closely with *absolute* space? Later, in the *Critique of Pure Reason,* Kant will insist only on the necessity of a transcendental setting in the form of a *commercium,* that is, "a thoroughgoing community of mutual interaction" (*Critique of Pure Reason* A 213 B 260, p. 235): a view that in effect reinstates the view first expressed in "Thoughts on the True Estimation of Living Forces" (see Gerd Buchdahl, *Metaphysics and the Philosophy of Science* [Oxford: Blackwell, 1969], 580–584). The crucial point, however, is that for Kant regions are not simply built up from positions; instead, positions depend on *regions:* "The position of the parts of space in reference to each other presuppose the region in which they are ordered in such a relation" ("Concerning the Differentiation," 365). "Region" here

translates *Gegend.* It is revealing that the Cambridge translation systematically replaces "region" by "direction" as a translation of the German word. Although I prefer
the literal translation, the choice of Walford and Meerbote has the merit of acknowledging the fact that the functional role of "region" in Kant's text is to *supply direction*
to the places and things located in a given region.

21. "Concerning the Differentiation," 366–367; his italics. I have again changed
"directions" to "regions" in the last sentence. The other two dimensional regions, front/
back and right/left, are deduced immediately thereafter on p. 367. For a discerning
treatment of the claim made in this passage, along with a useful diagram, see Hoke
Robinson, "Incongruent Counterparts and the Refutation of Idealism," *Kant-Studien*
72 (1981): 391–397.

22. "Concerning the Differentiation," 367; my italics. I have changed "directions
in general" to "regions in general" as a translation of *Gegenden überhaupt.* And I have
altered "the cardinal points of the compass" to "cosmic regions" as closer in meaning
to *Weltgegenden* in agreeing with Handyside's earlier translation (J. Handyside, ed.,
Kant's Inaugural Dissertation and Early Writings on Space [Chicago: Open Court,
1929], 22). It would take us too far afield to determine just how we know our own
bilaterality; Kant himself refers us only to "the distinct feeling of the right and the left
side" ("Concerning the Differentiation," 369). Heidegger takes Kant to task for this
claim: "Left and right are not something 'subjective' for which the subject has a feeling; they are directions of one's directedness into a world that is ready-to-hand already.
'By the mere feeling of a difference between my two sides' [i.e., citing Kant] I could
never find my way about in a world" (*Being and Time,* trans. J. Macquarrie and E.
Robinson [New York: Harper & Row, 1962], 143). For Heidegger, what matters is not
a bodily feeling but the whole arena constituted by being-in-the-world.

23. "Concerning the Differentiation," 367.

24. "The most precise map of the heavens, if it did not, in addition to specifying
the position of the stars relative to each other, also specify the direction by reference
to the position of the chart *relative to my hands,* would not enable me, no matter how
precisely I had it in mind, to infer from a known direction, for example, the north,
on which side of the horizon I ought to expect the sun to rise" ("Concerning the
Differentiation," 367; my italics). J. A. May remarks that "anyone who is used to
working with maps will know how true [Kant's] observation is. . . . Once one has located the north pointer, one orients oneself to the map by automatically associating
east with the right hand and west with the left hand. And by this very act of bodily
association, the concept north itself takes on meaning relative to the other directions"
(*Kant's Concept of Geography and Its Relation to Recent Geographical Thought* [To-
ronto: University of Toronto Press, 1970], esp. chap. 2).

25. "Concerning the Differentiation," 367–368. Note that "orientate" translates
nach den Gegenden stellen können. "Indeed" translates *ja,* which can also be rendered
as "even" or as "especially." On the latter translation, we could say that it is *especially*
our ongoing knowledge of the position of places around us that depends on the role of
our own body. It is the body that endows places (and regions) with a directionality
they would otherwise lack: otherwise, they would form nothing but an "entire system
of reciprocal positions" (*das ganze System der wechselseitigen Lagen*). This system of
reciprocal positions should be compared to the idea of a dynamical *commercium* of

substances in "thoroughgoing reciprocity" as discussed in the Third Analogy (*Critique of Pure Reason* A211 B256 ff.; see n. 25, above).

26. Such is the force of the phrase "our most ordinary knowledge" (*unserer gemeinsten Kenntnis*). Compare Seamus Heaney's lines: "the smells of ordinariness / were new on the night drive through France . . . / I thought of you continuously . . . / your ordinariness was renewed there" ("Night Drive," *New Yorker,* May 1994).

27. See Immanuel Kant, *Was heisst: Sich im Denken orientieren? (Gessammelte Schriften* [Berlin: Royal Prussian Academy of Sciences, 1902–66], 8:131–147). For a critical discussion of this example, see May, *Kant's Concept of Geography,* 71–72.

28. "One side of the body, the right side, namely, enjoys an indisputable advantage over the other in respect of skill and perhaps of strength, too" ("Concerning the Differentiation," 369). Anthropologists have explored comparable asymmetries of right vs. left valorization in cultural expressions and rituals: see R. Needham, ed., *Right & Left* (Chicago: University of Chicago Press, 1973), passim. I discuss the issue at more length in *Getting Back into Place: Toward a Renewed Understanding of the Place-World* (Bloomington: Indiana University Press, 1993), 88–97.

29. See Jacques Derrida, *Positions,* trans. A. Bass (Chicago: University of Chicago Press, 1981), 71. I owe this reference to Mary C. Rawlinson.

30. For this phrase and other descriptions of *durée réelle,* see Henri Bergson, *Time and Free Will* [French title: *Les données immédiates de la conscience,* first published in 1889], trans. F. L. Pogson (New York: Harper, 1960), chap. 2, esp. pp. 121–123. On space as "an empty homogeneous medium," see p. 95 ff. On the spatialization of time, see pp. 97–98. William James stands as a significant exception to the general neglect of space by nineteenth-century thinkers as anything other than uniform and quantitative. He was particularly impressed by the dimension of spatial *depth,* a dimension Bergson was willing to acknowledge in time alone. (William James, *Principles of Psychology* [New York: Dover (1890) 1950], 2:134 ff.) James also suspected the bodily basis of our experience of space by tracing this experience back to "the sensation of voluminousness." On James's treatment of depth and volume—and, implicitly, of place—see my essay, " 'The Element of Voluminousness': Depth and Place Re-Examined" (in M. Dillon, ed., *Merleau-Ponty Vivant* [New York: SUNY Press, 1991], 1–29). Kant had already pointed to the real possibility of alternative forms of space in "Thoughts on the True Estimation of Living Forces," in J. Handyside, *Kant's Inaugural Dissertation and Early Writings on Space,* secs. 10–11.

31. I have already cited Whitehead's view that the *Timaeus* ranks with Newton's *Scholium* as one of "the two statements of cosmological theory which have had the chief influence on Western thought" (*Process and Reality,* ed. D. R. Griffin and D. W. Sherburne [New York: Free Press, 1979], 93). On spatialization in Bergson, see *Process and Reality,* pp. 82, 114, 209, 220, 321, as well as Whitehead's *Science and the Modern World* (New York: Free Press, 1953), 51, 147.

32. Kant, "Concerning the Differentiation," 368. I have changed "referring" to "reference" in keeping with the nominative form of *Beziehung.* The citations in the previous sentence are from *Science and the Modern World,* pp. 52, 58. The phrase at the beginning of this sentence is from p. 52.

33. As Whitehead puts it somewhat technically: "If a region is merely a way of indicating a certain set of relations to other entities, then this characteristic, which I

call simple location, is that material [bodies] can be said to have just these relations of position to the other entities *without requiring for its explanation any reference to other regions constituted by analogous relations of position to the same entities*" (*Science and the Modern World,* 49; my italics; see also p. 58 for a restatement). In Leibniz's language, if *A* and *B* are located in relation to the fixed existents *C, D, F,* and *G,* the nexus thus formed is not *further* related to other nexuses—as they should be on a doctrine of *non*simple location.

34. *Science and the Modern World,* 49; my italics.

35. For a full discussion of region, see *Process and Reality,* 283–284, 300–302, 312–313.

36. "Concerning the Differentiation," 371. Handyside translates *Ursprünglichen Raum* as "primary space."

37. *Science and the Modern World,* 58; my italics.

38. *Process and Reality,* 51.

39. Ibid., 58.

40. Ibid.

41. Ibid., 59.

42. Ibid.

43. On this theme, see also Carolyn Merchant, *The Death of Nature: Women, Ecology, and the Scientific Revolution* (New York: Harper & Row, 1983), esp. chap. 12. Also Morris Berman, *The Reenchantment of the World* (Ithaca: Cornell University Press, 1980), passim.

44. *Process and Reality,* 64. At p. 81, Whitehead says that "the body . . . is only a peculiarly intimate bit of the world."

45. *Science and the Modern World,* 91.

46. "They [i.e., seventeenth-century philosophers] treat bodies on objectivist principles, and the rest of the world on subjectivist principles" (*Science and the Modern World,* 91).

47. *Science and the Modern World,* 92; my italics. In referring to "an aspect of the distant environment," Whitehead is self-consciously improving on simple location. It is striking that in undertaking this act of philosophical amelioration, Whitehead comes so close to Leibnizian thought, especially the notion that monads mirror and unify the world they express and represent.

48. *Science and the Modern World,* 91; my italics.

49. Ibid., 73.

50. On bodily efficacy, see *Process and Reality,* p. 312. Concerning prehensive unification, Whitehead says in *Science and the Modern World* that "this self-knowledge [of the body] discloses a prehensive unification of modal presences of entities beyond itself " (p. 73). On objectification (i.e., the converse of prehension), see *Process and Reality,* pp. 23–25. On "conformation" as entailed by causal efficacy, see A. N. Whitehead, *Symbolism, Its Meaning and Effect* (New York: Macmillan, 1927), 43 ff.

51. Both citations are from *Process and Reality,* p. 81. Whitehead is referring to what he terms technically "causal efficacy": ibid., 119–121 and 339, and especially the discussion in *Symbolism, Its Meaning and Effect,* pp. 39–49, where the contrast with presentational immediacy is borne out.

52. *Process and Reality,* 81.

53. Only in terms of presentational immediacy are secondary qualities the objects of (projected) "mental" prehensions. But Whitehead's express aim is to show that such qualities are ultimately grounded in the physical prehensions of the perceiver's own body: "The account here given traces back these secondary qualities to their root in physical prehensions expressed by the 'withness of the body' " (*Process and Reality*, 64; "withness" is underlined).

54. On repetition, see *Process and Reality*, pp. 133–137.

55. *Process and Reality*, 339. Nevertheless, adds Whitehead, the only use of repetition is to become "the organ of novelty" (ibid.) in the organism's future.

56. Ibid., 62; his italics. Notice how "withness" in this citation contests the primacy of vision. For further on withness, see pp. 81, 311–312, 333.

57. Ibid., 311; his italics.

58. Ibid., 63. On the basis of this claim, the close tie between the body's witness and causal efficacy—which is always a matter of the immediate past—becomes evident.

59. "Nexus" is defined by Whitehead as "a set of actual entities in the unity of the relatedness constituted by their prehensions of each other, or—what is the same thing conversely expressed—constituted by their objectifications in each other" (ibid., 24). The dialectic of prehensions and objectifications ensures that implacement in a nexus cannot be reduced to simple location.

60. Ibid., 93; his italics.

61. Ibid., 311; his italics. For further discussion of the here/there structure, see *Getting Back into Place*, chap. 3.

62. "A sense-object has *ingression* into space-time" (*Science and the Modern World*, 70; his italics).

63. *Science and the Modern World*, 70. At ibid., Whitehead gives as an example perceiving the green of a tree in a mirror: the green is present at the surface of the mirror in my "here," while having simultaneously the modal location of belonging to the tree in back of me "there," which is reflected in the same mirror.

64. On modal location, see *Science and the Modern World*, p. 71. For a discussion of the Spinozistic origin of the terms "mode" and "modal" as used by Whitehead, see p. 69. Compare also the treatment of "localization" in *Symbolism*, pp. 53–56. The phrase "location elsewhere" occurs at *Science and the Modern World*, p. 71.

65. *Process and Reality*, 7.

66. Ibid., 119. Beyond the obvious resemblance to Leibniz, such a claim as this also reflects Peirce's notion that human intuition (as exhibited in brilliant "abductive" hypotheses) shows itself to be part and parcel of the universe that it is attempting to grasp as well as the recently proposed "anthropic principle," according to which the universe is ultimately shaped in keeping with the structures of human understanding.

67. A "presented locus" is defined as "the contemporary nexus perceived in the mode of presentational immediacy, with its regions defined by sensa" (*Process and Reality*, 126).

68. "The presented locus [of any actual entity] is defined by some systematic relation to the human body" (*Process and Reality*, 126). It should be noted that the issue is not one of the relative priority of body *over* place, since the opposite can also be affirmed: "The [bodily] concrescence presupposes its basic region, and not the region

its concrescence" (ibid., 283). In the end, the situation is that of a bidirectional determination of body by place and vice versa, as we can see from the concomitance of prehension and objectification within any given actual entity.

69. Whitehead also criticizes Kant for making the forms of intuition *constitutive* of the experienced world rather than conforming to it: "Kant's 'form of intuition' . . . is derived from the actual world *qua datum,* and thus is not 'pure' in Kant's sense of that term. It is not productive of the ordered world, but derivative from it" (*Process and Reality,* 72).

70. Kant writes to Marcus Herz on February 21, 1772, concerning an early plan for the *Critique of Pure Reason*: the projected work will have two sections, namely, "Phenomenology in general" and "Metaphysics according to its nature and method" (translated in Kerferd and Walford, *Selected Pre-Critical Writings,* 111).

71. Edmund Husserl, *The Crisis of European Sciences and Transcendental Phenomenology,* trans. D. Carr (Evanston: Northwestern University Press, 1970), 98. Husserl underlines "I-myself" (*Ich-selbst*). The phrase "universal philosophy" also is found at p. 98. An alternative formulation of the transcendental project in philosophy is that it "goes back to knowing subjectivity as the primal locus of all objective formations of sense and ontic validities" (ibid., 99). The phrase "primal locus" (*Urstätte*) is suggestive of an implaced subjectivity but is not further pursued by Husserl.

72. Ibid., 99; his italics.

73. The title of section 28 of the *Crisis* is "Kant's Unexpressed 'Presupposition': The Surrounding World of Life, Taken for Granted as Valid." The phrase "rigorous science" (*strenge Wissenschaft*) is at p. 99. Husserl's essay of 1911, "Philosophy as a Rigorous Science," had stated its author's passionate commitment to such *Wissenschaft,* even though Husserl had not yet espoused a specifically transcendental form of it.

74. *Crisis,* 107. Husserl adds that "purely in terms of perception, physical body and living body [*Körper und Leib*] are essentially different; living body, that is, [understood] as the only one which is actually given [to me as such] in perception: my own living body" (ibid.). "The completely unique ontic meaning" is presumably the special way in which this same living body addresses itself to, and organizes, the perceptual life-world.

75. "I hold sway quite immediately, kinesthetically—[as] articulated into particular organs through which I hold sway, or potentially hold sway, . . . this 'holding-sway' [is] exhibited as functioning in all perception of bodies" (*Crisis,* 107). On participation, see p. 106: "Obviously and inevitably participating in this is our living body, which is never absent from the perceptual field, and specifically its corresponding 'organs of perception' (eyes, hands, ears, etc.)." The mention of "hands" is intriguing but is not focused on further.

76. *Crisis,* 106. Kinestheses are the basis of the deepest "correspondence" between the lived body and the life-world: "To the variety of appearances through which a [perceived] body is perceivable as this one-and-the-same body correspond, in their own way, the kinestheses which belong to this [lived] body" (p. 107). Even apart from the peculiarities of kinesthesia—to which we shall return below—there is a deep collusion between the sensible appearances of "bodies" in the environment and the lived body that is responsible for perceiving them: an appearance "exhibits itself perceptively only in seeing, in touching, in hearing, etc." (p. 106).

77. As in the phrase, "Jetzpunkt mit Vergangenheitshorizont" (Husserl, *The Phenomenology of Internal Time-Consciousness,* as published in the series *Husserliana,* ed. R. Boehm [The Hague: Nijhof, 1966], sec. 10).

78. I refer to manuscripts written at Seefeld in the summer of 1905 (when the idea of phenomenological reduction was also conceived): for example, the first text in volume 1 of the three volumes on intersubjectivity, which have been published as *Husserliana* 13: *Zur Phänomenologie der Intersubjektivität,* ed. Iso Kern (The Hague: Nijhof, 1973). See also Husserl's autobiographical comment at ibid., vol. 1, p. 490. (I owe this reference and many other valuable indications regarding Husserl's treatment of space to Elizabeth Behnke, director of the Jean Gebser Institute and editor of the *Newsletter for the Phenomenology of the Body.*) For Husserl's most concerted early treatment of the body in relation to space, see the lecture course and appendixes published under the title *Ding und Raum* (*Husserliana* 16, ed. Ulrich Claesges [The Hague: Nijhof, 1973]). For an account of these early inquiries, along with representative passages, see Ulrich Claesges, *Edmund Husserls Theorie der Raumkonstitution* (The Hague: Nijhof, 1964), and Elizabeth Ströker, *Investigations in Philosophy of Space,* trans. A. Mickunas (Athens: Ohio University Press, 1987).

79. Husserl, "The World of the Living Present and the Constitution of the Surrounding World External to the Organism," trans. F. A. Elliston and L. Langsdorf, in *Husserl: Shorter Works* (Notre Dame: University of Notre Dame Press, 1981), 246. (Hereafter "The World of the Living Present." This manuscript was written in 1931.)

80. Ibid., 247.

81. My own body (designated *Ichleib* by Husserl) "occupies a privileged position (*eine ausgezeichnete Stellung*) in the thing-world (*Dingwelt*) as it appears through perception" (*Ding und Raum,* 80).

82. On the *Leib* as a *Träger des Ich* and as localizing sensations, see *Ding und Raum,* p. 162. On the difference between my body as a *Körper* and as a *Leib,* see pp. 161–162, 279–280. This distinction, subsequently so celebrated, is already present in Husserl's earlier writings on the subject of space, i.e., those that stem from circa 1906–1907.

83. "To each distinguishable concrete element of sensation there corresponds its position (*Lage*), its here. And this here is a moment belonging to it, grounding relations of distance (*Abstand*)" (*Ding und Raum,* 283). Husserl describes this bodily "here" as located "in the eyes or behind the eyes" (p. 228). Elsewhere, Husserl says that "I constantly perceive [my *Leib*] as the bearer of the here" (*Intersubjectivity,* 1:236).

84. *Ding und Raum,* 80.

85. On the body's relation to the three dimensions—and thus to the directions they entail—see *Ding und Raum,* pp. 80, 231.

86. Ibid., 80: "Alles Erscheinende ist seine Umgebung."

87. The term "Ichzentrum" is found at *Ding und Raum,* p. 280. On the centrality of the *Ichpunkt,* see also pp. 238 and 281. According to Husserl's analysis, the lived body, the I, and the center of orientation all converge: indeed, they are aspects of the same entity. My body as *Eigenleib* is always absolutely proximal to myself: "My body is what is closest" (*Zur Phänomenologie der Intersubjektivität,* 2:546).

88. *Ding und Raum,* 280. See also p. 283: when I move in space, it appears that "the world has moved itself, while I rested; but after the movement it [the world] is

otherwise exactly the same as it was before—except that my body has another position (*Stellung*) in relation to it."

89. Ibid., 281: "der Leib bewegt sich, ohne sich zu 'entfernen.' "

90. As Husserl remarks in a text of 1931, "I cannot throw my hand so that it flies far away" ("The World of the Living Present and the Constitution of the Surrounding World External to the Organism," trans. F. A. Elliston and Lenore Langsdorf, in F. A. Elliston and P. McCormick, eds., *Husserl: Shorter Works* [Notre Dame: Notre Dame University Press, 1981), 249; hereafter "The World of the Living Present").

91. *Ding und Raum,* 80: "der immer bleibende Beziehungspunkt." This is not to deny that in some sense my body qua *Leib* does change place. It "wanders," as Husserl likes to put it: "When I move myself from place to place, the null-point of orientation wanders in a certain manner, coinciding with continually new points of objective space. My *Leibkörper* can wander only thanks to the fact that the null-point 'wanders' and with it my visual space" (ibid., 308). Such wandering appears to be a purely phenomenal movement, not to be confused with movement in "objective space."

92. Ibid., 83. For more on the idea of field, see secs. 23 and 48. On the distinction between *Sehraum* and objective *Raum,* see p. 367 (Beilage IX of 1916) and p. 304 (from Husserl's summary essay of 1916).

93. On these ideas, see *Ding und Raum,* sec. 53: "Das visuelle Feld als Ortssystem und seine möglichen Transformationen."

94. See *Ding und Raum,* 185, 275, 298–300.

95. Ibid., 179: "die Ortsmannigfaltigkeit ist etwas absolut Invariables, immer Gegebenes."

96. Ibid., 180. Husserl's point, however, is not that a particular kinesthetic sensation is associated with a particular place, but that there is a reliable correlation between "the whole extension of places and K in general" (ibid., 180).

97. On this point, see *Ideen II,* ed. M. Biemel (The Hague: Nijhof, 1952), 57–58; and a fragment of 1921 cited by Claesges, *Edmund Husserls Theorie,* 114 n. 1: "Originally, there belongs to every system of constitutive appearances of each (visual and tactile) 'world' a motivating system of kinesthetic occurrences, which have no meaning beyond this motivation."

98. On visual vs. other kinds of kinesthesia, see *Ding und Raum,* 299–300, 308.

99. "Der Ort ist verwirklicht durch die Kinäesthese, in der das Was des Ortes optimal erfarhen ist" (cited from a manuscript of 1932 in Claesges, *Edmund Husserls Theorie,* 82).

100. In a manuscript of 1931 Husserl writes, "In this way I have a core-sphere (*Kernsphäre*) of things constituted wholly originally, so to speak a core-world (*Kernwelt*): the sphere of things, to which I bring myself by means of my kinesthesias and which I can experience in optimal form" (cited in Claesges, *Edmund Husserls Theorie,* 83, n. 2).

101. As Claesges remarks, "The kinesthetic system is a system of enablement (*Vermöglichkeit*), which in a [given] kinesthetic situation is each time partially actualized. Enablement is a possibility in the sense of the 'I can' " (*Edmund Husserls Theorie,* 75).

102. From a manuscript of 1921 cited in Claesges, *Edmund Husserls Theorie,* 83. Nearness itself is defined by Husserl as "what I can see in a 'small' stretch of time—

in a unitary comprehensive intuition and in a kinesthetic aspect confined to a unified consciousness and bearing on a totality of sides" (from the same MS, ibid. n 4). For further discussion of the near-sphere, see Beilage 73, "Die Konstitution des Raumes im Synthetischen Übergang von Nahraum zu Nahraum" (Feb. 1927), *Zur Phänomenologie des Intersubjectivität* 2, where Husserl says that "der Raum [ist] konstituert im Übergang von Nahraum zu Nahraum durch Fernkinästhesen" (p. 546).

103. "Space as the 'form' of my intuitive world is thus the correlate of my kinesthetic system as a whole and its horizon-structure" (from the manuscript of 1921 as cited in Claesges, *Edmund Husserls Theorie,* 84).

104. From a manuscript of 1931; cited in Claesges, *Edmund Husserls Theorie,* 84. Even as he begins to notice the importance of place, Husserl never gives up the idea of a fully constituted, homogeneous objective space: "Space itself is a system of points and directions, and is homogeneous in itself " (*Zur Phänomenologie des Intersubjectivität,* 2:54). But see the statement cited next in my text above for a significant complication of this claim.

105. *Zur Phänomenologie des Intersubjectivität,* 1:239; his italics.

106. "*Leibhaftig*" means "bodily," "living," "animate," "corporeal," "in person"; Husserl uses it to characterize the unimpeachability of the evidence for eidetic insight.

107. Husserl, *Crisis,* 51; Husserl italicizes "garb of ideas." Husserl adds: "Mathematics and mathematical science, as a garb of ideas, or the garb of symbols of the symbolic mathematical theories, encompasses everything which, for scientists and the educated generally, *represents* the life-world, *dresses it up* as 'objectively actual and true' nature" (ibid.; his italics).

108. Ibid., 54; my italics. On the confusion of method with nature, see p. 51: "It is through the garb of ideas that we take for *true being* what is actually a *method* " (his italics).

109. Ibid., 55.

110. "The geometrical methodology of operatively determining some and finally all ideal shapes, beginning with basic shapes as elementary means of determination, points back to the methodology of determination by surveying and measuring in general" (ibid., 27). For a different but quite rigorous treatment of the genesis of geometry (most notably Euclidean geometry) out of phenomenological givens, see Oscar Becker, "Beiträge zur phänomenologischen Begründung der Geometrie und ihrer physikalischen Anwendungen," *Jahrbuch für Philosophie und phänomenologische Forschung* (1923) 6:385–560, as well as Becker's later book *Grösse und Grenze der mathematischen Denkweise* (Freiburg: München, 1959).

111. *Crisis,* 27–28.

112. On this domination and guidance, ibid., 28, 32.

113. Ibid., 38.

114. Ibid., 29. Husserl underlines "pure" and "abstract shape."

115. Ibid., 38.

116. "This universal idealized causality encompasses all factual shapes and plena in their idealized infinity" (ibid., 39).

117. For Husserl's statement of the subjectification of secondary qualities, see *Crisis,* p. 36, where "colors, tones, warmth, and weight," instead of being attributed to "the things themselves," are interpreted as "tone-vibrations," "warmth-vibrations," etc.

Husserl calls these latter "pure events in the world of shapes" (ibid.), but it is clear that such vibrations function only as registered in the physiology of the percipient organism, that is, as causally affecting that organism from within.

118. Ibid., 33; his italics.

119. On the indirect mathematization of secondary qualities, ibid., 37 ff.

120. Ibid., 34; his italics.

121. The first phrase comes from *Crisis,* p. 216; the second from p. 31.

122. Ibid., 50.

123. See *Process and Reality,* pp. 321, 316.

124. *Crisis,* 217.

125. On "Nahdinge," see "The World of the Living Present," p. 249.

126. Ibid., 107.

127. "The ensemble of things experienced at once in the living present is not a mere 'being experienced together' but a unity of a spatiotemporal 'ensemble', of [something] configuratively bound up in spatiotemporality" ("The World of the Living Present," 245–246).

128. "The World of the Living Present," 248.

129. Ibid., 249. In the language of the *Crisis,* particular bodily organs are what allow "the ego of affections and actions" to "hold sway": see *Crisis,* p. 107.

130. "The World of the Living Present," 249.

131. Ibid. I have altered "external" to "outer" as a translation of *äusseren.* "Flow" (*Verläufe*) in this sentence has connotations of moving, specifically, as running.

132. Ibid., 248. On this point, the formulation of the *Crisis* is clearer: "To the variety of appearances through which a body is perceivable as this one-and-the-same body correspond, in their own way, the kinestheses which belong to this body" (*Crisis,* 107).

133. "The World of the Living Present," 249–250. On the here/there relation, see *Crisis,* p. 216.

134. "From the beginning the animate organism has constitutively an exceptional position (*Ausnahmestellung*)" ("The World of the Living Present," 249).

135. "*Hiersein ist herrlich*" (Rilke, *Duino Elegies,* the Seventh).

136. "The World of the Living Present," 250.

137. Ibid.

138. On the achievement of persisting things, Husserl says that "walking thereby receives the sense of a modification of all coexistent subjective appearances whereby now the intentionality of the appearance of things first remains preserved, as self-constituting in the oriented things and in the change of orientation, as identical things (*identische Dinge*)" ("The World of the Living Present," 250). Put more clearly, "in the change of kinesthetically motivated modes of appearance every external thing (*Ausserding*) is constituted as the same" (p. 248). The "fixed system of places" is discussed at p. 250.

139. "The World of the Living Present," 240.

140. "Association is thus at work here—and this includes continual apperception, the synthetic unity which forms at *one* position (*die eine Stelle*) as the formation of adumbrations" (ibid., 246; his italics).

141. "The World of the Living Present," 250. The German is *feste Ortssystem,* which is rendered "fixed system of places" at p. 250, but *feste* connotes something

steady or stable, not pinpointed, and *System* connotes an organized whole—not a scientifically ordered totality. Elsewhere, Husserl adds this clarifying remark: "We have a surrounding space as a system of places—i.e., as a system of possible terminations of motions of bodies. In that system all earthly bodies certainly have their particular *loci* (*Stelle*)" ("Foundational Investigations of the Phenomenological Origin of the Spatiality of Nature," trans. F. Kersten, in Elliston and McCormick, *Husserl: Shorter Works,* 225; hereafter "The Origin of the Spatiality of Nature").

142. I borrow the term "basis-place" (*Bodenstätte*) from "The Origin of the Spatiality of Nature," where its semantic scope ranges from "home-place" (*Heimstätte*) to the earth as the ultimate "root-basis" (*Stammboden*): see pp. 226–227.

143. *Ortskontinuum.* The system of places and continuum of places are virtually identical, as is made clear from a passage in "The Origin of the Spatiality of Nature": "The earth has an inner space as a system of places or (even when not conceived mathematically) a continuum of places" (p. 225). Notice also Husserl's use of the somewhat more objectified phrase "continuum of positions": "Kinesthetic movement which has become a continuum (constitutively) is the continuum of positions (*Stelle*) of possible standing still" ("The World of the Living Present," 250).

144. "Jeder hat seinen Ort" ("The Origin of the Spatiality of Nature," 225).

145. "The World of the Living Present," 250; my italics.

146. Ibid.

147. Ibid., 248. Husserl adds that such "I move myself " is "taken purely in its subjective kinesthetic sense" (ibid.).

148. Ibid., 248.

149. On this point, see "The Origin of the Spatiality of Nature," pp. 224–226. On p. 230, Husserl says that "its rest is not a mode of motion." Indeed, so radically unmoving is the earth that in its case it is not perhaps even correct to call it "resting"—inasmuch as "rest" is correlated with "motion" in the case of ordinary physical bodies, and "the earth does not move" (p. 225)—just as it is not coherent to speak of the earth as a "body" in any usual sense.

150. "The Origin of the Spatiality of Nature," 224.

151. "The World of the Living Present," 245.

152. "The Origin of the Spatiality of Nature," 226. At pp. 225–226, Husserl maintains that the uniqueness of the lived body is such that for it we can even say that "in primordial experience [my *Leib*] has no motion away and no rest, only inner motion and inner rest unlike the outer bodies." But it remains that the lived body is felt to be *stationary* and does not experience itself as *in motion,* but as the still and unmoving center of motion. Part of the same radical line of thought implies that the lived body also has no proper *place.* A fragment of 1934—written in the same year in which "The Origin of the Spatiality of Nature" was composed—says that "my lived-physical body (*mein Leibkörper*) in its primordiality is so constituted (and thus has as a distinctive meaning) that for it change of place (*Ortsveränderung*) has no sense—and thus also place in space (*Ort im Raum*)" (*Zur Phänomenologie der Intersubjectivität,* 2:659). Notice that this last denial of a "place in space" is precisely what Husserl claims of the earth—suggesting a profound parallel between the earth and the body. (Perhaps this is not so surprising if the earth is the ultimate provider of the places on which the body, despite its inherent placelessness, is dependent.)

153. "The World of the Living Present," 239.

154. "The Origin of the Spatiality of Nature," 225; my italics.

155. Ibid., 250. I have again altered "fixed" to "steady" or "stable" in the translation. Irene Klaver, who pointed out this passage to me, also suggested the importance of rest in Husserl's later writings on body and motion.

156. Wallace Stevens, "Tea at the Palaz of Hoon."

157. "The Impenetrability of Bodies in Space Rests on the Fact that Spatial Determinations are Substantial and Individuating" (February 7, 1915), in *Franz Brentano: Philosophical Investigations on Space, Time, and the Continuum,* trans. B. Smith (London: Croom Helm, 1988), pp. 153, 152. In the same dictation, Brentano denies that there can be "an absolutely empty place": "for one could speak of absolute emptiness only if there was in reality no possible location at all" (ibid.). On the distinction of place from space, see the dictation of February 23, 1917, "What We Can Learn about Space and Time from the Conflicting Errors of the Philosophers," ibid., 156–181. By curious convergence, Jean-Paul Sartre rejoins Brentano in recognizing the importance of place (for Sartre, one of the main parameters of our factical "situation") independently of the role of the body (which Sartre treats separately). See *Being and Nothingness: A Phenomenological Essay on Ontology,* trans. H. Barnes (New York: Washington Square Press, 1992), 629–637 ("My Place").

158. For Merleau-Ponty's use of this term, see his *Phenomenology of Perception,* trans. C. Smith (New York: Humanities Press, 1962), 130.

159. Ibid., 146.

160. See *Phenomenology of Perception,* xvii–xix, on "operative intentionality" (a term borrowed from Husserl) and p. 387 on "original intentionality." These are two expressions of the same phenomenon: the uniquely corporeal intentionality of *le corps vécu.* On corporeal intentionality as a form of operative intentionality, see J. N. Mohanty, *The Concept of Intentionality* (St. Louis: Green, 1972), 139–143.

161. On Brentano's original formulation of the intentionality of consciousness, see his *Psychology from an Empirical Point of View,* first published in 1874 and translated by L. McAlister (New York: Humanities Press, 1973), 77 ff.

162. On the intentional arc, see *Phenomenology of Perception,* pp. 136, 157. For a clarifying treatment of this feature of lived experience, see Richard Zaner, *The Problem of Embodiment* (The Hague: Nijhof, 1971), 172–180; and David Michael Levin, *The Body's Recollection of Being* (London: Routledge & Kegan Paul, 1986), 140–142, 293–300. I have discussed various forms of arc in my *Getting Back into Place,* chaps. 5–8.

163. On such anchorage, see *Phenomenology of Perception,* 144.

164. The first phrase is from ibid., p. 250, the second from p. 251. "Gearing" translates *engrenage.*

165. *Phenomenology of Perception,* 387.

166. Ibid., 140.

167. Ibid., 267. Compare Husserl's use of the term "pre-phenomenal," for example, at *Ding und Raum,* pp. 85 ff.

168. Merleau-Ponty cites Kant as interpreted by P. Lachièze-Rey in the latter's "Réflexions sur l'activité spirituelle constituante" (*Recherches Philosophiques,* 1933–1934): 386–387.

169. *Recherches Philosophiques,* 387; my italics.

170. On spatializing vs. spatialized space, ibid., 244.

171. Ibid., 243.

172. "The Origin of the Spatiality of Nature," 225: "Die Erde bewegt sich nicht."

173. For Merleau-Ponty's rejection of these two interpretations of space, see ibid., 140, 243.

174. Ibid., 146. On orientedness, see pp. 102–103.

175. Ibid., 139–140; my italics. At p. 148, Merleau-Ponty says that "our body is not primarily *in* space: it is of it" (his italics); and at p. 250, it is remarked that "[one] inhabits the spectacle."

176. *Phenomenology of Perception,* 250.

177. On spatiality of situation vs. spatiality of position, see ibid., p. 100.

178. Ibid., 387. See also p. 244.

179. Ibid., 104. "Positional" here means *as explicitly posited in the mind,* that is, as a representation.

180. Ibid., 197. The conjunction of the "where" and the "what"—two of Aristotle's basic metaphysical categories—is striking in this sentence of Merleau-Ponty's.

181. Ibid., 5: "préjugé du monde."

182. Ibid., 249–250. The statement cited above is in effect a restatement of the bodily "I can" as conceived by Husserl. (See also p. 109.) On the notion of indefinite horizon, see p. 140, where Merleau-Ponty says: "The space and time which I inhabit are always in their different ways indeterminate horizons."

183. Ibid., 106. The phenomenal field is discussed at chapter 4 of the introduction.

184. On the body-as-place, see ibid., pp. 106, 154, 254. This claim contrasts with Husserl's conviction that the human body, like the earth, has no proper place. See also the view of Elisabeth Ströker: "My phenomenal place in attuned space is not ascertainable. As an attuned being, I have no determinable location in this space" (*Investigations in Philosophy of Space,* 27).

185. *Phenomenology of Perception,* 105.

186. Ibid., 104.

187. Ibid. On the customary body, see ibid., pp. 82, 146.

188. Ibid., 252. On the example of knowing one's own dwelling, see p. 129. Concerning the role of habit in bodily knowledge of place, see pp. 142–143, 146, 152. On the customary body, see pp. 82, 146. For Husserl's views on the habituality of the body, see Claesges, *Edmund Husserls Theorie,* p. 76. On habitual body memory, see my article "Habitual Body Memory in Merleau-Ponty," *Man and World* (1984) 17: 279–297.

189. *Phenomenology of Perception,* 106. I have replaced "part" with "region" as a translation of *région.*

190. *Process and Reality,* 41. On feelings as positive prehensions, see p. 23.

191. "An actual entity as felt is said to be 'objectified' for that subject" (ibid., 41). Here objectification does not connote the effects of undue theorizing, or the imposition of an *Ideenkleid.*

192. *Phenomenology of Perception,* 249. The Wertheimer experiment is discussed at pp. 248–251; the Stratton experiment (in which the experimental subject must adjust to the world through spectacles that invert the up-down axis) is treated at pp. 244–248.

193. Ibid., 250. On the notion of spatial level, see pp. 248–254.

194. "Every constitution of a level presupposes a different, pre-established level" (ibid., 249). For Merleau-Ponty, then, it is the *level of places,* not their "system" in Husserl's sense, that is preestablished.

195. Ibid., 251.

196. On these further dimensions, see *Phenomenology of Perception,* pp. 266–267.

197. For Heidegger's claim, see *Being and Time,* secs. 22–24, and my commentary in "In and Out of Place with Heidegger" (Pittsburgh: Simon Silverman Phenomenology Center, 1989), vol. 7. I return to a much more detailed discussion of Heidegger in chapter 11 below.

198. See M. Heidegger, *What Is Called Thinking?* trans. J. Glenn Gray (New York: Harper & Row, 1968), 16. "Work of [our] hands" translates *Handwerk.* See also Levin, *The Body's Recollection of Being,* 120–134 ("Thinking with Our Hands") and pp. 137–140 ("Lending a Hand to Being").

199. These are from the last two lines of Wallace Stevens's poem, "The Snow Man."

200. On the idea of "possible habitat" as this relates to the "virtual body," see Merleau-Ponty, *Phenomenology of Perception,* 250.

201. M. Merleau-Ponty, *The Visible and the Invisible,* trans. A. Lingis (Evanston: Northwestern University Press, 1968), 133–134. See also p. 148 and especially p. 261: "the touched-touching . . . the one [finger] encroaches upon the other; they are in a relation of real opposition (Kant)—Local *self* of the finger: its space is felt-feeling" (his italics). Already in *Phenomenology of Perception,* the right hand/left hand relation is treated with special attention: pp. 102, 141, 244, 266.

202. "My body is to the greatest extent what every thing is: a *dimensional this*" (*The Visible and the Invisible,* 260; his italics).

203. Ibid., 141; his italics.

204. Ibid., 260.

205. Ibid., 141; my italics.

206. Ibid. It is difficult to conceive since in fact "one eye, one hand, are capable of vision, of touch, and since what has to be comprehended is that these visions, these touches, these little subjectivities, these 'consciousnesses of . . .', could be assembled like flowers into a bouquet" (ibid.).

207. Ibid., 216–217; his italics.

208. The importance of the dyad at stake in right vs. left hands is emphasized not only by Merleau-Ponty in the above working note but also by Ströker: "In human activity the left 'need not know' what the 'right is doing'; the lived body is not only both-handed but two-handed" (*Investigations in Philosophy of Space,* 66).

209. *The Visible and the Invisible,* 261.

210. "Functional asymmetry" is Elizabeth Ströker's phrase in *Investigations in Philosophy of Space,* p. 65.

211. See, for example, Erwin Straus, "The Forms of Spatiality," in *Psychology of the Human World,* trans. Erling Eng (New York: Basic Books, 1966), and *The Primary World of Senses,* trans. J. Needleman (Glencoe: Free Press, 1963), 197–202, 246, 249, 316 ff., 340; Eugene Minkowski, "Toward a Psychopathology of Lived Space," in *Lived Time,* trans. N. Metzel (Evanston: Northwestern University Press, 1970), 399–433; Bruce Wilshire, *Role-Playing and Identity* (Bloomington: Indiana University Press, 1983); Otto Bollnow, "Lived-Space," trans. D. Gerlach, in *Philosophy Today*

(1961): 31–39; Herbert Plügge, *Der Mensch und sein Leib* (Tübingen: Niemeyer, 1967), 1–47; Elisabeth Ströker, *Investigations in Philosophy of Space,* passim; J. H. Van den Berg, "The Human Body and Movement," *Philosophy and Phenomenological Research* (1952); and M. A. C. Otto, *Der Ort: Phänomenlogische Variationen* (Freiburg: Alber, 1992).

212. On the literal invisibility of right vs. left, see Ströker, *Investigations in Philosophy of Space,* p. 65: "The left-right differentiation does not inhere in the visible symmetrical physical features. . . . To 'look at' my hands as members of my body is to find two completely, equally formed structures." It is for this reason that touch is strictly unreplaceable by sight: "It is important to see that touch, in its space-constituting activity, is not repeatable by any other sensory function, *not even by vision*" (p. 144; my italics).

213. Husserl's primary discussion of sedimentation and reactivation is in "The Origin of Geometry," an appendix to *The Crisis of European Sciences,* esp. at pp. 361 ff. Merleau-Ponty takes up this pair of terms in a working note of June 1, 1960: "It is a question of grasping the *nexus*—neither 'historical' nor 'geographic'—of history and transcendental geology, this very time that is space, this very space that is time, which I will have rediscovered by my analysis of the visible and the flesh, the simultaneous *Urstiftung* of time and space which makes there be a historical landscape and a quasi-geographical inscription of history. Fundamental problem: the sedimentation and the reactivation" (*The Visible and the Invisible,* 259; his italics). Although Merleau-Ponty does not here mention "place," it is operative throughout the note. Indeed, it is operative in the very word "sedimentation," which derives from *sedere,* Latin for "sit," "settle," and which is closely related to "seat" as well as to "reside."

214. Both factors also pertain specifically to the lived body: this, too, is something sedimented in its habituality, while being indefinitely reactivatable in its innovative actions. It is this doubleness of the lived body that allows it to be continuous with the life-world for Husserl and with the world-as-flesh for Merleau-Ponty. The two philosophers disagree only regarding the realist status of the body itself—Husserl considering the body to be both lived and extended in its implacing action, Merleau-Ponty finding the extendedness of the body to be an obstacle to implacement.

215. Merleau-Ponty, *Phenomenology of Perception,* 254. On the same page Merleau-Ponty points to this body-subject as "a system of anonymous 'functions' which draw every particular focus into a general project." Here Merleau-Ponty anticipates Foucault's thesis that institutionally passive or "docile" bodies inscribe and internalize the power-gaze of the other, who rob these bodies of the privacy and intimacy they might otherwise enjoy. (Michel Foucault, *Discipline and Punish,* trans. A. Sheridan [New York: Pantheon, 1977], 135–169.)

216. See Hannah Arendt, *The Human Condition* (New York: Anchor, 1959), chap. 1, "The Public and the Private Realm." For Arendt, the Greek *polis* is the original model of the public realm: "The public realm itself, the *polis,* was permeated by a fiercely agonal spirit. . . . It was the only *place* where men could show who they really and inexchangeably were" (p. 38; my italics).

217. See, for example, Beilage 70 of *Zur Phänomenologie der Intersubjektivität,* 2:515–516, where Husserl discusses the intimate ties between constituting the body of the other as a spatial thing in homogeneous space, along with Beilage 73, pp. 546–547, where the constitution of "near-space" is discussed in ways pertinent to

intersubjectivity. Husserl's extensive discussions of "home-world" vs. "alien-world" in the third *Intersubjectivität* volume (esp. Beilage 48) bear on this same problematic in an even more suggestive way. I am indebted to Anthony Steinbok for these references.

218. On "corpuscular societies," see Whitehead, *Process and Reality,* pp. 35, 63, 72, 92, 99.

219. See, for example, the working note entitled "Flesh—Mind" and dated June 1960, in *The Visible and the Invisible,* pp. 259–260. Two recent studies of the subtle interaction between body and social structure are Susan Bordo, *Unbearable Weight* (Berkeley: University of California Press, 1993), and Judith Butler, *Bodies that Matter: On the Discursive Limits of "Sex"* (New York: Routledge, 1993).

Chapter Eleven: Proceeding to Place by Indirection

1. Heidegger does occasionally allude to the body. In *Being and Time* he writes that "this 'bodily nature' hides a whole problematic of its own" (*Being and Time,* trans. J. Macquarrie and E. Robinson [New York: Harper & Row, 1962], 143). But this bare allusion and one other from the *Metaphysical Foundations of Logic,* to which I shall return in Section III, do not include the crucial assertion that the body plays an indispensable role in the experience of place. Indeed, as Dreyfus alleges, "Heidegger seems to suggest that having a body does not belong to Dasein's essential structure" (Hubert Dreyfus, *Being-in-the-World: A Commentary on Heidegger's Being and Time, Division I* [Cambridge: MIT Press, 1991], 41).

2. Heidegger, *Being and Time,* 456. The phrase "temporality as the ontological meaning of care" is the title of section 65, in which we read that "Temporality reveals itself as the meaning of authentic care" (p. 374; in italics in the text). Temporality (*Zeitlichkeit*) is defined as "the unity of a future which makes present in the process of having-been" (ibid.). As such, temporality is not to be confused with *time (Zeit),* which in its ordinariness and inner-worldly character is merely the leveled-down, homogenized residuum of temporality—much as space, in early modernity, is the *Nivellierung* of place. Modes of temporalizing are said expressly to enable "the basic possibility of authentic or inauthentic existence" (p. 377). See also *The History of the Concept of Time: Prolegomena,* trans. T. Kisiel (Bloomington: Indiana University Press, 1985), a lecture course of 1925; as well as a lecture of 1924, *The Concept of Time,* trans. W. McNeill (Oxford: Blackwell, 1992).

3. The last two sentences of *Being and Time* are as follows: "Is there a way that leads from primordial *time* to the meaning of *Being*? Does *time* manifest itself as the horizon of *Being*?" (*Being and Time,* 488; his italics).

4. *Being and Time,* 40; in italics in the text.

5. Ibid., 377; my italics. "Outside-of-itself " translates *Ausser-sich,* a phrase directly reminiscent of Kant's idea of space as the "outer sense" (*ausser Sinn*) and of the permanent spatial world as "outside" the subject. On the question of Heidegger's self-deconstruction in *Being and Time,* see my essay "Derrida's Deconstruction of Heidegger's Views on Temporality: The Language of Space and Time," in *Phenomenology of Temporality: Time and Language,* Third Annual Symposium of the Silverman Phenomenology Center (Pittsburgh: Duquesne University, 1987).

6. *Being and Time*, 79. On "insideness," see p. 134.

7. See *Being and Time*, p. 79. At p. 134, Heidegger says that "the entity inside and that which closes it round are both present-at-hand in space." By "categorial" Heidegger means having characteristics "of such a sort as to belong to entities whose kind of Being is not of the character of Dasein" (ibid.). The mention of "location-relationship" suggests how close this conception is to simple location in Whitehead's sense of the term.

8. Ibid., 79. Heidegger makes it clear that what is primarily lacking in the container relationship of two present-at-hand entities is the ability to "touch" each other in a *world*: "When two entities are present-at-hand . . . [they] are *worldless* in themselves, they can never 'touch' each other" (ibid., 81; his italics).

9. Ibid., 80; his italics.

10. Ibid. Even if Heidegger neglects the lived body as the vehicle of such actions of making familiar, surely it is involved in carrying out these actions.

11. Ibid., 83.

12. "Not until we understand Being-in-the-world as an essential structure of Dasein can we have any insight into Dasein's *existential spatiality*" (ibid., 83; his italics). This is one of the very few mentions in *Being and Time* of spatiality as "existential."

13. Ibid., 95; his italics. "Within-the-world" translates *innerweltlich,* that is, the special way in which *zuhanden* entities exist in the everyday world.

14. Ibid., 119. "The 'wherein' of an act of understanding which assigns or refers itself is that for which one lets entities be encountered in the kind of Being that belongs to involvements; and this 'wherein' is the phenomenon of the world. And the structure of that to which Dasein assigns itself is what makes up the *worldhood* of the world" (ibid.; mostly in italics in the text).

15. For further on the wherein as drawing together the basic practical relations of Dasein, see especially *Being and Time*, section 18.

16. On leeway, see *Being and Time*, section 23, especially this sentence: "Because Dasein is essentially spatial in the way of de-severance, its dealings always keep within an 'environment' which is de-severed from it with a certain leeway" (p. 141).

17. *Being and Time*, 141. The structure of "coming before" (*Vorkommen*) is the spatial analogue to the way that the future comes toward us as *Zu-kunft.* In both cases, a leeway of open possibilities is projected by Dasein, a leeway *wherein* it can realize its instrumental actions.

18. On the baneful role of determinate presence, see the Introduction to *Being and Time,* esp. section 6, "The Task of Destroying the History of Ontology."

19. The allusion to Aristotle is unmistakable in this passage, with which Part C opens: "This expression [i.e., "insideness"] means that an entity which is itself extended is closed round (*umschlossen*) by the extended boundaries of something that is likewise extended" (*Being and Time*, 134). The mention of "extended" draws in Descartes as well, making this statement a double critique of the two philosophers whom Heidegger sees as his main competitors—along with Kant—in the theory of space.

20. *Being and Time*, 135. See also p. 140: "*In Dasein there lies an essential tendency towards closeness*" (his italics). We shall return to this claim in Section III below.

21. Ibid., 136; his italics.

22. The "hither" (*Hier*) and "thither" (*Dorthin*) articulate the belongingness of a context of equipment to a region: see *Being and Time*, p. 145. Concerning the for-the-

sake-of-which (*das Worumwillen*), also see p. 145: "The 'whither' gets prescribed by a referential totality which has been made fast in a 'for-the-sake-of-which' of concern." For the other characteristics of the whither, the following passage is helpful: "In general the 'whither' to which the totality of places for a context of equipment gets allotted, is the underlying condition which makes possible the belonging-somewhere of an equipmental totality as something that can be placed. . . . Something like a region must first be discovered if there is to be any possibility of allotting or coming across places for a totality of equipment that is circumspectively at one's disposal" (p. 136). For a discerning discussion of the structures here at stake, see Dreyfus, *Being-in-the-World*, pp. 91 ff. See also chapter 7 of *Being-in-the-World*, "Spatiality and Space," pp. 128–140, for an account of the primary themes of sections 22–24 of *Being and Time*.

23. *Being and Time,* 136.

24. On inconspicuous familiarity and on becoming aware of a region by misplacement, see *Being and Time,* pp. 137–138. The operative premise here is that "anything constantly ready-to-hand of which circumspective Being-in-the-world takes account beforehand, *has its place*" (p. 137; my italics).

25. *Being and Time,* 137; my italics. "Individual places" translates *einzelnen Plätze.*

26. This example is given at ibid., p. 137. Less convincing are two other cases: the "places" of the sun on its daily journey (i.e., "sunrise, midday, sunset, midnight") as indicating certain celestial regions and the orientation of churches and graveyards toward the rising and setting sun—thereby indicating "the regions of life and death." (Both are given at p. 137.) These cases are less convincing because each mixes time—e.g., diurnal motion, or a lifetime—with regionality, whose atemporal specificity is here under discussion. For further treatment, see Maria Villela-Petit, "Heidegger's Conception of Space," in C. Macann, ed., *Martin Heidegger: Critical Assessments* (New York: Routledge, 1993), 124 ff.

27. "Dasein constantly takes these directions along with it, just as it does its deseverances" (*Being and Time,* 143).

28. *Being and Time,* 144. Heidegger's serious point is that there is never a "worldless subject" that becomes oriented from its mere feelings—or from external landmarks in the world. Orientation requires a Dasein who has being-in-the-world as a constitutive trait. Throughout, Heidegger's commitment is to the proposition that "Dasein understands itself proximally and for the most part in terms of its world" (p. 156).

29. Ibid., 144.

30. For an illuminating discussion of this public world as foundational to *Being and Time,* see Dreyfus, *Being-in-the-World,* chap. 8, esp. pp. 141–148.

31. *Being and Time,* 145; my italics. "At" here translates *bei,* usually rendered as "alongside" or even "in."

32. Ibid., 145. The phrase "its own discovered region," cited in the next sentence, is at ibid.

33. Both citations are at ibid., p. 145; his italics.

34. It was not, then, a contingent move when Heidegger first introduced "place" by allusion to the directionality of the closeness of equipment (see *Being and Time,* pp. 135–136). Nor is it arbitrary that he also claims in the same early passage that place, thus conceived, "must be distinguished in principle from just occurring at ran-

dom in some spatial position" (p. 135). The phrases "at random" and "in some spatial position" both signify circumstances entirely outside Dasein's range of intervention. It is to be noticed that directionality alone is shared by ready-to-hand things and Dasein. Direction, on the other hand, belongs only to the ready-to-hand—much as de–severance belongs only to Dasein.

35. If it is therefore the case that there is no place without Dasein, is there no Dasein without place? Heidegger never addresses this question, but I presume that his answer would be affirmative—given that Dasein's directional and de–severing powers (a) are part of Dasein's endowment and (b) constitute place as we know it. (I wish to thank Irene Klaver for bringing the pertinence of this question to my attention.)

36. *Richtung,* or "direction," is not the projection, or the product, of directionality, which on the contrary is guided by a direction—as when we "follow" a cardinal direction. Heidegger's rare invocation of the Latin locution *Form* reinforces further the predetermined status of what presents itself as already interinvolved in a region.

37. As Didier Franck remarks, "in the manner of tools, places are beings within reach of the hand (*les étants à portée-de-main*)" (Didier Franck, *Heidegger et le problème de l'espace* [Paris: Minuit, 1986], 69).

38. *Being and Time,* 145.

39. Concerning the autogenesis of positions from places, see ibid., p. 413: "In the 'physical' assertion that the 'hammer is heavy' . . . its place becomes a spatio-temporal position, a 'world-point,' which is in no way distinguished from any other."

40. *Being and Time,* 145. The locus of the *Worin* has thus shifted from "the world"—to which, as we have seen, the term was first attached—to "space." Hence it is "pure." But the interchangeability of world and space is precisely what Cartesian metaphysics (i.e., for Heidegger the quintessence of modern *vorhanden* thinking) entails.

41. Ibid., 145.

42. Ibid., 146; my italics.

43. Ibid., 146. The preceding sentences are also crucial: "Neither the region previously discovered nor in general the current spatiality is explicitly in view. In itself it is present for circumspection in the inconspicuousness of those ready-to-hand things in which that circumspection is concernfully absorbed. With being-in-the-world, space is proximally discovered in this spatiality" (ibid.).

44. On this conclusion, see ibid., p. 146, especially these sentences: "Space is not in the subject, nor is the world in space. Space is rather 'in' the world in so far as space has been disclosed by that being-in-the-world which is constitutive for Dasein. . . . Here '*apriority*' means the previousness with which space has been encountered (*as a region*) whenever the ready-to-hand is encountered environmentally" (my italics).

45. Heidegger here anticipates the thesis of Husserl's "Origin of Geometry," where, however, the genealogy is more carefully worked out. In a footnote Heidegger refers not to Husserl but to Oskar Becker as having blazed the way in his *Beiträge zur phänomenologischen Begründung der Geometrie und ihrer physicalischen Anwendungen* (1923). Becker himself, however, was a student of Husserl's and wrote this treatise under Husserl's watchful supervision.

46. Heidegger gives a more complete, and somewhat variant version, of the genealogy of space in his "Building Dwelling Thinking," p. 155. We shall return to this below.

47. For these developments, see *Being and Time,* p. 147.

48. Ibid., 147. I have changed "mere" to "sheer" as a translation of *reinen.*

49. Ibid., 147–148.

50. Ibid., 147. He adds: "Nor does the Being of space have the kind of Being which belongs to Dasein" (ibid.). Concerning this passage, Didier Franck comments: "Beyond the fact that de-temporalized space no longer manifests itself in the world, how can that which does not correspond to the modes of Being inventoried by universal ontology *be*? To say that space *is* not—does not *temporalize* itself—neither as *Dasein* nor as being within-reach-of-the-hand, is this not to presume that temporality does not deliver the constitutive sense of Dasein?" (*Heidegger et le problème de l'espace,* 98; his italics).

51. On the uncanny, see *Being and Time,* section 40. Heidegger expressly links the analysis of section 12 to the uncanny at p. 233.

52. "Anxiety does not 'see' any definite 'here' or 'yonder' from which it comes. That in the face of which one has anxiety is characterized by the fact that what threatens is *nowhere* (*nirgends*)" (*Being and Time,* 231; his italics). Thus it follows that "that in the face of which anxiety is anxious is nothing ready-to-hand within-the-world" (ibid.).

53. *Being and Time,* 230. Heidegger italicizes "turns thither." He also talks about these entities as part of trying to find solid ground again: "Everyday discourse tends towards concerning itself with the ready-to-hand and talking about it" (p. 231).

54. "The 'nothing' of readiness-to-hand [i.e., as experienced in anxiety] is grounded in the most primordial 'something'—in the *world.* Ontologically, however, the world belongs essentially to Dasein's Being as being-in-the-world. So if the 'nothing'—that is, the world as such—exhibits itself as that in the face of which one has anxiety, this means that *Being-in-the-world is that in the face of which anxiety is anxious*" (*Being and Time,* 232; his italics).

55. *Being and Time,* 232. Cf. p. 233: anxiety brings "Dasein face to face with its world as world, and thus bring[s] it face to face with itself as being-in-the-world." The strict parallelism of formulation only reflects the deep link between "world" and "being-in-the-world"—a link evident in another formulation: "Dasein *is* its world existingly" (p. 416; his italics).

56. Ibid., 232; his italics. Strictly speaking, "being-possible" is "that which Dasein is anxious *about*"—whereas it flees in the face of its *thrown* being-in-the-world. Cf. p. 235 for this distinction.

57. Ibid., 148. Heidegger adds: "Space is still *one* of the things that is constitutive for the world, just as Dasein's own spatiality is essential to its basic state of Being-in-the-world" (ibid.; his italics).

58. Ibid.

59. It is also to attain the pure "homogeneous space of Nature" (ibid., 147), which is the triumph of early modern science and which consists specifically, according to Heidegger, in being "deprived of worldhood" (ibid.). It is not surprising that Pascal was driven to profound anxiety in contemplating the silent infinity of just such space! (Yet the same planiform space can also be a source of metaphysical comfort—a point to which I return in the postface of this book.)

60. *"From an existential-ontological point of view, the 'not-at-home' must be conceived as the more primordial phenomenon"* (ibid., 234; his italics).

61. Ibid., 234.

62. Ibid., 231; my italics. One suspects that the nowhere of space is implicitly present in Kant's transcendental doctrine of space as an "infinite given magnitude" that is itself located nowhere in particular. I owe this observation to François Raffoul.

63. Ibid., 231.

64. "Only in so far as Dasein has the definite character of temporality, is the authentic potentiality-for-Being-a-whole of anticipatory resoluteness, as we have described it, made possible for Dasein itself. *Temporality reveals itself as the meaning of authentic care*" (ibid., 374; his italics). Care itself has the function of drawing Dasein's various *existentialia* into a first unification; but care depends on temporality for its own unification: "The primordial unity of the structure of care lies in temporality" (p. 375; in italics in the text).

65. "Dasein's spatiality is 'embraced' by temporality in the sense of being existentially founded upon it" (ibid., 418).

66. "Time and Being," in M. Heidegger, *On Time and Being,* trans. J. Stambaugh (New York: Harper, 1969), 23. Heidegger suggests that something like the converse must be the case: that is, "when we have previously gained insight into the origin of space in the properties peculiar to place (*Ort*) and have thought them adequately" (ibid.).

67. Ibid., 418.

68. As cited and translated in S. Sambursky, *The Concept of Place in Late Neoplatonism* (Jerusalem: Israel Academy of Sciences and Humanities, 1982), 37.

69. *Being and Time,* 418.

70. Ibid.

71. "The demonstration that [Dasein's] spatiality is existentially possible only through temporality cannot aim either at deducing space from time or at dissolving it into pure time" (ibid.). Concerning these matters, consult Franck, *Heidegger et le problème de l'espace,* especially Franck's eloquent argument that the role of hands and more particularly the flesh (*la chair*) in *Being and Time* exceeds and contests any temporal analysis of Dasein: "The intertwining of the hands, [i.e.] the originarily spatializing crisscrossing (*l'entrelacs*) of the flesh, has none of the modes of Being recognized by fundamental ontology. . . . It is because the spatiality of *Dasein* as a being in the world wherein [the mode of] Being is either present-at-hand or ready-to-hand presupposes the intertwining of the hands that [this spatiality] is irreducible to ecstatic temporality" (*Heidegger et le problème de l'espace,* 97).

72. *Being and Time,* 420.

73. Ibid.

74. Ibid., 419; my italics. The full sentence is: "Dasein takes space in (*einnehmt*); this is to be understood literally." *Einnehmen* means to occupy or take up space; but Heidegger is playing on *ein-nehmen,* that is, to "take in."

75. Ibid., 419. A few sentences later, Heidegger specifies that "Dasein's making room for itself is constituted by directionality and de-severance" (ibid.).

76. On breaking into (*Einbruch*) space, see *Being and Time,* p. 421. But does it help to add that "only on the basis of its ecstatico-horizonal temporality is it possible for Dasein to break into space" (ibid.; in italics in the text)?

77. Heidegger consistently uses *Platz* for "something that belongs to any ready-to-hand equipment" (p. 423). His employment of *Ort,* however, is not consistent. He

remarks that in considering a tool as something merely present-at-hand, "its place (*Platz*) becomes a matter of indifference" but that "this does not mean that what is present-at-hand loses its 'location' (*Ort*) altogether" (p. 413). Here *Ort* signifies something close to simple location in Whitehead's sense. But in the passage given above, *Ort* has genuine existential significance, since only Dasein can "determine its own location." This equivocation in terminology is revealing of Heidegger's ambivalence toward the importance of place in his early writings: only occasionally existential in status, it is all too often consigned to the realm of the ready-to-hand.

78. *Being and Time*, 420. Heidegger also discerns this same movement in his temporal analysis: "When we make something present by bringing it close from its 'thence,' the making-present forgets the 'yonder' and loses itself in itself " (p. 421).

79. Ibid., 420; my italics. Heidegger underlines "region."

80. *History of the Concept of Time*, 224. Heidegger's discussion of Dasein's "primary spatiality" in section 25 ("The Spatiality of the World") of this text of 1925 is of particular interest as an earlier version of the definitive formulations of sections 22–24 of *Being and Time*.

81. *The Metaphysical Foundations of Logic*, trans. M. Heim (Bloomington: Indiana University Press, 1984), 138.

82. Ibid.; his italics. I have kept with Heim's translation of *Zerstreuung* as "dissemination," even though "dispersion" (i.e., the choice of the English translators of *Being and Time*) is not invalid. "Dissemination"—now dignified by being given a specific noun form—rightly emphasizes the radicalness of the dispersive direction of the new analysis.

83. Ibid., 137–138.

84. Ibid., 138.

85. Ibid.; his italics.

86. Ibid.; my italics.

87. Ibid.

88. "To strew" derives from an Old Teutonic stem, *strau-*, that underlies German *streuen* (to spread, scatter) as well as *Zerstreuung*; one of the basic English meanings of "strew" is "to be spread or scattered upon" (*Oxford English Dictionary*)—a definition that combines the action of dissemination with the precondition of spread-outness.

89. *Metaphysical Foundations of Logic*, 221.

90. M. Heidegger, *An Introduction to Metaphysics*, trans. R. Manheim (New Haven: Yale University Press, 1959), 205; his italics. I have changed "site" to "place" as a translation of *Stätte*, and "man" to "Dasein." I have also capitalized "Being" when *Sein* is used by itself.

91. *An Introduction to Metaphysics*, 152; his italics.

92. "To this place and scene of history belong the gods, the temples, the priests, the festivals, the games, the poets, the thinkers, the ruler, the council of elders, the assembly of the people, the army and the fleet" (ibid., 152).

93. Ibid., 62.

94. Ibid., 60; his italics. I have rendered *Seiendes* as "being" rather than "essent."

95. "Building Dwelling Thinking," 154; his italics. "Presencing" translates *Wesen*. Hofstadter translates *Grenze* as "boundary." Heidegger has in mind *peras* in Greek discussions: "A space is something that has been made room for (*Eingeräumtes*),

something that is cleared and free, namely within a boundary, Greek *peras*" ("Building Dwelling Thinking," 154).

96. Indeed, both *zuhanden* and *vorhanden* entities arise precisely when "the end result is no longer that which is impressed into limits, that is, placed in its form" (*An Introduction to Metaphysics*, 62; I have taken the parentheses away from the phrase "placed in its form").

97. The phrase "place of history" as a description of the *polis* occurs at "Building Dwelling Thinking," p. 152. On the common meaning of *Anwesen* and *ousia* (presence) as real estate, see p. 61. The relation between German *Stätte* and English "estate" via Latin *status* is also to be noted.

98. Ibid., 37–38.

99. Ibid., 38.

100. Ibid., 38–39.

101. For further discussion of this dire direction—at once politically pernicious (given its apparent endorsement of Hitler) and philosophically dubious (have we not descended into the real of the *vorhanden* with talk of "nation," "center," etc.?)—see my essay "Heidegger in and out of Place," in *Heidegger: A Centenary Appraisal*, given in 1989 at the seventh annual symposium of the Silverman Phenomenology Center (Pittsburgh: Duquesne University, 1990), 62–98. For the link between "spirit," metaphysics, and Nazism—a link more explicitly evident in the *Rekoratsrede* of 1933—see Jacques Derrida, *Of Spirit: Heidegger and the Question,* trans. G. Bennington and R. Bowlby (Chicago: University of Chicago Press, 1989).

102. *An Introduction to Metaphysics*, 151.

103. Ibid., 151.

104. Ibid., 161. The first use of "violent one" is in italics.

105. Ibid., 152–153; his italics. "Statute" translates *Satzung*.

106. Ibid., 161. I have replaced "being-there" with "Dasein."

107. Heidegger cites the "specter" of "mass meetings attended by millions [which are] looked on as a triumph" (ibid., 38) with evident disdain—indeed, with as much chagrin as his learning that "a boxer is regarded as a nation's great man" (ibid.): an apparent reference to Joe Louis.

108. Heidegger takes his inspiration from a saying of Heraclitus: "War (*polemos*) is father of all and king of all" (Diels, fr. 53; Kahn translation). He remarks: "The *polemos* named here is a conflict that prevailed prior to everything divine and human, not a war in the human sense. . . . The struggle meant here is the original struggle, for it gives rise to the contenders as such" (ibid., 62).

109. Friedrich Nietzsche, *The Will to Power,* bk. 3, sec. 822 (1888), in Walter Kaufman's translation. Concerning this passage, see Erich Heller, "Nietzsche's Last Words about Art versus Truth," in Heller's *The Importance of Nietzsche* (Chicago: University of Chicago Press, 1988), 158–172.

110. "The Origin of the Work of Art," trans. A. Hofstadter, in *Poetry, Language, Thought* (New York: Harper & Row, 1971), 60–61.

111. Ibid., 61. "Present beings" translates *Anwesenden*. We recognize here the basic logic of a movement *from* leeway *back to* place that was first detected in section 70 of *Being and Time,* even if the word for "place" itself is *Stätte* and no longer *Platz*. But the place in question is no longer ready-to-hand.

112. Ibid., 41. Cf. p. 18: "We shall attempt to discover the nature of art in the place where (*dort wo*) art undoubtedly prevails in a real way."

113. The content of the last two sentences is found at ibid., p. 61. I have altered Hofstadter's translation at certain points to accord with earlier usage in this chapter.

114. Ibid., 41. At p. 42, Heidegger says that "standing there (*dastehend*), the building rests on the rocky ground."

115. Ibid., 56.

116. Ibid., 41–42. Cf. p. 62: "Truth wills to be established in the work as this conflict of world and earth."

117. Ibid., 55.

118. Ibid., 45. On the *Weite* of the world, see p. 42; on its "broad paths," p. 48; on "clearing of the paths," p. 55.

119. Ibid., 46.

120. Ibid., 47. See also p. 46: "That in which (*das Wohin*) the work sets itself back and which it causes to come forth in this setting back of itself we called the earth. Earth is that which comes forth and shelters. Earth, self-dependent, is effortless and untiring."

121. Ibid., 47; my italics.

122. Ibid., 46; in italics in the text.

123. Both phrases are at ibid., p. 47.

124. Ibid., 55. The earth "emerges as native ground (*der heimatische Grund*)" only when the world of the work is set back into the earth: ibid., 42.

125. Ibid., 42; my italics.

126. Ibid., 50. "Repose" translates *die Ruhe*. Heidegger stresses that it is not to be confused with mere peace or harmony.

127. The phrase "simplicity of intimacy" occurs at ibid., 49, "common cleft" and "rift" at p. 63.

128. Ibid., 63–64; my italics. I have changed "self-closing" to "self-secluding."

129. Ibid., 64; his italics.

130. Ibid., 64. "Fixing in place" here translates *feststellen* (i.e., ascertaining or establishing, but more particularly putting or making steady). *Stellen* itself means to arrange or set, put or place. Avoiding the noun form *Stelle* (perhaps out of his awareness of the derivative and hardened status of sheer "position" in early modern philosophy), Heidegger traces *stellen* back to the Greek *thesis*: "a setting up in the unconcealed" (ibid., 61). This formulation, however, favors world over earth, and in an addendum added in 1956 Heidegger revises himself. Now *thesis* is taken to mean "to let lie forth in its radiance and presence," signifying that "the 'fix' in 'fix in place' can never have the sense of rigid, motionless, and secure" (p. 83). To fix truth in place in a figure is not to pin it down to a determinate position; it is to put it in place in the Open, where it can move and radiate.

131. Ibid., 84.

132. Ibid., 83.

133. Ibid.

134. On "guiding measure" (*weisenden Mass*), see ibid., p. 44; on "setting of bounds" (*Aus-grenzen*), p. 47.

135. Ibid., 41.

136. Heidegger refuses to characterize the place of the work as an *Ort*, a term he

reserves for the simple location of, say, a temple: "We visit the temple in Paestum at its own location" (ibid., 40–41). Nor is the motion that is consonant with repose or rest a mere change of location (*Ortsveränderung*): p. 48. And the work's place is not at all to be reduced to the installing of art objects: " 'Setting up' no longer means a bare placing (*blosse Anbringen*)" (p. 44).

137. Ibid., 46.

138. For Heidegger's critique of the craft model of art, see ibid., pp. 58 ff., esp. p. 64. Regarding the denial of the work's instrumental character, see esp. pp. 29–30.

139. On the work's "self-sufficiency" (*Selbstgenugsamkeit*), see ibid., 29.

140. "In the work, the happening of truth is at work. But what is thus at work, is so *in* the work" (ibid., 58; his italics).

141. M. Heidegger, "Conversation on a Country Path," trans. J. M. Anderson and E. H. Freund, in *Discourse on Thinking* (New York: Harper, 1966), 64. I have altered the translation here and elsewhere. Horizon is paired with "transcendence," since representational thinking transcends objects *toward* an encircling horizon, which is the inner surface, as it were, of the all-englobing Open.

142. Ibid., 65; his italics. "Region" translates *Gegend;* "rests" translates *ruhe.* Notice that "belonging there" is decisively different from the "belongingness" of *zuhanden* regions as detailed in *Being and Time.*

143. Ibid., 66. On returning as remaining, see p. 68.

144. Ibid., 65. The coming-to-meet-us is analogous to the way that objects in a horizon come to meet us: "Out of the view which [a horizon] encircles, the appearance of objects comes to meet us" (ibid.). We recognize in this statement once again the basic spatial schema of *from/back to* that we have encountered several times before. We also detect an echo of the early claim that "only in thus 'coming before us' (*Vorkommen*) is the current world authentically ready-to-hand" (*Being and Time,* 141; in italics in the text).

145. "Conversation on a Country Path," 66. "Expanse" translates *Weite,* the same word used to describe the "breadth" of world in "The Origin of the Work of Art."

146. "Conversation on a Country Path," 68–69.

147. Ibid., 72. "Release" here translates *gelässt,* that is, literally "let be." *Gelassenheit* is letting things be by releasing oneself to them. The basic movement of "releasement" is found in that-which-regions—"in relation to which releasement is what it is" (p. 70). More specifically, in releasement one *receives* that-which-regions: "Releasement, thus composedly steadfast, would be a receiving of the regioning of that-which-regions" (p. 81). For a more explicit discussion of *Gelassenheit,* see the essay that precedes "Conversation on a Country Path," "Memorial Address."

148. Ibid., 72.

149. "Thinking is releasement to that-which-regions because its nature lies in the regioning of releasement" (ibid., 74). Truly spontaneous thinking, thanks to its regional ground, attains "in-dwelling" (*In-ständigkeit*). The Teacher says: "The in-dwelling in releasement to that-which-regions would then be the real nature of the spontaneity of thinking" (p. 82).

150. Ibid., 68.

151. Ibid., 86.

152. Ibid.

153. Ibid., 89. The fragment is Diels no. 122. Kahn remarks that "there is no reason

to doubt the authenticity of the single word listed as D. 122, but also no hint of a sentential context and hence no way to construe it as a meaningful fragment" (C. Kahn, *The Art and Thought of Heraclitus* [Cambridge: Cambridge University Press, 1979], 288).

154. "Conversation on a Country Path," 89. I have changed "oneself " to "yourself." On appropriation to that-which-regions, see p. 73: "Releasement comes out of that-which-regions because in releasement man stays released to that-which-regions and, indeed, through this itself. He is released to it in his being, insofar as he originally belongs to it. He belongs to it insofar as he is *appropriated* (*vereignet*) initially to that-which-regions and, indeed, through this itself " (his italics). For Heidegger, such appropriation is an instance of human beings' *being regioned* (*Vergegnis*), that is, being brought into the nearness of that-which-regions. Concerning the notion of coming into nearness, see David Michael Levin, *The Body's Recollection of Being* (London: Routledge & Kegan Paul, 1986), 134–137.

155. *Being and Time,* 140; in italics in the text. "Closeness" translates *Nähe.*

156. "Inwiefern und weshalb? Sein qua beständige Anwesenheit hat Vorrang, Gegenwärtigung."

157. M. Heidegger, "The Thing," in *Poetry, Language, Thought,* 165. "Nearness" again translates *Nähe.*

158. Ibid. "Despite all conquest of distances," adds Heidegger, "the nearness of things remains absent" (p. 166). "Distance" translates *Entfernung.*

159. Ibid., 166. In other words, everything "is, as it were, without distance" (ibid.).

160. For this last paradox, see ibid., p. 166.

161. Ibid., 181: "Dingen ist Nähern von Welt."

162. Ibid., 178.

163. Nearing is at once the nature of nearness and intrinsic to thinging. "Nearness is at work in bringing near, as the thinging of the thing" (ibid., 178). See also p. 181: "Nearing (*Nähern*) is the nature of nearness." The closely comparable participle *Näherung* is already employed in *Being and Time,* p. 140—but to very different effect. On the relationship between thing and place, see Heidegger's 1935–1936 lecture course entitled *What Is a Thing?* trans. W. B. Barton, Jr., and V. Deutsch (Chicago: Regnery, 1967), 14–28.

164. "The Thing," 177–178. It is striking that Heidegger here employs the same verb, *nahebringen* (to bring near) as he did in *Being and Time.*

165. Ibid., 181. The full statement is "The thing stays—gathers and unites—the fourfold. The thing things world. Each thing stays the fourfold into a happening of the simple onehood of world." World itself is now defined as "the simple onefold of earth and sky, divinities and mortals" (p. 179).

166. Ibid., 178.

167. *Being and Time,* 148.

168. "The Thing," 181; my italics.

169. "Building Dwelling Thinking," 151.

170. " 'Being alongside' (*Sein bei*) the world in the sense of being absorbed in the world (a sense which calls for still closer interpretation) is an *existentiale* founded upon Being-in" (*Being and Time,* 80–81). "Absorbed in the world" translates *Aufgehens in der Welt.*

171. Although Heidegger does not expressly invoke nearing at this juncture, it is

surely at stake in statements such as this: "Things themselves secure the fourfold *only when* they themselves *as* things are let be in their presencing" ("Building Dwelling Thinking," 151; his italics). To let things be in their presencing (*Wesen*) is to release them into their own nearness.

172. "Building Dwelling Thinking," 154. Heidegger's italics for the most part. I have changed "spots" to "positions" and "site" to "seat." For further discussion of the relation between building and dwelling, see my *Getting Back into Place: Toward a Renewed Understanding of the Place-World* (Bloomington: Indiana University Press, 1993), chaps. 4, 5.

173. "The location (*Ort*) makes room (*einräumt*) for the fourfold in a double sense. The location *admits* (*zulässt*) the fourfold and it *installs* (*einrichtet*) the fourfold" ("Building Dwelling Thinking," 158; his italics). The bridge-thing thus provides a *seat* for the fourfold, reminding us of Plato's characterization of *chōra* as a "seat" (*hedran*).

174. Cf. "Building Dwelling Thinking," 154.

175. Ibid. "Boundary" translates *Grenze*, and "cleared and free" renders *Freigegebenes*.

176. Ibid.; in italics in the text.

177. Ibid., 155.

178. Ibid., 155–156; my italics.

179. *Being and Time,* 148; his italics.

180. "The fact that they [i.e., such things as distances, spans, and directions] are *universally* applicable to everything that has extension can in no case make numerical magnitudes the *ground* (*Grund*) of the nature of spaces and locations that are measurable with the aid of mathematics" ("Building Dwelling Thinking," 156; his italics). Along with place, the ultimate grounding term is the *thing*: "The spaces through which we go daily are provided for by locations; their nature is grounded in things of the type of buildings" (p. 156). "Spaces" (*Räume*) in the last two citations are equivalent to places qua locations or localities.

181. "Building Dwelling Thinking," 157. "Provided for already" translates *schon eingeräumt.* " 'Space' " translates *'die' Raum.*

182. "And only because mortals pervade, persist through, spaces by their very nature are they able to go through spaces. But in going through spaces we do not give up our standing in them" (ibid., 157). I take "spaces" in this passage to be the conceptual equivalent of places.

183. Ibid., 156; his italics.

184. "From this spot right here, we are there at the bridge—we are by no means at some representational content in our consciousness" (ibid., 157). See my discussion of the here/there relationship in *Getting Back into Place,* pp. 50–54.

185. "Building Dwelling Thinking," 157.

186. "Time and Being," 11; my italics.

187. Ibid., 10.

188. Ibid., 12. On "time-space" (*Zeit-Raum*), see pp. 14 ff. In fact, the term is first used by Heidegger in his *Beiträge zur Philosophie* of 1936–1938, published in the Heidegger *Gesamtausgabe* (Frankfurt: Klostermann, 1989), vol. 65, esp. pp. 227 ff. and p. 323, where the compound phrase "Zeit-Spiel-Raum" is expressly employed. See Sections VI and VII below.

189. "Time and Being," 15: dimensionality "consists in a reaching out that opens

up (*lichtenden Reichen*) . . . not only as the area of possible measurement, but rather as reaching throughout, as giving and opening up." For further discussion of extensive magnitude, especially in view of determining spatial and temporal "parameters," see "The Nature of Language," in M. Heidegger, *On the Way to Language,* trans. P. Hertz (New York: Harper & Row, 1971), 102 f.

190. "Time and Being," 15. The full statement is "The unity of time's three dimensions consists in the interplay of each toward each. This interplay proves to be the true extending, playing in the very heart of time, the fourth dimension, so to speak—not only so to speak, but in the nature of the matter." "Zuspiel" is also discussed in the *Beiträge zur Philosophie,* pp. 169–170.

191. "Time and Being," 15. "Literally incipient extending" translates *an-fangende Reichen.*

192. "We may no longer ask in this manner for a where, for the place for time. For true time itself, the realm of its threefold extending determined by nearing nearness, is the pre-spatial locale (*vor-räumlich Ortschaft*) which first gives any possible 'where' " (ibid., 16; I have substituted "locale" for "region"). Here Heidegger rejoins Whitehead: "the place for time" signifies a simple location.

193. Ibid., 16.

194. Ibid., 15.

195. Ibid., 15–16. Nearing nearness "brings future, past, and present near to one another by distancing them" (p. 15).

196. Ibid., 22.

197. Ibid., 22–23. Heidegger adds: "Being vanishes in Appropriation" (p. 22). "Appropriation" here translates *Ereignis,* whose more complete rendition in English is "event of Appropriation."

198. See ibid., p. 202, where the epigraph to this section is to be found. The precise etymology of *Ereignis* (from *Ereignen*) derives from *er-äugnen,* that is, bring before the eye, to grasp, to make visible (*Auge* = eye). See the seminar on "Identität und Difference" (Pfullingen: Neske, 1957). I owe this reference to François Raffoul.

199. "Time and Being," 23. "Space" translates *Raum,* "origin" *Herkunft,* and "place" *Ort.*

200. "Building Dwelling Thinking," 157; my italics. The somatocentrism of Husserl's "absolute here" is thus contested once again. The term "free scope" is also found in "The Nature of Language," p. 106, as well as in the *Beiträge zur Philosophie,* as noted earlier; "throw open" is at ibid.: space "throws open locality and places."

201. "As a double space-making [*Einräumen:* as 'admitting' and 'installing'], the location is a shelter for the fourfold" ("Building Dwelling Thinking," 158).

202. It is in the *Introduction to Metaphysics* that Heidegger suggests that *chōra* adumbrates the infinite space of modernity: one boundaryless notion, ultimately rooted in the still more ancient idea of *apeiron,* leads to another. See *Introduction to Metaphysics,* p. 66, as well as Charles Kahn, *Anaximander and the Origins of Greek Cosmology* (New York: Columbia University Press, 1960), esp. pp. 232 ff., where the ancestry of *chōra* in *apeiron* is maintained.

203. Concerning the fourfold as "the world's four regions," see "The Nature of Language," 104. These regions are not just empty expanses but contain complex corners, including dark edges such as death, absence, night, and the underground.

204. "The Nature of Language," 93.

205. "The bridge *gathers* the earth as landscape around the stream" ("Building Dwelling Thinking," 152; his italics).

206. "Building Dwelling Thinking," 154.

207. For "nearhood," see "Time and Being," p. 15; for "nighness," see "The Nature of Language," p. 104: "we shall call nearness in respect of this, its movement, 'nighness.'"

208. As Heidegger says explicitly, "Space and time as parameters can neither bring about nor measure nearness" ("The Nature of Language," 104).

209. Neighborhood "does not first create nearness; rather, nearness brings about neighborhood" ("The Nature of Language," 101).

210. "The Nature of Language," 93.

211. Ibid., 82. Heidegger adds: "The two dwell face to face with each other . . . the one has settled facing the other, has drawn into the other's nearness (*Nähe*)" (ibid.).

212. M. Heidegger, *Hebel der Hausfreund* (Pfullingen: Neske, 1957), 13: "We call this multifarious between the *world,* for the world is the house in which mortals dwell" (his italics). Heidegger himself suggests in the very next sentence that particular places gather the multifarious between: "Yet the individual houses, villages, and cities are in each instance constructions (*Bauwerke*), which gather in and around themselves that multifarious between."

213. "The Nature of Language," 107.

214. Ibid., 106. The "all" in this sentence includes "time's removing and bringing to us" (ibid.). On this same page, Heidegger attempts to retrieve a more active sense of space and time—signified in the clauses "time times" and "space spaces"—such that the spacing of space "throws upon locality (*Ortschaft*) and places (*Orte*), vacates them and at the same time makes them free for all things and receives what is simultaneous as space-time." This sudden reversal of priority is consonant with the primacy of place: in order to do what Heidegger here assigns to it, space has to borrow properties from place itself, supposedly (on most modernist views) its own derivative.

215. "Die Kunst und der Raum," in *Gesamtausgabe,* vol. 13 (Frankfurt: Klostermann, 1983), 206–207.

216. "Doch was ist der Ort?" (ibid., 207).

217. Ibid., 207. He adds: "But this means at the same time: safeguarding, [by] gathering things in their belonging together" (pp. 207–208). "Gathering" (*Versammeln*) signifies "the freeing-up holding of things in their region" (p. 207).

218. Ibid., 208. *Walten* connotes exercising, prevailing, holding sway.

219. The full statement is: "Plastic [or three-dimensional art] would thus be the embodiment of places, which, opening and safeguarding a region, hold a Free [Open] gathered around itself, which [in turn] guards a constant lingering (*Verweilen*) for things and a dwelling for men in the midst of things" (ibid., 208).

220. Ibid., 209.

221. "The Nature of Language," 92–93. I omit the words "with language"—which is not to omit any delimited topic but that *topos* that is, in Heidegger's later thinking, the most encompassing region for other topics. For the *Erörterung* that language makes possible is uniquely suited to identify the "leading words" (*Grundworten*) of the saying of Being in the history of Western thought—a history that is itself to be conceived as a succession of places of such saying. For a lucid discussion of *Erörterung,* see Otto Pöggeler, *Der Denkweg Martin Heideggers* (Pfullingen: Neske, 1963), 280 ff.

222. *Being and Time,* 147. I have again changed "mere" to "sheer."

223. I have in mind this passage: "In principle the chair can never touch the wall, even if the space between them should be equal to zero. If the chair could touch the wall, this would presuppose that the wall is the sort of thing 'for' which a chair would be *encounterable*. . . . When two entities are present-at-hand within the world, and further are *worldless* in themselves, they can never 'touch' each other" (ibid., 81; his italics).

224. I am drawing on Heidegger's wordplay here: *Gegend* contains *gegen,* "against," "encountered"—whence "country" as what we encounter in a landscape. A characteristic passage is this: "The country (*die Gegend*) offers ways only because it is country" ("The Nature of Language," 92).

225. The full statement is the epigraph to this chapter. It comes from the 1925–1926 lectures on *Logik,* in the *Gesamtausgabe,* vol. 21, 267.

226. *Being and Time,* 148.

227. "But poetry that thinks is in truth the topology of Being. [This topology] gives to such poetry the locality of its essence (*die Ortschaft seines Wesens*)" (*Aus der Erfahrung des Denkens* [Pfullingen: Neske, 1967; written in 1947], 23). See Otto Pöggeler's discussion of this statement in *Der Denkweg Martin Heideggers,* pp. 294 ff. In the Thor seminar, Heidegger explains that the phrase *Ortschaft des Seins* implies "truth as the locality of Being" and that this "certainly presupposes a comprehension of the place-Being of place: hence the expression *Topologie des Seins*" (Seminar of September 2, 1969). In the seminar of September 6, Heidegger gives this explication of the move to the topology of Being: "In *Being and Time,* however, 'the question of Being' takes a very different direction. There it is a matter of the question of Being qua Being. This question bears thematically, in *Being and Time,* the name of 'the question of the meaning of Being.' This formulation is abandoned later for that of 'the question of the truth of Being'—and finally for that of 'the question of the place, or of the locality of Being'—whence the name *Topologie des Seins.* Three terms, which carry each other forward even as they mark the stages of the path of [my] thought: Meaning—Truth—Place (*topos*)" (cited in M. Heidegger, *Questions IV,* trans. J. Beaufret, F. Fédier, J. Lauxerois, and C. Roëls [Paris: Gallimard, 1976], 278; the first citation is at p. 269).

Chapter Twelve: Giving a Face to Place in the Present

1. Bachelard, *La terre et les rêveries de la volonté* (Paris: Corti, 1948), 379. Bachelard underlines "terrestrial."

2. On mind (*esprit*) versus soul (*âme*), see *The Poetics of Space,* trans. M. Jolas (New York: Orion, 1964), xiv–xviii.

3. Ibid., xi.

4. On psychic "reverberation" (*retentissement*), see Bachelard, *The Poetics of Space,* p. xii, where credit for the notion is given to Eugène Minkowski's *Vers une cosmologie,* chap. 9. Bachelard writes: "In this reverberation, the poetic image will have a sonority of being" (ibid.). The resulting resonance spreads out into the life of the reader: "The resonances are dispersed on the different planes of our life in the world, while the repercussions invite us to give greater depth to our own existence"

(ibid., xviii). Strictly speaking, resonance belongs to the image and reverberation to the effects on the reader's psyche. For discussion of the "resonance-reverberation doublet" see p. xix.

5. Bachelard, *The Poetics of Space*, xix. On psychic interiority versus exteriority, see chap. 9: "The Dialectics of Outside and Inside." Bachelard does not claim explicitly that psychic place or space is extended in a Cartesian or Philoponean sense. On the contrary, he says that such space "does not seek to become extended, but would like above all still to be possessed" (p. 10). Yet the soul has its own spread-outness, its own literal ex-tension, its "expanse" (*Weite*) in Heidegger's sense of the term.

6. "Space may be the projection of the extension of the psychical apparatus. No other derivation is probable. Instead of Kant's *a priori* determination of our psychical apparatus, *Psyche is extended;* knows nothing about it" (note of August 22, 1938; in S. Freud, *Standard Edition of the Complete Psychological Works* [London: Hogarth Press, 1964], 23:300; my italics). In his posthumously published *An Outline of Psychoanalysis,* Freud speaks of "the hypothesis we have adopted of a psychical apparatus extended in space, expediently put together, developed by the exigencies of life" (p. 196).

7. Bachelard inspects Jung's dream of a multistoried house as a symbol of the psyche in *The Poetics of Space*, p. xxxiii.

8. *The Poetics of Space*, 8. "Localities" translates *sites*—a term that, in French, has broader connotations than does "site" in English. "Psychological" is meant in the widest sense. On the convergence of several fields in topoanalysis, see p. xxxii. Bachelard is being ironic when he claims that topoanalysis is an "auxiliary of psychoanalysis" (p. 8). It is not at all subordinate to the latter inasmuch as it has its own objects of study: reveries and daydreams, rather than dreams or symptoms.

9. Ibid., xxxii.

10. Ibid., 8. I have changed "sequence" to "series" as a translation of *suite*. Embedded in this sentence are references to Bergson (time as "melting away" in the manner of a dissolving suger cube) and Proust ("in search of things past"). On Bachelard's continuing effort to distinguish his thought from Bergson's, see my essay "Image and Memory in Bachelard and Bergson," in *Spirit and Soul: Essays in Philosophical Psychology* (Dallas: Spring, 1991), 101–116.

11. *The Poetics of Space*, 9.

12. Ibid. Moreover, "hermeneutics, which is more profound than biography, must determine the centers of destiny by ridding history of its conjunctive temporal tissue, which has no action on our fates" (ibid.).

13. Ibid.

14. Ibid., 8. Bachelard adds: "That is what space is for" (ibid.).

15. Both citations are from *The Poetics of Space*, p. 9. The French reads: "Ici l'espace est tout . . . "l'inconscient séjourne." What Heidegger says of *Ereignis* Bachelard here says of the unconscious—perhaps not surprisingly, given that the unconscious is more of an appropriative *event* than it is a passively given thing. As J. D. Nasio writes (with reference to Lacan): "There is only an unconscious in the very event. . . . [It is] as if the speaking being [i.e., of the unconscious] existed only at the moment of the event, the place of a passage" (J. D. Nasio, *Laure: Le concept d'objet a dans la théorie de Jacques Lacan* [Paris: Aubier, 1987], 41, 29). I owe this reference to François Raffoul.

16. For the associated notions of felicitous, eulogized, and loved space in contrast with indifferent space, see *The Poetics of Space,* pp. xxxi–xxxii. The use of surveyed space as exemplary of objectified and homogenized space is common to Husserl, Heidegger, and Bachelard.

17. *The Poetics of Space,* 12. See also Yi-Fu Tuan, *Topophilia* (Englewood Cliffs, N.J.: Prentice-Hall, 1974), passim.

18. "Der Dichtungscharakter des Denkens ist noch verhüllt" (*Aus der Erfahrung des Denkens* [Pfullingen: Neske, 1965; written in 1947], 23). The German phrase for "still veiled over" is identical with that which describes space in *Being and Time,* section 22.

19. *Being and Time,* 138.

20. "But poetizing thinking is in truth the topology of Being (*Seyns*). It gives to this latter the proper place (*Ortschaft*) of its essence" (*Aus der Erfahrung des Denkens,* 23).

21. *The Poetics of Space,* xxxii. By "our intimate being" Bachelard means our innermost soul. I have explored a systematic comparison between Bachelard and Heidegger in regard to their shared stake in philosophical aspects of poetry in my dissertation, "Poetry and Ontology" (Northwestern University, 1967).

22. *Being and Time,* 62; in italics in the text.

23. Ibid., xxxii.

24. Heidegger, *Hebel der Hausfruend* (Pfullingen: Neske, 1957), 13; his italics. Individual houses, along with villages and towns, "gather" (*versammeln*) the multifarious between so as to make human inhabitation possible: ibid., 13–14.

25. These phrases are found in *The Poetics of Space,* p. 4 and p. 7, respectively. T. S. Eliot refers to "our first world" in "Burnt Norton," first stanza.

26. The first clause is from *The Poetics of Space,* p. 5 and the second from p. 31. "The real beginnings of images, if we study them phenomenologically, will give concrete evidence of the values of inhabited space" (p. 5).

27. "We are far removed from any reference to simple geometrical forms" (*The Poetics of Space,* 47); "house and space are not merely two juxtaposed elements of space" (p. 43).

28. Both citations are from *The Poetics of Space,* p. 47. On the primitive hut and its considerable imaginal potential, see pp. 31 ff. as well as Joseph Rykwert, *On Adam's House in Paradise: The Idea of the Primitive Hut in Architectural History* (New York: Museum of Modern Art, 1972).

29. "The house has its sunny side and its shady side; the way it is divided up into 'rooms' is oriented towards these, and so is the 'arrangement' (*Einrichtung*) within them, according to their character as equipment" (*Being and Time,* 137). A larger connotation of *Raum* is indicated in "Building Dwelling Thinking": "*Raum* means a place cleared or freed for settlement and lodging" (*Poetry, Language, Truth,* trans. A. Hofstadter [New York: Harper & Row, 1971], 154).

30. *The Poetics of Space,* 14.

31. Ibid., 15.

32. Ibid., 14–15.

33. Ibid., 46.

34. Ibid.

35. On the deep analogy between body and house, see Kent Bloomer and Charles

Moore, *Body, Memory, and Architecture* (New Haven: Yale University Press, 1977), 2–5, 46–49. I have explored the analogy in *Getting Back into Place: Toward a Renewed Understanding of the Place-World* (Bloomington: Indiana University Press, 1993), Pt. 3, "Built Places."

36. The first statement is from *The Poetics of Space*, p. 18; the second from p. 19.

37. Ibid., 19.

38. Ibid., 25–26. In contrast, one visualizes oneself moving both up and down in getting to a bedroom on the second floor of a house: see p. 26.

39. Ibid., 6.

40. Ibid., 25.

41. On this theme, see my essay "Toward an Archetypal Imagination," in *Spirit and Soul*, pp. 3–28, where I explore the idea of a systematic "arche-topology" of a priori structures of the imagination.

42. *The Poetics of Space*, 7: "Within the being, in the being of within (*l'être du dedans*), an enveloping warmth welcomes being."

43. Ibid., 5: "The real beginnings of images, if we study them phenomenologically, will give concrete evidence of *the values of inhabited space*, of the non-I that protects the I" (my italics). On "being-well" (*bien-être*) and "well-being" (*être-bien*), see p. 7: "When the human being is deposited in a being-well, in the well-being originally associated with being."

44. "Building Dwelling Thinking," 160; the phrase "the basic character (*die Grundzug*)" is in italics in the text.

45. The first citation is from "Building Dwelling Thinking," p. 147 (his italics); the second is from p. 160 (all in italics in the text). Moreover, "only if we are capable of dwelling, only then can we build" (p. 160). Bachelard considers *Being and Time* to be the work of a "metaphysician" (p. 212) and says about himself in contrast: "I only know how to work with a philosophy of detail" (p. 222).

46. *The Poetics of Space*, 216.

47. Ibid., 218.

48. Ibid., 212. They are especially unfortunate when the "there" becomes part of the compound adverbial phrase "être-là," the standard French translation of Heidegger's *Dasein*. With this phrase in mind, Bachelard speaks of the "geometrical cancerization of the linguistic tissue of contemporary philosophy" (p. 213). I have discussed here/there as well as in/out in *Getting Back into Place*, chap. 4, "Dimensions."

49. *The Poetics of Space*, 230.

50. From Milosz's *L'amoureuse initiation*, in *The Poetics of Space*, p. 190.

51. "The room is very deeply our room, it is in us. We no longer *see* it. It no longer *limits* us, because we are in the very ultimate depth of its repose, in the repose that it has conferred upon us. And all our former rooms come and fit into this one" (*The Poetics of Space*, 226; his italics). A striking case in point is provided by Rilke in *The Notebooks of Malte Laurids Brigge*, which evokes the vision of a last remaining wall of a torn-down house. Traces of previous rooms are manifest in this wall: "The tenacious life of these rooms refused to let itself be trampled on. . . . I recognize all of it here, and that's why it goes right into me: it's at home in me" (cited by Martin Heidegger, *The Basic Problems of Phenomenology*, trans. A. Hofstadter [Bloomington: Indiana University Press, 1982], 172–173). I thank David Michael Levin for this reference.

52. *The Poetics of Space*, 223.

53. "If there exists a border-line surface between such an inside and outside, this surface is painful on both sides" (ibid., 218). This passage indicates that Bachelard is not interested in felicitous space alone. For further on the "unsettled" character of intimate space—and human beings' "errancy" therein—see pp. 214–215.

54. "A space is something that has been made room for, something that is cleared and free, namely within a boundary, Greek *peras*" ("Building Dwelling Thinking," 154).

55. The phrase "reinforced geometrism" occurs at *The Poetics of Space,* p. 215. At p. 220 Bachelard speaks of "the lazy certainties of the geometrical intuition by means of which psychologists sought to govern the space of intimacy." See Eugène Minkowski's related idea of "morbid geometrism" (*Lived Time,* trans. N. Metzel [Evanston: Northwestern University Press, 1970], 277 ff.).

56. *The Poetics of Space,* 32.

57. Ibid., 203.

58. Ibid., 33. Notice the stress on living *in images*—and not the supposed psychological fact that images reside *in us.*

59. On the house as a "resting place" (*gîte*), see *The Poetics of Space,* p. 15. On the housing of motionless memories, see pp. 5, 8, 9.

60. Ibid., 215; his italics. On "intimate immensity," see all of chapter 8 of *The Poetics of Space.* In his *La terre et les rêveries de la volonté,* chap. 12, sec. 7 ("La terre immense"), Bachelard had treated of immensity in its sheer physical enormity, i.e., as an object of a "spectacle complex." Immensity in *The Poetics of Space* involves "a more relaxed participation in images of immensity, a more intimate relationship between small and large" (*The Poetics of Space,* 190).

61. "Miniature is an exercise that has metaphysical freshness; it allows us to be world conscious at slight risk" (*The Poetics of Space,* 161). Concerning miniaturization in art, especially in Southeast Asian art, see R. A. Stein, *Le monde en petit: Jardins en miniature et habitations dans la pensée religieuse d'extrême Orient* (Paris: Flammarion, 1987).

62. "Space, vast space, is the friend of being" (*The Poetics of Space,* 208). On the "absolute elsewhere," see p. 207. Ironizing on Heidegger, Bachelard remarks that "the *being-here* is maintained by a being from elsewhere" (p. 208; his italics). Pascal suffered from a surfeit of space. To the extent that he was *anxious* before it, he was constricted by it (as the etymological rooting of "anxiety" in 'narrow' suggests).

63. *The Poetics of Space,* 218. Bachelard adds: "In this ambiguous space, the mind has lost its geometrical homeland and the spirit is drifting" (ibid.).

64. On the virtual aspects of intimate space, see *The Poetics of Space,* pp. 5, 227; on the general status of the image, which encourages uninhibited imagining on the part of the reader, see p. 229.

65. Ibid., 218.

66. Ibid., 193.

67. See, for example, *La formation de l'esprit scientifique* (Paris: Vrin, 1938), and *The Poetics of Reverie,* trans. D. Russell (Boston: Beacon Press, 1971).

68. *The Poetics of Reverie,* 196. Bachelard italicizes "adheres." On the inhabitational properties of still water, see also *The Poetics of Space,* p. 210, and *Water and Dreams: An Essay on the Imagination of Matter,* trans. E. R. Farrell (Dallas: Pegasus Foundation, 1983), chap. 2.

69. *The Poetics of Space,* 191. One might compare Jung's method of "amplification," whereby dream images (and other images as well) are expanded in the course of the free associations of psychotherapy.

70. I borrow the term "multilocular" from Freud: "[The ego's] defense too becomes *multilocular*" (Draft N, May 31, 1897; in *Standard Edition of the Complete Psychological Works* [1960], 1:256; his italics).

71. The image, despite its evanescence, requires material elementarity: "The image is a plant which needs earth and sky, substance and form" (*Water and Dreams,* 3). Further: "If a reverie is to be pursued with the constancy of a written work . . . it must discover its *matter.* A material element must provide its own substance, its particular rules and poetics" (p. 3; his italics).

72. The first phrase is found in *La philosophie du non: Essai d'une philosophie du nouvel esprit scientifique* (Paris: Presses Universitaires de France, 1940), p. 41; the second is in *Water and Dreams,* p. 159 (in italics in the text). Sartre took up the term "coefficient of adversity" in his discussion of "situation" in *Being and Nothingness.*

73. "Being and the imaginary are for Sartre 'objects,' 'entities'—For me they are 'elements' (in Bachelard's sense), that is, not objects, but fields, subdued being, nonthetic being, being before being—and moreover involving their auto-inscription" (working note of November 1960; in *The Visible and the Invisible,* trans. A. Lingis [Evanston: Northwestern University Press, 1968], 267). For Merleau-Ponty's own creative appropriation of the Bachelardian idea of "element," see pp. 139–140.

74. *The Poetics of Space,* 210.

75. Michel Foucault, "Of Other Spaces," trans. J. Miskowiec, *Diacritics* (Spring 1986), 24.

76. Ibid., 22. The full sentence is "It is necessary to notice that the space which today appears to form the horizon of our concerns, our theory, our systems, is not an innovation: space itself has a history in Western experience and it is not possible to disregard the fatal intersection of time with space."

77. See ibid., 22–23.

78. Michel Foucault, "Questions on Geography," an interview that appeared in the Marxist geographic review *Hérodote* in 1976 and is reprinted in *Power/Knowledge: Selected Interviews and Other Writings 1972–1977,* ed. C. Gordon (New York: Pantheon, 1980), 69. See also Foucault's statement that "the spatializing description of discursive realities gives onto the analysis of related effects of power" (ibid., 70–71).

79. "Of Other Spaces," 23. The lecture opens with this sentence: "The great obsession of the nineteenth century was, as we know, history: with its themes of development and of suspension, of crisis and cycle, themes of the ever-accumulating past, with its great preponderance of dead men and the menacing glaciation of the world" (p. 22). The paradox, of course, is that Foucault borrows his own historicism—especially in its specifically Nietzschean, "genealogical" form—*from the nineteenth century* in order to apply it to the contemporary epoch. See Foucault's remark that "since Nietzsche this question of truth has been transformed. It is no longer, 'What is the surest path to Truth?' but 'What is the hazardous career that Truth has followed?' " ("Questions on Geography," 66). See also the interview "Truth and Power," in *Power/Knowledge,* pp. 109–133.

80. "Of Other Spaces," 22.

81. In Heidegger's language, the side-by-side is merely *vorhanden,* and it lacks the

closeness of genuine "touching" of the sort at stake in the *zuhanden.* As Merleau-Ponty says expressly: "If my arm is resting on the table I should never think of saying that it is *beside* the ash-tray in the way the ash-tray is beside the telephone. The outline of my body is a frontier which ordinary spatial relations do not cross. This is because its parts are interrelated in a peculiar way: they are not spread out side by side, but enveloped in each other" (*Phenomenology of Perception,* trans. C. Smith [New York: Humanities Press, 1962], 98; his italics). In addition to rejecting the model of juxtaposition for being-in-space, Merleau-Ponty here supplies the missing link in Heidegger's account of nearness: the lived body.

82. "Of Other Spaces," 23. I have slightly altered the translation.

83. The phrase "the hidden presence of the sacred" occurs in "Of Other Spaces," p. 23, where a series of undesanctified oppositions are also discussed.

84. Ibid. I have changed "quantities" to "qualities" to accord better with the sense of the claim.

85. Ibid.

86. Ibid. The reference to "colored with diverse shades of light" is to Bachelard's analysis of the aerian element in *L'air et les songes* (Paris: Corti, 1943).

87. "Of Other Spaces," 24. Again I have slightly altered the translation.

88. The phrase "sites with no real place" is found at ibid., p. 24. Elsewhere, Foucault distinguishes utopias and heterotopias on a different basis: the former respect syntax and order even as they project a perfect future society, the latter undermine the socially ordered: thus they "destroy syntax in advance," "dessicate speech," and "stop words in their tracks" (cf. *The Order of Things: An Archaeology of the Human Sciences* [New York: Random House, 1970], xviii).

89. "Places of this kind [i.e., heterotopias] are outside of all places, even though it may be possible to indicate their location in reality" ("Of Other Spaces," 24). I would say not only need it be "possible," but it is even *necessary* if heterotopias are to have the forcefulness Foucault assigns to them.

90. "As a sort of simultaneously mythic and real contestation of the space in which we live, this description [i.e., of countersites] could be called heterotopology" ("Of Other Spaces," 24).

91. "Of Other Spaces," 26.

92. For Foucault's analysis of Borges's passage, see the preface to *The Order of Things,* esp. pp. xv–xix.

93. The first principle is found in *The Order of Things,* p. 24; the second at p. 25. In one passage, Foucault blithely juxtaposes the two principles without acknowledging any tension between them: "[The first principle] is a constant of every human group. But the heterotopias obviously take quite varied forms, and perhaps no one absolutely universal form of heterotopia will be found" (p. 24). Reinforcing the latter direction of his thought—which I take to be his stronger commitment—he also says that "each heterotopia has a precise and determined function within a society and the same heterotopia can, according to the synchrony of the culture in which it occurs, have one function or another" (p. 25).

94. Gilles Deleuze and Félix Guattari, *A Thousand Plateaus,* trans. B. Massumi (Minneapolis: University of Minnesota Press, 1987), 354.

95. Ibid., 369. Husserl's own original discussion is at *Ideas* I, sec. 74, "Descriptive and Exact Sciences." Deleuze and Guattari discuss vague essences, that is, Husserl's

"morphological essences," at *A Thousand Plateaus,* p. 367. The authors take "round-ness" as a paradigm of a vague essence—in contrast with the eidetic perfection of the circle—and in so doing they inadvertently rejoin Bachelard's "phenomenology of roundness," the title of the last chapter of *The Poetics of Space.*

96. For the basic contrast between *gravitas* and *celeritas*—including an analysis of the law of gravitation versus the informal physics of hydraulics—see *A Thousand Plateaus,* pp. 370–371. On declination, see p. 489. "Anexact" is borrowed from Michel Serres, *La Naissance de la physique dans le texte du Lucrèce: Fleuves et turbulences* (Paris: Minuit, 1977). "Approximation" is a term taken over from Bachelard's early book, *Essai sur la connaissance approchée* (Paris: Vrin, 1927), and "inclination" here refers to the ancient Atomist idea of *clinamen,* that is, the swerve an atom takes as it deviates ever so slightly from a straight line. The distinction between metric and pro-jective and topological geometries is made at *A Thousand Plateaus,* pp. 361–362. Ultimately, it stems from Piaget's theory of the child's acquisition of spatial notions in an ordered sequence from topological to projective to metric geometries: see J. Piaget and B. Inhelder, *The Child's Conception of Space,* trans. F. J. Langdon and J. L. Lunzer (New York: Norton, 1967).

97. For this distinction in Boulez, see his *Boulez on Music Today,* trans. S. Brad-shaw and R. Bennett (Cambridge: Harvard University Press, 1971), 83 ff. For its ap-propriation by Deleuze and Guattari, see *A Thousand Plateaus,* pp. 477–478.

98. *A Thousand Plateaus,* 371. "The smallest deviation" refers to the *clinamen.* "Conduits or channels" make reference to the effort to control the flow of water in a predetermined and delimited manner, for example, by parallel watercourses—in con-trast with a certain receptivity to the vagaries of the flow of water itself. The important metaphor of the rhizome is analyzed in chapter 1, "Introduction: The Rhizome," pp. 3–25.

99. Smooth space is "a tactile space, or rather 'haptic,' a sonorous much more than a visual space. The variability, the polyvocality of directions, is an essential feature of smooth spaces of the rhizome type, and it alters their cartography" (*A Thousand Pla-teaus,* 382).

100. *A Thousand Plateaus,* 382. For further discussion of haecceity, see pp. 262–263, 276–277, 280.

101. Ibid., 382. Paradoxically, what is for the nomad a local absolute is for the person who reads of nomads an "absolute elsewhere"—in Bachelard's term for the sense of place engendered by reading about life on the desert. (See *The Poetics of Space,* p. 207: "An absolute elsewhere that bars the way to the forces that hold us imprisoned in the 'here'.") In contrast with the local absolute, "what is both limited and limiting is striated space, the *relative global*: it is limited in its parts, which are assigned constant directions, are oriented in relation to one another, divisible by bounds, and can interlink" (*A Thousand Plateaus,* 382; their italics).

102. *A Thousand Plateaus,* 383.

103. Only striated space or the relative global has precise perimeters; nomad space has no strict enclosures: "There is a strict difference between the [two] spaces: seden-tary space is striated, by walls, enclosures, and roads between enclosures, while nomad space is smooth, marked only by 'traits' that are effaced and displaced with the trajec-tory" (*A Thousand Plateaus,* 381). See also p. 380: nomad space "distributes people (or animals) in an open space, one that is indefinite and noncommunicating . . . without

borders or enclosure" (first clause in italics). Nevertheless, smooth spaces *in fact* exist between striated spaces, for example, between delimitable forests and fields: see p. 384.

104. The nomad has "no points, paths, or land" (*A Thousand Plateaus*, 381). Only in sedentary space are there points that *define* movement.

105. "Making the absolute appear in a particular place—is that not a very general characteristic of religion. . . . [T]he sacred place of religion is fundamentally a center that repels the obscure *nomos*" (p. 382). For this reason, religion is no less imperialistic than a secular state: "Religion is in this sense a piece in the State apparatus . . . even if it has within itself the power to elevate this model to the level of the universal or to constitute an absolute *Imperium*" (pp. 382–383).

106. *A Thousand Plateaus*, 380. The preceding sentence is "A path is always between two points, but the in-between has taken on all the consistency and enjoys both an autonomy and a direction of its own" (ibid.). See also p. 478: "In striated space, lines or trajectories tend to be subordinated to points: one goes from one point to another. In the smooth, it is the opposite: the points are subordinated to the trajectory."

107. "Nomad" derives from *nem-,* a root that signifies distribution rather than allocation, for example, of animals in a field. *Nomos* thus refers to a distributive model of law or justice, in contrast with that of the *polis,* which proceeds in terms of regulation and restriction. See *A Thousand Plateaus*, p. 557 n. 51, where the authors refer to Emmanuel Laroche, *Histoire de la racine 'nem' en grec ancien* (Paris: Klincksieck, 1949).

108. The first clause is from *Being and Time,* p. 138; the second is adapted from "Building Dwelling Thinking," p. 154: "Spaces receive their being from locations (*Orten*) and not from 'space' " (in italics in the text).

109. *A Thousand Plateaus*, 494. The authors link this thesis up with their overall stress on *becoming*: "It is an absolute that is one with becoming itself " (ibid.). On becoming, see chapter 10, "1730: Becoming-Intense, Becoming-Animal."

110. Ibid., 383. "A centered, oriented, globalization or universalization" refers to a religious experience of being at a sacred center of a "world religion." (Bachelard disagrees: the ordinary nomad is for him always at the center of the desert: "The nomad moves, but he is always at the *center* of the desert, at the center of the steppe" [*La terre et les rêveries de la volonté,* 379; his italics].) The "infinite succession of local operations" makes reference to the idea of "small tactile or manual actions of contact" and "the linking of proximities" within smooth space is construed as "the space of the smallest deviation" (all in the passage cited earlier from p. 371). The basic thesis is that smooth space is "a space constructed by local operations" (p. 478), for example, by "legwork."

111. For the nomad, "every point is a relay and exists only as a relay. . . . The nomad goes from point to point only as a consequence and as a factual necessity; in principle, points for him are relays along a trajectory" (*A Thousand Plateaus,* 380). See also p. 377: "The form of exteriority situates thought in a smooth space that it must occupy without counting, and for which there is no possible method, no conceivable reproduction, but only relays, intermezzos, resurgences."

112. *A Thousand Plateaus*, 479. Earlier, *Spatium* had been associated with the archaic state, whereas *Extensio* is allied with the modern state in its imperialistic, homogenizing tendencies: see p. 388. This interpretation of *Spatium* is at odds with

Heidegger's: "In a space that is represented purely as *spatium,* the bridge now appears as a mere something at some position, which can be occupied at any time by something else or replaced by a mere marker" ("Building Dwelling Thinking," 155). But Heidegger agrees that geometric or geographic dimensionality is what chiefly characterizes *extensio*: "Building Dwelling Thinking," 155.

113. "We can say of the nomads, following Toynbee's suggestion: *they do not move.* They are nomads by dint of not moving, not migrating, of holding a smooth space that they refuse to leave, that they leave only in order to conquer and die. Voyage in place: that is the name of all intensities, even if they also develop in extension" (*A Thousand Plateaus,* 482; their italics). On not moving while moving, see also p. 381.

114. "What distinguishes the two kinds of voyages [i.e., in smooth and striated space] is neither a measurable quantity of movement, nor something that would be only in the mind, but the mode of spatialization, the manner of being in space, of being for space" (*A Thousand Plateaus,* 482).

115. On the arc of vanishing, see *Getting Back into Place,* pp. 199, 207, 216–218.

116. *A Thousand Plateaus,* 479. On the "Unlimited," see p. 495.

117. Ibid., 494. "Where there is close vision, space is not visual, or rather the eye itself has a haptic, nonoptical function: no line separates earth from sky, which are of the same substance; there is neither horizon nor background nor perspective nor limit nor outline or form nor center" (ibid.). On the distinction between distance and magnitude, see p. 483.

118. Ibid., 493. The authors add: "Orientations are not constant but change according to temporary vegetation, occupations, and precipitation. There is no visual model for points of reference that would make them interchangeable and unite them in an inertial class assignable to an immobile outside observer" (ibid.).

119. Ibid., 494. For more on nomadic dwelling, see pp. 380–382, especially this claim: "Even the elements of [the nomad's] dwelling are conceived in terms of the trajectory that is forever mobilizing them" (p. 380). Once more, the importance of becoming is evident in this analysis.

120. Ibid., 381. They add: "It is the earth that deterritorializes itself, in a way that provides the nomad with a territory. The land ceases to be land, tending to become simply ground (*sol*) or support" (ibid.). This does not happen to the earth as a whole but at "specific locations, at the spot where the forest recedes, or where the steppe and the desert advance" (pp. 381–382). On landscape in relation to "faciality," see chapter 7, "Year Zero: Faciality."

121. Ibid., 476.

122. On the amorphous nature of smooth space, see *A Thousand Plateaus,* p. 477.

123. On the generation of homogeneity from striation, see *A Thousand Plateaus,* p. 488.

124. *A Thousand Plateaus,* 494.

125. On this effort to dominate the Unlimited and the Whole, see *A Thousand Plateaus,* pp. 379 and 495. Concerning segmentation, see the discussion of "segmentarity" at pp. 206–207, 211–212, 222–224.

126. *A Thousand Plateaus,* 474.

127. For this example, which draws on the analysis of Paul Virilio's idea of the "fleet in being" in Virilio's *L'insécurité du territoire* (Paris: Stock, 1975), see *A Thousand Plateaus,* pp. 363 and 480. Sea space is "the first [smooth space] to encounter

the demands of increasingly strict striation" (p. 479). Such striation is closely linked
to the determination of dimensionality. I have discussed the intriguing case of longitu-
dinal striation in *Getting Back into Place,* chap. 1.

128. *A Thousand Plateaus,* 500. On the smooth as something that "always possesses a greater power of deterritorialization than the striated," see p. 480.

129. Ibid., 372.

130. Ibid., 478.

131. Ibid., 486.

132. "The Column," in Jacques Derrida, *Dissemination,* trans. B. Johnson (Chicago: University of Chicago Press, 1981), 341: "The Tower of Babel, the text's spinal
column, is also a phallic column woven according to the thread of work." This citation
brings together body, building, and text.

133. "Philo-sophe, Archi-tecte," a public discussion at Cooper Union, New York,
September 28, 1988, p. 14 of transcript. I have changed "some" to "certain."

134. Ibid., 20. When Derrida addresses the architect Peter Eisenman, he asks char-
acteristically, "What are words for an architect? Or books?" and especially: "Why does
Peter Eisenman write such good *books*?" (J. Derrida, "Why Peter Eisenman Writes
Such Good Books," in *Eisenmanamnesie* [Tokyo: A+U Publishing, 1988]), 133–134.
The first two questions are posed on p. 114 of "Philo-sophe, Archi-tecte." In the third
question that provides the title of the article, Derrida is punning on a chapter title in
Nietzsche's *Ecce Homo*: "Why I Write Such Excellent Books."

135. "The field of beings, before being determined as the field of presence, is
structured according to the diverse possibilities—genetic and structural—of the trace"
(J. Derrida, *Of Grammatology,* trans. G. Spivak [Baltimore: Johns Hopkins University
Press, 1974], 47; I have changed "field of the entity" to "field of beings"). On the
importance of the "instituted trace," see p. 47: "Even before it is linked to incision,
engraving, drawing, or the letter, to a signifier referring in general to a signifier signi-
fied by it, the concept of the *graphie* [unit of a possible graphic system] implies the
framework of the *instituted trace*" (his italics). Concerning the "scene of writing," see
Derrida's "Freud and the Scene of Writing," in *Writing and Difference,* trans. A. Bass
(Chicago: University of Chicago Press, 1978), 196–231.

136. *Of Grammatology,* 65; his italics. On the cogeneration of space and time from
tracing, see also *"Ousia* and *Grammē,"* in *Margins of Philosophy,* trans. A. Bass
(Chicago: University of Chicago Press, 1982), 29–67.

137. Concerning the interiority of time and the infinity of space—the latter especially in the guise of God—See *Of Grammatology,* pp. 66–67, 70–71.

138. On the idea of "la zone spécifique," see *Of Grammatology,* p. 65. This zone,
which is that of protowriting (*archi-écriture*), is where texts arise as "the chains and
the systems of traces" (ibid.). Derrida remarks that "these chains and these systems
cannot be outlined except in the fabric of this trace or imprint" (ibid.). "Tissue," which
Derrida elsewhere links closely with text, also implies a place—the place of interweav-
ing. See also this statement in *Of Grammatology*: "Origin of the experience of space
and time, this writing of difference, this fabric of the trace, permits the difference
between space and time to be articulated, to appear as such, in the unity of an experience" (pp. 65–66).

139. See Derrida, "Freud and the Scene of Writing," pp. 206–215.

140. "It is absolutely impossible for two material and resistant [bodies] to occupy

the same place, but the immaterial ones are like light which, being emitted from different lamps, have interpenetrated throughout the same chamber" (Syrianus, as reported by Simplicius and translated by S. Sambursky, *The Concept of Place in Late Neoplatonism* [Jerusalem: Israel Academy of Sciences and Humanities, 1982], 59).

141. Derrida, "Point de Folie—Maintenant L'Architecture," trans. Kate Linker, *AA Files,* no. 12 (1986): sec. 13. He also points to the link between "fabrick"—"building" or "factory" in eighteenth-century English—and "fabric." (When citing "Point de Folie," I shall refer to section numbers rather than to pages.) Elizabeth Grosz points to the limitations of the textural metaphor as applied to architecture—preferring Deleuze's nomadological model of radical exteriority. See her essay "Architecture from the Outside" in E. Grosz, *Space, Time, and Perversion* (New York: Routledge, 1995), 125ff.

142. "Point de Folie," sec. 3: "une écriture de l'espace, un mode d'espacement qui fait sa place à l'événement."

143. Thus Derrida writes in "Point de Folie" that "we appear to ourselves only through an experience of spacing which is already marked by architecture" (sec. 3) and that the body "would receive from this other spacing [i.e., the buildings one inhabits] the invention of its gestures" (sec. 10).

144. Concerning these norms as they affect architecture, see "Point de Folie," esp. sec. 9.

145. Cited in Gregory Ulmer, "Electronic Monumentality," *Nomad* (1992). Derrida's own design, simple yet forceful, for the Villette project looks like this:

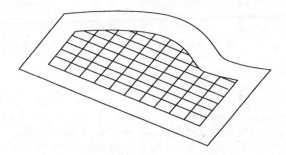

146. Irigaray and Butler both have argued that *chōra* cannot be directly shaped by anything not belonging to it intrinsically: thus there is a specific choric resistance to (male) imposition and subjection. See Irigaray, "Une Mère de Glace," in *Speculum of the Other Woman,* trans. G. C. Gill (Ithaca: Cornell University Press, 1985), 168–179, and Judith Butler, *Bodies that Matter: On the Discursive Limits of "Sex"* (New York: Routledge, 1993), 39–42.

147. "Point de Folie," sec. 3.

148. On the multiple meanings of *maintenant,* see "Point de Folie," esp. secs. 1–3, 15.

149. "Point de Folie," sec. 15; Derrida underlines "promised"; translation slightly altered.

150. Ibid., sec. 3; my italics. Bernard Tschumi specifies this point in a recent self-quoting statement: "Architecture is as much about the events that take place in space as about the spaces themselves" (*Event-Cities (Praxis)* [Cambridge: MIT Press, 1994],

13). More concretely put, "there is no architecture without action or without program" (*Event-Cities,* 117).

151. "Point de Folie," sec. 3. Derrida here makes reference to Tschumi's written work, especially his *Manhattan Transcripts* (London/New York: Academy Editions/ St. Martin's Press, 1981) in which Tschumi sets forth his ideas about architecture in a colorful and complex medley of images and words.

152. Referring again to Tschumi's *Manhattan Transcripts,* Derrida says elliptically: "Marked: provoked, determined *or* transcribed, captured, in any case always mobilized in a scenography of passage (transference, translation, transgression from one place to another, from a place of writing to another, graft, hybridisation)" ("Point de Folie," sec. 9).

153. Aphorism no. 37 in "Fifty-Two Aphorisms for a Foreword," in A. Papadakis, C. Cooke, and A. Benjamin, eds., *Deconstruction: Omnibus Volume* (New York: Rizzoli, 1989), 68. On the theme of event as the "there is (*il y a*)," see also Jean-François Lyotard, *The Differend: Phrases in Dispute,* trans. G. Van den Abbeele (Minneapolis: University of Minnesota Press, 1988), 59, 85, 164. The common ancestral concept for both Derrida and Lyotard is Heidegger's *Ereignis.*

154. "Point de Folie," sec. 8. The citation in the earlier part of this sentence is from section 4, and the point about subjection is found at section 3.

155. Theodor Lipps, cited by Rudolf Arnheim, *The Dynamics of Architectural Form* (Berkeley: University of California Press, 1971), 86.

156. On transarchitecture, see "Point de Folie," sec. 9. The phrase cited earlier in this sentence is from section 5.

157. "Point de Folie," sec. 9.

158. On "proto-place," "com-place," and "counter-place," see *Getting Back into Place,* chap. 3.

159. "Point de Folie," sec. 10.

160. Ibid., sec. 8. "Hyletics" refers to the strictly physical factor in architecture.

161. Ibid., sec. 10. Derrida continues: "Such opportunity is not given to the inhabitant or the believer, the user or the architectural theorist. . . . [Then one] would no longer simply be content to *walk,* circulate, stroll around *in* a place or *on* paths, but would transform its [i.e., the body's] motions by giving rise to them" (his italics). Tschumi adds that in his architecture "a new urban type results, based not on the static composition of building mass and urban axes but on the condition of the momentary and the constantly moving" (*Event-Cities,* 193).

162. "Point de Folie," sec. 6.

163. Ibid., sec. 14. For Tschumi's own statement on "dis-structuring," see his "Parc de la Villette, Paris" in *AA Files,* no. 12 (1986): 175 ff., as well as his *Architecture and Disjunction* (Cambridge: MIT Press, 1994). In *Event-Cities,* Tschumi underlines "the inherent disjunction of architecture—between space and event, between buildings and their use" (p. 279).

164. See "Anaximander's Saying," trans. D. Krell and F. Capuzzi, in M. Heidegger, *Early Greek Thinking* (New York: Harper & Row, 1975), 46–48. Derrida comments on this essay in *"Ousia* and *Grammē,"* pp. 34–35, 66–67.

165. Bernard Tschumi, "Madness and the Combinative," in *Précis V* (New York: Columbia University Press, 1984); cited by Derrida in "Point de Folie," sec. 14. The phrase "disjunctive force" occurs in aphorism no. 40 in "Fifty-Two Aphorisms": "The

disjunctive force can only be put in the architectural work at the moment where, by some secret or denied synergy, it can be integrated into the order of a narrative, whatever the dimension, in an uninterrupted history between the beginning and the end, the founding sub-foundation and the top of the house, the cellar and the roof, the ground and the point of the pyramid." What had been continuous and reassuring in the vertical dynamics of a house on Bachelard's analysis here becomes discontinuous and threatening.

166. "Madness and the Combinative," as cited in "Point de Folie," sec. 14. See also Derrida's statement that "the red *points space,* maintaining architecture in the dissociation of spacing. But this now (*maintenant*) does not only maintain a past and a tradition: it does not ensure a synthesis. It maintains the interruption, in other words the relation to the other *per se*" (ibid.; his italics).

167. "Point de Folie," sec. 15. Derrida adds: "But the inter-ruptor maintains together *both* the rupture *and* the relation to the other, which is itself structured as both attraction *and* interruption, interference *and* difference; a relation without relation" (ibid.; his italics).

168. On these properties of the point, see "Point de Folie," secs. 5 and 15. For the treatment of the point in "*Ousia* and *Grammē,*" see *Margins of Philosophy,* pp. 40 ff.

169. "The baseless ground (*le sans-fond*) of a 'deconstructive' and affirmative architecture can cause vertigo, but it is not the void (*le vide*), it is not the gaping and chaotic remainder, the hiatus of destruction" ("Fifty-Two Aphorisms," no. 50).

170. On the aphorism as monadic, see "Fifty-Two Aphorisms," no. 24: "An authentic aphorism must never refer to another. It is sufficient unto itself, world or monad." On the blindness, "Point de Folie," sec. 15: "This point of view does not see; it is blind to what happens *in the folie*" (his italics).

171. "Point de Folie," sec. 15.

172. "A Letter to Peter Eisenman," *assemblage,* no. 12 (1991): 11–12: "From fragility I turn to ashes, for me the other name or the surname for the essence (not the essential) of the step, of the trace, of writing, the place without place of deconstruction. There where deconstruction inscribes itself." Eisenman himself speaks of the atopic element within topos: "What is the 'between' in architecture? If architecture traditionally locates, then to 'be between' means to be between some place and no place. If architecture traditionally has been about 'topos', that is an idea of place, then to be between is to search for an 'atopos', the atopia within topos" (Peter Eisenman, "Blue Line Text," *assemblage,* no. 12 (1991): 150). Is it not precisely the point that introduces the atopic element—the disruptive force—into topos?

173. "Post/El Cards: A Reply to Jacques Derrida," in *assemblage,* no. 12 (1991): 17.

174. "Signature du corps" is Derrida's phrase in "Point de Folie," sec. 10. For the relationship between body and building, see Kent C. Bloomer and Charles W. Moore, *Body, Memory, and Architecture* (New Haven: Yale University Press, 1977), as well as chap. 5, secs. 3–4, of *Getting Back into Place.*

175. Peter Eisenman, *Eisenmanamnesie,* 121; my italics.

176. For a discussion of four invariants of Western architecture, see Derrida, "Point de Folie," sec. 8.

177. From an interview: "Jacques Derrida in Discussion with Christopher Norris," in *Deconstruction: Omnibus Volume,* p. 74.

178. "Fifty-Two Aphorisms," no. 29. In his interview with Norris, Derrida says that "the fact that architecture has always been interpreted as dwelling, or the element of dwelling—dwelling for human beings or dwelling for the gods—the place where gods or people are present or gathering or living and so on . . . [is] a value which can be questioned" (*Deconstruction,* 74).

179. "Fifty-Two Aphorisms," no. 41.

180. Tschumi, *Event-Cities,* 105.

181. Ibid., 246–247. About this design Tschumi has this to say: "We also extracted from the program the most particular or 'eventful' functions or activities, which in combination would produce the 'event'. Hence, we 'staged' a combination of image theater, sky lounge, wedding chapel, athletic club, amusement arcade, gourmet market, and historical museum into a new and composite architecture element invented by us: the programmatic extractor or 'skyframe' " (ibid., 223).

182. Interview with Norris, *Deconstruction,* 73. Deconstruction in architecture occurs "when you have deconstructed some architectural philosophy, some architectural assumptions—for instance, the hegemony of the aesthetic, of beauty, the hegemony of usefulness, of functionality, of living, of dwelling. But then you have to *reinscribe* these motifs within the work. You can't (or you shouldn't) simply dismiss those values of dwelling, functionality, beauty, and so on" (ibid.; his italics).

183. For a deconstructive look at, inter alia, the in/out pair, see "Fifty-Two Aphorisms," no. 49. See also my treatment of this binary as it pertains to architecture in part 3 ("Built Places") of *Getting Back into Place,* pp. 122–125. Certain of Eisenman's celebrated houses have *cuts* built into them: radical incisions in walls that disrupt the cozy continuity of domestic space, bringing inhabitants precipitously *out* of this space into the surrounding world.

184. See Tschumi, *Event-Cities,* 325 ff., esp. p. 329: "Transprogramming: combining several types of programs, regardless of incompatibilities, with their respective spatial configurations." An example is found in the combination of forum, running track, and reading room in Tschumi's proposal for the National Library of France, which "cannot be a frozen monument but must instead turn into an event, a movement" (ibid.).

185. For a critique of "projection" in architecture, see "Point de Folie," sec. 8, and "Fifty-Two Aphorisms," nos. 38, 39.

186. "Fifty-Two Aphorisms," no. 52. On the role of promise in architecture, see the talk at Trento, Italy, December 16, 1988, pp. 16–17: architecture "has to bind itself in an engagement, which has to be a promise. . . . Without any structure of promise there would not be this 'maintenant' of architecture." I thank Guillaume Ehrmann for showing me a copy of this transcript and of "Philo-sophe Archi-tecte."

187. This term, doubtless coined with the words "anachrony" and "anarchy" in mind, is discussed by Derrida in the talk at Trento, p. 15 in the transcript. See also "Point de Folie," sec. 9, where architecture, anarchitecture, and transarchitecture are briefly compared.

188. Tschumi, *Event-Cities,* 435.

189. Philipe Sollers, *Nombres,* cited in this typography by Derrida in *Dissemination,* p. 321.

190. Luce Irigaray, "Place, Interval: A Reading of Aristotle, *Physics* IV," in *An*

Ethics of Sexual Difference, trans. C. Burke and G. C. Gill (Ithaca: Cornell University Press, 1993), 54. She adds: "[Is it not the case that the two sexes are coupled] unless the one or the other claims to be the whole? And constructs his world into a closed circle. Total? Closed to the other. And convinced that there is no access to outside except by opening up a wound. Having no part in the construction of love, or of beauty, or the world" (pp. 54–55). The reference to wounding recalls Marduk's assumption that he can construct Babylon only by killing Tiamat. For Freud's invocation of Aristophanes (via Plato's *Symposium*), see his *Beyond the Pleasure Principle* (*Standard Edition of the Complete Psychological Works* [1955], xxi: 57–58). I should make it clear that throughout this section I do not make any systematic distinction between "sex" and "gender." This is out of deference to Irigaray's doubts about the validity of such a distinction—which on her view only reinscribes the problematic dichotomy between nature ("sex") and culture ("gender"). Her concern is with bodily bearings and practices that are sexually specific—"sexed" or "sexuated" as we might call them. (I owe this clarification to Elizabeth Grosz, who made several other valuable suggestions regarding this section.) Quite another approach is held by those who claim that *both* sex and gender are culturally determined—as effects of discourse, modes of performance, or stages in a coherent historical genesis. For the first of these three models of interpretation, see Michel Foucault, *The History of Sexuality,* trans. R. Hurley (New York: Vintage, 1980), I:154 ff.; for the second, Judith Butler, *Gender Trouble: Feminism and the Subversion of Identity* (New York: Routledge, 1990), esp. pp. 24–25, 33, 115, 134–141; for the third, Ivan Illich, *Gender* (New York: Pantheon, 1982), 14: "*Gender* and *sex* are ideal, limiting concepts to designate a polarity: the industrial transformation of society from a "gendering" into a "sexing" system. . . . Both gender and sex transform the genital organs into a social reality" (his italics). Illich also discusses the relation between "space/time and gender" at pp. 105–126, esp. p. 123: "Vernacular space [i.e., a collection of local milieus] not only shapes the landscape and the house, not only reaches into the past and beyond, it extends into the body itself, quite differently for women than for men."

191. For Bachelard's elegy, see *The Poetics of Reverie,* chap. 2, "Reveries on Reverie ('Animus'—'Anima')." Bachelard concentrates on *anima*-specific reveries, reserving for a future work—a work he did not live to write—a comparable treatment of *animus* themes. On *anima* in Jung, see *Anima: An Anatomy of a Personified Notion,* ed. James Hillman (Dallas: Spring, 1985), passim. For Deleuze and Guattari's discussion of "becoming-woman," see *A Thousand Plateaus,* pp. 275 ff. and p. 352. In the latter reference, the authors compare becoming-woman to the "war machine"—thus turning the tables on Mardukian models of war that are dogmatically masculinist in inspiration.

192. The full statement is "Fluidity is the fundamental condition, and the division into bodies is carried out—there being no obstacle to it—according to [our] need" (Leibniz, *New Essays on Human Understanding,* ed. P. Remnant and J. Bennett [Cambridge: Cambridge University Press, 1981], bk. 2, chap. 13, p. 151).

193. "Place, Interval," 52. Compare also this passage from an earlier work: *jouissance* is "indefinite flood in which all manner of developments can be inscribed" (*Speculum of the Other Woman,* 229). On the valorization of the birth-giving bodyplace, and its devalorization as a place-for-orgasm, see "Place, Interval," 52–53. Illich

attempts to justify the female body as place-of-fetation: "Both men and women make themselves at home through every move. . . . But only from women does bodily life come into the world" (*Gender*, 122).

194. "Place, Interval," 52. On the infinite regress entailed by place, see pp. 34–35. Archytas was reported to have said, "It is peculiar to place that while other things are in it, place is in nothing. For if it were in some place, this place again will be in another place, and this will go on without end. For this very reason it is necessary for other things to be in place, but for place to be in nothing." (As cited by Simplicius from *In Aristotelis categorias commentarium* and translated in S. Sambursky, *The Concept of Place in Late Neoplatonism*, p. 37.)

195. "Place, Interval," 52; her italics. The French is "un *sans lieu* féminin."

196. Ibid., 35; her italics.

197. Ibid.

198. Ibid., 34. Irigaray suggests that the "quest for infinity in God" is closely related to the "quest to infinity for the mother in women" and that the two quests "intersect ceaselessly": see p. 35. The theme of passage or "interval" as it relates to place and desire is taken up in "Sexual Difference," on pp. 8–10.

199. *Speculum of the Other Woman*, 227.

200. "Place, Interval," 35.

201. "She must lack—neither body,—nor extension within,—nor extension without, or she will plummet down and take the other with her (*elle s'abîme et abîme l'autre*)" ("Place, Interval," 35). For an insightful treatment of Irigaray in relation to Platonic *chōra*, see Elizabeth Grosz, "Woman, Chora, Dwelling" (in *Space, Time, and Perversion*), where the danger of employing *chōra* as a "silencing and endless metaphorization of femininity as the condition for men's self-representation and cultural production" (124) is pointed out with special reference to Plato and Derrida.

202. "Place, Interval," p. 48. In the enactment of sexual desire in intercourse, woman is thus "re-contained with place in place" (p. 53).

203. *Physics* 220a27 (Hardie and Gaye translation). Aristotle intends this axiom to apply to the "no longer" and the "not yet" of time. But in the case of place, the dyad of engagement is not constituted by two indifferently disposed and independent terms. In "Place, Interval" Irigaray asks, "[Are there] two motors of place? Two causes of place? And their coming together. Two pulses and their transformations. Of the one, of the other, and their interdeterminations. *At least two*. To infinity then?" (pp. 40–41; my italics).

204. On the theme of more-than-one as essential to female sexedness, see "This Sex Which Is Not One," trans. C. Reeder, in *New French Feminisms*, ed. E. Marks and I. Courtivron (New York: Schocken, 1981), 99–106, esp. p. 103: "*woman has sex organs just about everywhere. . . .* [What women desire] is always more and other than this *one*—of sex, for example" (her italics). The lack of self-engagement that results from lack of twoness is supported by Merleau-Ponty's observation that human flesh (*la chair*) is such that it is "reversible," that is, something that touches itself even as it touches other things. (See Merleau-Ponty, *The Visible and the Invisible*, 133–138.) Irigaray's lecture, given in the same series as "Place, Interval," discusses the chapter from which these same pages come. See "The Invisible of the Flesh: A Reading of *The Visible and the Invisible*, 'The Intertwining—the Chiasm,' " in *An Ethics of Sexual Difference*, pp. 151–184.

205. "Creating another space—outside any framework. The opening of openness" (*Elemental Passions,* trans. J. Collie and J. Still [New York: Routledge, 1992], 59).

206. "Place, Interval," 51. She adds: "There are two touches between boundaries; and these are not the same: the touch of one's body at the threshold; the touch of the contained other. There is also the internal touch of the body of the child" (ibid.).

207. "The Envelope: A Reading of Spinoza, *Ethics,* 'Of God,'" in *An Ethics of Sexual Difference,* 85; my italics.

208. "Man defines God who determines man" ("The Envelope," 88).

209. On "holey space"—posited as an important alternative to striated and smooth space yet not fully explored by the authors—see Deleuze and Guattari, *A Thousand Plateaus,* pp. 413–415.

210. Aristotle, *Physics* 212a19–20; Hussey translation.

211. Merleau-Ponty writes, "The flesh = the fact that the visible that I am is seer (look) or, what amounts to the same thing, has an *inside,* plus the fact that the exterior visible is also *seen,* i.e. has a prolongation, in the enclosure of my body, which is part of its being" (*The Visible and the Invisible,* working note of December 1960, p. 271; his italics). Irigaray would doubtless insist that this is also a situation in which tangibility figures—but so would Merleau-Ponty himself: see the working note of May 1960, p. 254 of *The Visible and the Invisible.*

212. For further discussion of the special character of lips, see Irigaray's "When Our Lips Speak Together," in *This Sex Which Is Not One,* trans. C. Porter (Ithaca: Cornell University Press, 1985). The mouth's lips are congruous counterparts; genital lips are incongruous counterparts—hence they (unlike buccal lips) can be designated "right" and "left." The idea of the "body without organs"—with allusions to the closely related idea of the body as a "desiring machine"—is first developed by Deleuze and Guattari in *Anti-Oedipus,* trans. R. Hurley, M. Seem, and H. R. Lane (Minneapolis: University of Minnesota Press, 1983), chaps. 1, 2, 5. The theme is taken up again in *A Thousand Plateaus,* pp. 149–166, 256.

213. Irigaray glosses Aristotle to the effect that "the place is in the thing, and the thing is in the place" ("Place, Interval," 40). The first clause reflects Aristotle's worry that if place is in a thing, then place is in place. Irigaray's own position is a variation on this Aristotelian conundrum and can be expressed thus: *place is in the sexed body, and (thus) such a body is in place.* She comments further: "Place is within and without and accompanies movement" (ibid.; in italics in the text). For a still more general account of the relation between place and body—one that does not attempt to take gender into account—see my *Getting Back into Place,* chap. 4, esp. pp. 104–105.

214. "The female, it seems, is pure disposable 'matter'. Pure receptacle that does not stay still. Not even a place, then? Always belonging to a threatening primitive chaos" ("The Envelope," 90). This claim is at least partly sardonic: the more woman is *only* matter or pure receptacle, the more she is merely chaotic—not even a place. But she *is* a place, as Irigaray continues to affirm.

215. *Elemental Passions,* 17.

216. "Place, Interval," 39.

217. "I will never be in a man's place, never will a man be in mine. Whatever identifications are possible, one will never exactly occupy the place of the other—they are irreducible one to the other" ("Sexual Difference," in *Elemental Passions,* 13).

218. "Sexual Difference." My italics.

219. "The outline of a womb-like maternal body is based upon your need for solidity. For a rock-solid home" (*Elemental Passions,* 80).

220. "Place, Interval," 39.

221. On woman as thing, Irigaray has this to say: "If traditionally, and as a mother, woman represents *place* for man, such a limit means that she becomes *a thing*" ("Sexual Difference," 10; her italics). I owe the line of thought in this last paragraph to conversation with my colleague Mary C. Rawlinson.

222. "Sexual Difference," 10–11; her italics.

223. Both sentences are from "Love of the Other," in *An Ethics of Sexual Difference,* 142; my italics. Irigaray adds: "His nostalgia for a first and last dwelling prevents him from meeting and living with the other. Nostalgia blocks the threshold of the ethical world" (ibid.). On the relation between nostalgia and place, see my article, "The World of Nostalgia," *Man and World* 20 (1987): 361–384.

224. "Love of the Other," 143.

225. "Place, Interval," 40.

226. "The Envelope," 93. The proposal of "conception" and "perception" as what men and women have "in common" occurs at p. 93, where the two terms are interpreted as "to suffer" and "to be active," respectively.

227. "Place, Interval," 54: "Between the one and the other there should be mutual enveloping in movement. For the one and the other move around within a whole." On "each giving the other necessity and freedom," see "The Envelope," 93.

228. "Place, Interval," 40. One must find and know one's own place before mutual implacement is possible, for such implacement cannot happen "unless each of us returns to his or her place to find his or her cause again and then returns toward the other place, the place of the other" (ibid.).

229. "The Envelope," 93.

230. On woman's body as cause, indeed in the position of *causa sui,* see "The Envelope," pp. 84–85, 92–93.

231. Thus, as Judith Butler remarks, for Irigaray "ethical relations ought to be based on relations of closeness, proximity, and intimacy that reconfigure conventional notions of reciprocity and respect. Traditional conceptions of reciprocity exchange such relations of intimacy for those characterized by violent erasure, substitutability, and appropriation" (Judith Butler, *Bodies that Matter,* 46). Butler's discussion of materiality in Irigaray—especially of the latter's treatment of Platonic *chōra*—is of special interest: see ibid., pp. 36–55).

232. "The Envelope," 93.

233. Ibid., 83; her italics. For a different treatment of God as a place, see my *Getting Back into Place,* pp. 17–18.

234. "Place, Interval," 53.

235. Ibid.

236. Ibid. The French text reads: "Ce lieu, production de l'intimité, est en quelque sorte une transmutation de la terre en ciel, ici maintenant." Alchemy is twice invoked in connection with woman's spirituality: p. 53, and p. 54.

237. Ibid., 50. The double tendency toward matrix and the infinite is also described at pp. 50–51.

238. Ibid., 51.

239. We have encountered before—most notably in Spinoza—the idea that God is

a physical entity. The idea of God as an actual entity who *becomes* is developed by Whitehead in *Process and Reality,* ed. D. R. Griffin and D. W. Sherburne (New York: Macmillan, 1978), esp. pt. 5, chap. 2, "God and the World."

240. "The Envelope," 84.

241. "Place, Interval," 55.

242. Ibid.; my italics. "Makes place" translates *fait lieu.* This phrase should be compared to Derrida's preferred phrase "donne lieu" as discussed in Section V above.

243. "The search for creation" is contrasted with the situation in which "the one and the other destroy the place of the other, believing in this way to have the whole (*le tout*); but they possess or construct only an illusory whole and destroy the meeting and the interval (of attraction) between the two. The world is destroyed in its essential symbol: the copula of the sex act. It is opened up to the abyss and not left slightly open (*entrouvert*) to welcome generation, the search for creation" ("Place, Interval," 54; translation slightly modified).

Postface: Places Rediscovered

1. For a discerning treatment of the feminist implications of Platonic *chōra*—implications denied by Derrida and affirmed, albeit often obliquely, by Irigaray—see Ann Bergren, "Architecture Gender Philosophy," in *Strategies in Architectural Thinking,* ed. J. Whiteman, J. Kipnis, and R. Burdett (Cambridge: MIT Press, 1992), 8–47.

2. Aristotle, *Physics* 209a25–26; Hussey translation.

3. The more complete statement is "if man and woman are both body and thought, they provide each other with . . . greater and greater envelopes, vaster and vaster horizons, but above all envelopes that are qualitatively more and more necessary and different. But always *overflowing (débordées)*" ("The Envelope," in *An Ethics of Sexual Difference,* trans. C. Burke and G. C. Gill [Ithaca: Cornell University Press, 1993], 86; her italics). At the same time, Irigaray cautions that man and woman *also* "provide each other with finiteness, limit, and the possibility of access to the divine by the development of envelopes" (ibid.).

4. This oxymoronic term of Deleuze and Guattari from *A Thousand Plateaus,* trans. B. Massumi (Minneapolis: University of Minnesota Press, 1987), 382, is presaged by Leibniz in his claim that " 'place' is either *particular,* as considered in relation to this or that body, or *universal*; the latter is related to everything, and in terms of it all changes of every body whatsoever are taken into account" (*New Essays on Human Understanding,* ed. P. Remnant and J. Bennett [Cambridge: Cambridge University Press, 1981], bk. 2, chap. 13, p. 149; his italics). Clearly, on the radically relationalist view, place is both particular and universal at once, as is made clear in an additional comment of Leibniz: "if there were nothing fixed in the universe, the place of each thing would still be determined by reasoning" (ibid.).

5. Irigaray, "Place, Interval," in *An Ethics of Sexual Difference,* 41. Eisenman's architecture, it might be noted, is often dependent on the twisting of axes around themselves, creating a visual torsion that can be considered the built analogue of the contortions of bodily bilaterality.

6. One of the clearest statements as to the significance of event in Derrida's thinking occurs in a recent interview: "[Event] is a name for the aspects of what happens that we will never manage either to eliminate or to deny (or simply never manage to

deny). It is another name for experience, which is always experience of the other. The event is what does not allow itself to be subsumed under any other concept, not even that of being." ("The Deconstruction of Actuality: An Interview with Jacques Derrida," in *Radical Philosophy* (Autumn 1994): 32.) It should be noted that Irigaray is critical of event qua "il y a" as something that "defers celebration" (*An Ethics of Sexual Difference,* 14).

7. Is it accidental that Foucault, a man, valorizes heterotopias that for the most part exist on the fringes of society, while Irigaray wishes to effect a radical change in attitudes toward sexual difference that are found in the very center of active social life?

8. "Place, Interval," 49.

9. Ibid., 50.

10. Alfred North Whitehead, *Science and the Modern World* (Cambridge: Cambridge University Press, 1926), 93.

11. Ibid.

12. Irigaray, *Elemental Passions,* trans. J. Collie and J. Still (New York: Routledge, 1992), 59. She adds: "the land cannot be laid waste if spatiality is produced by our bodies" (ibid.). This suggests, as with Whitehead, that the basis for the inclusive power of place is to be found in the body.

13. "The light dove, cleaving the air in her free flight, and feeling its resistance, might imagine that its flight would be still easier in empty space" (Immanuel Kant, *The Critique of Pure Reason,* trans. N. K. Smith [New York: Humanities Press, 1965], 47). Bachelard has explored the imagination of free movement in open space in his extraordinary book, *L'air et les songes* (Paris: Corti, 1943).

14. Cited by Ludwig Binswanger, "Freud's Conception of Man in the Light of Anthropology," in *Being-in-the-World,* trans. J. Needleman (New York: Basic Books, 1963), 178. See also Nietzsche, *The Gay Science,* trans. W. Kaufmann (New York: Vintage, 1974), secs. 124–125, for a similar line of thought. (I owe this last reference to Robert Gooding-Williams.)

15. As Husserl argues, however, to move through the outer atmosphere in spaceships is not to escape concrete implacement: it is only to carry a home-place (*Heimatstätte*) into outer space itself and to relocate place *in another place.* Throughout the journey, the earth remains as a "primitive home" (*Urheimat*). See Husserl's fragment, "Foundational Investigations of the Phenomenological Origin of the Spatiality of Nature," trans. F. Kersten, in P. McCormick and F. Elliston, eds., *Husserl: Shorter Works* (Notre Dame: University of Notre Dame Press, 1981), 228 ff.

16. See Jean-François Lyotard, *The Postmodern Condition: A Report on Knowledge,* trans. G. Bennington and B. Massumi (Minneapolis: University of Minnesota Press, 1985), 35, 66; Wallace Stegner, "Sense of Place," in W. Stegner, *Where the Bluebird Sings to the Lemonade Springs: Living and Writing in the West* (New York: Penguin, 1992), 199–206.

17. Jean-Luc Nancy, *The Inoperative Community,* trans. P. Connor (Minneapolis: University of Minnesota Press, 1991), 146; my italics.

18. Ibid., 146.

19. Recall Heidegger's observation that "the 'above' is what is 'on the ceiling'; the 'below' is what is 'on the floor'; the 'behind' is what is 'at the door' " (*Being and Time,* trans. J. Macquarrie and E. Robinson [New York: Harper & Row, 1962], 136).

20. I have in mind Merleau-Ponty's remarkable reinterpretation of depth in terms of body and place in *Phenomenology of Perception,* 254–267.

21. *Being and Time,* 137.

22. *A Thousand Plateaus,* 493. The authors add: "One can back away from a thing, but it is a bad painter who backs away from the painting he or she is working on. Or from the 'thing' for that matter: Cézanne spoke of the need to *no longer see* the wheat field, to be too close to it, to lose oneself without landmarks in smooth space" (ibid.; their italics). De Kooning has remarked similarly that his paintings of the late 1960s and early 1970s were done from a close-up glimpse taken at the surrounding landscape of eastern Long Island as he drove through it rapidly: "It's this glimpse which inspires [me]" (Willem De Kooning, *Sketchbook I: Three Americans* [New York: New York Times, 1979], 6). Note that in De Kooning's experience the dromocentric and the lococentric converge!

23. *The Inoperative Community,* 148. On the same page we read that "all that remains of the experience of the temple in the desert is destitution before the empty temples."

24. Ibid., 149. I have hyphenated "spacing out."

25. Ibid., 150.

26. "These places, spread out everywhere, yield up and orient new spaces; they are no longer temples, but rather the opening up and the spacing out of the temples themselves, a dis-location with no reserve henceforth, with no more sacred enclosures" (ibid., 150).

27. Ibid., 148: "Space is everywhere open, there is no place wherein to receive either the mystery or the splendor of a god."

28. Ibid., 148: "It is granted to us to see the limitless openness of that space, it falls to our age to know—with a knowledge more acute than even the most penetrating science, more luminous than any consciousness—how we are delivered up to that gaping naked face [of the absent god]."

Index